RON KALENUIK

SIMPLY DELICIOUS
C·O·O·K·I·N·G

MAGNANIMITY
HOUSE PUBLISHING

Project Coordinator
Dianna Kalenuik

Editor Lori Koch

Cuisine Coordinator / Food Stylist
Chef Ron Kalenuik

Cuisine Assistants
Mary Gifford
Jacqueline Hunt
Evelyn Hohn

Art Direction Sylvia Cook

Photography Kim Griffiths Photography, Edmonton

Design / Colour Separations / Film
Creative Edge Graphic Design, Edmonton

51 Glenthorne Dr., Scarborough, Ontario M1C 3S9

ISBN 0-9696683-2-5

This book is an Exclusive Edition for MINT Publishers Inc.

Printed in the United States of America.

CONTENTS

ABOUT THE AUTHOR

Mr. Kalenuik, affectionately known as Chef K (by those who could not pronounce his last name), began his culinary career in Jasper, Alberta, Canada, in 1973 at the world famous Jasper Park Lodge. Since then, he has established himself as Chef de Cuisine in many of the finer restaurants and hotels throughout Canada.

Ron has owned and operated several national award winning restaurants. He is a teacher and consultant to the hospitality industry as well as President of the North American Institute of Modern Cuisine Inc.

As an author, he expresses a uniqu` and creative flair in all areas of cookery. Whether classic or just down home family cookery, or in modern presentation, every style is simply given and easily prepared. This book is more than a collection of recipes; it is a collection of useable, delicious recipes that will become a standard in anyone's kitchen, from the homemaker to the professional chef.

With *Simply Delicious Cooking,* Mr. Kalenuik's career includes 8 cookery books to date. His international best selling series of *Simply Delicious Cooking* has sold over 850,000 copies the world over. His other books include *The Fundamentals of Taste, Cuisine Extraordinaire, Dining In, Championship Cooking, Chef K's Cheese Best* and *The Right Spice.*

A WORD FROM THE AUTHOR

The cooking passions of people run deep, whether they are in the latest trend or "just doing what Mom always did." People hold onto what they know works for them. That is why the *Simply Delicious Cooking* series is so important to more than 850,000 people. These are cookbooks they know they can hold onto, and trust for success in their kitchens. Now you, too, can enjoy that reliance with *Simply Delicious Cooking.*

Most want the best for their families and they deserve it. This is what we bring you in *Simply Delicious Cooking,* the best in simple and delightful recipes. No matter where you live these are sure to provide your family with exactly what you want for them: the very best.

The best cooks are the ones who are always seeking inspiration, looking to marry the old with the new so that creativity may flow. In *Simply Delicious Cooking,* the inspiration is defined and perfected. There is no recipe too hard or so different that one will pass it by. Every recipe has the taste of "just one more bite" leaving the guest with an immense desire for a new summons to the table.

No cook can resist the draw of his or her favourite recipes; nor could I. I've brought to you creations that have won awards and rave reviews from friends and critics alike. I've given to you more than just years of cooking experience. I've given you the tastes of culinary dreams. I hope you'll live the dream with me.

From my first international best-selling cookery book, I learned that my readers sought more international cuisine. We have answered the call, for within these pages you'll find cuisine from Africa to Asia, New Zealand to Newfoundland, from the U.S.A. to the U.K. and points between.

In *Simply Delicious Cooking,* we seek to give you years of enjoyment in food preparation. After all, food should be a pleasure to prepare and serve. This is accomplished here. Taste is the complete work of all the senses, not just the mouth, with all the senses working together for your enjoyment. To make the best use of taste, one must incorporate sight, touch, smell, hearing and flavour to yield taste. Here I have accomplished this for you; our pictures are but a prelude to the tastes that will follow. They are the appetizers for the eyes.

Your book looks like a coffee table book, something for show. However, beautiful as it is, it really belongs in the kitchen where your most reliable cooking tools are. Open the pages to a new world of delights that could change your world of culinary abilities forever.

Ron Kalenuik, Chef K

APPETIZERS

Chicken wings — someone let the chicken out and it has learned to fly! Appetizing "wings" are being served all over the world, and they are gaining popularity with each passing day.

Have you ever really wanted to know how they make those chicken wings Buffalo, N.Y. is famous for (they began in the Anchor Bar, a small restaurant bar in downtown Buffalo)? In this chapter of *Simply Delicious Cooking,* you will find out how to make them without going to Buffalo. Or, maybe you'd prefer the more exotic — they are within these pages as well. We have given you over 10 different kinds, ranging from Buffalo Style to a special Apricot Brandy Wing to the Smokin' Texas Wings. Why not enjoy them all?

Chicken wings, however, are not all you'll find. We have included some appetizing party starters and gourmet appetizers for the special occasions in your life. Why not make a meal from appetizers alone; they are extra special for your event nights.

The concept of appetizers began many years ago in Russia, where to whet the appetite one would nibble on something small and appealing. The French have always known that hors d'ouevres set the pace for all dishes to follow. If this first dish of adventure was of poor quality, then even the finest dishes following would be regarded in a poor light. But make it *Simply Delicious* and the praises for the following dishes will go on for weeks after the meal has ended.

Today, appetizers are more than just a nibble; they may be the best avenue to a successful, memory-making meal. Whether one chooses an extraordinary Shrimp in Apple Chocolate Sauce or the fascinating Tomato Capellini with Red Pepper Pesto and Shrimp, the result will always be the same — success! Count on the creativity of these extraordinary delights to bring out the best in your guests. They are sure to agree, these appetizers (like our Smoked Salmon Ravioli with Pepper Vodka Cheese Sauce) are the best that they have ever tasted, and they are the ones you have prepared. Their comment to you, and all they tell of your meal, will be "capriccioso," Italian for *Simply Delicious.*

Party Pickled Shrimp

Collector's Edition Radio

CRAB AND CASHEW CANAPÉS

1 lb	450 g	cooked crab meat
1 cup	250 ml	cashews, not salted
1 tbsp	15 ml	butter
2 tsp	10 ml	flour
¾ cup	180 ml	light cream
2 tbsp	30 ml	chopped parsley
¼ cup	60 ml	freshly grated Parmesan cheese
36	36	whole wheat crackers or toast points

Blend the crab and cashews. Heat the butter in a sauce pan, add the flour and cook for 2 minutes over low heat. Pour in the cream and simmer into a thick sauce. Blend in the parsley, cheese and crab.

Place on crackers and serve while hot.

SERVES 6

SHRIMP, SCALLOP AND ESCARGOT BUDDIES

24	24	peeled and deveined large shrimp
24	24	large bay scallops
24	24	extra large snails
3 tbsp	45 ml	butter
2	2	minced garlic cloves
¼ cup	60 ml	white wine
2 tbsp	30 ml	Pernod
1 tbsp	15 ml	chopped chives
1 tbsp	15 ml	chopped parsley

On bamboo skewers place 2 each, shrimp, scallops and snails alternating them. Place on a broiling pan.

Heat the butter in a sauce pan, add the remaining ingredients. Cook until mixture has reduced to half.

Brush the skewers with the butter. Broil for 2-3 minutes. Turn the skewers over, brush with the butter again. Broil for an additional 2-3 minutes. Remove from oven, brush a third time and serve at once.

SERVES 6

ARMADILLO EGGS

16	16	jalapeño peppers
1 cup	250 ml	grated Monterey Jack cheese
2	2	eggs
¼ cup	60 ml	milk
½ cup	125 ml	flour
1 cup	250 ml	seasoned bread crumbs
2 cups	500 ml	safflower oil
2 cups	500 ml	hot Creole Sauce (see page 121)
		curly lettuce leaves

Cut the tops from the peppers. Using a small knife remove the membranes and seeds from within the peppers.

Stuff each pepper with cheese, pack the cheese as tight as possible. Place on a baking tray.

Blend the eggs with the milk in a small mixing bowl.

Dust the peppers with the flour, dip into the eggs and dredge in the bread crumbs.

Heat the oil to 350°F (190°C). Fry the peppers in the oil until golden brown.

Place the Creole sauce in a small bowl, place the bowl on a large serving platter and arrange the lettuce leafs around the bowl. Place the Armadillo Eggs around the platter and serve at once.

SERVES 4

Shrimp, Scallop & Escargot Buddies

Armadillo Eggs

Spicy Yucatan Wings

SPICY YUCATAN WINGS

½ cup	125 ml	safflower oil
1	1	minced Spanish onion
1	1	finely diced green bell pepper
1	1	finely diced celery stalk
2	2	minced garlic cloves
2 tsp	10 ml	minced red chilies
1 cup	250 ml	crushed tomatoes
1 cup	250 ml	mashed bananas
½ tsp	3 ml	salt (optional)
½ tsp	3 ml	cayenne pepper
1 tsp	5 ml	oregano
¼ tsp	1 ml	white pepper
¼ tsp	1 ml	black pepper
2¼ lbs	1 kg	chicken wings

Heat the oil in a sauce pan. Add the onion, bell pepper, celery, garlic and chilies. Sauté until tender. Add the tomatoes, bananas and seasonings. Simmer for 15-20 minutes.

Wash and tip the chicken wings. Pat dry in paper towels. Place the wings in a large casserole dish. Cover with the sauce, than cover the dish with foil wrap. Bake in a preheated 350°F (180°C) oven for 45 minutes. Uncover and bake for 15 additional minutes. Transfer to a serving plate. Serve at once.

SERVES 4

Buffalo Chicken Wings

BUFFALO CHICKEN WINGS

2¼ lbs	1 kg	chicken wings
4 cups	1 L	oil
¼ cup	60 ml	butter
5 tbsp	75 ml	Franks-Durkees red hot cayenne pepper sauce: less for mild, more for hot
1 bunch	1	celery
1 cup	250 ml	blue cheese, crumbled
1 cup	250 ml	mayonnaise

Trim and separate the wing bone from the drumette. Heat the oil to 375°F (190°C). Fry the wings a few at a time, 10 minutes each batch. Be sure to maintain oil at set temperature. Reserve hot in the oven.

Melt the butter in a sauce pan and add the hot sauce. Place chicken wings in a serving bowl. Pour sauce over and toss to coat.

While wings are cooking cut the celery into sticks. Blend the blue cheese with the mayonnaise to serve as a dip for both the celery and wings.

Serve the wings with the celery.

SERVES 4

LOBSTER COCKTAIL

1 lb	450 g	cooked lobster meat
¼ cup	60 ml	tomato catsup
2 tbsp	30 ml	sherry
1 tbsp	15 ml	hot, grated horseradish
¼ tsp	1 ml	cayenne pepper
1 tbsp	15 ml	lemon juice
2 tsp	10 ml	chopped chives
1 tsp	5 ml	chopped capers
6	6	endive lettuce leaves
6	6	lobster claws – meat only

Dice the lobster meat.

In a mixing bowl blend the catsup, sherry, horseradish, cayenne, lemon juice, chives and capers. Add the diced lobster and mix.

Place mixture on the lettuce leaves on chilled plates or in chilled champagne glasses. Top with a lobster claw. Serve.

NOTE: Substitute shrimp or crab meats if desired.

SERVES 6

DIJON NUT WINGS

2¼ lbs	1 kg	chicken wings
1 cup	250 ml	Dijon mustard
1 cup	250 ml	powdered almonds
1 cup	250 ml	fine, seasoned bread crumbs
4 cups	1 L	safflower oil

Wash and tip the chicken wings. Pat dry with paper towels. Coat each wing with a layer of Dijon mustard.

Mix the almonds with the bread crumbs. Toss the wings in the bread crumb mixture.

Heat the oil to 375°F (180°C). Cook small batches of the wings in the oil for 10 minutes. Reserve hot in the oven while other batches cook. Serve hot.

SERVES 4

APRICOT BRANDY WINGS

1 cup	250 ml	dried apricots
1 cup	250 ml	water, hot
½ cup	125 ml	apricot brandy
3 tbsp	45 ml	sugar
½ tsp	3 ml	cinnamon
2¼ lbs	1 kg	chicken wings

In a sauce pan cook the apricots in the water until soft. Remove apricots to a food processor and process into a purée. Return to the sauce pan, add brandy, sugar and cinnamon. Simmer for 5 minutes.

Place chicken wings on a broiling pan. Broil in a preheated oven for 10 minutes. Turn the wings over and broil for an additional 10 minutes. During the last 3 minutes brush with sauce twice. Remove the wings from the oven and brush with sauce once more. Serve hot.

NOTE: You may exchange the brandy for apple juice or apricot nectar.

SERVES 4

CAJUN FRIED WINGS

2¼ lbs	1 kg	chicken wings
2 cups	500 ml	bread crumbs
2 tsp	10 ml	oregano
1 tsp	5 ml	basil
1 tsp	5 ml	salt
1 tsp	5 ml	chili powder
½ tsp	3 ml	onion powder
½ tsp	3 ml	paprika
½ tsp	3 ml	cayenne pepper
¼ tsp	1 ml	black pepper
¼ tsp	1 ml	white pepper
2	2	eggs
¼ cup	60 ml	milk
½ cup	125 ml	flour
4 cups	1 L	safflower oil

Preheat the oil to 375°F (190°C).

Wash and tip the chicken wings. Pat dry with paper towels. Blend the bread crumbs with the herbs and spices.

Beat the eggs into the milk, place the flour into a separate mixing bowl. Working quickly dip each wing piece into the flour then into the egg wash and roll in the seasoned bread crumbs.

Fry in the oil in small batches for 10-12 minutes. Reserve hot in the oven until all are ready to serve.

SERVES 4

Dijon Nut, Apricot Brandy & Cajun Fried Wings

Barbecued Chicken Wings

MASCARPONE BOUCHEES

¼ lb	115 g	Mascarpone cheese or cream cheese
1 tsp	5 ml	salt
¼ tsp	1 ml	white pepper
¼ cup	60 ml	finely chopped chives
2½ cups	625 ml	chopped walnuts

In a food processor combine the cheese, salt, pepper and chives, process until smooth.

Remove from food processor and roll into tiny balls.

Place the walnuts into a mixing bowl. Roll the cheese balls through to coat. Place the cheese balls on a waxed paper lined serving platter. Refrigerate for 1 hour before serving.

SERVES 6

BARBECUED CHICKEN WINGS

½ cup	125 ml	brown sugar
½ cup	125 ml	tomato catsup
2 tbsp	30 ml	Worcestershire sauce
1 tsp	5 ml	chili powder
½ tsp	3 ml	each of oregano, garlic powder, thyme, onion powder, paprika, salt, pepper, basil
2¼ lbs	1 kg	chicken wings

Blend together the brown sugar, catsup, Worcestershire, with the herbs and spices.

Wash and tip the wings (cutting the tip of each wing off). Pat dry in paper towels. Place on a broiling pan and broil in a preheated oven for 10 minutes. Turn the wings over and brush with the sauce. Broil for an additional 10 minutes. Brush once again during the last 2 minutes of cooking.

Serve hot with remaining sauce.

SERVES 4

CRÊPES FRUIT DE MER

¼ cup	60 ml	butter
½ lb	225 g	shrimp
½ lb	225 g	crab meat
½ lb	225 g	lobster meat
3 tbsp	45 ml	flour
1 cup	250 ml	Fish Stock (see page 76)
2 cups	500 ml	white wine
½ cup	125 ml	light cream
½ tsp	3 ml	salt (optional)
½ tsp	3 ml	pepper
⅓ cup	80 ml	freshly grated Parmesan cheese
16	16	Crêpes (see Crêpe Batter, page 469)
2 tbsp	30 ml	chopped parsley

Heat the butter in a skillet. Add the seafood and cook gently. Sprinkle with flour and cook for 2 additional minutes over low heat. Stir in the stock, wine and cream. Simmer until thick and smooth. Add the salt, pepper and Parmesan, continuing to cook the mixture for an additional 2 minutes.

Reserve 1 cup (250 ml) of filling, place equal amounts of the remaining filling in each crêpe and roll. Place on serving plates. Top with reserved filling. Sprinkle with parsley and serve.

SERVES 8

CRABBY MUSHROOMS

3 tbsp	45 ml	butter
3 tbsp	45 ml	flour
½ cup	125 ml	Chicken Broth (see page 77)
½ cup	125 ml	half and half cream
½ tsp	3 ml	salt
¼ tsp	1 ml	white pepper
1 tsp	5 ml	Dijon mustard
1	1	egg yolk
1 cup	250 ml	cooked crab meat
1 lb	454 g	large fresh mushroom caps
3	3	eggs
2 cups	500 ml	seasoned bread crumbs
4 cups	1 L	safflower oil

In a sauce pan heat the butter, add the flour, cook for 2 minutes over low heat. Add the broth, cream, salt, pepper and mustard. Simmer until sauce thickens, than beat in the egg yolk.

Stir the crab meat into the sauce, transfer to a food processor and purée, cool to room temperature. Place a small amount of the mixture in each mushroom cap. Place two caps together to sandwich in the filling. Dip the mushrooms into the remaining filling to coat them.

Beat the eggs until light. Dip the mushrooms into the eggs and dredge through the bread crumbs.

Heat the oil to 375°F (190°C) and fry the mushrooms in small batches until golden brown, reserve hot in the oven while the remainder cook. Serve at once very hot.

SERVES 6

FRENCH RISSOLES

1 quan	1	Puff Pastry (see page 689)
2 cups	500 ml	cooked, minced chicken
¾ cup	190 ml	Mornay Sauce (see page 111)
3	3	eggs
¼ cup	60 ml	half & half cream
4 cups	1 L	safflower oil

Roll the pastry out thin. Cut into small squares.

Blend the chicken with the mornay sauce. Place 1½ tsp (8 ml) in the centre of each square. Moisten the edges with a small amount of water, fold the pastry over to enclose the filling, pinch the edges to seal.

Blend the eggs with the cream.

Heat the oil to 375°F (190°C).

Dip the pastries into the egg mixture and then fry in small batches in the oil until golden brown. Transfer to a paper towel lined baking tray, reserve hot in the oven while completing the cooking of the remaining pastries. Serve at once very hot.

SERVES 6

BEEF FLAUTAS

1 tbsp	15 ml	chili powder
2 tsp	10 ml	paprika
1 tsp	5 ml	oregano
½ tsp	3 ml	each of basil, thyme, garlic powder, onion powder, salt, pepper
1 lb	450 g	thinly sliced sirloin steak
3 tbsp	45 ml	safflower oil
1	1	thinly sliced onion
1	1	thinly sliced green pepper
4 oz	120 g	thinly sliced mushrooms
12	12	soft corn tortillas

Blend all the herbs and spices together and lightly dust the meat with the mixture. Heat the oil and sauté the meat for 5 minutes. Remove the meat and reserve hot.

Sauté the vegetables quickly in the oil. Wrap the meat and vegetables in the tortillas. Serve with Salsa Sauce (see page 115).

SERVES 6

Crabby Mushrooms

Beef Flautas

Jezebel Wings

TOMATO CAPELLINI WITH RED PEPPER PESTO AND SHRIMP

1	1	garlic clove, minced
2 tbsp	30 ml	pine nuts
1 tbsp	15 ml	fresh chopped basil leaves
3 tbsp	45 ml	chopped parsley
1 cup	250 ml	seeded, diced red peppers
3 oz	90 ml	freshly grated Romano cheese
¼ cup	60 ml	olive oil
1 quan	1	Tomato Pasta Dough (see page 440)
1 lb	450 g	cooked bay shrimp

In a food processor, process the garlic and pine nuts until very fine. Add basil, parsley, peppers and cheese and process into a purée. Slowly add the oil and continue to process into a mayonnaise like sauce.

Cook the pasta al denté in 4 quarts (4 L) of boiling salted water. Drain.

Toss the sauce through noodles, place on warmed plates. Top with shrimp. Serve.

SERVES 6

FROGS' LEGS CHEF K

16 pairs	16	frogs' legs
2 cups	500 ml	beer
2 cups	500 ml	flour
1 tsp	5 ml	basil leaves
½ tsp	3 ml	each of thyme, paprika, oregano, salt, garlic powder, onion powder, pepper
3 tbsp	45 ml	butter
3 tbsp	45 ml	olive oil
2 tbsp	30 ml	lemon juice
2 tbsp	30 ml	chopped parsley

Soak the frogs' legs in the beer for 2 hours.

While frogs' legs are soaking, blend the flour, herbs and spices together.

Remove the frogs' legs from the beer. Pat dry with paper towels.

Dust the frogs legs' with seasoned flour. In a large skillet heat the butter and oil together. Sauté the frogs' legs in the butter and oil until golden brown on each side. Place on a serving plate, sprinkle with lemon and parsley and serve.

SERVES 4

JEZEBEL WINGS

½ cup	125 ml	apple jelly
½ cup	125 ml	pineapple preserves
1 tsp	5 ml	dry mustard
½ tsp	3 ml	red pepper flakes
1 tbsp	15 ml	hot horseradish
8 oz	225 g	cream cheese
2¼ lbs	1 kg	chicken wings
		salt & pepper to taste

Blend the apple jelly, pineapple preserves, mustard, red pepper and horseradish into the cream cheese.

Wash and tip the wings. Pat dry with paper towels. Place on a baking sheet. Sprinkle with salt and pepper. Bake in a preheated 350°F (180°C) oven for 45 minutes. Transfer to a casserole dish. Spoon the sauce over the wings. Cover with foil and bake for an additional 20 minutes. Serve hot.

SERVES 4

Tomato Capellini with Red Pepper Pesto & Shrimp

Honey Lemon Chicken Wings

HONEY LEMON CHICKEN WINGS

2¼ lbs	1 kg	chicken wings
3 tbsp	45 ml	grated lemon peel
3 tbsp	45 ml	lemon juice
1 cup	250 ml	honey
1 tsp	5 ml	cinnamon

Wash and tip the wings. Pat dry with paper towels.

Whip the lemon peel and lemon juice into the honey and cinnamon. Pour over wings and marinate for 2 hours. Place wings on a broiling pan. Reserve the marinade.

Broil in the oven for 10-12 minutes. Turn the wings, brush with the marinade. Broil for an additional 10 minutes. Serve at once.

SERVES 4

SMOKIN' TEXAS WINGS

2¼ lbs	1 kg	turkey wings
½ cup	125 ml	chili sauce
3 tbsp	45 ml	soya sauce
2	2	minced garlic cloves
½ tsp	3 ml	liquid smoke
½ tsp	3 ml	cayenne pepper
½ tsp	3 ml	black pepper
¼ cup	60 ml	brown sugar

Wash and tip the wings. Pat dry with paper towels. Place the wings into a casserole dish and cover with foil wrap. Bake in a preheated 350°F (180°C) oven for ½ hour.

While wings are baking blend the remaining ingredients together. Uncover wings. Pour the sauce over the wings. Recover and bake for 35-40 minutes until wings are tender. Serve at once.

SERVES 4

BERMUDA BURGERS

1 lb	454 g	very lean hamburger
¼ tsp	1 ml	each of salt, pepper, basil, thyme, oregano
2 tsp	10 ml	Worcestershire sauce
30	30	pickled pearl onions
1	1	egg yolk
½ cup	125 ml	ice water
¾ cup	190 ml	self-rising flour
4 cups	1 L	safflower oil
½ cup	125 ml	unbleached flour
2½ cups	625 ml	crushed corn flakes
2½ cups	625 ml	barbecue sauce

In a mixing bowl combine the hamburger, seasonings and Worcestershire sauce.

Wrap 1 tbsp (15 ml) of meat mixture around each onion.

Blend the egg yolk, water and self rising flour together in a mixing bowl.

Heat the oil to 375°F (190°C).

Dust the meatballs with flour, dip into the batter and then roll in the corn flakes. Fry in the oil in small batches until golden brown. Reserve hot in the oven while remaining meat balls are cooking.

Place the barbecue sauce in a small bowl in the centre of a serving platter. Arrange the cooked meatballs around serving platter, and serve at once.

SERVES 6

Smokin' Texas Wings

Crab Stuffed Mushrooms

HONEY & GARLIC WINGS

2¼ lbs	1 kg	chicken wings
4 cups	1 L	safflower oil
1 cup	250 ml	liquid honey
1 tbsp	15 ml	garlic powder

Wash and tip the chicken wings. Pat dry with a paper towel.

Heat the oil to 375°F (190°C). Fry the wings in small batches for 10 minutes. Reserve hot while others are cooking.

Blend the honey with the garlic powder, (if honey is hot this will work better).

Place wings in a serving bowl. Pour honey over the wings. Toss to coat the wings. Serve.

SERVES 4

STUFFED CUCUMBER SLICES

1	1	long English cucumber
1 cup	250 ml	olive oil
⅓ cup	80 ml	lemon juice
2 tsp	10 ml	salt
½ tsp	3 ml	white pepper
1 cup	250 ml	minced smoked salmon
¼ cup	60 ml	mayonnaise
2 tsp	10 ml	Dijon mustard
		watercress leaves

Pare the cucumber and cut it in ⅓ " lengths. Using an apple corer remove the centre pulp and seeds. Place into a large mixing bowl.

Blend the oil, lemon juice, salt and pepper together, pour over the cucumbers cover and refrigerate for 2 hours, drain.

Blend the salmon, mayonnaise and mustard together. Stuff this mixture into the cucumbers. Slice the cucumbers into bite size pieces, place on a serving platter, garnish with the watercress and serve.

SERVES 6

Stuffed Cucumber Slices

CRAB STUFFED MUSHROOMS

36	36	large mushrooms
3 tbsp	45 ml	butter
½ lb	225 g	crab meat
2 tbsp	30 ml	flour
1 tbsp	15 ml	chives
1 tbsp	15 ml	Dijon mustard
3 tbsp	45 ml	lemon juice
2 tsp	10 ml	Worcestershire sauce
2 tsp	10 ml	basil
¼ cup	60 ml	sherry
⅓ cup	80 ml	light cream
1 cup	250 ml	Béarnaise Sauce (see page 108)

Wash the mushrooms and remove the stems. Boil the caps in lightly salted water, drain and cool. Mince the stems.

Heat the butter in a large skillet. Sauté the crab meat and mushroom stems. Sprinkle with flour and cook for 2 minutes. Add the remaining ingredients except the béarnaise sauce. Simmer until very thick.

Preheat the ovens broiler.

Stuff the caps with the crab mixture, place caps on a cookie sheet. Top each cap with a dollop of béarnaise sauce. Place under the broiler of your oven and brown. Serve very hot.

SERVES 6

ITALIAN DELIGHTS

1	1	loaf Italian bread
2 cups	500 ml	Mascarpone cheese
¾ cup	190 ml	crumbled Gorgonzola cheese
15-20	15-20	anchovy fillets
15-20	15-20	stuffed green olives

Slice the bread into thin slices, trim the crusts from the slice. Cut the slices into various shapes.

Cream the cheeses together and spread over the slices.

Roll the anchovy fillets around the olives and place one rolled olive on each slice.

SERVES 6

DUCK LINGUINE A LA ORANGÉ

1 quan	1	Saffron Pasta (see page 436)
2-3 lbs	1 kg	duckling
1 cup	250 ml	Beef Broth (see page 85)
2 cups	500 ml	white wine
6	6	oranges
2	2	lemons
3 tbsp	45 ml	flour
¼ cup	60 ml	sugar
¼ tsp	1 ml	cinnamon
¼ cup	60 ml	orange brandy
2 tbsp	30 ml	red currant jelly

Process the pasta as directed and cut into linguine noodles.

Season the duckling with a little salt and pepper. Place in a roasting pan and pour the broth and wine over the duckling. Zest the rinds of 3 oranges and 1 lemon. Squeeze the juice of the zested fruit over the duckling. Cover the duckling and roast in a preheated 400°F (200°C) for 1¼ hours or until the juices of the thigh run clear when pricked with a fork. Remove the duckling from pan. Strain the fat from the juice, reserve 3 tbsp (45 ml) of fat and discard the remainder.

Heat the reserved fat in a sauce pan. Add the flour and cook for 2 minutes over medium heat. Reduce the heat, add the juices from the duckling and simmer. In a second sauce pan caramelize the sugar (brown it but watch not to burn it). Add the brandy and the juices of the remaining oranges and lemon.

Stir in the cinnamon and jelly, whip into the sauce. Add the orange and lemon zest, continue to simmer for 10 minutes.

Remove the meat from the duck and coarse dice it, reserve the meat hot.

Cook the pasta al denté in a kettle of boiling salted water, drain. Place on serving plates. Top with duck meat and smother with the sauce. Serve.

SERVES 6

Duck Linguine a la Orangé

Monte Cristo Canapes

ESCARGOT TORTELLINI

¼ quan	0.25	Basic Pasta Dough (see page 426)
18	18	large escargots
1 tbsp	15 ml	butter
1	1	minced garlic clove
1	1	minced small onion
1 tbsp	15 ml	lemon juice
1 tsp	5 ml	basil
2 tbsp	30 ml	sherry
2 tsp	10 ml	Pernod
3 tbsp	15 ml	chopped parsley
⅓ cup	80 ml	half & half cream

Roll the dough thin, using a 3" round cookie cutter, cut 36 rounds. Cover the rounds with a damp cloth to prevent drying.

Cut the snails in half. In a skillet heat the butter, sauté the garlic and onion until tender. Add the escargot and continue to sauté for 1 minute. Add the lemon, basil, sherry and Pernod. Reduce the heat and simmer for 3 minutes. Stir in the parsley and cream. Remove from the heat and reserve.

Transfer the snails to the bowl and cool. Brush the pasta rounds with water. Place a ½ escargot on each round, fold and press the edges together to seal the rounds. Curl the ends around the filling and pinch together.

In 3 quarts of boiling salted water cook the tortellini until they float.

Reheat the sauce. Stir in the drained tortellini and serve.

SERVES 6

MUSHROOM OINKS

1 lb	450 g	large mushrooms
⅓ lb	130 g	sausage meat
½ cup	125 ml	fine seasoned bread crumbs
1 tbsp	15 ml	melted butter
1 cup	250 ml	Béarnaise Sauce (see page 108)

Wash the mushrooms, remove the stems from the caps and chop the stems fine. In a large skillet brown the sausage meat, when almost cooked through add the chopped mushrooms, cook thoroughly. Remove from heat, and drain any excess fat. Transfer mixture to a mixing bowl and cool to room temperature.

Blend the bread crumbs and butter in cooled sausage mixture. Stuff the sausage mixture into the mushroom caps. Place on a baking sheet and bake in a preheated 350°F (180°C) oven for 15 minutes.

Top each mushroom with a ½ tsp (3 ml) of béarnaise sauce. Increase oven temperature to broil and broil mushrooms for 2-3 minutes until sauce has browned. Serve very hot.

SERVES 6

MONTE CRISTO CANAPÉS

16	16	slices white bread
16	16	slices Parma ham (Prosciutto)
1 cup	250 ml	grated Swiss cheese
4	4	eggs
¼ cup	60 ml	half & half cream
4 tbsp	60 ml	butter

Trim the crusts from the bread.

Place 2 slices of ham and a sprinkling of cheese between two slices of bread. Cut into four diagonally.

Blend the eggs with the cream. Dip the bread sections in the eggs.

Heat the butter in small amounts in a skillet and fry the sandwich sections in the butter until golden brown. Serve at once very hot.

SERVES 4

Chef K's Shrimp in Apple Chocolate Sauce

Honey Paprika Prawns

CHEF K'S SHRIMP IN APPLE CHOCOLATE SAUCE

1 lb	450 g	large shrimp, peeled and deveined
3 tbsp	45 ml	butter
2 tbsp	30 ml	safflower oil
1 cup	250 ml	apples, peeled, cored, diced
3 oz	80 g	mushrooms
2 tbsp	30 ml	flour
1 cup	250 ml	light cream
¼ cup	60 ml	apple brandy (Calvados)
3 oz	80 ml	grated white chocolate

Butterfly the shrimp by making an incision with a small knife down the back. Heat the butter and oil together in a large skillet. Quickly sauté the shrimp in the oil. Remove and reserve hot in the oven.

Add the apples and mushrooms to the skillet. Sauté 3 minutes. Sprinkle with flour, cook for 2 minutes over low heat. Add the cream and brandy, simmer to a smooth sauce. Blend in the chocolate and cook for 1 minute. Pour sauce over shrimp and serve.

SERVES 4

HONEY PAPRIKA PRAWNS

½ cup	125 ml	honey
1 tbsp	15 ml	sweet paprika
2 tbsp	30 ml	Worcestershire sauce
2 tbsp	30 ml	soya sauce
1 tsp	5 ml	dried thyme leaves
1 tsp	5 ml	chili powder
¼ cup	60 ml	safflower oil
¼ cup	60 ml	sherry
1½ lbs	675 g	large shrimp

Whisk together the honey, paprika, Worcestershire, soya, thyme, chili, oil and sherry.

Shell and devein the shrimp. Butterfly the shrimp by cutting a slit down the back of the shrimp. Rinse under cold water and pat dry in paper towels.

Cover shrimp with the marinade sauce and marinate for 1 hour.

Place shrimp on a large baking sheet. Broil in a preheated oven broiler for 3 minutes, turn and continue to broil for an additional 3 minutes.

Place on a serving platter and enjoy.

SERVES 6

OYSTERS MARINARA

36	36	oysters
10 oz	300 ml	spinach
2 tbsp	30 ml	butter
1½ cups	375 ml	Marinara Sauce (see page 111)
1 cup	250 ml	bread crumbs
¼ cup	60 ml	freshly grated Romano cheese
¼ cup	60 ml	freshly grated Parmesan cheese

Shuck the oysters, reserve the liquid for the marinara sauce and remove the meat.

Clean and trim the spinach. Heat the butter in a large skillet and sauté the spinach. Place a little spinach on each oyster shell. Top with an oyster. Place 1 tsp (5 ml) of marinara sauce over each oyster.

Sprinkle each oyster with the bread crumbs and cheese. Bake for 10-12 minutes in a preheated 450°F (230°C) oven. Serve very hot.

SERVES 6

Cheese 'n' Beef Pinwheels

CHICKEN & SPINACH RAMEKINS

2 cups	500 ml	fine diced, cooked chicken meat
2 cups	500 ml	diced, cooked spinach, drained
5	5	eggs
¾ cup	180 ml	heavy cream
2 tbsp	30 ml	chopped fine parsley
1 tsp	5 ml	chopped chives
½ tsp	3 ml	basil leaves
2 tbsp	30 ml	butter

Blend the chicken and spinach. Fold in the eggs one at a time. Blend in the cream and herbs.

Butter six ramekin dishes with the butter. Fill each dish with an even amount of mixture. Place the dishes in a shallow baking pan. Fill with water around the ramekins to half full, be sure to not pour any water into the ramekins.Place in a preheated 350°F (180°C) oven and bake for 45 minutes.

Turn out onto warm plates and serve. Suggestion: Serve a little Mornay Sauce (see page 111) with these — it is a great finishing to the dish.

SERVES 6

PISTACHIO CHEESE BALLS

2 cups	500 ml	ricotta cheese
¼ cup	60 ml	freshly chopped parsley
½ cup	125 ml	finely diced red pimento
¼ tsp	1 ml	salt
¼ tsp	1 ml	cracked black pepper
2 cups	500 ml	shelled, crushed pistachio nuts

In a food processor, combine the ricotta, parsley, pimento, salt and pepper, process until smooth.

Remove and roll into tiny balls.

Place the pistachio nut meats into a mixing bowl and roll the cheese balls through to coat.

Place cheese balls on a waxed paper lined serving platter, refrigerate for 1 hour before serving.

SERVES 6

CHEESE 'N' BEEF PIN WHEELS

½ lb	225 g	cold roast beef
1 cup	250 ml	cream cheese
3 tbsp	45 ml	creamed horseradish
3 tbsp	45 ml	finely chopped chives
¼ cup	60 ml	sliced stuffed olives

Slice the beef into very thin slices.

Cream the cheese, horseradish and chives together.

Spread the cheese mixture over the beef slices. Roll the slices together in a jelly roll fashion, slice into bite size pieces.

Place on a waxed paper lined serving platter. Garnish each pin wheel with one slice of olive placed in the centre. Refrigerate for 1 hour before serving.

SERVES 6

LOBSTER WRAPS

1 lb	450 g	lobster tail meat
18	18	bacon slices

Cut the lobster in 36 equal pieces. Divide each slice of bacon in two. Wrap the lobster chunks with a bacon piece. Skewer with a toothpick.

Bake in a preheated 500°F (250°C) oven for 8-10 minutes. Serve very hot.

SERVES 6

Pistachio Cheese Balls

PICKLE SANDWICHES

12	12	large dill pickles
24	24	sliced spicy salami
3 tbsp	45 ml	Dijon mustard

Cut a hole through the centre of the pickles, lengthwise. (Use a small hollow rod, sharpened at one end).

Spread the salami with a thin coat of mustard then roll tightly together. Stuff rolled salami into the end of each pickle.

Slice the pickles into rounds, place on a serving platter and serve at once or cover and refrigerate until required.

SERVES 6

Pickle Sandwiches

SWEET 'N' SPICY CHICKEN WINGS

2¼ lbs	1 kg	chicken wings
1 cup	250 ml	honey
3 tbsp	45 ml	soya sauce
3 tbsp	45 ml	Worcestershire sauce
½ tsp	3 ml	ginger powder
½ tsp	3 ml	garlic powder

Wash and tip the chicken wings. Pat dry with paper towels and place in a large mixing bowl.

Whip the honey, soya sauce, Worcestershire sauce, ginger and garlic together. Pour over the chicken wings. Marinate for 2 hours.

Place the wings on a broiling pan. Reserve marinade. Broil in a preheated oven for 10 minutes. Turn wings over and brush with reserved marinade. Broil for additional 10 minutes. Serve hot.

SERVES 4

SMOKED SALMON RAVIOLI, PEPPER VODKA CHEESE SAUCE

½ quan	0.5	Lemon Pepper Pasta (see page 432)
1 tbsp	15 ml	butter
8 oz	225 g	minced smoked salmon
1	1	minced celery stalk
1	1	minced small carrot
¼ tsp	1 ml	salt
¼ tsp	1 ml	cracked black pepper
1	1	egg
¼ cup	60 ml	vodka
¼ cup	60 ml	Marsala wine
¼ cup	60 ml	tomato paste
1½ cups	375 ml	Chicken Broth (see page 77)
¼ cup	60 ml	freshly grated Romano cheese
2 tsp	10 ml	green peppercorns
1 tbsp	15 ml	chopped parsley

Process the pasta as directed. Roll into thin sheets. Cut out rounds of pasta with a 3" (7.5 cm) round cookie cutter. Cover with a damp cloth and reserve.

Heat the butter in a skillet. Sauté the carrot and celery until tender. Place into mixing bowl and cool to room temperature. Blend in the salmon, salt, cracked pepper, egg and cooled vegetables.

Place 1 teaspoon (5 ml) of filling on each round. Moisten the edges with a little water. Fold the pasta round in half. Press the edges to seal. Curl the edges around the filling and pinch together. Cook the pasta in a large kettle of boiling salted water for 2 minutes after they float to the top.

For the sauce, place the vodka and wine in a sauce pan. Whip in the tomato paste and stock and simmer to reduce to ⅔ volume. Whip in the cheese, peppercorns and parsley. Toss in the ravioli and serve.

SERVES 6

Smoked Salmon Ravioli, Pepper Vodka Cheese Sauce

Mussels Provençale

PARTY PICKLED SHRIMP

8 cups	2 L	boiling water
1¼ lbs	625 g	peeled and deveined jumbo shrimp
1	1	lemon
1	1	lime
1	1	diced carrot
3 cups	750 ml	diced onion
1 cup	250 ml	diced celery
¼ cup	60 ml	pickling spice
6	6	bay leaves
1 cup	250 ml	safflower oil
½ cup	125 ml	vinegar
¼ cup	60 ml	sherry
2 tbsp	30 ml	capers
2 tsp	10 ml	salt
¼ tsp	1 ml	red pepper sauce

Pour the boiling water over the shrimp and place in a kettle. Quarter the lemon and lime, add to the shrimp. Place the carrot, 1 cup (250 ml) of onion, celery and pickling spice into the shrimp. Bring to a boil, cook for 5 minutes. Drain. Cool shrimp.

In a large bowl place alternate layers of shrimp and onions. Top with bay leaves. Blend the remaining ingredients, pour over shrimp. Cover and refrigerate 12-24 hours. Drain the marinade and serve.

SERVES 12

MUSSELS PROVENÇALE

48	48	fresh mussels
2 tbsp	30 ml	butter
2	2	minced garlic cloves
1	1	fine diced onion
1	1	fine diced celery stalk
1 cup	250 ml	red wine
2 cups	500 ml	stewed tomatoes
½ tsp	3 ml	salt
½ tsp	3 ml	basil leaves
¼ tsp	1 ml	black pepper

Scrub and debeard the mussels.

Heat the butter in a sauce pan, add the garlic, onion and celery, sauté until tender. Add the remaining ingredients and simmer for 15 minutes.

Add the mussels and continue to simmer an additional 10 minutes. Serve.

SERVES 6

PICKLE BOATS

16	16	small dill pickles
½ cup	125 ml	minced ham
½ cup	125 ml	cream cheese
1 tsp	5 ml	prepared mustard
16	16	slices smoked salmon

Slice the pickles in half lengthwise, using a small melon baller scoop the pulp out of the pickles.

Blend the ham, cheese and mustard together. Place into a piping bag fitted with a large star tip. Pipe the mixture into the hollowed out pickles.

Cut the smoked salmon slices in half diagonally. Skewer each slice with a tooth pick and place in the centre of the pickle as to form a sail. Serve at once or refrigerate until ready for service.

SERVES 6

Party Pickled Shrimp

ORIENTAL WINGS

¼ cup	60 ml	soya sauce
¼ cup	60 ml	safflower oil
⅔ cup	160 ml	brown sugar
¼ cup	60 ml	lemon juice
¼ cup	60 ml	sherry
½ tsp	3 ml	each of ground ginger, dry mustard, onion powder, garlic powder
1 tsp	5 ml	salt
1 tbsp	15 ml	Worcestershire sauce
2¼ lbs	1 kg	chicken wings

Combine all the ingredients except the wings.

Wash and tip the wings. Pat dry with paper towels. Place wings on a broiling pan. Brush with sauce and broil for 10 minutes brushing with sauce twice. Turn wings over, brush with sauce. Broil an additional 10 minutes brushing with sauce two more times. Serve hot.

SERVES 4

CHORIZO FRITTERS

1 lb	454 g	raw chorizo sausage meat*
3	3	eggs
¼ cup	60 ml	milk
¼ cup	60 ml	flour
2 cups	500 ml	crushed corn flakes
3 cups	750 ml	safflower oil
1½ cups	375 ml	hot Creole Sauce (see page 121)

Shape the sausage meat into tablespoon size pieces.

Mix the eggs with the milk.

Dust the sausage with the flour, dip into the milk, and dredge in the corn flakes.

Heat the oil to 375°F (190°C). Fry the fritters in small batches until golden brown, reserve hot in the oven while the remainder cook.

Place on serving platter and serve with the Creole sauce on the side.

SERVES 4

*Chorizo sausage is a highly seasoned Spanish sausage available at most Hispanic meat markets or through a special order from your grocer.

JUMBO SHRIMP COCKTAIL

1	1	lemon
1	1	celery stalk
1	1	small onion
4 cups	1 L	water
1 cup	250 ml	white wine
1 tsp	5 ml	salt
1	1	bouquet garni*
24	24	tiger prawns, cleaned, deveined
4	4	Romaine lettuce leaves, trimmed
4	4	lemon wedges

SAUCE		
½ cup	125 ml	chili sauce
⅓ cup	80 ml	tomato catsup
⅓ cup	80 ml	prepared horseradish
2 tbsp	30 ml	lemon juice
1 tsp	5 ml	Worcestershire sauce

Cut the lemon in half. Coarse dice the celery and onion. Place in a large pot along with the water, wine, salt, and bouquet garni. Bring to a boil, reduce to a simmer. Add the prawns, simmer for 8 minutes. Drain, cool, then refrigerate.

Blend the sauce ingredients together.

Place the lettuce leaves into four champagne glasses or on chilled plates, top with 30 ml (2 tbsp) of sauce. Arrange six prawns around each glass. Garnish with lemon wedges.

SERVES 4

*A bouquet garni is: thyme, marjoram, peppercorns, bay leaf and parsley, tied together in a cheesecloth.

Jumbo Shrimp Cocktail

Mozzarella & Zucchini Sticks

MOZZARELLA STICKS

1 cup	250 ml	flour
1/2 tsp	3 ml	baking powder
1/8 tsp	0.5 ml	baking soda
3/4 tsp	4 ml	salt
pinch	pinch	white pepper
1 cup	250 ml	beer
4 cups	1 L	safflower oil
1	1	egg white
1 lb	454 g	mozzarella cheese, cut into sticks

In a mixing bowl, sift the dry ingredients together. Slowly add the beer. Whisk briskly. Let stand for 1½ hours.

Heat the oil to 190°C (375°F).

Whip the egg white into the batter. Dip the cheese sticks into the batter allowing any excess to run off.

Using a slotted spoon, place cheese sticks into hot oil. Fry 2½ - 3 minutes or until golden brown. Serve at once. Try using the Onion Dip with these (see page 34). Very good.

SERVES 6

ZUCCHINI STICKS

2	2	zucchini
2 cups	500 ml	bread crumbs
1 tsp	5 ml	salt
1/2 tsp	3 ml	each of pepper, paprika, oregano leaves, thyme leaves, basil leaves, onion powder, garlic powder
2	2	eggs
1/2 cup	125 ml	milk
1/3 cup	80 ml	flour
4 cups	1 L	safflower oil
1 1/2 cups	375 ml	Ranch Dip (see page 34)

Wash and trim the zucchini, cut into sticks. Blend the bread crumbs with the seasonings.

Mix the eggs with the milk. Place the flour in a small mixing bowl. Dust the sticks with flour, dip into egg mixture. Dredge in bread crumbs.

Heat the oil to 190°C (375°F). Fry the sticks in the oil in small batches. Serve with ranch dip on the side.

SERVES 6

THREE CHEESE BUCKWHEAT LINGUINE

1 quan	1	Buckwheat Pasta (see page 428)
⅓ cup	80 ml	Gorgonzola cheese
1 cup	250 ml	Mascarpone cheese
⅓ cup	80 ml	grated Romano cheese
½ cup	125 ml	half & half cream

Process the pasta as directed and cut into linguine. Cook pasta al denté in a large kettle of boiling salted water. Drain.

Blend the cheeses with the cream. Toss the hot noodles through the cheese sauce. Serve.

SERVES 6

PARTY VEGETABLE PLATTER & DIPS

1	1	broccoli head
1	1	cauliflower head
3	3	large carrots
1	1	small zucchini
2 cups	500 ml	cherry tomatoes
2 cups	500 ml	mushrooms

Wash, trim and cut the vegetables into bite size pieces. Arrange on a large serving platter. Cover and refrigerate while you prepare the dips.

Consider serving these dips with chips, pretzels or crackers.

Party Vegetable Platter

ONION DIP

1 cup	250 ml	cream cheese
1 cup	250 ml	sour cream
1 pkg	1 pkg	onion soup mix
2 tbsp	30 ml	chopped chives
1 tsp	5 ml	chili powder
1 tsp	5 ml	Worcestershire sauce

Cream the cheese together with the remaining ingredients. Cover and refrigerate.

Yields 500 ml (2 cups).

MEXICALI DIP

1 cup	250 ml	cream cheese
1/2 cup	125 ml	sour cream
2 tbsp	30 ml	minced green bell pepper
2 tbsp	30 ml	minced red bell pepper
1 tsp	5 ml	minced jalapeño pepper
1 tsp	5 ml	chili powder
1 tsp	5 ml	Worcestershire sauce
1/2 tsp	3 ml	salt

Blend the cheese together with remaining ingredients. Cover and refrigerate.

Yields 375 ml (1½ cups).

RANCH DIP

1 cup	250 ml	cream cheese
¼ cup	60 ml	buttermilk
¼ cup	60 ml	mayonnaise
2 tbsp	30 ml	minced chives
1 tbsp	15ml	lemon juice
¼ tsp	1 ml	salt
pinch	pinch	white pepper

Cream the cheese together with the remaining ingredients. Cover and refrigerate.

Yields 375 ml (1½ cups)

CLAM DIP

2 cups	500 ml	cream cheese
1 cup	250 ml	can minced clams
2 drops	2 drops	Tabasco™ sauce
¼ tsp	1 ml	salt
2 tsp	10 ml	minced onion
1 tsp	5 ml	lemon juice

Blend the cheese with the remaining ingredients. Cover and refrigerate.

Yields 750 ml (3 cups).

TUNA PISTACHIO BITES

16	16	slices pumpernickel bread
1 cup	250 ml	cooked, flaked tuna
2 tsp	10 ml	Dijon mustard
¼ cup	60 ml	mayonnaise
¼ cup	60 ml	butter
1 tbsp	15 ml	minced chives
½ cup	125 ml	shelled, crushed pistachio nuts
2	2	grated, hard cooked eggs

Trim the bread of all crusts.

Blend the tuna, mustard and mayonnaise together in a small bowl.

Cream the butter with the chives. Spread thinly on the bread. Roll the edges in the nuts. Place onto a baking sheet and fill the centres with the tuna.

Sprinkle with the eggs, place on a serving platter and serve.

SERVES 4

COQUILLE ST. JACQUES

2¼ lbs	1 kg	scallops, large
½ lb	225 g	bay shrimp
4 tbsp	60 ml	butter
1 cup	250 ml	mushrooms, sliced
3 tbsp	45 ml	flour
½ cup	125 ml	cream
½ cup	125 ml	Chicken Broth (see page 77)
½ cup	125 ml	white wine
½ tsp	3 ml	salt
½ tsp	3 ml	white pepper
2 cups	500 ml	mashed potatoes, hot
2 cups	500 ml	Gruyére cheese, grated

Wash the scallops and pat dry with a paper towel. Rinse the shrimp under cold water, reserve.

In a large skillet, heat the butter. Sauté the mushrooms. Add the flour and cook for 2 minutes over low heat. Add the cream, chicken broth and wine, simmer to thicken. Add the seasonings.

Add the scallops and shrimp. Cook for 10 minutes.

Pipe the potatoes around large scallop shells. Fill with mixture. Sprinkle with cheese.

Place in oven at 190°C (375°F) for 10 minutes.

Serve at once.

SERVES 4

Coquilles St. Jacques

PÂTÉS

If ground meat could have a wish, it would wish to become a pâté. Known as the most noble of all ground meats, pâtés bring a special presence of excitement to the table. They speak immediately to your guest that you really care; after all, a pâté is not easy to make, right? Not so with those found in *Simply Delicious Cooking 2*.

When served as an appetizer, light entrée or on a buffet, a good pâté will always attract those who enjoy quality and the finer things in life. For that special "perfect" occasion, serve the Chicken & Rice in Pastry. It is the guarantee to the success of your event.

Pâtés are the correct, anytime, every occasion food. They are the starters for the exceptional dinners when "the best is only the beginning." Then too, they are for the times when they form the main entrée as in our Tourtiere. Why, there are even pâté types for dessert, the Chocolate Rocky Road Terrine (see page 542). Pâtés are great when the game's on and no one wants to cook (try the Cold Veal Loaf). Or, when it comes to the ladies' afternoon tea, a very special hot pâté like the French Veal & Basil Mousse is exactly right. Therefore, one may begin and even end a dinner by serving only pâtés.

The best comment to make about pâtés is that they are relatively inexpensive to prepare, and are therefore suitable to even the most parsimonious budgets. Preparation time is kept low in most cases, so you may spend your time and saved money on your guests.

We have offered only ten pâtés within our pages, but they are ten of the very best. A pâté should speak volumes in taste, texture and in pleasure bestowed on the diner. These ten do so—loudly! Venture forth and inhabit taste as you never have before with *Simply Delicious Cooking 2*.

Chicken & Rice in Pastry

COLD VEAL LOAF

1½ lbs	675 g	lean veal, ground twice
1 tsp	5 ml	salt
½ tsp	3 ml	each of white pepper, paprika, thyme, oregano, basil
1 tbsp	15 ml	chili powder
2 tsp	10 ml	Worcestershire sauce
¼ cup	60 ml	ground saltines
1	1	egg, beaten
½ cup	125 ml	fine diced green bell peppers
½ cup	125 ml	fine diced onion
½ cup	125 ml	fine diced celery
1 cup	250 ml	fine diced carrots
½ cup	125 ml	chili sauce
¼ cup	60 ml	barbecue sauce

Combine the veal, seasonings, Worcestershire sauce, saltines, egg, vegetables and chili sauce. Spoon into an 11" (28 cm) loaf pan. Spread the barbecue sauce on top.

Bake for 1¼ hours in a preheated 350°F (180°C) oven.

Remove from oven, cool to warm, unmold and chill. Serve cold.

SERVES 6

JOHNNY'S QUEBECOIS TOURTIERE

3 tbsp	45 ml	butter
2	2	fine diced onions
3	3	minced garlic cloves
2 cups	500 ml	peeled, seeded and diced tomatoes
¾ lb	345 g	lean ground pork
¾ lb	345 g	fine diced beef
1 cup	250 ml	Beef Stock (see page 85)
2	2	bay leaves
¼ tsp	1 ml	each of allspice, cinnamon, nutmeg
1 tsp	5 ml	salt
½ tsp	3 ml	pepper
⅓ cup	80 ml	fine bread crumbs
1 quan	1	double crust pie dough
3 tbsp	45 ml	milk
1	1	egg

In a large skillet, heat the butter and sweat the onion and garlic. Add the tomatoes and cook for 3 minutes, covered. Add the pork and cook thoroughly. Add beef, stock, bay leaves and seasonings. Cover and simmer for 30 minutes. Uncover and continue to simmer until most of the liquid has evaporated. Stir in the bread crumbs. Cool mixture to room temperature.

Preheat the oven to 400°F (200°C).

Roll out the pastry, divide in two and line a 10" (25 cm) pie shell with one part. Fill with the mixture and cover with the remaining pastry. Crimp edges and cut a 1" (2.5 cm) hole in top. Make a tin foil chimney and fit into hole.

Mix milk with the egg and brush over pastry.

Bake for 10 minutes, then reduce the heat to 350°F (180°C) and continue to bake for 25 minutes. Rest the pie for 20 minutes before cutting, or cool and chill and serve.

SERVES 8

Cold Veal Loaf

Johnny's Quebecois Tourtiere

French Veal & Basil Mousse

CHICKEN & RICE IN PASTRY

This dish will take some preparation. It is worth every effort — enjoy the pleasures of it.

1 quan	1	Gourmet Crust (see page 455)
2 lbs	900 g	chicken
2 tsp	10 ml	salt
3 tbsp	45 ml	chopped parsley
½ cup	125 ml	butter
1	1	large minced onion
¾ cup	180 ml	rice
2 cups	500 ml	Chicken Stock (see page 77)
½ tsp	3 ml	marjoram
½ tsp	3 ml	thyme
¾ cup	180 ml	Chicken Velouté (see page 105)
¼ lb	115 g	cooked chopped mushrooms
3	3	hard cooked chopped eggs
1	1	egg yolk
2 tbsp	30 ml	light cream

Cut the chicken into ¾" (2 cm) pieces. Sprinkle the chicken fillets with the salt and 1 tbsp (15 ml) of parsley. Chill.

Heat ½ of the butter in a sauce pan; sauté ¼ of the onion until tender. Add the rice and chicken stock, cook the rice to tender. Cool.

In a second sauce pan, heat the remaining butter and sauté the remaining onions and allow to cool. Combine the cooked rice, fried onion, remaining parsley, mushrooms, chopped egg herbs and velouté. Roll out half the pastry into a rectangle. Place ¼ of the rice mixture on the pastry, leaving a ¾" (2 cm) rim from each edge. Top the rice with strips of salmon. Continue to make layers of rice then chicken.

You should finish with 4 layers of rice and 3 layers of chicken.

Roll out the remaining pastry a little larger then the first. Mix the egg yolk with the cream. Brush on the bottom layer edges. Place the second piece of dough on top. Brush the edges firmly to seal the edges. Cut away any excess pastry. Brush with egg mixture.

Cut a hole in the very centre of the dough to allow steam to escape. Decorate with excess dough. Brush with egg one final time. Bake in a preheated 400°F (200°C) oven for 20 minutes, cover with foil wrap and continue to bake for an additional 15 minutes. Remove and serve hot, warm or cold.

SERVES 8

FRENCH VEAL & BASIL MOUSSE

1½ lbs	675 g	lean veal, ground twice
1 tsp	5 ml	salt
¼ tsp	1 ml	white pepper
2 tsp	10 ml	fresh chopped basil
3	3	egg whites
¾ cup	180 ml	light cream
¼ cup	60 ml	sherry

In a food processor, combine the veal, salt, pepper, basil and egg whites. With the machine running slowly, add the cream and sherry.

Preheat oven to 350°F (180°C).

Spoon mixture into a greased 9" (23 cm) loaf pan or ring mold. Cover with waxed paper and place in a second pan containing 1" (2.5 cm) of water. Bake for 45 minutes. Remove from the oven and allow to stand for 10 minutes.

Unmold and serve with Wild Mushroom Sherry Sauce (see page 105).

SERVES 6

Chicken & Rice in Pastry

PÂTÉ IN PASTRY

1 quan	1	Gourmet Pâté Pastry (recipe follows)
1 cup	250 ml	grated cheddar cheese
4	4	eggs
2 tbsp	30 ml	butter
4 oz	115 g	sliced mushrooms
1	1	minced onion
1	1	minced garlic clove
1¼ lbs	565 g	ground lean veal
1¼ lbs	565 g	ground lean pork
1 lb	450 g	ground raw sausage meat
1 tbsp	15 ml	salt
½ tsp	3 ml	each of pepper, thyme, marjoram
4	4	blanched, julienne cut carrots
6	6	hard boiled eggs

Mix the pastry together with ½ cup (125 ml) cheese. Add one egg and knead into a very smooth dough.

Line a 13" x 4" (32 x 10 cm) loaf pan with foil wrap. Lightly grease the foil. Roll out ⅔ of the pastry, and line the loaf pan, extending the dough over the edges. Chill.

Melt the butter and sauté the onion, mushrooms and garlic until tender. Place in a large mixing bowl. Add the veal, pork, sausage meat and spices; blend well.

Beat the 3 eggs and set aside ¼ cup (60 ml). Add the remaining eggs to the meat mixture. Fill half the loaf pan with mixture. Arrange the carrots and hard boiled eggs on top. Top with the remaining meat mixture. Add the remaining cheese.

Roll out the pastry. Top the loaf pan and seal the edges. Decorate with any remaining pastry. Brush with final beaten egg. Bake in a 350°F (180°C) oven for 2 hours or the dough is brown. Remove from pan. Discard the foil. Serve hot or chill and serve cold.

GOURMET PÂTÉ PASTRY

1 cup	250 ml	sifted all purpose flour
¼ tsp	1 ml	salt
1 tsp	5 ml	baking powder
¼ cup	60 ml	shortening
¼ cup	60 ml	hot water
¼ cup	60 ml	butter
1 tsp	5 ml	lemon juice
1	1	beaten egg yolk

Sift the flour, salt and baking powder together. Cut in the shortening. Combine the hot water with the butter and lemon juice, then beat in the egg yolk. Work into the dry ingredients. Chill and use as required.

Pâté in Pastry

Mousse au Jambon

THREE MEAT PÂTÉ

1 lb	450 g	chicken meat
1¼ lbs	565 g	boneless fatty pork
1¼ lbs	565 g	boneless veal
3 tbsp	45 ml	sherry
1	1	egg
1 tsp	5 ml	salt
½ tsp	3 ml	pepper
½ tsp	3 ml	paprika
1 tsp	5 ml	thyme
1 tsp	5 ml	basil
8 oz	225 g	bacon slices

Process the meats in a chilled food processor until very fine. Place in a bowl and combine the sherry, egg, herbs and salt.

Line a 9" (23 cm) loaf pan with foil wrap. Grease the foil and line with bacon slices. Fill with mousseline mixture. Cover with a piece of buttered wax paper.

Place in water bath and bake in a preheated 250°F (130°C) oven for 3 hours. Remove and allow to set for 30 minutes. Chill overnight in the refrigerator.

Unmold and remove bacon. Wipe away excess fat. Slice and serve.

SERVES 6

MOUSSE AU JAMBON

2 tbsp	30 ml	gelatin, unflavoured
⅔ cup	160 ml	water
1¼ cups	310 ml	hot Béchamel Sauce (see page 112)
1 tsp	5 ml	Dijon mustard, prepared
½ tsp	3 ml	Worcestershire sauce
2 cups	500 ml	ground cooked ham
¼ cup	60 ml	minced onion
½ cup	125 ml	mayonnaise
½ cup	125 ml	whipping cream, whipped

Soften the gelatin in the water. Blend into the béchamel sauce along with the mustard and Worcestershire. Cool.

Fold in the ham, onion, mayonnaise and whipped cream. Pour into an oiled 2 quarts (2 L) mold. Refrigerate and chill until firm. Unmold and serve.

SERVES 8

LAMB AND VEAL TERRINE

⅓ cup	80 ml	safflower oil
1	1	minced onion
3	3	minced garlic cloves
1½ lbs	675 g	boneless lean lamb
1½ lbs	675 g	boneless lean veal
1 lb	450 g	bacon slices
⅓ cup	80 ml	sherry
2 tsp	10 ml	each of thyme, rosemary, sage, oregano
1 tbsp	15 ml	salt
½ tsp	3 ml	pepper
½ cup	125 ml	seasoned bread crumbs
2	2	bay leaves
3	3	eggs

Heat the oil in a skillet. Sauté the onion and garlic until tender. Place in a large bowl.

In a food processor, process the lamb, veal and half the bacon to very smooth. Blend with the onion. Add the remaining ingredients and blend thoroughly.

Grease a 9" (23 cm) loaf pan. Line with the remaining bacon. Spoon mousseline mixture into the pan. Lay the bay leaves on top.

Butter a piece of wax paper, and lay the buttered side down on top of the pâté. Place in a water bath and bake for 2 hours in a preheated 350°F (180°C) oven. Remove from the oven and cool for 30 minutes.

Refrigerate for 1-4 days before using. Unmold and remove bacon lining. Wipe away the excess fat. Serve.

SERVES 6

Chicken Liver Pâté

CHICKEN LIVER PÂTÉ

2 tbsp	30 ml	unflavoured gelatin
1 cup	250 ml	tomato, beef or chicken bouillon, cold
6 tbsp	90 ml	butter
1 lb	450 g	chicken livers
3 tbsp	45 ml	minced onion
½ tsp	3 ml	salt
1 tbsp	15 ml	Dijon mustard
½ tsp	3 ml	allspice
½ tsp	3 ml	garlic powder
½ tsp	3 ml	pepper
¼ cup	60 ml	Madeira
½ cup	125 ml	whipping cream

Dissolve gelatin in bouillon; bring to a boil and remove from heat. Pour half the liquid into a loaf pan and chill. Decorate chilled aspic, if desired.

Melt the butter in a sauce pan. Add the chicken livers and onion; sauté 7 minutes. Pour into a food processor. Add the remaining broth and balance of the ingredients. Process until very smooth. Ladle mixture into the loaf pan and refrigerate, covered with plastic wrap, for 6-8 hours.

Unmold by quickly dipping pan into hot water and running spatula around the sides. Serve.

SERVES 8

CHICKEN 'N' SHRIMP PÂTÉ

1⅛ lbs	510 g	boneless chicken
½ lb	225 g	ham
¾ lb	340 g	bacon
1	1	small minced onion
1½ lbs	675 g	peeled and deveined shrimp
1 cup	250 ml	fine bread crumbs
¾ cup	180 ml	light cream
2 tbsp	30 ml	chopped parsley
1 tsp	5 ml	salt
½ tsp	3 ml	white pepper
¼ cup	60 ml	white sweet vermouth

In a food processor, grind the chicken, ham and ¼ lb (115 g) of bacon along with the onion.

Fold together the shrimp, bread crumbs, cream, seasonings and vermouth.

Line an 8 cup (2 L) loaf pan or mold with half of the remaining bacon. Fill the mold with the mixture.

Cover with the remaining bacon. Cover with foil and set into a second pan 1" (2.5 cm) filled with water.

Bake in a preheated 375°F (190°C) oven for 3 hours. Drain off the fat. Cool, then chill. Unmold, and remove bacon and serve. Excellent with Béarnaise Sauce (see page 108).

SERVES 8

Chicken 'n' Shrimp Pâté

BARBECUE

Have you ever wondered why a man who otherwise has no knowledge of cooking suddenly becomes an expert when it comes to the back yard barbecue? Why does food grilled over an open flame seemingly taste just that much better? Well, in the next few pages you will find the answers to these perplexing questions. In this chapter of *Simply Delicious Cooking 2*, we have refined the art of barbecuing for you. No man is superior to the next: it could just be that he has learned the simple rules of the barbecue. To ensure the best finished product for yourself and your guests, these rules, like most, should never be broken.

Use the finest ingredients. This first rule of all cooking applies not only to food ingredients, but to each component of the process, including the charcoal. Charcoals made from woods of mesquite, hickory, alder or apple are best suited to barbecuing and grilling, and are preferable to those which are oil-based. Charcoal alone produces a mild smoke flavour and is suitable for lamb, seafood and fish. To impart a stronger smoke taste to beef, pork and game meats, use wood chips as well, made from the same material as the charcoal. Soak the wood chips in water for a half hour or longer before using them. Then, place the chips evenly over the charcoal. For short-term cookery, this combination will give you plenty of smoke for that "just right" flavour.

Using a covered grill will guarantee that the smoke flavour penetrates into the food rather than escaping into the air before it has seasoned the food. In addition, it is important to plan ahead. Follow your recipe and be sure to begin your fire at least 40 minutes before you begin barbecuing. Use only a grill that has been cleaned well and oiled in the same manner, and allow food ingredients to come to room temperature before barbecuing them. Use a hot fire to seal meats quickly, then transfer them to a cooler part of the grill to finish cooking. Fattier cuts of meat should be cooked over a drip pan placed directly upon the coals. Barbecue fish and seafood on the cooler area of your grill as these foods require no sealing.

By following these simple rules, you'll be rewarded with far better results than the weekend chef ever imagined. Remember, too, that if you have the luxury of an indoor grill (such as a Jenn-Air®), these recipes will provide you the same culinary pleasure inside your home, despite the temperate outdoors.

There are many barbecue recipes found throughout this book but the ones specific to this chapter are a sure "fire" way to the hearts of your guests. These recipes will make you a champion barbecue master.

From *Simply Delicious Cooking 2*, you can select such exquisite barbecue dishes as our Red Snapper in Raspberry Sauce or the Gourmet T's for a heartier appetite. You will find Skewered Swordfish exceptional and have great fun with New York's Folly. Whatever you choose, you're assured of great times, fantastic memories, and wonderful food that will always be *Simply Delicious.*

Pacific Coast Seafood Kebabs & Rhineland Ribs

GAS GRILL

SALMON STEAK DIABLE

1¼ cups	310 ml	white wine
¼ cup	60 ml	minced green onions
1¼ cups	310 ml	Demi-Glace Sauce (see page 123)
1 tsp	5 ml	Worcestershire sauce
½ tsp	3 ml	dry mustard
6 – 10 oz	6 – 300 g	salmon steaks, 1" (2.5 cm) thick
2 tbsp	30 ml	olive oil

In a small sauce pan, boil the wine and green onions together. Reduce by ⅓ the wine volume. Add the remaining ingredients, reduce heat and simmer for 5 minutes. Pass sauce through a sieve, and reserve warm.

Brush the steaks with the oil then grill the steaks over medium coals for 10 minutes, serve covered with sauce.

SERVES 6

RED SNAPPER IN RASPBERRY SAUCE

1 lb	450 g	raspberries
2 tsp	10 ml	cornstarch
1 tbsp	15 ml	lemon juice
2 tbsp	30 ml	honey
4 – 6 oz	4 – 170 g	red snapper fillets
3 tbsp	45 ml	olive oil
½ tsp	3 ml	salt
½ tsp	3 ml	white pepper

Purée the raspberries in a food processor, pass through a fine sieve. Pour into a sauce pan, and bring to a boil. Blend the cornstarch with the lemon juice, whisk into the sauce along with the honey. Simmer until thick.

Brush the fillets with the oil, then season them lightly with salt and pepper. Grill over medium heat for 5-6 minutes per side, brushing with sauce frequently.

Serve with the remaining sauce.

SERVES 4

TERIYAKI BABY BACK RIBS

4 – 12 oz	4 – 340 g	Danish back ribs
1 tsp	5 ml	pepper, salt, paprika, chili powder, onion powder, thyme leaves, garlic powder, oregano leaves, basil
½ cup	125 ml	water
⅓ cup	80 ml	soya sauce
3 tbsp	45 ml	olive oil
4 tbsp	60 ml	sherry
2 tsp	10 ml	ground ginger
2	2	minced garlic cloves
½ tsp	3 ml	salt
3 tbsp	45 ml	honey

Trim the ribs of any excess fat, then place them in a shallow baking pan.

Blend the seasonings together, sprinkle over ribs, pour the water in along the side of the pan. Cover and bake in a preheated 350°F (180°C) oven for 1¼ hours. Remove the ribs, cool, drain and pull away the back skin.

Blend the remaining ingredients forming a sauce.

Grill the ribs for 7 minutes per side over medium heat, brushing with the sauce, several times.

SERVES 4

Red Snapper in Raspberry Sauce

Grilled Kal Bi Chicken

GRILLED KAL BI CHICKEN

6 – 6 oz	6 – 170 g	boneless, skinless chicken breasts
⅓ cup	80 ml	soya sauce
3 tbsp	45 ml	sesame oil
3 tbsp	45 ml	sherry
½ cup	125 ml	minced scallions
2	2	minced garlic cloves
2 tsp	10 ml	minced fresh ginger
3 tbsp	45 ml	brown sugar

Flatten the chicken breasts and place them in a large shallow pan.

Combine the remaining ingredients together to form a marinade. Pour the marinade over chicken, and marinate for 3 hours. Drain the chicken and reserve marinade.

Grill over medium heat for 5-6 minutes per side, basting frequently with marinade.

SERVES 6

SIRLOIN TIP ROTISSERIE

4½ lbs	2 kg	sirloin tip roast
6	6	garlic cloves
1 cup	250 ml	olive oil
½ cup	125 ml	red wine
1 cup	250 ml	onion slices
1	1	bay leaf
1 tbsp	15 ml	sugar
1 tsp	5 ml	garlic powder
1 tbsp	15 ml	Worcestershire sauce
1 tbsp	15 ml	soya sauce
4 drops	4 drops	Tabasco™ sauce
¼ cup	60 ml	lemon juice

Cut 12 small incisions evenly around the roast. Slice the garlic cloves in half and insert a half in each incision. Place the roast in a shallow roasting pan.

Blend the remaining ingredients together, pour into a sauce pan. Bring to a boil, remove from heat and cool. Pour over the roast and marinate for 8 hours.

Insert the rotisserie spit through the roast and roast over medium low heat for 1½ to 2 hours, basting with marinade frequently. Carve and serve.

SERVES 8

Apricot Glazed Seafood Kebabs

APRICOT GLAZED SEAFOOD KEBABS

1 lb	454 g	salmon, cut in large cubes
½ lb	225 g	large peeled & deveined shrimp
½ lb	225 g	sea scallops
2 tbsp	30 ml	olive oil
1 cup	250 ml	dried apricots
1 cup	250 ml	water
2 tbsp	30 ml	granulated sugar
2 tsp	10 ml	Dijon mustard
¼ cup	60 ml	apple juice

Skewer the seafood with water soaked bamboo skewers alternating the salmon, shrimp and scallops.

In a sauce pan boil the apricots in the water for 5 minutes. Transfer apricots to a food processor and purée. Reserve the water.

Stir the sugar and mustard into the water. Pour over the apricots and blend.

Return to sauce pan and stir in the apple juice, heat but do not boil.

Brush the skewers with the oil and grill on medium coals for 5 minutes per side, brushing frequently with the sauce. Brush with sauce one final time before serving.

SERVES 4

Asian Barbecued Ribs

ASIAN BARBECUED RIBS

Sauce:		
½ cup	125 ml	hoisin sauce*
3 tbsp	45 ml	orange juice
3 tbsp	45 ml	sherry
1 tbsp	15 ml	peeled, minced fresh ginger
1	1	minced garlic clove
½ tsp	3 ml	Chinese five spice
2 tbsp	30 ml	soya sauce
2 tbsp	30 ml	red wine vinegar
1 tbsp	15 ml	Dijon mustard
1 tbsp	15 ml	chili paste*

Ribs:		
2¼ lbs	1 kg	baby back pork ribs
1 tbsp	15 ml	salt
1 tsp	5 ml	Chinese five spice
1 tsp	5 ml	pepper

Sauce:

Combine all the ingredients together in a mixing bowl, cover and refrigerate.

Ribs:

Cut the ribs into 5 bone sections. Combine the seasonings and sprinkle over ribs. Roast in a preheated 350°F (180°C) oven for ½ hour.

Grill ribs for 15 minutes over medium coals, brushing frequently with sauce. Brush 1 final time before serving.

SERVES 4

* Available at Asian stores or in the Oriental food section of any supermarket.

GRILLED ZUCCHINI

1 lb	450 g	zucchini
½ cup	125 ml	olive oil
½ tsp	3 ml	each of garlic powder, onion powder, thyme leaves, basil, pepper, salt

Wash the zucchini and trim the ends from each. Blanch for 3-5 minutes in boiling salted water. Cool, slice in half lengthwise, place in a shallow pan.

Combine the remaining ingredients together, pour over the zucchini and marinate for 1 hour.

Broil over grill for 10 or 15 minutes, turning and basting frequently.

SERVES 4

BACALHAU

¼ cup	60 ml	lemon juice
⅔ cup	160 ml	olive oil
1 tbsp	15 ml	garlic, minced
1 tsp	5 ml	salt
2 tsp	10 ml	Worcestershire sauce
½ tsp	3 ml	each of thyme, basil, oregano
4 – 6 oz	4 – 170 g	cod fillets or steaks

Blend the lemon, oil, garlic, salt, Worcestershire and seasonings together.

Place the cod in a shallow pan, pour marinade over, cover and refrigerate for 4 hours. Drain, and reserve marinade.

Grill fish for 10 minutes per inch of thickness, basting frequently with marinade. Serve at once.

SERVES 4

BARBECUED CHICKEN SALAD

2 tsp	10 ml	garlic cloves, minced
1 tsp	5 ml	salt
1 tsp	5 ml	cracked black pepper
2 tbsp	30 ml	red wine
1 tbsp	15 ml	lemon juice
⅓ cup	80 ml	olive oil
1 tsp	5 ml	Worcestershire sauce
1 tsp	5 ml	dried leaves of thyme, basil, sage, oregano, rosemary each
1	1	red bell pepper
1	1	yellow bell pepper
1	1	green bell pepper
2	2	red onions
1	1	large zucchini
4 – 4 oz	4 – 115 g	boneless, skinless chicken breasts

In a mixing bowl blend the garlic, salt, pepper, wine, lemon juice, oil, Worcestershire and seasonings.

Cut the peppers into quarters and remove the membranes and seeds. Slice the onion and zucchini into large slices. Place the vegetables in a shallow pan and pour half the marinade over. Pour the remaining marinade over the chicken and marinate both for 2 hours.

Grill the chicken over medium coals for 5 minutes, turn over and grill for an additional 5 minutes.

While chicken cooks, grill the vegetables for 6 minutes. Serve together.

SERVES 4

Barbecued Chicken Salad

Gourmet T's

GOURMET T'S

4 – 12 oz	4 – 340 g	T-bone steaks
1 tbsp	15 ml	minced onion
½ cup	125 ml	red currant jelly
½ cup	125 ml	port
2 tbsp	30 ml	red wine vinegar
1 tsp	5 ml	orange zest
1 tsp	5 ml	lemon zest
1 tsp	5 ml	mustard, dry
pinch	pinch	cayenne

Trim the steaks of any excess fat.

Combine the remaining ingredients in a sauce pan, reduce to half of its volume.

Grill the steaks to desired doneness, brushing steak with sauce frequently. Serve.

SERVES 4

SPANISH PINCHO MORUNO

1½ lbs	675 g	beef tenderloin
2 tsp	10 ml	granulated sugar
1 tsp	5 ml	black pepper
1 tsp	5 ml	minced garlic
1 tsp	5 ml	onion powder
½ cup	125 ml	garlic vinegar
½ cup	125 ml	red wine
1 cup	250 ml	olive oil
½ tsp	3 ml	each of chopped basil, dried thyme leaves, dried marjoram leaves
1 tsp	5 ml	salt

Trim the tenderloin and cut it into 1" (2.5 cm) cubes. Skewer the meat with bamboo skewers, then place them into a shallow pan.

Blend the remaining ingredients together forming a marinade. Pour the marinade over the beef, marinate refrigerated and covered for 6-8 hours. Drain, reserve marinade.

Grill skewers over medium heat until desired doneness is reached, brushing frequently with marinade.

SERVES 4

HONEY GARLIC YOGURT LAMB CHOPS

8 – 3 oz	8 – 90 g	frenched lamb chops
2	2	minced garlic cloves
3 tbsp	45 ml	liquid honey
¼ cup	60 ml	plain yogurt
1 tsp	5 ml	cracked black pepper

Trim the chops of any excess fat, place in a shallow pan.

Combine the garlic, honey, yogurt and pepper together. Pour over the chops and marinate for 8 hours.

Grill the chops over medium coals for 3 minutes per side, brushing with marinade as chops cook. Serve.

SERVES 4

SMOKING CHOPS

4 – 6 oz	4 – 170 g	smoked pork or veal chops
½ cup	125 ml	white wine sauce
¼ cup	60 ml	dark soya sauce
2 tbsp	30 ml	olive oil
½ tsp	3 ml	Worcestershire sauce
½ tsp	3 ml	dry hot English mustard
¼ tsp	1 ml	each of ground cinnamon, allspice, cloves
2 tsp	10 ml	brown sugar

Trim the chops of any excess fat. Place them into a shallow pan.

Combine the remaining ingredients together and pour the marinade over chops, marinate 2 hours covered and refrigerated. Drain, reserve marinade.

Broil the chops over low heat for 6 minutes per side, basting frequently with the marinade.

SERVES 4

CILANTRO GRILLED LAMB CHOPS

12 – 2 oz	12 – 60 g	lamb chops
1 tbsp	15 ml	chili powder
½ tsp	3 ml	each of oregano leaves, thyme leaves, basil leaves, onion powder, garlic powder, salt, white pepper, black pepper
¼ tsp	1 ml	cayenne pepper
½ cup	125 ml	butter
4	4	minced garlic cloves
½ cup	125 ml	fresh chopped cilantro
1 tsp	5 ml	Dijon mustard
1 tsp	5 ml	lemon zest
2 tbsp	30 ml	olive oil

Trim the chops of excess fat.

Combine the seasonings and sprinkle on the chops. Cover chops and refrigerate for 1 hour.

Combine the butter with the garlic, cilantro, mustard and lemon. Spread on a sheet of wax paper and roll in cigar shape. Freeze for 1 hour.

Brush the chops with the oil. Grill for 3 minutes per side.

Slice the butter in thick rounds. Place one round on each serving of 2 chops. Serve at once.

SERVES 6

Honey Garlic Yogurt Lamb Chops

Smoking Chops

BARBECUED LEG OF LAMB

4½ lbs	2 kg	leg of lamb
2 tsp	10 ml	garlic cloves, minced
1	1	finely diced onion
1	1	finely diced carrot
1	1	finely diced celery stalk
1 tsp	5 ml	salt
1 tsp	5 ml	cracked black pepper
2 tbsp	30 ml	red wine
1 tbsp	15 ml	lemon juice
⅓ cup	80 ml	olive oil
1 tsp	5 ml	each of dried leaves of thyme, basil, sage, oregano, rosemary

Have the butcher remove the bone from the lamb. Spread the meat out flat, trim away any excess fat.

Spread the meat with the garlic, onion, carrot, celery, salt and pepper. Roll together and tie tightly. Place in a shallow casserole dish.

Blend the remaining ingredients together, pour over lamb and marinate for 8 hours or overnight.

Barbecue for 50 minutes over low heat, turning every 8-10 minutes and basting with the marinade. Carve and serve.

SERVES 6

CHICKEN SPECIAL GRILL

4 – 6 oz	4 – 170 g	boneless, skinless chicken breasts
⅓ cup	80 ml	papaya juice
⅓ cup	80 ml	safflower oil
2 tsp	10 ml	salt
½ tsp	3 ml	garlic powder
½ tsp	3 ml	cracked black pepper
1 tbsp	15 ml	fresh chopped mint
1 cup	250 ml	sour cream
1 tbsp	15 ml	curry powder
1 tbsp	15 ml	lemon juice
¼ tsp	1 ml	sugar

Place the chicken in a shallow pan.

Combine the papaya juice, oil, 1 tsp (5 ml) salt, garlic powder, black pepper and the mint, pour over the chicken and marinate for 4 hours.

Blend the remaining ingredients together and chill while chicken marinates. Broil the chicken over medium coals for 7-8 minutes per side, brushing several times with the sour cream sauce. Serve.

SERVES 4

BROILED LOBSTER

4 – 1 lb	4 – 450 g	lobsters
⅔ cup	160 ml	butter
2 tbsp	30 ml	lemon juice
1 tsp	5 ml	grated lemon peel
2 tsp	10 ml	chopped cilantro
½ tsp	3 ml	sweet basil leaves

Split the lobsters along the back, remove sac and sand vein. Loosen the meat from the shell, crack the claws.

Heat the butter in a skillet and add the remaining ingredients.

Brush the lobster with the butter and broil for 15-20 minutes. Brush and turn frequently.

Serve any remaining butter along with lobster for your guests to dip their meat into.

SERVES 4

Cilantro Grilled Lamb Chops

Pacific Coast Seafood Kebabs

PACIFIC COAST SEAFOOD KEBABS

1 lb	454 g	salmon
½ lb	225 g	large shrimp
½ lb	225 g	large sea scallops
¼ cup	60 ml	flour
2	2	yellow bell peppers
16	16	large mushrooms
16	16	cherry tomatoes
¼ cup	60 ml	olive oil
¼ cup	60 ml	lemon juice
¼ cup	60 ml	white vermouth
1	1	minced garlic clove
1 tsp	5 ml	each of thyme, basil, chervil, oregano, marjoram, salt
½ tsp	3 ml	cracked black pepper
½ tsp	3 ml	ground cumin
1 tsp	5 ml	Worcestershire sauce
3 drops	3 drops	Tabasco™ sauce

Soak 8 large bamboo skewers in warm water for 30 minutes.

Dice the salmon. Peel and devein the shrimp. Dust the scallops with the flour.

Cut the yellow pepper into large dice. Wash the mushroom caps.

Skewer the seafood alternating with the pepper, mushrooms and tomatoes.

Combine the oil and remaining ingredients together. Grill five minutes per side brushing frequently with marinade. Brush one final time before serving.

SERVES 4

BARBECUED TUNA

6 – 8 oz	6 – 250 g	tuna steaks
2 tsp	10 ml	garlic cloves,minced
2 tbsp	30 ml	red wine
1 tbsp	15 ml	lemon juice
⅓ cup	80 ml	olive oil
1 tsp	5 ml	Worcestershire sauce
1 tsp	5 ml	salt
1 tsp	5 ml	cracked black pepper
1 tsp	5 ml	dried leaves of thyme, basil, sage, oregano, rosemary each

SAUCE:		
1 cup	250 ml	tomato catsup
½ cup	125 ml	molasses
1	1	minced medium onion
¼ cup	60 ml	packed brown sugar
2 tbsp	30 ml	lemon juice
1 tbsp	15 ml	chili powder
1 tsp	5 ml	each of salt, thyme leaves, oregano leaves, basil leaves
½ tsp	3 ml	each of paprika, onion powder, garlic powder
¼ tsp	1 ml	Tabasco™ sauce

Wash and pat dry the tuna. Place in a shallow pan.Combine the garlic, wine, lemon juice, oil, Worcestershire sauce and seasonings in a small mixing bowl. Pour over the tuna and marinate for 4 hours.

SAUCE:

Combine all the ingredients together in a mixing bowl.

Grill the fish for 5-6 minutes per side depending on thickness, brushing often with the barbecue sauce. Brush one final time just before serving.

SERVES 6

Barbecued New York Striploins

HONEY GRILLED VEGGIES WITH HONEY GARLIC RANCH SAUCE

SAUCE:		
1	1	garlic clove
2	2	egg yolks
1 tsp	5 ml	dry mustard
pinch	pinch	cayenne pepper
¾ cup	190 ml	olive oil
2 tsp	10 ml	honey
1½ tbsp	28 ml	lemon juice
¼ cup	60 ml	buttermilk
⅓ cup	80 ml	freshly grated Parmesan cheese
1 tbsp	15 ml	minced chives
½ tsp	3 ml	cracked black pepper
VEGGIES:		
4	4	medium carrots
2	2	large zucchini
2 tbsp	30 ml	olive oil
2 tbsp	30 ml	liquid honey
1 tsp	5 ml	basil
1 tbsp	15 ml	toasted sesame seeds (optional)
16	16	cherry tomatoes

SAUCE:
Place the garlic, egg yolks, mustard, and cayenne in a blender or food processor. With the machine running, slowly add the oil in a thin stream until mixture reaches the consistency of mayonnaise.Stir in the honey, lemon juice, buttermilk, cheese, chives and pepper.

VEGGIES:
Pare the carrots. Slice the vegetables into thick lengthwise slices.Blend the oil, honey and basil together, pour over the vegetables and marinate for 30 minutes. Grill the vegetables for 8 minutes, transfer to a serving platter, sprinkle with sesame seeds, garnish with cherry tomatoes and serve with the sauce placed in the centre.

SERVES 4

Honey Grilled Veggies with Honey Garlic Ranch Sauce

BARBECUED NEW YORK STRIPLOINS

½ cup	125 ml	red wine vinegar
1 tbsp	15 ml	Worcestershire sauce
1 tsp	5 ml	each of basil leaves, thyme leaves, oregano leaves
½ cup	125 ml	tomato catsup
2	2	minced garlic cloves
½ tsp	3 ml	liquid smoke flavouring
1 tbsp	15 ml	sugar
6 – 8 oz	6 – 225 g	New York striploin steaks

In a sauce pan, combine all the ingredients except the steaks.

Trim all the fat from the steaks. Cut away the small gristle strip, this will prevent the steaks from curling while cooking. Pour marinade over steaks and refrigerate, covered for 6 hours.

Grill the steaks over medium coals to desired doneness. Brush frequently with marinade.

SERVES 6

SWEET AND SOUR BARBECUED MONKFISH

3 lbs	1.3 kg	monkfish fillets
½ cup	125 ml	olive oil
¼ cup	60 ml	tarragon vinegar
2 tsp	10 ml	Worcestershire sauce
½ tsp	3 ml	ground ginger
1 tbsp	15 ml	brown sugar
2 tbsp	30 ml	sherry
3 tbsp	45 ml	soya sauce
½ tsp	3 ml	garlic powder

Arrange the fish fillets in a shallow baking pan.

Combine the remaining ingredients together to form a marinade, pour the marinade over fish. Marinate covered and refrigerated for 1 hour. Drain and reserve marinade.

Grill the fish over medium coals for 10 minutes, brushing with the marinade. Place on a serving platter, brush one final time with marinade before serving.

SERVES 6

Honey Lemon Pork Steaks

RHINELAND RIBS

4½ lbs	2 kg	pork side or back ribs
2 tsp	10 ml	salt
1½ cups	375 ml	Beef Stock (see page 85)
¼ cup	60 ml	catsup
2 tbsp	30 ml	brown sugar
3 tbsp	45 ml	red wine
¼ tsp	1 ml	ground allspice
¼ tsp	1 ml	caraway seeds
2 tbsp	30 ml	Worcestershire sauce
pinch	pinch	cayenne
1 tsp	5 ml	grated lemon peel
1 tbsp	15 ml	cornstarch
2 tbsp	30 ml	cold water

Trim the ribs of any excess fat. Place them on a shallow baking sheet. Sprinkle with salt, then bake them in a preheated 300°F (160°C) oven for 2 hours.

In a sauce pan combine the remaining ingredients except the cornstarch and water. Heat to boiling, blend the cornstarch with the water and add to the sauce. Simmer until sauce thickens.

Transfer the ribs to a charbroiler, cook 10 minutes per side basting frequently with the sauce. Serve.

SERVES 6

EXOTIC PRAWN KEBABS

1½ lbs	675 g	prawns
⅓ cup	80 ml	soya sauce
⅓ cup	80 ml	olive oil
⅓ cup	80 ml	sherry
½ tsp	3 ml	each of onion powder, garlic powder, ground ginger, pepper

Peel and devein the prawns, skewer with bamboo skewers. Place in a shallow pan.

Blend the remaining ingredients together, pour over prawns and marinate for 30 minutes.

Grill over hot coals for 3-5 minutes per side.

SERVES 4

HONEY LEMON PORK STEAKS

½ cup	125 ml	chopped cilantro
1 tbsp	15 ml	olive oil
1 tbsp	15 ml	honey
1 tbsp	15 ml	lemon juice
1 tsp	5 ml	cracked black pepper
1 tsp	5 ml	grated lemon rind
4 – 6 oz	4 – 170 g	pork steaks

Combine the cilantro, oil, honey, lemon juice, pepper and rind in a small mixing bowl.

Grill the pork steaks over medium coals for 4 minutes. Turn steaks over, cover with sauce and continue to grill an additional 4 minutes. Cover with remaining sauce and serve.

SERVES 4

Rhineland Ribs

The Chef's Barbecued Ribs

GRILLED CHICKEN BREASTS

6 – 6 oz	6 – 170 g	boneless, skinless chicken breasts
½ cup	125 ml	olive oil
3 tbsp	45 ml	tarragon vinegar
1 tbsp	15 ml	lemon juice
1 tsp	5 ml	garlic salt
½ tsp	3 ml	chopped cilantro

Place the chicken breasts in a large shallow pan.

Combine the remaining ingredients, pour this marinade over the chicken, cover and refrigerate for 2 hours. Drain, reserving the marinade.

Grill the chicken for 7-8 minutes per side depending on the thickness of the breast, brushing with marinade. Serve.

SERVES 6

SKEWERED SWORDFISH

2 lbs	900 g	swordfish
3 tbsp	45 ml	garlic vinegar
⅓ cup	80 ml	olive oil
1 tsp	5 ml	grated lemon peel
½ tsp	3 ml	each of onion powder, garlic powder, oregano
1 tsp	5 ml	cracked bay leaves
1 tbsp	15 ml	chopped cilantro
1 tsp	5 ml	salt

Cut the swordfish into 1" (2.5 cm) cubes, skewer with bamboo skewers, place in a shallow pan.

Combine the remaining ingredients together and pour over fish. Marinate in the refrigerator covered for 2 hours.

Broil over medium heat for 10 minutes, turning and basting with marinade frequently.

SERVES 6

THE CHEF'S BARBECUED RIBS

RIBS:		
6 – 12 oz	6 – 340 g	Danish back ribs
3 tbsp	45 ml	olive oil
1 tsp	5 ml	each of salt, cracked black pepper, paprika, chili powder

SAUCE:		
3 tbsp	45 ml	olive oil
2 tbsp	30 ml	minced onion
2 tbsp	30 ml	minced green peppers
2 tbsp	30 ml	minced celery
1	1	minced garlic clove
¼ cup	60 ml	white wine
¼ tsp	1 ml	black pepper
½ tsp	3 ml	oregano leaves
½ tsp	3 ml	ground cumin
3 tbsp	45 ml	brown sugar
1¼ cups	310 ml	tomato purée
½ tsp	3 ml	hickory smoked salt

RIBS:

Place the ribs in a shallow pan, brush with oil and sprinkle with seasonings. Bake in a preheated 300°F (160°C) oven for 2 hours.

SAUCE:

While ribs cook, heat the oil in a sauce pan. Add the onion, green peppers, celery and garlic, sauté until tender. Blend in the remaining ingredients. Bring sauce to a boil, reduce heat and simmer for 20 minutes.

Remove ribs from oven, remove back skin and cut into serving portions. Grill the ribs over medium heat for 6-8 minutes per side. Brush heavily with sauce during cooking, and one final time just before serving.

SERVES 6

BUFFALO BURGERS

BURGERS:		
1 lb	450 g	lean ground buffalo meat
4 oz	120 g	ground pork, fatty
1	1	egg
2 tbsp	30 ml	fine bread crumbs
2 tbsp	30 ml	minced onion
1 tbsp	15 ml	Dijon mustard
1 tsp	5 ml	Worcestershire sauce

SAUCE:		
3 tbsp	45 ml	oil
¼ cup	60 ml	minced onion
¼ cup	60 ml	minced green pepper
¼ cup	60 ml	minced celery
3 cups	750 ml	tomatoes, peeled, seeded, chopped
1 tbsp	15 ml	hickory smoked salt
3 tbsp	45 ml	wine vinegar
½ tsp	3 ml	hot mustard
⅓ cup	80 ml	tomato paste
½ tsp	3 ml	each of basil, thyme, oregano, savory, paprika, garlic powder, pepper,
⅓ cup	80 ml	brown sugar

BURGER:

Place all the ingredients in a large mixing bowl and blend thoroughly. Form into patties, and place onto a baking sheet covered with wax paper. Cover with wax paper, and refrigerate until required.

SAUCE:

Heat the oil in a sauce pan, add the vegetables and sauté until tender. Add all of the remaining ingredients, reduce heat and simmer until liquid reaches one third its original volume. Grill the burgers over medium heat brushing with sauce frequently. Serve hot with extra sauce on your kaiser rolls.

SERVES 4

LIME VEAL CHOPS WITH TOMATO SALSA

CHOPS:		
4 – 6 oz	4 – 170 g	veal chops
3 tbsp	45 ml	lime juice
2 tbsp	30 ml	olive oil
2 tbsp	30 ml	sour cream
2 tsp	10 ml	sugar
¼ tsp	1 ml	salt
½ tsp	3 ml	crushed red chili peppers

SALSA:		
4	4	large peeled, seeded diced tomatoes
1	1	finely diced small onion
2	2	finely diced jalapeños
¼ cup	60 ml	fresh chopped cilantro
2 tbsp	30 ml	lime juice
½ tsp	3 ml	salt
¼ tsp	1 ml	cracked black pepper

CHOPS:

Trim the chops of any excess fat.

Combine the remaining ingredients together and pour over chops, marinate for 3 hours. Grill chops for 5 minutes per side over medium coals, brushing with marinade.

SALSA:

Combine the ingredients together in a mixing bowl. Cover and marinate for 3 hours.

Plate the chops, cover with salsa and serve.

SERVES 4

Lime Veal Chops with Tomato Salsa

Barbecued Ribs Cajun Style

STEAK 'N' LOBSTER

A perennial favourite, without the restaurant price.

4 – 4 oz	4 – 115 g	tenderloin fillets
4	4	bacon rashers
4 – 4 oz	4 – 115 g	rock lobster tails
⅓ cup	80 ml	melted butter
½ tsp	3 ml	each of onion powder, caraway seeds, coriander seeds, thyme leaves, oregano leaves, basil leaves, chervil, paprika
1 tsp	5 ml	garlic powder
1 tbsp	15 ml	chili powder
3 tbsp	45 ml	rock salt
1 cup	250 ml	Béarnaise Sauce (see page 108)

Wrap the filets with 1 rasher of bacon. Hold firm with toothpicks.

Split the lobster through the middle cutting through. Pull meat from shell and spread on top of shell. Brush with some of the butter. Bake in a preheated 400°F (200°C) oven for 15-20 minutes, or until cooked through.

While lobster cooks, combine the seasonings, sprinkle over the fillets. Broil the fillets for 7 minutes per side for medium done steaks. Less for rare, longer for well done.

Serve the steak with the béarnaise sauce. Serve the lobster with the remaining hot butter. Small lobster butter dishes work best to keep butter very hot.

SERVES 4

Steak 'n' Lobster

BARBECUED RIBS CAJUN STYLE

Sauce:

1 cup	250 ml	tomato catsup
½ cup	125 ml	molasses
1	1	minced medium onion
¼ cup	60 ml	packed brown sugar
2 tbsp	30 ml	lemon juice
1 tbsp	15 ml	chili powder
1 tsp	5 ml	each of salt, thyme leaves, oregano leaves, basil leaves
½ tsp	3 ml	each of paprika, onion powder, garlic powder
¼ tsp	1 ml	Tabasco™ sauce

Ribs:

2¼ lbs	1 kg	Danish or baby back pork ribs
½ tsp	3 ml	each of salt, paprika, thyme leaves, oregano leaves, white pepper, black pepper, cayenne pepper, onion powder, garlic powder
1 tbsp	15 ml	chili powder

Sauce:

In a food processor, combine all the ingredients thoroughly. Pour into a mixing bowl and reserve.

Ribs:

Cut the ribs into 5 bone sections.

Combine the seasonings. Sprinkle on the ribs and then rub into the meat. Refrigerate for 1 hour. Bake the ribs in a preheated 350°F (180°C) oven for ½ hour. Grill ribs for 15 minutes over medium coals brushing frequently. Brush 1 final time and serve.

SERVES 8

JUST PEACHY MONKFISH

6 – 6 oz	6 – 170 g	monkfish fillets
2 tbsp	30 ml	olive oil
2 tsp	10 ml	basil leaves
2 cups	500 ml	peach slices
1 cup	250 ml	water
2 tbsp	30 ml	sugar
2 tsp	10 ml	Dijon mustard
1 tsp	5 ml	cornstarch
1 tbsp	15 ml	lemon juice
¼ cup	60 ml	apple juice

Brush the fillets with the oil and sprinkle with basil.

In a sauce pan boil the peaches in the water for 5 minutes. Transfer peaches to a food processor and purée. Reserve the water. Stir the sugar and mustard into the water. Mix the cornstarch with the lemon juice, add to the water and simmer until thick. Pour over the peaches and blend.

Return to sauce pan and stir in the apple juice, heat but do not boil.

Grill the monkfish tails for 10 minutes brushing with sauce. Brush one final time with sauce just before serving.

SERVES 6

FRUIT VEAL STEAKS

6 – 6 oz	6 – 170 g	veal steaks
2 tbsp	30 ml	olive oil
1 tbsp	15 ml	basil
¼ cup	60 ml	sugar
¼ cup	60 ml	water
¼ tsp	1 ml	ground cinnamon
2	2	cloves
1 tbsp	15 ml	lemon zest
1 tbsp	15 ml	orange zest
1 cup	250 ml	sliced strawberries, fresh
1 cup	250 ml	sliced peaches, fresh
1 cup	250 ml	blueberries, fresh
2 tsp	10 ml	lemon juice

Trim the steaks of any excess fat. Brush with oil and sprinkle with basil. Grill over medium coals to desired doneness.

Combine the sugar, water, cinnamon, cloves and fruit zest together in a small sauce pan, bring to a boil, reduce heat and simmer into a thick syrup.

In a mixing bowl combine the remaining ingredients, add the syrup and spoon over the steaks and serve.

SERVES 6

HONEY BARBECUED SALMON

3 tbsp	45 ml	butter
3 tbsp	45 ml	oil
1	1	minced medium onion
1	1	minced garlic clove
⅔ cup	160 ml	tomato catsup
⅔ cup	160 ml	liquid honey
¼ cup	60 ml	cider vinegar
1 tbsp	15 ml	Worcestershire sauce
½ tsp	3 ml	each of thyme leaves, oregano leaves, basil leaves, paprika, pepper, chili powder, salt
½ tsp	3 ml	liquid smoke
4 – 6 oz	4 – 170 g	boneless salmon fillets 1" (2.5 cm) thick

Heat the butter with 2 tbsp (30 ml) of oil in a sauce pan. Add the onion and garlic and sauté until tender.

Add the catsup, honey, vinegar, Worcestershire, seasonings and smoke flavouring. Simmer until sauce is thick and glossy. Cool.

Brush the salmon with the remaining oil. Grill over medium coals 5 minutes per side, brushing frequently with sauce. Brush 1 final time before serving.

SERVES 4

Just Peachy Monkfish

Salmon with Cilantro Pesto

QUAGLIE ALLA TOSCANO (BARBECUED QUAIL)

12	12	quail
½ cup	125 ml	olive oil
3 tbsp	45 ml	white wine vinegar
1 tsp	5 ml	garlic powder
½ tsp	3 ml	cracked black pepper
2 tsp	10 ml	chopped cilantro
½ tsp	3 ml	each of fresh rosemary, tarragon, oregano, thyme, basil, chopped

Split the quail in half and place into a shallow pan.

Combine the remaining ingredients in a mixing bowl, pour over the quail, marinate 2 hours at room temperature. Drain and reserve the marinade.

Grill quail over medium heat for 10-15 minutes basting frequently with the marinade. Serve.

SERVES 6

SALMON WITH CILANTRO PESTO

SAUCE:		
1½ cups	375 ml	fresh cilantro chopped packed
6	6	minced garlic cloves
⅓ cup	80 ml	toasted pine nuts
⅔ cup	160 ml	grated Parmesan cheese
1 tsp	5 ml	salt
½ tsp	3 ml	pepper
¾ cup	180 ml	olive oil

FISH:		
4 – 6 oz	4 – 170 g	salmon fillets
2 tbsp	30 ml	olive oil
½ tsp	3 ml	salt
½ tsp	3 ml	white pepper

SAUCE:

Combine all the ingredients in a food processor except the oil, blend until well incorporated. Slowly add the oil until a thick mayonnaise type sauce is formed, reserve until required.

FISH:

Brush the fillets with oil and season with salt and pepper. Grill the fillets over medium heat for 5-6 minutes per side. Serve with a dollop of sauce on each fillet.

SERVES 4

Roasted Grilled Bell Peppers with Macadamia Pesto

Okey's Lamb Racks

OKEY'S LAMB RACKS

4	4	frenched lamb racks
¼ cup	60 ml	olive oil
¼ cup	60 ml	lemon juice
¼ cup	60 ml	white vermouth
1 tsp	5 ml	each of thyme, basil, chervil, oregano, marjoram, salt
½ tsp	3 ml	cracked black pepper
½ tsp	3 ml	ground cumin
1 tsp	5 ml	Worcestershire sauce
3 drops	3 drops	Tabasco™ sauce

Trim the lamb racks of any excess fat, place into a shallow pan.

Combine the remaining ingredients together, pour over the lamb racks and marinate for 8 hours.

Grill the lamb racks for 5 minutes per side over high coals. Insert a meat thermometer into one, transfer to a cooler part of the grill, cover grill and continue to cook until thermometer registers 160°F (66°C) for medium, longer for well done. Brush with marinade occasionally. Serve.

SERVES 4

NEW YORK'S FOLLY

4 – 8 oz	4 – 225 g	New York strip steaks
½ cup	125 ml	red wine
2 tbsp	30 ml	lemon juice
2	2	minced garlic cloves
¼ cup	60 ml	olive oil
1 tsp	5 ml	each of thyme leaves, basil leaves, oregano, paprika, onion powder
2 tsp	10 ml	cracked black pepper
½ tsp	3 ml	salt or ¼ tsp (1 ml) hickory smoked salt

Trim the steaks of excess fat, remove the strip of gristle along the fat edge to prevent the steak from curling while grilling. Place the steaks in a shallow pan.

Combine the remaining ingredients together pour over the steaks, marinate refrigerated and covered for 6-8 hours.

Drain steak, reserve marinade. Cook the steaks over medium heat on a charbroiler to desired doneness, brushing several times during cooking.

SERVES 4

ROASTED GRILLED BELL PEPPERS WITH MACADAMIA PESTO

2	2	red bell peppers
2	2	green bell peppers
2	2	yellow bell peppers
¾ cup	190 ml	olive oil
1 cup	250 ml	fresh chopped basil
2	2	minced garlic cloves
1 cup	250 ml	chopped, roasted, and salted macadamia nuts
¼ cup	60 ml	fresh grated Parmesan cheese

Place the peppers on a baking sheet and roast in a preheated 400°F (200°C) oven until the skins blister. Place in a paper bag and allow to steam for 20 minutes.

Remove from bag and peel away the skin. Cut into quarters, remove seeds.

In a food processor or blender, blend ¼ cup (60 ml) of oil, basil, garlic, nuts and cheese. With the machine running, slowly pour in the remaining oil.

Grill the quartered peppers over medium heat for 6 minutes. Place on serving plates and top with sauce. Serve.

SERVES 6

SALMON STEAKS WITH PIÑON BUTTER

4 – 6 oz	4 – 170 g	salmon steaks
¼ cup	60 ml	olive oil
2 tbsp	30 ml	red wine
2 tbsp	30 ml	lemon juice
2 tbsp	30 ml	minced chives
1	1	minced garlic clove
2 tbsp	30 ml	chopped cilantro
¼ cup	60 ml	butter
¼ cup	60 ml	finely chopped pine nuts

Wash and pat dry the salmon, place into a shallow pan.

Mix the oil, wine, lemon juice, chives, garlic and cilantro together in a small mixing bowl, pour over steaks and marinate for 3 hours covered and refrigerated.

Blend the butter with the pine nuts, spoon onto waxed paper and roll. Refrigerate for 3 hours.

Grill the fish for 5 minutes per side, brushing with marinade. Place onto serving plate, slice the butter and place a large dollop on each.

SERVES 4

HICKORY SMOKED 'TATERS

1½ lbs	675 g	new potatoes
½ cup	125 ml	olive oil
1 tbsp	15 ml	hickory smoked salt

Wash and brush the potatoes. Boil in a large kettle with salted water until tender but still firm. Drain the potatoes then cool them to room temperature. Slice them into ¼ inch slices. Place on a baking sheet.

Brush the potatoes with the oil and sprinkle with the salt.

Grill over a hot grill 3 minutes per side. Serve.

SERVES 4

FIRE STEAK

6 – 10 oz	6 – 300 g	New York striploin steaks
1 tsp	5 ml	garlic granules
2 tsp	10 ml	black pepper
½ tsp	3 ml	each of cayenne pepper, oregano leaves, thyme leaves, crushed rosemary, basil leaves, onion powder, salt

Trim the steaks of fat and remove the strip of grizzle along the edge (prevents curling while cooking).

Blend the seasonings together and rub into steak. Leave steaks for 30 minutes.

Cook over medium coals to desired doneness.

SERVES 6

Salmon Steaks with Piñon Butter

Fire Steak

SOUPS

The mark of a good cook is not how elegant a meal appears, from his or her labours, but how well the meal is prepared. Nothing expresses this excellence like a delicious bowl of soup.

The age-old expression "all of nature's goodness on one spoon" comes to mind when one is served a hearty bowl of soup. One could not express it truer, for as the meats, vegetables and seasonings simmer, the aroma alone gives the beholder a sense of goodness. After all, Mom has always known that a bowl of homemade chicken soup will make you feel better. Perhaps she didn't understand that the slow simmering of the meat and vegetables drew out all of the nutritional value into the broth. She just knew that it worked and this is what she cared about.

Today, soup still holds the foremost place in most cooks' hearts, for they know that the making of the soup is the best time spent in the kitchen. An entire meal may be prepared to have it consumed within an hour. Although soup may take only minutes to prepare, hours of simmering are often required to complete the exquisite process. All the while, the soup's fragrance wafts through the house like the king of potpourri.

Whether your soup is prepared as a starter course or as the main meal, those presented in this chapter are among the finest; they are both international and local in style, but all are out of this world in flavour! Your soups can be as memorable as any other dish, as they should be.

With the exception of shark's fin and alligator meat, all ingredients can be found at your local supermarket. Be sure to use the freshest and finest ingredients available. Soup is not a dish to compromise on quality. When an appetizer is not served, soup sets the pace for the remainder of the meal. Inferior soup suggests that the courses following it may be of the same lesser quality. One who compromises on soup will do so with the other dishes of the meal.

Whether your menu requires a purée, cream, bisque, chowder, or bouillon variety of soup, you'll find them all within the pages of this chapter. The soup du jour, when made with love, time and one of our recipes, will, as always, be *Simply Delicious*.

Ship to Shore Soup

POTAGES DOYEN

⅔ cup	170 ml	twice ground raw chicken
1 tsp	5 ml	grated onion
¼ tsp	1 ml	each of pepper, basil, thyme, paprika
½ tsp	3 ml	salt
1	1	egg white
⅛ cup	30 ml	whipping cream
6 cups	1.5 L	Chicken Broth (see page 77)
⅓ cup	90 ml	butter
⅓ cup	90 ml	flour, all purpose
2 cups	500 ml	half & half cream
1 tsp	5 ml	salt
¼ tsp	1 ml	white pepper
1½ cups	375 ml	diced cooked chicken
2 cups	500 ml	blanched peas

In a mixing bowl combine the ground chicken, onion, seasonings, egg white and cream. Press through a fine sieve and roll into small balls.

Bring 2 cups (500 ml) of the broth to a boil, drop the balls in the broth, reduce heat and simmer for 10 minutes. Remove the meatballs.

Heat the butter in a large sauce pan, stir in the flour and cook over low heat for 2 minutes.

Add the remaining broth, cream, salt and pepper, simmer for 10 minutes.

Divide the soup into two smaller pots, add the diced cooked chicken to one and 1 cup (250 ml) of peas to the other. Simmer each for 5 minutes, then purée in a food processor separately, return to soup pots and continue to simmer for an additional 5 minutes.

Stand a small saucer upright in a serving bowl, ladle the chicken soup on one side of the saucer and the pea soup on the other, remove the saucer quickly. Sprinkle with meat balls and the remaining peas, serve at once.

SERVES 6

Potages Doyen

MINESTRONE MILANESE

3 tbsp	45 ml	butter
2	2	minced garlic cloves
½ cup	125 ml	sliced onion
½ cup	125 ml	diced celery
½ cup	125 ml	diced green bell pepper
½ cup	125 ml	mushrooms
½ cup	125 ml	diced zucchini
3	3	pared, diced, medium potatoes
2 cups	500 ml	peeled, seeded, diced tomatoes
5 cups	1.25 L	Chicken Broth (see page 77)
2 cups	500 ml	cooked, diced chicken
2 tsp	10 ml	Worcestershire sauce
1 tsp	5 ml	basil
½ tsp	3 ml	thyme
½ tsp	3 ml	oregano
1 tsp	5 ml	salt
2 cups	500 ml	cooked penne noodles
1 cup	250 ml	freshly grated Parmesan cheese

Heat the butter in a large kettle or pan. Add the garlic, onion, celery, bell peppers, mushrooms and zucchini, sauté until tender.

Add the potatoes and tomatoes and sauté 5 minutes.

Pour in the chicken broth along with the diced chicken, Worcestershire sauce, basil, thyme, oregano and salt. Simmer gently 15-20 minutes (or until potatoes are cooked), yet firm.

Stir in the noodles and cheese. Cook for 2 minutes longer. Serve.

SERVES 8

Minestrone Milanese

Shrimp Bisque Bretonne

FISH BROTH OR STOCK

4½ lbs	2 kg	fish trimmings and bones
1	1	diced onion
3	3	large diced carrots
3	3	diced celery stalks
1	1	bouquet garni (see Glossary)
12 cups	3 L	water

Place the fish trimmings and bones into a large kettle or Dutch oven. Add the vegetables, bouquet and water.

Heat gently without boiling. Simmer for 2 hours. While stock simmers, remove any scum which may rise to the top.

Strain through a fine sieve then a second time through a cheesecloth.

Use as required.

YIELDS 8 CUPS (2 L)

SHRIMP BISQUE BRETONNE

3 tbsp	45 ml	grated onion
3 tbsp	45 ml	grated celery
3 tbsp	45 ml	grated carrot
4 tbsp	60 ml	finely diced red bell pepper
¼ cup	60 ml	thinly sliced mushrooms
½ cup	125 ml	butter
1 lb	450 g	peeled & deveined shrimp
2¼ cups	625 ml	Fish Stock (preceding recipe) or Chicken Stock (see page 77)
½ cup	125 ml	sherry
4 tbsp	60 ml	flour, all purpose
1 cup	250 ml	heavy cream
1 cup	250 ml	cooked, very small shrimp

In a large kettle sauté the onion, celery, carrot, pepper, mushroom in 4 tbsp (60 ml) butter until tender. Add the peeled shrimp, sauté for 5 minutes.

Add the stock and boil 15 minutes.

Purée in a food processor, and return to the kettle. Add the sherry, simmer 5 minutes.

Heat the remaining butter in a small sauce pan, add the flour and cook for 2 minutes over low heat. Whisk in the cream and simmer until very thick. Whip into the soup and simmer for an additional 5 minutes.

Ladle soup into bowls and garnish with the small shrimp. Serve at once.

SERVES 6

VELOUTÉ À LA CHAMPENOISE

2 cups	500 ml	pared, diced potatoes
1½ cups	375 ml	diced celery
½ cup	125 ml	butter
½ cup	125 ml	flour, all purpose
6 cups	1.5 L	Chicken Stock (see recipe this page)
1½ tsp	8 ml	salt
½ tsp	3 ml	white pepper
¾ cups	190 ml	fine diced ham
½ cup	125 ml	blanched, very fine diced carrots
½ cup	125 ml	blanched, very fine diced celery

Place the potatoes in a small sauce pot, fill with water and boil until tender, purée in a food processor.

Place the diced celery in a sauce pot, fill with water and boil until tender, purée in a food processor.

In a sauce pan, melt the butter, add the flour and stir, cooking for 2 minutes over low heat.

Add the chicken stock, salt and pepper and stir. Simmer for 30 minutes or until soup has thickened.

Divide the soup into two smaller pots, into one blend the potato purée. Blend the celery purée into the second. Simmer both for 10 minutes.

Stand a small saucer upright in a serving bowl, ladle the potato soup on one side of the saucer and the celery on the other, remove the saucer quickly. Sprinkle with ham, carrots and celery, serve at once.

SERVES 6

ARTICHOKE SOUP

4	4	artichokes
4 cups	1 L	Chicken Stock (see recipe this page)
3 tbsp	45 ml	butter
3 tbsp	45 ml	flour, all purpose
2 cups	500 ml	milk

Remove the stems from the artichokes. Remove the bottom leaves and trim the top. Par boil the artichokes in boiling water until tender. Plunge into cold water. Drain and spread the leaves. Open the artichokes with your fingers and remove the choke by scraping with a spoon.

Heat the chicken stock in a kettle. Add the artichokes and simmer for 1 hour. Transfer the artichokes to a food processor and process into a purée. Return the purée to the soup. Continue to simmer.

Heat the butter in a small sauce pan, add the flour and cook 2 minutes over low heat. Whip into the soup. Add the milk and simmer until thick. Taste, adjust seasonings if required, serve hot.

SERVES 4

CHICKEN BROTH OR STOCK

2¼ lbs	1 kg	meaty chicken bones
10 cups	2.5 L	cold water
2	2	coarsely chopped celery stalks
2	2	coarsely chopped large carrots
1	1	coarsely chopped onion
1	1	bouquet garni (see Glossary)
1 tsp	5 ml	salt

Place the bones in a large kettle or Dutch oven. Add the water and remaining ingredients; bring to a simmer. Simmer uncovered for 3-4 hours, skimming any scum or grease that may rise to the top.

Remove the meat (reserve and use as required), bones (discard), bouquet (discard) and vegetables (discard). Strain through a cheesecloth or fine sieve.

Chill the stock and remove any fat from the surface.

Allow stock to chill for 24 hours before using. Use for soups and sauces, or as required.

YIELDS 6 CUPS (1.5 L)

Velouté à la Champenoise

Tom Kar Gai

FRENCH CANADIAN PEA SOUP

This soup has a large yield, so freeze what you don't require.

1 lb	450 g	chick peas
1	1	ham bone
3½ qts	4 L	water
3	3	finely diced leeks
3	3	finely diced stalks celery
2	2	finely diced carrots
½ lb	225 g	diced ham
		salt, only if required
½ tsp	3 ml	white pepper

Soak the chick peas in water overnight or for 8 hours. Place into a large kettle with the ham bone and cover with the water. Bring to a boil, reduce to a simmer and add the vegetables. Simmer for 3½-4 hours.

Discard bone. Add the ham and simmer for 15 minutes more. Taste, adjust seasonings. Serve very hot.

SERVES 10

TOM KAR GAI

1 tsp	5 ml	minced ginger root
3 tbsp	45 ml	butter
3 tbsp	45 ml	flour, all purpose
4 cups	1 L	Chicken Broth (see page 77)
2 cups	500 ml	half & half cream
2 cups	500 ml	diced, cooked chicken meat
½ cup	125 ml	coconut milk
2 tbsp	30 ml	chopped cilantro (coriander)
		lime slices for garnish

In a sauce pan sauté the ginger root in the butter, stir in the flour and cook for 2 minutes.

Pour in the chicken broth and simmer until soup begins to thicken. Add the cream, chicken, coconut and continue to simmer for 20 minutes.

Stir in the cilantro and serve, garnish by floating lime slices on top.

SERVES 6

French Canadian Pea Soup

LE POT AU FEU

The traditional French stock pot. Is it a meal or is it a soup? Why not make it both.

1 lb	450 g	beef soup bones
4 tbsp	60 ml	oil
2¼ lbs	1 kg	roast beef – any cut
4	4	carrots
2	2	turnips
2	2	leeks
2	2	Spanish onions
3	3	celery stalk
1	1	parsnip
1 tsp	5 ml	salt
1	1	bouquet garni (see Glossary)

Place the bones in a roaster and roast in a preheated 400°F (200°C) oven until the bones brown.

Heat the oil in a large kettle, sear the roast on all sides in the oil. Transfer the bones to the kettle with the roast. Cover the roast with 12-16 cups (3-4 L) of water.

Pare and coarse dice the vegetables, add to the pot. Add the salt and bouquet garni.

Reduce the heat and simmer gently for 3½ – 4 hours. Skim any scum which will rise to the top to keep the broth clear.

Remove the meat and vegetables, reserve hot.

Strain the broth. Carve the roast and serve with the vegetables, pour the broth over.

SERVES 8

BISQUE D'ECREVISSES CARDINAL

5 lbs	2 kg	crayfish
10 cups	2.5 L	water
4 tbsp	60 ml	butter
1	1	finely diced medium onion
1	1	minced garlic clove
1	1	finely diced celery stalk
4 tbsp	60 ml	flour, all purpose
1 cup	250 ml	peeled, seeded, diced tomatoes
3 oz	80 ml	tomato paste
⅓ cup	80 ml	sherry
½ tsp	3 ml	salt
¼ tsp	1 ml	pepper
1 cup	250 ml	whipping cream

Place the crayfish in a large kettle. Cover with the water. Bring to a boil and boil for 30 minutes. Remove the crayfish and allow to cool. Remove the tail meat from the crayfish, reserve the meat, return the shells to water.

Simmer the crayfish shells until the water has reduced to 4 cups (1 L). Strain the broth reserving it. Discard the shells.

In a large sauce pan heat the butter. Sauté the onion, garlic and celery until tender. Sprinkle with flour and cook for 2 minutes over low heat.

Pour the crayfish broth over the vegetables. Add the tomatoes, tomato paste, crayfish tails, sherry, salt and pepper. Simmer for 15 minutes. Transfer the soup to a blender and purée. Return to the pot and continue to simmer for 5 minutes.

Whip in the cream and simmer for an additional 10 minutes. Serve very hot.

SERVES 4

Cream of Fennel

KUMMEL SUPPE

2 tbsp	30 ml	butter
1	1	finely diced Spanish onion
1	1	finely diced medium carrot
2	2	finely diced celery stalks
2 tbsp	30 ml	flour, all purpose
1 tsp	5 ml	caraway seeds
5 cups	1.25 L	Beef Broth (see page 85)
2 cups	500 ml	cooked elbow macaroni

Heat the butter in a large sauce pan. Add the vegetables and sauté until tender. Sprinkle with flour and caraway. Cook until the vegetables and flour turn brown.

Add the broth and simmer until soup thickens slightly. Stir in the macaroni and simmer for 5 minutes. Serve hot.

SERVES 4

CREAM OF FENNEL

2½ cups	625 ml	minced fennel
4 cups	1 L	Chicken Stock (see page 77)
3 tbsp	45 ml	butter
3 tbsp	45 ml	flour, all purpose
2 cups	500 ml	cream

Place the fennel in a large sauce pan cover with the chicken stock. Simmer for 30 minutes. Strain reserving the liquid and fennel.

Purée the fennel in a food processor or pass through a food mill. Return the fennel to the broth.

In a small sauce pan heat the butter and add the flour, cook for 2 minutes over low heat. Add the cream and cook into a thick sauce.

Whip the sauce into the soup. Reheat to very hot.

SERVES 6

SHIP TO SHORE SOUP

⅔ cup	170 ml	twice ground chicken
1 tsp	5 ml	grated onion
¼ tsp	1 ml	each of pepper, basil, thyme, paprika
½ tsp	3 ml	salt
1	1	egg white
⅛ cup	30 ml	whipping cream
6 cups	1.5 L	Fish Broth (see page 76) or Chicken Broth (see page 77)
1 tbsp	15 ml	butter
¾ cup	190 ml	diced lobster meat
1 cup	250 ml	peeled and deveined shrimp
½ cup	125 ml	button mushrooms
1 cup	250 ml	cooked long grain rice

In a mixing bowl combine the meat, onion, seasonings, egg white and cream. Press through a fine sieve and roll into small balls.

Bring 2 cups (500 ml) of the broth to a boil, drop the balls in the broth, reduce heat and simmer for 10 minutes. Remove the meatballs.

Heat the butter in a Dutch oven or large kettle, sauté the seafood and mushrooms together. Add the remaining broth, chicken and rice, reduce heat and simmer for 10 minutes. Serve.

SERVES 6

WATERCRESS SOUP

A nice peppery winter soup

10 oz	280 ml	washed and chopped watercress
4 tbsp	60 ml	butter
¼ cup	60 ml	onion – grated
3 tbsp	45 ml	flour, all purpose
3 cups	750 ml	Chicken Stock (see page 77)
2 cups	500 ml	whipping cream
½ tsp	3 ml	salt
¼ tsp	1 ml	pepper
⅛ tsp	pinch	cayenne

Sauté the watercress, butter and onions together. Sprinkle with flour and cook for 2 minutes over low heat.

Add stock, cream and seasonings. Simmer for 30 minutes. Serve very hot.

SERVES 4

CONSOMMÉ ANJOU

⅔ cup	170 ml	twice ground deer meat
1 tsp	5 ml	grated onion
¼ tsp	1 ml	each of pepper, basil, thyme, paprika
½ tsp	3 ml	salt
1	1	egg white
⅛ cup	30 ml	whipping cream
6 cups	1.5 L	Game Broth (see page 85)
1½ cups	375 ml	asparagus tips
1 cup	250 ml	cooked, long grain rice

In a mixing bowl combine the meat, onion, seasonings, egg white and cream. Press through a fine sieve and roll into small balls.

Bring 2 cups (500 ml) of the broth to a boil, drop the balls in the broth, reduce heat and simmer for 10 minutes. Remove the meatballs.

Heat the remaining broth in a large kettle or Dutch oven, add the asparagus, rice and meat balls, simmer for 10 minutes, serve.

SERVES 6

Ship to Shore Soup

TACO SOUP

2 lbs	900 g	lean ground beef
3 tbsp	45 ml	safflower oil
2	2	jalapeños seeded, diced
1	1	spanish onion, diced
2 cups	500 ml	tomatoes, peeled, seeded, diced
3 cups	750 ml	Beef Broth (see page 85)
2 cups	500 ml	V-8™ juice
1 tbsp	15 ml	cumin
1 tbsp	15 ml	chili powder
1 tsp	5 ml	salt
1½ cups	375 ml	cheddar cheese, grated
		tortilla chips

In a dutch oven or a large kettle, fry the beef in the oil. Add the peppers and onion. Sauté until tender.

Add the tomatoes, broth, juice and seasonings. Bring to a boil. Reduce heat and simmer for 15 minutes.

Pour soup into bowls, garnish with tortillas and cheese and serve

SERVES 6

BAKED BEAN SOUP

8 oz	225 g	navy beans
8 cups	2 L	Chicken Stock (see page 77)
2 cups	500 ml	tomato juice
¼ lb	125 g	diced bacon
1	1	finely diced Spanish onion
2	2	finely diced celery stalks
2	2	finely diced carrots
¼ cup	60 ml	tomato paste
1 tbsp	15 ml	chili powder
1 tsp	5 ml	salt
¼ tsp	1 ml	black pepper

Soak the beans in cold water for 6-8 hours. Drain. Place the beans in a large kettle, cover with chicken stock, simmer the beans for 2½ hours. Add the tomato juice.

Sauté the bacon in a skillet and add to it the onion, celery and carrots, continue to sauté until all are tender. Drain the excess fat and add the bacon and vegetables to the soup.

Stir in the tomato paste and seasonings. Continue to simmer for 1 hour longer. Serve very hot.

SERVES 8

CHEESE AND CHICKEN TORTELLINI IN BRODO

½ quan	0.5	Basic Pasta Dough (see page 426)
½ lb	225 g	finely diced, cooked chicken meat
1 cup	250 ml	ricotta cheese
1	1	egg
½ tsp	3 ml	basil
¼ tsp	1 ml	nutmeg
¼ tsp	1 ml	salt
¼ tsp	1 ml	pepper
8 cups	2 L	hot, strong Chicken Broth (see page 77)

Process the pasta as directed. Roll into thin sheets. Cut out pasta rounds with a 3" (7.5 cm) round cookie cutter. Cover with a damp cloth and reserve.

In a mixing bowl blend the chicken, ricotta, egg and seasonings. Place a teaspoon of filling on each pasta round. Moisten the edge with a little water. Fold the pasta round in half. Press the edges to seal. Curl the edges around the filling and pinch together. Place half the broth in a large kettle, bring to a boil and cook the pasta for 2 minutes or until they float.

Spoon equal amounts of tortellini into soup bowls. Cover with the remaining hot chicken broth. Serve.

SERVES 4

Cheese & Chicken Tortellini in Brodo

Taco Soup

Gulyasleves (Goulash Soup)

BEEF OR GAME BROTH OR STOCK

2¼ lbs	1 kg	meaty beef bones or veal bones**
¼ cup	60 ml	olive oil
10 cups	2.5 L	cold water
2	2	coarsely chopped celery stalks
2	2	coarsely chopped large carrots
1	1	coarsely chopped onion
1	1	bouquet garni (see Glossary)
1 tsp	5 ml	salt

Place the bones in a roaster and cover with the oil. Bake in a preheated 350°F (180°C) oven for 1 hour or until the bones are well browned. Transfer to a large kettle or Dutch oven.

Add the water and remaining ingredients; bring to a simmer. Simmer uncovered for 3-4 hours, skimming any scum or grease that may rise to the top.

Remove the meat (reserve and use as required), bones (discard), bouquet (discard) and vegetables (discard). Strain through a cheesecloth or fine sieve.

Chill the stock and remove any fat from the surface.

Allow stock to chill for 24 hours before using. Use for soups and sauces, or as required.

YIELDS 6 CUPS (1.5 L)

**For veal stock, do not brown the meat bones.

NOTE: To make game broth, substitute deer or moose bones for the beef or veal bones.

Old Fashion Alphabet Soup

GULYASLEVES (GOULASH SOUP)

½ lb	225 g	cooked beef roast
¼ lb	115 g	cooked pork roast
¼ lb	115 g	smoked ham
3 tbsp	45 ml	butter
3 tbsp	45 ml	oil
1	1	diced Spanish onion
1	1	diced celery stalk
1	1	diced red bell pepper
3 tbsp	45 ml	flour, all purpose
2 cups	500 ml	peeled, seeded and diced tomatoes
6 cups	1.5 L	rich Beef Stock (see recipe this page)
1 tsp	5 ml	caraway seeds

Slice the meats then shred.

Heat the butter and oil together in a large sauce pan. Add the vegetables and sauté until tender. Sprinkle with flour and cook 5 minutes or until the flour caramelizes.

Stir in the tomatoes and stock. Add the meats and simmer gently for 90 minutes. Sprinkle with caraway and simmer 5 minutes longer. Serve very hot.

SERVES 8

OLD FASHION ALPHABET SOUP

2 tbsp	30 ml	safflower oil
1	1	onion, diced fine
2	2	carrots, pared, diced fine
3	3	celery stalks, diced fine
2 cups	500 ml	cooked beef, diced
6 cups	1½ L	Beef Broth (see recipe this page)
2 cups	500 ml	tomatoes, peeled and seeded
½ tsp	3 ml	salt
¼ tsp	1 ml	pepper
⅓ cup	80 ml	alphabet noodles

Heat the oil in a large pot or dutch oven.

Add the vegetables and sauté until tender.

Add the beef, broth, tomatoes, salt and pepper. Bring to a boil. Add the noodles. Cover and reduce heat. Simmer for 10 minutes.

Serve very hot

SERVES 6

Cream of Chicken with Two Olives

Potages À L'Andalouse

CREAM OF CHICKEN WITH TWO OLIVES

3 tbsp	45 ml	butter
3 tbsp	45 ml	flour, all purpose
2½ cups	625 ml	Chicken Stock (see page 77)
2 cups	500 ml	half & half cream
2 cups	500 ml	diced, cooked chicken meat
¼ cup	60 ml	sliced, stuffed olives
¼ cup	60 ml	sliced, pitted black olives

Heat the butter in a 3 quart sauce pan. Sprinkle with flour and cook for 2 minutes over low heat. Add the chicken stock and simmer for 10 minutes. Add the cream, chicken meat, continue to simmer for an additional 10 minutes. Stir in the olives and simmer 1 additional minute.

Serve very hot or very cold. When serving cold stir in 2 tbsp (30 ml) of extra cream per serving just before serving.

SERVES 6

POTAGES À L'ANDALOUSE

4 cups	1 L	peeled, seeded, diced tomatoes
1	1	finely diced onion
2	2	bay leafs
2	2	cloves
2	2	sprigs parsley
2	2	sprigs marjoram
1	1	celery stalk
6	6	peppercorns
2 tsp	10 ml	sugar
1 tsp	5 ml	Worcestershire sauce
¼ tsp	1 ml	salt
¼ tsp	1 ml	white pepper
pinch	pinch	nutmeg
1 cup	250 ml	cooked long grain rice
3 tbsp	45 ml	finely diced red bell pepper
3 tbsp	45 ml	finely diced yellow bell pepper
3 tbsp	45 ml	finely diced green bell pepper

Simmer the tomatoes, onions, bay leaves, cloves, parsley, marjoram, celery, peppercorns and sugar together for 30 minutes. Press through a sieve, add the seasonings, and return to the pot to simmer for 5 minutes.

Stir in the rice and simmer for 3 minutes.

Ladle into soup bowls and garnish with the diced peppers.

SERVES 4

BROCCOLI & CHEDDAR SOUP

¼ cup	60 ml	butter
¼ cup	60 ml	flour, all purpose
3 cups	750 ml	Chicken Broth (see page 77)
3 cups	750 ml	milk
½ tsp	3 ml	salt
½ tsp	3 ml	white pepper
2 cups	500 ml	broccoli florets, blanched
3 cups	750 ml	sharp cheddar, graded

In a large pot or dutch oven, heat the butter, add the flour and reduce the heat. Cook 2 minutes.

Add the broth, milk, salt and pepper. Bring to a boil. Reduce heat and simmer for 10 minutes.

Stir in the broccoli and cheese. Continue to simmer for an additional 5 minutes.

Serve soup at once.

SERVES 6

CONSOMMÉ ADÈLE

⅔ cup	170 ml	twice ground chicken
1 tsp	5 ml	grated onion
¼ tsp	1 ml	each of pepper, basil, thyme, paprika
½ tsp	3 ml	salt
1	1	egg white
⅛ cup	30 ml	whipping cream
6 cups	1.5 L	Chicken Broth (see page 77)
¾ cup	190 ml	peas
2	2	pared, finely diced carrots

In a mixing bowl combine the meat, onion, seasonings, egg white and cream. Press through a fine sieve and roll into small balls.

Bring 2 cups (500 ml) of the broth to a boil, drop the balls in the broth, reduce heat and simmer for 10 minutes. Remove the meat balls.

Bring the remaining broth to a boil, reduce to simmer, add the peas and carrots and simmer, for 10 minutes. Add the meat balls and continue to simmer for an additional 5 minutes. Serve soup very hot.

SERVES 4

SEAFOOD GUMBO

¼ cup	60 ml	safflower oil
1	1	Spanish onion, diced
2	2	green bell peppers, diced
3	3	celery stalks, diced
½ lb	225 g	hot Italian sausage, sliced
3 tbsp	45 ml	flour
2 cups	500 ml	tomatoes, peeled, seeded, chopped
3 cups	750 ml	water or fish stock
1 cup	250 ml	raw rice
2 tsp	10 ml	salt
½ tsp	3 ml	each of oregano leaves, thyme leaves, paprika, black pepper, garlic powder, onion powder, chili powder
2 cups	500 ml	sliced okra
½ lb	225 g	shrimp, peeled and deveined
½ lb	225 g	crab meat
½ lb	225 g	lobster meat
½ lb	225 g	clams
2 tbsp	30 ml	gumbo filé*

In a large dutch oven, heat the oil, add the onion, bell peppers, celery and sausage. Cook until sausage is cooked through. Add the flour and cook for 3 minutes.

Add the tomatoes, water, rice, seasonings and okra, cover and simmer for 30 minutes.

Add the seafood and continue to simmer for 15 minutes. Stir in the gumbo filé and serve.

SERVES 6

* Gumbo filé is an herb made from ground sassafras leaves, available in most supermarkets' speciality food sections. It has a special thickening agent that is unique to the flavour and appearance of gumbo.

Seafood Gumbo

Broccoli & Cheddar Soup

Potages Crème de Volaille Supreme

CONSOMMÉ CHERBRUG

⅔ cup	170 ml	twice ground ham
1 tsp	5 ml	grated onion
¼ tsp	1 ml	each of pepper, basil, thyme, paprika
½ tsp	3 ml	salt
1	1	egg white
⅛ cup	30 ml	whipping cream
7 cups	1.75 L	Beef Broth (see page 85)
6	6	eggs
1 cup	250 ml	Madeira wine
1 cup	250 ml	brushed, sliced mushrooms
2 tbsp	30 ml	julienne, sliced truffles

In a mixing bowl combine the ham, onion, seasonings, egg white and cream. Press through a fine sieve and roll into small balls.

Bring 2 cups (500 ml) of the broth to a boil, drop the balls in the broth, reduce heat and simmer for 10 minutes. Remove the meat balls. Poach the eggs in an egg poacher until the whites are cooked but the yolks are still undercooked.

While the eggs poach, heat the remaining broth with the wine, meatballs, and mushrooms. Simmer for 10 minutes.

Place one poached egg in a serving bowl, cover with soup and garnish with truffles, serve at once.

SERVES 6

POTAGES CRÈME DE VOLAILLE SUPREME

½ quan	0.5	Puff Pastry (see page 689)
1	1	egg
⅓ cup	90 ml	butter
⅓ cup	90 ml	flour, all purpose
4 cups	1 L	Chicken Broth (see page 77)
1½ cups	375 ml	diced, cooked chicken
2 cups	500 ml	whipping cream
1 tsp	5 ml	salt
¼ tsp	1 ml	white pepper
6	6	parsley sprigs

Roll out the pastry as directed, cut into tiny various shapes, place onto a baking sheet. Beat the egg and brush onto pastry. Bake for 10 minutes in a preheated 400°F (180°C) oven.

In a large sauce pot heat the butter and add the flour, cook for 2 minutes over low heat. Add the chicken broth and cooked chicken, simmer for 15 minutes.

Whip in the cream, salt and pepper, continue to simmer for 10 minutes.

Ladle soup into bowls, garnish with the puff pastries and a sprig of parsley.

SERVES 6

CILANTRO CARROT SOUP

6	6	large carrots
4 cups	1 L	water
½ cup	60 ml	grated onion
4 tbsp	60 ml	butter
3 tbsp	45 ml	flour, all purpose
3 cups	750 ml	Chicken Stock (see page 77)
2 cups	500 ml	light cream
1 tsp	5 ml	salt
¼ tsp	1 ml	white pepper
⅛ tsp	pinch	cayenne
2 tbsp	30 ml	cilantro (coriander)

Pare and chop the carrots. Boil the carrots in the water until tender. Drain and purée the carrots in a food processor.

Sauté the onion in the butter, sprinkle with flour, and cook for 2 minutes over low heat. Add the chicken stock, cream and carrot purée. Simmer for 3 minutes. Stir in the seasonings. Simmer for 5 minutes longer. Sprinkle with cilantro and serve.

SERVES 6

Cilantro Carrot Soup

VEGETABLE BROTH OR STOCK

½ cup	60 ml	butter
2	2	onions
6	6	pared diced carrots
4	4	diced celery stalks
1	1	minced garlic clove
1 lb	450 g	peeled, seeded, diced tomatoes
1	1	bouquet garni (see Glossary)
12 cups	3 L	water

In a large kettle or Dutch oven heat the butter, add the onions, carrots and celery, sauté until tender.

Add the garlic, tomatoes, bouquet and water. Simmer uncovered until liquid has reduced by half its volume. Strain through a cheesecloth, use as required.

YIELDS 8 CUPS (2 L)

LA GRATINÉE LYONNAISE SOUPE

¼ cup	60 ml	butter
3	3	large onions, sliced
1 tsp	5 ml	granulated sugar
6 cups	1.5 L	Veal or Beef Broth (see page 85)
½ tsp	3 ml	each of thyme leaves, oregano leaves, salt
½ tsp	3 ml	Worcestershire sauce
1 tbsp	15 ml	soya sauce
6	6	bread rusks
2 cups	500 ml	Gruyére cheese, grated

Heat the butter in a large pot or dutch oven.

Add the onions and sugar, reduce heat and sauté until onions caramelize.

Add the broth, seasonings, worcestershire and soya. Simmer for 15 minutes.

Ladle soup into onion soup crocks, top with a bread rusk. Sprinkle with cheese.

Place soup crocks under the preheated oven broiler, grill until cheese is golden brown.

Serve at once.

SERVES 6

CONSOMMÉ ROYALE

2	2	eggs
4	4	egg yolks
1 cup	250 ml	Chicken Broth (see page 77)
⅛ tsp	pinch	each of salt, white pepper, cayenne, nutmeg
⅛ cup	30 ml	carrot purée
⅛ cup	30 ml	asparagus purée
⅛ cup	30 ml	tomato paste
6 cups	1.5 L	Beef or Game Broth (see page 85) or Chicken Broth (see page 77)

Beat the eggs with the egg yolks, add the broth and seasonings. Divide into three bowls.

Blend the carrot purée into one, asparagus into the second and tomato in the third.

Pour into three small pans, set into a large pan half filled with hot water and bake in a preheated 350°F (180°C) oven until very firm. Remove from oven and cool, then chill to completely set.

Once set cut into squares, diamonds, hearts or any other shape.

Heat the consommé, add the royale custard shapes, simmer for 5 minutes and serve.

SERVES 6

La Gratinée Lyonnaise Soupe

Consommé Royale

Wor Won Ton Soup

SORREL, LETTUCE, CHERVIL SOUP

¼ lb	115 g	sorrel
1	1	very small head bibb lettuce
1 tbsp	15 ml	chervil
2 tbsp	30 ml	butter
5 cups	1.25 L	cold Chicken Stock (see page 77)
2	2	egg yolk
1 cup	250 ml	croutons

Wash and pick through the sorrel, lettuce and chervil. Chop fine.

Heat the butter in a large sauce pan, add the vegetables and sauté until tender. Add all the chicken stock except ½ cup (125 ml). Simmer the soup for a half hour.

In a small mixing bowl blend the egg yolks with the cold stock, gradually whip in a little hot stock until a thick sauce is formed.

Remove soup from heat. Whip the sauce into the soup a little at a time. Serve at once.

SERVES 6

POTAGE ALLIGATOR AU SHERRY

2 tbsp	30 ml	butter
2 tbsp	30 ml	safflower oil
1 lb	450 g	diced alligator meat*
1	1	finely diced onion
2	2	finely diced carrots
2	2	finely diced celery stalks
2 quarts	2.5 L	Chicken Stock (see page 77)
2 cups	500 ml	cooked rice
½ cup	125 ml	cream sherry

In a large kettle heat the butter and the oil, brown the alligator meat, remove and reserve.

Add the vegetables and sauté until tender. Return the meat to the kettle. Cover with the chicken stock, reduce heat and simmer for 1½ hours uncovered. Skim soup for any impurities that rise to the top.

Add the cooked rice and sherry, and simmer for 15 minutes longer. Serve.

SERVES 8

* Alligator meat may be a little hard to find. Try special ordering it through your butcher or seafood supplies.

WOR WON TON SOUP

¼ lb	115 g	small shrimp, peeled and deveined
¼ lb	115 g	lean pork, ground
3	3	green onions, chopped
2 tbsp	30 ml	soya sauce
1	1	garlic clove, crushed
¼ tsp	1 ml	five spice blend
½ tsp	3 ml	salt
¼ lb	115 ml	won ton wrappers
6 cups	1.5 L	Chicken Broth (see page 77)
3	3	chives, chopped
1	1	medium onion, sliced
1 cup	250 ml	broccoli florets
1 cup	250 ml	button mushrooms
½ cup	125 ml	carrots, pared, sliced
¼ lb	115 g	large shrimp, peeled, deveined

In a food processor, place the small shrimp, pork, green onions, soya sauce, garlic, spice and salt. Process for 1 minute.

Place a small amount of the mixture on a won ton wrapper. Brush with water, fold over into a triangle. Pull the three corners together and press to seal. Repeat until all mixture is used.

Place the broth into a large pot and bring to a boil. Add the won tons and cook for 6 minutes. Add the remaining ingredients and continue to simmer for an additional 5 minutes.

Serve at once

SERVES 6

BLACK BEAN SOUP

1 cup	250 ml	black beans, turtle beans, dry
¼ lb	115 g	bacon, diced
2	2	onions, diced fine
1	1	carrot, diced fine
4 cups	1L	Chicken Broth (see page 77)
½ tsp	3 ml	each of marjoram leaves, thyme leaves, salt, pepper, paprika
pinch	pinch	cayenne pepper
½ tsp	3 ml	Worcestershire sauce
1	1	bay leaf
⅓ cup	80 ml	sherry
½ cup	125 ml	sour cream
¼ cup	60 ml	red onion, diced fine

Soak the beans for 8 hours or overnight in water.

In a large pot or dutch oven, fry the bacon. Add the vegetables and sauté until tender. Add the beans, chicken broth, seasonings, worcestershire and bay leaf. Cover and simmer for 1 ½ hours. Discard the bay leaf.

Pureé soup in small batches in a food processor or blender. Return to the pot and reheat. Add sherry.

Place in soup bowls and top with sour cream. Garnish with red onion.

SERVES 6

LA CREME MINESTRA DI DUE COLORI

Italian soup of two colours

1 cup	250 ml	milk
1½ tbsp	20 ml	butter
¼ tsp	1 ml	salt
⅛ tsp	pinch	nutmeg
1½ cups	375 ml	flour, all purpose
1	1	egg
1	1	egg yolk
¼ cup	60 ml	freshly grated Parmesan cheese
4 oz	120 g	washed and trimmed spinach
8 cups	2 L	Chicken Stock (see page 77)

Heat the milk in a sauce pan. Add the butter, salt and nutmeg. Gradually add the flour working it into a smooth paste. Remove from the heat, beat in the egg then the egg yolk. Stir in the Parmesan cheese. Divide the paste into two.

Steam the spinach. Purée the spinach in a food processor, drain well. Blend the spinach into 1 part of the paste.

Heat the chicken stock to a boil. Drop spoonfuls of green and yellow paste into the soup. Cook until the dumplings float and then serve very hot.

SERVES 6

SAN SI YU CHI SHARKS FIN SOUP

Shark has gained in favour during the last few years throughout the western world. Here we present the classic Chinese version of their most famous soup. Shark fin is available in Oriental food markets.

6 oz	170 g	shark fins, dried
1	1	minced garlic clove
½ oz	15 ml	minced ginger root
4 cups	1 L	Fish Stock (see page 76)
6 oz	170 g	chicken
3 cups	750 ml	bamboo shoots
⅛ tsp	2 drops	sesame oil
1 tbsp	15 ml	soya sauce

Place the shark fins in cold water and soak 12-20 hours. Transfer to a kettle and add the garlic and ginger. Bring to a boil, reduce to a simmer for 3½ – 4 hours. Drain and rinse under cool water. Remove the meat from the fins. Steam the meat for 1½ – 2 hours. Cut the fins in very fine strips.

Place the stock into a large kettle, add the fins and bring to a boil.

Slice the chicken into thin strips, place into the soup with bamboo shoots. Boil for 10 minutes.

Stir in the oil and soya sauce. Serve at once.

SERVES 6

Black Bean Soup

ASPARAGUS AND BRIÉ SOUP

⅓ cup	80 ml	butter
½ lb	225 g	asparagus, pared, blanched
¼ cup	60 ml	flour, all purpose
3 cups	750 ml	Chicken Broth (see page 77)
½ cup	125 ml	white wine, sweet
1 cup	250 ml	heavy cream
½ cup	125 ml	brié, rind removed

In a sauce pan, heat the butter. Add the asparagus and sauté until tender.

Stir in the flour, reduce heat and cook for 2 minutes.

Add the broth, wine and cream. Bring to a boil, reduce heat and simmer for 10 minutes.

Transfer soup to a food processor or blender, pureé. Return to pot and reheat.

Stir in the cheese, continue to simmer for 5 minutes.

Serve soup very hot.

SERVES 4

DAWN SOUP (MORGENROT)

6 cups	1.5 L	Chicken Stock (see page 77)
1 cup	250 ml	tapioca
½ cup	125 ml	tomato paste
2 cups	500 ml	julienne cut, cooked chicken

Heat the chicken stock in a 2 quart (2 L) sauce pan. Add the tapioca and simmer for 30-40 minutes.

Whip in the tomato paste and add the chicken, simmer for 5 minutes longer and serve.

SERVES 6

Le Waterzoie (Belgium Chicken Soup)

LE WATERZOIE (BELGIUM CHICKEN SOUP)

This is yet another version of a whole meal in a single pot.

1 – 5 lbs	1 – 2 kg	whole chicken
1	1	lemon
10 cups	2.5 L	cold Chicken Stock (see page 77)
1	1	onion, stuck with a clove
2	2	diced celery stalks
2	2	diced carrots
1	1	bouquet garni (see Glossary)
2 cups	500 ml	white wine
3 cups	750 ml	pared and diced potatoes

Rub the chicken with the lemon, place in a large kettle and cover with chicken stock.

Add the onion, celery, carrot and bouquet garni, cover and bring to a simmer. Skim the stock to remove any impurities that rise to the top during the 2½-4 hours of simmering. Discard bouquet garni.

Remove the chicken and reserve hot. Add the wine and potatoes, simmer for an additional 30 minutes (or until potatoes are cooked).

Carve the chicken, place into large serving bowls, cover with stock and vegetables and serve.

SERVES 6

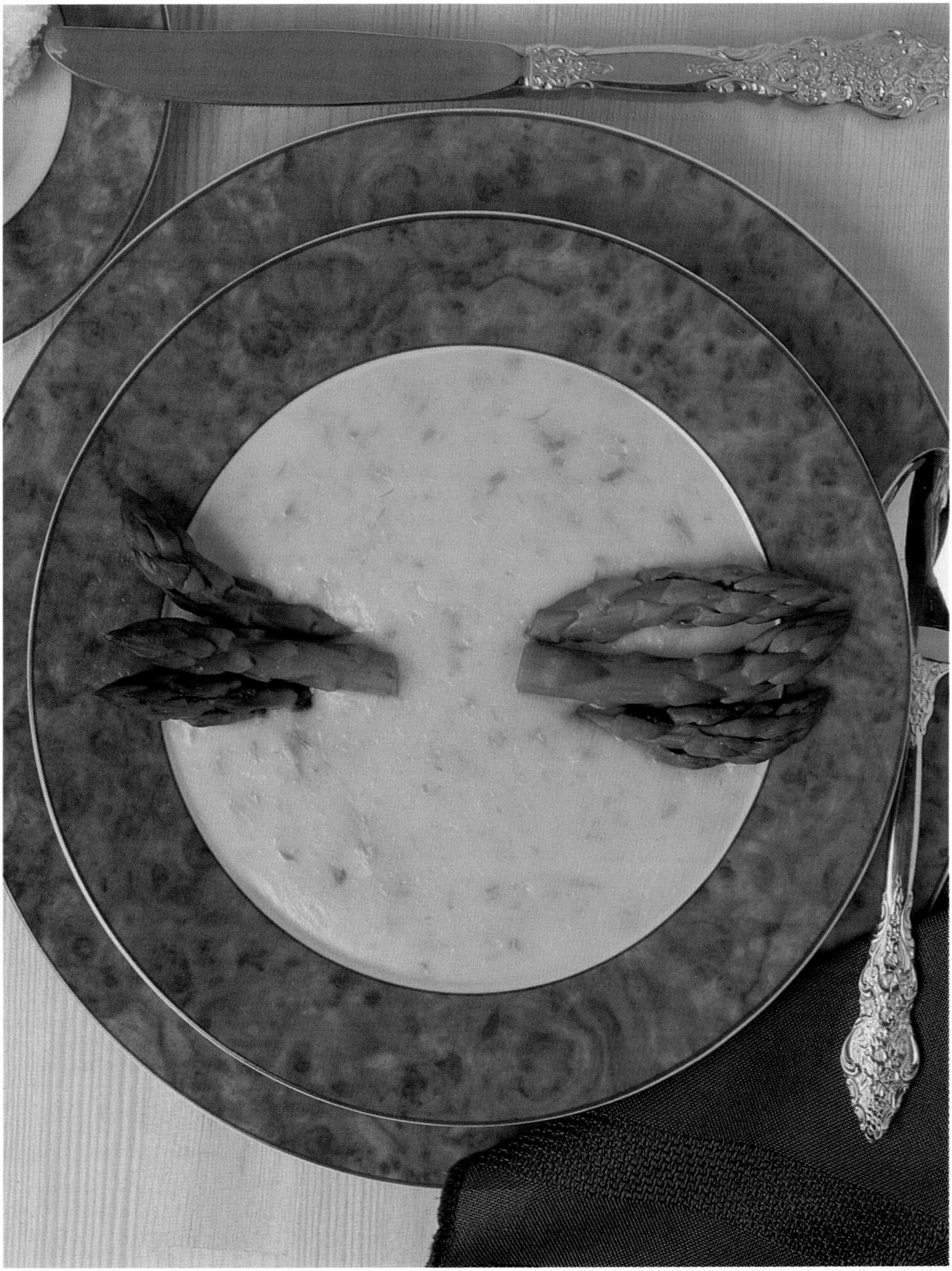

Asparagus & Brié Soup

Sopa de Quimgomba (South American Vegetable Soup)

Country Chicken Noodle Soup

SOPA DE QUIMGOMBA (SOUTH AMERICAN VEGETABLE SOUP)

3 tbsp	45 ml	butter
1	1	finely diced onion
2	2	finely diced celery stalks
2	2	finely diced carrots
3 tbsp	45 ml	flour, all purpose
2 cups	500 ml	sliced okra
4 cups	1 L	Vegetable Stock (see page 92)
2 cups	500 ml	peeled, seeded and diced tomatoes
¼ tsp	1 ml	each of oregano, thyme, basil, garlic powder, onion powder
1 tsp	5 ml	salt
½ tsp	3 ml	black pepper

In a large sauce pan heat the butter, add the onion, celery and carrots, sauté until tender. Sprinkle with flour and cook for 2 minutes.

Add okra and vegetable stock, simmer for 30 minutes. Add the tomato and seasonings, continue to simmer for 15 minutes. Serve very hot.

SERVES 6

COUNTRY CHICKEN NOODLE SOUP

5 lbs	2 kg	chicken, cut in pieces
12 cups	3 L	water
4	4	celery stalks, diced
4	4	carrots, pared, diced
2	2	medium onions, diced
1 cup	250 ml	tomatoes, peeled, seeded, diced
1 tbsp	15 ml	salt
1	1	bay leaf
2 cups	500 ml	flat egg noodles

Place the chicken in a large pot or dutch oven. Cover with water, add the celery, carrots and onions. Bring to a boil, reduce heat and simmer covered, for 8 hours.

Remove chicken pieces and clean all meat from them. Discard bones, dice the meat and return to the soup.

Add the remaining ingredients. Bring to a boil, reduce heat and simmer for 15 minutes longer. Discard the bay leaf. Serve soup very hot.

SERVES 6

MISOSHIRU

Japanese tuna vegetable soup.

6 cups	1.5 L	fish or chicken stock
18	18	pearl onions
1	1	julienne sliced leek
1	1	turnip – diced
2 cups	500 ml	bamboo shoots
1 cup	250 ml	diced firm tofu
6 oz	170 g	grated dried tuna*

Place the stock in a large kettle. Add the onion, leeks and turnip, bring to a boil. Boil until the turnip is tender. Add the bamboo, tofu and tuna. Simmer for 5 minutes. Serve very hot.

SERVES 6

*Dried tuna is available in Oriental food markets.

SAUCES

The chef responsible for the production of great sauces in the large commercial kitchens is a "saucier." He/she knows that the product that they make is usually the first item placed within their patrons' mouths. Therefore is called upon to perform several feats with the very first taste, and must be first rate.

A good sauce must stand on its own, yet not be so powerful that it overwhelms the item it is served with. It must complement what it accompanies. A good sauce must be made from scratch and can never be considered good if it comes out of some little package that one need only add hot water. There is no such thing as a good instant sauce; packaged sauces are meant to cover poor meals.

The saucier produces the most creative of dishes with the sauces he is called upon to make, such as taking a Hollandaise Sauce and turning it into a Raspberry Delight as found on Tournedos Dianna Lynn. Or perhaps, a sauce that can be used in various applications, as any of the five basic sauces are meant to do. Find and master these five sauces and you will have begun your journey into what the world recognizes as the culinary arts. As many know, cultures follow not after their rulers but rather their artists.

The five sauces of the artistic saucier are hollandaise, espagnole, velouté, tomato and béchamel, from which all sauces have their beginnings. You need not search any further than the pages of *Simply Delicious Cooking 2*. You'll also want to know how to prepare the fruit sauces that are now featured on many exciting dishes from appetizers to desserts. They, too, are found within this chapter.

With a sauce, you can take an old favourite and turn it into an all new preferred hit. For example, place a Loganberry Sauce over Apple Pie and see new joy in your family members' faces. Or, how about a Praline Sauce over Carrot Cake — something great! With *Simply Delicious* Sauces, you are sure to make every meal a parade of praise.

Espagnole Sauce

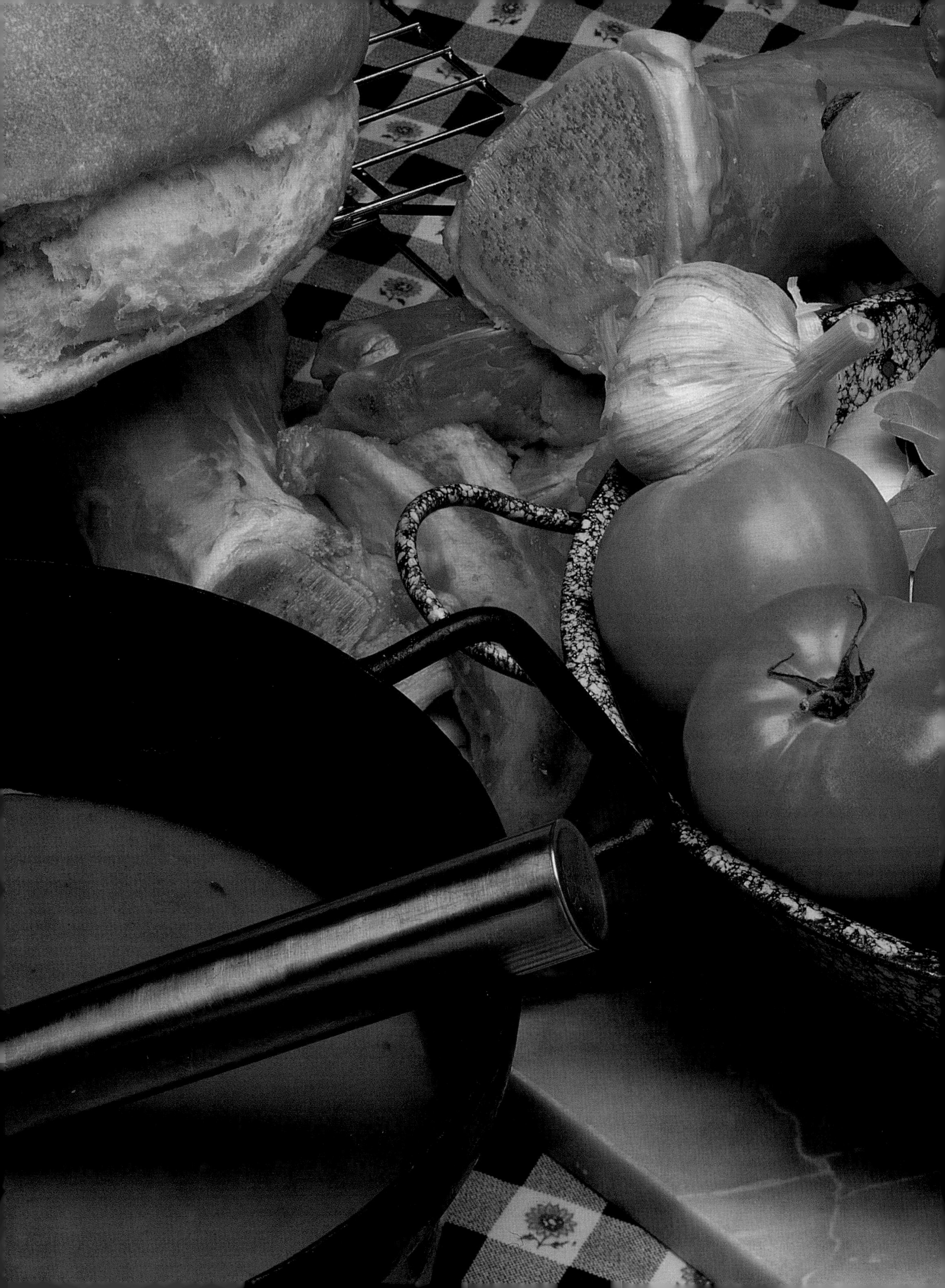

PRALINE SAUCE

½ cup	125 ml	butter
2 cups	500 ml	dark brown sugar
½ cup	125 ml	whipping cream
1 tbsp	15 ml	lemon juice
¼ cup	60 ml	chopped pecans
1 tsp	5 ml	vanilla extract

Melt the butter in a double boiler. Blend the sugar with the butter. Whisk in the cream until it is well blended. Stir in the lemon juice, cook for 45 minutes over simmering water. Stir occasionally.

Remove from heat, stir in the nuts and vanilla. Use hot as required.

YIELDS 2 CUPS (500 mL)

AILLOLI

2	2	garlic cloves, pounded into a paste
2	2	egg yolks
½ tsp	3 ml	salt
pinch	pinch	pepper
½ tsp	3 ml	Dijon mustard
1 cup	250 ml	olive oil
4 tsp	20 ml	wine vinegar

In a blender or food processor cream the garlic, egg yolks, salt, pepper and mustard.

With the machine running add the oil in a slow, thin stream. Add the vinegar.

Pour into a serving bowl or use as required.

1½ CUPS (375 mL)

CINNAMON BUTTER

4 tbsp	60 ml	butter
1 tbsp	15 ml	granulated sugar
1½ tsp	8 ml	ground cinnamon

Combine the ingredients together. Use as required.

YIELDS ⅓ CUP (90 mL)

CHAMPAGNE SAUCE

3 tbsp	45 ml	butter
3 tbsp	45 ml	flour, all purpose
½ cup	125 ml	Chicken Stock (see page 77)
½ cup	125 ml	heavy cream
½ cup	125 ml	champagne

Melt the butter in a sauce pan. Add the flour and stir into a paste (roux) cooking over low heat.

Add chicken stock, cream and champagne. Whisk all the ingredients together.

Simmer for 10 minutes over medium heat.

YIELDS 1¾ CUPS (430 mL)

Praline Sauce

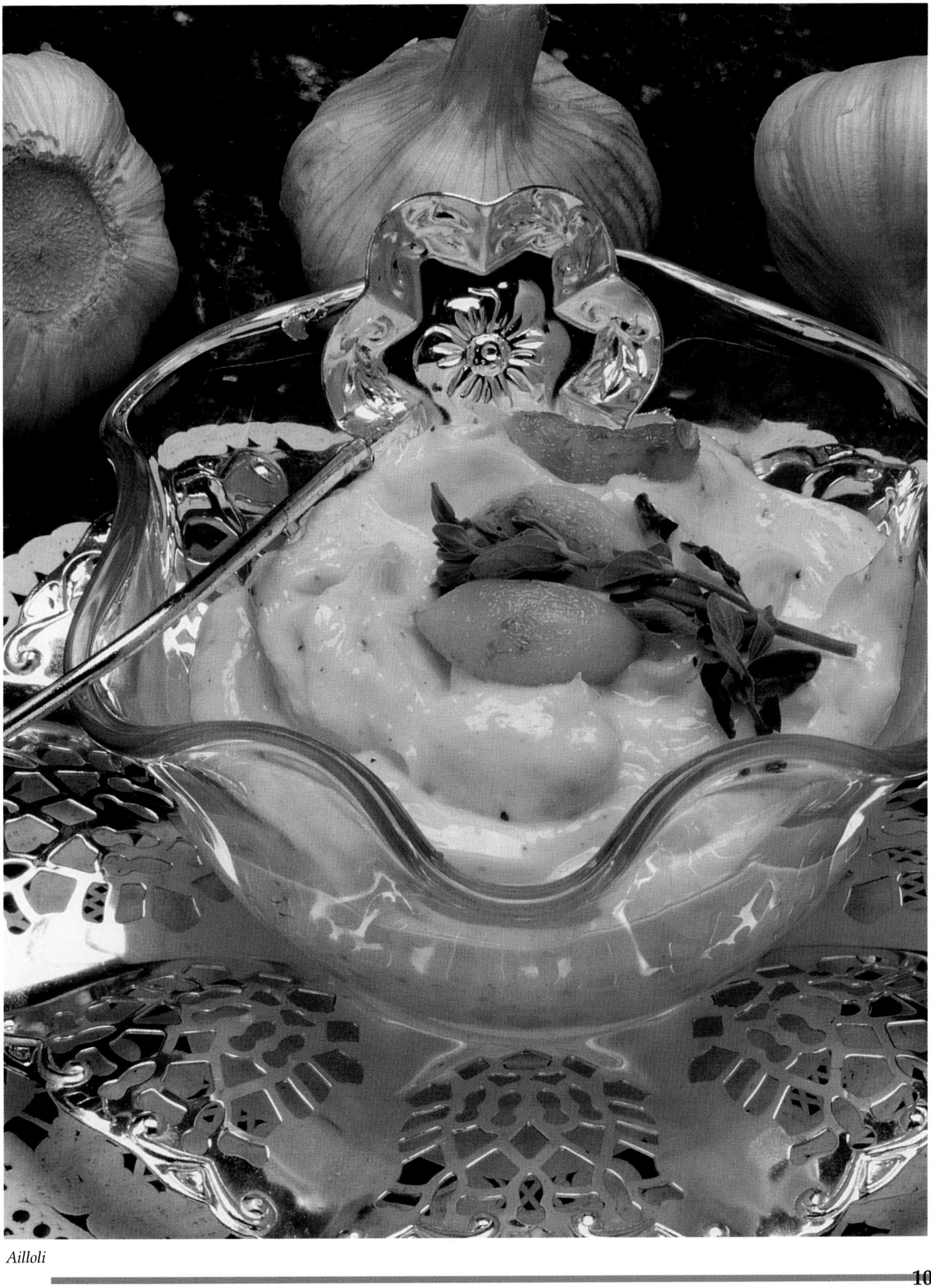

Ailloli

Wild Mushroom Sherry Sauce

APRICOT OR PEACH SAUCE

1 cup	250 ml	dried apricots
1 cup	250 ml	water
2 tbsp	30 ml	granulated sugar
1 tsp	5 ml	cornstarch
1 tbsp	15 ml	lemon juice
¼ cup	60 ml	apple juice

In a sauce pan boil the apricots in the water for 5 minutes. Transfer apricots to a food processor and purée.

Stir the sugar into the apricot water. Mix the cornstarch with the lemon juice, add to the water and simmer until thick. Pour over the apricots and blend.

Return to sauce pan and stir in the apple juice, heat but do not boil. Use as required.

YIELDS 1½ CUPS (310 mL)

WILD MUSHROOM SHERRY SAUCE

2 cups	500 ml	Espagnole Sauce (see page 111)
1 cup	250 ml	sherry
1½ cups	375 ml	wild mushrooms *
2 tbsp	30 ml	butter
1 tbsp	15 ml	flour, all purpose

Mix the espagnole sauce with the sherry, bring to a boil and reduce by half.

Sauté the mushrooms in the butter over high heat, sprinkle with flour, reduce heat and cook 2 minutes. Stir into the sauce. Simmer for 5 minutes.

* Use shiitake, straw, oyster, black forest, morels, chanterells, or porcini.

YIELDS 3 CUPS (750 mL)

MUSTARD SAUCE

2 tbsp	30 ml	butter
2 tbsp	30 ml	flour, all purpose
1 cup	250 ml	milk
¼ tsp	1 ml	salt
¼ tsp	1 ml	white pepper
pinch	pinch	nutmeg
¼ cup	60 ml	whipping cream
2 tbsp	30 ml	lemon juice
1 tsp	5 ml	prepared mustard
1 tsp	5 ml	Dijon mustard

Melt the butter in a sauce pan. Add flour and stir into a paste (roux) cook for 2 minutes over low heat.

Add the milk and stir; simmer until thickened. Add the salt, pepper and nutmeg and simmer 2 additional minutes.

Stir in the cream, lemon juice and mustards. Use as required.

YIELDS 1¾ CUPS (440 mL)

Velouté

VELOUTÉ

½ cup	125 ml	butter
½ cup	125 ml	flour, all purpose
4 cups	1 L	Chicken Stock (see page 77)

In a sauce pan, melt the butter, add the flour and stir, cooking for 2 minutes over low heat.

Add the chicken stock and stir. Simmer for 30 minutes or until sauce has thickened.

YIELDS 4 CUPS (1 L)

Sabayon

SABAYON

6	6	egg yolks
¾ cup	180 ml	granulated sugar
1¼ cups	310 ml	cream sherry
1 tsp	5 ml	lemon juice
⅛ tsp	pinch	nutmeg

Whisk the egg yolks and sugar together until very light. Place in a double boiler over simmering water. Whip the sherry in slowly. Cooking until thick, over cooking will curdle the eggs. Beat the lemon juice and nutmeg.

Serve at once, over fruit, frozen desserts or pour in champagne glasses and serve on its own.

YIELDS 2½ CUPS (625 mL)

TOMATO SAUCE

¼ cup	60 ml	butter
2	2	minced garlic cloves
2	2	diced carrots
1	1	diced onion
2	2	diced celery stalks
3¼ lbs	1.5 kg	peeled, seeded and chopped tomatoes
3	3	bay leaves
1 tsp	5 ml	thyme leaves
1 tsp	5 ml	oregano leaves
1 tsp	5 ml	basil leaves
1 tbsp	15 ml	salt
1 tsp	5 ml	pepper

In a large kettle heat the butter and sauté the garlic, carrots, onion and celery until tender. Add the tomatoes and seasonings. Reduce heat and simmer for 3 hours.

Strain the sauce and return to pot continuing to simmer to desired thickness.

YIELDS 4 CUPS (1 L)

KIWI PAPAYA SAUCE

6	6	pared, chopped kiwis
2 cups	500 ml	papaya pulp
¼ cup	60 ml	granulated sugar
1 ½ tbsp	24 ml	cornstarch
⅓ cup	80 ml	apple juice

Purée the kiwis with the papaya in a food processor. Press through a sieve into a small sauce pan. Stir in the sugar. Mix the cornstarch with the apple juice, add to the fruit. Heat over low heat until sauce is thick.

Use over fruit, ice cream, soufflés or as desired. Very nice with chocolate dishes.

YIELDS 3 CUPS (750 mL)

CHERRY BRANDY SAUCE

1¼ cups	310 ml	Bing cherries – fresh or tinned, pitted
¼ cup	60 ml	cherry brandy
3 tbsp	45 ml	cherry liquid or apple juice
1 tbsp	15 ml	lemon juice
2 tbsp	30 ml	granulated sugar

Heat the cherries in the cherry brandy over low heat until very tender. Press through the sieve into a sauce pan, return to the sauce pan.

Add the remaining ingredients, simmer until thick. Use hot or cold over fruit, sherbets, ice cream, crêpes, chocolate pasta or with soufflés.

YIELDS 1½ CUPS (375 mL)

ORANGE BRANDY SAUCE

2 tsp	10 ml	cornstarch
½ cup	125 ml	granulated sugar
1½ cup	375 ml	orange juice
½ cup	125 ml	Grand Marnier liqueur
2 tsp	10 ml	grated orange rind
1½ tbsp	24 ml	butter

Blend the cornstarch with the sugar. Heat the orange juice and liqueur to boiling. Stir in the sugar, reduce heat and simmer until thick. Remove from heat and stir in the rind and butter.

Use hot over ice cream, sorbets, crêpes, soufflés.

YIELDS 2¼ CUPS (560 mL)

STRAWBERRY COULIS

2 cups	500 ml	washed and hulled strawberries
⅓ cup	80 ml	apple juice
3 tbsp	45 ml	granulated sugar

Place the strawberries in a food processor with the apple juice and sugar, purée. Pour into a sauce pan, place over low heat simmering until sauce is thick. Press through a sieve into a mixing bowl.

Serve over fresh fruit, crêpes, ice cream, sorbets, chocolate pasta or with soufflés.

YIELDS 2 CUPS (500 mL)

RASPBERRY SAUCE

1½ lbs	675 g	fresh raspberries
¼ cup	60 ml	granulated sugar
1 tbsp	15 ml	lemon juice
2 tsp	10 ml	cornstarch

Purée the raspberries in a food processor, strain through a sieve (to remove seeds) into a sauce pan. Whisk in the sugar, heat to a boil reduce to simmering.

Blend the lemon and cornstarch add to sauce and simmer until thick.

YIELDS 2 CUPS (500 mL)

Raspberry Sauce

APRICOT RASPBERRY SAUCE

¾ lb	340 g	peeled, stoned apricots
1 lb	450 g	fresh raspberries
½ cup	125 ml	apple juice
2 tbsp	30 ml	lemon juice
¼ cup	60 ml	granulated sugar

Place the apricots and raspberries in a food processor, purée. Press through a sieve (to remove seeds) into a sauce pan.

Blend in the remaining ingredients and simmer into a thick sauce. Serve over fruit, cakes, ice cream or with soufflés.

YIELDS 3 CUPS (750 mL)

BÉARNAISE SAUCE

3 tbsp	45 ml	white wine
1 tbsp	15 ml	dried tarragon leaves
1 tsp	5 ml	lemon juice
½ cup	125 ml	butter
3	3	egg yolks
1 tsp	5 ml	fresh chopped tarragon

Combine the wine, tarragon and lemon juice in a small sauce pan. Over high heat reduce to 2 tbsp (30 ml), then strain.

In another small sauce pan, melt the butter and heat to almost boiling.

In a blender or food processor, process egg yolks until blended.

With machine running, add the butter in a slow thin stream.

With the machine on slow, add reduced wine mixture. Process just until blended, place in a serving bowl. Stir in the fresh tarragon.

YIELDS ¾ CUP (180 mL)

Jardinere Sauce

RASPBERRY HOLLANDAISE

½ lb	250 g	raspberries
½ cup	125 ml	butter
2	2	egg yolks

Purée the berries in a food processor, strain and discard pulp and seeds. In a sauce pan gently simmer the juice down to 2 tbsp (30 ml), cool.

Whisk the juice together with the egg yolks. Melt the butter and keep it hot. Place the egg yolks in a double boiler over low heat, cook whisking constantly until thick. Remove from heat, whisk in the warm butter until a nice creamy sauce is formed. Do not reheat. Use as required.

JARDINIERE SAUCE

1 cup	250 ml	Espagnole Sauce (see page 111)
2 tbsp	30 ml	finely diced blanched carrots
2 tbsp	30 ml	finely diced blanched zucchini
2 tbsp	30 ml	finely diced blanched celery
2 tbsp	30 ml	finely diced red bell pepper
1 tsp	5 ml	each of parsley, chervil, chives

Combine the ingredients together in a small sauce pan, bring to a boil, reduce heat and simmer for 5 minutes.

Use as required.

YIELDS 1½ CUPS (375 mL)

Apricot Raspberry Sauce

Marinara Sauce

ESPAGNOLE SAUCE

4½ lbs	2 kg	beef or veal bones
1	1	diced onion
4	4	diced carrots
3	3	diced celery stalks
3	3	bay leaves
3	3	minced garlic cloves
2 tsp	10 ml	salt
½ cup	125 ml	flour, all purpose
12 cups	3 L	water
1	1	bouquet garni (see Glossary)
1 cup	250 ml	tomato purée
¾ cup	180 ml	chopped leeks
3	3	parsley sprigs

Preheat oven to 450°F (230°C).

Put bones, onion, carrots, celery, bay leaves, garlic and salt in a roasting pan.

Bake 45 to 50 minutes until bones are nicely brown, take care not to let them burn. Sprinkle with flour and continue to bake another 15 minutes.

Transfer the ingredients to a stock pot. Swirl roasting pan with a little water. Pour drippings into stock pot. Add all the remaining ingredients, bring to a boil.

Reduce heat and simmer 3 to 4 hours or until half reduced. Skim off all impurities that rise to the top. Strain the sauce to remove bones, etc. Then strain a second time through a cheesecloth. Return to the pot and reduce until volume is achieved. Use as required.

YIELDS 6 CUPS (1.5 L)

Mornay Sauce

MARINARA SAUCE

3	3	red cascabel chilies
⅓ cup	80 ml	chopped black olives
2 tbsp	30 ml	capers
⅓ cup	80 ml	olive oil
1	1	finely diced onion
2	2	minced garlic cloves
1½ lbs	675 g	peeled, seeded and chopped tomatoes
2 tsp	10 ml	oregano leaves

Seed and dice the chilies, mix with the olives, capers and ½ the oil. Marinate for 1 hour.

Heat the remaining oil in a sauce pan. Sauté the onion and garlic until tender.

Drain the marinade and mix with the onion. Add the tomatoes and the oregano. Reduce heat to medium, cook until sauce has thickened. Serve over pasta.

YIELDS 3 CUPS (750 mL)

MORNAY SAUCE

3 tbsp	45 ml	butter
3 tbsp	45 ml	flour, all purpose
1¼ cups	310 ml	Chicken Broth (see page 77)
1¼ cups	310 ml	half & half cream
½ cup	125 ml	freshly grated Parmesan cheese

Heat the butter in a sauce pan. Add the flour and cook 2 minutes over low heat.

Stir in the chicken broth and cream. Reduce heat and simmer until thickened. Stir in the cheese and simmer for 2 more minutes.

Use as required.

YIELDS 3 CUPS (750 mL)

MADEIRA WINE SAUCE

2 cups	500 ml	Espagnole Sauce (see page 111)
1 cup	250 ml	sherry

Mix the espagnole sauce with the sherry, bring to a boil and reduce by half.

YIELDS 1½ CUPS (375 mL)

GARLIC BUTTER

1	1	minced garlic clove
⅓ cup	80 ml	butter
½ tsp	3 ml	each of chives, parsley, chervil, basil, shallots
1 tbsp	15 ml	Pernod liqueur

Place the ingredients in a food processor or blender and process until very smooth. Use as required.

YIELDS ½ CUP (125 mL)

BÉCHAMEL SAUCE

2 tbsp	30 ml	butter
2 tbsp	30 ml	flour, all purpose
1 cup	250 ml	milk
¼ tsp	1 ml	salt
¼ tsp	1 ml	white pepper
pinch	pinch	nutmeg

Melt the butter in a sauce pan. Add the flour and stir into a paste (roux) cook for 2 minutes over low heat.

Add the milk and stir; simmer until thickened. Add the seasonings and simmer 2 additional minutes.

YIELDS 1¼ CUPS (310 mL)

CRAYFISH OR SHRIMP BUTTER

¼ cup	60 ml	cooked crayfish or shrimp meat
¼ cup	60 ml	butter

Place both ingredients in a blender and blend until very smooth. Use as required.

YIELDS ½ CUP (125 mL)

COFFEE MINT SAUCE

¼ cup	60 ml	granulated sugar
4	4	egg yolks
2 cups	500 ml	scalded milk
2 tbsp	30 ml	strong coffee
½ tsp	3 ml	mint extract

Beat the sugar into the egg yolks until light and pale. Stir the milk into the eggs, transfer to a double boiler, stirring constantly until thick. Remove from the heat, stir in the coffee and extract. Use hot over ice cream, soufflés or berries.

YIELDS 2 CUPS (500 mL)

COFFEE CHOCOLATE SAUCE

1 cup	250 ml	boiling water
2 tsp	10 ml	instant coffee crystals
2 tbsp	30 ml	granulated sugar
4	4	egg yolks
⅓ cup	80 ml	whipping cream
1½ tsp	8 ml	cornstarch
2 tbsp	30 ml	milk
2 oz	60 g	chocolate chips

Dissolve the coffee crystals in the boiling water. Place in a double boiler. Add the sugar and stir until dissolved. Whip in the egg yolks one at a time. Add the cream and cook 2 minutes.

Mix the cornstarch into the milk and add to the sauce along with the chocolate. Gently cook until sauce thickens. Remove from the heat. Use as required.

YIELDS 2 CUPS (500 mL)

Béchamel Sauce

Coffee Mint Sauce

Hollandaise Sauce

BUTTERSCOTCH CREAM SAUCE

3 oz	80 g	butterscotch chips
¾ cup	180 ml	confectioners' sugar
¼ cup	60 ml	boiling water
1 cup	250 ml	whipping cream
1	1	egg white
1 tsp	5 ml	vanilla extract

In a double boiler melt the butterscotch, stir in the sugar and water. Remove from the heat and cool.

Whip the cream and fold into the butterscotch. Whip the egg white and fold into the mixture along with vanilla. Use as required.

YIELDS 2 CUPS (500 mL)

MALTAISE SAUCE

½ cup	125 ml	butter
2	2	egg yolks
2 tsp	10 ml	lemon juice
⅛ tsp	pinch	cayenne pepper
3 tbsp	45 ml	fresh strained orange juice
1 tsp	5 ml	grated orange peel

Melt the butter to very hot.

Place the egg yolks in a double boiler over low heat.

Add the lemon juice slowly, be sure its thoroughly incorporated.

Remove from heat, slowly whisk in the hot butter.

Add the cayenne, fold in the orange juice and grated rind. Use sauce as required with fish, seafood or vegetables.

YIELDS 1 CUP (250 mL)

VERONIQUE

1 cup	250 ml	Fish Stock (see page 76)
¼ cup	60 ml	white wine
4 tsp	20 ml	green onions
1 tsp	5 ml	cornstarch
1 tbsp	15 ml	cold water
½ cup	125 ml	whipping cream
¼ tsp	1 ml	salt
¼ tsp	1 ml	pepper
1	1	egg yolk
16	16	green seedless grapes

Combine the stock, wine and green onion in a sauce pan. Bring to a boil, reduce to half volume. Strain, return the liquid to the pan.

Mix cornstarch with the cold water, blend into sauce. Reheat and whisk in the cream, add the salt and pepper.

Blend the egg yolk with a little cooled sauce, whisk into the sauce and remove from heat.

Stir in the grapes. Use as required.

YIELDS 1 CUP (250 mL)

HOLLANDAISE SAUCE

½ cup	125 ml	butter
2	2	egg yolks
2 tsp	10 ml	lemon juice
pinch	pinch	cayenne pepper

Melt the butter to very hot.

Place the egg yolks in a double boiler over low heat.

Add lemon juice slowly, be sure its thoroughly incorporated.

Remove from heat, slowly whisk in the hot butter.

Add the cayenne and use sauce at once.

YIELDS ¾ CUP (180 mL)

CHOCOLATE RASPBERRY SAUCE

1 lb	450 g	fresh raspberries
2 tbsp	30 ml	lemon juice
3 tbsp	45 ml	granulated sugar
3 oz	80 g	grated semi-sweet chocolate
1 tbsp	15 ml	butter

Purée the raspberries in a food processor, press through a sieve (to remove seeds) into a small sauce pan.

Add the lemon juice and sugar, bring to a boil, reduce the heat and simmer to 1 cup (250 ml). Stir in the chocolate. Remove from the heat whip in the butter, use as required.

YIELDS 1½ CUPS (375 mL)

GUACAMOLE

2	2	avocados
1	1	peeled, seeded and chopped tomatoes
1	1	chopped red onion
3 tbsp	45 ml	chopped cilantro
2 tbsp	30 ml	lime juice
1 tsp	5 ml	Worcestershire sauce
¼ tsp	1 ml	salt

Peel and seed the avocados, place into a food processor with the remaining ingredients. Blend until smooth. Use as required.

YIELDS 2 CUPS (500 mL)

SALSA

1 lb	450 g	peeled and seeded tomatoes
1	1	Spanish onion
3	3	crushed garlic cloves
1	1	bunch chopped cilantro
2	2	jalapeños
1	1	green bell pepper
2 tbsp	30 ml	lime juice
½ tsp	3 ml	salt

Chop the tomatoes, mince the onion. Place in a mixing bowl along with the garlic and cilantro.

Seed the jalapeños and dice fine, blend into the tomatoes.

Remove the seeds and membrane from the green peppers, dice fine, stir into the tomatoes along with the lime juice, add the salt.

Chill 30 minutes before serving.

YIELDS 4 CUPS (1 L)

Salsa & Guacamole

Lemon Sauce

LEMON SAUCE

2 tsp	10 ml	cornstarch
¾ cup	180 ml	granulated sugar
1¾ cup	430 ml	boiling water
¼ cup	60 ml	lemon juice
1 tbsp	15 ml	grated lemon rind
2 tbsp	30 ml	butter

Blend the cornstarch with the sugar. Whisk into the boiling water, simmer until thick. Whip in the juice, and rind, simmer until the sauce thickens again.

Remove from heat. Whip in the butter. Use hot or cold with fruit, sorbets, crêpes, cakes, soufflés.

YIELDS 1¾ CUPS (430 mL)

GRAND MARNIER CHOCOLATE SAUCE

2 oz	60 g	grated semi-sweet chocolate
3 tbsp	45 ml	butter
3	3	egg yolks
3 tbsp	45 ml	granulated sugar
¼ cup	60 ml	half & half
⅓ cup	80 ml	Grand Marnier liqueur
1 tsp	5 ml	grated orange rind

Melt the chocolate in a double boiler, add the butter and stir until melted. Beat in the egg yolks one at a time, then the sugar. Whip in the cream and cook until thickened. Add the liqueur and orange rind, remove from heat and use as required.

YIELDS 1½ CUPS (375 mL)

Chunky Tomato Sauce

CHUNKY TOMATO SAUCE (TOMATO SAUCE II)

2 tbsp	30 ml	olive oil
2	2	minced garlic cloves
1	1	diced green bell pepper
1	1	diced onion
2	2	diced celery stalks
4 oz	120 g	sliced mushrooms
1 tsp	5 ml	salt
½ tsp	3 ml	pepper
1 tsp	5 ml	basil leaves
½ tsp	3 ml	oregano leaves
½ tsp	3 ml	thyme leaves
½ tsp	3 ml	paprika
¼ tsp	1 ml	cayenne
3 lbs	1.35 kg	peeled, seeded, and chopped tomatoes

In a sauce pan heat the oil. Sauté the garlic, green pepper, onion, celery and mushrooms until tender. Add the seasonings and tomatoes. Simmer for 3 hours or until desired thickness. Use as required.

YIELDS 4-6 CUPS (1-1.5 L)

COURT BOUILLON

16 cups	4 L	water
1 tbsp	15 ml	green peppercorns
1 tbsp	15 ml	salt
1	1	sliced onion
2	2	chopped carrots
1	1	chopped celery stalk
1	1	lemon, cut in half
1 cup	250 ml	white wine
1	1	bouquet garni (see Glossary)

Combine all the ingredients. Bring to a boil. Boil 30 minutes.

Strain through a cheesecloth. Reserve the liquid and discard bouquet.

Use the broth for cooking fish and shellfish.

YIELDS 16 CUPS (4 L)

FRANGIPANE CUSTARD CREAM

1	1	egg
3	3	egg yolks
½ cup	125 ml	granulated sugar
1 tbsp	15 ml	flour, all purpose
1¼ cups	310 ml	milk
¾ cup	180 ml	ground almonds
1 tbsp	15 ml	butter
2 tsp	10 ml	orange extract
1 tsp	5 ml	rum extract

Beat the egg, egg yolks, sugar and flour together until very smooth. Mix the milk and almonds together in a sauce pan, bring to a boil. Remove from heat and steep 10 minutes.

Sieve the almonds from the milk and mix into the eggs. Pour the milk slowly into the eggs stirring. Place in a double boiler and cook sauce until thick.

Remove from heat and blend in the butter and extract.

Use to fill cakes when cold, serve hot or cold over fruit, or with frozen desserts.

YIELDS 3 CUPS (750 mL)

BERRY BERRY SAUCE

1 lb	450 g	washed and hulled strawberries
½ lb	225 g	washed and hulled raspberries
½ lb	225 g	washed and hulled blackberries
1 cup	250 ml	granulated sugar
2 tsp	10 ml	lemon juice
1 tsp	5 ml	lemon peel – grated

Place the berries in a food processor. Process into a purée. Press through a fine sieve and place into sauce pot, stir in the sugar until dissolved. Add the lemon juice and peel. Bring to a boil, reduce heat and simmer until sauce has yielded 2 cups (500 ml).

Serve on crêpes, ice cream, or on banana pasta.

YIELDS 2 CUPS (500 mL)

MARCHAND DE VINS SAUCE

2 tbsp	30 ml	butter
½ cup	125 ml	diced ham
½ cup	125 ml	diced mushrooms
½ cup	125 ml	green onions
1½ cups	375 ml	Demi-Glace (see page 123)
½ cup	125 ml	sherry
¼ cup	60 ml	heavy cream – optional

In a sauce pan melt the butter, sauté the ham, mushrooms and green onions.

Add the demi-glace and sherry. Reduce heat and simmer to half of the sauce's volume.

Add cream and simmer for 2 minutes longer if using.

YIELDS 1¾ CUPS (430 mL)

COUNTRY GRAVY

4 tbsp	60 ml	butter
3 tbsp	45 ml	flour, all purpose
1 cup	250 ml	milk
1 cup	250 ml	Chicken Broth (see page 77)
½ tsp	3 ml	salt
¼ tsp	1 ml	cracked black pepper

In a sauce pan heat the butter, add the flour and cook for 2 minutes over low heat. Whisk in the milk. broth, salt and pepper, reduce heat and simmer until smooth.

YIELDS 2 CUPS (500 mL)

Marchand de Vins Sauce

Country Gravy

Pineapple Mango Sauce

PINEAPPLE MANGO SAUCE

1 cup	250 ml	crushed pineapple, drain and reserve juice
1 cup	250 ml	mango pulp
¼ cup	60 ml	granulated sugar
1½ tbsp	24 ml	cornstarch

Purée the pineapple with the mangoes in a food processor, press through the sieve into a small sauce pan. Stir in the sugar.

Blend the cornstarch into ¼ cup (60 ml) of reserved pineapple juice. Add to fruit. Cook over low heat until sauce thickens.

Use hot or cold over fruit, ice cream or with chocolate dishes.

YIELDS 2¼ CUPS (560 mL)

LOGANBERRY OR BLACKBERRY SAUCE

2 lbs	900 g	fresh berries
1½ tbsp	25 ml	cornstarch
1 tbsp	15 ml	apple juice
¼ cup	60 ml	granulated sugar

Purée the berries in a food processor, strain through a sieve into a small sauce pan. Blend the cornstarch, apple juice and sugar into the berries. Heat over low heat until thick.

Use hot or cold over fruit, ice cream, crêpes, soufflés or as directed.

YIELDS 2 CUPS (500 mL)

CREME ANGLAISE

¾ cup	180 ml	granulated sugar
6	6	egg yolks
2 cups	500 ml	scalded milk
¼ tsp	2 ml	vanilla

In the top of a double boiler whisk the sugar with the egg yolks until light and pale, place over simmering water. Slowly whip in the milk and cook until thick, stirring constantly.

Remove from the heat, stir in the vanilla. Use hot or cold, with fruit, ice sorbets, chocolate dishes, floating islands, white chocolate pasta or as desired.

YIELDS 2 CUPS (500 mL)

CREOLE SAUCE

3 tbsp	45 ml	safflower oil
3	3	finely diced onions
2	2	finely diced green bell peppers
3	3	finely diced celery stalks
20	20	peeled, seeded and chopped tomatoes
2 tsp	10 ml	salt
2 tsp	10 ml	paprika
1 tsp	5 ml	garlic powder
1 tsp	5 ml	onion powder
1 tsp	5 ml	cayenne pepper
½ tsp	3 ml	white pepper
½ tsp	3 ml	black pepper
1 tsp	5 ml	basil leaves
½ tsp	3 ml	oregano leaves
½ tsp	3 ml	thyme leaves
6	6	diced green onions
1	1	bunch chopped parsley

Heat the oil in a large sauce pan. Sauté the onion, celery and green pepper until tender. Add the tomatoes and seasoning, simmer gently until the desired thickness has been achieved (about 4 hours).

Add the green onion and parsley. Simmer 15 minutes longer. Sauce is ready for use.

YIELDS 4-6 CUPS (1-1.5 L)

MAPLE WALNUT SAUCE

2	2	egg yolks
½ cup	125 ml	maple syrup
½ cup	125 ml	whipping cream – whipped
¼ cup	60 ml	broken walnut pieces

Beat the egg yolks. Whip in the syrup, place over a double boiler and cook until thick, remove from heat and cool.

Fold in the cream and nuts. Use as required.

YIELDS 1½ CUPS (375 mL)

HERB BUTTER

¼ cup	60 ml	butter
½ tsp	3 ml	each of chives, parsley, chervil, tarragon, shallots
1 tbsp	15 ml	whipping cream

Place the ingredients in a blender and process until very smooth.

YIELDS ⅓ CUP (90 mL)

Creole Sauce

Chocolate Sauce

Californian Sauce

CHOCOLATE SAUCE

3 oz	80 g	semi-sweet chocolate
1 cup	250 ml	granulated sugar
½ cup	125 ml	water
½ tsp	1 ml	salt
1 tsp	5 ml	vanilla
3 tbsp	45 ml	butter

Melt the chocolate in a double boiler.

In a sauce pan heat the sugar, water, salt and vanilla, reduce to ¾ cup (180 ml) or half its volume. Stir in the chocolate and remove from the heat.

Whip in the butter and use as required.

YIELDS 1¾ CUPS (430 mL)

DEMI-GLACE

3 cups	750 ml	Espagnole Sauce (see page 111)
1¼ cups	310 ml	brown Beef Stock (see page 85)
¼ cup	60 ml	sherry

Combine the Espagnole sauce and the beef stock. Simmer until sauce is reduced in volume by two thirds.

Add sherry and use as required.

YIELDS 1¾ CUPS (430 mL)

REMOULADE SAUCE

2 tbsp	30 ml	prepared mustard
2 tbsp	30 ml	paprika
2 tbsp	30 ml	creamed horseradish
2 cups	500 ml	olive oil
½ cup	125 ml	tarragon vinegar
2 tsp	10 ml	Worcestershire sauce
1 tsp	5 ml	Tabasco™ sauce
2 tsp	10 ml	salt
2 tbsp	30 ml	chopped parsley
¾ cup	180 ml	finely diced red bell pepper
¾ cup	180 ml	finely diced green bell pepper
½ cup	125 ml	finely diced green onions
½ cup	125 ml	finely diced dill pickles

In a blender combine the mustard, paprika and horseradish. With the machine running, very slowly add the oil.

Blend in the remaining ingredients, process until smooth. Recipe may be divided for smaller quantities.

YIELDS 4 CUPS (1 L)

CALIFORNIAN SAUCE

3 tbsp	45 ml	olive oil
3 tbsp	45 ml	flour, all purpose
⅔ cup	160 ml	Chicken Broth (see page 77)
⅔ cup	160 ml	light cream
⅓ cup	80 ml	tomato catsup
2 tsp	10 ml	Worcestershire sauce
1 tsp	5 ml	paprika
3 drops	3 drops	Tabasco™ sauce
1 tbsp	15 ml	lemon juice

Heat the oil in a sauce pan, add the flour and cook for 2 minutes over low heat.

Whisk in the broth and cream and simmer until thick. Whisk in the remaining ingredients, continue to simmer for 2 additional minutes.

Remove from the heat, use as required.

YIELDS 2 CUPS (500 mL)

SALADS

What a remarkable thing a well-made salad is. The ability to refresh the appetite and to make the taste buds dance with coolness cannot be surpassed by any other menu item.

The memorable salad is not always one with several ingredients. All too often, salads represent an intermingling of indistinguishable components that leave the diner wondering what he has just consumed. A good salad must bestow the impression of coolness and refreshment to the palette. It must prepare the diner for courses to follow, leaving anticipation and exhilaration for all new taste sensations in its wake.

It seems redundant to say that in preparing a salad one must use the freshest, finest ingredients available. However, nowhere do inferior products show their ugliness more quickly than in those dishes that are supposed to be fresh. A wilted leaf, a wrinkled vegetable or an air-dried piece of browning fruit implies disdain for the dish being served as well as a cavalier attitude toward the diner. This attitude is not appropriate in matters of the culinary arts, and most certainly not in grade manger (the specialty area of cold food preparation), of which salad preparation is an integral part.

We have taken salads to new heights in *Simply Delicious Cooking 2*. This chapter includes a wide variety of salads to suit every taste. There are recipes for hot, cold and frozen salads. Some salads may be served from the back yard barbecue or at a family gathering picnic. Others will find their way into the menus of your formal, elegant dinner parties. We have also presented multicultural salads which allow you to sample the exquisite cuisines of other countries without ever leaving your home. From popular, bistro type varieties to classic salads that have been the standard of good restaurants the world over for many years, whatever your taste, you will find the perfect salad within this chapter. For your guests, the greatest draw to our salads is that they will always be *Simply Delicious*.

A Salad of Many Colours

RED CURRANT DRESSING

1 cup	250 ml	mayonnaise
3 tbsp	45 ml	red currant preserves
2 tbsp	30 ml	confectioners' sugar
1 tsp	5 ml	grated orange rind

Combine all the ingredients together in a small mixing bowl.

Use as required or desired.

YIELDS 1¼ CUPS (310 ML)

MAYONNAISE

½ tsp	3 ml	prepared mustard
½ tsp	3 ml	granulated sugar
⅛ tsp	pinch	cayenne pepper
1	1	egg yolk
1 tbsp	15 ml	lemon juice
⅔ cup	170 ml	olive oil

Blend the mustard, sugar and pepper together.

Beat in the egg yolk thoroughly, add the lemon juice, blending completely.

Beat in the oil a few drops at a time until the sauce is very thick.

YIELDS 1 CUP (250 ML)

SUZETTE DRESSING

8 oz	225 g	cream cheese
½ cup	125 ml	red currant preserves
3 tbsp	45 ml	orange juice
1 tsp	5 ml	grated orange rind
1 cup	250 ml	whipped cream
3 tbsp	45 ml	chopped pistachio nuts

Soften the cream cheese and beat until very light. Add the preserves, juice and orange rind, beat to incorporate.

Fold in the whipped cream and nuts.

Use as required or desired.

YIELDS 3 CUPS (750 ML)

Raspberry Cream, Mayonnaise, Suzette & Red Current Dressings

ITALIAN SEAFOOD SALAD

2	2	garlic cloves, pounded into a paste
2	2	egg yolks
½ tsp	3 ml	salt
pinch	pinch	pepper
½ tsp	3 ml	Dijon mustard
1 cup	250 ml	olive oil
4 tsp	20 ml	wine vinegar
16	16	cherry tomatoes
1	1	julienne sliced red bell pepper
1	1	julienne sliced yellow bell pepper
1	1	julienne sliced green bell pepper
1	1	sliced Spanish onion
1 cup	250 ml	diced cooked lobster
1 cup	250 ml	cooked sea scallops
1 cup	250 ml	cooked large shrimp

In a blender or food processor cream the garlic, egg yolks, salt, pepper and mustard.

With the machine running add the oil in a slow thin stream. Add the vinegar, blend.

In a large mixing bowl combine the remaining ingredients. Pour the sauce over and toss to coat, serve chilled.

SERVES 6

Italian Seafood Salad

RASPBERRY CREAM DRESSING

1 cup	250 ml	raspberries
¼ cup	60 ml	raspberry vinegar
2 tbsp	30 ml	granulated sugar
½ cup	125 ml	safflower oil
⅓ cup	80 ml	heavy cream

Wash and hull the berries. Press through a sieve set over a bowl.

Stir in the vinegar and sugar. Whisk in the oil.

Whisk in the cream just before serving.

YIELDS 1¾ CUPS (430 ML)

INSALADA PRIMAVERA

1 cup	250 ml	broccoli flowerettes
1 cup	250 ml	cauliflower buds
1	1	julienne cut large carrot
1	1	julienne cut celery stalk
1	1	julienne cut red bell pepper
1 cup	250 ml	peel, seeded and chopped tomatoes
4	4	chopped green onions
4 cups	1 L	cooked rotini
1½ cups	375 ml	mayonnaise
1½ tsp	8 ml	each of basil, thyme, oregano, salt, pepper
1 cup	250 ml	grated cheddar

Mix the vegetables with the rotini.

Blend the mayonnaise, seasoning and cheese together. Thoroughly mix throughout the salad and serve.

SERVES 8

Peach and Almond Salad

Classic Greek Salad

PEACH AND ALMOND SALAD

10 oz	300 g	spinach, washed and trimmed
8	8	large, sliced mushrooms
1 cup	250 ml	grated Gruyère cheese
1 cup	250 ml	red seedless grapes
1½ cup	375 ml	fresh peach slices
¼ cup	60 ml	toasted almonds
1 cup	250 ml	mayonnaise
½ cup	125 ml	orange juice concentrate
¼ tsp	1 ml	ground cinnamon

Tear the spinach into bite pieces and place on chilled serving plates. Top with mushrooms, cheese, grapes, peach slices and almonds.

In a mixing bowl, blend together the mayonnaise, juice and cinnamon. Serve with the salad, to the side.

SERVES 4

CLASSIC GREEK SALAD

4	4	large tomatoes, chopped
1	1	Spanish onion, chopped
1	1	small cucumber, pared, chopped
2	2	green bell peppers, chopped
24	24	mushrooms, quartered
24	24	black olives
1 cup	250 ml	Feta cheese
½ cup	125 ml	olive oil
2 tbsp	30 ml	lemon juice
2 tbsp	30 ml	white wine vinegar
1 tbsp	15 ml	oregano leaves
1 tsp	5 ml	salt
½ tsp	3 ml	cracked black pepper

In a large mixing bowl, combine the vegetables, olives, and cheese.

In a small mixing bowl, blend together the remaining ingredients. Pour over salad, toss to coat. Serve at once.

SERVES 4

ANOTHER BEAN SALAD

1 lb	450 g	green beans, sliced lengthwise
¼ lb	115 g	bacon
1	1	Spanish onion
3	3	peeled, seeded, and chopped tomatoes
½ cup	125 ml	olive oil
3 tbsp	45 ml	vinegar
2 tbsp	30 ml	lemon juice
½ tsp	3 ml	salt
¼ tsp	1 ml	black pepper
½ cup	125 ml	freshly grated Parmesan cheese
2	2	grated, hard boiled eggs

Blanch the beans in boiling salted water for 5 minutes. Rinse under cold water. Drain, place in a large mixing bowl.

Dice the bacon, sauté it until crisp then drain the fat and reserve the bacon.

Dice the onion and mix into the beans along with the tomatoes.

Blend the oil, vinegar, lemon, salt and pepper. Pour over the salad and marinate 1 hour.

Sprinkle with cheese, egg and bacon and serve.

SERVES 6-8

LOBSTER SALAD A LA LIECHTENSTEIN

2 oz	60 g	button mushrooms
1 tbsp	15 ml	butter
1 lb	450 g	cooked and diced lobster meat
⅓ cup	80 ml	extra virgin olive oil
3 tbsp	45 ml	lemon juice
½ tsp	3 ml	dry mustard
¼ tsp	1 ml	each of salt, pepper, paprika
1 cup	250 ml	whipping cream
4	4	curly lettuce leaves
1	1	red onion, sliced in rings

Wash the mushrooms, remove the stems.

Heat the butter in a skillet and sauté the mushrooms.

Place the cooked lobster meat in a mixing bowl.

Blend the oil together with the lemon juice, mustard and seasonings. Whip the cream, fold into it the vinaigrette. Pour over the lobster.

Cool. Place the lettuce leaves on chilled plates. Scoop the lobster onto the lettuce, garnish with the fried mushrooms and onion rings. Serve.

SERVES 4

FROZEN FRUIT FLIP

8 oz	225 g	softened cream cheese
1 cup	250 ml	mayonnaise
¼ cup	60 ml	confectioners' sugar
1–3 oz pkg	1–80 g	cherry gelatin
½ cup	125 ml	boiling water
1 cup	250 ml	tangerine segments
1 cup	250 ml	diced pears
1 cup	250 ml	crushed pineapple
1 cup	250 ml	diced peaches
1 cup	250 ml	whipping cream

Whip the cream cheese together with the mayonnaise and icing sugar.

Mix the gelatin together with the water and fold into the cheese mix.

Blend in the fruit.

Whip the cream and fold into the salad.

Pour the mixture into a bundt pan or mold. Freeze covered.

Unmold by immersing the pan into very hot water. Turn onto a serving platter. Serve.

SERVES 6-8

GRANNY'S POTATO SALAD

8	8	large potatoes
¼ lb	115 g	bacon
1 tbsp	15 ml	safflower oil
2 tbsp	30 ml	vinegar
3	3	chopped green onions
5	5	diced radishes
2	2	diced celery stalks
1 cup	250 ml	mayonnaise
1 tbsp	15 ml	mustard
3	3	chopped hard cooked eggs
1 tsp	5 ml	salt
½ tsp	3 ml	white pepper

Pare and dice the potatoes. Place in a pot and boil until tender. Drain and rinse under cold water to cool.

Dice the bacon and fry until crisp. Drain and reserve.

Place the potatoes in a large mixing bowl. Sprinkle with the oil and vinegar.

Stir in the onions, radishes and celery.

In a small mixing bowl, blend the mayonnaise, mustard, eggs, salt and pepper. Fold into the potatoes, along with the bacon.

Serve as required.

SERVES 6

Granny's Potato Salad

Frozen Fruit Flip

Crab and Chicken Salad in Tomato

CRAB AND CHICKEN SALAD IN TOMATO

⅓ lb	125 g	cooked crab meat
⅓ lb	125 g	cooked chicken meat
3	3	chopped green onions
1	1	finely diced celery
¼ cup	60 ml	finely diced green bell pepper
¼ cup	60 ml	finely diced red bell pepper
1 cup	250 ml	plain yogurt
1 tbsp	15 ml	lemon juice
½ tsp	3 ml	salt
¼ tsp	1 ml	fresh cracked black pepper
1 tsp	5 ml	granulated sugar
1 tsp	5 ml	dill weed
1 tsp	5 ml	sweet basil
6	6	large tomatoes
2 cups	500 ml	alfalfa sprouts
6	6	endive lettuce leaves
1 tbsp	15 ml	chopped cilantro

Fine dice the meats and place into a mixing bowl. Mix in the diced vegetables.

Blend the yogurt, lemon, and seasonings together.

Cut the tops from the tomatoes. Scoop out the pulp. Dice the tops and mix into the crab along with the pulp.

Pour half the dressing into the salad and blend well. Fill the tomato cavity with the salad.

Place the alfalfa and endive onto chilled plates to form nests.

Place a tomato in each nest. Spoon over each a little dressing. Sprinkle with cilantro and serve.

SERVES 6

INSALADTA D'INDIVIA

1 head	1 head	endive lettuce
⅓ cup	80 ml	olive oil
1	1	minced garlic clove
2 tbsp	30 ml	lemon juice
2 tsp	10 ml	fresh chopped mint
¼ tsp	1 ml	salt
⅛ tsp	pinch	pepper
2	2	chopped hard cooked eggs
⅓ cup	80 ml	crisp cooked bacon bits
⅓ cup	80 ml	freshly grated Romano cheese

Thoroughly wash the lettuce. Trim and chop into bite size pieces.

Blend the oil, garlic, lemon and seasonings. Pour over the lettuce place in a serving bowl. Sprinkle with egg, bacon and cheese, serve at once.

SERVES 4

ORANGE AND ALMOND SALAD

10 oz	300 g	spinach, washed and trimmed
8	8	mushrooms, large, sliced
1 cup	250 ml	Gruyére cheese, grated
1 cup	250 ml	red seedless grapes
1 cup	250 ml	canned Mandarin orange sections, drained
¼ cup	60 ml	toasted almonds
1 cup	250 ml	mayonnaise
¼ cup	60 ml	juice from orange sections
¼ cup	60 ml	orange juice concentrate
¼ tsp	1 ml	cinnamon

Tear the spinach into bite size pieces and place on chilled serving plates. Top with mushrooms, cheese, grapes, orange sections and almonds.

In a mixing bowl, blend together the mayonnaise, juices and cinnamon. Serve with the salad, to the side.

SERVES 4

Orange and Almond Salad

A Salad of Many Colours

A SALAD OF MANY COLOURS

1 head	1 head	butter lettuce
1 head	1 head	small radicchio
2	2	Belgian endives
1	1	large carrot
1	1	fine cut julienne red bell pepper
16	16	yellow and orange nasturtiums
8	8	red and white rose buds or rose petals
1	1	mashed garlic clove
⅓ cup	80 ml	extra virgin olive oil
2 tbsp	30 ml	lemon juice
¼ tsp	1 ml	salt
¼ tsp	1 ml	black pepper
1 tbsp	15 ml	chopped chives
1 tsp	5 ml	freshly chopped thyme

Wash, trim and dry the lettuce, radicchio and endives. Mix in a large bowl.

Pare the carrot and cut into thin star shape slices. Sprinkle on lettuce along with the bell pepper.

Place the flowers and rose pedals around the salad.

Blend the garlic together with the olive oil, lemon juice and seasoning. Serve the salad with the vinaigrette separately.

SERVES 4-6

TUNA NIÇOISE SALAD

¾ cup	180 ml	olive oil
¼ cup	60 ml	vinegar
½ tsp	3 ml	each of pepper, dry mustard
1 tsp	5 ml	salt
2 tbsp	30 ml	lemon juice
8	8	pared, cooked, and diced medium potatoes
1	1	diced finely green onion
½ lb	225 g	blanched, French cut green beans
4	4	lettuce leaves
4	4	tomatoes
4	4	hard cooked eggs
2 cups	500 ml	canned tuna, drained
12	12	black olives, pitted
8	8	anchovy fillets
1 tbsp	15 ml	fresh basil leaves

Combine the oil, vinegar, pepper, mustard, lemon juice and salt.

Pour ½ of the dressing over the potatoes. Chill for 1 hour.

Toss the onions and beans with ¼ of the dressing.

Toss the beans with the potatoes.

Place lettuce leaves on chilled plates. Top with equal portions of salad.

Arrange equal portions of tomato, egg, tuna, olives and anchovy on top of salad. Pour remaining sauce over salad. Sprinkle with basil and serve.

SERVES 4

Tuna Niçoise Salad

Warm Kohlrabi Salad

WARM KOHLRABI SALAD

20 oz	560 g	kohlrabi leaves
3 oz	80 g	sliced mushrooms
⅓ cup	80 ml	extra virgin olive oil
3 tbsp	45 ml	lemon juice
2 tbsp	30 ml	vinegar
2 tsp	10 ml	Dijon mustard
1 tsp	5 ml	Worcestershire sauce
¼ tsp	1 ml	salt
¼ tsp	1 ml	fresh cracked black pepper
½ cup	125 ml	cooked crumbled bacon
½ cup	125 ml	freshly grated Parmesan cheese
2	2	hard boiled, grated eggs

Wash and trim the kohlrabi leaves. Place in a mixing or salad bowl. Sprinkle with mushrooms.

Heat the oil in a sauce pan, whip in the lemon juice, vinegar, mustard, Worcestershire sauce, salt and pepper. Heat for 2 minutes. Pour at once over kohlrabi.

Sprinkle with bacon, cheese and eggs and serve immediately.

SERVES 4

SALADE ASTORIA

1	1	yellow grapefruit sections
1	1	pink grapefruit sections
3	3	pared, cored and julienne cut Bartlett pears
1	1	julienne cut green bell pepper
1	1	julienne cut red bell pepper
½ cup	125 ml	silvered hazelnuts (filberts)
½ cup	125 ml	extra virgin olive oil
3 tbsp	45 ml	lemon juice
1 tsp	5 ml	basil
¼ tsp	1 ml	salt
⅛ tsp	pinch	pepper
4	4	curly endive lettuce leaves

Mix the grapefruits, pears, bell peppers and hazelnuts.

Blend the oil, lemon juice, and seasonings.

Place the lettuce leaves on chilled plates, top with salad, pour vinaigrette over salad and serve.

SERVES 4

Salade Astoria

BLUE CHEESE DRESSING

¼ cup	60 ml	blue cheese
1½ cups	375 ml	mayonnaise
1 tbsp	15 ml	lemon juice
½ tsp	3 ml	salt
¼ tsp	1 ml	white pepper

Melt the cheese over a double boiler. Remove from heat.

Place in a mixing bowl. Fold in the mayonnaise, lemon juice and seasonings.

Refrigerate, use as required. You may wish to crumble additional blue cheese into dressing before serving.

YIELDS 2 CUPS (500 mL)

HONEY PEPPERCORN DRESSING

1½ cups	375 ml	safflower oil
¼ cup	60 ml	lemon juice
¼ cup	60 ml	white vinegar
1 tsp	5 ml	each of salt, granulated sugar, paprika
2 tsp	10 ml	pink peppercorns
2 tsp	10 ml	green peppercorns
¼ cup	60 ml	liquid honey

Blend all the ingredients together thoroughly. Refrigerate. Use as required.

YIELDS 2¼ CUPS (560 mL)

CRACKED BLACK PEPPER RANCH DRESSING

1 cup	250 ml	mayonnaise
½ cup	125 ml	buttermilk
3 tbsp	45 ml	minced chives
1 tsp	5 ml	cracked black pepper
1 tbsp	15 ml	lemon juice
¼ tsp	1 ml	salt

Fold the mayonnaise and buttermilk together. Stir in the remaining ingredients. Refrigerate. Use as required.

YIELDS 2 CUPS (500 mL)

Italian, Cracked Black Pepper Ranch, Blue Cheese, Thousand Island & Honey Peppercorn Dressings

THOUSAND ISLAND DRESSING

1 cup	250 ml	mayonnaise
⅓ cup	80 ml	chili sauce
⅓ cup	80 ml	tomato catsup
¼ cup	60 ml	sweet pickle relish
½ tsp	3 ml	Dijon mustard
½ tsp	3 ml	basil leaves
½ tsp	3 ml	Worcestershire sauce
3 drops	3	Tabasco™ sauce
1 tbsp	15 ml	red pimento
2	2	grated hard cooked eggs

Blend all the ingredients together thoroughly. Refrigerate. Use as required.

YIELDS 2 CUPS (500 mL)

Country Tossed Garden Salad

ITALIAN DRESSING

1½ cups	375 ml	olive oil
1	1	minced garlic clove
3 tbsp	45 ml	minced onion
2 tbsp	30 ml	minced red pimiento
2 tbsp	30 ml	granulated sugar
2 tsp	10 ml	Worcestershire sauce
1 tsp	5 ml	each of salt, dry mustard, paprika
½ tsp	3 ml	each of thyme leaves, basil leaves, oregano leaves, marjoram leaves, chervil
¼ cup	60 ml	lemon juice
¼ cup	60 ml	white vinegar

Blend all the ingredients together thoroughly. Refrigerate. Use as required.

YIELDS 560 mL (2¼ CUPS)

COUNTRY TOSSED GARDEN SALAD

1	1	head bibb lettuce
1	1	bunch green onions
3	3	celery stalks
4	4	large radishes
½ cup	125 ml	brushed, sliced mushrooms
1	1	red bell pepper
1	1	small cucumber
1	1	small radicchio
1½ cups	375 ml	broccoli florets
1½ cups	375 ml	cauliflower florets
24	24	cherry tomatoes

Wash and tear the lettuce into bite size pieces. Place into a large serving bowl.

Cut the onions, celery, radishes, mushrooms, pepper, cucumber and radicchio into coarse dice. Add to the lettuce.

Mix in the remaining vegetables. Serve with one or a combination of Italian, Cracked Black Pepper Ranch, Blue Cheese, Thousand Island and Honey Peppercorn Dressings (previous page).

SERVES 6

PAMELA KRYSTAL'S SALAD

4 oz	120 g	white chocolate
8 oz	225 g	softened cream cheese
1–3 oz pkg	1–80 g	strawberry gelatin
½ cup	125 ml	light cream
2 cups	500 ml	whipping cream
½ cup	125 ml	confectioners' sugar
2 cups	500 ml	sliced strawberries
		whole strawberries for garnish

Melt the chocolate in a double boiler.

Whip the cream cheese.

Fold the chocolate into the cheese.

Place the gelatin in the light cream, scald, stirring until the gelatin dissolves. Allow to cool. Fold into the cheese mix. Cool and chill but do not allow to set.

Whip the whipping cream. Blend in the confectioners' sugar.

Wash and hull the berries then slice, fold into the cheese. Pour salad into a bundt pan or a mold. Freeze covered.

Unmold salad by immersing the pan quickly in hot water. Turn out on a serving platter. Garnish with strawberries. Serve.

SERVES 6

HAVE A HEART SALAD

8 oz	225 g	softened cream cheese
1 cup	250 ml	mayonnaise
¼ cup	60 ml	confectioners' sugar
¼ tsp	1 ml	red liquid food colouring
1 cup	250 ml	boiling water
1 tbsp	15 ml	unflavoured gelatin
⅔ cup	160 ml	candy cinnamon hearts
2 cups	500 ml	whipping cream
2 cups	500 ml	miniature marshmallows

Whip the cream cheese, mayonnaise, icing sugar and food colour together.

Dissolve the gelatin and half the candy hearts in the boiling water. Cool. Blend into the cheese mixture. Chill but do not allow to set.

Whip the cream and fold into the cheese mixture with the marshmallows. Pour into a heart shape mold and freeze covered.

Unmold by immersing pan in hot water. Turn out onto a serving platter. Sprinkle with the remaining candy hearts and marshmallows. Serve.

SERVES 6-8

SEAFOOD SALAD

4	4	very large tomatoes
¼ lb	115 g	cooked, peeled, deveined shrimp
¼ lb	115 g	cooked lobster meat
¼ lb	115 g	cooked crab meat
¼ lb	115 g	small cooked scallops
2	2	chopped green onions
3 tbsp	45 ml	finely diced red bell pepper
3 tbsp	45 ml	finely diced celery
1 cup	250 ml	Cracked Black Pepper Ranch Dressing (see page 138)
2 cups	500 ml	alfalfa sprouts

Cut the tops from the tomatoes, scoop out the pulp and set aside.

In a mixing bowl, blend the seafood, vegetables and dressing together.

Fill the tomato cavity with the seafood mixture.

Place the sprouts on four chilled serving plates, top with a tomato and serve.

SERVES 4

CRAB & ORZO NOODLE SALAD

1 lb	450 g	cooked crab meat
3	3	peeled, seeded, and chopped tomatoes
1	1	pared diced fine carrot
1	1	finely diced red bell pepper
1	1	finely diced green bell pepper
3	3	chopped green onions
4 cups	1 L	cooked and chilled orzo*
½ cup	125 ml	mayonnaise
3 tbsp	45 ml	chili sauce
1 tbsp	15 ml	lemon juice
1 tsp	5 ml	salt
½ tsp	3 ml	white pepper
3 drops	3	Tabasco™ sauce

Mix the crab meat, tomatoes, carrots, peppers and green onions together with the orzo in a large mixing bowl.

In a small mixing bowl, blend the mayonnaise, chili sauce, lemon juice, salt, pepper and Tabasco. Pour over salad. Toss to coat, serve.

SERVES 6

*Orzo is a noodle, shaped very much like a grain of rice, found in the pasta section of the supermarket.

Crab & Orzo Salad

Have a Heart Salad

Russian Salad

Creamy Ranch Caesar

CREAMY RANCH CAESAR

1	1	garlic clove
2	2	egg yolks
1 tsp	5 ml	dry mustard
2 tsp	10 ml	granulated sugar
⅛ tsp	pinch	cayenne pepper
1½ cups	375 ml	olive oil
3 tbsp	45 ml	lemon juice
¼ cup	60 ml	buttermilk
⅓ cup	80 ml	freshly grated Parmesan cheese
2 tbsp	30 ml	minced chives
½ tsp	3 ml	cracked black pepper
2	2	heads Romaine lettuce, washed
⅓ cup	80 ml	cooked diced bacon
⅓ cup	80 ml	croutons

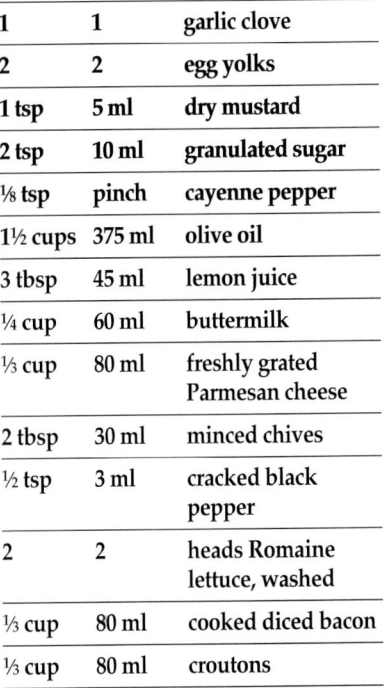

Place the garlic, egg yolks, mustard, sugar and cayenne in a blender or food processor. With the machine running, very slowly add the oil in a thin stream until mixture reaches the consistency of mayonnaise.

Stir in the lemon juice, buttermilk, cheese, chives and pepper.

Cut the lettuce into bite size pieces and place into a large bowl. Cover lettuce with dressing and toss to coat.

Serve the salad on chilled plates and garnish with bacon and croutons.

SERVES 6

SALAD AIDA

1 head	1 head	curly endive lettuce
8	8	julienne cut marinated artichokes
4	4	tomatoes cut in wedges
1	1	julienne cut green bell peppers
1	1	julienne cut red bell pepper
3	3	chopped hard boiled eggs
½ cup	125 ml	extra virgin olive oil
3 tbsp	45 ml	red wine vinegar
1 tsp	5 ml	each of basil, tarragon
¼ tsp	1 ml	salt
¼ tsp	1 ml	cracked black pepper

Wash, trim and cut the lettuce. Place in a salad serving bowl. Arrange the artichoke, tomatoes, peppers and eggs around the lettuce.

Blend the oil, vinegar and seasonings. Pour over the salad and serve.

SERVES 6

RUSSIAN SALAD

½ lb	225 g	cooked, diced lobster meat
½ lb	225 g	boneless, cooked, diced chicken meat
½ cup	125 ml	blanched peas
½ cup	125 ml	fine diced, blanched carrots
3 oz	80 g	French cut, blanched green beans
3	3	pared, diced, blanched potatoes
1	1	pared, diced, blanched turnip
1½ cups	375 ml	mayonnaise
1 tbsp	15 ml	lemon juice
½ tsp	3 ml	each of salt, pepper and paprika
6-8	6-8	washed romaine leaves

Blend the lobster, chicken and vegetables in a mixing bowl.

Blend the mayonnaise with the lemon and seasonings. Mix into the salad. Refrigerate for 30 minutes.

Place the romaine leaves around a salad bowl. Scoop the salad into the centre of the leaves. Serve.

SERVES 6

Grilled Chicken Garlic Caesar

SALADE DIVINE

2	2	blanched julienned artichokes
2	2	julienne cut celery stalks
1 oz	30 ml	finely diced truffles
3 cups	750 ml	blanched asparagus tips
⅓ cup	80 ml	extra virgin olive oil
3 tbsp	45 ml	lemon juice
¼ tsp	1 ml	each of salt, pepper, basil, chervil
½ cup	125 ml	mayonnaise
1 cup	250 ml	whipped cream
¼ cup	60 ml	ice wine or sweet sherry
1 head	1 head	butter lettuce
½ lb	225 g	cooked baby shrimp

Mix the artichokes, celery, truffles, and asparagus together.

Blend the oil together with the lemon and seasonings. Pour over the salad and marinate for 2 hours in the refrigerator. Drain.

Blend the mayonnaise together with the whipped cream and sherry.

Wash and trim the lettuce. Place the lettuce leaves on chilled plates. Top with salad.

Spoon over the salad 4 tbsp (60 ml) of mayonnaise dressing.

Sprinkle on the shrimp and serve.

SERVES 6

GRILLED CHICKEN GARLIC CAESAR

4 – 4 oz	4 – 115 g	boneless, skinless chicken breasts *
4 oz	115 g	diced bacon
1	1	garlic clove
2	2	egg yolks
1 tsp	5 ml	dry mustard
2 tsp	10 ml	granulated sugar
⅛ tsp	pinch	cayenne pepper
1½ cups	375 ml	olive oil
3 tbsp	45 ml	lemon juice
1 tbsp	15 ml	minced parsley
¼ tsp	1 ml	each of thyme, basil, oregano, salt, pepper
⅓ cup	80 ml	freshly grated Parmesan cheese
1	1	head romaine lettuce, washed
12	12	cherry tomatoes

Grill the chicken breast for 6 minutes per side or until cooked through.

Fry the bacon until crisp, drain the fat and cool the meat.

While chicken cooks, place the garlic, egg yolks, mustard, sugar and cayenne in a food processor or blender. With the machine running slowly, add the oil in a thin, steady stream until mixture reaches the consistency of mayonnaise.

Stir in the lemon juice and seasonings.

Cut the lettuce into bite size pieces and place in a large bowl. Cover with dressing and toss to coat.

Place on chilled serving plates.

Cut the chicken into julienne strips and place on top of the salad. Sprinkle with cheese, tomatoes and bacon.

SERVES 4

* Note: Substitute large, peeled and deveined cooked shrimp for the chicken to make Shrimp Caesar.

ORIGINAL FRENCH DRESSING

1½ cups	375 ml	olive oil
¼ cup	60 ml	lemon juice
¼ cup	60 ml	vinegar
1 tbsp	15 ml	grated onion
1 tsp	5 ml	salt
½ tsp	3 ml	pepper

Combine all the ingredients together thoroughly.

YIELDS 2 CUPS (500 ML)

HOT SPINACH SALAD

½ lb	225 g	bacon
10 oz	300 g	spinach
1½ cups	375 ml	mushrooms
⅓ cup	80 ml	freshly grated Parmesan cheese
2	2	grated hard cooked eggs

Dressing:

4 tsp	20 ml	Dijon mustard
2 tsp	10 ml	granulated sugar
¼ cup	60 ml	white wine vinegar
2 tsp	10 ml	Worcestershire sauce
1 tsp	5 ml	seasoned salt
½ cup	125 ml	olive oil
2	2	chopped green onions

Dice the bacon and fry until crisp. Drain, reserving the drippings.

Wash the spinach and trim the leaves. Tear into bite size pieces. Place on serving plates. Top with the bacon, mushrooms, cheese and eggs.

Heat 3 tbsp (45 ml) of the bacon drippings in a sauce pan. Add the mustard and sugar and bring to a boil.

Whisk in the vinegar, Worcestershire and salt.

Slowly add the oil, stirring constantly. Stir in the green onions. Pour sauce over the salad and serve at once.

SERVES 4

Hot Spinach Salad

Salade Crispi

THE GENGHIS KHAN SALAD

1 cup	250 ml	bulgar (cracked) wheat
1 cup	250 ml	finely diced zucchini
3	3	peeled, seeded and chopped tomatoes
6	6	chopped fine green onions
4 tbsp	60 ml	chopped parsley
1	1	finely diced celery stalks
1	1	finely diced red bell pepper
1	1	minced garlic clove
4 tbsp	60 ml	chopped fresh mint
1 tbsp	15 ml	sweet basil
¼ cup	60 ml	extra virgin olive oil
1 tsp	5 ml	salt
½ cup	125 ml	lemon juice

Soak the wheat in cold water for 1 hour. Drain well. Place into a mixing bowl, add the vegetables and garlic, blend thoroughly.

Blend the mint, basil, oil, salt and lemon juice together. Pour over the salad. Chill for 2½ hours. Serve.

NOTE; This salad will not keep well overnight. It should be served immediately after refrigeration.

SERVES 8

JENNY K'S SALAD

1 lb	450 g	diced, cooked chicken
2 cups	500 ml	pared, cored julienne cut apples
4 oz	120 g	button mushrooms
1 lb	450 g	blanched asparagus tips
1½ cups	375 ml	mayonnaise
¼ cup	60 ml	confectioners' sugar
1 tsp	5 ml	curry powder
6 oz	170 g	watercress

Place the chicken, apples and vegetables in a mixing bowl.

Blend the mayonnaise, sugar and curry powder together.

Wash and trim the watercress. Place the salad on chilled plates, surround with watercress. Serve.

SERVES 8

SALADE CRISPI

8	8	curly endive leaves
2	2	peeled avocados
1	1	pink grapefruit segments
2	2	oranges segments
2 cups	500 ml	cherries, stoned
½ cup	125 ml	pine nuts
1 cup	250 ml	mayonnaise
¼ cup	60 ml	confectioners' sugar
½ tsp	3 ml	ground cinnamon
⅓ cup	80 ml	toasted, shredded coconut

Place the endive on chilled salad plates.

Cut the avocados in half. Place thin cuts down the avocado halves from ¼-inch (6 mm) of the narrow end through the thick end. Fan the avocado halves.

Mix the fruit and pine nuts. Blend the mayonnaise with the sugar and cinnamon. Thoroughly mix through the fruit.

Divide the fruit salad among the plates. Place an avocado fan on each. Sprinkle with coconut. Serve.

SERVES 4

The Genghis Khan Salad

TNRK SALAD

6	6	large navel oranges
4 oz	120 g	cream cheese
2 tbsp	30 ml	mayonnaise
¼ cup	60 ml	confectioners' sugar
1-3 oz pkg	1-80 g	tangerine gelatin
1½ cups	375 ml	half & half cream
3	3	large pared, cored, diced apples
1	1	julienne cut celery stalk
1	1	pared julienne cut carrot
2 cups	500 ml	seedless green grapes – cut in half
1 cup	250 ml	mayonnaise
1 head	1 head	butter lettuce
⅓ cup	80 ml	toasted slivered almonds

Cut the tops from the oranges, hollow out the pulp and juice, set aside in small mixing bowl.

Blanch the orange cavities for 3 minutes in boiling water, drain and chill.

Whip the cream cheese, 2 tbsp (30 ml) of mayonnaise and sugar together. Fold in the orange pulp and juice.

Scald the cream, dissolve the gelatin in the cream. Allow to cool. Stir into the cheese mix. Spoon this blend into the orange cavities. Cover with wax paper and freeze.

Blend the apples, celery, carrots, grapes and mayonnaise together.

Wash and trim the lettuce, break into small leaves. Place on chilled plates. Top with apple salad mix and sprinkle with almonds. Place an orange in the centre of the plate. Serve.

SERVES 6

TNRK Salad

ROSEANNE'S ROAST BEEF ORZO SALAD

1 lb	450 g	cooked, diced roast beef
3	3	peeled, seeded and chopped tomatoes
1	1	pared, finely diced carrot,
1	1	finely diced red bell pepper
1	1	finely diced green bell pepper
3	3	chopped green onions
4 cups	1 L	chilled cooked orzo*
½ cup	125 ml	mayonnaise
3 tbsp	45 ml	chili sauce
1 tbsp	15 ml	lemon juice
½ tsp	3 ml	each of onion powder, garlic powder
1 tsp	5 ml	chili powder
3 drops	3 drops	Tabasco™ sauce
6	6	large curly lettuce leaves
		parsley sprigs

Mix the roast beef, vegetables and orzo together in a mixing bowl.

Blend the mayonnaise, chili sauce, lemon juice, seasoning and Tabasco together. Pour over salad and toss.

Place the lettuce leaves on chilled plates, top with salad, garnish with parsley and serve.

SERVES 6

*Orzo is a dried, rice-shaped pasta found in the pasta section of your grocery store.

Roseanne's Roast Beef Orzo Salad

A Pasta Salad of Sorts

A PASTA SALAD OF SORTS

3 cups	750 ml	broccoli flowerettes
2	2	chopped green onions
1	1	diced red bell pepper
1	1	diced green bell pepper
2	2	peeled, seeded and diced tomatoes
4 cups	1 L	cooked multicoloured rotini
¼ cup	60 ml	granulated sugar
1 tsp	5 ml	dry mustard
1 tsp	5 ml	paprika
½ tsp	3 ml	celery seeds
½ tsp	3 ml	salt
⅓ cup	80 ml	honey
2 tbsp	30 ml	vinegar
2 tbsp	30 ml	lemon juice
⅔ cup	160 ml	safflower oil

Blanch the broccoli and chill in cold water, drain and place in a mixing bowl.

Mix in the vegetables and rotini.

Blend the sugar, seasoning, honey, vinegar, lemon and the oil. Pour over the salad, chill for 1 hour before serving.

SERVES 6-8

PARISIAN BEEF SALAD

1 lb	450 g	cooked, lean roast beef
3	3	cooked, diced large potatoes
1	1	sliced red onion
½ cup	125 ml	olive oil
3 tbsp	45 ml	garlic vinegar
2 tbsp	30 ml	lemon juice
½ tsp	3 ml	each of salt, pepper, oregano, thyme
¼ tsp	1 ml	each of basil, garlic powder, onion powder
6-8	6-8	lettuce leaves
2	2	quartered tomatoes
2	2	quartered hard boiled eggs

Thin slice the roast beef, place in a bowl. Mix in the potatoes and onion.

Blend the oil, vinegar, lemon and seasonings together. Pour over the beef. Marinate refrigerated for 1 hour.

Arrange lettuce leaves on a platter, and spoon the salad on top of the leaves. Garnish with tomato and egg. Serve very cold.

SERVES 6-8

SALADE DE POMMES

6	6	large apples
1½ cups	375 ml	granulated sugar
4 cups	1 L	water
½ lb	225 g	baby shrimps
1	1	fine diced celery stalk
2	2	chopped green onions
¼ cup	60 ml	fine diced red bell pepper
¼ cup	60 ml	fine diced green bell pepper
1 cup	250 ml	mayonnaise
6	6	curly endive lettuce leaves
1 tbsp	15 ml	chopped parsley

Pare and core the apples. Whip the sugar into the water. Heat the water in a sauce pan. Poach the apples in sugar syrup until tender. Remove and chill.

While the apples are chilling, blend the shrimp, celery, green onion, peppers and mayonnaise.

Stuff the shrimp mixture into the apple centers. Place a lettuce leaf on chilled plates, form small nests of the remaining shrimp mixture. Top with an apple and sprinkle with parsley. Serve.

SERVES 6

SALAD BOMBAY

12	12	curly endive lettuce leaves
1 lb	450 g	large peeled and deveined cooked shrimp
3 cups	750 ml	cooked long grain rice
1	1	finely diced green bell pepper
1	1	finely diced red bell pepper
4	4	chopped green onions
2 cups	500 ml	peeled, seeded and chopped tomatoes
2	2	finely diced celery stalks
½ cup	125 ml	extra virgin olive oil
4 tbsp	60 ml	lemon juice
½ tsp	3 ml	salt
1 tsp	5 ml	curry powder
¼ tsp	1 ml	black pepper
2 tbsp	30 ml	chopped parsley

On a large serving platter place the lettuce leaves. Put the shrimp around the leaves toward the edge of the platter.

Mix the rice with the vegetables.

Blend the oil, lemon juice, salt, curry and pepper. Pour into the rice and mix thoroughly.

Place the rice into the centre of the shrimp ring. Sprinkle with parsley and serve.

SERVES 6

SALADE A L' EGYPTIAN

¼ lb	115 g	chicken livers
2 tbsp	30 ml	butter
¼ lb	115 g	julienne cut cooked ham
1	1	julienne cut blanched artichoke
1 cup	250 ml	sliced mushrooms
1 cup	250 ml	blanched peas
1	1	julienne cut red bell pepper
4	4	chopped green onions
4 cups	1 L	cooked long grain rice
½ cup	125 ml	safflower oil
3 tbsp	45 ml	lemon juice
¼ tsp	1 ml	each of salt, pepper, garlic powder, basil, onion powder, thyme
1 tsp	5 ml	Worcestershire sauce
8	8	washed, trimmed romaine leaves
3	3	tomatoes cut into wedges

Sauté the chicken livers in the butter, and place on a paper towel to absorb excess fat. Cool.

Blend with the ham, vegetables and rice.

Mix the oil, lemon, seasonings and Worcestershire. Mix throughout the salad.

Place the romaine leaves around a salad bowl, fill with the salad. Garnish with tomato wedges. Serve.

SERVES 8

Salade a l'Egyptian

Cherry Salad

CHERRY SALAD

3 cups	750 ml	fresh stoned, halved cherries
1 cup	250 ml	broken walnuts pieces
1 cup	250 ml	coarse diced celery
1 cup	250 ml	mayonnaise
¼ cup	60 ml	confectioners' sugar
1 tsp	5 ml	white vanilla extract

Mix the cherries, walnuts and celery in a mixing bowl.

Blend the mayonnaise with the sugar and vanilla.

Pour over cherries and stir to mix. Chill for 1 hour before serving.

SERVES 4

CHEF'S SALAD

4 oz	115 g	ham
4 oz	115 g	turkey
4 oz	115 g	roast beef
4 oz	115 g	cheddar cheese
1 quan	1	Country Tossed Garden Salad (see page 139)
4	4	sliced hard cooked eggs
12	12	cherry tomatoes

Cut the ham, turkey, beef and cheese into julienne strips.

Divide the salad onto four chilled dinner plates.

Top the salad with equal amounts of meats, 1 egg and 3 tomatoes.

Serve with your choice of dressing.

SERVES 4

Chef's Salad

SALADE CHAMBERRY

6	6	large tomatoes
1 cup	250 ml	Honey Vinaigrette (recipe follows)
½ lb	225 g	cooked, diced lobster meat
¼ lb	115 g	julienne cut smoked salmon
2	2	trimmed, blanched, cut fine artichokes
¼ lb	115 g	blanched French green beans
3 tbsp	45 ml	diced gherkins
1 cup	250 ml	mayonnaise
½ head	0.5 head	shredded bibb lettuce

Cut the tops from the tomatoes, carefully hollow out the centres.

Marinate the tomatoes in the vinaigrette for 1 hour.

While the tomatoes marinate mix the lobster, salmon, artichokes, green beans and gherkins, bind together with the mayonnaise.

Remove the tomatoes from the marinade, and fill the tomato cavity with the salad.

Place nests of lettuce on chilled plates and set a tomato upon the nests. Pour the marinade over the salad and serve.

HONEY VINAIGRETTE

¾ cup	180 ml	safflower oil
3 tbsp	45 ml	lemon juice
¼ cup	60 ml	honey
¼ tsp	1 ml	each of basil, thyme, garlic powder, oregano, onion powder, salt, black pepper, chervil

Blend all the ingredients together well.

SERVES 6

SALADE DAME CHARMANTE

1	1	honeydew melon
6 oz	170 g	cooked, diced chicken meat
2	2	peeled, seeded and chopped tomatoes
2	2	tangerine segments
1 cup	250 ml	mayonnaise
2 tbsp	30 ml	catsup
2 tbsp	30 ml	orange juice
1	1	fine cut sweet red bell pepper

Cut the melon in half. Scoop out the seeds and filaments. Remove the flesh and dice it, reserve the cavities. Mix it together with the chicken, tomatoes and tangerines.

Blend the mayonnaise with the catsup and orange juice. Bind together the salad with the mayonnaise. Refill the melon cavities with the salad. Sprinkle with red bell pepper and serve.

SERVES 2

INSALADA DELLE 24 ORE

½ head	0.5 head	bibb lettuce
½ head	0.5 head	bibb lettuce
1 oz	30 g	sliced black truffles
2	2	egg yolks
⅓ cup	80 ml	olive oil
2	2	anchovy fillets
½ tsp	3 ml	Dijon mustard
3 tbsp	45 ml	vinegar
2 tbsp	30 ml	lemon juice
3 tbsp	45 ml	black caviar
12	12	yellow and orange nasturtium flowers

Blend the two lettuces. Sprinkle with the chopped truffles. Place the egg yolks into a blender. On high speed slowly incorporate the oil into the egg forming a thick mayonnaise. Blend in the anchovy, mustard, vinegar, and lemon.

Pour this dressing over the lettuce and toss. Plate lettuce on well chilled plates. Sprinkle with caviar and garnish with flowers. Serve.

SERVES 4

CLASSIC CAESAR

1 tsp	5 ml	salt
1	1	minced garlic clove
3	3	anchovy fillets
½ tsp	3 ml	dry mustard
1 tbsp	15 ml	lemon juice
¼ tsp	1 ml	Worcestershire sauce
3	3 drops	Tabasco™ Sauce
1 tbsp	15 ml	red wine vinegar
½ tsp	3 ml	cracked black pepper
¼ cup	60 ml	olive oil
1	1	egg yolk
1	1	head Romaine lettuce, washed
1	1	hard cooked, grated egg
⅓ cup	80 ml	freshly grated Parmesan cheese
⅓ cup	80 ml	diced, cooked bacon
½ cup	125 ml	croutons

Rub the bottom of a large wooden bowl with the salt. Add the garlic and anchovy fillets, mash with two forks.

Add the mustard, lemon juice, Worcestershire, Tabasco, vinegar, pepper and oil. Blend thoroughly. Add the egg yolk and mix well.

Cut the lettuce into bite size pieces. Toss lettuce with dressing.

Serve the salad on chilled plates. Garnish with egg, cheese, bacon and croutons. Serve at once.

SERVES 4

Classic Caesar Salad

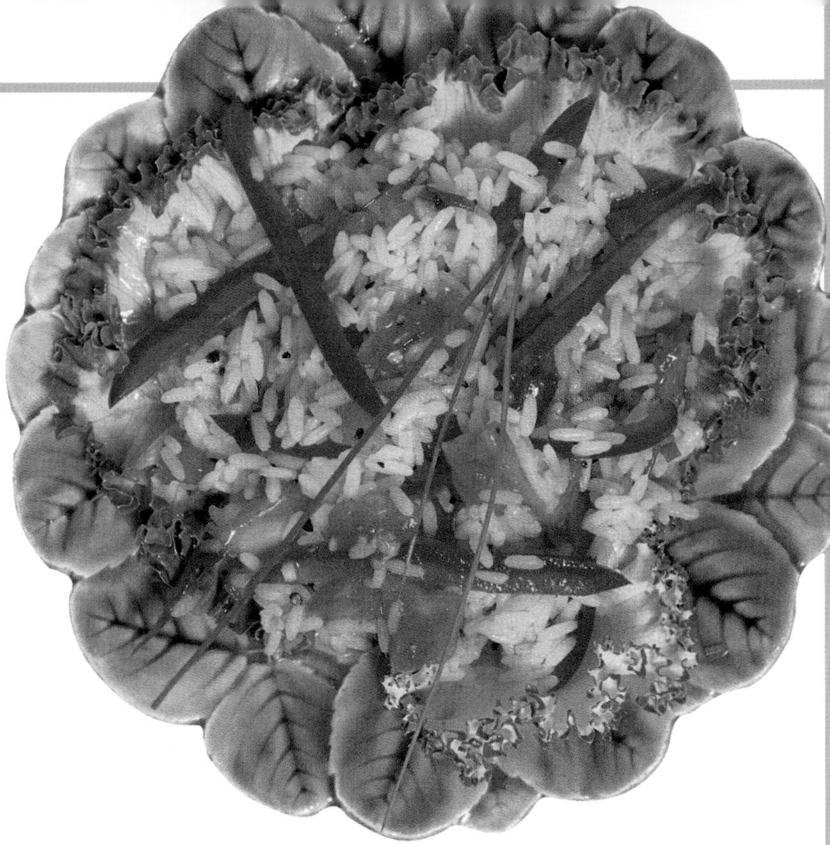

Ensalada Andaluza

ENSALADA ANDALUZA

1	1	red bell peppers
2 cups	500 ml	peeled, seeded and diced tomatoes
3 cups	750 ml	long grain rice, cooked, chilled
3 tbsp	45 ml	chopped chives
⅓ cup	80 ml	safflower oil
2 tbsp	30 ml	lemon juice
2 tbsp	30 ml	vinegar
1 tsp	5 ml	minced garlic
½ tsp	3 ml	salt
½ tsp	3 ml	fresh cracked black pepper
4	4	lettuce leaves

Core the red pepper, remove the seeds and membranes. Cut into a fine dice.

In a mixing bowl, blend the red pepper, tomatoes, rice and chives.

Whip the oil together with the remaining ingredients except lettuce leaves. Pour over the rice. Marinate for 2 hours refrigerated.

Place the washed lettuce leaves on chilled plates. Top with salad and serve.

SERVES 4

WARM CHICKEN DINNER SALAD

1 lb	450 g	boneless chicken breasts
⅛ tsp	pinch	each of oregano, basil, thyme, salt, pepper, paprika, onion powder, garlic powder
1 head	1 head	romaine lettuce
1	1	minced garlic clove
1	1	egg yolk
⅓ cup	80 ml	olive oil
3 tbsp	45 ml	lemon juice
¼ tsp	1 ml	each of basil, thyme, pepper, salt, dry mustard
½ tsp	3 ml	Worcestershire sauce
1 cup	250 ml	bread croutons
⅛ cup	60 g	cooked crumbled bacon
1 cup	250 ml	grated cheddar cheese

Place the chicken on a broiling pan.

Blend the first seasoning list and sprinkle over the chicken. Broil under the oven's preheated broiler for 6 minutes per side or until cooked through. Remove and reserve hot.

While chicken cooks, cut and wash the lettuce and thoroughly dry it. Place the garlic and the egg yolk into a blender. Blend on medium speed. Slowly pour the oil into the blender forming a mayonnaise. Add the lemon juice, second seasoning list and the Worcestershire sauce.

Toss the dressing through the lettuce. Place on chilled plates. Sprinkle with croutons, bacon and cheese.

Julienne slice the chicken and place on top. Serve at once.

SERVES 4

SEAFOOD

With today's supermarkets featuring fresh fish counters, selections of fish and seafood for your table can be original every night. So vast and diverse are the varieties of fish that one could have a different meal every day for a year without repeating the same recipe. All that is required is to allow your creativity to flow.

That's exactly what we have done for you in *Simply Delicious Cooking 2*. It doesn't matter whether you're in the mood for fish or crustacean, your 'depth' of mind will be satisfied by the recipes within this chapter.

Fish meets the high nutritional requirements of the modern family, and exceeds those found in many cuts of meat. Delicate and light meals are made better when prepared with fish and seafood. The adventurous know that when it comes to a dish such as Hazelnut Red Snapper, they have met not only the requirements of nutrition, but also the requirements of great cuisine. There is never a compromise with fresh seafood.

Look not only to salmons and soles to bring satisfaction, but to all types of fish. Snapper and bass are as good as their more costly counterparts; less expensive types of fish often rival the bigger name results without the tremendous budgets. Many recipes that call for salmon, for example, may be prepared with less costly fish, but the same fathomless praise will still be the result.

The fascination found in serving seafood will only deepen as you venture into this chapter. With one new recipe for every day of the month, no one could ever be bored with your catch of the day. We have presented such interesting dishes as Gamberi Piccanti (Spicy Shrimp) or Macadamia Nut Mako Shark. Everyone has heard of monk fish but when you place an Italian name on it, it becomes that much more exciting; thus monk fish with tomatoes becomes Rana Pescatrice al Forno.

Of course, the fresher the fish, the better. If you catch it yourself you'll enjoy it even more. So catch the fresh recipes here and enjoy seafood and fish that are *Simply Delicious*.

Red Wine Tuna Stew & Shrimp Stuffed Trout

Apricot Raspberry Shrimp

SHARK IN TOMATO GINGER SAUCE

1 lb	454 g	boneless shark
3 tbsp	45 ml	olive oil
2 tbsp	30 ml	soya sauce
2 tbsp	30 ml	sherry
1	1	minced garlic clove
1 tsp	5 ml	minced ginger
6	6	dried Chinese mushrooms, soaked 1 hour in warm water
2 tbsp	30 ml	tomato paste

Cut the shark in thin strips.

Blend 1 tsp (5 ml) of oil with the soya, sherry, garlic and ginger and pour over the shark and marinate 2 hours.

Slice the mushrooms.

Heat the remaining oil in a wok. Quickly fry the shark undrained with the mushrooms. Stir in the tomato paste and cook 1 minute longer. Serve.

SERVES 4

APRICOT RASPBERRY SHRIMP

¾ lb	345 g	peeled, stoned apricots
1 lb	450 g	fresh raspberries
½ cup	125 ml	apple juice
2 tbsp	30 ml	lemon juice
¼ cup	60 ml	sugar
4 cups	1 L	Court Bouillon (see page 117)
2¼ lbs	1 kg	large peeled and deveined shrimp

Place the apricots and raspberries in a food processor, purée. Press through a sieve (to remove seeds) into a sauce pan.

Blend in the apple juice, lemon juice and sugar, simmer into a thick sauce.

While sauce simmers, heat the court bouillon to boiling, add the shrimp and reduce the heat, simmer for 15 minutes.

Place shrimp on a large platter and send the sauce to the table on the side.

SERVES 6

Crab Stuffed Sole

CRAB STUFFED SOLE

¼ cup	60 ml	butter
2	2	minced green onions
½ tsp	3 ml	fresh chopped basil
1 tbsp	15 ml	chopped parsley
½ tsp	3 ml	salt
¼ tsp	1 ml	white pepper
½ cup	125 ml	cream
½ lb	225 g	cooked crab meat
4 tsp	20 ml	lemon juice
2 cups	500 ml	seasoned bread crumbs
6 – 6 oz	6 – 170 g	sole fillets

Sauce:		
3 tbsp	45 ml	butter
3 tbsp	45 ml	flour
1 cup	250 ml	Chicken Broth (see page 77)
¼ cup	60 ml	cream
½ cup	125 ml	grated cheddar cheese

In a small sauce pan, heat the butter. Add the onions with the basil, parsley, salt, pepper, cream, crab meat and lemon juice. Pour into a mixing bowl, stir in the bread crumbs.

Place the fish on a greased baking sheet. Top with stuffing. Bake in a preheated 375°F (190°C) oven for 25 minutes.

Sauce:

While fish bakes, heat the butter in a small sauce pan. Add the flour, reduce the heat and cook for 2 minutes. Stir in the broth and cream and simmer until thick. Blend in the cheese. Place fish on a serving plate. Smother with sauce and serve.

SERVES 6

SOGLIOLA AL LIMONE "SOLE IN LEMON BUTTER"

¼ cup	60 ml	unsalted butter
1 tbsp	15 ml	lemon juice
1 tbsp	15 ml	chopped parsley
4 – 6 oz	4 – 170 g	sole fillets or ocean perch
1 tbsp	15 ml	olive oil

Cream the butter, blend in the lemon juice and parsley. Place on a sheet of wax paper and roll in a tube shape. Refrigerate at least one hour.

Brush the fillets of sole with the oil and sauté each lightly for 7½ to 8 minutes over medium heat. Place fillets on a serving plate, top with a thick slice of butter, serve.

SERVES 4

MACADAMIA NUT MAKO SHARK

6 – 6 oz	6 – 170 g	mako shark or swordfish steaks
½ cup	125 ml	ground macadamia nuts
¼ cup	60 ml	freshly grated Parmesan cheese
1 cup	250 ml	fine dry bread crumbs
¼ cup	60 ml	melted butter

Wash and pat dry the mako shark.

Combine the nuts, cheese and bread crumbs in a small mixing bowl.

Dip the steaks in the melted butter then dredge through the crumb mixture. Place into a small casserole dish. Bake in a preheated 350°F (180°C) oven for 15 minutes or until shark is golden brown. Serve at once with an Apricot Raspberry Sauce (see page 108).

SERVES 6

POACHED ORANGE ROUGHY MOUSSELINE

4 cups	1 L	water
2 cups	500 ml	white wine
1	1	chopped onion
1	1	chopped large carrot
1	1	chopped celery stalk
1	1	bouquet garni*
6 – 6 oz	6 – 170 g	orange roughy fillets
3	3	egg yolks
1 tbsp	15 ml	water
1 tbsp	15 ml	lemon juice
¾ cup	180 ml	melted butter
½ cup	125 ml	whipping cream
¼ tsp	1 ml	each of salt and pepper
pinch	pinch	cayenne pepper

In a large sauce pan, bring the water, wine, onion, carrot, celery and bouquet garni to a boil. Reduce to half the liquid's volume. Reduce temperature, place fish into liquid and simmer for 10 minutes.

While fish poaches, blend the eggs with 15 ml (1 tbsp) of water and lemon juice. place in a double boiler. Cook, stirring constantly until eggs thicken but do not over cook. Remove from heat and whip in the butter until sauce is very smooth and thick. Whip the cream and fold into the sauce, add seasonings.

Place poached fish on serving plates. Cover with sauce and serve.

SERVES 6

*The bouquet garni for this dish is; a bay leaf, 8 sprigs of parsley, 2 sprigs of thyme, 6 peppercorns and 1 small, chopped leek tied together in a cheesecloth.

Sogliola al Limone "Sole in Lemon Butter"

Macadamia Nut Mako Shark

GAMBERI PICCANTI

1½ lbs	675 g	tiger prawns
¼ cup	60 ml	olive oil
1 tsp	5 ml	salt
½ tsp	3 ml	each of garlic powder, onion powder, cayenne pepper, oregano, thyme, basil, white pepper, black pepper

Shell and devein the prawns, skewer them lengthwise so they won't curl during cooking. Brush them with oil and place them on a baking sheet.

Blend the herbs, spices and season the prawns heavily. Broil the prawns for 2½-3 minutes on each side, over a grill above medium coals or under the oven broiler. Serve at once.

SERVES 4

BEER BATTERED SHARK

1½ lbs	675 g	boneless shark
2	2	eggs
1 ½ cup	375 ml	flour, all purpose
½ cup	125 ml	ice cold beer
1 tsp	5 ml	baking powder
3 cups	750 ml	safflower oil

Cut the shark into 1" strips. Whip the eggs, 1 cup (250 ml) flour, beer, and baking powder together.

Heat the oil to 375°F (190°C).

Dust the shark with remaining flour. Dip into the batter then deep fry in small batches to golden brown, reserve hot. Once all the shark has been cooked, serve with Remoulade Sauce (see page 123).

SERVES 6

POACHED SALMON GRIBICHE

4 cups	1 L	water
1 cup	250 ml	white wine
1	1	lemon
1	1	celery stalk
1	1	chopped onion
1	1	chopped carrot
1 ¼ tsp	6 ml	salt
1	1	bouquet garni*
6 – 6 oz	6 – 170 g	salmon fillets
3	3	hard cooked eggs
½ tsp	3 ml	Dijon mustard
¼ tsp	1 ml	dry mustard
1 cup	250 ml	olive oil
¼ cup	60 ml	white wine vinegar
1	1	minced garlic clove
1 tsp	5 ml	each of freshly chopped tarragon, basil, chervil, marjoram
2 tsp	10 ml	freshly chopped parsley
8	8	capers

In a large shallow pan, bring the water and the wine to a boil. Cut the lemon in half. Squeeze in the juice and then drop the lemon into water, along with the celery, onion, carrot, 1 tsp (5 ml) salt and bouquet garni. Boil until broth is reduced by half.

Reduce heat and poach the salmon in the simmering broth for 10-12 minutes.

While salmon poaches, separate the eggs, reserve the whites and place the yolks into a food processor. Blend in the mustards and remaining salt.

With the machine running, very slowly add the oil in a steady stream a couple of tablespoons at a time. Once sauce is very thick, add the vinegar in the same slow, steady stream fashion, keeping the sauce very thick. Blend in the remaining ingredients.

Cut the egg whites into julienne strips.

Place the poached fish on serving plates. Place a dollop of sauce on fish, sprinkle with egg white and serve.

SERVES 6

* The bouquet garni for this should be parsley, bay leaf, thyme, chervil and 5 peppercorns tied together in a cheesecloth. (J-Cloth works fine).

Gamberi Piccanti

SHARK STEAK MARCHAND DE VINS

6 tbsp	90 ml	butter
⅔ cup	160 ml	chopped green onions
1 cup	250 ml	red wine
½ cup	125 ml	cream style sherry
¼ tsp	1 ml	crushed rosemary
¼ tsp	1 ml	marjoram
4 tbsp	60 ml	chopped parsley
2 tbsp	30 ml	flour, all purpose
½ cup	125 ml	Beef Stock (see page 85)
1 tbsp	15 ml	lemon juice
6 – 6 oz	6 – 170 g	shark steaks, 1" thick

Heat 2 tbsp (30 ml) of butter in a sauce pan, sauté the green onions for 3 minutes. Add the wine, sherry and herbs. Bring to a boil, reduce heat and simmer to ¾ cup (160 ml) of liquid. Strain through a fine sieve.

In a second sauce pan heat 2 tbsp (30 ml) of butter, add the flour and cook over low heat for 8 minutes or until hazelnut in colour. Add the strained sauce, beef stock and lemon juice, continue to simmer for an additional 7 minutes. Sprinkle with remaining parsley.

Heat the remaining butter and brush on the steaks, broil the steaks for 5 minutes per side. Place on serving plates, pour sauce over the steaks and serve.

SERVES 6

Lemon Pepper Tuna Steak

LEMON PEPPER TUNA STEAK

4 – 6 oz	4 – 170 g	tuna steaks, 1" thick
¼ cup	60 ml	lemon pepper
2 tbsp	30 ml	safflower oil
2 tbsp	30 ml	butter
1 cup	250 ml	Wild Mushroom Sherry Sauce (see page 105)
⅓ cup	80 ml	sour cream

Roll each steak in the lemon pepper.

Heat the oil with the butter in a large skillet and sauté the tuna for 5 minutes per side.

While steaks cook, heat the sauce in a sauce pan. Whip in the sour cream.

When the steaks are ready place on serving platters, pour the sauce over the steaks and serve.

SERVES 4

HAZELNUT RED SNAPPER

¾ cup	180 ml	ground hazelnuts (filberts)
¼ cup	60 ml	fine bread crumbs
¼ cup	60 ml	Romano cheese
¼ cup	60 ml	milk
1	1	egg
4 – 6 oz	4 – 170 g	red snapper fillets
3 tbsp	45 ml	butter
¼ cup	60 ml	flour, all purpose
3 tbsp	45 ml	safflower oil

Mix the hazelnuts, crumbs and cheese. Blend the milk with the egg. Dust the red snapper with flour, dip in the milk and dredge through nut mixture.

Heat the butter and oil together in a large skillet. Sauté the fillets over medium heat for 5-6 minutes per side, depending on thickness.

Serve with a Raspberry Hollandaise (see page 108)

SERVES 4

Cajun Scallops with Chili Pepper Mayonnaise

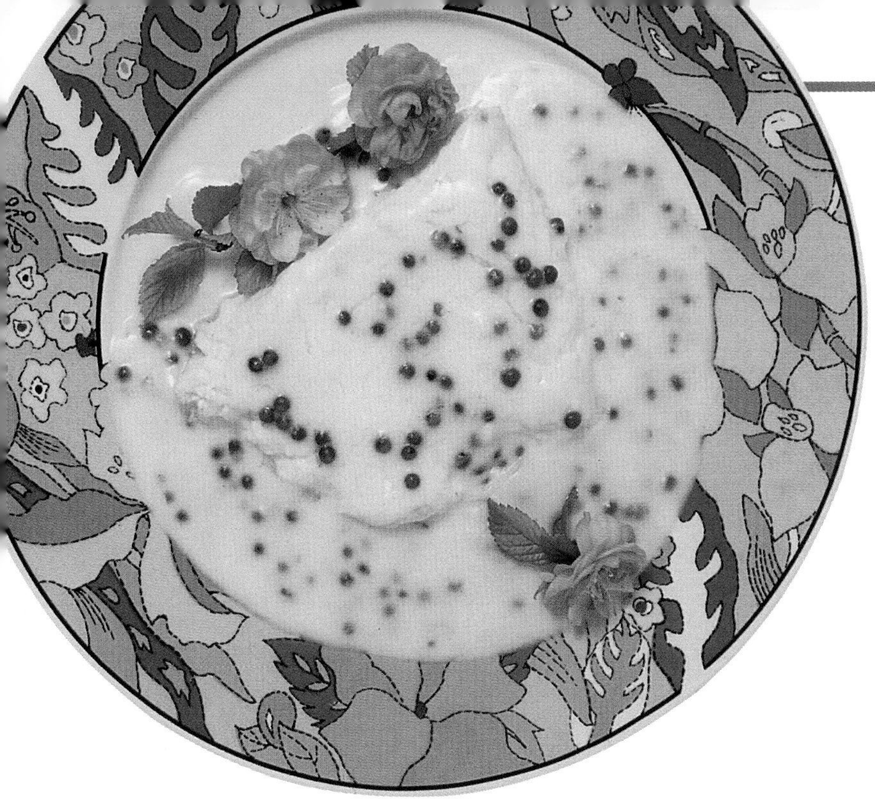

Monkfish with Pink and Green Peppercorn Sauce

CAJUN SCALLOPS WITH CHILI PEPPER MAYONNAISE

MAYONNAISE:		
2	2	egg yolks
1 cup	250 ml	safflower oil
1 tbsp	15 ml	lemon juice
¼ tsp	1 ml	salt
1 tbsp	15 ml	chili powder
3 drops	3 drops	Tabasco™ sauce

Place the egg yolks in a blender. With the machine running, very slowly add the oil until a thick sauce is formed.

Add the lemon juice, salt, chili powder and Tabasco. Turn machine off, pour sauce in a bowl and serve with the scallops.

SCALLOPS:		
1 lb	450 g	large scallops
½ tsp	3 ml	each of oregano leaves, thyme leaves, basil leaves, cayenne pepper, black pepper, onion powder, garlic powder
1 tsp	5 ml	each of paprika, salt, chili powder
1 ½ cups	375 ml	flour, all purpose
¾ cup	180 ml	milk
2 cups	500 ml	safflower oil

Wash and pat dry the scallops.

Blend all the seasonings into the flour. Dip the scallops in the milk, then dust with the seasoned flour.

Heat the oil in a large pan to 375°F (190°C) fry the scallops (a few at a time) for 3-4 minutes until golden brown. Serve at once with the mayonnaise.

SERVES 4

MONKFISH WITH PINK AND GREEN PEPPERCORN SAUCE

2 tbsp	30 ml	butter
2 tbsp	30 ml	flour, all purpose
½ cup	125 ml	Fish Broth (see page 76) or Chicken Broth (see page 77)
½ cup	125 ml	light cream
3 tbsp	45 ml	brandy
1 tbsp	15 ml	pink peppercorns
1 tbsp	15 ml	green peppercorns
1 tbsp	15 ml	chopped green onions
1 tbsp	15 ml	chopped parsley
4 – 6 oz	4 – 170 g	monkfish fillets
2 tbsp	30 ml	butter – melted
½ tsp	3 ml	salt
¼ tsp	1 ml	white pepper

Heat the butter in a sauce pan and add the flour, then cook for 2 minutes over low heat. Stir in the broth, cream, brandy and simmer until thickened. Stir in the peppercorns, green onions and parsley.While sauce simmers brush the fillets with the melted butter. Season with salt and pepper, and bake in a preheated 375°F (190°C) oven for 10 minutes. Remove and place on a serving plate. Cover with sauce and serve at once.

SERVES 4

ASIAN SALMON

4 – 6 oz	4 – 170 g	salmon fillets
½ cup	125 ml	yogurt
2 tsp	10 ml	flour, all purpose
1 tbsp	15 ml	curry powder
2 tbsp	30 ml	fine bread crumbs
2 tbsp	30 ml	water

Place the salmon in a small casserole dish.

In a small mixing bowl blend the yogurt, flour and curry powder. Spread over the salmon. Sprinkle with bread crumbs and pour the water in along the sides.

Place in a preheated 350°F (180°C) oven and bake for 15 minutes.

Remove and serve with a rice pilaf.

SERVES 4

POMPANO MONTMORENCY

1 ¼ cups	310 ml	Bing cherries – fresh or tinned, pitted
¼ cup	60 ml	cherry brandy
3 tbsp	45 ml	cherry liquid or apple juice
1 tbsp	15 ml	lemon juice
2 tbsp	30 ml	granulated sugar
6 – 6 oz	6 – 170 g	pompano fillets
2 tbsp	30 ml	melted butter

Heat the cherries in the cherry brandy over low heat until very tender. Press through the sieve into a sauce pan, return to the sauce pan.

Add the cherry juice, lemon juice and sugar, simmer until thick.

Place the fish on a baking sheet and brush with butter. Bake in a preheated 375°F (180°C) oven for 8 minutes.

Plate the fish and smother with sauce. Serve.

SERVES 6

Barbecue Shark Steak

BARBECUE SHARK OR TUNA STEAKS

2	2	minced garlic cloves
1	1	minced Spanish onion
2 tbsp	30 ml	butter
2 tbsp	30 ml	olive oil
1 cup	250 ml	brown sugar
2 tsp	10 ml	Worcestershire sauce
½ tsp	3 ml	each of thyme leaves, oregano leaves, chervil, cumin, paprika, black pepper, white pepper
1 tbsp	15 ml	chili powder
1 tsp	5 ml	salt
2 cups	500 ml	tomato catsup
2 tsp	10 ml	lemon juice
6 – 6 oz	6 – 170 g	shark or tuna steaks, 1" thick
2 tbsp	30 ml	melted butter

In a sauce pan, sauté the garlic and onion in the butter and olive oil. Combine the sugar, Worcestershire, seasonings, catsup and lemon juice, add to the sauce pan. Reduce heat and simmer 15-20 minutes, stirring occasionally.

Brush the fish with butter and grill over medium coal for 5 minutes per side, brushing frequently with sauce. Brush with sauce one final time before serving.

SERVES 6

Pompano Montmorency

ORANGE ROUGHY MEUNIÈRE

6 – 6 oz	6 – 175 g	orange roughy fillets
½ cup	125 ml	butter
1 tbsp	15 ml	lemon juice
2 tbsp	30 ml	fresh chopped parsley

Place the fillets on a baking sheet.

Heat the butter in a small sauce pan. Brush the fillets with butter and bake in a preheated 375°F (190°C) oven for 10 minutes.

While fillets bake, continue to cook the butter over low heat until it turns a hazelnut colour. Add the lemon juice and parsley.

Remove fish from oven, place on serving plates. Pour butter sauce over and serve.

SERVES 6

COQUILLE ST. JACQUES ALFONSO XII

3 tbsp	45 ml	butter
1 lb	450 g	scallops
1 cup	250 ml	diced dry figs
1	1	finely diced red bell pepper
3 tbsp	45 ml	flour
2 cups	500 ml	Fish Broth (see page 76) or Chicken Broth (see page 77)
1 cup	250 ml	banana slices
1 ½ cups	375 ml	Béarnaise Sauce (see page 108)

Heat the butter in a large skillet. Sauté the scallops, figs and pepper until tender. Sprinkle with flour and continue to sauté for 2 minutes. Add the broth and simmer until thickened. Stir in the banana slices.

Spoon into four coquille shells. Top with béarnaise sauce.

Place in a 500°F (250°C) preheated oven for 5-6 minutes or until golden brown. Serve at once with rice.

SERVES 4

California Tuna & Shark Kebabs

CALIFORNIA TUNA & SHARK KEBABS

1 lb	454 g	large cubed tuna
1 lb	454 g	large cubed shark
½ cup	125 ml	apricot nectar
1 tbsp	15 ml	lemon juice
1 tbsp	15 ml	lime juice
¼ cup	60 ml	olive oil
1 tbsp	15 ml	Worcestershire sauce
½ tsp	3 ml	salt
½ tsp	3 ml	thyme leaves
1 tbsp	15 ml	chopped cilantro
2	2	green bell peppers, cubed
1	1	yellow bell pepper, cubed
12	12	mushrooms
12	12	cherry tomatoes
1	1	Spanish onion, cubed
1	1	thick sliced zucchini

Cut the fish into ¾" (2 cm) cubes. Place the cubes in a mixing bowl.

Blend the apricot, lemon, lime, oil, Worcestershire, salt, thyme and cilantro, pour this marinade over the fish and marinate in the refrigerator for 12 hours or overnight.

On bamboo skewers alternate fish, peppers, mushrooms, tomatoes, onions and zucchini. Grill these over medium heat on a broiler for 8-10 minutes, brushing with marinade. Serve.

SERVES 6

TUNA CURRY

1½ lbs	675 g	tuna
2 tbsp	30 g	onion
¼ cup	60 ml	bread crumbs
1	1	egg
½ tsp	3 ml	each of, cayenne, turmeric, ginger powder, black pepper, basil, thyme leaves, oregano, paprika
1 tsp	5 ml	salt
1	1	minced garlic clove
3 tbsp	45 ml	safflower oil
2 tbsp	30 ml	butter
2 tbsp	30 ml	flour, all purpose
1 tsp	5 ml	curry powder
1 ½ cup	375 ml	Chicken Stock (see page 77)
¾ cup	180 ml	light cream

In a food processor coarse chopped the tuna. Add the onion, bread crumbs, egg, seasonings and garlic. Process into a fine mix. Remove and shape into small balls.

Heat the oil in a large skillet and brown the meat balls. Drain all oil. Transfer the meatballs to a casserole dish.

Heat the butter in a sauce pan, add the flour and curry powder cook for 2 minutes over low heat. Add the stock and cream, simmer for 5 minutes. Pour the sauce over the meatballs.

Cover the dish and bake in a preheated 350°F (180°C) oven for 25 minutes. Serve with rice.

SERVES 6

Oriental Scallops

ORIENTAL SCALLOPS

½ cup	125 ml	soya sauce
¼ cup	60 ml	oyster sauce
¼ cup	60 ml	sherry
1 tbsp	15 ml	Worcestershire sauce
1 lb	454 g	large sea scallops
¼ cup	60 ml	flour, all purpose
3 tbsp	45 ml	safflower oil
2	2	crushed garlic cloves
1 tbsp	15 ml	finely julienne cut ginger root
2	2	dried red chili peppers

In a mixing bowl combine the soya sauce, oyster sauce, sherry and Worcestershire sauce.

Wash the scallops and pat dry. Dust with the flour.

In a wok or large skillet heat the oil, sauté the garlic, ginger and red chilies for 30 seconds. Add the scallops and cook for 2 minutes. Pour in the sauce, reduce heat and cook until most of the liquid has evaporated.

Serve at once.

SERVES 4

SOLE ALMANDINE

4 – 6 oz	4 – 175 g	sole fillets
⅓ cup	90 ml	milk
⅓ cup	90 ml	flour, all purpose
⅓ cup	90 ml	butter
2 tbsp	30 ml	fresh parsley
2 tbsp	30 ml	lemon juice
⅓ cup	90 ml	toasted almond slices

Dip the sole in the milk then dust with flour.

Heat the butter in a large skillet. Sauté the fillets in the butter for 2½ minutes per side. Remove the fish to a heated platter.

Add the parsley, lemon and almonds. Cook for 1 minute. Pour sauce over fillets and serve at once.

SERVES 4

Prawn, Scallop & Halibut Souvlakia

PRAWN, SCALLOP AND HALIBUT SOUVLAKIA

½ lb	225 g	large shelled and deveined prawns
½ lb	225 g	large sea scallops
½ lb	225 g	coarse diced halibut
⅓ cup	80 ml	olive oil
3 tbsp	45 ml	lemon juice
1	1	minced garlic clove
¼ tsp	1 ml	salt
¼ tsp	1 ml	pepper
2 tsp	10 ml	oregano

Skewer the seafood alternating with the halibut, place skewers in a shallow baking pan.

Blend the oil with the lemon juice, garlic and seasonings. Pour over the seafood and marinate 4-6 hours.

Broil the kebabs for 10 minutes over medium heat, turning and basting with the marinade. Serve hot with rice.

SERVES 4

BASS AND LOBSTER MOUSSE VERONIQUE

2 tbsp	30 ml	unflavoured gelatin
¼ cup	60 ml	white wine
¾ cup	180 ml	Fish Broth (see page 76) or Chicken Broth (see page 77)
¼ cup	60 ml	mayonnaise
½ tsp	3 ml	salt
½ tsp	3 ml	paprika
½ tsp	3 ml	white pepper
2 tsp	20 ml	grated lemon peel
1 ¾ cups	430 ml	flaked cooked bass
¾ cup	180 ml	heavy cream
⅓ cup	80 ml	finely ground saltine crackers
1 cup	250 ml	minced, cooked lobster meat
1 ½ cups	375 ml	Sauce Veronique (see page 114)

Soften the gelatin in the wine. Add the broth and bring to a boil. Cool to room temperature.

In a mixing bowl combine the mayonnaise, salt, paprika, pepper, and lemon peel. Fold in ⅔ rds of the broth, stir in the bass, cream and crackers.

In a second bowl mix the lobster with the remaining broth. Pour half the mixture into 6 (1 cup – 250 ml) molds.

Spread the lobster mixture on top of the bass mixture. Then pour the remaining bass mixture on top of the lobster.

Chill 5-6 hours or overnight, unmold. Place on a serving platter and cover with veronique sauce and serve.

SERVES 6

Bass & Lobster Mousse Veronique

AILLOLI CHILLED SHRIMP

2¼ lbs	1 kg	small shrimp
4 cups	1 L	Court Bouillon (see page 117)
2	2	garlic cloves, pounded into a paste
2	2	egg yolks
½ tsp	3 ml	salt
pinch	pinch	pepper
½ tsp	3 ml	Dijon mustard
1 cup	250 ml	olive oil
4 tsp	20 ml	wine vinegar

Cook the shrimp in simmering court bouillon for 15 minutes, drain, place in a mixing bowl and chill.

In a blender or food processor cream the garlic, egg yolks, salt, pepper and mustard.

With the machine running add the oil in a slow thin stream. Add the vinegar.

Pour into a serving bowl, serve as dip in the centre of a platter surrounded by the chilled shrimp.

SERVES 6

Ailloli Chilled Shrimp

LOBSTER MORNAY

1 lb	454 g	lobster meat
¼ cup	60 ml	butter
¼ cup	60 ml	flour, all purpose
1 cup	250 ml	Fish Broth (see page 76) or Chicken Broth (see page 77)
1 cup	250 ml	light cream
½ tsp	3 ml	white pepper
½ cup	125 ml	freshly grated Parmesan cheese

Dice the lobster meat.

Heat the butter in a small sauce pan. Sauté the lobster, remove and reserve.

Add the flour to the pan and reduce heat. Cook 2 minutes.

Add the broth, cream and pepper. Simmer until sauce thickens.

Add the cheese and lobster and continue to cook for 5 minutes.

Serve with a rice pilaf.

SERVES 4

DIJON PRAWNS

¼ cup	60 ml	oil
¼ cup	60 ml	flour, all purpose
1	1	finely diced Spanish onion
2	2	finely diced green bell peppers
3	3	finely diced celery stalks
2 cups	500 ml	peeled, seeded, and chopped tomatoes
2 tsp	10 ml	salt
1 tsp	5 ml	each of oregano leaves, thyme leaves, basil leaves
2 tbsp	30 ml	stone ground prepared Dijon mustard
1 ½ cups	375 ml	Fish Broth (see page 76) or Chicken Broth (see page 77)
1 tbsp	15 ml	brown sugar
1 ½ lbs	675 g	peeled and deveined tiger prawns
¼ cup	60 ml	chopped green onions
3 tbsp	45 ml	chopped parsley

Heat the oil in a large pan or Dutch oven. Add the flour, reduce the heat and cook into a light brown roux (paste). Add the onions, peppers and celery, sauté until tender, stirring constantly.

Add the tomatoes, seasonings, mustard, broth and sugar. Simmer, covered for 20 minutes.

Add the prawns and continue to simmer uncovered for 10 minutes. Stir in the green onion and parsley and serve at once over cooked rice.

SERVES 4

Dijon Prawns

COCONUT BEER SHRIMP WITH JALAPEÑO MARMALADE

½ cup	125 ml	flour, all purpose
¼ tsp	1 ml	baking powder
⅛ tsp	pinch	baking soda
½ tsp	3 ml	salt
½ cup	125 ml	beer
2 cups	500 ml	vegetable oil
1	1	egg white
1 lb	450 g	large peeled and deveined shrimp
¼ cup	60 ml	coconut flakes
1 cup	250 ml	Jalapeño Marmalade*

In a mixing bowl sift together the dry ingredients. Slowly add the beer. Whisk briskly and let stand for 1 hour.

Heat the oil to 375°F (190°C).

Whip the egg white and fold into the batter. Roll the shrimp in the coconut, then dip into the batter. Fry in the oil for 2½-3 minutes or until golden brown. Serve at once with the marmalade on the side.

*Use our Jalapeño Marmalade (see page 701) or blend 3 seeded, stemmed, minced jalapeño peppers with 1 cup (250 ml) lemon or orange marmalade.

SERVES 4

Coconut Beer Shrimp with Jalapeño Marmalade

SALMON NADINE IN CRUST

4 oz	120 g	peeled and deveined shrimp
4 oz	120 g	bay scallops
2 tbsp	30 ml	butter
1 quan	1	Puff Pastry (see page 689)
4 – 4 oz	4 – 120 g	salmon fillets
4 oz	120 g	cream cheese
2 tbsp	30 ml	red peppercorns
1 cup	250 ml	Wild Mushroom Sherry Sauce (see page 105)

Sauté the shrimp and scallops in the butter, drain and cool.

Roll out the pastry for the final stage, and cut into four equal sizes. Top with a salmon fillet, and equal portions of shrimp, scallops, cheese and sprinkle with red peppercorns.

Carefully wrap the pastry around the fillets. Seal the edges and decorate with the remaining pastry. Place the filet sealed side down.

Bake in a preheated 425°F (220°C) oven for 20 minutes or until pastry is golden brown. Serve with the Wild Mushroom Sherry Sauce on the side.

SERVES 4

Salmon Nadine in Crust

GRAND MARNIER ORANGE ROUGHY

⅔ cup	160 ml	dried apricots
1 cup	250 ml	water
1 tbsp	15 ml	granulated sugar
1 tsp	5 ml	cornstarch
¼ cup	60 ml	Grand Marnier liqueur
4 – 6 oz	4 – 170 g	orange roughy fillets
2 tbsp	30 ml	melted butter
½ tsp	3 ml	salt
½ tsp	3 ml	white pepper

In a small sauce pan cook the apricots with the water until they are soft. Remove the apricots and reserve.

Add the sugar to the liquid, combine the cornstarch into the Grand Marnier. Transfer to a food processor with the apricots. Purée and reserve warm.

Wash and pat dry the fillets. Heat the butter in a skillet and gently sauté the fillets for 2½-3 minutes per side. Season with salt and pepper. Transfer to a serving plate, cover with sauce and serve.

SERVES 4

GINGERSNAP PEAR CIDER SALMON

3 cups	750 ml	pear cider
4 – 6 oz	4 – 170 g	salmon fillets
3 tbsp	45 ml	butter
¼ cup	60 ml	finely ground gingersnaps
½ cup	125 ml	heavy cream

Heat 2 cups (500 ml) of cider in a large shallow pot. Reduce to simmer, add the salmon and poach for 12-15 minutes.While salmon poaches, heat the butter in a sauce pan. Add the gingersnaps and cook for 2 minutes. Add the remaining cider and cream, simmer until thickened.

Remove the salmon to serving plates, cover with sauce and serve.

SERVES 4

Grand Marnier Orange Roughy

BARBECUE SEAFOOD SAUTÉ

2	2	minced garlic cloves
1	1	minced Spanish onion
2 tbsp	30 ml	butter
2 tbsp	30 ml	olive oil
1 cup	250 ml	brown sugar
2 tsp	10 ml	Worcestershire sauce
½ tsp	3 ml	each of thyme leaves, oregano leaves, chervil, cumin, paprika, black pepper, white pepper
1 tbsp	15 ml	chili powder
1 tsp	5 ml	salt
2 cups	500 ml	tomato catsup
2 tsp	10 ml	lemon juice
½ lb	225 g	diced lobster meat
½ lb	225 g	large peeled and deveined shrimp
½ lb	225 g	large scallops
2 tbsp	30 ml	butter
2 tbsp	30 ml	safflower oil

In a sauce pan, sauté the garlic and onion in the butter and olive oil. Combine the sugar, Worcestershire, seasonings, catsup and lemon juice, add. Reduce heat and simmer 15-20 minutes, stirring occasionally.

Fry the seafood in the butter and oil in a large skillet. Pour the sauce over and simmer for 10 minutes. Serve over rice or noodles.

SERVES 6

Salmon Dianna Lynn

SALMON DIANNA LYNN

4 – 6 oz	4 – 170 g	salmon fillets
3	3	egg yolks
1 tsp	5 ml	cold water
pinch	pinch	cayenne pepper
2 tbsp	30 ml	fresh lemon juice
½ cup	125 ml	melted butter
⅔ cup	160 ml	cooked bay shrimp
½ cup	125 ml	fresh peach pulp

Broil or poach the salmon for 10 minutes per inch of thickness.

Blend the egg yolks, cold water, pepper, lemon juice, while constantly whipping, place the egg over gently simmering water. Whip until thick.

Remove from heat and slowly whip in the butter, a little at a time. Once thick, hollandaise is formed, fold in the shrimp and peach.

Place cooked salmon on serving plates and cover with sauce. Serve with choice of vegetables.

SERVES 4

COCONUT TUNA

1½ lbs	675 g	cubed fresh tuna
1 tsp	5 ml	each of salt, paprika, pepper
6 tbsp	90 ml	butter
1	1	diced Spanish onion
1	1	minced garlic clove
3 tbsp	45 ml	flour, all purpose
¾ cup	180 ml	blanched, grated almonds
1 tsp	5 ml	crushed red chilies
½ tsp	3 ml	thyme leaves
1	1	bay leaf
¼ cup	60 ml	lemon juice
¼ cup	60 ml	honey
2 cup	500 ml	coconut milk
1 cup	250 ml	grated fresh coconut

Sprinkle the tuna pieces with salt, paprika and pepper.

Heat the butter in a large skillet and fry the onion and garlic with the tuna to brown. Sprinkle with flour and cook for 2 minutes. Add the remaining ingredients. Cover, reduce heat and simmer for 30 minutes. Serve with rice pilaf.

SERVES 6

BAKED STUFFED SALMON 2

4½ lbs	2 kg	Coho, pink or Chinook salmon
2 tbsp	30 ml	olive oil
¼ lb	115 g	Black Forest ham, diced
1	1	diced onion
1	1	diced celery stalk
2	2	pared, diced carrots
2 cups	500 ml	seasoned bread crumbs
1 cup	250 ml	tiny shrimp
1 tsp	5 ml	paprika
¼ tsp	1 ml	pepper
½ cup	125 ml	white wine

Preheat the oven to 375°F (190°C).

Thoroughly wash and clean the salmon.Heat the oil in a sauce pan. Add the ham, onion, celery and carrot. Sauté until tender. Cool.

Mix the bread crumbs with the shrimp, seasoning and wine. Stir into the fried mixture. Stuff into the cavity of the fish. Tie with a string. Bake on a greased, covered pan for 40-45 minutes.Carve and serve.

SERVES 8

HONEY MUSTARD SEAFOOD KEBABS

1 lb	454 g	large, peeled and deveined shrimp
1 lb	454 g	large sea scallops
½ cup	125 ml	safflower oil
¼ cup	60 ml	chopped parsley
2 tbsp	30 ml	lemon juice
2 tbsp	30 ml	liquid honey
½ tsp	3 ml	cracked black pepper
2	2	minced garlic cloves
2 tsp	10 ml	Dijon mustard

Skewer the shrimp and scallops alternating each on a water soaked bamboo skewers, place in a shallow casserole dish.

Combine the remaining ingredients together in a blender and process for 30 second, pour over the kebabs and marinate for 1 hour, covered and refrigerated.

Broil the kebabs over medium coals for 5 minutes per side, brushing frequently with marinade. Brush one final time before serving.

SERVES 6

KHARIA SWORDFISH

¾ lb	375 g	swordfish
3 tbsp	45 ml	olive oil
1	1	garlic clove
2 tsp	10 ml	peeled, sliced fresh ginger
1	1	thinly sliced red bell pepper
1	1	thinly sliced green bell pepper
1	1	small thinly sliced onion
2 tbsp	30 ml	flour, all purpose
2 tbsp	30 ml	soya sauce
1 tsp	5 ml	Worcestershire sauce
⅓ cup	90 ml	Gewürztraminer wine
¾ cup	190 ml	Chicken Broth (see page 77)
1	1	egg

Slice the fish into strips.

Heat the oil in a large skillet and fry the fish thoroughly, remove and reserve.

Add the garlic, ginger, peppers and onions, sauté until tender, discard the garlic clove. Sprinkle with flour and cook for 2 minutes over low heat. Add the soya, Worcestershire, wine and broth, simmer until sauce thickens.

Stir in the fish and continue to simmer for 5 minutes.

Beat the egg with a little sauce and slowly add this to the mixture, simmer for 1 minute, do not boil, remove from heat and serve over rice or noodles.

SERVES 4

Kharia Swordfish

Honey Mustard Seafood Kebabs

SHRIMP FRICASSEE

2 tbsp	30 ml	butter
2 tbsp	30 ml	finely chopped onion
2 tbsp	30 ml	finely chopped green bell peppers
2 tbsp	30 ml	finely chopped red bell peppers
1	1	minced garlic clove
2 tbsp	30 ml	flour, all purpose
1½ cups	375 ml	crushed tomatoes
¼ tsp	1 ml	each of, pepper, paprika, basil, chervil, marjoram
1 tbsp	15 ml	chopped parsley
1 tsp	5 ml	salt
⅛ tsp	5 drops	Tabasco™ sauce
½ tsp	3 ml	Worcestershire sauce
1 lb	454 g	peeled, deveined shrimp
2½ cups	625 ml	cooked long grain rice

In a large skillet heat the butter and sauté the vegetables until tender, sprinkle with flour and cook for 2 minutes over low heat.

Add the tomatoes, seasonings, Tabasco sauce and Worcestershire, cover and simmer for 15 minutes.

Stir in the shrimp and continue to simmer for an additional 10 minutes.

Place the rice on a serving platter, cover with shrimp, then sauce and serve at once.

SERVES 4

SALMON ROSÉ

4 – 6 oz	4 – 170 g	salmon fillets
3 cups	750 ml	rosé wine
3 tbsp	45 ml	butter
3 tbsp	45 ml	flour, all purpose
½ cup	125 ml	heavy cream
3 tbsp	45 ml	chopped shallot
1 tbsp	15 ml	chopped fresh basil

Wash and pat dry the salmon fillets. Pour 2 cups (500 ml) of rosé into a large pan or skillet. Bring to a boil, reduce to simmer. Poach the salmon in the wine for 10-12 minutes.

In a sauce pan heat the butter, add the flour and cook for 2 minutes over low heat. Add the remaining cup of rosé and the cream. Simmer until sauce thickens. Stir in the shallots and basil.

Plate the salmon and serve smothered with the sauce.

SERVES 4

SALMON OSCAR

4 – 6 oz	4 – 170 g	salmon fillets
2 tbsp	30 ml	melted butter
8 oz	225 g	cooked snow crab meat
12	12	asparagus spears
1 cup	250 ml	Béarnaise Sauce (see page 108)

Place the salmon fillets on a baking dish. Brush with melted butter. Bake in a 350°F (180°C) preheated oven for 10-12 minutes.

Remove the salmon from the oven and turn the oven to broil.

Top each fillet with 2 oz (30 g) crab meat, 4 asparagus spears and equal amounts of béarnaise sauce. Return to oven for 3-4 minutes or until sauce is golden. Serve at once.

SERVES 4

Salmon Rosé

Salmon Oscar

RED WINE TUNA STEW

4 tbsp	60 ml	safflower oil
8	8	slices of bacon
20	20	button mushrooms
20	20	pearl onions
3	3	celery stalks, diced
3	3	carrots, diced
4 tbsp	60 ml	flour, all purpose
1 cup	250 ml	tomatoes, peeled, seeded, chopped
2 cup	500 ml	red wine
1 cup	250 ml	Beef Stock (see page 85)
2 tsp	10 ml	Worcestershire sauce
1 tbsp	15 ml	soya sauce
½ tsp	3 ml	Dijon mustard
¼ tsp	1 ml	salt
¼ tsp	1 ml	cracked black pepper
1 ½ lbs	675 g	boneless cubed fresh tuna

Dice the bacon, fry in a large kettle, add the oil and the vegetables, sauté for 3 minutes. Sprinkle with flour and cook for 3 minutes. Add the remaining ingredients except tuna. Cover and simmer gently for 20 minutes.

Add the tuna and continue to simmer for 30 minutes, covered. Serve with rice or over noodles.

SERVES 6

LOBSTER OH MY

¼ tsp	1 ml	salt
¼ tsp	1 ml	cracked black pepper
3 tbsp	45 ml	soya sauce
3 tbsp	45 ml	sherry
1 tsp	5 ml	minced green onion
¼ tsp	1 ml	garlic powder
¼ tsp	1 ml	ground ginger or Chinese 5 spice
2 tsp	10 ml	brown sugar
1 lb	450 g	lobster meat
2 tbsp	30 ml	sesame oil
1 tbsp	15 ml	water
1 tsp	5 ml	cornstarch

Blend the salt, pepper, soya sauce, sherry, green onion, garlic, ginger and sugar.

Coarse dice the lobster meat.

Heat the oil in a large skillet or wok and fry the lobster in the oil quickly for 3 minutes. Add the sauce and reduce the heat.

Blend the water with the cornstarch and add to the lobster and simmer until thickened. Serve at once with Bombay Rice (see page 709).

SERVES 4

CALIFORNIAN CRAB SURPRISE

3 tbsp	45 ml	olive oil
3 tbsp	45 ml	flour, all purpose
⅔ cup	160 ml	Chicken Broth (see page 77)
⅔ cup	160 ml	light cream
¼ cup	80 ml	tomato catsup
2 tsp	10 ml	Worcestershire sauce
1 tsp	5 ml	paprika
3 drops	3 drops	Tabasco™ sauce
1 tbsp	15 ml	lemon juice
1¾ lbs	800 g	shelled crab claws
3 cups	750 ml	Spanish Rice (see page 749)

Heat the oil in a sauce pan, add the flour and cook for 2 minutes over low heat.

Whisk in the broth and cream and simmer until thick. Whisk in the catsup, Worcestershire, paprika, Tabasco and lemon juice continue to simmer for 2 additional minutes. Add the crab claws, simmer for an additional 10 minutes.

Place the rice on serving plates, cover with mixture and serve.

SERVES 6

Red Wine Tuna Stew

Chef K Barbecued Shrimp

CHEF K BARBECUED SHRIMP

3 tbsp	45 ml	butter
3 tbsp	45 ml	oil
1	1	minced onion
1	1	garlic clove, minced
⅔ cup	160 ml	tomato catsup
⅔ cup	160 ml	orange brandy
½ cup	125 ml	cider vinegar
½ cup	125 ml	orange juice
½ cup	125 ml	orange juice concentrate
⅓ cup	80 ml	light molasses
1 tbsp	15 ml	Worcestershire sauce
½ tsp	3 ml	each of thyme leaves, basil leaves, chervil, oregano leaves, garlic powder, cracked black pepper, white pepper, paprika, salt
¼ tsp	1 ml	Tabasco™ sauce
½ tsp	3 ml	liquid smoke flavouring
2 ¼ lbs	1 kg	tiger prawns or very large shrimp
1 quan	1	Court Bouillon (see page 117)
3 tbsp	45 ml	melted butter

Heat the butter in a sauce pan with the oil, add the onion and garlic. Sauté until tender.

Stir in the catsup, brandy, vinegar, orange juice, concentrate, molasses, Worcestershire, seasonings, Tabasco and smoke flavouring and bring to a boil. Reduce heat and simmer until sauce is very thick. Cool.

Peel and devein the prawns. Bring the court bouillon to a boil and simmer the prawns until cooked. Toss the prawns in the barbecue sauce and serve.

Or, brush the prawns with melted butter and grill over medium coals for 10 minutes brushing often with sauce.

SERVES 6

Port & Raspberry Orange Roughy

TERIYAKI SALMON

⅓ cup	80 ml	brown sugar
1 tsp	5 ml	ground ginger
1 cup	250 ml	Beef Broth (see page 85)
⅓ cup	80 ml	soya sauce
2 tbsp	30 ml	cornstarch
¼ cup	60 ml	white wine
4 – 6 oz	4 – 170 g	salmon steaks, 1" (2.5 cm) thick

Dissolve the sugar and ginger in the broth and soya sauce in a sauce pan. Bring to a boil. Blend the cornstarch in the wine. Add to the broth and simmer until thickened. Cool.

Place salmon in a shallow tray, cover with the sauce and marinade 1 hour, refrigerate.

Grill the salmon steaks on a charbroiler over medium coals, or in the oven for 10 minutes, turning once. Brush with sauce several times during grilling.

SERVES 4

MUSHROOM TROUT

6 – 8 oz	6 – 225 g	trout
5 tbsp	75 ml	butter
1¾ cups	440 ml	finely sliced mushrooms
2 tbsp	30 ml	minced chives
1½ cup	375 ml	fresh bread crumbs
2 tbsp	30 ml	chopped parsley
1 tsp	5 ml	each of basil, chervil and salt
½ tsp	3 ml	cracked black pepper
¾ cup	190 g	small cooked shrimp
¼ cup	60 ml	heavy cream

Wash and pat dry the trout.

Heat 3 tbsp (45 ml) of butter in a skillet, sauté the mushrooms until all liquid has evaporated.

Combine the mushrooms with the remaining ingredients in a mixing bowl thoroughly. Stuff into the cavity of the trout.

Place trout into a small casserole dish, brush with the remaining butter. Bake in a preheated 375°F (190°F) oven for 20 minutes. Serve.

SERVES 6

PORT & RASPBERRY ORANGE ROUGHY

½ cup	125 ml	red currant preserves
¼ cup	60 ml	port
2 tsp	10 ml	lemon juice
1½ cups	375 ml	raspberries
2 tsp	10 ml	cornstarch
¼ tsp	1 ml	cracked black pepper
4 – 6 oz	4 – 170 g	orange roughy fillets
1 tbsp	15 ml	melted butter

Place the red currant preserves into a small sauce pan, add the port and lemon juice, simmer over low heat.

Press the raspberries through a sieve to remove the seeds, pour into the sauce. Bring sauce to a boil.

Blend the cornstarch with 1 tbsp (15 ml) of water, add to the sauce and simmer until thick. Remove from heat and stir in the black pepper.

Brush the orange roughy with the butter, bake in a preheated 350°F (180°C) oven for 8 minutes.

Plate the fish, pour the sauce over and serve.

SERVES 4

Teriyaki Salmon

NEW ORLEANS TIGER PRAWNS

3 tbsp	45 ml	safflower oil
3	3	finely diced onions
2	2	finely diced green bell peppers
3	3	finely diced celery stalks
20	20	peeled, seeded and chopped tomatoes
2 tsp	10 ml	salt
2 tsp	10 ml	paprika
1 tsp	5 ml	each of garlic powder, onion powder, cayenne pepper, basil leaves
½ tsp	3 ml	each of white pepper, black pepper, oregano leaves, thyme leaves
2 tsp	10 ml	Worcestershire sauce
¼ tsp	1 ml	Tabasco™ sauce
6	6	diced green onions
1	1	bunch chopped parsley
2 ¼ lbs	1 kg	tiger prawns or very large shrimp
1 quan	1	Court Bouillon (see page 117)
1 quan	1	Rice Matriciana (see page 757)

Heat the oil in a large sauce pan. Sauté the onion, celery and green pepper until tender. Add the tomatoes and seasoning, Worcestershire sauce, Tabasco and simmer gently until the desired thickness has been achieved (about 4 hours).

Add the green onion and parsley. Simmer 15 minutes longer.

During the last half hour of simmering of the sauce bring the court bouillon to a boil. Peel and devein the tiger prawns, simmer gently until cooked, 12 minutes approximately.

Plate the rice, smother with sauce and top with prawns.

Serve at once.

SERVES 6

New Orleans Tiger Prawns

FILLETS OF SOLE FLORENTINE STYLE "FILETTI DI SOGLIOLA ALLA FIORENTINA"

4 – 6 oz	4 – 170 g	sole fillets
3 cups	750 ml	fish stock
10 oz	280 g	fresh chopped spinach
3 tbsp	45 ml	dry white wine
1 cup	250 ml	cooked bay shrimp meat
1 ¼ cups	310 ml	Mornay Sauce (see page 111)
¼ cup	60 ml	freshly grated Parmesan cheese
¼ cup	60 ml	freshly grated Romano cheese
3 tbsp	45 ml	pitted, sliced black olives
¼ cup	60 ml	peeled, seeded, chopped tomatoes

Wash and pat dry the fillets. Place the fish stock in a large pan, bring to a boil, reduce heat to simmer. Gently poach the sole in the broth for 5-6 minutes, then remove and reserve.

Steam the spinach and drain. Then place in a casserole dish. Top with the fillets. Sprinkle with the wine and spread with the shrimp meat.

Cover casserole with mornay sauce and sprinkle on the cheeses.

Bake in a preheated oven 400°F (200°C) for 10 minutes. Garnish with the olives and tomatoes. Serve at once.

SERVES 4

Salmon & Shrimp Pie

SALMON & SHRIMP PIE

½ quan	0.5 quan	Plain Pastry (see page 616)
1 cup	250 ml	finely diced cooked salmon
1 cup	250 ml	finely diced cooked shrimp
2 cups	500 ml	Velouté (see page 105)
¼ tsp	1 ml	each of salt, pepper, nutmeg
1 tbsp	15 ml	parsley
1 tbsp	15 ml	grated onion
3	3	eggs, separated

Roll out the pie dough and fit into a 9" deep dish pie shell.

In a mixing bowl blend the salmon, shrimp and Velouté. Add the seasonings and onion.

Beat the egg yolks and fold into the mixture. Beat the egg whites stiffly, fold into the mixture.

Pour mixture into the pie shell and bake 25-30 minutes in a preheated 400°F (200°C) oven or until the mixture has risen and is golden brown. Serve at once.

SERVES 6

LEMONADE BARBECUE SWORDFISH

¾ cup	190 ml	lemonade concentrate
¼ cup	60 ml	catsup
3 tbsp	45 ml	brown sugar
3 tbsp	45 ml	white vinegar
¼ tsp	1 ml	ground ginger
1 tsp	5 ml	soya sauce
¼ tsp	1 ml	each of paprika, chili powder, garlic powder, onion powder, thyme, basil, oregano, salt and pepper
1 – 2¼ lb	1 – 1 kg	swordfish, cut in pieces
½ cup	125 ml	flour, all purpose
¼ cup	60 ml	safflower oil

In a mixing bowl combine the concentrate, catsup, sugar, vinegar, ginger, soya and seasonings.

Dredge the swordfish in the flour. Heat the oil in a large kettle or Dutch oven, brown the swordfish. Drain any excess oil. Pour the sauce over the swordfish, cook over low heat for 15 minutes covered.

SERVES 4

GOURMET CATFISH

8 – 4 oz	8 – 115 g	catfish fillets
2	2	eggs
¼ cup	60 ml	milk
½ cup	125 ml	flour, all purpose
1⅓ cups	325 ml	bread crumbs
1 tbsp	15 ml	paprika
1 tsp	5 ml	each of oregano, thyme, sage, garlic powder, onion powder, black pepper, marjoram, chili powder
2 cups	500 ml	safflower oil
3 tbsp	45 ml	butter
3 tbsp	45 ml	flour, all purpose
½ cup	125 ml	Chicken Stock (see page 77)
½ cup	125 ml	heavy cream
½ cup	125 ml	champagne

Wash the catfish and pat dry.

In a mixing bowl, combine the eggs and the milk. Place the flour in a second bowl and the bread crumbs in a third. Blend the seasonings into the bread crumbs.

Dust the catfish with the flour, dip into the eggs and dredge in the bread crumbs.

Heat the oil to 325°F (160°C). Fry the catfish to golden brown in small batches being sure that the fish is cooked thoroughly. Cooking time is dependent on the size of the fish pieces.

Reserve hot until all fish is cooked.

Melt the butter in a sauce pan. Add the remaining flour and stir into a paste (roux) cooking over low heat.

Add chicken stock, cream and champagne. Whisk all the ingredients together.

Simmer for 10 minutes over medium heat.

Plate the fish and smother with sauce, serve.

SERVES 4

OCEAN PERCH ROLLUPS

6 – 4 oz	6 – 120 g	ocean perch fillets
1 cup	250 ml	green seedless grapes
6 oz	170 g	rindless Brie cheese
1 cup	250 ml	baby shrimp
2	2	eggs
⅓ cup	80 ml	milk
⅓ cup	80 ml	ground pine nuts
½ cup	125 ml	fine seasoned bread crumbs
⅓ cup	80 ml	freshly grated Romano cheese
½ cup	125 ml	flour, all purpose
⅓ cup	80 ml	safflower oil

Place the perch between two pieces of waxed paper, pound flat with a meat mallet.

Cut the grapes in half and place a few grapes on the perch along with 1 oz (30 g) of cheese and a sprinkling of shrimp. Roll the perch to enfold the filling inside. Place on a baking pan and refrigerate for 1 hour.

Blend the eggs and milk together. Mix the nuts with the bread crumbs and cheese. Dust the rolled chicken with flour. Dip the perch into the egg wash then roll in the bread crumbs.

In a large skillet heat the oil, fry the perch to golden brown on each side. Serve with a Blackberry Brandy Sauce (see Roast Veal with Blackberry Brandy Sauce, page 214)

SERVES 6

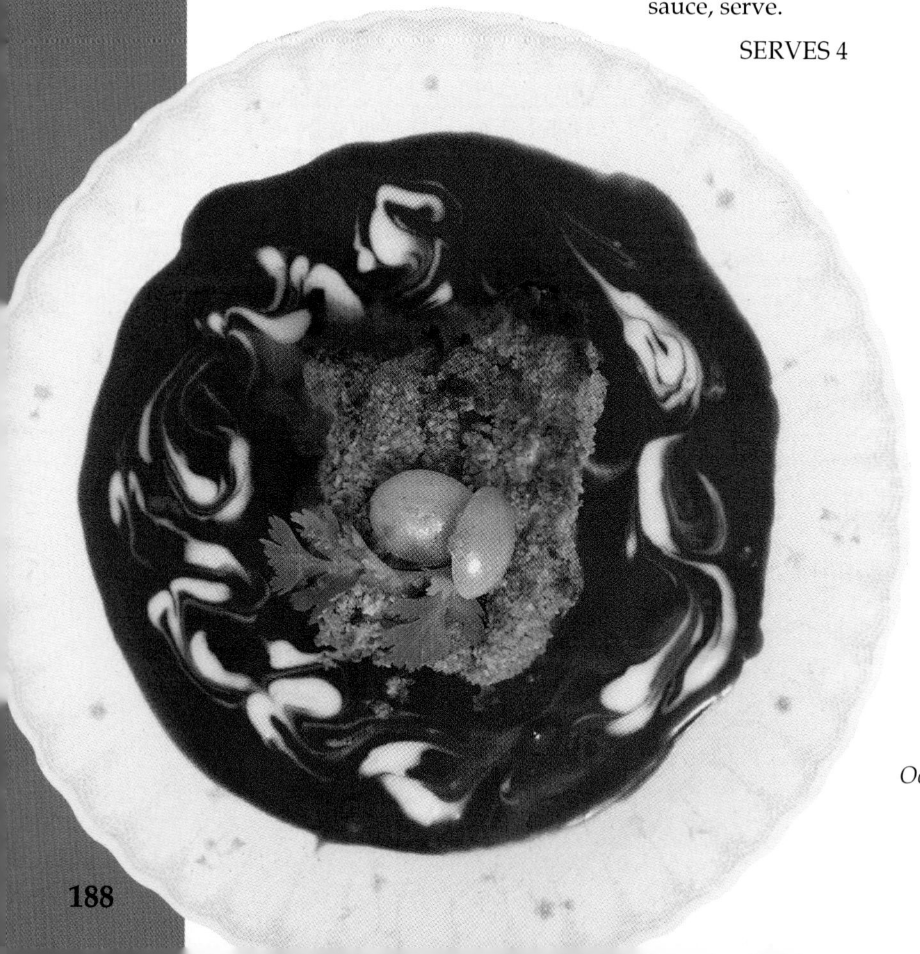

Ocean Perch Rollups

Gourmet Catfish

Smoked Canadian Black Cod with Herb Lemon Butter

SMOKED CANADIAN BLACK COD

1 cup	250 ml	Riesling white wine
2 cups	500 ml	water
10	10	black peppercorns
1	1	bay leaf
1	1	sprig parsley
½ tsp	3 ml	each of thyme, basil, marjoram
1	1	small diced Spanish onion
2	2	pared, diced carrots
2	2	diced celery stalks
1	1	lemon, cut in half
4 – 6 oz	4 – 170 g	black cod fillets (sablefish)

In a large stock pot or Dutch oven combine the wine and water.

Tie the peppercorns, bay leaf, parsley and herbs together in a cheesecloth and place in the pot. Add the vegetables and lemon. Bring to a boil, reduce heat and simmer for 10 minutes.

Place the fillets in the pot and coddle, very gentle simmer for 15 minutes. Remove to serving plates and serve at once with Herb Lemon Butter (recipe follows), fresh steamed carrots, broccoli and a rice pilaf.

SERVES 4

HERB LEMON BUTTER

1 cup	250 ml	softened butter
½ tsp	3 ml	each of basil, thyme, oregano, marjoram
1 tbsp	15 ml	lemon zest
3 tbsp	45 ml	lemon juice

Blend the ingredients together. Place on a sheet of waxed paper and roll together. Refrigerate for 1 hour. Remove waxed paper and slice. Place 2 slices on each fillet.

SHRIMP STUFFED TROUT

6 – 8 oz	6 – 225 g	trout
2 tbsp	30 ml	minced chives
1½ cup	375 ml	fresh bread crumbs
2 tbsp	30 ml	chopped parsley
1 tsp	5 ml	each of basil, chervil and salt
½ tsp	3 ml	cracked black pepper
¾ cup	190 g	small cooked shrimp
¼ cup	60 ml	heavy cream
3 tbsp	45 ml	melted butter

Wash and pat dry the trout.

Combine the remaining ingredients in a mixing bowl thoroughly. Stuff into the cavity of the trout.

Place trout into a small casserole dish, brush with butter. Bake in a preheated 375°F (190°C) oven for 20 minutes. Serve.

SERVES 6

Shrimp Stuffed Trout

BÉARNAISE RED SNAPPER CASSEROLE

1½ lbs	675 g	red snapper fillets
¾ cup	190 ml	butter
1	1	small, finely diced onion
¼ cup	60 ml	finely diced red bell pepper
¼ cup	60 ml	finely diced yellow bell pepper
¼ cup	60 ml	finely diced green bell pepper
2⅔ cups	675 ml	cooked long grain rice
3 tbsp	45 ml	white wine
1 tbsp	15 ml	dried tarragon leaves
1 tsp	5 ml	lemon juice
3	3	egg yolks
1 tsp	5 ml	fresh chopped tarragon

Cut the red snapper into large cubes.

Heat 3 tbsp (45 ml) of the butter in a large skillet and sauté the fish, remove and reserve. Add the onions, and peppers to the skillet and sauté until tender. Mix in the rice and cook for 8 minutes. Place into a greased casserole dish.

Place fish on top, cover with waxed paper and bake in a preheated 350°F (180°C) for 15 minutes.

While fish bakes combine the wine, tarragon and lemon juice in a small sauce pan. Over high heat reduce to 2 tbsp (30 ml), then strain.

In another small sauce pan, melt the butter and heat to almost boiling.

In a blender or food processor, process egg yolks until blended.

With machine running, add the butter in a slow thin stream.

With the machine on slow, add reduced wine mixture. Process just until blended, place in a serving bowl. Stir in the fresh tarragon.

Remove waxed paper, spread sauce over fish, increase the oven temperature to 450°F (230°C) and bake for 10 minutes or until sauce is golden brown.

SERVES 6

Oysters Casino

OYSTERS CASINO

36	36	oysters
6	6	slices diced bacon
1	1	finely diced small onion
¼ cup	60 ml	finely diced green bell pepper
¼ cup	60 ml	finely diced celery
1 tbsp	15 ml	lemon juice
1 tsp	5 ml	salt
¼ tsp	1 ml	pepper
1 tsp	5 ml	Worcestershire sauce
⅛ tsp	5 drops	Tabasco™ sauce
½ cup	125 ml	grated Provolone cheese

Shuck the oysters and place on a baking sheet.

In a sauce pan fry the bacon and drain all but 2 tsp (10 ml) of fat. Sauté the onion, bell pepper and celery until tender. Add the remaining ingredients and simmer for 5 minutes.

Ladle equal amounts of mixture onto the oysters, bake in a preheated 350°F (180°C) oven for 10 minutes, sprinkle with cheese and continue to bake for 5 minutes or until golden brown. Serve very hot.

SERVES 6

Great for clams as well.

Salmon Vol au Vént

SALMON VOL AU VÉNT

1 quan	1	Puff Pastry (see page 689)
2	2	beaten eggs
1½ lbs	675 g	salmon fillets
4 tbsp	60 ml	butter
2 tbsp	30 ml	flour
1 cup	250 ml	milk
¼ tsp	1 ml	salt
¼ tsp	1 ml	white pepper
1 tsp	5 ml	basil
2 tbsp	30 ml	finely diced red pimento

Roll the pastry out as directed. Cut out 6 – 4" (10 cm) rounds, and 6 – 3" (7.5 cm) rounds with a 2" (5 cm) hole in the middle. Place the 4" (10 cm) rounds on a baking sheet, brush with egg and top with the 3" (7.5 cm) round and brush with egg. Bake in a 425°F (215°C) oven for 5 minutes, reduce heat to 350°F (180°C) and continue to bake for an additional 20-25 minutes. Remove from heat and cool, remove and reserve the centre.

Dice the salmon into small pieces. Heat 2 tbsp (30 ml) of butter in a skillet and sauté the salmon.

Melt the remaining butter in a sauce pan. Add flour and stir into a paste (roux) cook for 2 minutes over low heat.

Add the milk and stir; simmer until thickened. Add the seasonings and pimento, simmer 2 additional minutes. Stir in the salmon and simmer for 5 minutes.

Ladle the salmon into the pastry shells, top with the reserved pastry centre and serve.

SERVES 6

PISZTRANG — TROUT WITH WHITE WINE MAYONNAISE

4 tbsp	60 ml	white wine
3	3	egg yolks
½ cup	125 ml	oil
4 – 8 oz	4 – 225 g	trout – dressed or cleaned
3 tbsp	45 ml	butter
1 tbsp	15 ml	lemon juice

Reduce the wine in a sauce pan to 2 tbsp (30 ml). In a blender or food processor, process egg yolks until blended. With machine running add the oil in a slow thin stream. With machine on low add the wine. Process until blended, pour into a sauce boat.

Sauté the trout over medium heat for 4-6 minutes per side in the butter and lemon juice. Serve with the mayonnaise on the side.

SERVES 4

Zuppa Di Pesce

Salmon Jambalaya

SALMON JAMBALAYA

2 tbsp	30 ml	safflower oil
2 tbsp	30 ml	butter
½ lb	225 g	andouille sausage (see Glossary)
½ cup	125 ml	diced onions
2	2	minced garlic cloves
3 tbsp	45 ml	chopped parsley
1½ cups	375 ml	diced green bell pepper
2	2	diced celery stalks
2 cups	500 ml	peeled, seeded, chopped tomatoes
1 tsp	5 ml	salt
½ tsp	3 ml	each of white pepper, black pepper, oregano leaves, basil, thyme leaves, garlic powder, onion powder, chili powder
2 tsp	10 ml	Worcestershire sauce
⅛ tsp	5 drops	Tabasco™ sauce
1 ½ cup	375 ml	water
1 cup	250 ml	raw long grain rice
1 ½ lbs	670 g	coarse diced boneless salmon
2 cups	500 ml	cooked crayfish tails

In a Dutch oven or large kettle, sauté the sausage in the oil and butter. Add the vegetables, continue to sauté until vegetables are tender.

Stir in all the remaining ingredients except the salmon and cray fish, reduce heat, cover and simmer on low heat for 40 minutes. Stir in the fish and continue to cook for 15 minutes. Serve.

SERVES 6

ZUPPA DI PESCE

2 tbsp	30 ml	olive oil
4 oz	120 g	halved mushrooms
1	1	diced medium onion
2	2	diced carrots
2	2	diced celery stalks
4 cups	1 L	Fish Broth (see page 76)
1 ½ cups	375 ml	peeled, seeded and chopped tomatoes
8 oz	225 g	coarse diced red snapper
8 oz	225 g	coarse diced lobster meat
8 oz	225 g	peeled and deveined shrimp
8 oz	225 g	scallops
16	16	debearded, washed mussels
16	16	washed, brushed clams
½ cup	125 ml	white wine
½ tsp	3 ml	salt
1 tsp	5 ml	fresh chopped basil

Heat the oil in a large Dutch oven or kettle. Add the vegetables and sauté until tender.

Add the tomatoes and broth, simmer for 5 minutes.

Add all remaining ingredients, simmer gently for 15 minutes, serve at once.

SERVES 4

Salmon Grandduke Style

SALMON GRANDDUKE STYLE

4 – 6 oz	4 – 170 g	salmon fillets, 1" (2.5 cm) thick
5 tbsp	75 ml	butter
3 cups	750 ml	chicken broth
3 tbsp	45 ml	flour, all purpose
½ cup	125 ml	heavy cream
¼ cup	60 ml	Crayfish Butter (see page 112)
1 cup	250 ml	cooked crayfish tails
1 cup	250 ml	blanched asparagus tips
⅓ cup	90 ml	freshly grated Parmesan cheese
4	4	large slices of truffles

Wash and pat dry the salmon fillets. Place on a baking sheet. Melt 2 tbsp (30 ml) of the butter and brush on fish. Bake in a preheated 350°F (180°C) oven for 10 minutes.

Heat the chicken broth to a boil, reduce to 1½ (375 ml) cups of liquid.

Heat the remaining butter in a sauce pan and add the flour, cook over low heat for 2 minutes. Add the reduced broth and cream, simmer until thick. Stir in the crayfish butter, crayfish tails and asparagus tips, simmer for 3 minutes and add the cheese.

Place the fish on serving plates, smother with sauce and top with a truffle slice.

Serve at once.

SERVES 4

SCALLOP FRITTERS

1¼ cups	310 ml	flour, all purpose
2	2	separated eggs
¾ cup	190 ml	beer
¼ tsp	1 ml	each of thyme, cayenne, salt, pepper, basil
3 cups	750 ml	safflower oil
2¼ lbs	1 kg	large sea scallops
2 cups	500 ml	Remoulade Sauce (see page 123)

Combine the 1 cup (250 ml) flour and the egg yolks in a mixing bowl. Pour in sufficient beer to make a smooth batter. Beat in the seasonings. Allow batter to rest for 1 hour.

Beat the egg whites stiff and fold into the batter.

Heat the oil to 375°F (180°C).

Dust the scallops with the remaining flour and dip into the batter and fry in small batches to golden brown, reserve hot while others batches cook.

Serve with Remoulade Sauce.

SERVES 6

SAUTÉED ORANGE ROUGHY WITH CLEMENTINE SAUCE

6 – 6 oz	6 – 170 g	orange roughy fillets
3 tbsp	45 ml	oil
		salt and pepper
⅓ cup	80 ml	tangerine or orange juice concentrate
½ cup	125 ml	Chicken Stock (see page 77)
¼ cup	60 ml	whipping cream
1 tsp	5 ml	butter
¼ tsp	1 ml	cracked black pepper
1 tsp	5 ml	lime juice

Heat the oil in a large skillet. Sauté the fillets for 6-8 minutes. Season with salt and pepper and reserve hot.

Heat the tangerine juice in a sauce pan with the chicken stock, bring to a boil and reduce heat. Add the cream and simmer until sauce coats a spoon. Remove from heat. Whip in the butter, pepper and lime juice.

Place the fillets on a serving plate, cover with sauce and serve.

SERVES 6

Scallop Fritters

SHRIMP CHASSEUR

1 lb	454 g	peeled and deveined large shrimp
¼ cup	60 ml	butter
1 tbsp	15 ml	safflower oil
4 oz	115 g	sliced mushrooms
1 tsp	5 ml	minced green onions
3 tbsp	45 ml	brandy
⅓ cup	90 ml	white wine
1 ¼ cups	310 ml	Demi-Glace (see page 123)
2 tbsp	30 ml	tomato paste
1 tsp	5 ml	fresh chopped parsley
3 cups	750 ml	steamed rice

Wash the shrimp and drain.

Heat 1 tbsp (15 ml) butter with the oil in a small sauce pan and sauté the mushrooms with the onions. Add the brandy and wine, reduce to half its volume. Add the demi-glace and tomato paste. Bring to a boil, reduce heat and simmer for 5 minutes. Stir in the parsley.

In a skillet, heat the remaining butter and sauté the shrimp. Pour sauce over shrimp. Place rice on serving plates, top with shrimp and sauce and serve.

SERVES 4

TUNA AND RICE

¼ cup	60 ml	butter
1½ lbs	680 g	boneless diced tuna
½ lb	225 g	sliced mushrooms
¼ cup	60 ml	fine diced onions
3 tbsp	45 ml	flour, all purpose
1½ cups	375 ml	Chicken Broth (see page 77)
½ cup	125 ml	light cream
¼ cup	60 ml	sherry
⅓ cup	90 ml	toasted sliced almonds
2 cups	500 ml	cooked long grain rice
		parsley sprigs

In a large kettle or Dutch oven heat the butter, add the tuna and brown. Remove the tuna and reserve.

Add the mushrooms and onions and sauté until tender. Sprinkle with flour and cook for 2 minutes over low heat. Add the broth, cream and sherry, simmer for 3 minutes.

Return the tuna and continue to simmer for an additional 35 minutes.

Stir the almonds into the rice and spoon the rice around the edges of a serving platter. Ladle the tuna into the centre and serve garnished with parsley.

SERVES 4

SEAFOOD À L'ÉTOUFFÉE

⅓ cup	90 ml	butter
¾ cup	190 ml	diced onions
1	1	diced green bell pepper
2 cups	500 ml	peeled, seeded, diced tomatoes
1 tsp	5 ml	each of salt, pepper, paprika
½ tsp	3 ml	each of oregano leaves, thyme leaves, cayenne pepper, garlic powder, onion powder, chili powder
1 tsp	5 ml	Worcestershire sauce
⅛ tsp	5 drops	Tabasco™ sauce
¼ cup	60 ml	chopped green onions
2 tbsp	30 ml	chopped parsley
1 lb	454 g	peeled and deveined shrimp
½ lb	225 g	crab meat
¼ lb	115 g	lobster meat
4 cups	1 L	steamed rice

Melt the butter in a sauce pan. Add the onion and pepper, sauté until tender. Add the tomatoes, seasonings, Worcestershire and Tabasco. Reduce heat and simmer for 30 minutes.

Add the chopped onion, parsley and seafood, cover and simmer for 15 minutes.

Place rice on serving plates, cover with mixture and serve.

SERVES 6

Seafood à l'Étouffée

Shrimp Chasseur

OCEAN PERCH WITH STRAWBERRY ITALIAN WINE CREAM

6 – 4 oz	6 – 120 g	ocean perch fillets
1 tbsp	15 ml	olive oil
¼ tsp	1 ml	each of basil, salt, pepper, paprika
6	6	egg yolks
½ cup	125 ml	granulated sugar
½ cup	125 ml	Marsala or sweet sherry
1½ cups	375 ml	sliced strawberries

Brush the perch with the oil, sprinkle with seasonings. Broil in the oven for 3-5 minutes per side. Reserve warm.

Beat the egg yolks with the sugar in the top of a double boiler until foamy and pale in colour. Place over the boiling water. Slowly add the sherry beating continuously until mixture becomes thick and foamy. Remove from heat, stir in the strawberries.

Place perch on a serving platter and pour half the sauce over the perch and serve with the remaining sauce on the side.

SERVES 6

SEA BASS FINOCCHIO

1½ lbs	675 g	boneless sea bass fillets
3 cups	750 ml	Chicken Broth (see page 77)
6 tbsp	90 ml	butter
1½ cups	375 ml	finely chopped fennel
1	1	julienne cut carrot
1	1	julienne red bell pepper
3 tbsp	45 ml	flour, all purpose
¾ cup	190 ml	light cream
1 quan	1 quan	Risotto Alla Certosian (see page 740)

Dice the bass into large cubes.

Heat the broth in a large kettle or Dutch oven and gently poach the bass for 10 minutes. Remove and reserve the bass, strain the broth. Return the broth to the pot and bring to a boil, reduce to 1½ cups.

In a sauce pan heat the butter and sauté the vegetables until tender. Sprinkle with flour and cook over low heat for 2 minutes. Add the broth and the cream and simmer until sauce thickens. Stir in the bass and continue to simmer for 5 minutes.

Place the risotto around the rim of a serving dish, ladle the bass into the centre and serve.

SERVES 4

RANA PESCATRICE AL FORNO

1 ½ lbs	750 g	monk fish tails – skinless
2 tbsp	30 ml	olive oil
1	1	finely diced small onion
1	1	finely diced celery stalk
1 cup	250 ml	sliced mushrooms
1 tbsp	15 ml	flour, all purpose
1 cup	250 ml	seeded, peeled, and diced tomatoes
½ cup	125 ml	Fish Broth (see page 76) or Chicken Broth (see page 77)
½ tsp	3 ml	basil leaves

Place the monkfish in a large casserole dish. Heat the oil in a large skillet, sauté the onion, celery and mushroom until tender. Sprinkle with flour, reduce heat, cook for 2 minutes.

Add the tomatoes, broth and basil. Simmer for 5 minutes. Pour over fish, cover the casserole and bake in a preheated 350°F (180°C) oven for 30 minutes.

SERVES 4

Sea Bass Finocchio

Rana Pescatrice Al Forno

BEEF AND VEAL

Like all other chapters in this book, we offer to you some of the most creative of all recipes. There can never be boredom cooking from *Simply Delicious Cooking 2*. You may choose Cajun, Oriental, German, or any other food style; you will always find a great selection here. Creative use of recipes such as Paupiettes De Veau—Veal Birds or Beef Ribs Diable will always leave a guest with an aspiration of returning.

Use the best cuts suited to your task and never compromise on quality. After all, you have to eat it as well. Trim away excess fat and follow the cooking methods for best results. The grain fed beef of western Canada and the corn fed beef of mid-west America are the finest in the world. Purchase them above all else. Always use the finest in ingredients, as they will make all the difference in the final offering. Aged meats are preferred (21-30 days of aging) and they are usually not what one receives from the supermarket, so buy them from a good, reliable butcher. That would be the first step in preparing your recipe.

Salting and seasoning of grilled meats should be done when one is almost finished. Adding these to the cooking of meats any earlier will tend to dry the food. Avoid salting, if possible; try using herbs and spices instead. You'll find they provide a far superior product.

Slow, long roasting will always provide an incomparable product over that of quick, high heat. Try braising, grilling, sautéing or even boiling your meats. If people would be more creative in the fashion in which they cook, they would not require so many trends in their food, for they would achieve all their dietary goals just by using creativity.

This, then, is what we have offered you within *Simply Delicious Cooking 2*. Whether you choose a Tomato and Veal Stew, a grilled California Kebab or a Roast Veal with Blackberry Brandy Sauce, your creativity will shine forth.

In France, one may say, "les plaísírs de la bonne table," that they have enjoyed the pleasures of a fine table, especially when it is of your cooking derived from this book. In English, like always, they say "it was just *Simply Delicious*."

Baron of Roast Beef

Tom's Steak Lasagna

TOM'S STEAK LASAGNA

1 quan	1	Basic Pasta Dough (see page 426)
1 lb	454 g	thin sliced sirloin steak
3 tbsp	45 ml	olive oil
1	1	sliced Spanish onion
1	1	sliced red bell pepper
1	1	sliced green bell pepper
3	3	diced celery stalks
2	2	minced garlic cloves
2 cups	500 ml	peeled, seeded, diced tomatoes
½ tsp	3 ml	each of oregano leaves, thyme leaves, basil, marjoram, chervil, paprika, pepper, onion powder, garlic powder
1 tsp	5 ml	salt
2 tsp	10 ml	chili powder
1 cup	250 ml	ricotta cheese
1½ cups	375 ml	grated cheddar
2	2	eggs
1	1	chopped green onion
1½ cups	375 ml	grated mozzarella

Process the dough as per instructions. Cut into lasagna noodles. Reserve.

In a large skillet, fry the steak in the oil. Add the onion, bell peppers, celery and garlic. Sauté until tender. Add the tomatoes and seasonings, cover and simmer for 30 minutes.

Blend together the ricotta, cheddar, eggs and green onions.

In a large, greased casserole dish, alternate layers of pasta, steak sauce, and cheese mixture. Finish with a layer of sauce. Cover with mozzarella cheese.

Bake in a preheated 375°F (190°C) oven for 50-60 minutes or until cheese is golden brown. Serve at once.

SERVES 6

HONEY BARBECUED VEAL STEAKS

3 tbsp	45 ml	butter
3 tbsp	45 ml	oil
1	1	minced medium onion
1	1	minced garlic clove
⅔ cup	160 ml	tomato catsup
⅔ cup	160 ml	liquid honey
¼ cup	60 ml	cider vinegar
1 tbsp	15 ml	Worcestershire sauce
½ tsp	3 ml	each of thyme leaves, oregano leaves, basil leaves, paprika, pepper, chili powder, salt
½ tsp	3 ml	liquid smoke
4 – 6 oz	4 – 170 g	veal round steaks

Heat the butter with 30 ml (2 tbsp) of oil in a sauce pan. Add the onion and garlic and sauté until tender.

Add the catsup, honey, vinegar, Worcestershire, seasonings and smoke flavouring. Simmer until sauce is thick and glossy. Cool.

Brush the steaks with the remaining oil. Grill over medium coals 6 minutes per side, brushing frequently with sauce. Brush 1 final time before serving.

SERVES 4

Honey Barbecued Veal Steaks

RED WINE STEW

1½ lbs	675 g	boneless lean veal
5 tbsp	75 ml	butter
1	1	minced garlic clove
3 tbsp	45 ml	flour, all purpose
1 tbsp	15 ml	chopped fresh parsley
¼ cup	60 ml	red wine
1 cup	250 ml	peeled, seeded, chopped tomatoes
½ cup	125 ml	Veal Stock (see page 85) or Chicken Stock (see page 77)
½ tsp	3 ml	each of salt, pepper, paprika
1 tsp	5 ml	oregano
2 tsp	10 ml	capers
2 tsp	10 ml	lemon zest

Coarse dice the veal. Heat the butter in a large sauce pan. Add the veal and garlic; cook until meat browns. Sprinkle with flour and continue cooking for 3 minutes over low heat.

Add the remaining ingredients. Cover and simmer for 30 minutes.

Serve with rice.

SERVES 6

PEPPERED VEAL CHOPS

6 – 6 oz	6 – 180 g	veal chops
¼ cup	60 ml	crushed black peppercorns
¼ cup	60 ml	butter
2 tbsp	30 ml	brandy
1 cup	250 ml	Demi-Glace (see page 123)
2 tbsp	30 ml	sherry
¼ cup	60 ml	heavy cream

Pat the peppercorns into the veal chops.

Heat the butter in a large skillet and sauté the veal chops to the desired doneness. Remove and reserve hot.

Pour in the brandy and flame. Add the demi-glace and sherry. Simmer 1 minute. Add the cream, blending well.

Pour sauce over the chops and serve.

SERVES 6

BLANQUETTE DE VEAU A L'INDIENNE

1½ lbs	675 g	veal shoulder, diced in ¾" cubes
4 cups	1 L	Chicken Stock (see page 77)
2 tsp	10 ml	salt
20	20	pearl onions
4	4	carrots, julienned
2 tbsp	30 ml	butter
2 tbsp	30 ml	flour, all purpose
2 tbsp	30 ml	curry powder
2 tbsp	30 ml	lemon juice
2	2	egg yolks
1 tbsp	15 ml	chopped parsley

In a Dutch oven, place the veal, chicken stock and salt. Cover and simmer for 1½ hours. Add the onions and carrots. Continue cooking for 15 minutes. Remove 2 cups (500 ml) of liquid.

Melt the butter in a small sauce pan. Add the flour and curry powder; cook for 3 minutes over low heat. Slowly add the 2 cups of liquid, stirring until thickened.

Whisk the lemon juice in the egg yolks. Blend into the sauce. Do not boil.

Add the sauce to the veal. Reheat, but do not boil. Pour into a serving dish. Garnish with parsley. Serve over cooked egg noodles.

SERVES 6

Red Wine Stew

COUNTRY SIMMERING BEEF

2¼ lbs	1 kg	beef round
3 tbsp	45 ml	olive oil
3 tbsp	45 ml	flour, all purpose
3	3	diced onions
1	1	minced garlic clove
3	3	large diced carrots
4	4	diced celery stalks
20	20	button mushrooms
3 cups	750 ml	Beef Broth (see page 85)
⅓ cup	90 ml	tomato paste
1 tbsp	15 ml	Worcestershire sauce
2 tbsp	30 ml	soya sauce
½ tsp	3 ml	each of salt, pepper, paprika, chili powder, thyme, oregano
6	6	large potatoes

Cut the beef in large cubes. Heat the oil in a large kettle or Dutch oven. Add the beef and brown. Remove the beef.

Sprinkle with flour and cook over low heat for 5 minutes or until golden brown.

Add the onion, garlic, carrots, celery and mushrooms. Sauté until tender. Stir in the beef, broth, tomato paste, Worcestershire, soya and seasonings. Cover and simmer for 45 minutes.

Pare and dice the potatoes. Add to the stew and continue to simmer for an additional 30 minutes. Serve with Grandma's Best Dumplings (recipe follows) or fresh biscuits.

SERVES 6

Country Simmering Beef

GRANDMA'S BEST DUMPLINGS

1 cup	250 ml	unbleached flour
1½ tsp	8 ml	baking powder
½ tsp	3 ml	salt
½ cup	125 ml	buttermilk

Sift the flour, baking powder and salt together in a mixing bowl. Gradually add the milk until a light soft dough is formed

Drop into a stew or fricassee in small spoonfuls. Cover and simmer for 15 minutes before serving. Do not uncover during the simmering process.

SERVES 6

VEAL OSCAR

1½ lb	675 g	veal shoulder
2	2	eggs
¼ cup	60 ml	milk
½ cup	125 ml	flour
1 cup	250 ml	fine bread crumbs seasoned
¼ cup	60 ml	safflower oil
1½ cup	375 ml	cooked crab meat
18	18	blanched asparagus spears
¾ cup	180 ml	Béarnaise Sauce (see page 108)

Cut the veal shoulder into 6, 4 oz (120 g) pieces. Flatten and tenderize each piece with a meat mallet.

Blend the eggs into the milk. Dust each cutlet with flour, dip into egg wash and dredge with bread crumbs.

Heat the oil in a large skillet and fry until golden brown on each side.

Transfer the cutlets to a pastry sheet. Top each with equal amounts of crab meat, 3 asparagus spears and 2 tbsp (30 ml) of béarnaise sauce. Place under the preheated oven broiler for 1½ minutes. Serve.

SERVES 6

Chicken Fried Steak

CHICKEN FRIED STEAK

6 – 4 oz	6 – 115 g	top round steaks
2	2	eggs
¼ cup	60 ml	milk
1 cup	250 ml	fine bread crumbs
¼ tsp	1 ml	each of salt, pepper, basil, thyme leaves, chili powder, onion powder, oregano, paprika
⅓ cup	80 ml	flour, all purpose
¼ cup	60 ml	safflower oil
2 cups	500 ml	Country Gravy (see page 118)

Pound the steaks with a meat mallet to tenderize.

Blend the eggs with the milk. Mix the bread crumbs together with the seasonings.

Dust the steaks with flour, then dip them into the egg wash, then dredge the steaks through the bread crumbs.

Heat the oil in a large skillet. Fry the steaks for 3 minutes per side. Serve with gravy on the side.

SERVES 6

LEMON PEPPER STEAK

1 lb	450 g	beef tenderloin
¼ cup	60 ml	lemon pepper
2 tbsp	30 ml	safflower oil
2 tbsp	30 ml	butter
1 cup	250 ml	Wild Mushroom Sherry Sauce (see page 105)
⅓ cup	80 ml	sour cream

Trim the tenderloin and cut into steaks. Roll each steak in the lemon pepper.

Heat the oil with the butter in a large skillet and sauté the tenderloin to desired doneness.

While steaks cook, heat the sauce in a sauce pan. Whip in the sour cream.

When the steaks are ready place on serving platters, pour the sauce over the steaks and serve.

SERVES 4

BEEF AND TOMATO ON NOODLES

½ tsp	3 ml	baking soda
3 tbsp	45 ml	peanut oil
2	2	minced garlic cloves
2 tsp	10 ml	granulated sugar
1 tsp	5 ml	salt
3 tbsp	45 ml	soya sauce
2 tbsp	30 ml	sherry
1 lb	454 g	flank steak
½ cup	125 ml	sliced mushrooms
1	1	sliced medium onion
1 cup	250 ml	peeled, seeded, chopped tomatoes
1 tsp	5 ml	cornstarch
1 tbsp	15 ml	water
12 oz	345 g	Chinese noodles

Blend the baking soda with 1 tbsp (15 ml) of oil and the garlic, sugar, salt, soya sauce and sherry.

Slice the steak thin; place in a large mixing bowl. Pour marinade over beef and set aside for 20 minutes.

In a large wok or skillet, heat the remaining oil. Drain the beef and reserve the marinade. Fry the beef, mushrooms and onion for 3 minutes. Add the reserved marinade and tomatoes; reduce heat and simmer for 1 minute.

Mix the cornstarch with the water and add to the beef. Simmer until sauce thickens.

While cooking the beef, cook the noodles in a large kettle of boiling, salted water. Drain and transfer to a large platter. Pour beef over noodles and serve.

SERVES 6

Lemon Pepper Steak

CRANBERRY VEAL CHOPS

6 – 6 oz	6 – 170 g	boneless veal chops
3 tbsp	45 ml	olive oil
2 cups	500 ml	fresh cranberries
¾ cup	180 ml	granulated sugar
½ tsp	3 ml	salt
⅓ cup	80 ml	water

Brown the chops in the oil in a large skillet. Drain off fat.

Add the remaining ingredients. Bring to a boil. Reduce heat and cook simmering for ½ hour covered. Serve the chops covered with the sauce.

SERVES 6

APPLESAUCE BURGERS

1 lb	450 g	lean ground beef
1	1	minced, small onion
½ cup	125 ml	apple sauce
2 tbsp	30 ml	brown sugar
¼ cup	60 ml	tomato catsup
½ cup	125 ml	bread crumbs
6	6	kaiser rolls

Mix the ground beef thoroughly with the remaining ingredients. Form into six patties.

Place on a broiling pan; bake 15 minutes in a preheated 400°F (200°C) oven.

Place each patty in a roll, top as desired. Serve hot.

SERVES 6

DEVILED VEAL CHOPS

2 tbsp	30 ml	butter
¼ tsp	1 ml	each of cayenne pepper, black pepper, white pepper
6 – 6 oz	6 – 170 g	boneless veal chops
½ cup	125 ml	chili sauce
½ cup	125 ml	catsup
¼ tsp	1 ml	each of salt, basil, paprika, chili powder, thyme, oregano
2 tbsp	30 ml	Worcestershire sauce
2 tbsp	30 ml	Dijon mustard
½ cup	125 ml	water

Make a smooth paste of the butter and peppers.

Place the veal chops into a casserole dish and spread the butter over them. Place under the oven broiler for 3 minutes, turn the veal over and broil for an additional 3 minutes.

While veal broils, combine the remaining ingredients together in a small mixing bowl. Pour over veal and bake at 350°F (180°C) for 20-25 minutes in a preheated oven.

Serve with rice pilaf.

SERVES 6

Cranberry Veal Chops

CALIFORNIA KEBABS

2 lbs	900 g	sirloin tip
½ cup	125 ml	apricot nectar
1 tbsp	15 ml	lemon juice
1 tbsp	15 ml	lime juice
¼ cup	60 ml	olive oil
1 tbsp	15 ml	Worcestershire sauce
½ tsp	3 ml	salt
½ tsp	3 ml	thyme leaves
1 tbsp	15 ml	chopped cilantro
2	2	green bell peppers, cubed
1	1	yellow bell pepper, cubed
12	12	mushrooms
12	12	cherry tomatoes
1	1	Spanish onion, cubed
1	1	thick sliced zucchini

Trim any fat from the sirloin and cut the meat into ¾" (2 cm) cubes. Place the cubes in a mixing bowl.

Blend the apricot, lemon, lime, oil, Worcestershire, salt, thyme and cilantro. Pour this marinade over the beef and marinate in the refrigerator for 12 hours or overnight.

On bamboo skewers, alternate beef, peppers, mushrooms, tomatoes, onions and zucchini. Grill these over medium heat on a broiler for 8-10 minutes, brushing with marinade. Serve.

SERVES 6

California Kebabs

CREOLE VEAL TURKEYS

8	8	¾" double veal chops
2¾ cups	680 ml	bread cubes
5 tbsp	75 ml	butter
1	1	minced small onion
½ tsp	3 ml	Worcestershire sauce
½ tsp	3 ml	salt
½ tsp	3 ml	pepper
4 tbsp	60 ml	oil
2 cups	500 ml	Creole Sauce (see page 121)

Mix the bread, butter, onion, Worcestershire sauce, salt and pepper into a stuffing. Stuff into the chops.

Heat the oil in a large skillet. Brown chops in oil. Drain excess oil. Pour sauce over the chops. Cover and reduce heat. Simmer for 1 hour.

Serve with rice.

SERVES 6

LIVER ORIENTAL

1 lb	450 g	calf's liver
¼ cup	80 ml	flour, all purpose
4 tbsp	60 ml	safflower oil
4 oz	115 g	button mushrooms
3 oz	80 g	snow peas
1	1	minced garlic clove
1	1	sliced onion
1 tsp	5 ml	minced ginger root
¼ tsp	1 ml	Chinese five spice
½ cup	125 ml	Beef Stock (see page 85)
1 tbsp	15 ml	soya sauce
1 tsp	5 ml	Worcestershire sauce

Remove any membranes from the liver. Slice into thin strips. Dust the liver slices with flour.

Heat the oil to very hot in a wok. Add the liver and fry for 3 minutes. Add the mushrooms, peas, garlic, onion and ginger; fry for an additional 4 minutes. Add the remaining ingredients. Reduce heat and simmer until sauce thickens.

Serve with Bombay Rice (see page 709).

SERVES 4

Calf's Liver with Citrus Peppercorn Sauce

Veal with Shrimp and Cashews

CALF'S LIVER WITH CITRUS PEPPERCORN SAUCE

6 – 4 oz	6 – 115 g	calf's liver slices
⅓ cup	80 ml	flour, all purpose
¾ cup	180 ml	butter
½ cup	125 ml	fine sugar
3	3	oranges
2	2	grapefruit
1 tbsp	15 ml	green peppercorns

Remove any veins from the livers, then dust the slices with flour.

Heat 4 tbsp (60 ml) of butter in a skillet; sauté the livers for 3 minutes per side.

Heat the remaining butter in a sauce pan. Add the sugar and caramelize it. Add the juice from 2 oranges and 1 grapefruit. Zest the remaining orange and grapefruit, then section each. Add 2 tsp (10 ml) of lemon zest and 1 tsp (5 ml) of grapefruit zest to the sauce. Cook for 1 minute. Remove from heat, and add the fruit sections and peppercorns.

Place sautéed liver on serving plates. Cover with sauce and serve.

SERVES 6

NEW YORK STRIPLOIN DIABLE

6 – 10 oz	6 – 300 g	New York striploin steaks
1¼ cups	310 ml	white wine
¼ cup	60 ml	minced green onions
1¼ cups	310 ml	Demi-Glace Sauce (see page 123)
1 tsp	5 ml	Worcestershire sauce
½ tsp	3 ml	dry mustard

Trim the steak of fat and the gristle strip along the edge to prevent curling while meat cooks.

In a small sauce pan, boil the wine and green onions together. Reduce by ⅓ the wine volume. Add the remaining ingredients. Reduce heat and simmer for 5 minutes. Pass sauce through a sieve, and reserve warm.

Grill the steaks over medium coals to desired doneness. Serve covered with sauce.

SERVES 6

VEAL WITH SHRIMP AND CASHEWS

2 lbs	900 g	boneless veal shoulder
3 tbsp	45 ml	safflower oil
1	1	sliced onion
2	2	coarse diced carrots
2	2	coarse diced celery stalks
3 tbsp	45 ml	all purpose flour
2 cups	500 ml	Chicken Stock (see page 77)
1 cup	250 ml	light cream
1 lb	450 g	cooked baby shrimp
1 cup	250 ml	cashews

Dice the veal into ¾" (2 cm) cubes.

Heat the oil in a Dutch oven. Add the veal and brown. Add the onion, carrot and celery; sauté until tender. Sprinkle with flour and cook for 2 minutes. Add the chicken stock and cream. Reduce heat and simmer gently for 1 hour.

Pour into a serving dish. Sprinkle with shrimp and nuts. Serve with noodles.

SERVES 6

Chili Con Carne & Cheese

FILET AU POIVRE

6 – 8 oz	6 – 225 g	tenderloin filets
¼ cup	60 ml	crushed black peppercorns
¼ cup	60 ml	butter
2 tbsp	30 ml	brandy
1 cup	250 ml	Demi-Glace (see page 123)
2 tbsp	30 ml	sherry
¼ cup	60 ml	heavy cream

Trim the filets of any fat. Pat the peppercorns over the filets.

Heat the butter and sauté until desired doneness. Remove and reserve hot.

Pour the brandy into the pan and carefully flame. Add the demi-glace, sherry and cream. Blend well. Pour sauce over steaks and serve.

SERVES 6

ROAST VEAL WITH BLACKBERRY BRANDY SAUCE

1½ lbs	675 g	veal shoulder, boned and tied
1	1	garlic clove
¼ tsp	1 ml	each of thyme leaves, oregano leaves, salt, pepper, paprika, dry mustard
1 tbsp	15 ml	olive oil

SAUCE:		
1¼ lbs	625 g	blackberries
4 tsp	20 ml	cornstarch
¼ cup	60 ml	blackberry brandy
2 tbsp	30 ml	fine sugar

Preheat the oven to 350°F (180°C).

Rub the roast with the garlic clove. Blend the seasonings together.

Place roast in a small roasting pan and sprinkle with the seasonings. Drizzle the oil over the roast. Roast, uncovered, for 35-45 minutes depending on required doneness.

While the roast cooks, purée the blackberries in a food processor. Strain to remove pulp and seeds. Place the juice into a small sauce pan. Blend in the cornstarch, brandy and sugar. Slowly heat until sauce thickens.

Remove the roast from the oven and carve. Place on a serving platter and pour sauce over. Serve.

SERVES 4

CHILI CON CARNE & CHEESE

2¼ lbs	1 kg	lean ground beef
3 tbsp	45 ml	safflower oil
1	1	diced onion
1	1	diced green bell pepper
1	1	diced red bell pepper
3 oz	90 g	sliced mushrooms
3	3	diced celery stalks
1	1	minced garlic clove
3 cups	750 ml	peeled, seeded, chopped tomatoes
1 tsp	5 ml	each of salt, pepper, paprika, thyme leaves
1 tbsp	15 ml	chili powder
2 tsp	10 ml	Worcestershire sauce
3 drops	3 drops	Tabasco™ sauce
2¼ cups	560 ml	canned red kidney beans, drained
¼ cup	60 ml	tomato paste
1½ cups	375 ml	grated cheddar cheese

In a large Dutch oven or kettle, brown the beef in the oil. Add the vegetables and garlic and sauté until tender.

Stir in all the remaining ingredients except the cheese. Lower the heat, and simmer for 1 hour or until desired thickness is achieved.

Place into serving bowls, sprinkle with cheese and serve.

SERVES 6

BEEF IN TOMATO GINGER SAUCE

1 lb	450 g	beef tenderloin
3 tbsp	45 ml	olive oil
2 tbsp	30 ml	soya sauce
2 tbsp	30 ml	sherry
1	1	minced garlic clove
1 tsp	5 ml	minced ginger
6	6	dried Chinese mushrooms, soaked 1 hr. in warm water
2 tbsp	30 ml	tomato paste

Trim the beef of any fat and cut in thin strips.

Blend 1 tsp (5 ml) of oil with the soya, sherry, garlic and ginger and pour over the beef. Marinate 2 hours.

Slice the mushrooms.

Heat the remaining oil in a wok. Quickly fry the beef, undrained, with the mushrooms. Stir in the tomato paste and cook 1 minute longer. Serve.

SERVES 4

VEAL SCALOPPINE

1½ lbs	675 g	veal cutlets
¼ cup	60 ml	flour, all purpose
1 tsp	5 ml	salt
¼ tsp	1 ml	white pepper
1	1	garlic clove
3 tbsp	45 ml	olive oil
⅔ cup	170 ml	Veal Broth (see page 85) or Chicken Broth (see page 77)
2 tbsp	30 ml	lemon juice
⅓ cup	90 ml	white wine
2 tbsp	30 ml	chopped parsley

Cut the veal into small serving pieces.

Mix the flour with the salt and pepper and dust the veal.

Heat the oil in a large skillet and fry the garlic to golden brown, then remove and discard it. Fry the veal in the oil until golden brown.

Reduce the heat and add the broth, lemon juice and wine. Cover and simmer for 45 minutes.

Sprinkle with the parsley and serve.

SERVES 6

Filet au Poivre

BEEF IN PINEAPPLE SAUCE

1 lb	450 g	beef tenderloin
1 tbsp	15 ml	brown sugar
½ tsp	3 ml	minced ginger
2 tbsp	30 ml	soya sauce
2 tbsp	30 ml	sherry
2 tbsp	30 ml	safflower oil
1 cup	250 ml	pineapple chunks
½ cup	125 ml	pineapple juice
1 tsp	5 ml	cornstarch
2 tbsp	30 ml	water

Trim the tenderloin, remove all fat, and cut into thin strips.

Blend the sugar with the ginger, soya and sherry; pour over the beef and marinate for 2 hours.

Heat the oil in a wok. Add the beef, undrained, along with the pineapple chunks. Cook for 3 minutes. Pour in the pineapple juice. Blend the cornstarch with the water and add to the beef. Simmer until sauce thickens. Serve.

SERVES 6

GRILLED T-BONE WITH MUSHROOMS

1 cup	250 ml	olive oil
4	4	minced garlic cloves
1 tbsp	15 ml	basil leaves
1 tsp	5 ml	chervil
2 tsp	10 ml	crushed rosemary
½ tsp	3 ml	crushed black pepper
3 tbsp	45 ml	lemon juice
½ cup	125 ml	dry red wine
4 – 8 oz	4 – 225 g	T-bone steaks
6 oz	175 g	fresh oyster mushrooms
6 oz	175 g	rehydrated Chinese mushrooms
3 tbsp	45 ml	butter

In a sauce bowl, combine the oil, garlic, basil, chervil, rosemary, pepper, lemon juice, and red wine.

Place steaks in a shallow pan. Pour marinade over steaks and marinate 1 hour. Drain steaks. Grill over hot coals for 7 minutes per side for medium, longer for well done, less for rare.

While steaks grill, slice the mushrooms. Heat the butter in a skillet and sauté the mushrooms. Serve on top of the steaks.

SERVES 4

VEAL SATAY

2 lbs	900 g	boneless lean veal, coarse diced
4 tbsp	60 ml	peanut oil
1¼ tbsp	20 ml	ground Brazilian nuts
½ tsp	3 ml	ground ginger
1½ tsp	8 ml	ground coriander
¼ tsp	1 ml	each of cayenne, garlic powder
½ tsp	3 ml	each of pepper, onion powder
2 tsp	10 ml	molasses
4 tsp	20 ml	lime juice
4 tsp	20 ml	lemon juice
3 tbsp	45 ml	hot water

Skewer the meat with bamboo skewers. Place in a large shallow pan.

In a mixing bowl, blend the remaining ingredients. Pour over the skewered beef. Marinate, covered, in the refrigerator 3½ to 4 hours.

Grill the skewers over high heat for 10-12 minutes, or until meat is cooked through, brushing frequently with marinade.

Serve with Bombay Rice (see page 709).

SERVES 6

Beef in Pineapple Sauce

Veal Satay

VEAL CHOPS FRICASSEE II

4½ lbs	1-2 kg	small veal chops
½ cup	125 ml	seasoned flour
4 tbsp	60 ml	olive oil
2	2	chopped onions
2	2	chopped carrots
2	2	chopped celery stalks
1	1	bouquet garni*
4 cups	1 L	cold Veal Broth (see page 85) or Chicken Broth (see page 77)
½ tsp	3 ml	each of salt, pepper, paprika, chili powder, basil
½ cup	125 ml	tomato paste
3 tbsp	45 ml	butter
3 tbsp	45 ml	flour, all purpose

Wash and pat dry the chops.

Dust the chops in the seasoned flour.

Heat the oil in a large kettle or Dutch oven. Brown the chops on all sides and drain the excess oil. Add the onions, carrots, celery and bouquet. Cover with the broth and bring to a boil. Reduce temperature and simmer gently for 45 minutes.

Remove the chops and reserve warm. Strain the broth and discard the vegetables and bouquet. Return to the pot, and add the seasonings and tomato paste. Bring to a boil and reduce the liquid to 2 cups (500 ml).

In a small sauce pan, heat the butter, add the flour and cook over low heat for 2 minutes. Add the reduced broth and simmer into a thick sauce. Pour sauce over chops and serve with rice or noodles.

SERVES 4

**The bouquet garni for this dish is; a bay leaf, 8 sprigs of parsley, 2 sprigs of thyme, 6 peppercorns and 1 small, chopped leek tied together in a cheesecloth.

Veal Steaks with Herb Butter

VEAL STEAKS WITH HERB BUTTER

1	1	minced garlic clove
½	0.5	lemon
½	0.5	lime
2 tsp	10 ml	each of parsley, basil, marjoram, thyme
¼ lb	115 g	sweet butter
6	6	slices maple bacon
6 – 6 oz	6 – 170 g	lean veal steaks

In a food processor, combine the garlic, lemon and lime juices, herbs and butter until smooth. Form butter into a dowel shape. Wrap in wax paper and freeze for 1 hour.

Wrap the bacon around the veal steaks. Broil on a charbroiler over medium coals or in the oven until cooked thoroughly.

Plate the steaks and top with a slice of herb butter.

SERVES 6

BEEF RIBS DIABLE

18	18	standing rib roast ribs
¼ cup	60 ml	French Dijon mustard
2 tsp	10 ml	English dry mustard
¼ cup	60 ml	white wine
4 tbsp	60 ml	molasses
1 tbsp	15 ml	cider vinegar
¼ cup	60 ml	Worcestershire sauce
1 tsp	5 ml	Tabasco™ sauce
¼ tsp	1 ml	each of ground ginger, onion powder, garlic powder

Place the ribs in a large oven roaster.

Blend the remaining ingredients together thoroughly; pour over the ribs. Bake the ribs in a preheated 350°F (180°C) oven for 1¼ to 1½ hours or until fork tender. Serve.

SERVES 6

SALISBURY STEAK LYONNAISE

1½ lbs	675 g	lean ground beef
⅓ cup	80 ml	seasoned bread crumbs
1	1	egg
2 tsp	10 ml	Worcestershire sauce
2 tbsp	30 ml	minced onions
2 tbsp	30 ml	minced carrots
2 tbsp	30 ml	minced celery
¼ cup	60 ml	butter
1	1	sliced Spanish onion
2 tsp	10 ml	granulated sugar
3 tbsp	45 ml	flour, all purpose
¼ cup	60 ml	sherry
1½ cups	375 ml	Beef Broth (see page 85)
3 tbsp	45 ml	tomato paste
½ tsp	3 ml	salt
¼ tsp	1 ml	black pepper

In a large mixing bowl, combine the beef, crumbs, egg, Worcestershire sauce, minced onion, carrot and celery. Shape into 6 even size patties. Place on a broiling pan and bake in a preheated 400°F (200°C) oven for 15-20 minutes. Time is dependent on thickness of patties.

While patties cook, heat the butter in a sauce pan. Add the sliced onions and sugar. Sauté over low heat until onions caramelize. Sprinkle in the flour and continue to cook for 4 minutes. Add the sherry, broth, tomato paste and seasonings. Simmer until sauce thickens.

Place patties on serving plates, smother with sauce and serve.

SERVES 6

SZECHUAN SHREDDED BEEF

1½ lbs	675 g	sirloin steak, sliced 1/8" thick
3 tbsp	45 ml	sherry
3 tbsp	45 ml	soya sauce
1 tsp	5 ml	minced garlic
1 tsp	5 ml	minced ginger root
¼ tsp	2 ml	cayenne pepper
2 tbsp	30 ml	safflower oil

Cut the steak into thin strips.

Blend the sherry, soya, garlic, ginger and cayenne together. Pour over the steak and mix through. Marinate 30 minutes.

Heat the oil to very hot in a wok or large skillet. Add the undrained beef. Fry, stirring constantly, for 5 minutes. Serve.

SERVES 6

Salisbury Steak Lyonnaise

Beef Goulash Revisited

BEEF GOULASH REVISITED

3 tbsp	45 ml	butter
3 tbsp	45 ml	minced onions
2 tsp	10 ml	salt
1 tsp	5 ml	pepper
1 tbsp	15 ml	paprika
2¼ lbs	1 kg	cubed beef round
3 tbsp	45 ml	flour, all purpose
4 cups	1 L	hot Beef Broth (see page 85)
1	1	bouquet garni (see Glossary)
1½ cups	375 ml	diced potatoes
1	1	sprig fresh marjoram
1 cup	250 ml	sour cream
¼ cup	60 ml	tomato paste
1 tsp	5 ml	caraway seeds

In a large kettle or Dutch oven, heat the butter and add the onions. Cook until tender without browning.

Blend the salt, pepper and paprika together. Dust the beef with the seasonings and add to the pot. Cook the beef until brown. Sprinkle with flour and continue to cook for 3 minutes over low heat.

Add the broth and bouquet. Simmer for 1¼ hours.

Add the potatoes and marjoram. Continue to simmer for an additional 30 minutes. Discard the bouquet. Stir in the sour cream, tomato paste and caraway seeds. Simmer 5 minutes longer and serve at once with Goulash Dumplings (recipe follows).

SERVES 6

Beef Satay

GOULASH DUMPLINGS

4 cups	1 L	flour, all purpose
1 tsp	5 ml	salt
2	2	eggs
¼ cup	60 ml	water
2	2	slices of bacon
2 cups	500 ml	Beef Broth (see page 85)

Sift the flour with the salt. Place in a mixing bowl and knead in the eggs. Add the water (just enough to form a stiff paste).

Roll the dough out on a flour dusted surface and allow to dry very hard. Once dry, break into pieces and grate with a coarse vegetable grater. Fry the bacon in a skillet and strain the meat (use the bacon for some other cuisine), reserving 2 tbsp (30 ml) of bacon fat.

Pour the bacon fat into a small sauce pot, add the broth and bring to a boil. Cook the dumplings for 4-5 minutes. Serve with Goulash.

SERVES 6

BEEF SATAY

1 lb	450 g	flank steak
3 tbsp	45 ml	peanut oil
1 tbsp	15 ml	ground Brazil nuts
¼ tsp	1 ml	ground ginger
1 tsp	5 ml	ground coriander
¼ tsp	1 ml	each of pepper, onion powder
¼ tsp	1 ml	each of cayenne, garlic powder
1 tsp	5 ml	molasses
1 tbsp	15 ml	lime juice
1 tbsp	15 ml	lemon juice
3 tbsp	45 ml	hot water

Trim and slice the beef into thin slices.

Skewer the meat with bamboo skewers. Place them into a large shallow pan.

In a mixing bowl blend the remaining ingredients; pour over the skewered beef. Marinate covered in the refrigerator for 3½ to 4 hours.

Grill the skewers over high heat for 2 minutes per side, brushing frequently with the marinade while cooking. Serve at once.

SERVES 4

VEAL STEAKS WITH PINK AND GREEN PEPPERCORN SAUCE

2 tbsp	30 ml	butter
2 tbsp	30 ml	flour, all purpose
½ cup	125 ml	Veal Broth (see page 85) or Chicken Broth (see page 77)
½ cup	125 ml	light cream
3 tbsp	45 ml	brandy
1 tbsp	15 ml	pink peppercorns
1 tbsp	15 ml	green peppercorns
1 tbsp	15 ml	green onion, minced
1 tbsp	15 ml	parsley, chopped
4 – 6 oz	4 – 170 g	veal round steaks
2 tbsp	30 ml	melted butter
½ tsp	3 ml	salt
¼ tsp	1 ml	white pepper

Heat the butter in a sauce pan and add the flour. Reduce heat and cook 2 minutes.

Stir in the broth, cream and brandy. Simmer until sauce thickens. Stir in the peppercorns, onion and parsley.

Brush the veal with melted butter. Season with salt and pepper. Bake in a preheated 375°F (190°C) oven for 15-20 minutes.

Remove and place on a serving plate. Cover with sauce and serve.

SERVES 4

BRAISED SHORT RIBS

2¼ lbs	1 kg	short ribs of beef
2 cups	500 ml	flour, all purpose
½ tsp	3 ml	each of garlic powder, onion powder, salt, pepper
¼ tsp	1 ml	each of thyme, oregano, chili powder, paprika
1	1	minced garlic clove
½ cup	60 ml	soya sauce
½ tsp	3 ml	ground ginger
½ cup	60 ml	brown sugar
½ cup	60 ml	sherry
¾ cup	180 ml	water

Cut the ribs into desired serving portions.

Blend the flour with the seasonings; dust the ribs with flour. Brown in a preheated 350°F (180°C) oven.

Mix the garlic, soya, ginger, sugar, sherry and water together and pour this mixture over the ribs. Cover the ribs. Reduce the temperature of the oven to 300°F (150°C) and bake for 2 hours.

Serve with Spanish Rice (see page 749).

SERVES 6

SOUR CREAM BEEF

2 tbsp	30 ml	safflower oil
2 tbsp	30 ml	butter
1	1	diced celery stalk
1	1	diced small onion
1	1	diced green bell pepper
1 lb	454 g	thinly sliced sirloin
3 tbsp	45 ml	flour, all purpose
1½ cups	375 ml	Beef Broth (see page 85)
¼ cup	60 ml	sherry
½ tsp	3 ml	each of salt, pepper, paprika
1 tsp	5 ml	Dijon mustard
1 cup	250 ml	sour cream
3 cups	750 ml	steamed rice or noodles

In a large skillet, heat the oil and butter. Sauté the vegetables. Add the beef and sauté. Sprinkle with flour. Cook for 3 minutes.

Add the beef broth, sherry, seasonings and mustard. Reduce heat and simmer, covered, for 1¼ hours.

Blend in the sour cream and mix thoroughly. Place rice or noodles on a serving plate. Cover with stroganoff and serve.

SERVES 4

Braised Short Ribs

Cloved Veal Stew

STUFFED ROAST VEAL

1½ lbs	675 g	veal shoulder roast, boned
1	1	finely diced onion
2	2	finely diced celery stalks
2	2	finely diced carrots
2 tbsp	30 ml	butter
¼ cup	60 ml	raisins
⅓ cup	80 ml	cashews
3 cups	750 ml	bread cubes
1 tsp	5 ml	each of salt, pepper, sugar, basil, thyme leaves
2	2	eggs

Preheat the oven to 350°F (180°C).

Butterfly the veal by making an incision down the centre. Using a meat mallet, flatten the veal.

Sauté the onion, celery and carrots in a skillet with the butter. Cool to room temperature. Place in a mixing bowl. Add the raisins, cashews, cubed bread and seasonings. Bind all the ingredients together with the eggs.

Pat the stuffing on the veal. Roll and tie the veal. Place it into a roasting pan. Roast, uncovered, for 45-50 minutes. Remove and carve. Place on a serving platter. Serve with Wild Mushroom Sherry Sauce (see page 105).

SERVES 4

CLOVED VEAL STEW

2 tbsp	30 ml	olive oil
2 lbs	900 g	diced boneless veal
1 lb	450 g	peeled, seeded and chopped tomatoes
6	6	cloves
1 cup	250 ml	Chicken Stock (see page 77)
2	2	minced garlic cloves
¼ tsp	1 ml	each of basil, thyme, marjoram
½ tsp	3 ml	salt and pepper
1 tbsp	15 ml	chopped parsley

Heat the olive oil in a Dutch oven. Add the veal and brown. Add the tomatoes, cloves, stock, garlic and seasoning.

Cover, reduce heat and simmer for 2 hours.

Serve over noodles or rice. Sprinkle with parsley as a garnish.

SERVES 6

TOMATO & VEAL STEW

1½ lbs	675 g	veal shoulder, coarsely diced
3 cups	750 ml	Chicken Stock (see page 77)
2 tsp	10 ml	salt
1 tsp	5 ml	each of thyme and oregano leaves
3 tbsp	45 ml	butter
20	20	pearl onions
2	2	carrots, julienned
2	2	celery stalks, julienned
1	1	minced garlic clove
20	20	button mushrooms
3 tbsp	45 ml	flour, all purpose
1½ cup	375 ml	tomato purée

In a Dutch oven, place the veal, stock, salt, thyme and oregano. Cover and simmer for 1½ hours.

Heat the butter in a sauce pan. Add the carrots, celery, onions, mushrooms and garlic. Sauté for 5 minutes. Sprinkle with flour and cook for 3 minutes without browning.

Pour into the veal and blend. Add the tomato purée and simmer for 10 minutes. Serve with rice.

SERVES 6

SAUTÉED VEAL CHOPS WITH CLEMENTINE SAUCE

6 – 6 oz	6 – 170 g	boneless veal chops
3 tbsp	45 ml	oil
		salt, pepper to taste
⅓ cup	80 ml	tangerine or orange juice concentrate
½ cup	125 ml	Veal Broth (see page 85) or Chicken Broth (see page 77)
¼ cup	60 ml	whipping cream
1 tbsp	15 ml	butter
1 tsp	5 ml	lime juice

Heat the oil in a large skillet. Sauté the veal for 6-8 minutes. Season with salt and pepper and reserve hot.

Heat the tangerine juice in a sauce pan with the broth, bring to a boil and reduce heat. Add the cream and simmer until sauce coats a spoon. Remove from heat. Whip in the butter and lime juice.

Place veal chops on a serving plate. Cover with sauce and serve.

SERVES 6

BEEF IN RED WINE MUSHROOM SAUCE

2¼ lbs	1 kg	sirloin, sliced into thin strips
3 tbsp	45 ml	butter
3 tbsp	45 ml	safflower oil
4 oz	115 g	sliced mushrooms
3 tbsp	45 ml	finely diced carrots
3 tbsp	45 ml	finely diced celery
¼ cup	60 ml	flour, all purpose
½ cup	125 ml	red wine
2 cups	500 ml	Beef Broth (see page 85)
3 tbsp	45 ml	tomato paste
1 tsp	5 ml	each of black pepper, garlic powder, onion powder

In a large Dutch oven or kettle, sauté the beef in the butter and oil. Add the vegetables and continue to cook until tender. Sprinkle with flour, reduce the heat and cook for 5 minutes.

Add the wine, broth, tomato paste and seasonings. Simmer for 50 minutes covered.

Serve over noodles.

SERVES 6

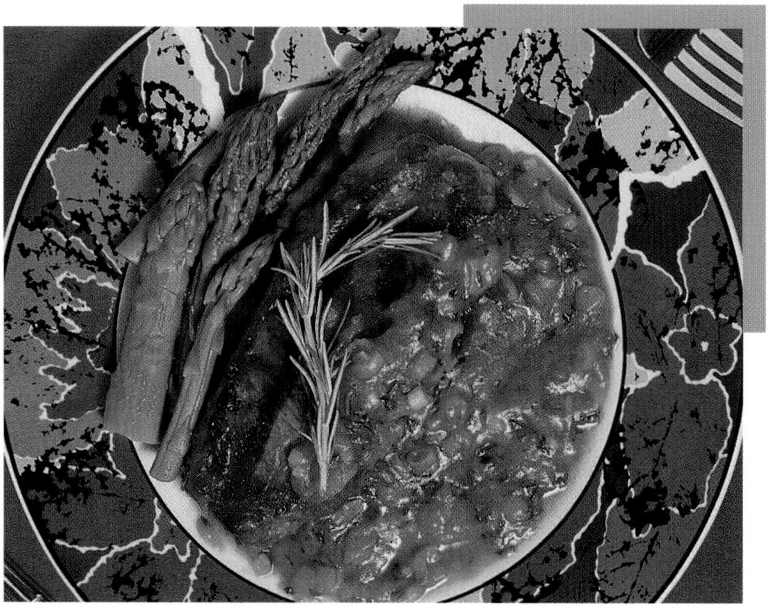

Bifteck Marchand de Vins

BIFTECK MARCHAND DE VINS

4 tbsp	60 ml	butter
⅔ cup	160 ml	chopped green onions
1 cup	250 ml	red wine
½ cup	125 ml	cream style sherry
¼ tsp	1 ml	crushed rosemary
¼ tsp	1 ml	marjoram
4 tbsp	60 ml	chopped parsley
2 tbsp	30 ml	flour, all purpose
½ cup	125 ml	Beef Stock (see page 85)
1 tbsp	15 ml	lemon juice
6 – 6 oz	6 – 150 g	New York strip steaks

Heat 2 tbsp (30 ml) of butter in a sauce pan. Sauté the green onions for 3 minutes. Add the wine, sherry and herbs. Bring to a boil, reduce heat and simmer to ¾ cup (160 ml) of liquid. Strain through a fine sieve.

In a second sauce pan, heat the remaining butter. Add the flour and cook over low heat for 8 minutes or until hazelnut in colour. Add the strained sauce, beef stock and lemon juice. Continue to simmer for an additional 7 minutes. Sprinkle with remaining parsley.

Trim the steaks of any excess fat. Remove the gristle along the fat strip as this will prevent the steaks from curling while they cook. Broil the steaks to the desired doneness. Place on serving plates. Pour sauce over the steaks and serve.

SERVES 6

Beef in Red Wine Mushroom Sauce

TOURNEDOS DIANNA LYNN

12	12	slices maple bacon
12	12	3 oz (80 g) filet steaks
12 oz	360 g	cooked crab meat
⅓ cup	90 ml	Raspberry Hollandaise sauce (see page 108)

Wrap a slice of bacon around each steak. Broil to the desired doneness. Top with crab meat. Pour over each steak 1 tbsp (15 ml) of Raspberry Hollandaise. Place on a baking sheet. Broil for 1 minute or until golden brown. Serve.

SERVES 6

BEEF VIENNOISE

1½ lbs	675 g	top round
3 tbsp	45 ml	safflower oil
2	2	sliced Spanish onion
2 tsp	10 ml	paprika
¼ cup	60 ml	sherry
20	20	button mushrooms
¼ lb	115 g	oyster mushrooms – fresh or rehydrated, sliced
1	1	crushed garlic clove
1 tbsp	15 ml	Worcestershire sauce
1 tsp	5 ml	basil
¼ cup	60 ml	wine vinegar
¼ cup	60 ml	flour, all purpose
4	4	large potatoes – pared, cubed
2 cups	500 ml	Beef Stock (see page 85)

Dice the top round into ¾" (2 cm) cubes.

Heat the oil in a large Dutch oven. Add the onion and paprika. Sauté until tender. Add the beef and continue to sauté until the beef has browned. Add the sherry, mushrooms, garlic, Worcestershire, basil and vinegar. Simmer until most of the liquid has evaporated.

Sprinkle with flour and cook 3 minutes. Add the potatoes and stock. Cover and simmer until sauce has thickened and potatoes are tender. Serve.

SERVES 4

Tournedos Dianna Lynn

Beef Viennoise

South African Beef

Ceylon Beef

VEAL A LA RHINE

1½ lbs	675 g	veal shoulder
2	2	eggs
¼ cup	60 ml	milk
½ cup	125 ml	flour, all purpose
1 cup	250 ml	fine bread crumbs, seasoned
¼ cup	60 ml	safflower oil
1½ cup	375 ml	baby shrimp
18	18	blanched asparagus spears
¾ cup	180 ml	Hollandaise Sauce (see page 114)

Cut the veal shoulder into 6, 4 oz (120 g) pieces. Flatten and tenderize each piece into a cutlet with a meat mallet.

Blend the eggs into the milk. Dust each cutlet with flour, dip into the egg wash and dredge with bread crumbs.

Heat the oil in a large skillet. Fry each cutlet to golden brown on each side. Place on a baking sheet.

Divide the shrimp over each cutlet. Top with 3 asparagus spears and 2 tbsp (30 ml) of hollandaise sauce. Place under the oven broiler for 1½ minutes or until golden brown. Serve.

SERVES 6

CEYLON BEEF

3 tbsp	45 ml	safflower oil
2 lb	900 g	shoulder beef, cut into thin strips
1 cup	250 ml	sliced onions
1 cup	250 ml	sliced mushrooms
2	2	minced garlic cloves
3 tbsp	45 ml	flour , all purpose
½ tsp	3 ml	salt
2 tsp	10 ml	curry powder
4 cups	1 L	tomatoes, seeded, peeled, diced
¼ cup	60 ml	sherry
½ cup	125 ml	almonds, blanched, sliced
2 cups	500 ml	snow peas

Heat the oil in a large skillet or sauce pan. Add the beef and sauté to brown.

Add the onions, mushrooms and garlic and continue cooking until vegetables are tender. Sprinkle with flour; reduce heat and cook for an additional 2 minutes. Add the salt, curry, tomatoes and sherry. Bring to a boil; reduce heat and simmer for 15-20 minutes. Add the almonds and peas. Continue cooking for an additional 3 minutes. Serve with rice.

SERVES 6

SOUTH AFRICAN BEEF

6 – 6 oz	6 – 150 g	shoulder steaks
½ cup	125 ml	flour, all purpose
½ tsp	3 ml	each of basil, oregano leaves, thyme leaves, salt
¼ tsp	1 ml	each of chili powder, paprika, pepper
3 tbsp	45 ml	safflower oil
1 cup	250 ml	sliced mushrooms
1 cup	250 ml	sliced green bell pepper
1 cup	250 ml	sliced onion
2 cups	500 ml	chopped tomatoes
½ cup	125 ml	water
½ tsp	3 ml	Worcestershire sauce

Have the butcher tenderize the steaks or pound thin with a meat mallet.

Blend the flour with the spices, then dredge the steaks in the seasoned flour.

Heat the oil in a large skillet. Brown the steaks. Remove to a large casserole dish. Sauté the mushrooms, green pepper and onion in the oil. Add the tomato, water and Worcestershire. Simmer for 5 minutes. Pour over the steaks, cover and bake in a preheated 350°F (180°C) oven for 1 to 1¼ hours.

Remove from the oven and serve with rice pilaf.

SERVES 6

PAUPIETTES DE VEAU — VEAL BIRDS

6 – 4 oz	6 – 115 g	provimi veal cutlets
4 oz	115 g	ground veal
2 oz	60 g	bacon
1	1	small onion
1	1	carrot
1	1	celery stalk
¼ tsp	1 ml	lemon rind
½ tsp	3 ml	each of salt, basil leaves, pepper, thyme leaves
2 cup	500 ml	fine bread crumbs
1	1	egg
3 tbsp	45 ml	oil
3 tbsp	45 ml	butter
4 tbsp	60 ml	flour, all purpose
1½ cups	375 ml	Chicken Stock (see page 77)
¾ cup	180 ml	heavy cream
2 tbsp	30 ml	chopped parsley

Pound the cutlets very thin. In a food processor, place the ground veal, bacon, onion, carrot, and celery, grind very fine. Transfer to a mixing bowl and add the lemon, seasonings and bread crumbs, mixing thoroughly. Add the egg to bind. Spread the stuffing over the cutlets, then roll and tie together.

Heat the oil and butter in a sauce pan. Sear the veal on each side then transfer them to a casserole dish. Sprinkle the flour into the skillet. Reduce heat and cook 2 minutes. Add the chicken stock and cream. Simmer for 5 minutes. Pour the sauce over the veal.

Bake in a preheated 350°F (180°C) oven for 1 hour. Remove the paupiettes, untie, place upon a platter, pour sauce over and sprinkle with parsley for garnish before serving.

SERVES 6

FILET MIGNON STÉFANIE BLAIS

2 tbsp	30 ml	butter
1 tsp	5 ml	olive oil
1 tsp	5 ml	minced onion
1 tsp	5 ml	minced chives
½ lb	225 g	ground mushrooms
6 – 4 oz	6 – 115 g	filet mignons
½ quan	0.5 quan	Puff Pastry (see page 689)
½ lb	225 g	cooked crayfish tails or small shrimp
1	1	egg
1½ cups	375 ml	Béarnaise Sauce (see page 108) or Demi-Glace (see page 123)

Heat 1 tsp (5 ml) of butter and the oil together in a large skillet. Sauté the onion, chives and mushrooms until all liquid has evaporated.

Heat the remaining butter in a second skillet and brown the filet on all sides. Pat dry on a paper towel.

Roll the pastry out as directed; cut into 6 even pieces. Place some of the mushroom duxelles on the pastry, top with crayfish and a filet. Wrap the pastry around to completely seal in the filling. Trim any excess pastry.

Roll out the remaining pastry and use it to decorate the steaks. Mix the egg with a little water and brush over the pastry. Bake in a preheated 375°F (190°C) oven for 15-18 minutes.

Serve with béarnaise sauce on the side.

SERVES 6

Filet Mignon Stéfanie Blais

Paupiettes de Veau — Veal Birds

Sour Cream Herb Meat Loaf

BARON OF ROAST BEEF

¼ cup	60 ml	flour, all purpose
2 tbsp	30 ml	dry mustard
1 tsp	5 ml	basil
½ tsp	3 ml	each of thyme leaves, chervil, salt
5 lbs	2.2 kg	baron of beef
2 tbsp	30 ml	Worcestershire sauce
1	1	chopped onion
2	2	chopped carrots
2	2	chopped celery stalks
1	1	bay leaf
1 cup	250 ml	red wine
1 cup	250 ml	Beef Broth (see page 85) or water

Preheat the oven to 325°F (160°C).

Mix the flour, mustard and seasonings together.

Rub into the roast. Place roast into a roasting pan. Pour Worcestershire over roast.

Surround roast with the vegetables and bay leaf. Pour in the red wine and water.

Bake to desired doneness (see chart below), basting often.

Use the pan juices to make gravy.

SERVES 8

Roasting Chart:

Rare	Medium	Well Done
27	34	44 minutes per lb (454 g)

SOUR CREAM HERB MEATLOAF

1 lb	454 g	lean ground beef
¾ lb	345 g	ground veal
½ lb	225 g	lean ground pork
2	2	eggs
1 cup	250 ml	soda cracker crumbs
1 cup	250 ml	sour cream
⅓ cup	80 ml	chopped parsley
3 tbsp	45 ml	chopped chives
½ tsp	3 ml	each of thyme leaves, chervil, basil leaves
1 tsp	5 ml	salt
¾ tsp	4 ml	cracked black pepper
½ cup	125 ml	Mornay Sauce (see page 111)

Preheat oven to 350°F (180°C).

In a large mixing bowl, combine all the ingredients except Mornay Sauce.

Line a large loaf pan with tin foil. Pack the mixture into the pan. Bake for 1½ hours.Turn loaf out, remove the foil wrap. Slice and serve with Mornay Sauce.

SERVES 6

VEAL CUTLETS WITH TOMATO JAM AND CHEESE

1 cup	250 ml	crushed tomatoes
1 cup	250 ml	granulated sugar
¼ cup	60 ml	sherry
6 – 4 oz	6 – 120 g	veal cutlets
1	1	egg
¼ cup	60 ml	milk
½ cup	125 ml	flour, all purpose
1 cup	250 ml	seasoned bread crumbs
3 tbsp	45 ml	safflower oil
2 cups	500 ml	grated Havarti cheese

Mix the tomatoes, sugar and sherry in a sauce pan. Heat on low, stirring constantly. Reduce until the tomato mixture is very thick and resembles the consistency of jam.

Pound the cutlets thin with a meat mallet. Mix the egg with the milk. Dust the cutlets with flour, dip into the egg wash, and dredge in bread crumbs.

Heat the oil in a large skillet. Fry the cutlets until golden brown on both sides. Place each cutlet on a baking sheet, top with tomato jam, and sprinkle with cheese. Place in a preheated 450°F (230°C) oven until cheese is melted and golden.

Serve at once.

SERVES 6

Baron of Roast Beef

HONEY LEMON VEAL CUTLETS

6–4 oz	6–115 g	veal cutlets
½ cup	125 ml	flour, all purpose
3 tbsp	45 ml	safflower oil
2 tbsp	30 ml	butter
2 tbsp	30 ml	flour, all purpose
⅔ cup	160 ml	light cream
¼ cup	60 ml	lemon juice
¼ cup	60 ml	liquid honey
12	12	lemon slices
		parsley sprigs for garnish

Pound the cutlets flat with a meat mallet. Dust the cutlets with ½ cup (125 ml) of flour.

Heat the oil in a skillet and fry the cutlets for 3 minutes per side or until golden brown.

Heat the butter in a sauce pan. Add the flour and cook over low heat for 2 minutes. Add the cream and simmer into a thick sauce. Whip in the lemon juice and honey. Continue to simmer for 2 minutes.

Place cutlets on a serving platter, pour sauce over and garnish with lemon slices and parsley. Serve.

SERVES 6

VEAL CHOPS WITH LIME CILANTRO CREAM

1	1	egg
¼ cup	60 ml	milk
6 – 4 oz	6 – 120 g	boneless veal chops
½ cup	125 ml	flour, all purpose
1 cup	250 ml	seasoned bread crumbs
6 tbsp	90 ml	olive oil
3 tbsp	45 ml	butter
2 tbsp	30 ml	flour, all purpose
½ cup	125 ml	Chicken Stock (see page 77)
½ cup	125 ml	light cream
¼ cup	60 ml	lime juice
2 tbsp	30 ml	chopped cilantro (coriander)
1 cup	250 ml	julienned bell peppers

Mix the egg with the milk. Dust the chops with ½ cup (125 ml) of flour, dip into egg, then dredge through the bread crumbs.

Heat the oil in a large skillet. Fry the chops for 3 minutes per side or until golden brown. Reserve hot in the oven.

Heat the butter in a sauce pan. Add the flour and cook 2 minutes over low heat. Add the chicken stock and cream; simmer into a light sauce. Whip in the lime juice and cilantro; continue to simmer 5 minutes.

Place chops on serving plates and pour the sauce over the chops. Garnish with bell peppers.

SERVES 6

Veal Chops with Lime Cilantro Cream

Honey Lemon Veal Cutlets

The Gourmet's Breakfast Steak

VEAL CUTLETS CHERBOURG

6 – 4 oz	6 – 120 g	veal cutlets
1	1	egg
¼ cup	60 ml	milk
½ cup	125 ml	flour, all purpose
1 cup	250 ml	seasoned bread crumbs
3 tbsp	45 ml	safflower oil
6 tbsp	90 ml	butter
3 tbsp	45 ml	flour, all purpose
1 cup	250 ml	Chicken Stock (see page 77)
1 cup	250 ml	light cream
1½ cups	375 ml	cooked crayfish tails
¼ tsp	2 ml	salt
pinch	pinch	each of white pepper, paprika

Pound the cutlets thin with a meat mallet.

Mix the egg into the milk. Dust the cutlets in the ½ cup (125 ml) of flour. Dip into the egg wash, then dredge with bread crumbs. Heat the oil in a large skillet and fry the cutlets until golden brown. Reserve hot.

Heat half the butter in a sauce pan. Add the flour and cook for 2 minutes over low heat. Add both the chicken stock and cream and simmer 15 minutes or until sauce thickens.

In a food processor, purée the remaining butter and half the crayfish tails. Remove sauce from heat; whisk in the purée. Add the remaining crayfish and seasonings.

Place cutlets on serving plate. Smother with sauce and serve.

SERVES 6

THE GOURMET'S BREAKFAST STEAK

6 – 6 oz	6 – 170 g	tenderloin filets
2 tbsp	30 ml	butter
¾ cup	190 ml	sliced mushrooms
3 tbsp	45 ml	chopped chives
1½ cups	375 ml	Demi-Glace (see page 123)
3 tbsp	45 ml	brandy
3 tbsp	45 ml	sherry
¼ cup	60 ml	heavy cream
6	6	eggs
3	3	English muffins

Season the steaks as you like and broil them to your desired doneness.

While steaks cook, heat the butter in a small sauce pan. Add the mushrooms and sauté until all moisture has evaporated. Add the onions, demi-glace, brandy and sherry. Bring to a boil and reduce sauce to half its volume. Swirl in the cream.

Poach the eggs and toast the muffins. Place a half muffin on serving plates, top with a steak and smother with sauce. Place an egg on top. Garnish as desired.

SERVES 6

VEAL STEAKS SAUTÉ PROVENÇALE

6 – 6 oz	6 – 170 g	veal round steaks
4 tbsp	60 ml	butter
3	3	minced garlic cloves
1	1	sliced green bell pepper
1	1	sliced onion
3 cups	750 ml	peeled, seeded, chopped tomatoes
¼ cup	60 ml	sherry
1 tsp	5 ml	paprika
½ tsp	3 ml	salt
¼ tsp	1 ml	pepper

In a skillet, fry the veal in the butter for 4-6 minutes per side (depending on the thickness). Remove and reserve hot.

Add the garlic, bell pepper and onions to the skillet and sauté until tender. Add the tomatoes and bring to a boil. Reduce heat and simmer for 10 minutes. Add the sherry and seasonings; continue to simmer until liquid has evaporated.

Place veal steaks on the platter, pour sauce over and serve with lemon rice pilaf.

SERVES 6

Veal Steaks Sauté Provençale

Veal Steak Cumberland

VEAL STEAK CUMBERLAND

6	6	slices of bacon
6 – 6 oz	6 – 170 g	veal steaks
3	3	shallots
¼ cup	60 ml	water
1	1	orange
1	1	lemon
pinch	pinch	each of ground ginger, cayenne pepper
⅓ cup	80 ml	red currant jelly
¼ cup	60 ml	port wine

Wrap the bacon around the veal steaks and fasten with toothpicks. Broil on a charbroiler over medium coals, or in the oven until well done.

Chop the shallots and place in the water in a sauce pan.

Zest the orange and lemon. Place in the shallots, parboil for 3 minutes, and drain.

Add the juice of the orange and ½ lemon, the seasonings, jelly and port. Bring to a boil and reduce to half.

Pour over steaks and serve.

SERVES 6

VEAL CUTLETS VERDE

6 – 4 oz	6 – 120 g	veal cutlets
1	1	egg
¼ cup	60 ml	milk
½ cup	125 ml	flour, all purpose
1 cup	250 ml	seasoned bread crumbs
4 tbsp	60 ml	oil
3 tbsp	45 ml	butter
1	1	minced garlic clove
2 tbsp	30 ml	flour, all purpose
2 cups	500 ml	Veal Stock (see page 85) or Chicken Stock (see page 77)
1 cup	250 ml	peas
¼ tsp	1 ml	each of salt and pepper

Pound the cutlets with a meat mallet thin.

Mix the egg with milk. Dust with ½ cup of flour, dip into egg wash, and dredge in bread crumbs.

Heat the oil in a skillet and fry the cutlets to golden brown on each side. Reserve hot.

Heat the butter along with the garlic. Sprinkle with flour and cook for 2 minutes over low heat. Add the stock, peas and seasonings. Simmer until sauce thickens. Pour in a food processor and process until smooth.

Plate the cutlets and cover with sauce. Serve.

SERVES 6

SPICED PRIME RIB OF BEEF

¼ cup	60 ml	flour, all purpose
2 tbsp	30 ml	dry mustard
1 tsp	5 ml	basil
½ tsp	3 ml	each of thyme leaves, chervil, salt, chili powder, paprika, oregano leaves, garlic granules, onion powder
5 lbs	2.2 kg	standing rib roast (4 bones on)
2 tbsp	30 ml	Worcestershire sauce
1 tbsp	15 ml	soya sauce
1	1	chopped onion
2	2	chopped carrots
2	2	chopped celery stalks
1	1	bay leaf
1 cup	250 ml	red wine

Preheat the oven to 325°F (160°C).

Mix the flour, mustard and seasonings together.

Rub into roast. Place roast into a roasting pan. Pour Worcestershire and soya sauce over.

Surround roast with the vegetables and bay leaf. Pour in the wine.

Bake to desired doneness (see chart on Baron of Roast Beef, page 233), baste often.

Use the pan juices to make gravy.

SERVES 8

Spiced Prime Rib of Beef

Veal Chops Creole Style

Veal with Mushrooms

BEEF CROQUETTES

2 tbsp	30 ml	butter
4 tbsp	60 ml	flour, all purpose
1 cup	250 ml	milk
2 cups	500 ml	cooked lean ground beef, fat drained
½ tsp	3 ml	each of salt, paprika, chili powder
¼ tsp	1 ml	pepper
1 tsp	5 ml	Worcestershire sauce
2 tsp	10 ml	soya sauce
1 tsp	5 ml	finely chopped parsley
1	1	egg
2 tbsp	30 ml	water
½ cup	125 ml	seasoned flour
1½ cups	375 ml	fine bread crumbs
1 cup	250 ml	safflower oil

Heat the butter in a sauce pan. Add the flour and cook over low heat for 2 minutes. Stir in the milk and simmer into a very thick sauce. Stirring constantly, stir in the beef, seasonings, Worcestershire, soya and parsley. Cool to room temperature. Shape into equal size patties.

Blend the egg with the water. Dust each patty with flour, dip into the egg, then coat with bread crumbs.

Heat the oil in a large skillet. Fry the patties to golden brown on each side. Serve.

SERVES 4

VEAL WITH MUSHROOMS

1½ lbs	675 g	boneless veal
8	8	dried Chinese black mushrooms or wild mushrooms
1½ tsp	8 ml	cornstarch
4 tsp	20 ml	light soya sauce
1	1	egg white
¼ cup	60 ml	safflower oil
1	1	minced garlic clove
2 tsp	10 ml	granulated sugar
3 tbsp	45 ml	oyster sauce
2 tbsp	30 ml	red wine

Cut the veal into thin slices.

Soak the mushrooms in warm water for 1 hour.

Blend the cornstarch with soya sauce and egg white. Pour over the veal and marinate an additional hour.

Drain the mushrooms and slice into thin strips.

Heat the oil in a wok. Stir fry the garlic. Add the veal and fry 2 minutes. Add the sugar, oyster sauce, and wine. Continue to fry until most of the liquid has evaporated.

Serve with steamed rice.

SERVES 6

VEAL CHOPS CREOLE STYLE

12	12	small veal chops
¼ tsp	1 ml	each of thyme, basil, oregano, salt, cayenne pepper, black pepper, white pepper
½ tsp	3 ml	paprika
1 tsp	5 ml	chili powder
1½ cups	375 ml	fine dry bread crumbs
2	2	eggs
¼ cup	60 ml	milk
½ cup	125 ml	flour, all purpose
¼ cup	60 ml	olive oil
2 cups	500 ml	hot Creole Sauce (see page 121)

Trim the chops of any excess fat.

In a mixing bowl, blend the seasonings with the bread crumbs.

Blend the eggs with the milk.

Dust the chops in the flour, dip into the eggs and dredge through the bread crumbs.

Heat the oil in a large skillet and fry the chops for 8 minutes or less depending on their size. Plate the chops and smother with Creole sauce. Serve at once.

SERVES 6

Veal Rollups L.T.

VEAL ROLLUPS L.T.

6 – 4 oz	6–120 g	veal cutlets
18	18	blanched asparagus spears
18	18	large peeled, deveined shrimp
3 oz	80 g	grated Havarti cheese
1½ cups	375 ml	fresh clementine or tangerine juice
1 cup	250 ml	Veal Stock (see page 85) or Chicken Stock (see page 77)
½ cup	125 ml	heavy cream
2 tbsp	30 ml	butter
¼ tsp	1 ml	fresh ground pepper
½ cup	125 ml	Mandarin oranges

Pound the veal very thin with a meat mallet. Place 3 asparagus, 3 large shrimp, and ½ oz (15 g) of cheese in each. Fold in the ends and roll together. Secure with tooth picks. Place on a baking sheet.

Brush with oil. Bake in a preheated 350°F (180°C) oven for 25-30 minutes.

While veal bakes, combine the orange juice with the chicken stock in a sauce pan. Heat and reduce to half. Add the cream and reduce again to half. Remove from heat. Whip in the butter. Add the pepper and Mandarin orange sections.

Place the rollups on serving plate. Pour sauce over rollups and serve.

SERVES 6

VEAL FORESTIERE

1½ lbs	675 g	veal shoulder
2	2	eggs
¼ cup	60 ml	milk
½ cup	125 ml	flour, all purpose
1 cup	250 ml	fine bread crumbs, seasoned
¼ cup	60 ml	safflower oil
½ lb	225 g	sliced mushrooms
1	1	finely diced Spanish onion
3 tbsp	45 ml	butter
1½ cups	375 ml	Mornay Sauce (see page 111)
¼ cup	60 ml	Parmesan cheese, freshly grated

Cut the veal shoulder into 6, 4 oz (120 g) pieces. Flatten and tenderize each piece with a meat mallet.

Mix the eggs with the milk. Dust each cutlet with flour, dip into egg wash and dredge with bread crumbs.

Heat the oil and fry the cutlets for 3 minutes per side. Place on a baking sheet.

Sauté the mushrooms and onion in the butter until all the moisture has evaporated. Spread onto the cutlets. Pour the mornay sauce over each, sprinkle with Parmesan and place beneath the preheated oven broiler for 2 minutes. Serve.

SERVES 6

Veal Forestiere

POULTRY

More than chicken alone, poultry on today's menu represents creativity and tastefulness at their best. The limitless ways of preparing the bird range from traditional stuffed birds to all new, never before seen dishes such as a Strawberry Italian Wine Cream Chicken.

International in scope, local in flavour, the recipes here are easily prepared and a pleasure to serve. No recipe can be preferred over another, for they all are too good not to try. However, when considering something different for the special function, consider this chapter first. Dishes like Duck Lasagna are sure to be a pleasure to any group. Or, perhaps it's more of a formal affair. Then plan the Roast Guinea Fowl with Blueberry Hollandaise and fly away with the praise you receive.

The ideas for poultry are endless. From grilling and roasting to sautéing, just let your creativity flow, and enjoy. With *Simply Delicious Cooking 2*, your meals will always keep your guests coming back for more.

No longer is the chicken a lowly bird. It has reached new pinnacles of success and, unfortunately, so has its price as purveyors drive the price ever higher. What is exciting, however, is that whatever can be done with chicken can also be accomplished with any other type of bird. Turkey, for example, has come into its own. No longer just the holiday meal centre piece, many new turkey dishes are showing a renewed love for an old friend, with such dishes as Turkey Fillets Creole or Smoked Turkey in Cherry Sauce.

Everyone loves a meal prepared with love, and everyone loves the person who prepares the meal they love the most. That usually means a *Simply Delicious* poultry dish.

Roast Christmas Goose

Strawberry Italian Wine Cream Chicken

CORNISH HENS GREEK ISLAND STYLE

4	4	Cornish hens
1	1	eggplant
1	1	minced garlic clove
3 tbsp	45 ml	olive oil
1 cup	250 ml	Tomato Sauce (see page 106)
2 tsp	10 ml	oregano leaves
1 tsp	5 ml	basil
¼ tsp	1 ml	cracked black pepper
¾ lb	340 g	crumbled Feta cheese

Split the hens in half down the back.Using a very sharp small knife remove the bones from the hens.

Pare the eggplant and slice into ¾" (2 cm) slices, place into a 8 x 8" (20 x 20 cm) casserole dish and broil for 10 minutes per side.

Rub the hens with the garlic. Heat the oil in a skillet and brown the hens, transfer to the casserole dish.

Combine the tomato sauce, oregano, basil and pepper, pour over the hens. Sprinkle with the cheese and bake in a preheated 350°F (180°C) oven for 25 minutes covered. Remove cover and bake for an additional 15 minutes.

Serve with a side dish of Linguine with Olive Oil, Garlic and Fresh Herbs (see page 448).

SERVES 4

Cornish Hens Greek Island Style

STRAWBERRY ITALIAN WINE CREAM CHICKEN

6 – 4 oz	6 – 120 g	boneless chicken breasts
1 tbsp	15 ml	olive oil
¼ tsp	1 ml	each of basil, salt, pepper, paprika
6	6	egg yolks
½ cup	125 ml	granulated sugar
½ cup	125 ml	Marsala or sweet sherry
1½ cups	375 ml	sliced strawberries

Brush the chicken with the oil, sprinkle with seasonings. Broil in the oven for 3-5 minutes per side. Reserve warm.

Beat the egg yolks with the sugar in the top of a double boiler until foamy and pale in colour. Place over the boiling water. Slowly add the sherry beating continuously until mixture becomes thick and foamy. Remove from heat, stir in the strawberries.

Place chicken on a serving platter and pour half the sauce over the chicken and serve with the remaining sauce on the side.

SERVES 6

BLACKBERRY BRANDY GRILLED CHICKEN & SHRIMP

2 cups	500 ml	blackberries
1½ cups	375 ml	granulated sugar
½ cup	125 ml	blackberry brandy
2 – 6 oz	2 – 170 g	boneless cubed chicken
1 lb	454 g	large, peeled, deveined shrimp
1 tbsp	15 ml	oil

Purée berries in a food processor. Pass through a sieve to remove seeds.

Mix the blackberry pulp, sugar and brandy together in a sauce pan. Heat to a boil, reduce heat and simmer until sauce thickens.

Skewer the chicken and shrimp with water soaked bamboo skewers. Brush the oil over the skewers. Grill skewers for 5 minutes per side, brushing frequently with the sauce. Brush one final time before serving.

SERVES 4

CORNISH HENS WITH PEPPERCORN SAUCE

3 – 1 lb	3 – 450 g	Cornish game hens
¼ tsp	1 ml	each of, salt, basil, oregano, pepper, paprika
1	1	garlic clove
1 tbsp	15 ml	olive oil
2 tbsp	30 ml	butter
2 tbsp	30 ml	flour, all purpose
1 cup	250 ml	Chicken Stock (see page 77)
½ cup	125 ml	light cream
1 tbsp	15 ml	green peppercorns
1 tsp	5 ml	Dijon mustard
1 tbsp	15 ml	chopped chives
1 tbsp	15 ml	chopped parsley

Split the hens in half.

Blend the seasonings together. Rub the hens with the garlic clove. Brush the hens with the olive oil and sprinkle them with the seasonings. Place on a broiling pan and bake in a preheated 350°F (180°C) oven for 45 minutes.

While hens bake, heat the butter in a sauce pan and add the flour, cook for 2 minutes over low heat. Whip in the stock, cream, peppercorns, mustard and chives. Simmer for 10 minutes.

Transfer the hens to a serving platter, cover with sauce, sprinkle with parsley and serve.

SERVES 6

FLORENCE DEVILED CHICKEN

6 – 6 oz	6 – 170 g	chicken breast, bone in
¼ cup	60 ml	olive oil
1	1	minced garlic clove
2 tsp	10 ml	minced ginger root
1 tbsp	15 ml	lemon juice

Flatten the chicken breasts leaving the bones in and place in a shallow baking pan.

Blend the remaining ingredients together, pour over the chicken and marinate for 6 hours.

Broil the chicken over a charcoal or gas barbecue for 7 minutes per side on medium heat. Serve very hot.

SERVES 6

Cornish Hens with Peppercorn Sauce

Pecan Rice Chicken

PECAN RICE CHICKEN

¼ cup	60 ml	butter
1½ lbs	675 g	boneless, diced chicken
½ lb	225 g	sliced mushrooms
¼ cup	60 ml	fine diced onions
3 tbsp	45 ml	flour, all purpose
1½ cups	375 ml	Chicken Broth (see page 77)
½ cup	125 ml	light cream
¼ cup	60 ml	sherry
⅓ cup	80 ml	pecans
2 cups	500 ml	cooked long grain rice
		parsley sprigs

In a large kettle or Dutch oven heat the butter, add the chicken and brown. Remove the chicken and reserve.

Add the mushrooms and onions and sauté until tender. Sprinkle with flour and cook for 2 minutes over low heat. Add the broth, cream and sherry, simmer for 3 minutes.

Return the chicken and continue to simmer for an additional 35 minutes.

Stir the pecans into the rice and spoon the rice around the edges of a serving platter. Ladle the chicken into the centre and serve garnished with parsley.

SERVES 4

BROILED CORNISH HEN WITH WALNUT MARINADE

4	4	Cornish hens
2 tsp	10 ml	Dijon mustard
1 tbsp	15 ml	lemon juice
¼ tsp	1 ml	salt
¼ tsp	1 ml	cracked black pepper
2 tsp	10 ml	walnut oil
¼ cup	60 ml	olive oil

Wash the hens and split them down the back. Place hens in a shallow baking pan.

In a small mixing bowl combine the remaining ingredients, pour over the hens and marinate covered and refrigerate for 8 hours.

Broil the hens over medium heat on a charbroiler for 20-25 minutes, brushing frequently with the marinade. Serve at once, with one final brushing of the marinade.

SERVES 4

PARMESAN BAKED CHICKEN

¾ cup	180 ml	fine dry bread crumbs
¼ cup	60 ml	dried parsley flakes
⅓ cup	80 ml	freshly grated Parmesan cheese
¼ cup	60 ml	butter
1	1	minced clove garlic
4 – 6 oz	4 – 170 g	boneless, skinless chicken breasts
½ tsp	3 ml	salt
¼ tsp	1 ml	pepper

Combine the bread crumbs, parsley and cheese together in a small mixing bowl.

Melt the butter in a skillet and add the garlic, cook for 1 minute over low heat.

Dip the chicken in the butter then dredge through the bread crumbs, place in a small casserole dish. Season with the salt and pepper and brush with the remaining butter. Bake in a preheated 350°F (180°C) oven for 45 minutes.

SERVES 4

SAUTÉ CHICKEN WITH CLEMENTINE SAUCE

6 – 6 oz	6 – 170 g	boneless chicken breasts
3 tbsp	45 ml	oil
		salt and pepper
⅓ cup	80 ml	tangerine or orange juice concentrate
½ cup	125 ml	Chicken Stock (see page 77)
¼ cup	60 ml	whipping cream
1 tsp	5 ml	butter
1 tsp	5 ml	lime juice

Heat the oil in a large skillet. Sauté the chicken for 6-8 minutes. Season with salt and pepper and reserve hot.

Heat the tangerine juice in a sauce pan with the chicken stock, bring to a boil and reduce heat. Add the cream and simmer until sauce coats a spoon. Remove from heat. Whip in the butter and lime juice.

Place chicken on a serving plate, cover with sauce and serve.

SERVES 6

CHICKEN & SHRIMP PIE

½ quan	0.5 quan	Plain Pastry (see page 616)
1 cup	250 ml	finely diced cooked chicken
1 cup	250 ml	finely diced cooked shrimp
2 cups	500 ml	Béchamel sauce (see page 112)
¼ tsp	1 ml	each of salt, pepper, nutmeg
1 tbsp	15 ml	parsley
1 tbsp	15 ml	grated onion
3	3	eggs, separated

Roll out the pie dough and fit into a 9" deep dish pie shell.

In a mixing bowl blend the chicken, shrimp and Béchamel sauce. Add the seasonings and onion.

Beat the egg yolks and fold into the mixture. Beat the egg whites stiffly, fold into the mixture.

Pour mixture into the pie shell and bake 25-30 minutes in a preheated 400°F (200°C) oven until the pie is golden brown. Serve at once.

SERVES 6

Chicken & Shrimp Pie

CHICKEN JAMBALAYA

1½ lbs	675 g	diced boneless chicken
2 tbsp	30 ml	safflower oil
2 tbsp	30 ml	butter
½ lb	225 g	andouille sausage*
½ cup	125 ml	diced onions
2	2	minced garlic cloves
3 tbsp	45 ml	chopped parsley
1½ cups	375 ml	diced green bell pepper
2	2	diced celery stalks
2 cups	500 ml	peeled, seeded, chopped tomatoes
½ tsp	3 ml	each of white pepper, black pepper, oregano leaves, basil, thyme leaves, garlic powder, onion powder, chili powder.
2 tsp	10 ml	Worcestershire sauce
3 drops	3 drops	Tabasco™ sauce
2¼ cups	625 ml	water
1 cup	250 ml	raw long grain rice

In a Dutch oven or large kettle, sauté the chicken in the oil and butter. Add the sausage and vegetables, continue to sauté until vegetables are tender.

Stir in the remaining ingredients, reduce heat, cover and simmer on low heat for 40-45 minutes. Serve.

SERVES 6

*If you cannot find andouille sausage, use hot Italian sausage.

Chicken Jambalaya

Spanish Tarragon Chicken

JENNIFER'S CHICKEN

6 – 4 oz	6 – 120 g	boneless chicken breasts
1 cup	250 ml	green seedless grapes
6 oz	170 g	rindless Brie cheese
1 cup	250 ml	baby shrimp
2	2	eggs
⅓ cup	80 ml	milk
⅓ cup	80 ml	ground pine nuts
½ cup	125 ml	fine seasoned bread crumbs
⅓ cup	80 ml	freshly grated Romano cheese
1⁄2 cup	125 ml	flour, all purpose
1⁄3 cup	80 ml	safflower oil

Pound the chicken flat with a meat mallet.

Cut the grapes in half and place a few grapes on the chicken along with 1 oz (30 g) of cheese and a sprinkling of shrimp. Roll the chicken to enfold the filling inside. Place on a baking pan and refrigerate for 1 hour.

Blend the eggs and milk together. Mix the nuts with the bread crumbs and cheese. Dust the rolled chicken with flour. Dip the chicken into the egg wash then roll in the bread crumbs.

In a large skillet heat the oil, fry the chicken to golden brown on each side. Transfer to the baking sheet and bake in a preheated 350°F (180°C) oven for 15-18 minutes.

Serve with a Blackberry Brandy Sauce (see Roast Veal with Blackberry Brandy Sauce page 214).

SERVES 6

SPANISH TARRAGON CHICKEN

1 tbsp	15 ml	olive oil
1 – 3 lb	1 – 1 kg	chicken
8 oz	225 g	thin strips of sliced ham
2	2	sliced onion
2	2	coarse dice celery stalks
3	3	coarse dice carrots
1½ cups	375 ml	chicken stock
1 tbsp	15 ml	chopped fresh tarragon
2 tbsp	30 ml	butter
2 tbsp	30 ml	flour, all purpose

Rub the oil over the chicken. Place in a earthenware cocotte (casserole dish). Place uncovered in a preheated 350°F (180°C) oven. Bake for 30 minutes.

Add the ham, onion, celery, carrots, stock and tarragon. Cover and continue to bake for 1 hour. Remove from oven, strain the broth and carve chicken.

Return the chicken to the cocotte and reserve warm with the vegetables.

Heat the butter in a sauce pan, stir in the flour and pour in 2 cups (500 ml) of the strained broth. Simmer until sauce thickens, pour over chicken and vegetables. Serve in the cocotte.

SERVES 6

Jennifer's Chicken

CHICKEN WALNUT

1 lb	450 g	boneless chicken strips
3 tbsp	45 ml	sherry
⅔ cup	160 ml	Chicken Stock (see page 77)
2 tbsp	30 ml	soya sauce
1 tbsp	15 ml	cornstarch
3 tbsp	45 ml	safflower oil
1½ cups	375 ml	snow peas
4 oz	120 g	button mushrooms
1 cup	250 ml	sliced celery
1	1	sliced onion
1	1	sliced green bell pepper
¾ cup	180 ml	walnut pieces

Toss the chicken with the sherry and marinate for 30 minutes.

Blend the chicken stock, soya sauce and cornstarch together in a mixing bowl. Heat 2 tbsp (30 ml) of oil in a wok, add the chicken, and fry thoroughly. Remove the meat, add the remaining oil and fry the vegetables.

Return the chicken and add the broth. Simmer for 2 minutes. Stir in the walnuts and serve with steamed rice.

SERVES 6

CHICKEN 'N' CHESTNUTS

4 tbsp	60 ml	safflower oil
1½ lbs	675 g	boneless chicken meat
1	1	finely diced Spanish onion
1	1	finely diced red bell pepper
1	1	fine diced green bell pepper
3 oz	80 g	sliced mushrooms
3 oz	80 g	chestnuts, peeled, diced
4 tbsp	60 ml	flour, all purpose
1 tbsp	15 ml	curry powder
2 cups	500 ml	Chicken Stock (see page 77)
1 cup	250 ml	heavy cream

Heat the oil in a large Dutch oven. Add the chicken, vegetables and chestnuts. Sauté until chicken browns. Sprinkle with flour and curry powder, reduce heat and cook for 2 minutes. Pour in stock and cream and simmer for 35-45 minutes.

Serve over noodles or rice.

SERVES 6

CHICKEN FRICASSEE

1 – 4 ½ lb	1 – 2 kg	chicken, cut into 8 pieces
2	2	chopped onions
2	2	chopped carrots
2	2	chopped celery stalks
1	1	bouquet garni *
4 cups	1 L	cold Chicken Broth (see page 77)
1 tsp	5 ml	celery salt
½ tsp	3 ml	white pepper
3 tbsp	45 ml	butter
3 tbsp	45 ml	flour, all purpose

Wash and pat dry the chicken.

Place the chicken in a large kettle or Dutch oven along with the onions, carrots and celery and bouquet. Cover with the broth and bring to a boil, reduce temperature simmer gently for 1½ hours.

Remove the chicken and reserve warm. Strain the broth and discard the vegetables and the bouquet. Return the broth to the pot, add the salt and pepper, bring to a boil, reduce the liquid to 2 cups (500 ml).

In a small sauce pan heat the butter, add the flour and cook over low heat for 2 minutes. Add the reduced broth and simmer into a thick sauce. Pour sauce over chicken and serve with rice or noodles.

SERVES 4

*The bouquet garni for this dish is; a bay leaf, 8 sprigs of parsley, 2 sprigs of thyme, 6 peppercorns and 1 small, chopped leek tied together in a cheesecloth.

Chicken Walnut

Chicken Rolls

ROAST CHRISTMAS GOOSE

3	3	apples pared, cored, diced
2	2	grated carrots
1	1	finely diced Spanish onion
2	2	finely diced celery stalks
1 cup	250 ml	seedless raisins
1 cup	250 ml	blanched and peeled walnuts
½ cup	125 ml	milk
½ tsp	3 ml	each of salt, pepper
1 tsp	5 ml	marjoram
3 cups	750 ml	cubed stale bread
1 – 9 lb	1 – 4 kg	goose
1	1	garlic clove
1 tbsp	15 ml	safflower oil
½ tsp	3 ml	paprika
1 tsp	5 ml	cornstarch

Mix the apples, carrots, onion, celery, raisins, walnuts, bread, milk and seasonings together. Stuff the mixture into the goose, truss the goose.

Place in a large roaster. Rub goose with garlic and brush with the oil. Sprinkle with paprika.

Place in a preheated 350°F (180°C) oven for 3½ to 4 hours. Baste several times during cooking. When the goose is cooked remove from the roaster, place on a serving platter and keep warm.

Deglaze the pan juices, mix the cornstarch with 2 tbsp (30 ml) of water. Pour into pans juices. Bring to a boil. Strain into a sauce boat and serve with the goose.

CHICKEN ROLLS

3	3	slices of diced bacon
1	1	finely diced carrot
1	1	finely diced stalk of celery
1	1	finely diced small onion
1 cup	250 ml	grated Havarti cheese
4 – 6 oz	4 – 170 g	boneless, skinless chicken breasts pounded flat
2 tbsp	30 ml	melted butter
2 cups	500 ml	hot Mornay Sauce (see page 111)

In a large skillet fry the bacon, add the carrot, celery and onion and sauté until tender, drain excess fat, place in a small mixing bowl and cool to room temperature.

Combine the sautéed mixture together with the cheese, and press onto the chicken breasts. Roll the chicken as to encase the filling. Place in a small baking dish, brush with butter and bake in a preheated 350°F (180°C) oven for 25-30 minutes.

Transfer chicken to serving plates, smother with mornay sauce and serve.

SERVES 4

AUSTRIAN STUFFED CHICKEN

3 oz	80 g	sliced mushrooms
1	1	fine diced medium onion
1 tbsp	15 ml	safflower oil
2½ cups	625 ml	cooked rice, cold
½ cup	125 ml	peas
1½ tsp	7 ml	each of salt, pepper, thyme leaves, basil
¼ tsp	1 ml	cinnamon
1	1	egg
1 – 5 lb	1 – 2 kg	chicken
2 cups	500 ml	Tomato Sauce (see page 106)

Sauté the mushrooms and onions in a large skillet with the oil until all the liquid has evaporated. Cool to room temperature. Blend into the cooked rice along with the peas, seasonings and egg.

Stuff this mixture into the chicken, truss the chicken. Place the chicken into a roaster and roast in a 325°F (160°C) oven for 1½ hours. Check for doneness. Remove chicken from oven. Scoop the stuffing into a serving dish, carve the chicken and serve with tomato sauce on the side.

SERVES 6

CHICKEN MEATBALL CURRY

2 lbs	900 g	chicken meat
2 tbsp	30 ml	onion
¼ cup	60 ml	bread crumbs
1	1	egg
½ tsp	3 ml	each of, cayenne, turmeric, ginger powder, black pepper, basil, thyme leaves, oregano, paprika
1 tsp	5 ml	salt
1	1	minced garlic clove
3 tbsp	45 ml	safflower oil
2 tbsp	30 ml	butter
2 tbsp	30 ml	flour, all purpose
1 tsp	5 ml	curry powder
1½ cups	375 ml	Chicken Stock (see page 77)
¾ cup	180 ml	light cream

In a food processor coarse chop the chicken. Add the onion, bread crumbs, egg, seasonings and garlic. Process into a fine mix. Remove and shape into small balls.

Heat the oil in a large skillet and brown the meat balls. Drain all oil. Transfer the meatballs to a casserole dish.

Heat the butter in a sauce pan add the flour and curry powder. Cook for 2 minutes over low heat. Add the stock and cream, simmer for 5 minutes. Pour the sauce over the meatballs.

Cover the dish and bake in a preheated 350°F (180°C) oven for 45 minutes. Serve with rice.

SERVES 6

Lemonade Chicken

LEMONADE CHICKEN

¾ cup	190 ml	lemonade concentrate
¼ cup	60 ml	catsup
3 tbsp	45 ml	brown sugar
3 tbsp	45 ml	white vinegar
¼ tsp	1 ml	ground ginger
1 tsp	5 ml	soya sauce
¼ tsp	1 ml	each of paprika, chili powder, garlic powder, onion powder, thyme, basil, oregano, salt and pepper
1 – 2¼ lb	1 – 1 kg	chicken, cut into 8 pieces
½ cup	125 ml	flour, all purpose
¼ cup	60 ml	safflower oil

In a mixing bowl combine the concentrate, catsup, sugar, vinegar, ginger, soya and seasonings.

Dredge the chicken in the flour. Heat the oil in a large kettle or Dutch oven, brown the chicken. Drain any excess oil. Pour the sauce over the chicken, cook over low heat for 35-40 minutes covered. Serve with Hickory Smoked 'Taters (see page 70).

SERVES 4

MACADAMIA NUT CHICKEN

6 – 6 oz	6 – 170 g	boneless, skinless chicken breasts
½ cup	125 ml	ground macadamia nuts
¼ cup	60 ml	freshly grated Parmesan cheese
1 cup	250 ml	fine dry bread crumbs
¼ cup	60 ml	melted butter

Wash and pat dry the chicken breasts.

Combine the nuts, cheese and bread crumbs in a small mixing bowl.

Dip the chicken in the melted butter, then dredge through the crumb mixture. Place into a small casserole dish. Bake in a preheated 350°F (180°C) oven for 40-45 minutes or until chicken is golden brown. Serve at once with an Apricot Raspberry Sauce (see page 108).

SERVES 6

Chicken Meatball Curry

BEER BATTERED CHICKEN

1½ lbs	675 g	boneless chicken breasts
2	2	eggs
1½ cups	375 ml	flour, all purpose
½ cup	125 ml	ice cold beer
1 tsp	5 ml	baking powder
3 cups	750 ml	safflower oil

Cut the chicken into 1" (2.5 cm) strips. Whip the eggs, 1 cup (250 ml) flour, beer, and baking powder together.

Heat the oil to 375°F (190°C).

Dust the chicken with remaining flour. Dip into the batter then deep fry in small batches to golden brown, reserve hot. Once all the chicken has been cooked, serve.

SERVES 6

GUINEA HENS WITH RASPBERRY, KIWI AND GREEN PEPPERCORN SAUCE

4	4	small guinea hens
2 tbsp	30 ml	melted butter
1 tsp	5 ml	salt
½ tsp	3 ml	black pepper
1 cup	250 ml	raspberries
½ cup	125 ml	heavy cream
¼ cup	60 ml	powdered sugar
1 tbsp	15 ml	green peppercorns
2	2	kiwis

Place the hens in a shallow baking dish, brush with butter and season with salt and pepper. Bake in a preheated 350°F (180°C) oven for 45-50 minutes.

While hens bake, purée the raspberries and press through a fine sieve to remove the seeds.

Heat the cream, raspberries and sugar together in a small sauce pan. Add the peppercorns and simmer for 5 minutes.

Pare the kiwis and dice them, stir into the sauce.

Remove hens from the oven and place upon serving plates and smother with the sauce. Serve at once.

SERVES 4

Beer Battered Chicken

CHICKEN FRICASSEE II

1 – 4½ lb	1 – 2 kg	chicken, cut into 8 pieces
½ cup	125 ml	seasoned flour
4 tbsp	60 ml	olive oil
2	2	chopped onions
2	2	chopped carrots
2	2	chopped celery stalks
1	1	bouquet garni (see Glossary)
4 cups	1 L	cold Chicken Broth (see page 77)
½ tsp	3 ml	each of salt, pepper, paprika, chili powder, basil
½ cup	125 ml	tomato paste
3 tbsp	45 ml	butter
3 tbsp	45 ml	flour, all purpose

Wash and pat dry the chicken.

Dust the chicken in the seasoned flour.

Heat the oil in a large kettle or Dutch oven, brown the chicken on all sides, drain the excess oil. Add the onions, carrots, celery and bouquet, cover with the broth and bring to a boil, reduce temperature and simmer gently for 1½ hours.

Remove the chicken and reserve warm. Strain the broth and discard the vegetables and bouquet. Return the broth to the pot, add the seasonings and tomato paste, bring to a boil, reduce the liquid to 2 cups (500 ml).

In a small sauce pan heat the butter, add the flour and cook over low heat for 2 minutes. Add the reduced broth and simmer into a thick sauce. Pour sauce over chicken and serve with rice or noodles.

SERVES 4

Chicken Fricasse II

CHICKEN IN THREE PEPPERCORN SAUCE

5 lbs	2 kg	chicken, cut into pieces
⅓ cup	80 ml	flour, all purpose
½ tsp	3 ml	each of onion powder, paprika, thyme leaves, oregano leaves, black pepper, chervil
2 tsp	10 ml	each of salt, chili powder
¼ cup	60 ml	safflower oil
3 oz	85 g	mushrooms, sliced
2 tsp	10 ml	green peppercorns
2 tsp	10 ml	pink peppercorns
1 tsp	5 ml	black peppercorns
2 cups	500 ml	Demi-Glace (see page 123)
⅓ cup	80 ml	whipping cream
¼ cup	60 ml	Marsala wine
1 tbsp	15 ml	butter

Wash the chicken and pat dry.

Combine the flour with the seasonings. Dust the chicken with the flour.

Heat the oil in a large skillet. Fry the chicken until golden brown. Remove and reserve.

Fry the mushrooms until tender. Return the chicken to the pan. Add the peppercorns and demi-glace. Reduce heat. Cover and simmer for 1 hour. Transfer chicken to a serving platter.

Increase the heat and reduce sauce by half its volume. Stir in the cream and wine. Whisk in the butter, pour sauce over chicken and serve.

SERVES 6

Duck Lasagna

POLLO FINOCCHIO

1½ lbs	675 g	boneless chicken
3 cups	750 ml	Chicken Broth (see page 77)
6 tbsp	90 ml	butter
1½ cups	375 ml	finely chopped fennel
1	1	julienne cut carrot
1	1	julienne red bell pepper
3 tbsp	45 ml	flour, all purpose
¾ cup	180 ml	light cream
1 quan	1 quan	Risotto Alla Certosina (see page 740)

Dice the chicken into large cubes.

Heat the broth in a large kettle or Dutch oven and gently poach the chicken for 35 minutes. Remove and reserve the chicken, strain the broth. Return the broth to the pot and bring to a boil, reduce to 1½ cups (375 ml).

In a sauce pan heat the butter and sauté the vegetables until tender. Sprinkle with flour and cook over low heat for 2 minutes. Add the broth and the cream and simmer until sauce thickens. Stir in the chicken and continue to simmer for 5 minutes.

Place the risotto around the rim of a serving dish, ladle the chicken into the centre and serve.

SERVES 4

Pollo Finocchio

DUCK LASAGNA

2 lbs	900 g	boneless duck meat
1	1	large Spanish onion
1	1	red bell pepper
1	1	green bell pepper
3	3	celery stalks
1	1	minced garlic clove
¼ cup	60 ml	olive oil
3 cups	750 ml	crushed tomatoes
½ tsp	3 ml	each of salt, basil, marjoram
¼ tsp	1 ml	each of pepper, paprika
1 tsp	5 ml	Worcestershire sauce
1½ lbs	625 g	mafalda noodles (a 1" wide pasta)
¾ lb	345 g	grated mozzarella cheese

Cut the duck meat into ½" (1.5 cm) cubes. Medium dice the vegetables.

Heat the oil in a Dutch oven. Add the duck and vegetables and sauté until the duck has cooked through. Add the tomato, seasonings and Worcestershire. Reduce the heat and simmer for 1½ to 2 hours until sauce is very thick. Skim any grease from sauce as it floats to the top.

Cook the noodles in a large Dutch oven with plenty of salted water until they are al dente, drain and cool.

Alternate layers of noodles and sauce in a large greased casserole dish. Cover with cheese. Bake in a preheated 350°F (180°C) oven for 15 minutes or until cheese is golden brown. Serve.

SERVES 8

BLANQUETTE DE POULET

1½ lbs	675 g	boneless chicken meat
3 cups	750 ml	Chicken Stock (see page 77)
1 tsp	5 ml	salt
¼ tsp	1 ml	thyme leaves
1	1	bay leaf
20	20	pearl onions
4	4	carrots, julienned
2 tbsp	30 ml	butter
2 tbsp	30 ml	flour, all purpose
2 tbsp	30 ml	lemon juice
2	2	egg yolks
pinch	pinch	cayenne pepper
1 tbsp	15 ml	chopped parsley

In a Dutch oven or a large kettle, put the chicken, stock, salt, thyme, and bay leaf; cover and simmer for 45 minutes. Add the onions and carrots and continue to simmer for an additional 10 minutes.

Remove 2 cups (500 ml) of liquid. Melt the butter in a small sauce pan, add the flour and cook for 2 minutes over low heat (do not brown it). Slowly add the 2 cups (500 ml) of liquid stirring until thickened.

Whisk the lemon juice in the egg yolks. Blend into the sauce. Reheat but do not boil the sauce as this will curdle the eggs. Blend the sauce with the chicken. Stir in the cayenne. Pour into a serving bowl.

Sprinkle with parsley and serve over noodles or rice.

SERVES 6

Chicken Florentine Twist

SMOKED TURKEY IN CHERRY SAUCE

1½ lbs	675 g	smoked turkey breast
1½ lbs	675 g	fresh stoned sour cherries
¼ cup	60 ml	granulated sugar
¼ cup	60 ml	sweet sherry or apple juice
¼ tsp	1 ml	ground cinnamon
⅛ tsp	pinch	allspice
1 tsp	5 ml	cornstarch

Place the turkey in a roaster, cover and bake for 1 hour in a preheated 350°F (180°C) oven. Remove, slice and reserve hot.

While the turkey is roasting combine the remaining ingredients except the cornstarch in a food processor, process into a purée.

Transfer to a sauce pan and simmer gently for 1 hour. Mix the cornstarch with 2 tbsp (30 ml) of cold water. Add to sauce and simmer until sauce thickens.

Place turkey on a serving platter, pour the sauce over the turkey and serve.

SERVES 6

CHICKEN FLORENTINE TWIST

6 – 4 oz	6 – 120 g	chicken breasts
10 oz	280 g	spinach leaves
6 oz	170 g	Havarti cheese
6 oz	170 g	smoked salmon
2 tbsp	30 ml	melted butter
2 cups	500 ml	Chicken Velouté (see page 105)

Pound the chicken breasts flat with a meat mallet.

Chop the spinach fine.

Place 1½ oz (45 g) of spinach, 1 oz (30 g) of cheese, and 1 oz (30 g) of salmon on each breast. Roll chicken and secure with toothpicks.

Brush with melted butter, place on a baking sheet. Bake for 20 minutes in a preheated 350°F (180°C) oven.

Place on serving dished with the velouté poured over them. Serve.

SERVES 6

CHICKEN FRITTERS GRAND'MERE

1 cup	250 ml	flour, all purpose
1½ tsp	6 ml	salt
¼ tsp	1 ml	each of marjoram and paprika
1 tsp	5 ml	baking powder
2	2	eggs, separated
⅓ cup	80 ml	cold milk
2 tbsp	30 ml	sherry
1 cup	250 ml	cooked, diced chicken
1 cup	250 ml	cooked peas
3 cups	750 ml	safflower oil

Sift the flour together with the salt, herbs and baking powder.

Beat the egg yolks until creamy then beat in the milk and sherry. Slowly beat the flour into the liquid. Beat the egg whites until they are stiff and fold into the batter. Fold in the chicken and peas.

Heat the oil to 375°F (190°C). Drop small batches of spoonful size batter into the oil and cook until golden brown. Reserve hot while remainder cook. Serve very hot, good with Mornay Sauce (see page 111).

SERVES 4

CHICKEN STIR FRY

8 oz	225 g	boneless skinless chicken
2 tbsp	30 ml	safflower oil
1	1	small diced onion
½ cup	125 ml	diced green bell pepper
½ cup	125 ml	diced red bell pepper
20	20	button mushrooms
2 tbsp	30 ml	oyster sauce*
2 tbsp	30 ml	soya sauce
1 tsp	5 ml	cornstarch
1 tbsp	15 ml	sherry or water

Dice the chicken into bite size pieces.

Heat the oil in a wok or large skillet. Fry the chicken for 3 minutes. Add the vegetables and fry until tender.

Add the oyster sauce and soya sauce. Simmer for 2 minutes.

Mix the cornstarch with sherry and stir into chicken. Simmer until thick. Serve over rice or noodles.

SERVES 2

*Available in the Oriental section of your supermarket

Chicken Fritters Grand'Mere

CHICKEN SAUTÉ BOURGUIGNONNE

3 – 2¼ lb	3 – 1 kg	chickens
¼ cup	60 ml	clarified butter (see Glossary)
1 tbsp	15 ml	shallots
1 tbsp	15 ml	flour, all purpose
1	1	bouquet garni*
¼ lb	115 g	diced cooked bacon
20	20	pearl onions
20	20	button mushrooms
¾ cup	180 ml	red wine

Cut the chicken into quarters.

Heat the butter in a large kettle or Dutch oven, fry the chicken until golden brown, remove and reserve the chicken. Stir in the shallots and flour, reduce heat and cook for 4 minutes.

Add the remaining ingredients along with the chicken. Reduce the heat and simmer gently for 40-45 minutes or until the chicken is cooked through. Discard the bouquet garni and serve with rice or noodles.

SERVES 6

*The bouquet garni for this dish is; a bay leaf, 8 sprigs of parsley, 2 sprigs of thyme, 6 peppercorns and 1 small, chopped leek tied together in a cheesecloth.

CHICKEN TIA JUANA

1 – 4½ lb	1 – 2 kg	chicken, cut into 8 pieces
¼ cup	60 ml	flour, all purpose
2 tsp	10 ml	salt
¼ tsp	1 ml	each of black pepper, white pepper, cloves
2 tsp	10 ml	each of chili powder, paprika
⅓ cup	80 ml	olive oil
1	1	large sliced onion
2	2	minced garlic cloves
1	1	sliced green bell pepper
1	1	sliced red bell pepper
1½ cups	375 ml	sliced mushrooms
3 cups	750 ml	peeled, seeded, chopped tomatoes
½ cup	125 ml	sherry
⅓ cup	80 ml	green stuffed olives

Wash and pat dry the chicken.

Combine the flour with the seasonings. Dredge the chicken through the flour.

Heat the oil in a large kettle or Dutch oven, brown the chicken in the oil. Transfer the chicken to a large casserole dish.

Sauté the onion, garlic, peppers and mushrooms in the pan until tender. Stir in the tomatoes and sherry, simmer for 5 minutes. Pour over the chicken and bake in a preheated 350°F (180°C) oven for 45-50 minutes covered. Remove the cover and stir in the olives and continue to bake for an additional 15 minutes.

Serve with rice.

SERVES 4

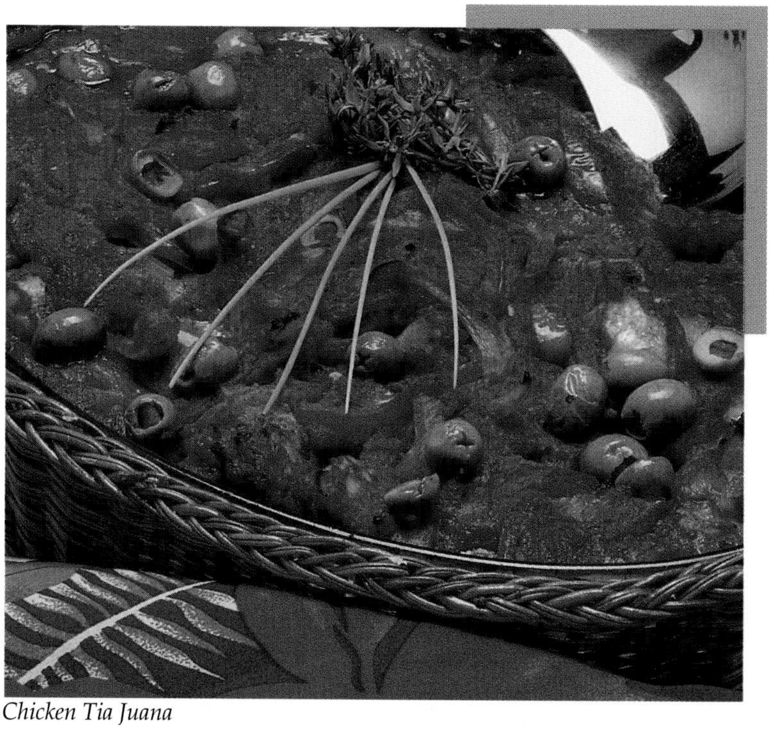

Chicken Tia Juana

TURKEY FILLETS CREOLE

1½ lbs	675 g	turkey breast
½ cup	125 ml	seasoned flour
2	2	diced Spanish onion
2	2	diced green bell peppers
1	1	diced red bell pepper
3 tbsp	45 ml	safflower oil
½ tsp	3 ml	each of basil, oregano, thyme, paprika, garlic powder, onion powder, chili powder
¼ tsp	1 ml	each of black pepper, white pepper, cayenne
1 tsp	5 ml	salt
1 tbsp	15 ml	Worcestershire sauce
3 cups	750 ml	crushed tomatoes
½ cup	125 ml	chopped green onions
2 tbsp	30 ml	chopped parsley

Cut the turkey in ¾" (2 cm) wide strips, dust with flour.

In a large Dutch oven fry the turkey, onions and peppers in the oil until the turkey is cooked through. Add the seasoning, Worcestershire and tomatoes, reduce heat and simmer for 1¼ hours.

Add the green onion and parsley simmer for 5 minutes longer. Serve over noodles or rice.

SERVES 6

Turkey Fillets Creole

Chicken Marchand de Vin

CHICKEN MARCHAND DE VIN

1 – 2¼ lb	1 – 1 kg	chicken, cut in 8 pieces
2 tbsp	30 ml	olive oil
½ tsp	3 ml	each of salt, pepper, paprika, chili powder, basil, thyme, oregano
2 tbsp	30 ml	butter
½ cup	125 ml	diced ham
½ cup	125 ml	diced mushrooms
½ cup	125 ml	green onions
1½ cups	375 ml	Demi-Glace (see page 123)
½ cup	125 ml	sherry
¼ cup	60 ml	heavy cream – optional

Place the chicken in a shallow baking pan, brush with oil and sprinkle with the seasonings. Bake in a preheated 350°F (180°C) oven for 45 minutes.

In a sauce pan melt the butter, sauté the ham, mushrooms and green onions. Add the demi-glace and sherry. Reduce heat and simmer to half of the sauce's volume.

Add cream and simmer for 2 minutes longer if using.

Pour sauce over chicken and continue to bake for an additional 10 minutes. Serve with rice or noodles.

SERVES 4

Deviled Chicken Breasts

DEVILED CHICKEN BREASTS

2 tbsp	30 ml	butter
¼ tsp	1 ml	each of cayenne, black pepper, white pepper
6 – 6 oz	6 – 170 g	boneless, skinless chicken breasts
½ cup	125 ml	chili sauce
½ cup	125 ml	catsup
¼ tsp	1 ml	each of salt, basil, paprika, chili powder, thyme, oregano
2 tbsp	30 ml	Worcestershire sauce
2 tbsp	30 ml	Dijon mustard
½ cup	125 ml	water

Make a smooth paste of the butter and peppers. Place the chicken breasts into a casserole dish and spread the butter over them. Place under the preheated oven broiler for 3 minutes, turn the breasts over and broil for an additional 3 minutes.

While chicken broils combine the remaining ingredients together in a small mixing bowl. Pour over chicken and bake for 20-25 minutes in a 350°F (180°C) oven.

Serve with a rice pilaf.

SERVES 6

CHICKEN CREOLE AU GRATIN

3 cups	750 ml	Chicken Broth (see page 77)
1½ lbs	675 g	boneless coarse diced chicken
2 cups	500 ml	cooked drained fettucini noodles
1½ cups	375 ml	Creole Sauce (see page 121)
½ cup	125 ml	grated mild cheddar cheese
½ cup	125 ml	grated sharp cheddar cheese
½ cup	125 ml	grated Havarti cheese

Preheat the oven to 400°F (200°C).

Bring the broth to a boil. Add the chicken and simmer gently for 30 minutes. Drain and reserve the chicken.

Place the noodles in a greased casserole dish. Spread the chicken over the noodles and smother with sauce. Combine the cheeses and sprinkle over the casserole. Bake for 15-20 minutes or until cheese is melted and is golden brown, serve at once.

SERVES 4

Chicken Pistachio

CHICKEN PROVENÇALE

3 tbsp	45 ml	olive oil
1	1	minced garlic clove
1½ lbs	675 g	boneless chicken strips
3 oz	80 g	button mushrooms
20	20	pearl onions
¾ lb	345 g	julienned zucchini
2 cups	500 ml	crushed tomatoes
3 tbsp	45 ml	lemon juice
¼ tsp	1 ml	each of thyme leaves, basil, paprika, salt
½ tsp	3 ml	cracked black pepper

Heat the oil in a Dutch oven, add the garlic, chicken, mushrooms and onions, sauté until chicken is cooked thoroughly. Add the zucchini and continue cooking 5 minutes. Add the tomatoes, lemon juice and seasonings, reduce heat and simmer for 30 minutes.

Serve with rice.

SERVES 6

CHICKEN PISTACHIO

6 – 4 oz	6 – 120 g	boneless chicken breasts
2 oz	60 g	suet
1 lb	450 g	ground chicken meat
3 tbsp	45 ml	grated onion
3 tbsp	45 ml	minced carrot
3 tbsp	45 ml	minced celery
¼ tsp	1 ml	each of, basil, thyme leaves, marjoram, salt, pepper
1 cup	250 ml	shelled pistachio nuts
1	1	egg
2 tbsp	30 ml	melted butter

Pound the chicken breast flat with a meat mallet.

Blend the suet, ground chicken, vegetables, seasonings, nuts and egg together in a large mixing bowl. Divide the mixture evenly over the chicken breasts. Roll the chicken breasts to enfold the filling. Fasten together with toothpicks or tie.

Brush with melted butter and place on a baking tray. Bake for 35-40 minutes in a preheated 350°F (180°C) oven. Serve with a Wild Mushroom Sherry Sauce (see page 105).

SERVES 6

APRICOT CHICKEN

1 cup	250 ml	boiling water
10 oz	280 g	preserved dry apricots
⅔ cup	160 ml	safflower oil
⅓ cup	80 ml	lemon juice
¼ tsp	1 ml	each of garlic powder, onion powder, basil, thyme leaves, oregano leaves, salt, white pepper
⅓ cup	80 ml	minced onion
¼ cup	60 ml	minced sweet red bell pepper
2 tbsp	30 ml	butter
1	1	sliced Spanish onion
1 cup	250 ml	Chicken Broth (see page 77)
4½ lbs	2 kg	chicken pieces

Pour the boiling water over the apricots and soak for 10 minutes. Drain and place into a food processor with the oil, lemon juice, and seasonings. Process for 1 minute. Pour into a mixing bowl and stir in the minced onion and pepper.

Heat the butter in a skillet and sauté the onion. Add the broth, bring to a boil reducing the stock to ⅓ cup (80 ml). Add the apricot mixture.

Place the chicken pieces in a large casserole dish. Pour sauce over, cover and bake in a preheated 350°F (180°C) oven for 45 minutes. Uncover and continue to bake for 15 additional minutes. Serve with rice pilaf.

SERVES 8

FRUIT STUFFED CHICKEN BREASTS

¼ cup	60 ml	currants
¼ cup	60 ml	chopped dates
¼ cup	60 ml	chopped dried apples
½ cup	125 ml	dry bread crumbs
6 – 6 oz	6 – 170 g	boneless, skinless chicken breasts, pounded flat
¼ cup	60 ml	seasoned flour
2 tbsp	30 ml	olive oil
½ cup	125 ml	orange juice
¼ cup	60 ml	water

Combine the currants, dates, apples and bread crumbs together. Place equal amounts of filling on the chicken breasts. Fold and roll the breasts to encase the filling. Hold together with toothpicks, refrigerate for 1 hour.

Dust the breasts with the flour. Heat the oil in a large skillet and brown the breast on all sides. Transfer to a casserole dish.

Pour the orange juice and water over the chicken and bake in a preheated 350°F (180°C) oven for 35-30 minutes.

Serve with a Orange Cashew Rice Pilaf (see page 724).

SERVES 6

ROAST CHICKEN AILLOLI

1 – 5 lb	1 – 2 kg	chicken
1	1	garlic clove
¼ tsp	1 ml	salt
½	0.5	lemon
¾ cup	180 ml	Ailloli Sauce (see page 102)

Truss the chicken.

Rub the chicken all over with the garlic clove. Sprinkle with salt and the juice of the lemon. Place in a roasting pan and roast in a preheated 325°F (160°C) oven for 1¾ to 2½ hours or until thoroughly cooked.

Remove chicken and carve. Place on a serving platter with ailloli sauce to the side.

SERVES 6

Roast Chicken Ailloli

ROASTED ROSEMARY CHICKEN

2 cups	500 ml	Chicken Broth (see page 77)
⅓ cup	80 ml	lemon juice
3 tbsp	45 ml	liquid honey
5 lbs	2.2 kg	chicken
8	8	fresh sprigs rosemary
		salt and pepper
1	1	head of garlic
2 tbsp	30 ml	butter
2 tbsp	30 ml	flour, all purpose
¼ cup	60 ml	white wine

Place 1 cup (250 ml) of the chicken broth, lemon juice and honey into a sauce pan. Bring to a boil. Reduce heat and simmer until liquid is reduced by half.

With a small knife, cut a pocket between the skin and breasts on both sides of the chicken. Insert a sprig of rosemary in each. Thoroughly rub the chicken with the garlic then season generously with salt and pepper. Place the remaining rosemary, along with the garlic, into the cavity.

Place in a roaster, roast for 2¾ to 3½ hours, basting often during the last hour of cooking.

Remove chicken from roaster, strain the drippings through a fine sieve.

Heat the butter in a sauce pan and add the flour. Reduce heat and cook until roux* is golden brown. Add the wine, drippings and remaining chicken broth. Reduce heat and simmer until sauce thickens.

Carve the chicken and serve with the gravy.

SERVES 6

*Roux is any fat to which flour has been added and cooked for 2 or more minutes.

Cornish Hens Catalane

CORNISH HENS CATALANE

3 – 12 oz	3 – 340 g	Cornish game hens
1 tbsp	15 ml	safflower oil
3 tbsp	45 ml	butter
1	1	finely diced Spanish onion
3 oz	80 g	sliced mushrooms
2 tbsp	30 ml	flour, all purpose
1½ cups	375 ml	tomatoes, peeled, seeded, chopped
1 oz	30 g	grated bittersweet chocolate
1½ cups	375 ml	Espagnole Sauce (see page 111)

Split the hens in half. Brush with oil. Place on a baking sheet. Roast for 45 minutes in preheated 350°F (180°C) oven.

While the hens roast, heat the butter in a sauce pan, add the onion and mushrooms and sauté until all the liquid has evaporated. Sprinkle with flour and cook for 2 minutes longer. Add the tomatoes, chocolate and espagnole sauce. Reduce heat and simmer for 30 minutes.Remove hens from the oven, place on a serving platter, cover with sauce and serve.

SERVES 6

CHICKEN DIANNE

⅓ cup	80 ml	butter
4 – 6 oz	4 – 170 g	boneless, skinless chicken breasts
4 oz	115 g	mushrooms, sliced
2	2	minced green onions
¼ cup	60 ml	brandy
1½ cup	375 ml	Demi-Glace Sauce (see page 123)
¼ cup	60 ml	sherry
¼ cup	60 ml	cream

In a large skillet, heat the butter. Fry the chicken in the butter for 6 minutes per side. Remove and reserve hot.

Add the mushrooms to the pan and sauté until tender. Add the green onions and carefully flame with the brandy. Stir in the demi-glace, sherry and cream, reduce the liquid to ¾ of a cup (175 ml).

Place the chicken onto serving plates, pour the sauce over the chicken and serve.

SERVES 4

Roasted Rosemary Chicken

CHICKEN VELVET

1½ lbs	675 g	boneless chicken breast
3 oz	80 g	mushrooms
3 tbsp	45 ml	safflower oil
3 tbsp	45 ml	flour, all purpose
1½ cup	375 ml	Chicken Stock (see page 77)
⅔cup	160 ml	heavy cream
¼ tsp	1 ml	salt
¼ tsp	1 ml	white pepper
8 oz	225 g	grated cheddar cheese

Cut the chicken breasts into strips.

Fry with the mushrooms in the oil in a large skillet. Sprinkle with flour, reduce heat and continue to cook for 2 minutes. Pour in the chicken stock and cream. Add the seasonings and continue simmering for 35 minutes.

Stir in the cheese and simmer an additional 5 minutes longer. Serve over rice or noodles.

SERVES 6

SPICY CHICKEN WITH COCONUT

1½ lbs	675 g	chicken pieces
1 tsp	5 ml	each of salt, paprika, pepper
6 tbsp	90 ml	butter
1	1	diced Spanish onion
1	1	minced garlic clove
¾ cup	180 ml	blanched, grated almonds
1 tsp	5 ml	crushed red chilies
½ tsp	3 ml	thyme leaves
1	1	bay leaf
¼ cup	60 ml	lemon juice
¼ cup	60 ml	honey
2 cups	500 ml	coconut milk
1 cup	250 ml	grated fresh coconut

Sprinkle the chicken pieces with salt, paprika and pepper.

Heat the butter in a large skillet and fry the onion with the chicken to brown. Add the remaining ingredients. Cover, reduce heat and simmer for 45 minutes.

Serve with rice pilaf.

SERVES 6

GRILLED CHICKEN BURGER

4 – 3 oz	4 – 90 g	boneless, skinless chicken breasts
4 tbsp	60 ml	olive oil
1 tbsp	15 ml	sherry
1	1	minced garlic clove
½ tsp	3 ml	each of salt, cracked black pepper, thyme leaves, oregano leaves, basil leaves, paprika
¼ tsp	1 ml	Worcestershire sauce
12	12	bacon rashers
4	4	large kaiser rolls
1	1	large hot house tomato, sliced thick
4	4	lettuce leaves
4 tbsp	60 ml	ranch dressing

Wash and pat dry the chicken breasts. Place in a shallow sided pan.

In a mixing bowl, blend together the oil, sherry, garlic, seasonings and Worcestershire. Pour over chicken and marinate for 3 hours, covered and refrigerated.

Grill the chicken breast for 4 minutes per side, brushing frequently with the marinade.

Fry the bacon crisp and place on a paper towel to absorb any excess fat.

Slice the rolls in half, place a tomato slice and lettuce leaf on one half. On the other, place 1 tbsp (15 ml) of dressing. Top with one breast of chicken and 3 slices bacon. Serve at once.

SERVES 4

Grilled Chicken Burger

HONEY BARBECUED CHICKEN

3 tbsp	45 ml	butter
3 tbsp	45 ml	oil
1	1	minced medium onion
1	1	minced garlic clove
⅔ cup	160 ml	tomato catsup
⅔ cup	160 ml	liquid honey
¼ cup	60 ml	cider vinegar
1 tbsp	15 ml	Worcestershire sauce
½ tsp	3 ml	each of thyme leaves, oregano leaves, basil leaves, paprika, pepper, chili powder, salt
½ tsp	3 ml	liquid smoke
4 – 6 oz	4 – 170 g	boneless, skinless chicken breasts

Heat the butter with 2 tbsp (30 ml) of oil in a sauce pan. Add the onion and garlic and sauté until tender.

Add the catsup, honey, vinegar, Worcestershire, seasonings and smoke flavouring. Simmer until sauce is thick and glossy. Cool.

Brush the chicken with the remaining oil. Grill over medium coals 8 minutes per side, brushing frequently with sauce. Brush 1 final time before serving.

SERVES 4

Honey Barbecued Chicken

CHICKEN PROVENÇALE II

1 – 4½ lb	1 – 2 kg	chicken, cut into 8 pieces
⅓ cup	80 ml	flour, all purpose
¼ cup	60 ml	olive oil
3	3	minced garlic cloves
20	20	pearl onions
20	20	button mushrooms
2	2	julienne cut carrots
2 cups	500 ml	peeled, seeded, chopped tomatoes
1 cup	250 ml	double Chicken Broth (see page 77)
1 cup	250 ml	red wine
½ tsp	3 ml	each salt, pepper, basil, chervil, marjoram

Wash and pat dry the chicken.

Dust the chicken with the flour. Heat the oil in a large kettle or Dutch oven, brown the chicken and remove.

Add the garlic, onions, mushrooms and carrots sauté until tender, sprinkle with the remaining flour and cook for 2 minutes over low heat.

Return the chicken to the kettle and add the remaining ingredients, stir to blend well. Cover the chicken and simmer very gently for 1½ hours.

Serve with rice or pasta.

SERVES 4

Rosemary & Orange Chicken

Chicken St. Jacques A L'Indienne

CHICKEN ST. JACQUES Á L'INDIENNE

1 cup	250 ml	white wine
1 lb	450 g	boneless, coarse diced chicken
¼ cup	60 ml	butter
1	1	small diced onion
1	1	diced green bell pepper
1	1	diced celery stalk
3 tbsp	45 ml	flour, all purpose
1 cup	250 ml	heavy cream
⅓ cup	90 ml	sherry
½ tsp	3 ml	salt
2 tsp	10 ml	curry powder
1 cup	250 ml	peeled, seeded, chopped tomatoes

Heat the wine in a small sauce pan, add the chicken and simmer gently for 20 minutes. Drain and reserve the chicken and the broth.

In a second sauce pan heat the butter, sauté the onion, green pepper and celery until tender. Add the flour and cook 2 minutes over low heat. Stir in the cream, sherry and seasoning, simmer until thick.

Add the tomatoes and chicken, simmer for 5 minutes. If sauce is too thick, thin it slightly with the broth.

Place on serving plates and serve with Aloo Madarasi (see page 710).

SERVES 4

ROSEMARY & ORANGE CHICKEN

2	2	oranges
1 tbsp	15 ml	butter
4 – 6 oz	4 – 170 g	boneless, skinless chicken breasts
2 tsp	10 ml	rosemary
1 quan	1 quan	Orange Cashew Rice (see page 724)

Peel and slice one orange, squeeze the juice from the other.

In a large skillet heat the butter and add the chicken, fry until cooked through. Sprinkle with rosemary and add the juice, and orange slices. Reduce heat and simmer for 2 minutes.

Spoon the rice onto serving plates, cover with chicken and sauce, serve at once.

SERVES 4

COTTAGE COUNTRY CHICKEN

4 – 6 oz	4 – 170 g	boneless, skinless chicken breasts
½ cup	125 ml	yogurt
2 tsp	10 ml	flour, all purpose
1 tbsp	15 ml	curry powder
2 tbsp	30 ml	fine bread crumbs
2 tbsp	30 ml	water

Place the chicken in a small casserole dish.

In a small mixing bowl blend the yogurt, flour and curry powder. Spread over the chicken. Sprinkle with bread crumbs and pour the water in along the sides.

Place in a preheated 350°F (180) oven and bake for 40 minutes or until the chicken is tender.

Remove and serve with a rice pilaf.

SERVES 4

HAWAIIAN ROAST CHICKEN

1–4½ lb	1–2 kg	roasting chicken
2	2	minced garlic clove
¼ tsp	1 ml	pepper
½ tsp	3 ml	salt
¼ cup	60 ml	soya sauce
3 tbsp	45 ml	liquid honey
¼ cup	60 ml	catsup

Place the chicken in a roaster, rub with half the garlic, season with the salt and pepper. Roast in a preheated 350°F (180°C) oven for 2½ hours or until cooked through. Combine the remaining ingredients in a small mixing bowl and brush the chicken at least 6 times during roasting. Brush one final time before carving and serving.

SERVES 6

TURKEY SAUTÉ PROVENÇALE

6 – 6 oz	6 – 170 g	boneless turkey breasts
4 tbsp	60 ml	butter
3	3	minced garlic cloves
1	1	sliced green bell pepper
1	1	sliced onion
3 cups	750 ml	peeled, seeded, chopped tomatoes
¼ cup	60 ml	sherry
1 tsp	5 ml	paprika
½ tsp	3 ml	salt
¼ tsp	1 ml	pepper

In a skillet, fry the turkey in the butter for 4-6 minutes per side (depending on the thickness of the breast). Remove and reserve hot.

Add the garlic, bell pepper and onion to the skillet, sauté until tender. Add the tomatoes and bring to a boil, reduce heat and simmer for 10 minutes. Add the sherry and seasonings, continue to simmer until the liquid has evaporated.

Place the turkey breasts on a platter, pour sauce over and serve with lemon pilaf.

SERVES 6

CHICKEN WITH PINK AND GREEN PEPPERCORN SAUCE

2 tbsp	30 ml	butter
2 tbsp	30 ml	flour, all purpose
½ cup	125 ml	Chicken Broth (see page 77)
½ cup	125 ml	light cream
3 tbsp	45 ml	brandy
1 tbsp	15 ml	pink peppercorns
1 tbsp	15 ml	green peppercorns
1 tbsp	15 ml	green onion, minced
1 tbsp	15 ml	parsley, chopped
4 – 6 oz	4 – 170 g	boneless, skinless chicken breasts
2 tbsp	30 ml	melted butter
½ tsp	3 ml	salt
¼ tsp	1 ml	white pepper

Heat the butter in a sauce pan and add the flour. Reduce heat and cook 2 minutes.

Stir in the broth, cream and brandy. Simmer until sauce thickens. Stir in the peppercorns, onion and parsley.

Brush the chicken with melted butter. Season with salt and pepper. Bake in a preheated 375°F (190°C) oven for 15-20 minutes.

Remove and place on a serving plate. Cover with sauce and serve.

SERVES 4

Chicken with Pink & Green Peppercorn Sauce

Smoked Turkey Cheddar Crêpes

BROILED CHICKEN

⅔ cup	160 ml	olive oil
⅓cup	80 ml	lemon juice
⅓ cup	80 ml	sherry
2 tbsp	30 ml	crushed rosemary
2 tbsp	30 ml	basil leaves
1 tbsp	15 ml	thyme leaves
½ tsp	3 ml	each of granulated sugar, pepper, salt
4 – 6 oz	4 – 170 g	boneless, skinless chicken breasts

Combine all the ingredients except the chicken in a mixing bowl.

Place the chicken in a shallow pan and pour sauce over. Cover and refrigerate for 6 hours.

Grill chicken over medium coals on charbroiler for 6 minutes per side.

SERVES 4

SMOKED TURKEY CHEDDAR CRÊPES

CRÊPES:

3	3	eggs
⅔ cup	160 ml	flour, all purpose
¼ tsp	1 ml	salt
1 cup	250 ml	milk
1 tbsp	15 ml	safflower oil

Whip the eggs, add the flour, salt and milk, and blend thoroughly with the oil. Heat an 8" (20 cm) skillet and spray with non-stick food spray. Add 3-4 tbsp (45 ml-60 ml) batter, fry to golden brown over medium heat. Turn out and cool.

FILLING:

1½ lbs	675 g	smoked turkey breast
2 tbsp	30 ml	butter
1 cup	250 ml	sliced mushrooms
2 tbsp	30 ml	flour, all purpose
1 cup	250 ml	Chicken Stock (see page 77)
1 cup	250 ml	grated medium cheddar

Fry the turkey and the mushrooms in the butter in a large skillet. Sprinkle with flour and cook for 2 minutes. Add the chicken stock and reduce heat, simmer for 5 minutes. Stir in the cheese and continue cooking for 3 minutes.

Place equal amounts of filling in crêpes, roll and serve.

SERVES 6

Teriyaki Grilled Chicken

SOUTHERN FRIED CHICKEN

4½ lbs	2 kg	chicken, cut into pieces
4	4	eggs
¾ cup	180 ml	milk
1½ cups	375 ml	flour, all purpose
3 cups	750 ml	bread crumbs
1 tbsp	15 ml	paprika
1 tsp	5 ml	each of oregano, thyme, sage, garlic powder, onion powder, black pepper, marjoram, chili powder
4 cups	1 L	safflower oil

Wash the chicken and pat dry.

In a mixing bowl, combine the eggs and the milk. Place the flour in a second bowl and the bread crumbs in a third. Blend the seasonings into the bread crumbs.

Dust the chicken with the flour, dip into the eggs and dredge in the bread crumbs.

Heat the oil to 325°F (160°C). Fry the chicken to golden brown in small batches being sure that the chicken is cooked thoroughly. Cooking time is dependent on the size of the chicken pieces.

Reserve hot until all chicken is cooked.

SERVES 6

Southern Fried Chicken

TERIYAKI GRILLED CHICKEN

⅓ cup	80 ml	brown sugar
1 tsp	5 ml	ground ginger
1 cup	250 ml	Beef Broth (see page 85)
⅓ cup	80 ml	soya sauce
2 tbsp	30 ml	cornstarch
¼ cup	60 ml	sherry
1 tbsp	15 ml	oil
4 – 6 oz	4 – 175 g	boneless, skinless chicken breasts

In a sauce pan, dissolve the sugar and ginger in the broth and soya sauce, bring to a boil.

Mix the cornstarch with the sherry and add to the sauce. Reduce heat and simmer until sauce thickens. Cool.

Brush the oil over the chicken breasts. Grill over medium heat for 8 minutes per side. Brush frequently with sauce while cooking. Brush 1 final time and serve.

SERVES 4

SMOKED TURKEY SOUR CREAM CHEESE SAUCE

1½ lbs	675 g	smoked turkey breast
2 tbsp	30 ml	butter
2 tbsp	30 ml	flour, all purpose
1½ cup	375 ml	Chicken Stock (see page 77)
¾ cup	180 ml	sour cream
¼ tsp	1 ml	each of salt, pepper
½ tsp	3 ml	paprika
6 oz	170 g	grated Gruyere cheese
2 tbsp	30 ml	chopped parsley

Place the turkey in a roaster, bake in a preheated 350°F (180°C) oven for 1 hour. Remove, carve and reserve hot.

Melt the butter in a sauce pan; add the flour and cook for 2 minutes over low heat. Pour in the chicken stock, and simmer for 5 minutes. Whip in the sour cream, seasonings and cheese, continue to simmer for an additional 5 minutes.

Place turkey on a serving platter, pour sauce over turkey, sprinkle with parsley and serve.

SERVES 6

POULET FARCI EN COCOTTE

1 – 3 lb	1 – 1 kg	chicken
¼ lb	115 g	chicken livers
2	2	shallots
2 tbsp	30 ml	chopped parsley
¼ cup	60 ml	butter
2 cups	500 ml	bread crusts
¼ cup	60 ml	milk
¼ tsp	1 ml	each of thyme leaves, basil, oregano, salt, pepper

Wash the chicken. Clean the livers of any membranes then fine dice them. Fine dice the shallots and mix with the parsley.

Heat 1 tbsp (15 ml) of butter in a skillet, sauté the livers and shallots for 10 minutes, cool to room temperature.

In a mixing bowl blend the bread crumbs, milk, seasonings and livers together. Stuff into the chicken. Heat the remaining butter in a earthenware cocotte (casserole dish) add the chicken browning it on all sides. Place the lid on the cocotte and bake in a preheated 350°F (180°C) oven for 1½ hours. Carve the chicken and serve in the cocotte.

SERVES 6

ROAST GUINEA FOWL WITH BLUEBERRY HOLLANDAISE

2 – 1½ lb	2 – 675 g	guinea hens
6	6	slices bacon
¼ tsp	1 ml	each of rosemary, thyme, salt, pepper
2 cups	500 ml	blueberries
2	2	egg yolks
½ cup	125 ml	very hot butter

Split the guinea fowl in half and place them on a baking sheet. Layer the bacon over the birds, and sprinkle with seasonings. Roast them in a preheated 350°F (180°C) oven for 45 minutes. Remove from oven and remove the bones while hot.

While birds roast purée the blueberries in a food processor, strain to remove pulp and seeds. Place the juice in a sauce pan and heat to a boil reducing to 2 tbsp (30 ml) of thick liquid. Cool.

Place the egg yolks in a double boiler, whisk in the blueberry syrup, slowly whisk in the hot butter forming a thick sauce. Serve the guinea fowl on a large serving platter with the sauce on the side.

SERVES 4

CHICKEN ATLANTA

6 – 6 oz	6 – 175 g	boneless chicken breasts
6 oz	175 g	shrimp meat
6 oz	175 g	Swiss cheese
6 oz	175 g	sliced peaches
2	2	eggs
¼ cup	60 ml	milk
½ cup	125 ml	flour
2 cups	500 ml	seasoned bread crumbs
½ cup	125 ml	safflower oil
1 cup	250 ml	apricot brandy sauce

Pound the chicken breasts flat. Place 1 oz (28 g) of shrimp and 1 oz (28 g) of cheese and 1 oz (28 g) of peaches on the chicken. Fold the breast to encase the filling. Place on a baking sheet and freeze for ½ hour.

Mix the eggs with the milk. Dust the chicken with flour, dip into milk. Dredge in bread crumbs.

Heat the oil in a large skillet. Brown the chicken on all sides. Transfer to a baking sheet.

Bake in a preheated 350°F (180°C) oven for 5 minutes. Serve with sauce.

SERVES 6

POACHED CHICKEN MOUSSELINE

4 cups	1 L	water
2 cups	500 ml	white wine
1	1	chopped onion
1	1	chopped large carrot
1	1	chopped celery stalk
1	1	bouquet garni*
6 – 6 oz	6 – 170 g	boneless, skinless chicken breasts
3	3	egg yolks
1 tbsp	15 ml	water
1 tbsp	15 ml	lemon juice
⅔ cup	180 ml	melted butter
½ cup	125 ml	whipping cream
¼ tsp	1 ml	each of salt and pepper
pinch	pinch	cayenne pepper

In a large sauce pan, bring the water, wine, onion, carrot, celery and bouquet garni to a boil. Reduce to half the liquid's volume. Reduce temperature. Place chicken into liquid and simmer for 12 minutes.

While chicken poaches, blend the eggs with 15 ml (1 tbsp) of water and lemon juice. Place in a double boiler. Cook, stirring constantly until eggs thicken but do not over cook. Remove from heat and whip in the butter until sauce is very smooth and thick. Whip the cream and fold into the sauce, add seasonings.

Place poached chicken on serving plates. Cover with sauce and serve.

SERVES 6

*The bouquet garni for this dish is; a bay leaf, 8 sprigs of parsley, 2 sprigs of thyme, 6 peppercorns and 1 small, chopped leek tied together in a cheesecloth.

Grilled Chicken Cacciatore

GRILLED CHICKEN CACCIATORE

1 quan	1 quan	Basic Pasta Dough (see page 426)
3 tbsp	45 ml	olive oil
2	2	minced garlic cloves
1	1	diced green bell pepper
1	1	diced onions
2	2	diced celery stalks
4 oz	115 g	sliced mushrooms
1 tsp	5 ml	each of salt, basil leaves
½ tsp	3 ml	each of pepper, thyme leaves, oregano leaves, paprika
½ tsp	3 ml	Worcestershire sauce
3 lbs	1.5 kg	tomatoes, peeled, seeded and chopped
6 – 6 oz	6 – 170 g	boneless chicken breasts

Process the pasta as directed, cut into fettucini noodles, cover with a moist towel and reserve.

In a large sauce pan, heat 2 tbsp (30 ml) of oil. Add the garlic, pepper, onion, celery and mushrooms, sauté until tender.

Add the seasonings, Worcestershire and tomatoes, reduce heat and simmer for 3 hours or until a thick sauce is formed.

Brush the chicken breasts with the remaining oil. Grill 7 minutes per side.

Boil the pasta in a large kettle of salted water. Drain, place on plates, cover with sauce and top with a breast of chicken. Serve at once.

SERVES 6

PORK AND LAMB

Pork is the white meat being examined in a whole new culinary light. Pork has shown itself to be the versatile alternative to beef, chicken, veal and even seafood.

Not to be left behind, lamb is taking a good run at every gastronomic stronghold found within any kind of cuisine, from nouvelle bistro or Thai through to classic French.

Between the two, they are capturing an ever-growing, select group of those who know that these two meats are *Simply Delicious* at first bite. Not restricted by their culinary counterparts, pork and lamb allow the creative person to show his abilities and yet keep cost to minimum. The ordinary become extraordinary when something as simple as switching the main menu feature to pork or lamb is involved.

What is absolutely fabulous about these two features is that by using a recipe for beef, veal or chicken and exercising some ingenuity, one may create an entirely new dish. Or, create some new adventures on your own, like Creole Pork Turkeys or Lamb Cutlets Cherbourg.

Pork and lamb lend themselves to making a classic dinner original and memorable, and casual dinner exciting. When it has to be just right, dazzle your guests with a pork steak smothered with crab and a raspberry peppercorn hollandaise. Or, when the party is reaching its crescendo, push it over the edge with a hearty helping of Fresh Peach BBQ Ribs.

A skillfully prepared meal of pork or lamb means you really do care that your guests have the best, and it will show. Theoretically a red meat, pork is now considered a white meat, because it is as nutritious and adaptable as any white meat. So when your guests decide to come to dinner, and they ask "what are we having?", tell them "Pork Chops Charcutiere" and watch the compliments come regarding how your meal is absolutely *Simply Delicious.*

Pork Satay

INTOXICATED PORK

3 tbsp	45 ml	oil
1 - 5 lb	1 - 1.75 kg	centre cut boneless pork loin, tied
3	3	minced garlic cloves
¼ cup	60 ml	chopped parsley
4 cups	1 L	red wine
½ tsp	3 ml	salt
1 tsp	5 ml	peppercorns
2 tbsp	30 ml	butter
2 tbsp	30 ml	flour, all purpose

Heat the oil in a Dutch oven. Sear the meat in the oil to brown on all sides.

Add the garlic, parsley, wine, salt and peppercorns. Reduce heat and simmer covered for 3 hours. Remove meat and reduce stock to ⅓ its volume. Strain.

Heat the butter in a smaller sauce pan. Add the flour and cook 2 minutes, pour in the stock and simmer until thicken.

Carve the pork and serve with sauce separately.

SERVES 8

HAM LOAF

LOAF:

1 lb	450 g	ground ham
1 lb	450 g	fresh ground pork
1 cup	250 ml	seasoned bread crumbs
¼ cup	60 ml	minced onion
1	1	minced carrot
1	1	minced celery stalk
½ cup	125 ml	milk

SAUCE:

½ cup	125 ml	brown sugar
1 tbsp	15 ml	Dijon mustard
2 tbsp	30 ml	vinegar
1 tbsp	15 ml	water

Combine all the ingredients together. Press into a greased ring mold (bundt pan) place in a 350°F (180°C) oven and bake 45 minutes. Drain excess fat.

Blend the sauce ingredients together. Pour over meat. Continue to bake for 30 minutes. Turn out onto a serving platter.

Serve with rice pilaf.

SERVES 6

LAMB CHOPS GRANDDUKE STYLE

4 – 6 oz	4 – 170 g	lamb chops
2 tbsp	30 ml	olive oil
3 cups	750 ml	Chicken Broth (see page 77)
3 tbsp	45 ml	butter
3 tbsp	45 ml	flour, all purpose
½ cup	125 ml	heavy cream
¼ cup	60 ml	Crayfish Butter (see page 112)
1 cup	250 ml	cooked crayfish tails
1 cup	250 ml	blanched asparagus tips
⅓ cup	90 ml	freshly grated Parmesan cheese
4	4	large slices of truffles

Wash and pat dry the chops.

Heat the oil in a skillet and brown the chops.

Add the chicken broth, gently poach the chops for 15 minutes, remove and reserve hot.

Strain the broth, return it to the heat and bring to a boil, reduce to 1½ cups (375 ml) of liquid.

Heat the butter in a sauce pan and add the flour, cook over low heat for 2 minutes. Add the reduced broth and cream, simmer until thick. Stir in the crayfish butter, crayfish tails and asparagus tips, simmer for 3 minutes and add the cheese.

Place the chops on serving plates, smother with sauce and top with a truffle slice. Serve at once.

SERVES 4

Ham Loaf

Intoxicated Pork

Pork Steaks with Crab & Raspberry Peppercorn Hollandaise

PORK STEAKS WITH CRAB & RASPBERRY PEPPERCORN HOLLANDAISE

2 cups	500 ml	raspberries
6	6	bacon slices
6 – 4 oz	6 – 120 g	pork steaks
6 oz	170 g	crab meat
2	2	egg yolks
½ cup	125 ml	hot melted butter
1 tsp	5 ml	pink peppercorns

Pick through and wash the berries. Purée in a food processor then strain to remove pulp and seeds. Pour into a sauce pan and bring to a boil, reduce heat and simmer until only 4 tbsp (60 ml) of liquid remain.

Wrap the bacon around the pork steaks. Broil over charbroiler or in the oven thoroughly. Top with crab.

Place the egg yolks in a food processor. With the machine running, slowly add the butter. Add the raspberry liquid in a slow steady stream. Stir in the peppercorns.

Place a dollop of sauce on each steak, place steaks on a baking sheet. Place under a preheated oven broiler and glaze.

Serve at once.

SERVES 6

ROSEMARY & ORANGE PORK STEAKS

2	2	oranges
1 tbsp	15 ml	butter
4 – 6 oz	4 – 170 g	boneless pork steaks
2 tsp	10 ml	rosemary
1 quan	1 quan	Orange Cashew Rice (see page 724)

Peel and slice one orange, squeeze the juice from the other.

In a large skillet heat the butter and add the pork steaks, fry until cooked through. Sprinkle with rosemary and add the juice and orange slices. Reduce heat and simmer for 2 minutes.

Spoon the rice onto serving plates, cover with pork steak and sauce, serve at once.

SERVES 4

HERB BROILED LAMB CHOPS

⅔ cup	160 ml	olive oil
⅓ cup	80 ml	lemon juice
⅓ cup	80 ml	sherry
2 tbsp	30 ml	crushed rosemary
2 tbsp	30 ml	basil leaves
1 tbsp	15 ml	thyme leaves
½ tsp	3 ml	each of granulated sugar, pepper, salt
8 – 3 oz	8 – 90 g	lamb chops, 1" (2.5 cm) thick

Combine all the ingredients except the chops in a mixing bowl.

Place the chops in a shallow pan and pour sauce over. Cover and refrigerate for 6 hours.

Grill chops over medium coals on charbroiler for 5 minutes per side.

SERVES 4

Rosemary & Orange Pork Steaks

Lamb Crowns with Raspberry, Kiwi & Green Peppercorn Sauce

LAMB CROWNS WITH RASPBERRY, KIWI AND GREEN PEPPERCORN SAUCE

2	2	lamb crowns*
2 tbsp	30 ml	melted butter
1 tsp	5 ml	salt
½ tsp	3 ml	black pepper
1 cup	250 ml	raspberries
½ cup	125 ml	heavy cream
¼ cup	60 ml	powdered sugar
1 tbsp	15 ml	green peppercorns
2	2	kiwis

Place the lamb crowns in a shallow baking dish, brush with butter and season with salt and pepper. Bake in a preheated 350°F (180°C) oven for 35-40 minutes.

While racks bake, purée the raspberries and press through a fine sieve to remove the seeds.

Heat the raspberries and sugar together in a small sauce pan. Reduce to ⅓rd volume. Add the cream, peppercorns and simmer for 5 minutes.

Pare the kiwis and dice them, stir into sauce.

Remove racks from the oven and place upon serving plates and smother with the sauce. Serve at once.

SERVES 4

* A crown is two racks tied together to form a circle. Place a large ball of tin foil in the center while cooking to hold its form.

Broiled Pork Steaks with Walnut Marinade

LAMB TRATTORIA

1½ lbs	675 g	boneless, lean lamb
5 tbsp	75 ml	butter
1	1	minced garlic clove
3 tbsp	45 ml	flour, all purpose
1 tbsp	15 ml	chopped fresh parsley
¼ cup	60 ml	red wine
1 cup	250 ml	tomatoes – peeled, seeded, chopped
½ cup	125 ml	Chicken Stock (see page 77)
½ tsp	3 ml	each of salt, pepper, paprika
1 tsp	5 ml	oregano
2 tsp	10 ml	capers
2 tsp	10 ml	lemon zest

Coarse dice the lamb. Heat the butter in a large sauce pan. Add the lamb and garlic, cook until meat browns. Sprinkle with flour and continue cooking for 3 minutes over low heat.

Add the remaining ingredients, simmer for 30 minutes.

Serve with rice.

SERVES 6

BROILED PORK STEAKS WITH WALNUT MARINADE

6 – 6 oz	6 – 170 g	boneless pork steaks
2 tsp	10 ml	Dijon mustard
1 tbsp	15 ml	lemon juice
¼ tsp	1 ml	salt
¼ tsp	1 ml	cracked black pepper
2 tsp	10 ml	walnut oil
¼ cup	60 ml	olive oil

Place the steaks in a shallow baking pan.

In a small mixing bowl combine the remaining ingredients, pour over the steaks and marinate covered and refrigerated for 8 hours.

Broil the steaks over medium heat on a charbroiler for 10-15 minutes, brushing frequently with the marinade. Serve at once with one final brushing of the marinade.

SERVES 4

CASHEW LAMB CUTLETS

6 – 6 oz	6 – 170 g	lamb cutlets
½ cup	125 ml	ground cashew nuts
¼ cup	60 ml	freshly grated Parmesan cheese
1 cup	250 ml	fine dry bread crumbs
¼ cup	60 ml	melted butter

Wash and pat dry the cutlets.

Combine the nuts, cheese and bread crumbs in a small mixing bowl.

Dip the cutlets in the melted butter then dredge through the crumb mixture. Place into a small casserole dish. Bake in a preheated 350°F (180°C) oven for 45-50 minutes or until cutlets are golden brown. Serve at once with an Apricot Raspberry Sauce (see page 108).

SERVES 6

LAMB DELIGHTS

1 cup	250 ml	flour, all purpose
1 tsp	5 ml	salt
¼ tsp	1 ml	each of marjoram and paprika
1 tsp	5 ml	baking powder
2	2	eggs separated
⅓ cup	90 ml	cold milk
2 tbsp	30 ml	sherry
1 cup	250 ml	cooked, diced lamb
1 cup	250 ml	cooked peas
3 cups	750 ml	safflower oil

Sift the flour together with the salt, herbs and baking powder.

Beat the egg yolks until creamy then beat in the milk and sherry.

Slowly beat the flour into the liquid. Beat the egg whites until they are stiff and fold into the batter. Fold in the lamb and peas.

Heat the oil to 375°F (190°C). Drop small batches of spoonful size batter into the oil and cook until golden brown. Reserve hot while remainder cook. Serve very hot, good with Mornay Sauce (see page 111).

SERVES 4

ITALIAN SAUSAGE LASAGNA

1 lb	450 g	coarse chopped Italian sausage
1	1	minced garlic clove
2 tsp	10 ml	each of oregano, thyme, basil
½ tsp	3 ml	each of salt and pepper
4 cups	1 L	peeled, seeded and chopped tomatoes
1 ¼ cups	310 ml	tomato paste
1 quan	1 quan	Basic Pasta Dough (see page 426), cut in wide noodles
3 cups	750 ml	creamed cottage cheese
2	2	beaten eggs
½ cup	125 ml	freshly grated Parmesan cheese
1 lb	450 g	grated mozzarella

Brown the sausage slowly in a Dutch oven. Drain the excess fat. Add the garlic, herbs, tomatoes and tomato paste. Simmer for one hour.

Line a large buttered casserole dish with a layer of noodles. Blend the cottage cheese, eggs and Parmesan together.

Place a layer of meat sauce on the noodles, then add a layer of noodles covering them with the cheese blend. Alternate sauce, cheese blend and mozzarella layers. Finish with a final layer of sauce covered with the mozzarella. Bake in a preheated 375°F (190°C) oven for 40 minutes.

Stand 15 minutes and serve.

SERVES 12

Italian Sausage Lasagna

Pork & Chicken Stir Fry

PORK & CHICKEN STIR FRY

8 oz	225 g	boneless pork
8 oz	225 g	boneless skinless chicken
2 tbsp	30 ml	safflower oil
1	1	small, diced onion
½ cup	125 ml	diced red bell pepper
20	20	button mushrooms
¼ cup	60 ml	oyster sauce
2 tbsp	30 ml	soya sauce
1 tsp	5 ml	cornstarch
1 tbsp	15 ml	sherry or water

Dice the pork and chicken into bite size pieces.

Heat the oil in a wok or large skillet. Fry the meats for 3 minutes. Add the vegetables and fry until tender.

Add the oyster sauce and soya sauce. Simmer for 2 minutes.

Mix the cornstarch with the sherry and stir into chicken. Simmer until thick. Serve over rice or noodles.

SERVES 2

PORK ROULADENS

3	3	slices of diced bacon
1	1	finely dice carrot
1	1	finely diced stalk of celery
1	1	finely diced small onion
1 cup	250 ml	grated Havarti cheese
4 – 6 oz	4 – 170 g	boneless, pork cutlets , pounded flat
2 tbsp	30 ml	melted butter
2 cups	500 ml	hot Mornay Sauce (see page 111)

In a large skillet fry the bacon, add the carrot, celery and onion and sauté until tender, drain excess fat, place in a small mixing bowl and cool to room temperature.

Combine the sautéed mixture together with the cheese, and press onto the cutlets. Roll the cutlets as to encase the filling. Place in a small baking dish, brush with butter and bake in a preheated 350°F (180°C) oven for 25-30 minutes.

Transfer cutlets to serving plates, smother with Mornay Sauce and serve.

SERVES 4

PORK CUTLETS VERDE

6 – 4 oz	6 – 120 g	pork cutlets
1	1	egg
¼ cup	60 ml	milk
½ cup	125 ml	flour, all purpose
1 cup	250 ml	seasoned bread crumbs
3 tbsp	45 ml	oil
3 tbsp	45 ml	butter
1	1	minced garlic clove
2 tbsp	30 ml	flour, all purpose
2 cups	500 ml	Chicken Stock (see page 77)
1 cup	250 ml	peas
¼ tsp	1 ml	each of salt and pepper

Pound the cutlets with a meat mallet thin.

Mix the egg with milk. Dust with flour, dip into the egg wash, dredge in bread crumbs.

Heat the oil in a skillet and fry the cutlets to golden brown on each side. Reserve hot.

Heat the butter along with the garlic, sprinkle with flour and cook for 2 minutes over low heat. Add the stock, peas and seasonings, simmer until sauce thickens. Pour in a food processor and process until smooth.

Plate the cutlets and cover with sauce, serve.

SERVES 6

ASIAN PORK

1½ cups	375 ml	short grain rice
¼ cup	60 ml	currants
8 – 4 oz	8 – 115 g	boneless pork steaks
2 tbsp	30 ml	safflower oil
1	1	diced onion
1 cup	250 ml	finely diced, pared apples
2	2	minced garlic cloves
2 tbsp	30 ml	curry powder
1 cup	250 ml	Chicken Broth (see page 77)
½ cup	125 ml	chutney
1 cup	250 ml	whipping cream
3 tbsp	45 ml	fresh chopped cilantro

Sprinkle the rice in a large casserole dish, add the currants. Layer the pork over the rice.

In a skillet heat the oil and sauté the onion, apples and garlic until tender. Stir in the curry powder, reduce the heat and cook for 3 minutes longer.

Stir in the chicken broth, chutney, and whipping cream, boil 2 minutes. Pour over the pork, cover, and bake in a preheated 350°F (180°C) oven for 1¼ hours.

Remove cover and sprinkle with cilantro, serve at once.

SERVES 8

CHINESE PORK TENDERLOIN

1½ lbs	675 g	pork tenderloin
⅓ cup	80 ml	safflower oil
1 tsp	5 ml	peeled, minced ginger root
2	2	minced garlic clove
¼ cup	60 ml	light soya sauce
⅓ cup	80 ml	honey, liquid
2 tbsp	30 ml	sherry
4 drops	4	red food colouring (optional)

Trim and slice the pork.

Blend 2 tbsp (30 ml) of oil with the remaining ingredients. Pour over the pork, marinate for 4-6 hours.

Heat the remaining oil in a wok. Drain the pork but reserve the marinade. Fry the pork thoroughly. Drain any excess oil. Add the marinade and continue to fry until all the liquid has evaporated.

Serve with rice.

SERVES 6

LAMB HOMESTYLE

8 – 3 oz	8 – 90 g	lamb chops
½ cup	125 ml	yogurt
2 tsp	10 ml	flour, all purpose
1 tbsp	15 ml	curry powder
2 tbsp	30 ml	fine bread crumbs
2 tbsp	30 ml	water

Place the lamb in a casserole dish.

In a small mixing bowl blend the yogurt, flour and curry powder. Spread over the lamb. Sprinkle with bread crumbs and pour the water in along the sides.

Place in a preheated 350°F (180°C) oven and bake for 40 minutes or until the lamb is tender.

Remove and serve with a rice pilaf.

SERVES 4

Lamb Homestyle

Chinese Pork Tenderloin

Yucatan Pork Chops

YUCATAN PORK CHOPS

4½ lbs	2 kg	large pork chops
¼ cup	60 ml	flour, all purpose
2 tsp	10 ml	salt
¼ tsp	1 ml	each of black pepper, white pepper, cloves
2 tsp	10 ml	each of chili powder, paprika
⅓ cup	90 ml	olive oil
1	1	large sliced onion
2	2	minced garlic cloves
1	1	sliced green bell pepper
1	1	sliced red bell pepper
1½ cups	375 ml	sliced mushrooms
3 cups	750 ml	peeled, seeded, chopped tomatoes
½ cup	125 ml	sherry
⅓ cup	90 ml	green stuffed olives

Wash and pat dry the chops.

Combine the flour with the seasonings. Dredge the chops through the flour.

Heat the oil in a large kettle or Dutch oven, brown the chops in the oil. Transfer the chops to a large casserole dish.

Sauté the onion, garlic, peppers and mushrooms in the pan until tender. Stir in the tomatoes and sherry, simmer for 5 minutes. Pour over the chops and bake in a preheated 350°F (180°C) oven for 45-50 minutes covered. Remove the cover and stir in the olives and continue to bake for an additional 15 minutes.

Serve with rice.

SERVES 4

LAMB CUTLETS GLORIA BLAIS

6 – 3 oz	6 – 90 g	lamb cutlets
7 tbsp	105 ml	butter
¾ lb	340 g	ground turkey
1 tsp	5 ml	minced chives
1 tbsp	15 ml	minced onion
1 tsp	5 ml	each of chervil, parsley, tarragon
3 tbsp	45 ml	minced mushrooms
2 ¼ cups	560 ml	fine bread crumbs
3 tbsp	45 ml	sherry
2	2	eggs
¼ cup	60 ml	milk
¼ cup	60 ml	flour, all purpose
4 cups	1 L	safflower oil

Pound the lamb cutlets flat.

In a food processor mix 3 tbsp (45 ml) of butter along with the turkey chives, onions, seasonings, mushroom, ¾ cup (180 ml) bread crumbs and the sherry.

Heat the remaining butter in a skillet and sauté the mixture for 5 minutes over medium heat. Cool to room temperature, spread over the lamb cutlets and roll them up in jelly roll fashion.

Mix the eggs with milk. Dust the rolls with the flour, then dip into the eggs and dredge through the remaining bread crumbs.

Heat the oil to 375°F (190°C), and fry the rolls until golden brown. Serve with Madeira Wine Sauce (see page 112).

SERVES 6

Lamb Cutlets Gloria Blais

Chinese Sweet & Sour Ribs

Fruit Stuffed Lamb Cutlets

FRUIT STUFFED LAMB CUTLETS

¼ cup	60 ml	currants
¼ cup	60 ml	chopped dates
¼ cup	60 ml	chopped dried apples
½ cup	125 ml	dry bread crumbs
6 – 3 oz	6 – 90 g	lamb cutlets, pounded flat
¼ cup	60 ml	seasoned flour, all purpose
2 tbsp	30 ml	olive oil
½ cup	125 ml	orange juice
¼ cup	60 ml	water

Combine the currants, dates, apples and bread crumbs together. Place equal amounts of filling on the cutlets. Fold and roll the breasts to encase the filling. Hold together with tooth picks, refrigerate for 1 hour.

Dust the cutlets with the flour. Heat the oil in a large skillet and brown the breast on all sides. Transfer to a casserole dish.

Pour the orange juice and water over the cutlets and bake in a preheated 350°F (180°C) oven for 30-35 minutes.

Serve with a Orange Cashew Rice Pilaf (see page 724).

SERVES 6

CHINESE SWEET & SOUR RIBS

4 lbs	1.75 kg	spare ribs
⅓ cup	80 ml	soya sauce
1 cup	250 ml	brown sugar
¾ cup	180 ml	vinegar
½ cup	125 ml	sherry
2 tbsp	30 ml	oyster sauce
1	1	thin sliced green bell pepper
1 tbsp	15 ml	chopped candied ginger
¾ cup	180 ml	pineapple chunks
2 tsp	10 ml	cornstarch
2 tbsp	30 ml	water

Cut the ribs into 2" (5 cm) size pieces. Place on a baking sheet. Bake in a preheated 325°F (160°C) oven for 1½ hours or until crisp.

Blend the soya sauce, sugar, vinegar, sherry, oyster sauce, green peppers in a sauce pan. Bring to a boil. Add the ginger and pineapple chunks.

Blend the cornstarch with the water, add the sauce. Remove from the heat as soon as the sauce thickens. Pour over the ribs and serve.

SERVES 4

PORK CHOPS CHARCUTIERE

6 – 6 oz	6 – 170 g	pork shoulder chops
2 tbsp	30 ml	safflower oil
1	1	diced Spanish onion
2 tbsp	30 ml	butter
2 tbsp	30 ml	flour, all purpose
1 cup	250 ml	white wine
1 cup	250 ml	Chicken Stock (see page 77) or Veal Stock (see page 85)
2 tbsp	30 ml	chopped gherkins
1 tsp	5 ml	Dijon mustard

Brush the chops with the oil. Season with a little salt and pepper if desired. Broil in the oven until cooked through.

Fry the onion in the butter in a sauce pan until brown. Sprinkle with flour and continue to cook for 2 minutes over low heat. Add the wine, stock, gherkins and mustard, simmer 15 minutes.

Place chops on a serving plate, pour sauce over chops and serve.

SERVES 6

CREOLE PORK TURKEYS

8	8	¾" double pork chops
2 ¾ cups	680 ml	bread cubes
5 tbsp	75 ml	butter
1	1	minced small onion
½ tsp	3 ml	Worcestershire sauce
½ tsp	3 ml	salt
½ tsp	3 ml	pepper
4 tbsp	60 ml	oil
2 cups	500 ml	Creole Sauce (see page 121)

Cut a deep incision in each chop.

Blend the bread, butter, onion, Worcestershire sauce, salt and pepper into a stuffing. Stuff into the chops.

Heat the oil in a large skillet. Brown chops in oil, drain excess oil. Pour sauce over the chops. Cover and reduce heat, simmer for 1 hour.

Serve with rice.

SERVES 6

LAMB OLIVES

1½ lbs	675 g	lamb cut into thin slices
3 oz	80 g	anchovies
2 tbsp	30 ml	capers
¼ cup	60 ml	red pimento
1 cup	250 ml	flour, all purpose
⅔ cup	160 ml	cornstarch
1 tsp	5 ml	baking powder
1	1	egg
2 tbsp	30 ml	olive oil
1 tbsp	15 ml	lemon juice
1½ cups	375 ml	ice water
3 cups	750 ml	safflower oil

Pound the lamb to very thin.

In a food processor purée the anchovies, capers and pimento, place a little purée in the centre of each lamb slice. Wrap the meat around, shape in a olive shape. Refrigerate 1 hour.

Sift the flour, cornstarch and baking powder together.

Mix the egg, olive oil, lemon juice and water together. Whisk into the flour to form a thin batter.

Heat the safflower oil to 375°F (190°C). Dip the lamb into the batter and fry in the oil until golden brown. Serve very hot.

SERVES 6

LAMB CHOPS WITH LIME CILANTRO CREAM

1	1	egg
¼ cup	60 ml	milk
6 – 4 oz	6 – 120 g	boneless blade lamb chops
½ cup	125 ml	flour, all purpose
1 cup	250 ml	seasoned bread crumbs
6 tbsp	90 ml	olive oil
3 tbsp	45 ml	butter
2 tbsp	30 ml	flour, all purpose
½ cup	125 ml	Chicken Stock (see page 77)
½ cup	125 ml	light cream
¼ cup	60 ml	lime juice
2 tbsp	30 ml	chopped cilantro (coriander)

Mix the egg with the milk, dust the lamb chops with the flour, dip into egg then dredge through the bread crumbs.

Heat the oil in a large skillet, fry the chops for 3 minutes per side or until golden brown. Reserve hot in the oven.

Heat the butter in a sauce pan, add the flour and cook 2 minutes over low heat. Add the chicken stock and cream, simmer into a light sauce. Whip in the lime juice and cilantro, continue to simmer 5 minutes.

Place chops on serving plates and pour the sauce over the chops.

SERVES 6

Lamb Chops with Lime Cilantro Cream

Lamb Sauté Provençale

PORK AND LAMB WITH A DIFFERENCE

6 oz	170 g	lean, ground pork
4 oz	120 g	lean, ground lamb
2 oz	60 g	minced bacon
3 tbsp	45 ml	minced green onions
¼ tsp	1 ml	minced garlic
1 tbsp	15 ml	fresh chopped parsley
2 tbsp	30 ml	sherry
¼ tsp	1 ml	each of paprika, oregano, thyme, basil
½ tsp	3 ml	salt
1	1	extra large beaten egg
2 – 1 lb	2 – 450 g	whole boneless chicken breasts, with skins
2 tbsp	30 ml	olive oil

In a food processor (chill the bowl and blade first) process the pork, lamb, bacon, green onions, garlic, parsley, sherry, seasonings and egg into a smooth paté mixture.

With a sharp knife trim the chicken of any fat, etc. Gently pull the skin away from the chicken taking care not to separate the skin from the edges. Stuff the mixture under the skin. Skewer the skin to keep intact.

Brush the chicken with oil, bake in a preheated 375°F (190°C) oven for 25 minutes. Remove skewers, carve and serve.

SERVES 6

DEVILED PORK CHOPS

2 tbsp	30 ml	butter
¼ tsp	1 ml	each of cayenne pepper, black pepper and white pepper
6 – 6 oz	6 – 170 g	boneless, pork chops
½ cup	125 ml	chili sauce
½ cup	125 ml	catsup
¼ tsp	1 ml	each of salt, basil, paprika, chili powder, thyme, oregano
2 tbsp	30 ml	Worcestershire sauce
2 tbsp	30 ml	Dijon mustard
½ cup	125 ml	water

Make a smooth paste of the butter and peppers.

Place the chops into a casserole dish and spread the butter over them. Place under the oven broiler for 3 minutes, turn the chops over and broil for an additional 3 minutes.

While chops broils combine the remaining ingredients together in a small mixing bowl. Pour over chops and bake for 20-25 minutes.

Serve with rice pilaf.

SERVES 6

LAMB SAUTÉ PROVENÇALE

12 – 3oz	12 – 90 g	boneless or bone in lamb chops
4 tbsp	60 ml	butter
3	3	minced garlic cloves
1	1	sliced green bell pepper
1	1	sliced onion
3 cups	750 ml	peeled seeded, chopped tomatoes
¼ cup	60 ml	sherry
1 tsp	5 ml	paprika
½ tsp	3 ml	salt
¼ tsp	1 ml	pepper

In a skillet, fry the chops in the butter for 4-6 minutes per side (depending on the thickness). Remove and reserve hot.

Add the garlic, bell pepper and onions to the skillet and sauté until tender. Add the tomatoes and bring to a boil, reduce heat and simmer for 10 minutes. Add the sherry and seasonings, continue to simmer until liquid has evaporated.

Place chops on a serving platter, pour sauce over and serve with lemon rice pilaf.

SERVES 6

FRESH PEACH BBQ RIBS

2 cups	500 ml	pared diced peaches
¼ cup	60 ml	vinegar
½ cup	125 ml	peach juice
¼ cup	60 ml	brown sugar
1 tsp	5 ml	Worcestershire sauce
1 tsp	5 ml	salt
½ tsp	3 ml	oregano
4 drops	4 drops	Tabasco™ sauce
4 lbs	1.75 kg	baby back ribs

Place all the ingredients except the ribs in a food processor. Purée, then transfer to a sauce pan. Simmer into a very thick sauce.

Parboil the ribs in boiling salted water until tender.

Transfer to a charbroiler and grill over medium coals. Brush with plenty of sauce. Serve with a final brushing of sauce.

SERVES 4

PORK & LAMB KEBABS NOUVELLE

2 cups	500 ml	blackberries
1½ cups	375 ml	granulated sugar
½ cup	125 ml	blackberry brandy
1 lb	450 g	cubed lean pork
1 lb	450 g	cubed lean lamb
1 tbsp	15 ml	oil

Purée the berries in a food processor. Pass through a sieve to remove seeds.

Mix the blackberry pulp, sugar and brandy together in a sauce pan. Heat to a boil, reduce heat and simmer until sauce thickens.

Skewer the pork and lamb with water soaked bamboo skewers. Brush the oil over the skewers. Grill skewers for 5 minutes per side, brushing frequently with the sauce. Brush 1 final time before serving.

SERVES 4

Fresh Peach BBQ Ribs

LAMB CUTLETS CHERBOURG

6 – 4 oz	6 – 120 g	lamb cutlets
1	1	egg
¼ cup	60 ml	milk
½ cup	125 ml	flour, all purpose
1 cup	250 ml	seasoned bread crumbs
3 tbsp	45 ml	safflower oil
6 tbsp	90 ml	butter
3 tbsp	45 ml	flour, all purpose
1 cup	250 ml	Chicken Stock (see page 77)
1 cup	250 ml	light cream
1 ½ cups	375 ml	cooked crayfish tails
¼ tsp	2 ml	salt
pinch	pinch	each of white pepper, paprika

Pound the cutlets thin with a meat mallet.

Mix the egg into the milk. Dust the cutlets in the flour, dip into the egg wash, then dredge with bread crumbs. Heat the oil in a large skillet and fry the cutlets until golden brown. Reserve hot.

Heat ½ the butter in a sauce pan, add the flour and cook for 2 minutes over low heat. Add both the chicken stock and cream and simmer 15 minutes or until sauce thickens.

In a food processor purée the remaining butter and ½ the crayfish tails. Remove sauce from heat whisk in the purée. Add the remaining crayfish and seasonings.

Place cutlets on serving plate smother with sauce and serve.

SERVES 6

Pork & Lamb Kebabs Nouvelle

Pork Stew with Three Peppercorn Sauce

PORK STEW WITH THREE PEPPERCORN SAUCE

5 lbs	2 kg	large cubes of pork
⅓ cup	80 ml	flour, all purpose
½ tsp	3 ml	each of onion powder, paprika, thyme leaves, oregano leaves, black pepper, chervil
2 tsp	10 ml	each of salt, chili powder
¼ cup	60 ml	safflower oil
3 oz	90 g	mushrooms sliced
2 tsp	10 ml	green peppercorns
2 tsp	10 ml	pink peppercorns
1 tsp	5 ml	black peppercorns
2 cups	500 ml	Demi-Glace (see page 123)
⅓ cup	80 ml	whipping cream
¼ cup	60 ml	Marsala wine
1 tbsp	15 ml	butter

Wash the pork and pat dry.

Combine the flour with the seasonings. Dust the pork with the flour.

Heat the oil in a large skillet. Fry the pork until golden brown. Remove and reserve.

Fry the mushrooms until tender. Return the pork to the pan. Add the peppercorns and demi-glace. Remove heat. Cover and simmer for 1 hour. Transfer pork to a serving platter.

Increase the heat and reduce sauce by half its volume. Stir in the cream and wine. Whisk in the butter, pour sauce over pork and serve.

SERVES 6

PEPPERED LAMB CHOPS

6 – 6 oz	6 – 180 g	lamb chops
¼ cup	60 ml	crushed black peppercorns
¼ cup	60 ml	butter
2 tbsp	30 ml	brandy
1 cup	250 ml	Demi-Glace (see page 123)
2 tbsp	30 ml	sherry
¼ cup	60 ml	heavy cream

Pat the peppercorns into the lamb chops.

Heat the butter in a large skillet and sauté the lamb chops to the desired doneness. Remove and reserve hot.

Pour in the brandy and flame, add the demi glace and sherry. Simmer 1 minute. Add the cream blending well.

Pour sauce over the lamb chops and serve.

SERVES 6

GOURMET PORK STEW

¼ cup	60 ml	butter
1½ lbs	675 g	boneless diced lean pork
½ lb	225 g	sliced mushrooms
¼ cup	60 ml	fine diced onions
3 tbsp	45 ml	flour, all purpose
1½ cups	375 ml	Chicken Broth (see page 77)
½ cup	125 ml	light cream
¼ cup	60 ml	sherry
⅓ cup	80 ml	toasted sliced almonds
2 cups	500 ml	cooked long grain rice
		parsley sprigs

In a large kettle or Dutch oven heat the butter, add the pork and brown. Remove the pork and reserve.

Add the mushrooms and onions and sauté until tender. Sprinkle with flour and cook for 2 minutes over low heat. Add the broth, cream and sherry, simmer for 3 minutes.

Return the pork and continue to simmer for an additional 45 minutes.

Stir the almonds into the rice and spoon the rice around the edges of a serving platter. Ladle the pork into the centre and serve garnished with parsley.

SERVES 4

PARMESAN BAKED PORK CHOPS

¾ cup	180 ml	fine dry bread crumbs
¼ cup	60 ml	dried parsley flakes
⅓ cup	80 ml	freshly grated Parmesan cheese
¼ cup	60 ml	butter
1	1	minced clove garlic
4 – 6 oz	4 – 170 g	boneless pork chops
½ tsp	3 ml	salt
¼ tsp	1 ml	pepper

Combine the bread crumbs, parsley and cheese together in a small mixing bowl.

Melt the butter in a skillet and add the garlic, cook for 1 minute over low heat.

Dip the pork chops in the butter then dredge through the bread crumbs, place in a small casserole dish. Season with the salt and pepper and brush with the remaining butter. Bake in a preheated 350°F (180°C) oven for 45 minutes.

SERVES 4

PORK STEAK CUMBERLAND

6	6	slices of bacon
6 – 6 oz	6 – 170 g	lean pork steaks
3	3	shallots
¼ cup	60 ml	water
1	1	orange
1	1	lemon
pinch	pinch	each of ground ginger, cayenne pepper
⅓ cup	80 ml	red currant jelly
¼ cup	60 ml	port wine

Wrap the bacon around the pork steaks and fasten with toothpicks. Broil on a charbroiler over medium coals, or in the oven until well done.

Chop the shallots and place in the water in a sauce pan.

Zest the orange and lemon, place in the shallots, parboil for 3 minutes, drain.

Add the juice of the orange and ½ lemon, the seasonings, jelly and port. Bring to a boil and reduce to half.

Pour over steaks and serve.

SERVES 6

Gourmet Pork Stew

Lamb Cutlets with Tomato Jam & Cheese

GRILLED LAMB CACCIATORE

1 quan	1 quan	Basic Pasta Dough (see page 426)
3 tbsp	45 ml	olive oil
2	2	minced garlic cloves
1	1	diced green bell pepper
1	1	diced onions
2	2	diced celery stalks
4 oz	115 g	sliced mushrooms
1 tsp	5 ml	each of salt, basil leaves
½ tsp	3 ml	each of pepper, thyme leaves, oregano leaves, paprika
½ tsp	3 ml	Worcestershire sauce
3 lbs	1.5 kg	tomatoes, peeled, seeded and chopped
6 – 6 oz	6 – 170 g	boneless lamb chops

Process the pasta as directed, cut into fettuccini noodles, cover with a moist towel and reserve.

In a large sauce pan, heat 2 tbsp (30 ml) of oil. Add the garlic, pepper, onion, celery and mushrooms, sauté until tender.

Add the seasonings, Worcestershire and tomatoes, reduce heat and simmer for 3 hours or until a thick sauce is formed.

Brush the chops with the remaining oil. Grill 5 minutes per side.

Boil the pasta in a large kettle of salted water. Drain, place on plates, cover with sauce and top with a lamb chop. Serve at once.

SERVES 6

LAMB CUTLETS WITH TOMATO JAM AND CHEESE

1 cup	250 ml	crushed tomatoes
1 cup	250 ml	granulated sugar
¼ cup	60 ml	sherry
6 – 4 oz	6 – 120 g	lamb cutlets
1	1	egg
¼ cup	60 ml	milk
½ cup	125 ml	flour, all purpose
1 cup	250 ml	seasoned bread crumbs
3 tbsp	45 ml	safflower oil
2 cups	500 ml	grated Havarti cheese

Mix the tomatoes, sugar and sherry in a sauce pan. Heat on low, stirring constantly, reduce until the tomato mixture is very thick – the consistency of jam.

Pound the cutlets thin with a meat mallet. Mix the egg with the milk. Dust the cutlets with flour, dip into the egg wash, dredge in bread crumbs.

Heat the oil in a large skillet. Fry the cutlets until golden brown on both sides.

Place each cutlet on a baking sheet, top with tomato jam, sprinkle with cheese, place in a 450°F (230°C) oven until cheese is melted and golden.

Serve at once.

SERVES 6

PORK & LAMB IN CRUST

½ quan	0.5 quan	Plain Pastry (see page 616)
1 cup	250 ml	finely diced cooked pork
1 cup	250 ml	finely diced cooked lamb
2 cups	500 ml	Béchamel sauce (see page 112)
½ tsp	3 ml	each of salt, pepper, nutmeg
1 tbsp	15 ml	parsley
3	3	eggs, separated
¼ cup	60 ml	diced onions

Roll out the pie dough and fit into a 9" (23 cm) deep dish pie shell.

In a mixing bowl blend the pork, lamb and cream sauce. Add the seasonings and onion.

Beat the egg yolk and fold into the mixture. Beat the egg whites stiffly, fold into the mixture.

Pour mixture into the pie shell and bake 25-30 minutes in a preheated 400°F (200°C) oven until golden brown. Serve at once.

SERVES 6

Pork & Lamb in Crust

LAMB FRICASSEE

4½ lbs	2 kg	lamb, cut into large cubes
2	2	chopped onions
2	2	chopped carrots
2	2	chopped celery stalks
1	1	bouquet garni*
4 cups	1 L	cold Chicken Broth (see page 77)
1 tsp	5 ml	celery salt
½ tsp	3 ml	white pepper
3 tbsp	45 ml	butter
3 tbsp	45 ml	flour, all purpose

Wash and pat dry the lamb.

Place the lamb in a large kettle or Dutch oven along with the onions, carrots, celery and bouquet. Cover with the broth and bring to a boil, reduce temperature and simmer gently for 1½ hours.

Remove the lamb and reserve warm. Strain the broth and discard the vegetables and the bouquet. Return the broth to the pot, add the salt and pepper, bring to a boil, reduce the liquid to 2 cups (500 ml).

In a small sauce pan heat the butter, add the flour and cook over low heat for 2 minutes. Add the reduced broth and simmer into a thick sauce. Pour sauce over lamb and serve with rice or noodles.

SERVES 8

*The bouquet garni for this dish is; a bay leaf, 8 sprigs of parsley, 2 sprigs of thyme, 6 peppercorns and 1 small, chopped leek tied together in a cheesecloth.

Lemonade Pork Chops

LEMONADE PORK CHOPS

¾ cup	180 ml	lemonade concentrate
¼ cup	60 ml	catsup
3 tbsp	45 ml	brown sugar
3 tbsp	45 ml	white vinegar
¼ tsp	1 ml	ground ginger
1 tsp	5 ml	soya sauce
¼ tsp	1 ml	each of paprika, chili powder, garlic powder, thyme, basil, oregano, salt and pepper
2¼ lb	1 kg	pork chops
½ cup	125 ml	flour, all purpose
¼ cup	60 ml	safflower oil

In a mixing bowl combine the concentrate, catsup, sugar, vinegar, ginger, soya and seasonings.

Dredge the chops in the flour. Heat the oil in a large kettle or Dutch oven, brown the chops. Drain any excess oil. Pour the sauce over the chops, cook over low heat 35-40 minutes covered.

Serve with Hickory Smoked 'Taters (see page 70).

SERVES 4

PORK CREOLE AU GRATIN

3 tbsp	45 ml	olive oil
1½ lbs	675 g	boneless coarse diced lean pork
3 cups	750 ml	Chicken Broth (see page 77)
2 cups	500 ml	cooked drained fettuccini noodles
1½ cups	375 ml	Creole Sauce (see page 121)
½ cup	125 ml	grated mild cheddar cheese
½ cup	125 ml	grated sharp cheddar cheese
½ cup	125 ml	grated Havarti cheese

Preheat the oven to 400°F (200°C).

Heat the oil in a large kettle, brown the pork. Add the broth and bring to a boil, simmer gently for 30 minutes. Drain and reserve the pork.

Place the noodles in a greased casserole dish. Spread the pork over the noodles and smother with sauce.

Combine the cheeses and sprinkle over the casserole. Bake for 25-30 minutes or until cheese is melted and is golden brown, serve at once.

SERVES 4

Lamb Fricassee

PORK & LAMB SAUTÉ

1½ lbs	675 g	lean pork
1½ lbs	675 g	lean lamb
¼ cup	60 ml	clarified butter*
1 tbsp	15 ml	shallots
1 tbsp	15 ml	flour, all purpose
1	1	bouquet garni**
¼ lb	115 g	diced cooked bacon
20	20	pearl onions
20	20	button mushrooms
¾ cup	180 ml	red wine

Cut the pork and lamb into large cubes.

Heat the butter in a large kettle or Dutch oven, fry the meats until golden brown, remove and reserve. Stir in the shallots and flour, reduce the heat and cook for 4 minutes.

Add the remaining ingredients along with the meats. Reduce the heat and simmer gently for 1¼ hours or until the meats are cooked through. Discard the bouquet garni and serve with rice or noodles.

SERVES 6

*Clarified butter is butter which has been melted, the curd removed leaving only the golden fat.

**The bouquet garni for this dish is: a bay leaf, 8 sprigs of parsley, 2 sprigs of thyme, 6 peppercorns and 1 small chopped leek tied together in a cheesecloth.

Pork & Lamb Sauté

HONEY BARBECUED PORK STEAK

3 tbsp	45 ml	butter
3 tbsp	45 ml	oil
1	1	minced medium onion
1	1	minced garlic clove
⅔ cup	160 ml	tomato catsup
⅔ cup	160 ml	liquid honey
¼ cup	60 ml	cider vinegar
1 tbsp	15 ml	Worcestershire sauce
½ tsp	3 ml	each of thyme leaves, oregano leaves, basil leaves, paprika, pepper, chili powder, salt
½ tsp	3 ml	liquid smoke
4 – 6 oz	4 – 170 g	pork steaks

Heat the butter with 2 tbsp (30 ml) of oil in a sauce pan. Add the onion and garlic and sauté until tender.

Add the catsup, honey, vinegar, Worcestershire, seasonings and smoke flavouring. Simmer until sauce is thick and glossy. Cool.

Brush the steaks with the remaining oil. Grill over medium coals 6 minutes per side, brushing frequently with sauce. Brush 1 final time before serving.

SERVES 4

PORK CUTLET WITH APPLE RICE AND ORANGE BUTTER SAUCE

6 – 4 oz	6 – 120 g	pork cutlets
½ quan	0.5	Apple Rice with Dates and Nuts (see page 710)
1	1	egg
¼ cup	60 ml	milk
½ cup	125 ml	flour, all purpose
1 cup	250 ml	seasoned fine bread crumbs
¼ cup	60 ml	safflower oil
2 tbsp	30 ml	minced shallots
⅓ cup	80 ml	orange juice
3 tbsp	45 ml	dry sherry
4 tbsp	60 ml	sweet butter
2 tbsp	30 ml	julienned orange peel

Pound the cutlets very thin with a meat mallet. Place 4 tbsp (60 ml) of rice on each, fold in the ends and roll together.

Blend the egg with the milk. Dust the cutlets with flour. Dip into the egg, dredge in bread crumbs. Heat the oil in a large skillet, brown the cutlets in the oil.

Transfer to a baking sheet. Bake in a preheated 350°F (180°C) oven for 25 minutes.

While cutlets bake, heat shallots, orange juice and sherry together. Reduce to 3 tbsp (45 ml). Over very low heat whisk in the butter a little at a time. Add the orange peel.

Transfer the cutlets to a serving platter, pour butter sauce over the cutlets and serve.

SERVES 6

Pork Cutlet with Apple Rice & Orange Butter Sauce

PORK STEAKS DIANNE

4	4	slices of bacon
4 – 6 oz	4 – 170 g	pork steaks
⅓ cup	80 ml	butter
4 oz	115 g	mushrooms, sliced
2	2	minced green onions
¼ cup	60 ml	brandy
1½ cups	375 ml	Demi-Glace Sauce (see page 123)
¼ cup	60 ml	sherry
¼ cup	60 ml	cream

Wrap the bacon around the steaks.

In a large skillet, heat the butter. Fry the steaks in the butter for 6 minutes per side. Remove and reserve hot.

Add the mushrooms to the pan and sauté until tender. Add the green onions and carefully flame with the brandy. Stir in the demi-glace, sherry and cream, reduce the liquid to ¾ of a cup (175 ml).

Place the steaks onto serving plates, pour the sauce over the steaks and serve.

SERVES 4

PORK STEAKS WITH HERB BUTTER

1	1	minced garlic clove
½	0.5	lemon
½	0.5	lime
2 tsp	10 ml	each of parsley, basil, marjoram, thyme
¼ lb	115 g	sweet butter
6	6	maple bacon slices
6 – 6 oz	6 – 170 g	lean pork steaks

In a food processor combine the garlic, lemon and lime juices, herbs and butter until smooth. Form butter into a dowel shape. Wrap in wax paper, freeze for 1 hour.

Wrap the bacon around the pork steaks. Broil on a charbroiler over medium coals or in the oven until cooked thoroughly.

Plate the steaks and top with a slice of herb butter.

SERVES 6

Teriyaki Grilled Lamb

PORK STEW II

4½ lbs	2 kg	boneless pork
⅓ cup	80 ml	flour, all purpose
¼ cup	60 ml	olive oil
3	3	minced garlic cloves
20	20	pearl onions
20	20	button mushrooms
2	2	julienne cut carrots
2 cups	500 ml	peeled, seeded, chopped tomatoes
1 cup	250 ml	double Chicken Broth (see page 77)
½ tsp	3 ml	each of salt, pepper, basil, chervil, marjoram

Dice the pork into very large cubes.

Dust the pork with the flour. Heat the oil in a large kettle or Dutch oven, brown the pork and remove. Add the garlic, onions, mushrooms and carrots, sauté until tender, sprinkle with the remaining flour and cook for 2 minutes over low heat.

Return the pork to the kettle and add the remaining ingredients, stir to blend well. Cover the pork and simmer very gently for 1½ hours.

Serve with rice or pasta.

SERVES 8

TERIYAKI GRILLED LAMB

⅓ cup	80 ml	brown sugar
1 tsp	5 ml	ground ginger
1 cup	250 ml	Beef Broth (see page 85)
⅓ cup	80 ml	soya sauce
2 tbsp	30 ml	cornstarch
¼ cup	60 ml	sherry
1 tbsp	15 ml	oil
8 – 3 oz	8 – 90 g	boneless lamb chops

In a sauce pan. dissolve the sugar and ginger in the broth and soya sauce, bring to a boil.

Mix the cornstarch with the sherry and add to the sauce. Reduce heat and simmer until sauce thickens. Cool.

Brush the oil over the chops. Grill over medium coals for 5 minutes per side. Brush frequently with sauce while cooking. Brush 1 final time and serve.

SERVES 4

LAMB ROLLUPS WITH CLEMENTINE SAUCE

6 – 4 oz	6 – 120 g	lamb cutlets
18	18	blanched asparagus spears
18	18	large peeled and deveined shrimp
2 tbsp	30 ml	olive oil
1½ cups	375 ml	fresh clementine or tangerine juice
1 cup	250 ml	Chicken Stock (see page 77)
½ cup	125 ml	heavy cream
2 tbsp	30 ml	butter
¼ tsp	1 ml	fresh ground pepper
1 cup	250 ml	orange segments

Pound the lamb very thin with a meat mallet. Place 3 asparagus and 3 large shrimp in each. Fold in and roll together. Secure with tooth picks. Place on a baking sheet.

Brush with oil. Bake in a preheated 350°F (180°C) oven for 25-30 minutes.

While lamb bakes, combine the orange juice with the chicken stock in a sauce pan. Heat and reduce to half. Add the cream and reduce again to half. Remove from heat. Whip in the butter. Add the pepper and orange segments.

Place the rollups on a serving plate pour sauce over rollups and serve.

SERVES 6

Lamb Roll Ups with Clementine Sauce

Hawaiian Pork Roast

HAWAIIAN PORK ROAST

1 – 4½ lbs	1 – 2 kg	boneless pork top loin
2	2	minced garlic clove
¼ tsp	1 ml	pepper
½ tsp	3 ml	salt
¼ cup	60 ml	soya sauce
3 tbsp	45 ml	liquid honey
¼ cup	60 ml	catsup

Place the top loin in a roaster, rub with half the garlic and season with the salt and pepper. Roast in preheated 350°F (180°C) oven for 2½ hours or until cooked through.

Combine the remaining ingredients in a small mixing bowl and brush the roast at least 6 times during roasting. Brush one final time before carving and serving.

SERVES 6

SMOKED PORK LOIN WITH PLUM SAUCE

1 – 2 lbs	1 – 900 g	centre cut smoked pork loin
1 cup	250 ml	orange juice
¼ cup	60 ml	Hungarian plum brandy
1 cup	250 ml	plum jam
¼ tsp	1 ml	ground ginger
1 tsp	5 ml	cornstarch
2 tbsp	30 ml	cold water

Cut the loin into six even pieces. Place in a casserole dish.

In a sauce pan combine the orange juice, brandy, jam and ginger. Bring to a boil. Blend the cornstarch with the water, pour into the sauce, once the sauce returns to a boil remove from the heat.

Pour over the pork, cover and bake in a preheated 350°F (180°C) oven for 30 minutes. Remove and serve.

SERVES 6

PORK SATAY

2 lbs	900 g	boneless lean pork coarse diced
4 tbsp	60 ml	peanut oil
1½ tbsp	20 ml	ground Brazilian nuts
½ tsp	3 ml	ground ginger
1½ tsp	8 ml	ground coriander
¼ tsp	1 ml	each of cayenne, garlic powder
½ tsp	3 ml	each of pepper, onion powder
2 tsp	10 ml	molasses
4 tsp	20 ml	lime juice
4 tsp	20 ml	lemon juice
3 tbsp	45 ml	hot water

Skewer the meat with bamboo skewers, place in a large shallow pan.

In a mixing bowl blend the remaining ingredients. Pour over the skewered pork marinade, covered in the refrigerator 3½ - 4 hours.

Grill the skewers over high heat for 10-12 minutes, or until meat is cooked through, brushing frequently with marinade.

Serve with Bombay Rice (see page 709).

SERVES 6

Smoked Pork Loin with Plum Sauce

ROAST LEG OF LAMB

1 5-7 lbs	1 2-3 kg	lamb leg – shank off
1	1	garlic clove
½ tsp	3 ml	each of onion powder, paprika, salt, pepper, thyme, marjoram, basil, dry mustard
2 tbsp	30 ml	olive oil

Preheat the oven to 350°F (180°C).

Make a small incision in the meat near the bone and insert the garlic clove. Blend the seasonings. Brush the lamb with the oil, sprinkle with the seasonings. Roast for 2½-3 hours.

Carve and serve.

SERVES 8

SAUTÉ PORK STEAKS WITH CLEMENTINE SAUCE

6 – 6 oz	6 – 170 g	pork steaks
3 tbsp	45 ml	oil
		salt and pepper to taste
¼ cup	60 ml	tangerine or orange juice concentrate
½ cup	125 ml	Chicken Stock (see page 77)
¼ cup	60 ml	whipping cream
1 tsp	5 ml	butter
1 tsp	5 ml	lime juice

Heat the oil in a large skillet. Sauté the steaks for 6-8 minutes. Season with salt and pepper and reserve hot.

Heat the tangerine juice in a sauce pan with the chicken stock, bring to a boil and reduce heat. Add the cream and simmer until sauce coats a spoon. Remove from heat. Whip in the butter and lime juice.

Place steaks on a serving plate cover, with sauce, serve.

SERVES 6

LAMB WITH CHINESE MUSHROOMS

1½ lbs	675 g	boneless lamb
8	8	dried Chinese black mushrooms or fresh oyster mushrooms
1½ tsp	8 ml	cornstarch
4 tsp	20 ml	light soya sauce
1	1	egg white
¼ cup	60 ml	safflower oil
1	1	minced garlic clove
2 tsp	10 ml	granulated sugar
3 tbsp	45 ml	oyster sauce
2 tbsp	30 ml	rice wine

Cut the lamb into thin slices.

Soak the mushrooms in warm water for 1 hour. Blend the cornstarch with soya sauce and egg white. Pour over the lamb, and marinate 1 hour.

Drain the mushrooms and slice into thin strips.

Heat the oil in a wok. Stir fry the garlic. Add the lamb and mushrooms, fry 2 minutes. Add the sugar, oyster sauce, and wine. Continue to fry until most of the liquid has evaporated. Serve with steamed rice.

SERVES 6

Roast Leg of Lamb

Lamb with Chinese Mushrooms

Lamb Salad with Wild Mushrooms

LAMB SRI LANKA

1 cup	250 ml	white wine
1 lb	450 g	coarse diced lamb
¼ cup	60 ml	butter
1	1	small diced onion
1	1	diced green bell pepper
1	1	diced celery stalk
3 tbsp	45 ml	flour, all purpose
1 cup	250 ml	heavy cream
⅓ cup	80 ml	sherry
½ tsp	3 ml	salt
2 tsp	10 ml	curry powder
1 cup	250 ml	peeled, seeded, chopped tomatoes

Heat the wine in a small sauce pan, add the lamb and simmer gently for 20 minutes. Drain and reserve the lamb and the broth.

In a second sauce pan heat the butter, sauté the onion, green pepper and celery, add the flour, reduce heat and cook for 2 minutes. Add cream, sherry and seasoning, simmer until thick.

Add the tomatoes and lamb, simmer for 5 minutes. If sauce is too thick, thin slightly with the broth.

Place on serving plates and serve with Aloo Madarasi (see page 710).

SERVES 4

LAMB SALAD WITH WILD MUSHROOMS

1½ lbs	675 g	julienne cut cooked lamb
⅔ lb	300 g	wild mushrooms
2 tbsp	30 ml	chopped basil leaves
1 tbsp	15 ml	parsley
¼ cup	60 ml	chopped green onion
½ tsp	3 ml	salt
1 tsp	5 ml	cracked black pepper
⅓ cup	80 ml	lemon juice
1 cup	250 ml	olive oil
1	1	small head Boston bibb lettuce
1	1	small head radicchio
1	1	egg yolk
		edible flowers for garnish

Mix the lamb with the mushrooms in a mixing bowl.

In a blender combine the basil, parsley, green onion, salt, pepper and lemon juice. With the machine running on low, slowly pour in the oil. Blend thoroughly.

Pour half the dressing over the lamb and mushrooms, marinate in the refrigerator 1 hour.

Wash the lettuce and radicchio. Chop into coarse pieces. Place on plates. Top with the marinated lamb.

Place the egg yolk in a blender. With the machine running, slowly pour in the remaining dressing. Once a thin mayonnaise is formed pour over the salad and serve. Garnish with flowers.

NOTE: For wild mushrooms, use chanterelles, shiitake, morels, or enokitake mushrooms; otherwise use cultivated ones.

SERVES 6

Lamb Sri Lanka

GAME

Those who hunt for food supply and sustain life. Those who kill for sport are mislead. To participate in the killing of defenseless animals for the hunt's sake with no intent of consumption will not serve anyone but a warped sense of greed. Those who hunt for the sake of provision must be able to prepare the food that they kill. The most fitting way to honour that which has given its life to sustain another's is to prepare the game tastefully and with flair.

Preparing great food is our focus in *Simply Delicious Cooking 2*. Preparing game meats skillfully and simply enhances this focus. Having never hunted myself, I had to purchase the meats used in the recipes in this chapter. Most are commercially raised throughout most countries, making them as readily available as beef or chicken. If you ask your local meat purveyor (butcher), he or she will likely be able to obtain what you require.

Cooking with game brings outdoor adventure into the home and treats the guest with the delights of earthy, natural tasting food at its best. Traditionally, game meats were served at formal state dinners from the woods where they were caught. We have chosen to focus our selections on casual dining. Whether your choice is Moose Stroganoff or a Pheasant in Red Wine Sauce, your guests will enjoy delights they have not previously associated with this style of dining.

As new varieties of game meat become available, the creative cook is able to expand his menu choices, astonishing his guests with the distinctive flavours of these meats. Not only are they exquisite to the palette, but overall are more nutritionally sound choices than more traditional selections. Buffalo or musk ox, for example, contain less fat, calories and cholesterol than do beef or pork. Deer, moose or caribou meats provide unique flavours only obtainable from such selections.

For the preparation of the uncommon with a truly distinctive flair, the selection must be game meat. Your guest will agree that your menu choice was absolutely *Simply Delicious*.

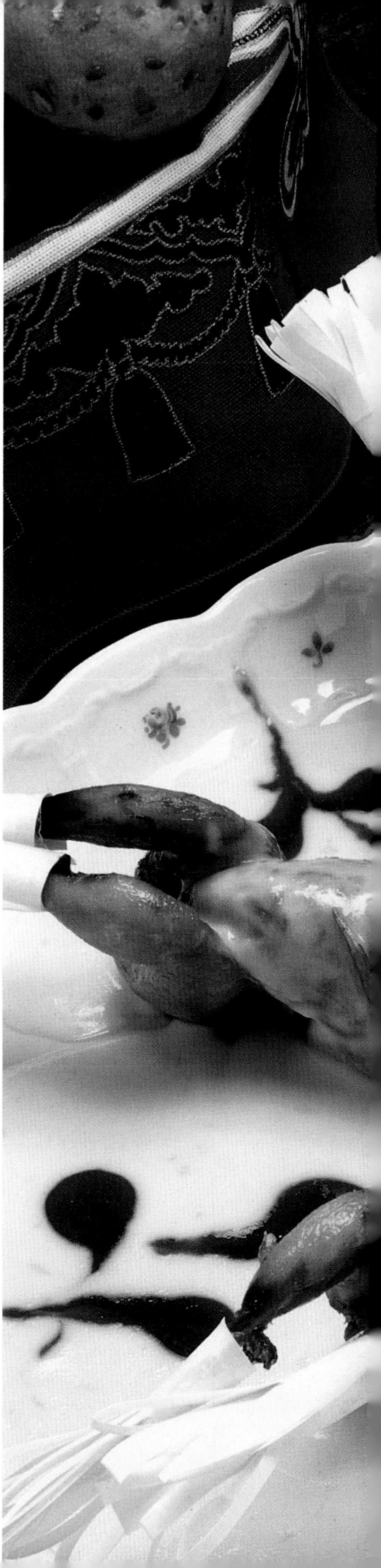

Sautéed Quail with Clementine Sauce

QUALITÄTSWEIN
L. A. P. Nr. 1 640 888 184
1992

GUINEA HENS MARENGO

2	2	guinea hens, cut in quarters
⅓ cup	80 ml	safflower oil
4	4	pared and sliced carrots
2	2	diced celery stalks
1	1	small diced onion
6	6	slices of bacon
⅓ cup	80 ml	flour, all purpose
4 cups	1 L	peeled, seeded, diced tomatoes
¼ cup	60 ml	sherry
½ tsp	3 ml	salt
¼ tsp	1 ml	pepper
1	1	bouquet garni (see Glossary)
¼ lb	115 g	sliced mushrooms
2 tbsp	30 ml	chopped parsley
3 cups	750 ml	steamed rice

Preheat the oven to 350°F (180°C).

Sauté the hens in the oil for 5 minutes. Remove and place in casserole dish.

Dice the bacon and sauté in a sauce pan, add flour, reduce heat and cook for 4 minutes. Add the vegetables and continue to cook until vegetables are tender. Add tomatoes, sherry and seasonings, cook for 10 minutes over low heat.

Pour sauce and bouquet garni over the hens, top with mushroom, cover and bake for 1 hour.

Sprinkle with parsley and serve with hot rice.

SERVES 4

ALMOND PARMESAN PHEASANT

¼ cup	60 ml	flour, all purpose
⅛ tsp	pinch	each of salt, pepper, paprika, thyme, basil
1	1	egg
¼ cup	60 ml	milk
¼ cup	60 ml	ground almonds
¼ cup	60 ml	freshly grated hard Parmesan cheese
½ cup	125 ml	fine bread crumbs
6 – 4 oz	6 – 120 g	boneless pheasant breasts
3 tbsp	45 ml	melted butter

Mix the flour and seasonings together. Mix the egg with the milk. Mix the almonds, Parmesan, and bread crumbs. Dust the pheasant breasts with flour, dip into egg wash and dredge in bread crumbs.

Heat the butter in a large skillet, sauté the pheasant for 4-5 minutes per side or until golden brown. Excellent when served with a Wild Mushroom Sherry Sauce (see page 105)

SERVES 6

BUFFALO MINCEMEAT

1 lb	450 g	ground buffalo meat
⅓ lb	150 g	beef suet
5	5	large, pared and chopped apples
7 lbs	3 kg	raisins
2 cups	500 ml	apple cider
1 cup	250 ml	molasses
4 tbsp	60 ml	fine julienne cut lemon rind
4 tbsp	60 ml	fine julienne cut orange rind
1 tsp	5 ml	ground cinnamon – or more to taste

Cook the buffalo in the suet. Cool and remove all the fat.

Mix all the remaining ingredients with the meat in a Dutch oven. Cook gently for 2 hours. Cool and use in pies or tartlets.

MAKES 3 – 9" PIES

Almond Parmesan Pheasant

MOOSE STROGANOFF

2¼ lbs	1 kg	moose meat, diced into ¾" cubes
¼ cup	60 ml	oil
3 tbsp	45 ml	butter
2	2	sliced celery stalk
1	1	sliced onion
1	1	sliced green bell pepper
½ lb	225 g	mushrooms
⅓ cup	90 ml	flour, all purpose
1¼ cups	310 ml	Beef Stock (see page 85)
¾ cup	180 ml	sherry
2 tbsp	30 ml	Worcestershire sauce
2 tbsp	30 ml	Dijon mustard
¼ cup	60 ml	tomato paste
1	1	bay leaf
2 tsp	10 ml	paprika
½ tsp	3 ml	thyme
¼ tsp	1 ml	pepper
1 cup	250 ml	sour cream

Heat the oil and butter together. Brown the moose meat and sauté the vegetables. Add the flour and stir, cooking for 2 minutes. Add the beef stock, sherry, Worcestershire sauce, mustard, tomato paste and seasonings.

Cover and simmer for 1¼ hours. Blend in the sour cream. Serve over egg noodles.

SERVES 8

Moose Stroganoff

SPICY BUFFALO SHORT RIBS

2¼ lbs	1 kg	buffalo short ribs
4 tbsp	60 ml	safflower oil
2 tbsp	30 ml	butter
1	1	finely diced onion
2 tbsp	30 ml	lemon juice
1 tbsp	15 ml	brown sugar
½ cup	125 ml	catsup
1 tbsp	15 ml	Worcestershire sauce
1 tsp	5 ml	Dijon mustard
¼ tsp	1 ml	each of white pepper, black pepper, salt, paprika
½ tsp	3 ml	each of basil, thyme, marjoram
⅛ tsp	pinch	cayenne

Brown the ribs in the oil. Drain excess oil. In a sauce pan heat the butter, fry the onion and add the remaining ingredients. Pour over the ribs.

Cover and simmer over low heat for 2 hours or until tender.

Serve with rice.

SERVES 4

DEER PEPPER STEAK

2 lbs	900 g	deer round steak
3 tbsp	45 ml	safflower oil
1 tsp	5 ml	pared, minced ginger root
2	2	julienned green bell peppers
1 cup	250 ml	sliced mushrooms
¼ cup	60 ml	soya sauce
1 tbsp	15 ml	sugar
2 tbsp	30 ml	sherry
1 tsp	5 ml	cornstarch

Cut the meat into thin strips.

Heat the oil in a wok. Add the ginger and cook 1 minute. Brown the meat then add the peppers and mushrooms. Fry for 5 minutes. Add the soya and sugar. Mix the sherry with the cornstarch and blend into the stir fry. Cook 1 minute.

Serve with rice.

SERVES 6

BUFFALO CHILI

3 tbsp	45 ml	safflower oil
2¼ lbs	1 kg	ground buffalo meat
3	3	diced large onions
1	1	diced green bell pepper
3	3	diced jalapeño peppers
8 cups	2 L	peeled, seeded and diced tomatoes
2 tbsp	30 ml	chili powder
2	2	minced garlic cloves
1 tbsp	15 ml	granulated sugar
2 tsp	10 ml	salt
8 cups	2 L	canned kidney beans
2 cups	500 ml	V-8™ juice

Heat the oil in a Dutch oven. Brown the meat. Add the onions and peppers, sauté until tender. Add the remaining ingredients, cover and simmer 4 hours, stirring occasionally.

Serve with garlic cheese bread.

SERVES 8

REINDEER MEATBALLS

2 lbs	900 g	ground reindeer meat
3	3	beaten eggs
3 tbsp	45 ml	freshly grated Parmesan cheese
2 tbsp	30 ml	bread crumbs
1 tsp	5 ml	basil
1	1	minced garlic clove
½ tsp	3 ml	salt
½ tsp	3 ml	pepper

Mix all the ingredients together thoroughly. Shape into meatballs, golf ball size.

Bake for 15 minutes in a preheated 350°F (180°C) oven. Serve with a Tomato Sauce (see page 106) or mushroom sauce on noodles or rice.

SERVES 6

NOTE: If reindeer is unavailable in your area use deer, caribou, wapiti or moose meats.

CARIBOU BOURGUIGNON

3 lbs	1.5 kg	thinly sliced lean caribou meat
¼ cup	60 ml	olive oil
1	1	crushed garlic clove
3 cups	750 ml	red wine – burgundy
20	20	pearl onions
20	20	button mushrooms
1 tsp	5 ml	salt
⅛ tsp	pinch	pepper
2	2	bay leaves
2	2	cloves
1 tsp	5 ml	marjoram
½ tsp	3 ml	rosemary
2 tbsp	30 ml	butter
2 tbsp	30 ml	flour

Brown the meat in the oil in a Dutch oven with the garlic. Drain any excess fat. Add the wine, onions, mushrooms, and seasonings, simmer covered for 2½ hours.

Heat the butter in a small sauce pan, add the flour and cook 4 minutes over low heat, or until flour turns hazelnut brown. Stir into the sauce. Continue to simmer for 15 minutes.

Serve over egg noodles.

SERVES 6

Caribou Bourguignon

Buffalo Chili

Buffalo Schnitzel

VENISON ROULADEN

4 – 6 oz	4 – 170 g	boneless venison steaks
¼ tsp	1 ml	each of salt, pepper, paprika, garlic powder
1 lb	450 g	lean ground venison
8	8	slices bacon
8	8	dill pickle spears
4 tbsp	60 ml	safflower oil
2 cups	500 ml	Beef Broth (see page 85)
2 tbsp	30 ml	butter
1 cup	250 ml	sliced mushrooms
2 tbsp	30 ml	flour

Pound the venison steaks very thin with a meat mallet.

Blend the seasonings with the ground meat, spread over the steaks. Layer 2 slices of bacon and 2 pickle spears over each steak. Roll together and tie to secure.

Heat the oil in a large skillet. Brown the steak on all sides then pour off excess fat. Pour the beef broth over, cover and simmer for 3 hours.

Remove rouladen and the strings. Reserve hot. Heat the butter in a sauce pan, sauté the mushrooms and sprinkle with flour. Reduce heat and cook for 2 minutes. Add the broth and simmer into a sauce.

Place rouladen on a serving platter, pour sauce over and serve.

SERVES 4

FAISAN CACCIATORE

4	4	boneless pheasant breasts
½ cup	125 ml	flour
¼ cup	60 ml	olive oil
1	1	garlic clove
½ tsp	3 ml	each of salt, thyme, oregano, basil
¼ tsp	1 ml	pepper and paprika
1	1	julienne cut green bell pepper
1	1	sliced Spanish onion
3 cups	750 ml	tomatoes
1 cup	250 ml	sliced mushrooms

Dust the pheasant breasts with flour. Heat the oil in a large skillet and brown the breasts, add the garlic, seasonings and vegetables. Simmer for 1¾ hours covered.

Uncover the pan and continue to simmer for an additional 30 minutes.

Serve with rice or noodles.

SERVES 4

BUFFALO SCHNITZEL

6 – 4 oz	6 – 120 g	buffalo cutlets
1	1	egg
¼ cup	60 ml	milk
½ cup	125 ml	flour
1 cup	250 ml	seasoned bread crumbs
¼ cup	60 ml	safflower oil
1	1	lemon cut in wedges

Pound the cutlets very thin.

Mix the egg with milk. Dust the cutlets in the flour, dip into the egg, dredge in the bread crumbs.

Heat the oil in a skillet. Fry the cutlets to golden brown on each side. Serve with lemon wedge.

SERVES 6

Venison Rouladen

BLACKBERRY BRANDY GRILLED PHEASANT BREASTS

2 cups	500 ml	blackberries
1½ cups	375 ml	granulated sugar
½ cup	125 ml	blackberry brandy
1 tbsp	15 ml	safflower oil
4 – 6 oz	4 – 175 g	boneless pheasant breasts

Purée the berries in a food processor. Pass through a sieve to remove seeds.

Mix the blackberry pulp, sugar and brandy together in a sauce pan. Heat to a boil, reduce heat and simmer until sauce thickens.

Brush the oil over the pheasant and grill for 6 minutes per side, brushing frequently with the sauce. Brush 1 final time before serving.

SERVES 4

BUFFALO FILET AU POIVRE

6 – 8 oz	6 – 225 g	buffalo filet steaks
¼ cup	60 ml	three peppercorn blend
¼ cup	60 ml	butter
2 tbsp	30 ml	brandy
1 cup	250 ml	Demi-Glace (see page 123)
2 tbsp	30 ml	sherry
¼ cup	60 ml	whipping cream

Trim the filets of any fat. Pat the peppercorns over the filets.

Heat the butter and sauté until desired doneness. Remove and keep hot.

Pour the brandy into the pan and carefully flame. Add the demi-glace, sherry and cream. Blend well, pour sauce over steaks and serve.

SERVES 6

WILD TURKEY SAUTÉ PROVENÇALE

6 – 6 oz	6 – 175 g	boneless wild turkey breast slices
4 tbsp	60 ml	butter
3	3	minced garlic cloves
1	1	sliced green bell pepper
1	1	sliced onion
3 cups	750 ml	peeled, seeded, chopped tomatoes
¼ cup	60 ml	sherry
1 tsp	5 ml	paprika
½ tsp	3 ml	salt
¼ tsp	1 ml	pepper

In a skillet, fry the turkey in the butter for 4-6 minutes per side depending on the thickness of the breast. Remove and reserve hot.

Add the garlic, bell pepper and onions to the skillet and sauté until tender. Add the tomatoes and bring to a boil, reduce heat and simmer for 10 minutes. Add the sherry and seasonings, continue to simmer until liquid has evaporated.

Place turkey breasts on the platter, pour sauce over turkey and serve with lemon rice pilaf.

SERVES 6

Buffalo Filet au Poivre

Wild Turkey Sauté Provençale

FRENCH CANADIAN TOURTIERE

2	2	slices bacon – diced
1½ lbs	675 g	lean, ground venison or pork of half of each
½ cup	125 ml	chopped onion
½ cup	125 ml	chopped celery
1	1	minced garlic clove
2 tbsp	30 ml	flour, all purpose
1 cup	250 ml	Beef Stock (see page 85)
1 tsp	5 ml	salt
½ tsp	3 ml	chervil
¼ tsp	1 ml	mace
1	1	crushed bay leaf
1 quan	1	Plain Pastry (see page 616)
1	1	beaten egg

Heat the bacon in a large skillet. Add the meat, onion, celery and garlic, cook until meat has browned. Sprinkle with flour and cook for 2 minutes over low heat. Add the beef stock and seasonings. Blend and cook covered 30 minutes. Cool to room temperature.

Roll out half the pastry and fit into a 9" (23 cm) pie pan. Fill with meat mixture. Roll out the remaining pastry, moisten the pie crust rim with the beaten egg. Fit on the top. Fold the edges under to seal and flute the top. Slit the top of the pastry to allow steam to escape. Brush with egg.

Bake in a preheated 375°F (190°C) oven for 40 minutes.

Serve hot or cold.

SERVES 6

Deer Burgers

DEER BURGERS

1½ lbs	675 g	lean, ground deer meat
1	1	egg
¼ cup	60 ml	milk
½ cup	125 ml	seasoned bread crumbs
1 tsp	5 ml	Worcestershire sauce
1 tsp	5 ml	Dijon mustard
1 tbsp	15 ml	soya sauce
1 tsp	5 ml	salt
½ tsp	3 ml	each of basil, marjoram, pepper, paprika
6	6	kaiser rolls

Blend all the ingredients together, form into patties. Broil to desired doneness over medium heat on a charbroiler.

Serve on kaiser rolls. Garnish after the fashion of hamburgers.

SERVES 6

NOTE: You may use any wild deer meat, elk, caribou, wapiti, etc.

WILD TURKEY STIR FRY

8 oz	225 g	boneless wild turkey meat
2 tbsp	30 ml	safflower oil
1	1	small diced onion
½ cup	125 ml	diced green bell pepper
½ cup	125 ml	diced red bell pepper
20	20	button mushrooms
¼ cup	60 ml	oyster sauce*
2 tbsp	30 ml	soya sauce
1 tsp	5 ml	cornstarch
1 tbsp	15 ml	sherry or water

Dice the turkey into bite size pieces.

Heat the oil in a wok or large skillet. Fry the turkey for 3 minutes. Add the vegetables and fry until tender.

Add the oyster sauce and soya sauce. Simmer for 2 minutes.

Mix the cornstarch with the sherry and stir into turkey, simmer until thick. Serve over rice or noodles.

SERVES 2

*Oyster sauce is a commercial product found in the Oriental food section of many supermarkets.

MOOSE MEAT STEW

2¼ lbs	1 kg	moose meat, cut into ¾" cubes
1 cup	250 ml	flour
3 tbsp	45 ml	oil
20	20	pearl onions
1 cup	250 ml	coarse diced carrots
1 cup	250 ml	coarse diced turnips
1 cup	250 ml	coarse diced celery
2 cups	500 ml	Beef Stock (see page 85)
1 cup	250 ml	red wine
2 cups	500 ml	peeled, seeded and diced tomatoes
¼ tsp	1 ml	each of salt, pepper, basil, thyme, paprika
1 tsp	5 ml	Worcestershire sauce
4 cups	1 L	coarse diced potatoes

Dust the moose meat with the flour. Heat the oil in a Dutch oven, add the meat and brown. Add the remaining ingredients, except the potatoes. Reduce heat, cover and simmer gently for 1½ to 2 hours. Add the potatoes and continue to simmer for 30 additional minutes.

Serve with a green salad.

SERVES 8

BROILED GUINEA HENS

⅔ cup	160 ml	olive oil
⅓ cup	80 ml	lemon juice
⅓ cup	80 ml	sherry
2 tbsp	30 ml	crushed rosemary
2 tbsp	30 ml	basil leaves
1 tbsp	15 ml	thyme leaves
½ tsp	3 ml	each of sugar, pepper, salt
4 – 6 oz	4 – 175 g	boneless guinea hen breasts

Combine all the ingredients except the breasts in a mixing bowl.

Place the guinea hen in a shallow pan and pour sauce over. Cover and refrigerate for 6 hours.

Grill hens over medium coals for 6 minutes per side, brushing with marinade frequently. Brush one final time before serving.

SERVES 4

GRILLED MOOSE CHEF K

1 cup	250 ml	brown sugar
½ cup	125 ml	chili sauce
½ cup	125 ml	safflower oil
¼ cup	60 ml	vinegar
¼ cup	60 ml	lemon juice
1 tsp	5 ml	Dijon mustard
1 tsp	5 ml	onion juice
¼ tsp	1 ml	Tabasco™ sauce
1 tsp	5 ml	Worcestershire sauce
¼ tsp	1 ml	each of garlic powder, paprika, chili powder
½ tsp	3 ml	salt and pepper
4½ lbs	2 kg	moose steaks, ½" thick

Place all the ingredients except the moose steak in a blender and mix well.

In a large shallow pan layer the meat and sauce, marinate covered and refrigerated for 24 hours.

Grill on a charbroiler over medium coals for 20 minutes (10 per side) or to desired doneness. Brush several times with the marinade during grilling, serve at once.

SERVES 8

Moose Meat Stew

Broiled Deer Steak

GRILLED PHEASANT BREASTS CUMBERLAND

6 – 6 oz	6 – 170 g	boneless pheasant breasts
3 tbsp	45 ml	melted butter
		salt and pepper, to taste
Sauce:		
¾ cup	180 ml	red currant preserves
¾ cup	180 ml	orange juice
¼ cup	60 ml	lemon juice
¼ tsp	1 ml	ground ginger
2 tbsp	30 ml	cornstarch
2 tbsp	30 ml	water

Brush the pheasant breasts with the butter. Season with salt and pepper. Grill over medium heat or coals for 6-7 minutes per side.

While the pheasant grills, heat the red currant preserves in a sauce pan. Add the orange and lemon juices with the ginger. Bring to a boil. Blend the cornstarch with the water, add to sauce. Simmer until sauce is thickened.

Brush sauce over pheasant as it grills and 1 time before serving.

This is a very nice luncheon dish when served with an Orange and Almond Salad (see page 133).

SERVES 6

BROILED DEER STEAK

1 cup	250 ml	safflower oil
¼ cup	60 ml	garlic vinegar
2 tbsp	30 ml	lemon juice
2 tbsp	30 ml	minced onion
1	1	minced garlic clove
1 tsp	5 ml	each of salt, marjoram, basil, thyme
½ tsp	3 ml	cracked black pepper
6 – 8 oz	6 – 225 g	deer steaks

Blend all the ingredients except the steaks together. Place the steaks in a large shallow baking pan, pour the marinade over the steaks, marinate 4-6 hours covered and refrigerated.

Broil the steaks on a charbroiler over medium coals or flame to desired doneness.

SERVES 6

BUFFALO LOAF

4 lbs	1.75 kg	ground buffalo meat
1	1	minced onion
½	½	minced green bell pepper
3	3	minced celery stalks
3	3	beaten eggs
1 cup	250 ml	cooked oatmeal
½ cup	125 ml	cracker crumbs
½ cup	125 ml	catsup
1 tbsp	15 ml	Worcestershire sauce

Mix all the ingredients together, and shape into a loaf. Bake on a shallow baking sheet in a preheated 350°F (180°C) oven for 1¼ hours.

Serve with a Wild Mushroom Sherry Sauce (see page 105).

SERVES 8

Buffalo Loaf

VENISON GOULASH

2 tbsp	30 ml	butter
½ cup	125 ml	finely diced onion
3	3	minced garlic cloves
3 tbsp	45 ml	paprika
2¼ lbs	1 kg	deer meat, diced
4 cups	1 L	Beef Stock (see page 85)
1 tsp	5 ml	caraway seeds
½ tsp	3 ml	black pepper
2 cups	500 ml	peeled, seeded and chopped tomatoes
8 oz	225 g	button mushrooms
½ tsp	3 ml	oregano
1 tbsp	15 ml	cornstarch

Heat the butter in a large Dutch oven. Add the onion, garlic and paprika, sauté until the onion is tender. Brown the meat in the pan, then add the stock, caraway and pepper. Simmer covered for 1½ hours.

Add the tomatoes, mushrooms and oregano, continue to simmer for 40 minutes. Blend the cornstarch with a little water. Add to goulash and simmer until thickened.

Serve over noodles or rice.

SERVES 8

BARBECUED MUSK OX STEAKS WITH GARLIC CILANTRO BUTTER

6 – 8 oz	6 – 225 g	musk ox tenderloin steaks
1 tbsp	15 ml	chili powder
½ tsp	3 ml	each of oregano leaves, thyme leaves, basil leaves, onion powder, garlic powder, salt, white pepper, black pepper
¼ tsp	1 ml	cayenne pepper
½ cup	125 ml	butter
4	4	minced garlic cloves
½ cup	125 ml	fresh chopped cilantro
1 tsp	5 ml	Dijon mustard
1 tsp	5 ml	lemon zest
2 tbsp	30 ml	olive oil

Trim the steaks and place in a shallow pan.

Combine the seasonings and sprinkle over the steaks, cover and refrigerate for 1 hour.

Combine the butter with the garlic, cilantro, mustard and lemon. Spread on a sheet of wax paper and roll in cigar shape. Freeze for 1 hour.

Brush the steaks with the oil. Grill over medium coals until desired doneness (medium is best for ox).

Slice the butter in thick rounds. Place one round on each steak serving. Serve at once.

SERVES 6

Venison Goulash

Faisan au Vin

SAUTÉED QUAIL WITH CLEMENTINE SAUCE

12	12	quail
		salt and pepper to taste
3 tbsp	45 ml	safflower oil
⅓ cup	80 ml	clementine, tangerine or other orange juice concentrate
½ cup	125 ml	Chicken Stock (see page 77)
¼ cup	60 ml	whipping cream
1 tsp	5 ml	butter
1 tsp	5 ml	lime juice

Split the quail down the back, season lightly with salt and pepper.

Heat the oil in a large skillet. Sauté the quail for 6 minutes per side, reserve hot.

Heat the clementine juice in a sauce pan with the chicken stock, bring to a boil and reduce heat. Add the cream and simmer until sauce is reduced enough to coat a spoon. Remove from heat. Whip in the butter and lime juice.

Place chicken on a serving plate and cover with sauce and serve.

SERVES 6

FAISAN AU VIN

4 lbs	8 kg	pheasant – cut into pieces
4 tbsp	60 ml	flour, all purpose
¼ cup	60 ml	butter
¼ cup	60 ml	brandy
½ cup	125 ml	red wine
1 tsp	5 ml	thyme
1 tsp	5 ml	paprika
2 tsp	10 ml	salt
1½ cups	375 ml	Chicken Stock (see page 77)
4	4	slices of bacon
20	20	pearl onions
20	20	button mushrooms

Dust the pheasant with the flour. In a large skillet brown the pheasant in the butter over low heat. Tilt the pan away from you and flame with the brandy. Add the red wine, seasoning and chicken stock. Cover and simmer until the pheasant is tender, about 40 minutes.

In a sauce pan, brown diced bacon and sauté the onions and mushrooms. Drain any oil. Add to the pheasant and simmer 5 additional minutes. Cover and simmer until pheasant is tender about 40 minutes.

Serve with steamed rice or noodles.

SERVES 8

PHEASANT CORDON BLEU

6 – 6 oz	6 – 175 g	boneless pheasant breasts
6 oz	175 g	Black Forest ham
6 oz	175 g	Swiss cheese
2	2	eggs
¼ cup	60 ml	milk
½ cup	125 ml	flour, all purpose
2 cups	500 ml	seasoned bread crumbs
½ cup	125 ml	safflower oil
1 cup	250 ml	Mornay Sauce (see page 111)

Pound the breasts flat.

Place 1 oz (28 g) of ham and 1 oz (28 g) of cheese on the pheasant. Fold the breast to encase the ham and cheese. Place on a baking sheet and freeze for ½ hour.

Mix the eggs with the milk. Dust the pheasant with flour, dip into milk. Dredge in bread crumbs.

Heat the oil in a large skillet. Brown the pheasant on all sides. Transfer to a baking sheet.

Bake in preheated 350°F (180°C) oven for 10 minutes, place on serving plates and cover with sauce, serve at once with a rice pilaf.

SERVES 6

EASY GOURMET

I've entitled this chapter Easy Gourmet because within these pages there are some of the easiest and tastiest features that you will ever have wowed your guests with. I have attempted to give a cross section for exceptional dining no matter what time of day you may be entertaining.

For the gourmet dinner, impress the most fastidious guest with such dishes as Chicken Dermott or Cornish Hens in Wine Sauce. At lunch you can win over every critic with entrées like Louisiana Cioppino or Barbecued Shrimp with Chili Pepper Mayonnaise. At Sunday dinner your guests will flip over a Coca Cola Roast Beef, or a Smoked Turkey & Gorgonzola Lasagna. Perhaps you have been given the assignment of presenting the after party snacks; a spread of Chicken Apple Nuggets or Barbecued Scallops is certainly the party pleaser. Go oriental and serve a variety of sushi such as a California Roll, or Temaki Grilled Salmon, or give them a real Thai treat like Grilled Chicken and Shrimp Satay.

Being a gourmet doesn't mean being a stuffy perfectionist; it is the art of cooking what is right at the right time for the right people. Easy Gourmet allows you to serve exceptional cuisine that's just right all the time.

Perhaps it is a pasta your guests have a craving for. Serve them a Fettuccini Vongolé or a Spaghetti Ragu a la Bolognese. Whatever gourmet selection you choose, know for a certainty that it will be easy and *Simply Delicious.*

Hamburger Satay

SALMON À LA KING

¼ cup	60 ml	butter
½ cup	125 ml	diced green bell pepper
½ cup	125 ml	diced red bell pepper
4 oz	115 g	sliced mushrooms
½ cup	125 ml	flour
½ tsp	3 ml	salt
¼ tsp	1 ml	white pepper
1 cup	250 ml	Chicken Broth (see page 77)
1 cup	250 ml	milk
3 cups	750 ml	cooked salmon
1	1	egg yolk
3 cups	750 ml	steamed rice

In a large sauce pan, heat the butter. Sauté the peppers and mushrooms. Sprinkle with flour and cook 2 minutes.

Add the salt, pepper, broth and milk, reduce heat and simmer until sauce is thick.

Add the salmon and continue to simmer for 5 minutes.

Remove from heat and whisk in the egg yolk. Serve over rice.

SERVES 4

BARBECUED NEW YORK STRIPLOINS

½ cup	125 ml	red wine vinegar
1 tbsp	15 ml	Worcestershire sauce
1 tsp	5 ml	each of basil leaves, thyme leaves, oregano leaves
½ cup	125 ml	tomato catsup
2	2	minced garlic cloves
½ tsp	3 ml	liquid smoke flavouring
1 tbsp	15 ml	granulated sugar
6 – 8 oz	6 – 225 g	New York Striploin steaks

In a sauce pan, combine all the ingredients except the steaks of course.

Trim all the fat from the steaks. Cut away the small gristle strip, this will prevent the steaks from curling while cooking. Pour marinade over steaks and refrigerate, covered for 6 hours.

Grill the steaks over medium coals to desired doneness. Brush frequently with marinade.

SERVES 6

Salmon à la King

BARBECUE SAUTÉ

½ lb	225 g	pork tenderloin, diced
½ lb	225 g	large shrimp, peeled and deveined
½ lb	225 g	large scallops
2 tbsp	30 ml	butter
2 tbsp	30 ml	safflower oil
1 cup	250 ml	Barbecue Sauce (recipe follows)

Fry the meat and seafood in the butter and oil in a large skillet. Pour the sauce over the meat and simmer for 10 minutes. Serve over rice or noodles.

SERVES 6

Sauce:		
2	2	garlic cloves
1	1	Spanish onion, minced
2 tbsp	30 ml	butter
2 tbsp	30 ml	oil
1 cup	250 ml	brown sugar
2 tsp	10 ml	Worcestershire sauce
½ tsp	3 ml	each of thyme leaves, oregano leaves, chervil, cumin, paprika, black pepper, white pepper
1 tbsp	15 ml	chili powder
1 tsp	5 ml	salt
2 cups	500 ml	tomato catsup
2 tsp	10 ml	lemon juice

In a sauce pan, sauté the garlic and onion in the butter and oil. Combine the remaining ingredients and add. Reduce heat and simmer 15-20 minutes, stirring occasionally.

YIELDS 3 CUPS (750 ML)

Barbeque Sauté

Lasagna Roll Ups

LASAGNA ROLL UPS

Sauce:		
3 tbsp	45 ml	olive oil
1	1	minced garlic clove
1	1	finely diced medium onion
2	2	finely diced celery stalks
4 oz	115 g	sliced mushrooms
1 tsp	5 ml	each of salt, basil leaves
½ tsp	3 ml	each of thyme leaves, oregano leaves, paprika, pepper
¼ tsp	1 ml	cayenne pepper
3 lb	1.3 kg	peeled, seeded and chopped tomatoes

Pasta:		
1 quan	1	Pasta Verde (see page 436)
1½ cups	375 ml	ricotta cheese
1½ cups	375 ml	grated cheddar cheese
3 tbsp	45 ml	chopped chives
1 tsp	5 ml	basil leaves
½ tsp	3 ml	each of cracked black pepper, salt
2	2	eggs

Sauce:

In a large sauce pan, heat the oil. Add the garlic, onion, celery, and mushrooms, sauté until tender.

Add the seasonings and tomatoes. Simmer over low heat for 3 hours or until desired thickness is achieved.

Pasta:

Process pasta as directed, cut into lasagna noodles.

In a mixing bowl, blend the cheeses with the seasonings and eggs.

Spoon mixture onto noodles and roll in a jelly roll fashion.

Place in a baking dish, cover with sauce and bake in a 375°F (190°C) preheated oven for 30 minutes, covered. Remove cover and continue to bake for an additional 15 minutes. Serve.

SERVES 6

Blackberry Brandy Grilled Chicken

BLACKBERRY BRANDY GRILLED CHICKEN

2 cups	500 ml	blackberries
1½ cups	375 ml	granulated sugar
½ cup	125 ml	blackberry brandy
1 tbsp	15 ml	oil
4 – 6 oz	4 – 175 g	boneless chicken breasts

Purée the berries in a food processor. Pass through a sieve to remove seeds.

Mix the blackberry pulp, sugar and brandy together in a sauce pan. Heat to a boil, reduce heat and simmer until sauce thickens.

Brush the oil over the chicken. Grill chicken for 8 minutes per side, brushing frequently with the sauce. Brush 1 final time before serving.

SERVES 4

SUSHI

Here is a selection of 4 different varieties of the famous Japanese food.

SUSHI RICE

1 cup	250 ml	water
¾ cup	180 ml	short grain rice
1½ tbsp	25 ml	vinegar
1½ tbsp	25 ml	lemon juice
2 tbsp	30 ml	sugar
½ tsp	3 ml	salt

Bring the water to a boil and add the rice. Reduce heat. Cover and cook until rice absorbs the liquid.

In a small sauce pan, combine the vinegar, lemon juice, sugar and salt. Bring to a boil, reduce heat and simmer until sugar is dissolved.

Pour into rice. Let stand until liquid is absorbed by rice. Cool.

CALIFORNIA ROLL SUSHI

1	1	sheet of nori, cut in half
1 cup	250 ml	Sushi Rice (see recipe, this page)
1 tsp	5 ml	Dijon mustard
1 small	1 small	finely sliced cucumber
1	1	sliced fine avocado
1 cup	250 ml	cooked crab meat

Lay the nori flat, spread with a thin layer of rice.

Turn over and spread with mustard.

Layer with cucumber, avocado and crab meat. Roll in jelly roll fashion.

Wrap with a piece of plastic wrap. Roll tightly, remove wrap and cut into 8 slices. Serve.

SERVES 4

EBI PRAWNS

1 lb	454 g	large prawns
4 cups	1 L	water
1 cup	250 ml	white wine
1	1	lemon
1	1	small onion
1	1	celery stalk
1 tsp	5 ml	salt
½ tsp	3 ml	peppercorns
1½ cups	375 ml	Sushi Rice (see recipe, this page)

Skewer the prawns with bamboo skewers along the underside of the prawn.

In a large pot, bring to a boil the water, wine, lemon, onion, celery and seasonings.

Place the skewered shrimp into boiling liquid. Remove the shrimp once they float. Drop them into ice cold water. Once cooled, remove skewer and peel away the shell, leaving the tail tip.

Butterfly the shrimp by cutting along the middle from the underside. Do not cut through.

Place small amounts of rice in the cut and wrap the shrimp around it.

Serve at once.

SERVES 4

California Roll Sushi, Ebi Prawns & Temaki Grilled Salmon Sushi

CREAM CHEESE SMOKED SALMON SUSHI

1	1	piece nori 7" x 8" (18 x 20 cm)
1½ cups	375 ml	Sushi Rice (recipe on previous page)
2 oz	60 g	smoked salmon
4 oz	115 g	cream cheese
1	1	julienne cut spring onion

Place a piece of nori on a slightly damp tea towel. Top with rice. Pack down firmly.

Place a generous portion of salmon along a short end. Beside it, place a strip of cream cheese and onion.

Roll in jelly roll fashion. Using a very sharp knife, cut into 1" (2.5 cm) slices. Serve.

YIELDS 8 SLICES

TEMAKI GRILLED SALMON SUSHI

8 oz	225 g	salmon fillet
1	1	sheet nori
1 cup	250 ml	Sushi Rice (recipe on previous page)
1	1	pared, julienne cut carrot
1 small	1 small	julienne cut cucumber
1 oz	28 g	alfalfa sprouts

Grill or broil the salmon, skin side down. Once cooked, cut the fish into julienne strips.

Cut the nori into 8 pieces. Place small amounts of the remaining ingredients on the nori and wrap in a conical shape. Serve.

SERVES 4

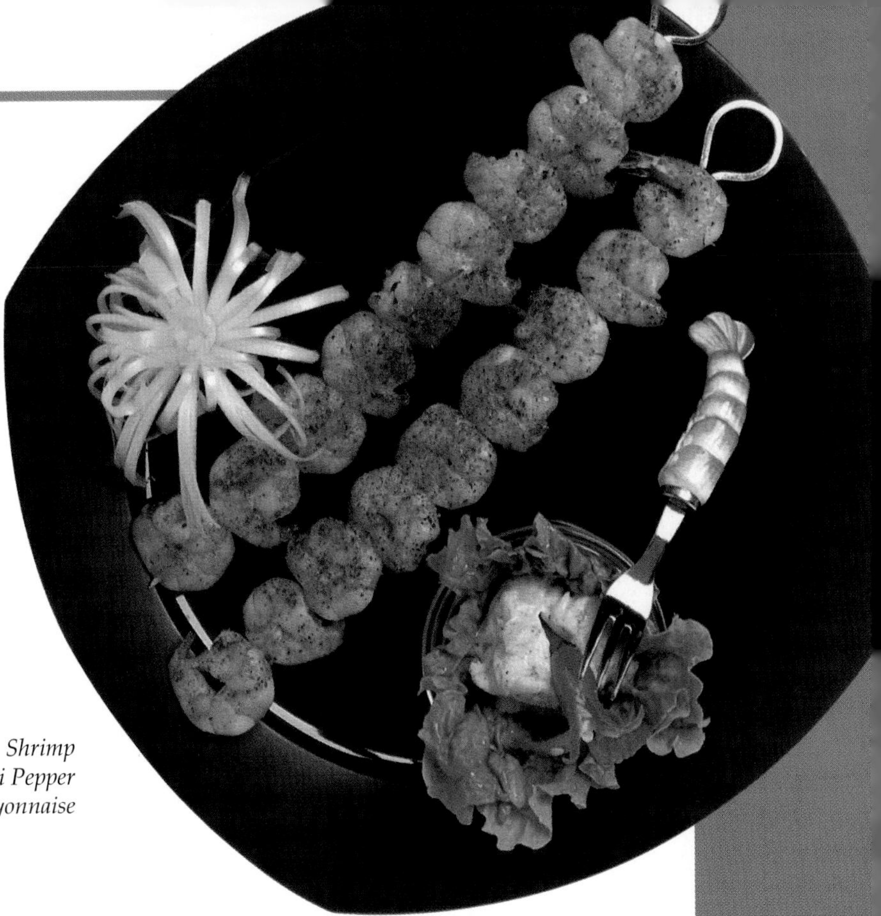

Barbecued Shrimp with Chili Pepper Mayonnaise

BARBECUED SHRIMP WITH CHILI PEPPER MAYONNAISE

Shrimp:		
2 lb	900 g	large shrimp
1 tbsp	15 ml	chili powder
½ tsp	3 ml	each of basil leaves, oregano leaves, thyme leaves, onion powder, garlic powder, cayenne pepper, black pepper
1 tsp	5 ml	salt

Mayonnaise:		
2	2	egg yolks
1 cup	250 ml	safflower oil
1 tbsp	15 ml	lemon juice
¼ tsp	1 ml	salt
1 tbsp	15 ml	chili powder
3 drops	3 drops	Tabasco™ sauce

Shrimp:

Peel and devein the shrimp. Skewer with bamboo skewers.

Mix the seasonings together.

Sprinkle seasoning on shrimp and grill for 4 minutes on each side. Serve with mayonnaise.

Mayonnaise:

Place the egg yolks in a blender. With the machine running very slowly, add the oil until a thick sauce is formed. Add the lemon juice, salt, chili powder and Tabasco. Turn machine off, pour sauce into a small bowl, serve with shrimp.

SERVES 6

Chicken Dermott

Louisiana Cioppino

CHICKEN DERMOTT

6 – 6 oz	6 – 175 g	boneless chicken breasts
½ cup	125 ml	crab meat
4 oz	115 g	smoked salmon cream cheese
1	1	egg
¼ cup	60 ml	milk
⅓ cup	80 ml	flour
1½ cups	375 ml	seasoned bread crumbs
½ cup	125 ml	safflower oil
½ cup	125 ml	red currant preserves
¼ cup	60 ml	Marsala wine
2 tsp	10 ml	lemon juice
12 oz	345 g	raspberries
1 tbsp	15 ml	cornstarch
2 tbsp	30 ml	water
½ tsp	3 ml	cracked black pepper

Place the chicken breasts between two sheets of waxed paper and pound thin.

Top chicken with 2 tbsp (30 ml) each of crab meat and cheese. Roll together and freeze for 30 minutes.

Combine the egg with the milk. Dust the chicken in the flour, dip into the milk and dredge through the bread crumbs.

Heat the oil in a skillet and fry the chicken to golden brown. Place on a baking sheet and bake in a preheated 375°F (190°C) oven for 35 minutes.

While chicken bakes, place the red currant preserves in a small sauce pan. Add the wine and lemon juice and simmer over low heat.

Purée the berries in a food processor, then pass through a sieve to remove the seeds. Add to sauce and bring to a boil.

Mix the cornstarch with the water, add to sauce and simmer until sauce thickens. Stir in the pepper.

Remove chicken from oven, place on serving plates. Cover chicken with sauce and serve.

SERVES 6

LOUISIANA CIOPPINO

3 tbsp	45 ml	butter
1	1	sliced red bell pepper
1	1	sliced green bell pepper
1	1	sliced small onion
1	1	minced garlic cloves
1 tbsp	15 ml	chopped fresh parsley
2 cups	500 ml	peeled, seeded, chopped tomatoes
4 cups	1 L	Fish Broth (see page 76)
2 cups	500 ml	white wine
¼ lb	115 g	peeled and deveined shrimp
½ lb	225 g	sliced red snapper
¼ lb	115 g	crayfish tails
¼ lb	115 g	clams, in shell
¼ lb	115 g	crab claws
1	1	bouquet garni (see Glossary)

In a large Dutch oven or kettle, heat the butter. Add the vegetables and sauté until tender. Add the parsley, tomatoes, broth and wine. Bring to a boil, reduce heat and simmer for 10 minutes.

Add the fish, seafood, and bouquet garni. Cover and simmer for 15 minutes.

Discard the bouquet garni and serve the stew.

SERVES 6

CHICKEN FINGERS

1 lb	450 g	chicken breasts, boneless
2 cups	500 ml	fine bread crumbs
2 tsp	10 ml	oregano leaves, dried
2 tsp	10 ml	basil leaves, dried
1 tsp	5 ml	salt
1 tbsp	15 ml	chili powder
1 tsp	3 ml	each of paprika, pepper, onion powder, garlic powder
2	2	eggs
¼ cup	60 ml	milk
½ cup	125 ml	flour
4 cups	1 L	safflower oil
1 cup	250 ml	plum sauce, commercial type

Cut the chicken breasts into 1" (2.5 cm) strips.

Mix the bread crumbs with the seasonings.

Beat the eggs into the milk. Place the flour into a small bowl.

Preheat the oil to 375°F (190°C).

Dust the chicken strips with flour. Dip them into the egg mixture. Dredge through the bread crumbs.

Fry the strips in the oil for 10 minutes. Place on a paper towel to absorb excess oils. Transfer to a serving platter. Serve with plum sauce on the side.

SERVES 4

Blackened Shrimp with Garlic Parmesan Linguini

BLACKENED SHRIMP WITH GARLIC PARMESAN LINGUINI

Do this outside on your gas barbecue; it's very smoky.

1 quan	1	Cracked Black Pepper Pasta (see page 432)
1 lb	454 g	peeled and deveined large shrimp
1 tbsp	15 ml	each of salt, chili powder
1 tsp	5 ml	each of thyme leaves, oregano leaves, basil, black pepper, paprika, chervil,
½ tsp	3 ml	each of white pepper, cayenne pepper
¼ cup	60 ml	safflower oil
⅓ cup	80 ml	butter
3	3	minced garlic cloves
3 tbsp	45 ml	lemon juice
½ cup	125 ml	grated Parmesan cheese
2 tbsp	30 ml	fresh chopped parsley

Prepare pasta as per instructions, cut into linguini.

Rinse the shrimp under cold water, drain. Blend the seasonings together.

Dust the shrimp in the seasonings. Heat the oil to very hot just before the smoking point. Fry the shrimp in the hot oil for 3 minutes. Transfer to a platter and reserve.

Cook the pasta in a large kettle of boiling water. While the pasta cooks, heat the butter in a skillet. Add the garlic and lemon juice and cook for 3 minutes. Drain pasta and pour butter over, sprinkle with cheese and toss to coat.

Place on serving plates, top with shrimp and sprinkle with parsley. Serve.

SERVES 4

Chicken Fingers

Jack Daniel's Sour Mash Ribs

HAMBURGER SATAY

1 lb	454 g	lean ground beef
¼ cup	60 ml	seasoned bread crumbs
1	1	egg
¼ cup	60 ml	peanut oil
1½ tbsp	20 ml	ground Brazil nuts
½ tsp	3 ml	ground ginger
½ tsp	3 ml	ground coriander
2 tsp	10 ml	molasses
½ tsp	3 ml	each of black pepper, paprika, cayenne pepper, salt, thyme leaves, oregano leaves, red pepper flakes
4 tsp	20 ml	lime juice
3 tbsp	45 ml	hot water

In a mixing bowl, blend the beef with the bread crumbs and egg. Shape into small balls and skewer with bamboo skewers. Place on a baking sheet.

Blend the remaining ingredients together in a mixing bowl. Pour over the meat balls. Refrigerate for 3½ hours.

Grill the skewers over medium high heat for 10-12 minutes or until meat is cooked through.

Serve at once.

SERVES 4

JACK DANIEL'S SOUR MASH RIBS

Sauce:		
3 tbsp	45 ml	butter
3 tbsp	45 ml	oil
1	1	minced onion
1	1	garlic clove, minced
⅔ cup	160 ml	tomato catsup
⅔ cup	160 ml	Jack Daniels Sour Mash Whiskey
½ cup	125 ml	cider vinegar
½ cup	125 ml	peach juice
½ cup	125 ml	peach syrup
⅓ cup	80 ml	light molasses
1 tbsp	15 ml	Worcestershire sauce
½ tsp	3 ml	each of thyme leaves, basil leaves, chervil, oregano leaves, garlic powder, cracked black pepper, white pepper, paprika, salt
½ tsp	3 ml	liquid smoke flavouring

Ribs:		
10 lb	4.4 kg	Danish or baby back pork ribs
½ tsp	3 ml	each of thyme leaves, oregano leaves, basil, savory, sage
1 tsp	5 ml	each of pepper, paprika, chili powder, salt

Sauce:

Heat the butter in a sauce pan with the oil, add the onion and garlic. Sauté until tender. Stir in the remaining ingredients and bring to a boil. Reduce heat and simmer until sauce is very thick. Cool.

Ribs:

Cut the ribs into 5 bone sections.

Combine the seasonings and sprinkle over ribs.

Bake in a preheated 350°F (180°C) oven for ½ hour.

Grill over medium coals, brushing frequently with sauce for 10 minutes. Brush one final time then serve.

SERVES 8

Hamburger Satay

CHICKEN MARENGO

1	1	chicken fryer, cut into 8 pieces
⅓ cup	80 ml	safflower oil
4	4	pared, sliced carrots
2	2	diced celery stalks
1	1	diced small onion
6	6	rashers of bacon
⅓ cup	80 ml	flour
4 cups	1 L	peeled, seeded, diced tomatoes
¼ cup	60 ml	sherry
½ tsp	3 ml	salt
¼ tsp	1 ml	pepper
1	1	bouquet garni*
¼ lb	115 g	sliced mushrooms
2 tbsp	30 ml	chopped parsley
3 cups	750 ml	steamed rice

Preheat the oven to 350°F (180°C).

Sauté the chicken in the oil for 5 minutes. Remove and place in casserole dish.

Dice the bacon and sauté in a sauce pan, add flour, reduce heat and cook for 4 minutes. Add the vegetables and continue to cook until vegetables are tender. Add tomatoes, sherry and seasonings, cook for 10 minutes over low heat. Pour sauce and bouquet garni over chicken, top with mushrooms, cover and bake for 1 hour.

Sprinkle with parsley and serve with hot rice.

SERVES 4

* Bouquet garni for chicken is thyme leaves, oregano leaves, basil, a bay leaf, rosemary sprig, marjoram and 6 peppercorns tied together in a cheesecloth. J Cloth also works well.

Chicken Marengo

PAUL NORTHCOTT'S COCA-COLA ROAST BEEF

5 lbs	2 kg	bottom round
1 tbsp	15 ml	each of salt, chili powder
1 tsp	5 ml	each of thyme leaves, basil leaves, oregano leaves, paprika, black pepper, chervil, dry mustard
1 tbsp	15 ml	Worcestershire sauce
2 cups	500 ml	Coca-Cola soft drink – do not use diet cola

Place the roast in a large roasting pan. Blend the seasonings together. Pour Worcestershire over the beef and sprinkle with the seasonings. Pour the coke along the side of the beef.

Bake in a preheated 375°F (190°C) oven for 30 minutes, reduce temperature to 300°F (150°C) and continue to bake for 3 hours.

Remove beef, slice and serve.

SERVES 8

Paul Northcott's Coca-Cola Roast Beef

FETTUCCINI VONGOLÉ

1 quan	1	Pasta Verde (see page 436)
3 tbsp	45 ml	butter
3 tbsp	45 ml	flour
1¼ cups	310 ml	clam nectar or Chicken Broth (see page 77)
1¼ cups	310 ml	half & half cream
1½ cups	375 ml	chopped clams
½ tsp	3 ml	salt
½ tsp	3 ml	white pepper
⅔ cup	160 ml	freshly grated Romano cheese

Process the pasta as directed, cut into fettuccini.

In a sauce pan, heat the butter and add the flour. Reduce heat and cook for 2 minutes.

Add the clam nectar and cream, simmer into a thick sauce. Add the clams and seasonings, continue to simmer for 10 minutes.

Cook the noodles in a large kettle of salted water. Drain and place on serving plates.

Add half the cheese to the sauce, ladle sauce over noodles. Sprinkle with remaining cheese and serve at once.

SERVES 6

STEAK 'N' CHICKEN FAJITAS

12 oz	340 g	top sirloin
12 oz	340 g	boneless chicken
3	3	minced garlic cloves
2	2	sliced Spanish onions
2	2	minced serrano chilies
¼ cup	60 ml	chopped cilantro
⅓ cup	80 ml	lime juice
⅓ cup	80 ml	lemon juice
3 tbsp	45 ml	butter
1	1	sliced green bell pepper
1	1	sliced red bell pepper
1	1	sliced yellow bell pepper
3 oz	85 g	sliced mushrooms
1 tbsp	15 ml	each of salt, chili powder
2 tsp	10 ml	each of paprika, onion powder, garlic powder, basil leaves,
1 tsp	5 ml	each of dry mustard, cumin, black pepper, white pepper, thyme leaves
12	12	large tortillas
½ cup	125 ml	sour cream
1 cup	250 ml	Salsa Sauce (see page 115)

Slice the steak and chicken in thin strips. Place each in separate mixing bowls. Cover each with half the onions slices, chilies, cilantro, lemon and lime juice. Marinate for 4 hours.

Grill meats over medium coals for 2-3 minutes.

In a large skillet, melt the butter and sauté the remaining onion, peppers and mushrooms.

Blend the seasonings together and season both the meats and vegetables while they cook.

Place meats and vegetables on very hot serving platters, serve with tortillas, sour cream and salsa so that your guests may construct their own. Also good with Guacamole Sauce (see page 115).

SERVES 6

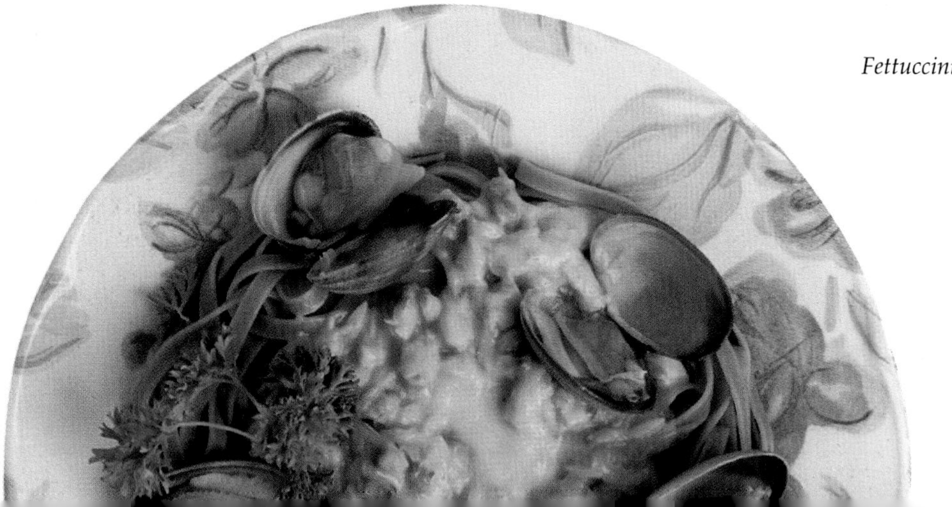

Fettuccini Vongolé

Steak 'n' Chicken Fajitas

GRILLED CHICKEN AND SHRIMP SATAY

12 oz	340 g	peeled and deveined large shrimp
12 oz	340 g	cubed boneless chicken
3 tbsp	45 ml	butter
¼ cup	60 ml	olive oil
4	4	chopped green onions
2	2	minced garlic cloves
1 tbsp	15 ml	chopped parsley
1 cup	250 ml	white wine
2 tbsp	30 ml	lemon juice
2 tbsp	30 ml	lime juice

Sauce:

¼ cup	60 ml	butter
1	1	diced finely Spanish onion,
1 tsp	5 ml	each of thyme leaves, basil, salt, crushed rosemary
¼ tsp	1 ml	cayenne pepper
2 cups	500 ml	Chicken Broth (see page 77)
1 tbsp	15 ml	lemon juice
1 tbsp	15 ml	lime juice
2 cups	500 ml	chunky style peanut butter – use no substitute
3 tbsp	45 ml	brown sugar

Skewer the shrimp and chicken with water soaked bamboo skewers. Place into a large shallow pan.

Heat the butter and oil in a sauce pan and sauté the green onions and garlic until tender. Place into a mixing bowl, combine with the parsley, white wine and juices. Pour over skewers. Marinate for 4 hours.

Sauce:

Heat the butter in a small sauce pan and sauté the onion until tender. Add the remaining ingredients and simmer 20 minutes, stirring constantly.

Grill skewers for 3 minutes per side over medium coals. Brush with sauce and serve. Serve remaining sauce on the side.

SERVES 6

SHEPHERD'S PIE

3 tbsp	45 ml	safflower oil
1 lb	450 g	lean ground beef
1	1	minced onion
2	2	minced celery stalks
2	2	pared, minced carrots
3 oz	85 g	sliced mushrooms
1	1	minced garlic clove
¼ cup	60 ml	flour
1½ cups	375 ml	Beef Broth (see page 85)
2 tbsp	30 ml	tomato paste
1 tsp	5 ml	Worcestershire sauce
½ tsp	3 ml	each of thyme leaves, chervil, salt, paprika, pepper
2 cups	500 ml	creamed corn
4 cups	1 L	hot mashed potatoes
2 cups	500 ml	grated sharp cheddar

In a large skillet, heat the oil. Fry the ground beef. Add the vegetables and sauté until vegetables are tender.

Sprinkle with flour and continue to cook for 2 minutes. Add the broth, tomato paste, Worcestershire and seasonings. Simmer until thick.

Spoon into a large casserole dish. Cover mixture with the creamed corn. Spread mashed potatoes over the corn. Sprinkle cheese over top.

Bake in a preheated 400°F (200°C) oven for 15 minutes or until cheese is golden brown.

SERVES 6

Shepherd's Pie

Grilled Chicken & Shrimp Satay

Smoked Turkey & Gorgonzola Lasagna

SMOKED TURKEY & GORGONZOLA LASAGNA

1 quan	1	Basic Pasta Dough (see page 462)
3 tbsp	45 ml	butter
3 tbsp	45 ml	olive oil
1	1	Spanish onion
3	3	diced stalks celery
1	1	diced red bell pepper
1	1	diced green bell pepper
3 oz	85 g	sliced mushrooms
¼ lb	115 g	hot Italian sausage
3 cups	750 ml	peeled, seeded, chopped tomatoes
½ tsp	3 ml	each of thyme leaves, basil leaves, onion powder, garlic powder, paprika, black pepper
1 tsp	5 ml	each of salt, chili powder
2 tsp	10 ml	Worcestershire sauce
½ lb	225 g	diced smoked turkey
1 cup	250 ml	ricotta cheese
¾ cup	180 ml	crumbled Gorgonzola
2	2	eggs
2 cups	500 ml	grated mozzarella cheese
¾ cup	180 ml	grated cheddar cheese
⅓ cup	80 ml	grated Parmesan cheese

Process the pasta dough as per instructions. Cut into lasagna noodles.

In a large Dutch oven or kettle, heat the butter and oil. Add the vegetables and sausage. Sauté until vegetables are tender. Add the tomatoes, seasonings and Worcestershire. Reduce heat and simmer for 35 minutes. Add the turkey and continue to simmer for 25 minutes.

Combine the ricotta, Gorgonzola and eggs.

In a large, greased casserole dish, alternate layers of pasta, sauce and cheese mixture. Be sure to finish with a layer of sauce.

Sprinkle the remaining cheeses over the top. Bake for 45 minutes in a preheated 375°F (190°C) oven. Remove from oven and serve.

SERVES 8

Barbecued Scallops

BARBECUED SCALLOPS

24	24	scallops, large
12	12	bacon rashers, hickory smoked
½ cup	125 ml	onion, minced
3 tbsp	45 ml	canola oil
1 cup	250 ml	tomato sauce
⅓ cup	80 ml	water
3 tbsp	45 ml	lemon juice
2 tsp	10 ml	Worcestershire sauce
½ tsp	3 ml	Tabasco™ sauce
1 tsp	5 ml	basil leaves
½ tsp	3 ml	each of chili powder, paprika, thyme, pepper, salt

Wash and pat dry the scallops.

Slice the bacon in half. Wrap one scallop with a piece of bacon. Skewer six scallops on bamboo skewers. Broil on a grill or in the oven for 10 minutes, turning frequently.

Sauté the onions in a small pan with the oil. Add the remaining ingredients. Bring to a boil, reduce heat and simmer for 15 minutes. Brush scallops with sauce. Serve at once.

SERVES 4

CORNISH HENS IN WINE SAUCE

4 – 12 oz	4 – 345 g	Cornish game hens split in half
24	24	pearl onions
4	4	julienne cut carrots
¼ cup	60 ml	butter
1 cup	250 ml	red wine
½ cup	125 ml	sherry
¼ cup	60 ml	brandy
½ cup	125 ml	Chicken Stock (see page 77)
24	24	button mushrooms
½ tsp	3 ml	salt
¼ tsp	1 ml	pepper
¼ lb	115 g	diced bacon
3 tbsp	45 ml	flour

In a large kettle or Dutch oven, heat the butter. Sauté the hens until they turn brown, remove and reserve. Add the vegetables to the butter and sauté. Sprinkle with flour, reduce heat and cook for 4 minutes or until golden brown.

Return the hens, pour the liquids over. Add the mushrooms and seasonings. Simmer for 20 minutes.

In a skillet, fry the bacon. Sprinkle with flour and cook for 2 minutes, stir into chicken.

Pour chicken into a large casserole dish, cover and bake in a preheated oven for 1 hour. Serve with rice, and a half hen per person.

SERVES 8

CHICKEN APPLE NUGGETS

2 lbs	900 g	boneless chicken
½ tsp	3 ml	each of oregano leaves, thyme leaves, basil, garlic powder, onion powder, paprika,
2 tsp	10 ml	each of salt, chili powder
2 cups	500 ml	flour
1½ cups	375 ml	milk
4 cups	1 L	safflower oil
1 lb	454 g	pared, cored, diced apples
3 tbsp	45 ml	butter
1 tbsp	15 ml	lemon juice
1 tbsp	15 ml	lime juice
¼ cup	60 ml	granulated sugar

Dice the chicken into even size cubes. Combine the seasonings with the flour.

Dip the chicken into the milk then into the flour. Heat the oil to 375°F (190°C). Drop the chicken into the oil and fry 2-3 minutes. Reserve hot.

Place the apples in a large sauce pan. Add the butter, juices and sugar. Cover and cook over low heat until apples are tender. Purée in a food processor.

Serve chicken with apple sauce on the side.

SERVES 8

Chicken Apple Nuggets

SPAGHETTI RAGÙ A LA BOLOGNESE

3 tbsp	45 ml	olive oil
10 oz	280 g	extra lean ground beef
4 oz	115 g	ground pork
4 oz	115 g	ground veal
4 oz	115 g	bacon diced
1	1	large finely diced Spanish onion
2	2	large, pared, finely, diced carrots
2	2	finely diced stalks celery
1	1	minced garlic clove
½ cup	125 ml	fresh chopped parsley
¼ cup	60 ml	tomato paste
1 cup	250 ml	Beef Broth (see page 85)
1½ cups	375 ml	white wine
1 tsp	5 ml	salt
½ tsp	3 ml	each of oregano, thyme, basil, black pepper
1	1	bay leaf
1 tsp	5 ml	Worcestershire sauce
4 cups	1 L	salted water
½ quan	0.5	Basic Pasta Dough (see page 426), cut into spaghetti
⅓ cup	80 ml	Parmesan cheese, grated

In a large skillet heat the oil. Fry the meats thoroughly, drain excess oil. Add the vegetables and continue to cook until vegetables are tender. Add the parsley, tomato, broth, wine, seasonings and Worcestershire. Reduce heat and simmer for 30 minutes. Discard the bay leaf.

While sauce simmers boil the water in a large pot or Dutch oven. Cook the spaghetti for 9 minutes or until al denté, if using dried pasta; half the time for fresh pasta, drain and place on serving plates. Spoon sauce over, sprinkle with cheese and serve at once.

SERVES 4

Cornish Hens in Wine Sauce

*E*GG DISHES

Eggs—for breakfast, lunch and dinner. Eggs have come into their rightful culinary position and have cracked their way to the top of delightful cuisine. Many who have regimented the egg to a place where it only comes out at breakfast or perhaps during baking have thought of it in a very limited way. Egg-citing new culinary treats created by imaginative cooks are making the humble egg more egg-ceptional than any other food item.

Eggs are being offered to guests in more and more egg-travagant ways, showing the guest the classic and novelle possibilities of what was held in ignominy. Eggs have risen to new heights that even the most perfect of soufflés could not imagine.

In *Simply Delicious Cooking 2*, we have given you new ways to show your guest what is really egging you on. They will eggs-claim your praises while they bite into such dishes as Oeufs Poches a la Bourguignonne or an Omelette a la Jardiniere.

Eggs are not complicated to prepare; it takes but minutes to offer your guest the eggs-perience of a life time. So get cracking, and make your next egg meal one that is *Simply Delicious*.

Eggs Bellay

EGGS NERO

1 lb	450 g	minced cooked chicken meat
¼ cup	60 ml	chopped green onion
2 tbsp	30 ml	butter
½ cup	125 ml	flour
½ cup	125 ml	heavy cream
¼ cup	60 ml	sherry
1 tbsp	15 ml	chopped parsley
1 tsp	5 ml	chopped chervil
7	7	eggs
¼ cup	60 ml	milk
1½ cups	375 ml	seasoned bread crumbs
½ cup	125 ml	safflower oil
2 cups	500 ml	hot Tomato Sauce II (see page 117)

Mix the chicken with the green onion in a mixing bowl.

Heat the butter in a sauce pan. Add 2 tbsp (30 ml) of flour. Cook 2 minutes over low heat. Add the cream, sherry, parsley and chervil. Cook into a very thick sauce. Pour over the chicken and blend well. Cool.

Once cooled, shape into round, flat croquettes. Mix one egg with the milk. Dust the croquettes with remaining flour, dip into the egg wash, then roll in the seasoned bread crumbs.

Heat the oil in a skillet and fry the croquettes until golden brown on each side.

While croquettes fry, poach the remaining eggs. Place a little sauce on a serving plate, float a croquette on the sauce. Top with an egg and serve.

SERVES 6

Eggs Nero

EGGS DUBARRY

1 cup	250 ml	minced cauliflower
1½ cups	375 ml	hot Mornay Sauce (see page 111)
8	8	eggs
8- 3"	8- 7.5 cm	blind baked tart shells
1 cup	250 ml	grated medium cheddar

Steam the cauliflower until very tender.

Stir the cauliflower into the mornay sauce.

Poach the eggs. Place an egg in each tart shell and smother with sauce. Sprinkle with cheese. Place on a baking sheet. Broil in a preheated oven until cheese melts. Serve very hot.

SERVES 4

EGGS BALTIC STYLE

8	8	eggs
8 – 3"	8 – 3"	blind baked tart shells
2 tbsp	30 ml	red caviar
2 tbsp	30 ml	black caviar
1½ cups	375 ml	hot Mornay Sauce (see page 111)
1 cup	250 ml	grated sharp cheddar

Poach the eggs, place in a tart shell, and sprinkle with caviar. Place shell on a baking sheet.

Cover the eggs with mornay sauce and sprinkle with cheddar. Place beneath a preheated oven broiler. Broil until cheese melts. Serve very hot.

SERVES 4

Eggs Dubarry

Bombay Eggs

EGGS CHEF K STYLE

8 - 3"	8 - 7.5 cm	baked blind tart shells
1 cup	250 ml	cooked crayfish tails or shrimp meat
1 cup	250 ml	grated medium cheddar cheese
8	8	eggs
1½ cups	375 ml	hot cheese sauce
2 tbsp	30 ml	red caviar
2 tbsp	30 ml	black caviar

Place the crayfish tails into the tart shells. Sprinkle with cheese and bake in a preheated 400°F (200°C) oven for 4-5 minutes.

While shells bake, poach the eggs. Place 1 egg in each tart shell. Cover with cheese sauce, sprinkle with caviar and serve at once.

SERVES 4

FARMER'S OMELETTE

2	2	eggs
2 tbsp	30 ml	light cream
1 tbsp	15 ml	chopped sorrel
1 tbsp	15 ml	safflower oil
4	4	diced bacon slices
⅓ cup	80 ml	cold, sliced, boiled potatoes
⅓ cup	80 ml	grated medium cheddar

Beat the eggs with the cream and sorrel.

Heat the oil in a skillet, add the bacon and fry until crisp. Remove bacon and reserve the fat. Fry the potatoes in the fat until the potatoes are golden brown. Fold in the egg mixture. Sprinkle with bacon. Cook on 1 side until omelette is set, turn over and complete cooking.

Sprinkle with cheese and broil for 1 minute in a preheated oven broiler. Serve flat.

SERVES 1

Farmer's Omelette

BOMBAY EGGS

RICE:		
2 tbsp	30 ml	butter
1	1	small, finely diced onion
¼ cup	60 ml	finely diced red bell pepper
¼ cup	60 ml	finely diced green bell pepper
½ cup	125 ml	sliced mushrooms
¼ cup	60 ml	finely diced celery
1 tsp	5 ml	curry powder
1 cup	250 ml	short grain rice
3½ cups	875 ml	Chicken Broth (see page 77) or Vegetable Broth (see page 92)

Heat the butter in a large sauce pan. Add the vegetables and curry powder. Sauté until tender. Add the rice and stock, cover and simmer until rice is completely cooked.

EGGS:		
1 tsp	5 ml	curry powder
2 cups	500 ml	hot Mornay Sauce (see page 111)
8	8	eggs

Whip the curry powder into the mornay sauce. Poach the eggs. Place the rice on a serving platter as a bed for the eggs, top with the eggs, cover with sauce and serve at once.

SERVES 4

PASTOR'S EGGS

6 - 3"	6 - 7.5 cm	blind baked tart shells
2 cups	500 ml	cooked shrimp meat
6	6	eggs
1 cup	250 ml	Hollandaise Sauce (see page 114)
1 cup	250 ml	grated Havarti cheese

Divide the shrimp meat into the tart shells.

Poach the eggs and place on top of the shrimp. Smother with sauce and sprinkle with cheese. Place on a baking sheet. Place under a preheated oven broiler until golden brown. Serve hot.

SERVES 6

OMELETTE OF FINE HERBS AND CHEESE

3	3	eggs
3 tbsp	45 ml	light cream
¼ tsp	1 ml	each of chives, chervils, basil, parsley
⅛ tsp	pinch	salt and pepper
1 tsp	5 ml	butter
¼ cup	60 ml	grated medium cheddar

Beat the eggs with the cream and seasoning.

Heat the butter in a skillet. Pour in the egg mixture and fry until eggs are set. Turn over. Sprinkle with cheese. Place beneath a preheated oven broiler and cook until cheese melts. Fold in half. Transfer to a serving plate and serve very hot.

SERVES 1

EGGS BUTCHER STYLE

1½ lbs	675 g	beef tenderloin
1 tsp	5 ml	each of salt, sugar, basil, oregano, thyme, chili powder
½ tsp	3 ml	each of onion powder, garlic powder, paprika, coriander seeds
¼ tsp	1 ml	each of white pepper, black pepper, cayenne pepper
3 tbsp	45 ml	extra virgin olive oil
½ cup	125 ml	sliced mushrooms
1 tbsp	15 ml	butter
½ cup	125 ml	chopped green onions
1 cup	250 ml	Demi-Glace (see page 123)
¼ cup	60 ml	sherry
⅓ cup	80 ml	heavy cream
12	12	eggs

Trim and slice the tenderloin into very thin slices.

Blend the herbs and spices, making a steak spice. Sprinkle on the beef. Heat the oil very hot in a large skillet. Fast fry the tenderloin. Remove and reserve hot.

Add the mushrooms to the skillet along with the butter. Sauté until tender. Add the green onions, demi-glace, sherry and cream. Reduce heat and simmer for 5 minutes.

While the sauce simmers, poach the eggs. Place the tenderloin on serving plates. Top with an egg. Smother with sauce. Serve very hot.

SERVES 6

Omelette of Fine Herbs & Cheese

Eggs Butcher Style

Oeufs Poches a la Hollandaise

SCRAMBLED EGGS ARCHDUCHESS

POTATO:		
2 cups	500 ml	hot mashed potatoes
3 tbsp	45 ml	light cream
¼ tsp	1 ml	paprika
¼ cup	60 ml	freshly grated Parmesan cheese

Whip the potatoes with cream, paprika and cheese, then pipe the potatoes around an oven proof platter.

EGGS:		
3 tbsp	45 ml	butter
1 cup	250 ml	diced ham
1 cup	250 ml	sliced mushrooms
9	9	eggs
½ cup	125 ml	cream
¼ tsp	1 ml	paprika
½ tsp	3 ml	salt
⅛ tsp	pinch	pepper

Heat the butter in a skillet. Add the ham and mushrooms and sauté for 3 minutes. Beat the eggs with the cream and seasonings. Add to the skillet and sauté the eggs scrambling. Place the eggs in the centre of the piped potatoes.

SAUCE:		
½ tsp	3 ml	paprika
2 cups	500 ml	hot Mornay Sauce (see page 111)
2 cups	500 ml	blanched asparagus tips

Whip the paprika into the mornay sauce. Pour over the eggs. Sprinkle the asparagus tips over. Bake in a preheat 500°F (250°C) oven for 3-4 minutes.

SERVES 4

Oeufs Poches a la Bourguignonne

OUEFS POCHES A LA HOLLANDAISE

8	8	slices bread
3 tbsp	45 ml	butter
6 oz	170 g	smoked salmon
8	8	eggs
1½ cups	375 ml	Hollandaise Sauce (see page 114)
1 cup	250 ml	cooked shrimp meat
1	1	small, sliced red onion
1 tbsp	15 ml	capers

Trim the bread crusts. Cut the bread into rounds. Heat the butter in a skillet and fry the bread until golden on each side.

Place 1 oz (30 g) of salmon sliced very thin on each crouton. Poach the eggs and place on top of the salmon.

Smother with hollandaise. Sprinkle with shrimp, onion rings and capers. Serve at once.

SERVES 4

OEUFS POCHES A LA BOURGUIGNONNE

4	4	slices of bread
4 tbsp	60 ml	butter
8	8	eggs
2 cups	500 ml	sweet white wine
4 tsp	20 ml	flour
1 cup	250 ml	hot Demi-Glace (see page 123)

Trim the crust off the bread. Heat 2 tbsp (30 ml) of butter in a skillet and fry the bread to a golden on each side.

Heat the wine to boiling in a sauce pan. Poach the eggs in the wine. Place 2 eggs on each bread crouton and reserve hot. Strain the wine.

Heat the remaining butter and add the flour. Cook 2 minutes over low heat. Add 1 cup (250 ml) of wine; simmer for 2 minutes. Whip in the demi-glace; simmer until sauce thickens.

Pour the sauce over the eggs and serve very hot.

SERVES 4

EGGS BELLAY

8	8	eggs
2 cups	500 ml	hot Mornay Sauce (see page 111)
2 tbsp	30 ml	butter
1 cup	250 ml	grated sharp cheddar cheese
1 cup	250 ml	fine diced lobster meat
1 cup	250 ml	minced mushrooms
¼ cup	60 ml	freshly grated Parmesan cheese

Boil the eggs hard.

Blend the mornay sauce with the cheddar cheese.

Sauté the lobster and mushrooms in the butter.

Cut the eggs in half lengthwise. Scoop out the yolks. Blend the yolks with ½ cup (125 ml) of cheese sauce along with the lobster and mushrooms. Refill the cavities of the eggs.

Place on oven proof serving plates and cover with the remaining cheese sauce. Sprinkle with Parmesan cheese. Broil in a preheated oven for 1 minute. Serve very hot.

SERVES 4

OEUFS BROUILLES A' ITALIENNE

RICE:		
3 tbsp	45 ml	butter
2 oz	60 g	julienne cut prosciutto
2 oz	60 g	julienne cut ham
½ cup	125 ml	sliced mushrooms
½	0.5	finely diced red bell pepper
½	0.5	finely diced green bell pepper
1	1	finely diced small onion
1	1	finely diced celery stalk
1¼ cups	310 ml	long grain rice
1 cup	250 ml	white wine
4 cups	1 L	Chicken Stock (see page 77)
1 cup	250 ml	Tomato Sauce II (see page 117)
½ cup	125 ml	freshly grated Romano cheese

In a sauce pan, heat the butter. Add the prosciutto and ham along with the vegetables. Sauté until the vegetables are tender. Add the rice, wine and chicken stock. Cover and simmer until the rice has absorbed the liquid.

Remove from heat, stir in the tomato sauce and cheese. Place in a ring on a round, heat proof platter.

EGGS:		
9	9	eggs
½ cup	125 ml	light cream
3 tbsp	45 ml	butter
1 cup	250 ml	grated mozzarella
1 cup	250 ml	grated sharp cheddar

Beat the eggs with the cream. Heat the butter in a skillet and cook the eggs thoroughly. Place the eggs within the risotto ring. Sprinkle with the cheeses. Broil in a preheated oven just until cheese melts. Serve very hot.

SERVES 4

Eggs Bellay

Eggs Mercedes

EGGS MERCEDES

6	6	oval dinner rolls
1 cup	250 ml	peeled, seeded and chopped tomatoes
2 tbsp	30 ml	chopped chives
1 tbsp	15 ml	safflower oil
8	8	eggs
⅓ cup	80 ml	light cream
3 tbsp	45 ml	butter
¼ tsp	1 ml	salt
⅛ tsp	pinch	pepper
1½ cups	375 ml	hot Tomato Sauce II (see page 117)
1 cup	250 ml	grated medium cheddar cheese

Cut the tops from the dinner rolls and hollow them out.

Mix the tomatoes together with chives.

Heat the oil in a skillet and cook the tomatoes until most of the liquid has evaporated. Divide the tomatoes among the dinner rolls.

Beat the eggs together with the cream. Heat the butter in a skillet and cook the eggs thoroughly. Fill the dinner rolls with the eggs. Season with salt and pepper. Top with tomato sauce and cheese; place on a baking sheet. Broil in a preheated oven until cheese melts. Serve very hot.

SERVES 6

OMELETTE A LA JARDINIERE

1 tbsp	15 ml	julienne cut blanched carrot
1 tbsp	15 ml	julienne cut red bell pepper
1 tbsp	15 ml	julienne cut celery
1 tbsp	15 ml	sliced mushroom
2 tsp	10 ml	chopped green onion
2 tbsp	30 ml	butter
2 tsp	10 ml	flour
½ cup	125 ml	light cream
¼ tsp	1 ml	basil leaves
¼ tsp	1 ml	salt
⅛ tsp	pinch	pepper
2 tbsp	30 ml	freshly grated Parmesan cheese
2	2	eggs

Sauté the vegetables in 1 tbsp (15 ml) of butter. Sprinkle with flour and cook for 2 minutes over low heat. Pour in all the cream but 2 tbsp (30 ml). Add the seasoning and cheese; simmer into a thick sauce.

Blend the remaining cream into the eggs.

Heat the remaining butter in a skillet. Fry the eggs until set. Turn over and cover with half the sauce. Fold the omelette in half. Transfer to a serving plate. Cover with the remaining sauce and serve.

SERVES 1

ADMIRAL'S EGGS

3 tbsp	45 ml	butter
3 oz	85 g	mushrooms
4 tsp	20 ml	flour
1 cup	250 ml	light cream
¼ cup	60 ml	sherry
2	2	chopped green onions
½ lb	225 g	cooked, diced lobster meat
8	8	eggs
4	4	English muffins
1 tbsp	15 ml	chopped cilantro

Heat the butter in a small sauce pan. Sauté the mushrooms until cooked through. Sprinkle with flour and cook for 2 minutes over low heat. Blend in the cream and sherry; simmer until sauce thickens.

Add the green onions and lobster meat continuing to simmer for 5 additional minutes.

While sauce is simmering, poach the eggs and toast the muffins. Place muffins on a serving plate, place a poached egg upon each muffin half and cover with sauce.

Sprinkle with cilantro and serve.

SERVES 4

EGGS JASON GRAHAM

5	5	eggs
2 tbsp	30 ml	butter
½ cup	125 ml	flour
½ cup	125 ml	light cream
½ cup	125 ml	cooked shrimp meat
½ tsp	3 ml	chervil
¼ tsp	1 ml	salt
⅛ tsp	pinch	pepper
¼ cup	60 ml	milk
1½ cups	375 ml	seasoned bread crumbs
2 cups	500 ml	safflower oil

Hard boil four eggs. Cool and cut in half lengthwise.

Heat the butter in a sauce pan, add 2 tbsp (30 ml) of flour and cook 2 minutes over low heat. Add the cream, shrimp and seasonings; simmer into a very thick sauce. Cool to room temperature.

Blend the egg yolks into the sauce. Fill the egg cavity with the shrimp sauce.

Blend the remaining egg with milk. Dip the eggs into the remaining flour, then into the egg wash. Dredge in the seasoned bread crumbs.

Heat the oil to 375°F (190°C). Fry for 3-4 minutes or until golden brown. Serve very hot.

SERVES 4

Eggs Jason Graham

Admiral's Eggs

CHEF K'S SPECIALTIES

In the last restaurant I operated, once a month we had a five course gourmet dinner that was always sold out three months in advance. The reason was creative, delicious gastronomic delights unavailable anywhere, but there. Price was no object, and enjoyment never restrained.

Within this chapter you and your guest can enjoy some of the very best, most creative presentations, to delight your taste buds. These dishes have been created to honour people well respected or to honour the dish itself; either way, honour is the principal ingredient within each recipe.

Many include the use of fresh fruit that gladdens the heart, pleases the taste buds and delights the eyes—in other words, accomplishes all of what taste is about.

True, you will find seafood, lamb, beef and pork, but the discoveries go far deeper. Offering your guest such exquisite dishes such as Poulet Kenneth & Gloria or Tiger Prawns Peri-Peri will cause such taste buds revolution that they may never want to depart from your residence.

The recipes in this chapter are not for the everyday cook, and are the recipes that will entertain your guest the most. When the occasion is extra special, these are the recipes to delight one's self with.

Forget going out — stay in, and enjoy a gourmet treat that can't be beat!

19
THE CANADIAN FEDERATION OF CHEFS DE CUISINE
LA FÉDÉRATION CANADIENNE DES CHEFS DE CUISINE
63

TOURNEDOS ĔPIMĔLĔIA

8 – 4 oz	8 – 115 g	tenderloin filets
½ tsp	3 ml	each of oregano leaves, thyme leaves, basil leaves, cayenne pepper, black pepper, onion powder, garlic powder
1 tsp	5 ml	each of paprika, salt, chili powder
5 tbsp	75 ml	butter
½ cup	125 ml	diced mushrooms
½ cup	125 ml	green onions
1 cup	250 ml	rehydrated sundried tomatoes
1½ cups	375 ml	Demi-Glace (see page 123)
½ cup	125 ml	sherry
¼ cup	60 ml	heavy cream
2 cups	500 ml	cooked crayfish tails
8	8	bread rusks

Trim the blue skin and fat from the filets. Combine the seasonings and rub into the filets.

Heat 3 tbsp (45 ml) of butter in a large skillet and sauté the filets to desired tenderness; reserve hot.

While the filets cook, melt the butter in a sauce pan; sauté the mushrooms, green onions and tomatoes.

Add the demi-glace and sherry. Reduce heat and simmer to half of the sauces volume. Add cream and crayfish tail; simmer for 5 minutes longer.

Place the filets on the bread rusks, smother with sauce and serve.

SERVES 4

TOURNEDOS SHERWOOD

8 – 4 oz	8 – 115 g	tenderloin filets
½ tsp	3 ml	each of oregano leaves, thyme leaves, basil leaves, cayenne pepper, black pepper, onion powder, garlic powder, salt
5 tbsp	75 ml	butter
1 cup	250 ml	blanched, diced, artichoke hearts
½ cup	125 ml	green onions
1 cup	250 ml	rehydrated sundried tomatoes
1½ cups	375 ml	Demi-Glace (see page 123)
½ cup	125 ml	sherry
¼ cup	60 ml	heavy cream
2 cups	500 ml	blanched, julienne cut, red bell pepper
8	8	bread rusks

Trim the blue skin and fat from the filets. Combine the seasonings and rub into the filets.

Heat 3 tbsp (45 ml) of butter in a large skillet and sauté the filets to desired tenderness; reserve hot.

While the filets cook, melt the butter in a sauce pan; sauté the artichoke, green onions and tomatoes.

Add the demi-glace and sherry. Reduce heat and simmer to half of the sauces volume. Add cream and bell pepper; simmer for 5 minutes longer.

Place the filets on the bread rusks, smother with sauce and serve.

SERVES 4

ESCALOPE OF VEAL WITH SMOKED SALMON

6 – 3 oz	6 – 90 g	veal cutlets
12 oz	340 g	smoked salmon
6 oz	170 g	Camembert cheese
1	1	egg
¼ cup	60 ml	milk
⅓ cup	80 ml	seasoned flour, all purpose
1½ cups	375 ml	dry bread crumbs
1½ cups	375 ml	safflower oil
1½ cups	375 ml	Mornay Sauce (see page 111)

Preheat the oven to 350°F (180°C).

Pound the cutlets very flat. Top with salmon and cheese, fold and roll to encase the filling. Chill in refrigerator for 1 hour.

Mix the egg with the milk. Dust with flour, dip into egg and dredge in bread crumbs.

Heat the oil to 375°F (190°C); fry the cutlets to golden brown. Place on a baking sheet and bake in the oven for 15-20 minutes.

Place cutlets on serving plates and pour the Mornay Sauce over. Serve.

SERVES 6

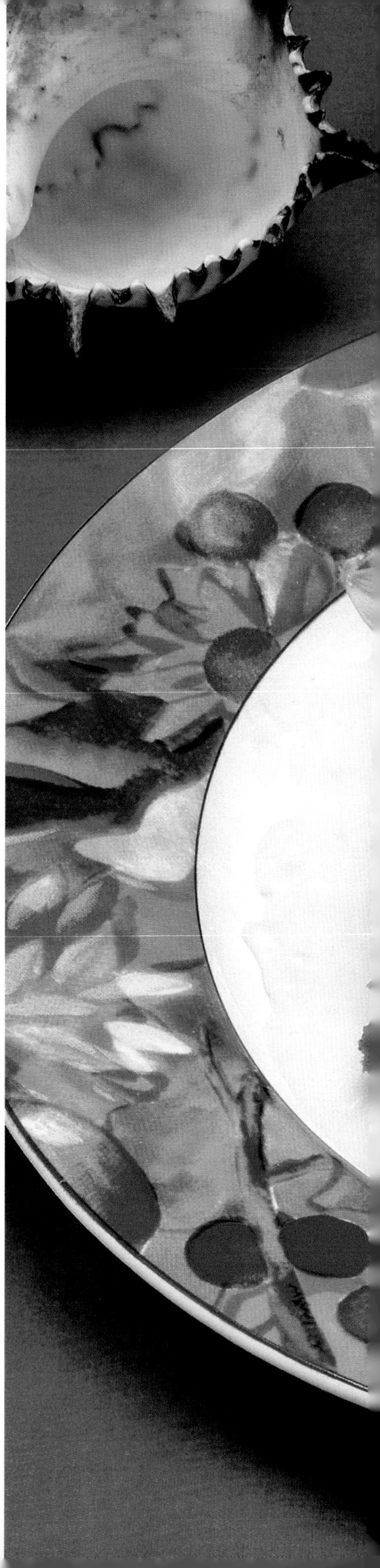

MJ's GRILLED FILLETS OF SNAPPER

1	1	each of red, green, yellow bell peppers
6 – 6 oz	6 – 170 g	red snapper fillets
1	1	minced garlic clove
2 tsp	10 ml	minced ginger root
¼ cup	60 ml	sherry
¼ cup	60 ml	soya sauce
1 tbsp	15 ml	Worcestershire sauce
½ tsp	3 ml	Chinese five spice
2 tbsp	30 ml	Brown Sugar
1 tsp	5 ml	cornstarch
1 tbsp	15 ml	cold water
2 tbsp	30 ml	safflower oil
2 tbsp	30 ml	oil
2 tbsp	30 ml	butter
4 oz	115 g	oyster mushrooms
8 oz	225 g	peeled, deveined large shrimp

Place the peppers on a baking sheet and roast in a preheated 400°F (200°C) oven until the skins blister. Remove from oven, place in a paper bag and allow to steam for 20 minutes.

Remove from bag and peel away the skin. Cut into quarters, remove seeds and slice the quarters into julienne strips.

Place the snapper fillets into a shallow pan. Blend the garlic, ginger, sherry, soya, Worcestershire and five spice. Pour over the fish and marinate for 30 minutes.

Remove fish and pour marinade into a small sauce pan with the brown sugar; heat to boil. Combine the cornstarch with the water and simmer until thick.

Brush the fillets with oil and grill over medium coals for 10 minutes, brushing frequently with sauce.

While fish grills, heat the oil and the butter in a large skillet; sauté the mushrooms and shrimp until shrimp are just cooked. Add the peppers and continue to sauté for 3 minutes.

Brush the fillets one final time and place on serving plates. Top with sauté and serve at once.

SERVES 6

PORK TENDERLOIN ASKENCHUCK

½ quantity	0.5	Puff Pastry (see page 689)
4 – 4 oz	4 – 115 g	pork tenderloin
2 tbsp	30 ml	butter
1 cup	250 ml	thinly sliced mushrooms
1 cup	250 ml	cooked crayfish tails
6 oz	170 g	Camembert cheese
1¼ cups	310 ml	Bing cherries – fresh or tinned, pitted
¼ cup	60 ml	cherry brandy
3 tbsp	45 ml	cherry liquid or apple juice
1 tbsp	15 ml	lemon juice
2 tbsp	30 ml	granulated sugar

Roll the pastry into ¼" (6 mm) thick square. Cut into 4 even pieces.

Trim the tenderloin of any fat and blue skin.

Heat half the butter in a skillet and sear the pork. Add the remaining butter and mushrooms; sauté until all liquid has evaporated.

Layer the pork, mushrooms, crayfish tails and cheese onto the puff pastry. Roll and fold to encase the filling. Pinch the edges to seal in filling. Bake in a preheated 375°F (190°C) oven for 35-40 minutes or until golden brown.

While pork bakes, heat the cherries in the cherry brandy over low heat until very tender.

Add the cherry juice, lemon juice and sugar. Simmer until thick.

Place pork on serving plates and cover with sauce.

SERVES 4

BON
APPETIT

AIGUILLETTE DE VOLAILLE NOUVEAU

6 – 6 oz	6 – 170 g	chicken breasts
1 cup	250 ml	cooked crayfish tails
6 oz	170 g	Camembert cheese
½ tsp	3 ml	each of oregano leaves, thyme leaves, basil leaves, cayenne pepper, black pepper, onion powder, garlic powder, salt, paprika
2 cups	500 ml	fine dry bread crumbs
½ cup	125 ml	milk
1	1	egg
¾ cups	180 ml	flour, all purpose
3 tbsp	45 ml	olive oil
1 cup	250 ml	dried apricots
1 cup	250 ml	water
2 tbsp	30 ml	granulated sugar
1 tsp	5 ml	cornstarch
1 tbsp	15 ml	lemon juice
¼ cup	60 ml	apple juice
¾ cup	180 ml	whipping cream
1 cup	250 ml	chopped fresh figs
1 tbsp	15 ml	fresh chopped tarragon

Pound the chicken breasts flat, top with crayfish tails and 1 oz (30 ml) of cheese. Fold and roll to encase filling. Refrigerate for 1 hour.

Blend the seasonings with the bread crumbs. Combine the milk and the egg. Dust the chicken with the flour, dip into the milk and dredge with bread crumbs.

Place on a baking sheet and brush with oil. Bake in a preheated 350°F (180°C) oven for 25-30 minutes.

In a sauce pan, boil the apricots in the water for 5 minutes. Transfer apricots to a food processor and purée. Reserve the water. Stir the sugar into the water. Mix the cornstarch with the lemon juice, add to the water and simmer until thick. Pour over the apricots and blend.

Return to sauce pan and stir in the apple juice; heat but do not boil. Add the cream, figs, and tarragon; simmer gently for 10 minutes.

Place cutlets on serving plates, cover with sauce and serve.

SERVES 6

CHICKEN LEDGISTER

6 – 6 oz	6 – 170 g	boneless, skin-on chicken breasts
½ cup	125 ml	orange segments
6 oz	170 g	rindless Brie cheese
5 tbsp	75 ml	butter
1 cup	250 ml	thinly sliced mushrooms
3 tbsp	45 ml	flour, all purpose
½ cup	125 ml	orange juice
½ cup	125 ml	Chicken Broth (see page 77)
½ cup	125 ml	whipping cream
4 tbsp	60 ml	Jalapeño Marmalade (see page 701)
¼ cup	60 ml	liquid honey

Pound the chicken breasts flat. Lay the breasts on a flat surface skin side down. Layer with orange segments and cheese. Wrap and roll the breasts to encase the filling.

Melt 2 tbsp (30 ml) of butter and brush on the chicken. Bake in a preheated 350°F (180°C) oven for 20 minutes, or until cooked through.

While the chicken bakes, heat the remaining butter in a sauce pan. Add the mushrooms and sauté until tender. Stir in the flour and cook over low heat for 2 minutes.

Add the orange juice and chicken broth; simmer for 10 minutes. Stir in the cream, marmalade and honey. Continue to simmer for an additional 10 minutes.

Remove chicken from oven, place on serving plates and smother with sauce.

SERVES 6

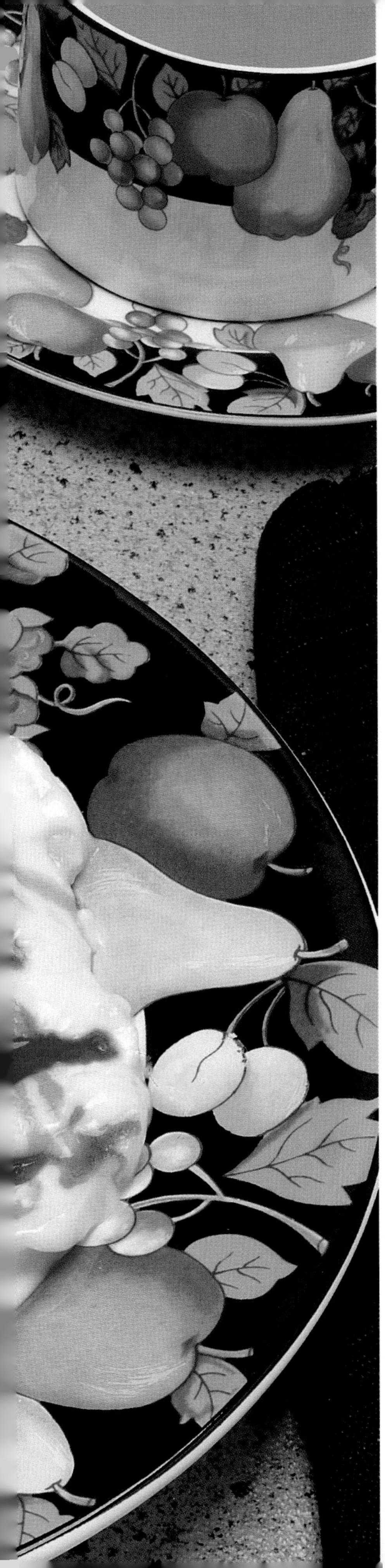

PORK TENDERLOIN PECHÂH

1 lb	450 g	pork tenderloin
¼ cup	60 ml	raspberry jam
3 tbsp	45 ml	cracked black pepper
6 tbsp	90 ml	butter
4	4	pared, sliced cooking apples
3 tbsp	45 ml	flour, all purpose
4 tbsp	60 ml	granulated sugar
¾ cup	180 ml	apple juice
¾ cup	180 ml	whipping cream

Trim the tenderloin of all blue skin and fat. Spread the jam on the tenderloin, then roll in the cracked black pepper. Place on a buttered waxed paper lined baking sheet. Melt 2 tbsp (30 ml) of butter and brush on tenderloin. Bake in a preheated 350°F (180°C) oven for 20 minutes.

While tenderloin bakes, heat the remaining butter in a sauce pan. Add the apple and sauté until tender. Sprinkle with flour and cook for 2 minutes over low heat. Add the sugar and apple juice; simmer until thick. Fold in the cream and simmer for 5 minutes.

Remove tenderloin from oven and carve. Spread the sauce on serving plates, top with tenderloin slices and serve.

SERVES 4

BEEF TENDERLOINS IN ROAST BELL PEPPER ARUGULA SAUCE

1	1	each of red, green, yellow bell peppers
6 – 6 oz	6 – 170 g	tenderloin filets
½ tsp	3 ml	each of oregano leaves, thyme leaves, basil leaves, cayenne pepper, black pepper, onion powder, garlic powder
1 tsp	5 ml	each of paprika, salt, chili powder
3 tbsp	45 ml	butter
1½ cups	375 ml	thinly sliced mushrooms
1	1	minced garlic clove
1½ cups	375 ml	Demi-Glace (see page 123)
¾ cup	180 ml	whipping cream
3 tbsp	45 ml	tomato paste
2	2	bunches chopped arugula
½ tsp	3 ml	cracked black pepper

Place the peppers on a baking sheet and roast in a preheated 400°F (200°C) oven until the skins blister. Remove from oven, place in a paper bag and allow to steam for 20 minutes.

Remove from bag and peel away the skin. Cut into quarters, remove seeds and slice the quarters into julienne strips.

Trim the tenderloin of any fat. Combine the season blends and rub into the beef. Broil the beef to desired doneness.

While steaks broil, heat the butter in a small sauce pan and sauté the mushrooms with the garlic. Add the demi-glace, reduce the heat and simmer for 15 minutes. Fold in the cream and tomato paste; simmer for 5 minutes. Add the arugula, pepper and bell peppers; continue to simmer for 10 minutes.

Plate the steaks and smother with sauce. Serve.

SERVES 6

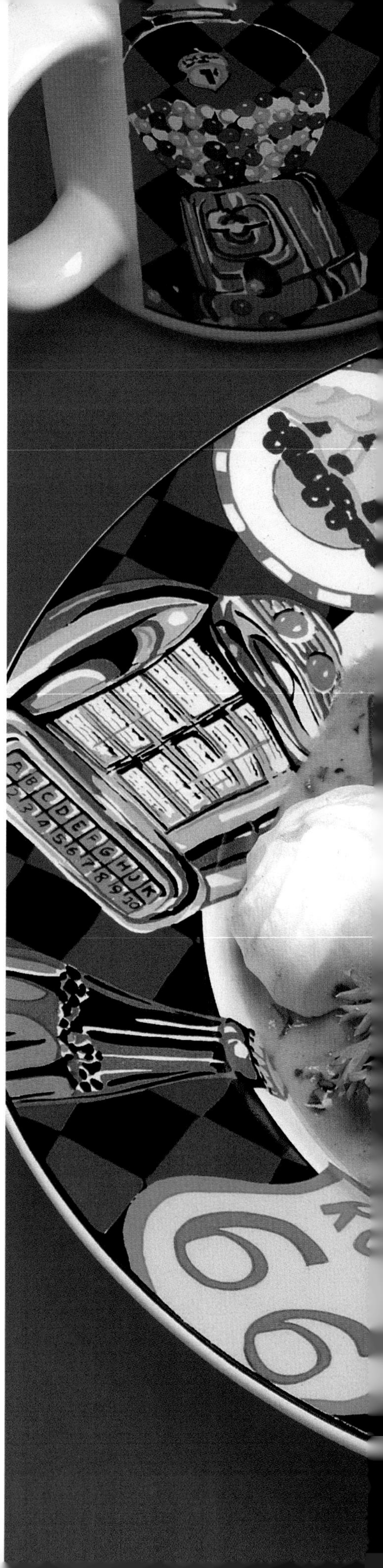

Kodak

TIGER PRAWNS PERI-PERI

1 cup	250 ml	pared, sliced apples
3 tbsp	45 ml	flour, all purpose
2 tsp	10 ml	curry powder
½ cup	125 ml	apple juice
½ cup	125 ml	Chicken Broth (see page 77)
½ cup	125 ml	heavy cream
3 tbsp	45 ml	Jalapeño Marmalade (see page 701)
16	16	tiger prawns
5 tbsp	75 ml	butter
½ tsp	3 ml	paprika

Heat 3 tbsp (45 ml) butter in a sauce pan and sauté the apples until soft. Sprinkle with the flour and curry and continue to cook for 2 minutes over low heat.

Add the apple juice and chicken broth, and simmer for 10 minutes. Add the cream and marmalade, and simmer for 10 minutes longer.

While sauce simmers, peel, devein and butterfly the tiger prawns. Melt 2 tbsp (30 ml) of butter, brush over shrimp, sprinkle with paprika and place on a baking sheet. Bake prawns in a preheated 350°F (180°C) oven for 10 minutes or until cooked through.

Spread serving plates with sauce and float the prawns on top. Serve at once.

SERVES 4

CUTLETS NICK KALENUIK

6 – 4 oz	6 – 115 g	veal cutlets
6 oz	170 g	rindless Brie cheese
6 oz	170 g	lobster meat
18	18	green seedless grapes
1	1	egg
¼ cup	60 ml	milk
¼ cup	60 ml	flour, all purpose
1½ cups	375 ml	seasoned bread crumbs
2 cups	500 ml	safflower oil
12	12	peeled, stoned apricots
½ cup	125 ml	water
1 tbsp	15 ml	butter
¼ cup	60 ml	finely diced red bell pepper
1	1	minced garlic clove
¼ cup	60 ml	brown sugar
1 tsp	5 ml	Dijon mustard
1 tsp	5 ml	paprika

Pound the cutlets very thin, place on top 1 oz (30 g) of cheese, 1 oz (30 g) of lobster meat and 3 grapes. Fold and roll the meat to encase the filling. Place on a baking sheet and refrigerate for 1 hour.

Blend the egg with the milk.

Dust the veal rolls in the flour. Dip into the milk and dredge in the bread crumbs. Heat the oil and brown the rolls on all sides.

Bake in a preheated 350°F (180°C) oven for 20 minutes.

While cutlets bake, cut the apricots in half and place in a saucepan. Add the water and simmer until the apricots are tender. Place into a food processor and purée.

Heat the butter in a sauce pan and sauté the red pepper and garlic. Stir in the purée, brown sugar, mustard and paprika; simmer for 5 minutes.

Ladle sauce onto serving plates and top with veal. Serve at once.

SERVES 6

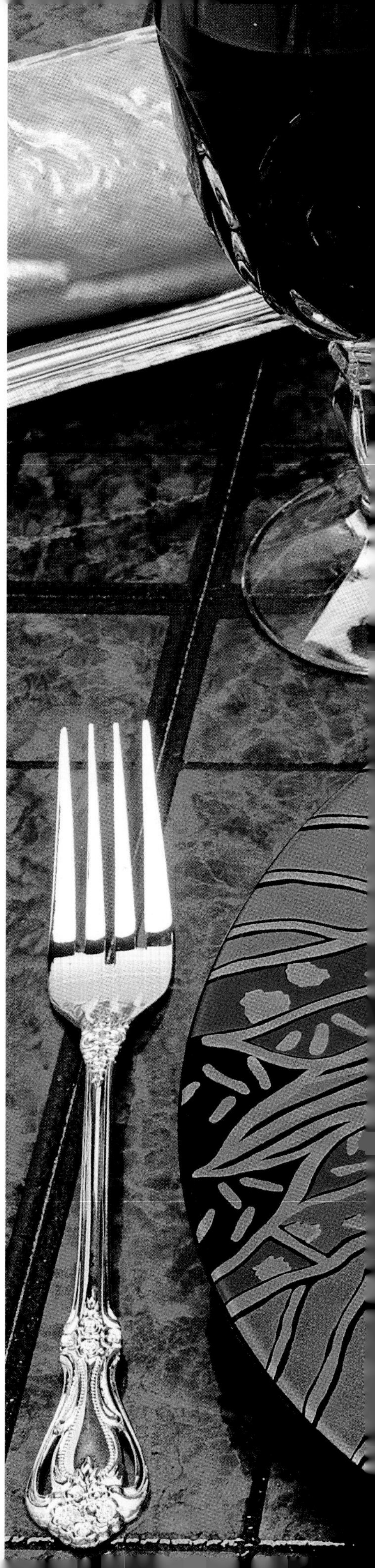

SCALLOPS PROVENÇALE

½ tsp	3 ml	each of oregano leaves, thyme leaves, basil leaves, cayenne pepper, black pepper, onion powder, garlic powder
1 tsp	5 ml	each of paprika, salt, chili powder
3 tbsp	45 ml	butter
3	3	minced garlic cloves
1	1	large minced onion
1	1	finely diced red bell pepper
1	1	finely diced green bell pepper
6	6	large peeled, seeded, chopped tomatoes
1 cup	250 ml	Demi-Glace (see page 123)
½ cup	125 ml	whipping cream
1½ cups	375 ml	flour, all purpose
¾ cup	180 ml	milk
1½ lbs	675 g	large sea scallops
¼ cup	60 ml	olive oil

Combine the seasonings in a mixing bowl.

Heat the butter in a sauce pan. Add the garlic, onion, and peppers and sauté until tender. Add the tomatoes and continue to cook for 20 minutes over low heat. Stir in half the season blend and demi-glace; continue to simmer for 20 minutes. Add the cream and simmer 5 additional minutes.

Combine the remaining seasonings with the flour. Dip the scallops into the milk and dust with the flour. Heat the oil in a large skillet and fry the scallops to golden brown. Place on serving plates, smother with sauce and serve.

SERVES 6

BLUE CHEESE WHITE CHOCOLATE VEAL CHOPS

6-8 oz	6-225 g	veal chops
½ tsp	3 ml	each of salt, pepper, paprika, oregano, thyme, basil, chervil
1½ cups	375 ml	dry bread crumbs
2	2	eggs
⅓ cup	90 ml	milk
½ cup	125 ml	flour, all purpose
3 tbsp	45 ml	olive oil
4 tbsp	60 ml	butter
½ cup	125 ml	sliced mushrooms
1	1	small, finely diced onion
¾ cup	180 ml	Chicken Broth (see page 77)
¾ cup	180 ml	light cream
2 oz	60 g	grated white chocolate
3 oz	90 g	crumbled blue cheese
¼ cup	60 ml	each of red, green, yellow julienned bell pepper

Wash and pat dry the veal chops.

Blend the seasoning with the flour. Beat the egg into the milk. Dust the chops with ¼ cup (60 ml) of flour. Dip into the eggs and dredge in the bread crumbs. Place on a baking sheet and brush with the oil. Bake in a preheated 350°F (180°C) oven for 25 minutes.

While chops bake, prepare the sauce by heating the butter in a sauce pan. Add the mushrooms and onion and sauté until tender. Add the remaining flour and cook for 2 minutes over low heat. Stir in broth and cream and simmer for 15 minutes. Fold in the chocolate and cheese; continue to simmer for an additional 5 minutes.

Blanch the peppers.

Plate the chops, smother with sauce and serve with a sprinkling of the peppers.

SERVES 6

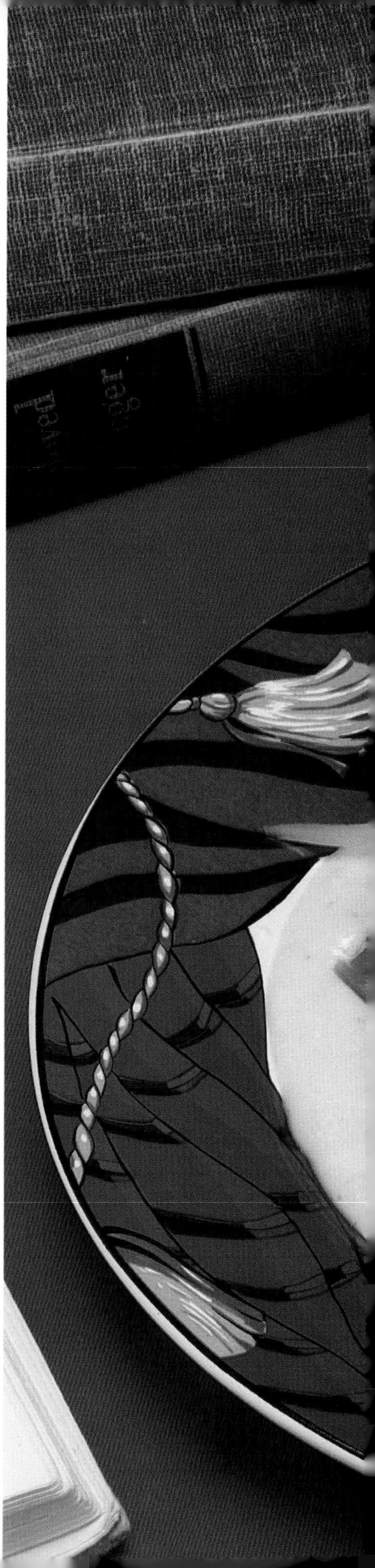

POULET KENNETH & GLORIA

1 lb	450 g	washed and hulled strawberries
½ lb	225 g	washed and hulled raspberries
½ lb	225 g	washed and hulled blackberries
1 cup	250 ml	sugar
2 tsp	10 ml	lemon juice
1 tsp	5 ml	lemon peel – grated
6-6 oz	6-170 g	boneless, skinless chicken breasts
2	2	peeled, diced mangos
6 oz	170 g	Camembert cheese
2 tbsp	30 ml	melted butter

Place the berries in a food processor. Process into a purée. Press through a fine sieve and place into sauce pot. Stir in the sugar until dissolved. Add the lemon juice and peel. Bring to a boil, reduce heat and simmer until sauce has yielded 1½ cups (375 ml).

Pound the chicken breasts very flat; top with mango and 1 oz (30 g) cheese. Fold and roll to completely encase the filling; hold together with tooth picks.

Brush with melted butter and cover with wax paper. Bake in a preheated 350°F (180°C) oven for 20 minutes; remove toothpicks.

Plate the chicken, smother with sauce and serve.

SERVES 6

CHEF K'S STUFFED SHRIMP

12	12	tiger shrimp
4 tbsp	60 ml	butter
1¾ cups	430 ml	flour, all purpose
1½ cups	375 ml	milk
2½ cups	625 ml	cooked crab meat
½ tsp	3 ml	each of oregano leaves, thyme leaves, basil leaves, cayenne pepper, black pepper, onion powder, garlic powder, salt, paprika
2	2	eggs
2 cups	500 ml	fine dry bread crumbs
3 tbsp	45 ml	olive oil

SAUCE:

3 tbsp	45 ml	butter
3 tbsp	45 ml	flour, all purpose
½ cup	125 ml	Chicken Stock (see page 77)
½ cup	125 ml	heavy cream
½ cup	125 ml	champagne
1 cup	250 ml	rehydrated sundried tomatoes
1	1	bunch chopped arugula

Peel and devein the shrimp. Slice down the centre ¾'s through, flat with a meat mallet. Place on a baking sheet.

Heat the butter in a sauce pan; add the flour, reduce heat and cook for 2 minutes. Add 1 cup (250 ml) of milk. Cook, stirring until a very thick sauce is formed. Cool to room temperature. Stir in the crab meat. Place 2 tbsp (30 ml) of filling on each shrimp. Chill for 2 hours.

Blend the seasoning with the remaining flour. Beat the eggs in the remaining milk. Dust the shrimp with the seasoned flour, dip in the egg milk and dredge in the bread crumbs.

Brush with the oil. Bake in a preheated 350°F (180°C) oven for 15 minutes. Plate the shrimp and serve with the sauce.

SAUCE:

Melt the butter in a sauce pan. Add the flour and stir into a paste (roux), cooking over low heat.

Add chicken stock, cream and champagne. Simmer for 10 minutes over medium heat. Stir in the tomatoes and arugula and simmer for 5 additional minutes.

SERVES 4

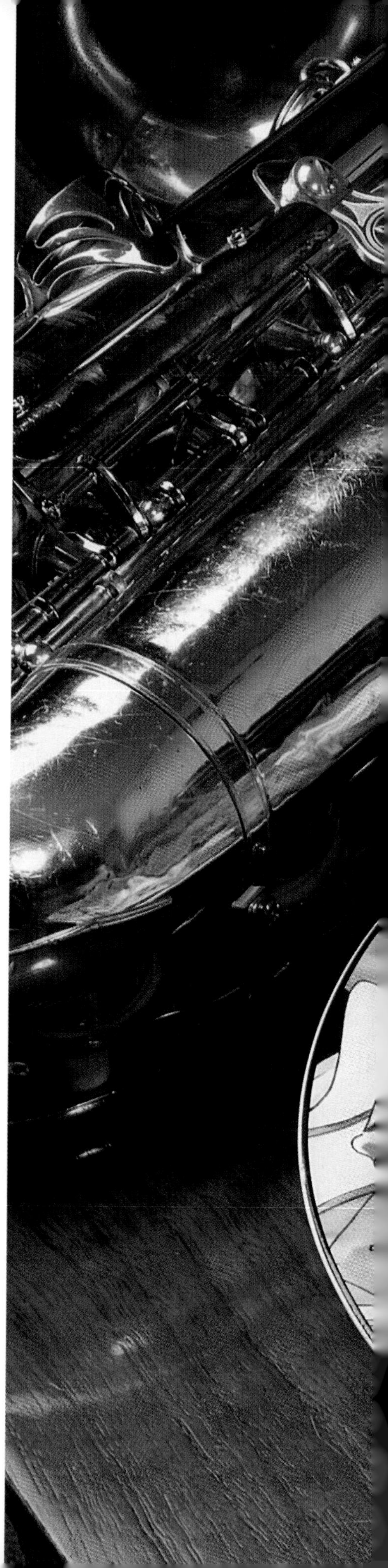

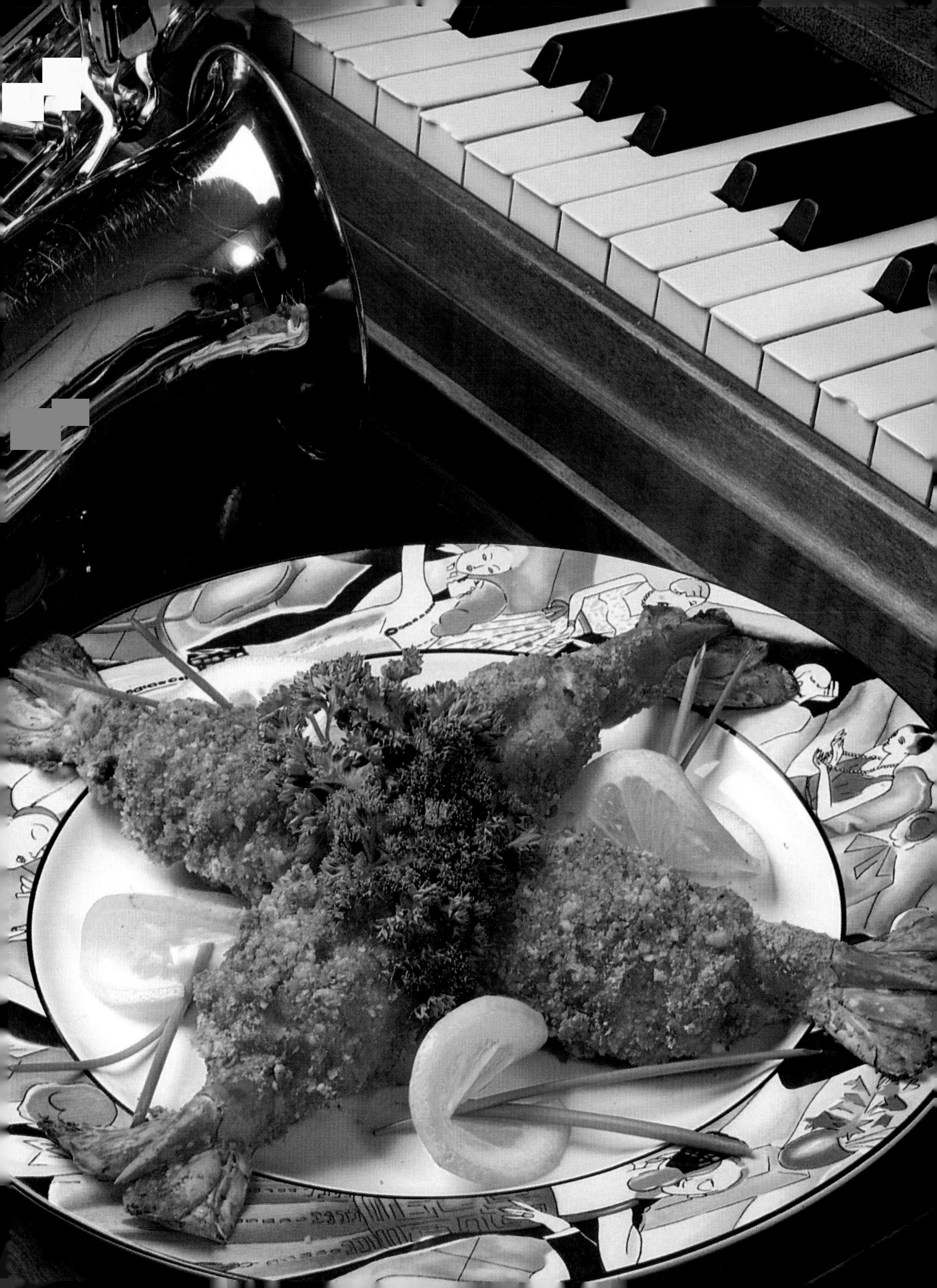

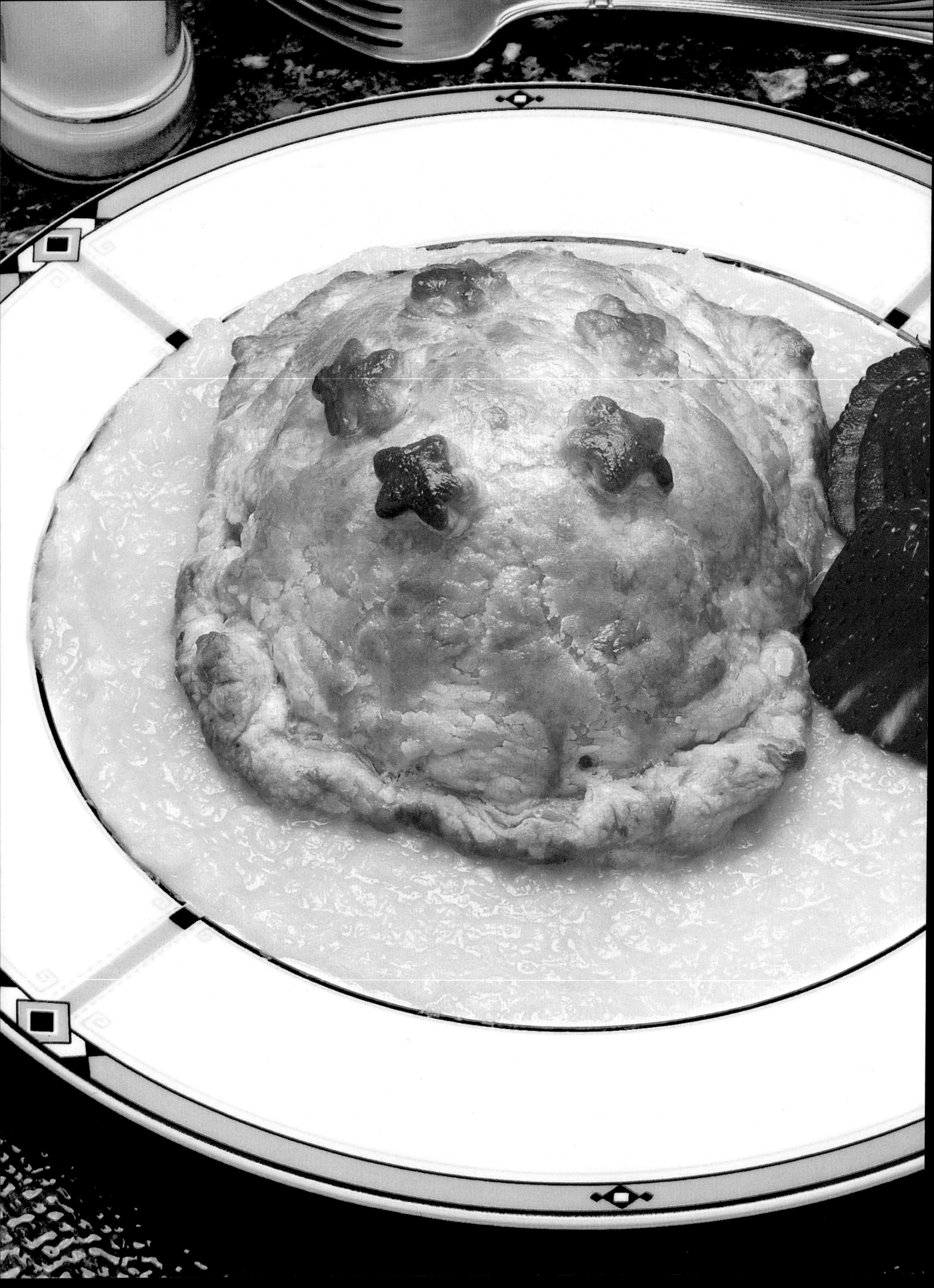

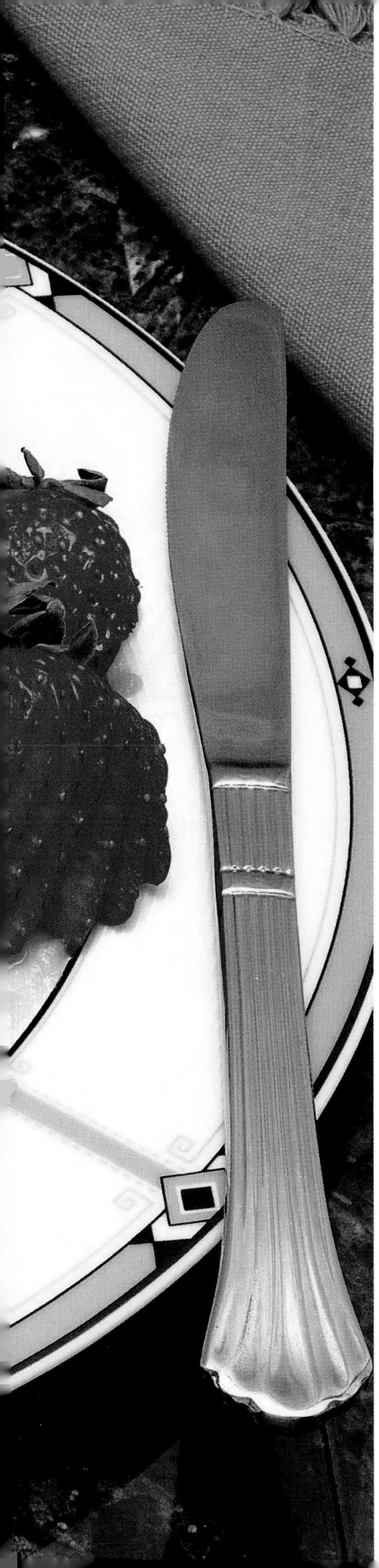

LAMB FIJI ISLAND SURPRISE

2-14 oz	2-420 g	lamb rib roasts (lamb racks)
½ quantity	0.5	Puff Pastry (see page 689)
3 tbsp	45 ml	butter
1½ cups	375 ml	diced mangos
6 oz	170 g	Mascarpone cheese
⅓ cup	90 ml	seedless raisins
⅓ cup	90 ml	cashews
1 cup	250 ml	crushed pineapple, drain and reserve juice
1 cup	250 ml	mango purée
¼ cup	60 ml	granulated sugar
1½ tbsp	25 ml	cornstarch

Have the butcher remove all the bones from the lamb racks and trim all the fat. Preheat the oven to 375°F (190°C).

Roll the pastry out on a lightly floured surface to ¼" (6 mm) thick. Cut into two squares.

Heat the butter in a large skillet and sear the lamb. Place on the pastry squares. Cover with diced mango, cheese, raisins and nuts. Fold and roll the pastry as to encase the meat and filling completely. Bake in the oven for 25-30 minutes.

While the lamb bakes, purée the pineapple with the mangoes in a food processor; press through the sieve into a small sauce pan. Stir in the sugar.

Blend the cornstarch into ¼ cup (60 ml) of reserved pineapple juice. Add to fruit. Cook over low heat until sauce thickens.

Remove lamb from oven, carve and place on serving plates. Cover with sauce or serve separately.

SERVES 4

CHICKEN DIJONNAISE

6 – 6 oz	6 – 170 g	boneless, skinless chicken breasts
3 tbsp	45 ml	butter
¾ cup	180 ml	mayonnaise
3 tbsp	45 ml	Dijon mustard
¼ cup	60 ml	Parmesan cheese
¼ cup	60 ml	dry seasoned bread crumbs

Wash and pat dry the chicken.

Heat the butter and sauté the chicken until cooked through; time depends on the thickness of the chicken breasts. Place on a baking sheet and preheat the oven to 400°F (200°C).

Combine the mayonnaise, mustard and cheese and spread thickly over the breasts. Sprinkle with bread crumbs and bake 10 minutes or until golden brown. Serve.

SERVES 6

VEAL STEAKS WITH TWO SAUCES

SAUCE 1:

2 tbsp	30 ml	butter
¾ cup	180 ml	chopped fennel
2 tbsp	30 ml	flour, all purpose
½ cup	125 ml	light cream
½ cup	125 ml	Chicken Broth (see page 77)
¼ tsp	1 ml	salt
¼ tsp	1 ml	white pepper
pinch	pinch	nutmeg

SAUCE 2:

3 tbsp	45 ml	olive oil
3 tbsp	45 ml	flour, all purpose
⅔ cup	160 ml	Chicken Broth (see page 77)
⅔ cup	160 ml	light cream
⅓ cup	80 ml	tomato catsup
2 tsp	10 ml	Worcestershire sauce
1 tsp	5 ml	paprika
3 drops	3 drops	Tabasco™ sauce
1 tbsp	15 ml	lemon juice
3 tbsp	45 ml	chopped arugula

STEAKS:

6 – 6 oz	6 – 170 g	veal steaks
½ tsp	3 ml	each of oregano leaves, thyme leaves, basil leaves, cayenne pepper, black pepper, onion powder, garlic powder, salt, paprika
4 tbsp	60 ml	butter
4 oz	115 g	chanterelles, shiitake, oyster or other mushrooms

SAUCE 1:
Melt the butter in a sauce pan; sweat the fennel. Add flour and stir into a paste (roux). Cook for 2 minutes over low heat. Add the cream and broth. Stir. Simmer until thickened. Add the seasonings and simmer 2 additional minutes.

SAUCE 2:
Heat the oil in a sauce pan, add the flour and cook for 2 minutes over low heat. Whisk in the broth and cream and simmer until thick. Whisk in the remaining ingredients; continue to simmer for 2 additional minutes. Remove from the heat. Use as required.

STEAK:
Rub the steaks with the blended seasonings. Heat half the butter in a skillet and sauté the steaks to desired doneness; remove and reserve hot.In a second skillet, heat the remaining butter and sauté the mushrooms. Ladle the sauces onto the plate, half on each side. Top with the steaks and surround with mushrooms.

SERVES 6

CREVETTES EN AMOUR

16	16	tiger prawns
5 tbsp	75 ml	butter
½ tsp	3 ml	paprika
½ cup	125 ml	thin sliced mushrooms
3 tbsp	45 ml	flour, all purpose
½ cup	125 ml	Chicken Stock (see page 77)
½ cup	125 ml	heavy cream
½ cup	125 ml	champagne
¼ cup	60 ml	Pernod
¾ cup	190 ml	tiny cooked shrimp

Peel, devein and butterfly the tiger prawns. Melt 2 tbsp (30 ml) of butter, brush over shrimp, sprinkle with paprika and place on a baking sheet. Bake prawns in a preheated 350°F (180°C) oven for 10 minutes or until cooked through.

Melt the remaining butter in a sauce pan. Sauté the mushrooms. Add the flour and stir into a paste (roux), cooking over low heat for 2 minutes.

Add chicken stock, cream, champagne and Pernod. Whisk all the ingredients together. Simmer for 10 minutes over medium heat.

Place the prawns on serving plates, smother with sauce and sprinkle with tiny shrimp. Serve.

SERVES 4

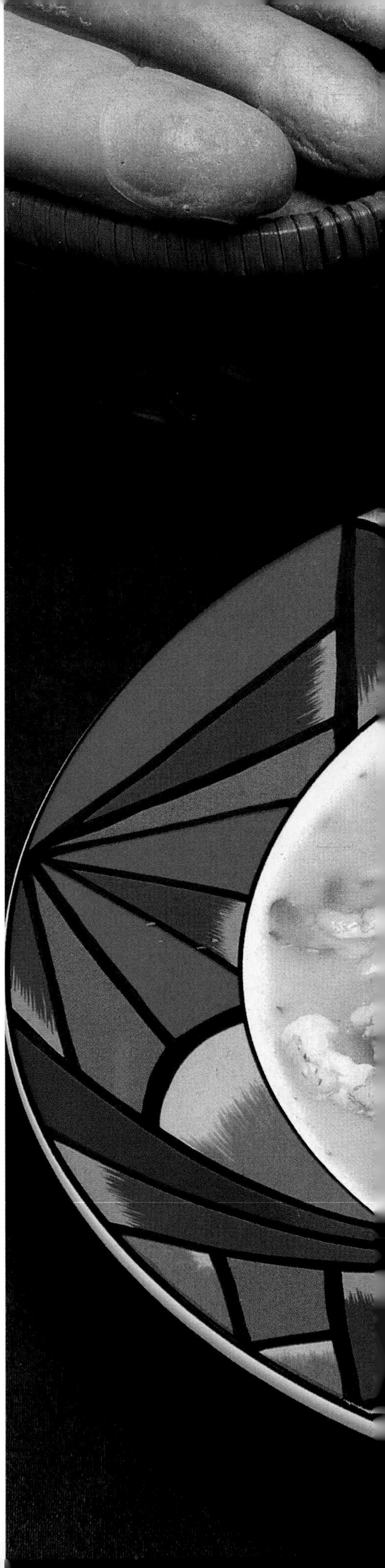

246
11

SCAMPI PROVENÇALE

5 tbsp	75 ml	butter
3	3	minced garlic cloves
1	1	large minced onion
1	1	finely diced red bell pepper
1	1	finely diced green bell pepper
6	6	large peeled, seeded, chopped tomatoes
1 cup	250 ml	Demi-Glace (see page 123)
½ cup	125 ml	whipping cream
1½ lbs	675 g	scampi tails
½ tsp	3 ml	paprika

Heat 3 tbsp (45 ml) butter in a sauce pan. Add the garlic, onion, and peppers and sauté until tender. Add the tomatoes and continue to cook for 20 minutes over low heat. Stir in demi-glace; continue to simmer for 20 minutes. Add the cream and simmer 5 additional minutes.

While sauce simmers, split the scampi down the back, pull meat from shell and butterfly it across the top of the shell. Melt the remaining butter and brush the scampi. Sprinkle with paprika and bake in a preheated 350°F (180°C) oven for 15 minutes.

Place scampi in sauce and simmer for 5 minutes. Serve with rice.

SERVES 4

CHICKEN SCHOLAZŌ

6-6 oz	6-170 g	boneless, skinless chicken breasts
6 tbsp	90 ml	butter
¼ cup	60 ml	red currant preserves
6	6	large peeled, stoned peaches
¼ cup	60 ml	brown sugar
¾ cup	190 ml	apple juice
1	1	cinnamon stick
3	3	cloves
3 tbsp	45 ml	flour, all purpose
¾ cup	190 ml	whipping cream
1 lb	450 g	fresh raspberries
2 tbsp	30 ml	lemon juice
3 tbsp	45 ml	granulated sugar
3 oz	80 g	grated semi-sweet chocolate

Wash and pat dry the chicken breasts. Place on a baking sheet. Melt 2 tbsp (30 ml) of butter; brush on the chicken. Bake in a preheated 350°F (180°C) oven for 30 minutes. Brush the chicken with the red currant preserves and continue to bake for an additional 5 minutes.

While chicken bakes, slice the peaches; place in a sauce pan. Add the brown sugar, apple juice, cinnamon stick and cloves. Simmer for 20 minutes. Discard the cinnamon stick and cloves.

Heat 3 tbsp (45 ml) of butter in a sauce pan. Add the flour and cook for 2 minutes over low heat. Whip in the cream and simmer for 5 minutes. Stir into the peaches.

Purée the raspberries in a food processor. Press through a sieve (to remove seeds) into a small sauce pan.

Add the lemon juice and sugar; bring to a boil. Reduce the heat and simmer to 1 cup (250 ml). Stir in the chocolate. Remove from the heat and whip in the remaining butter.

Remove chicken from oven.

Ladle the peach sauce onto plates, top with chicken and cover with chocolate sauce.

SERVES 6

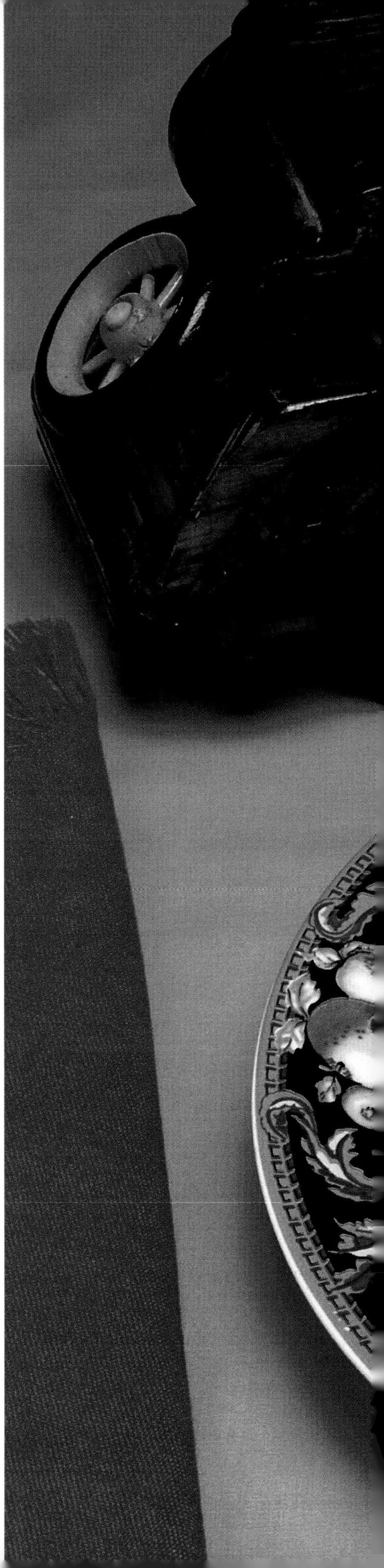

PRODUIT DE FRANCE

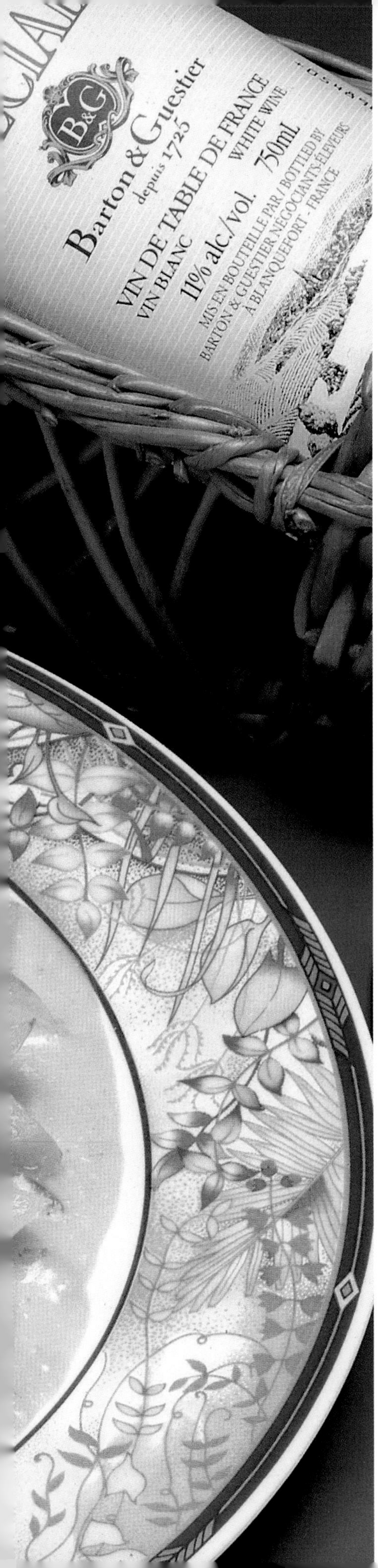

SHRIMP PÂTÉ WITH LOBSTER MORNAY SAUCE

2	2	pared, diced, medium potatoes
1 lb	450 g	shrimp meat
1¾ cups	440 ml	light cream
½ tsp	3 ml	fresh chopped basil
½ tsp	3 ml	salt
¼ tsp	1 ml	white pepper
1	1	minced garlic clove
½ cup	125 ml	butter
3	3	eggs
3 tbsp	45 ml	flour, all purpose
¾ cup	190 ml	Chicken Broth (see page 77)
¾ cup	190 ml	cooked chopped lobster meat
½ cup	125 ml	freshly grated Parmesan cheese

Place the potatoes in a sauce pan and cover with water. Bring to a boil and cook for 15 minutes. Add the shrimp and continue to cook until potatoes are tender. Drain and place in a food processor. Add a ½ cup (125 ml) of cream, basil, salt, pepper, and garlic; process until smooth. Melt half the butter and add; process with the eggs until just blended.

Spoon in lightly buttered molds, place into a pan half filled with water and bake in a 350°F (180°C) oven for 30 minutes.

While pâté bakes, heat the remaining butter in a sauce pan. Add the flour and cook 2 minutes over low heat.

Stir in the chicken broth and remaining cream. Reduce heat and simmer until thickened. Stir in the lobster and cheese; simmer for 2 more minutes.

Remove pâté from oven, unmold, and place on serving plates. Smother with sauce and serve.

SERVES 4

ORANGE ROUGHY ANDERSON

½ lb	225 g	raspberries
½ cup	125 ml	butter
2	2	egg yolks
6-6 oz	6-170 g	orange roughy fillets
2 cups	500 ml	Court Bouillon (see page 117)
24	24	blanched asparagus tips
12 oz	340 g	cooked crab meat

Purée the berries in a food processor, strain and discard pulp and seeds. In a sauce pan, gently simmer the juice down to 2 tbsp (30 ml). Cool.

Whisk the juice together with the egg yolks. Melt the butter and keep it hot. Place the egg yolks in a double boiler over low heat; cook, whisking constantly, until thick. Remove from heat and whisk in the warm butter until a nice creamy sauce is formed. Do not reheat.

Coddle the orange roughy in the court bouillon. Place onto a baking sheet; top with asparagus and crab meat. Cover with raspberry hollandaise (see page 108) and place in a preheated 500°F (260°C) oven until the sauce is golden brown. Serve at once.

SERVES 6

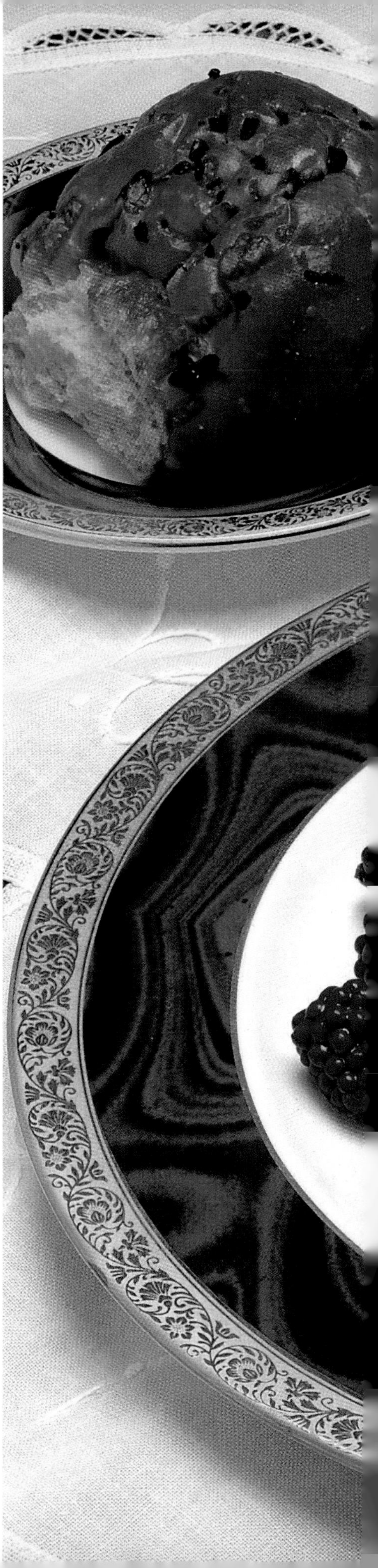

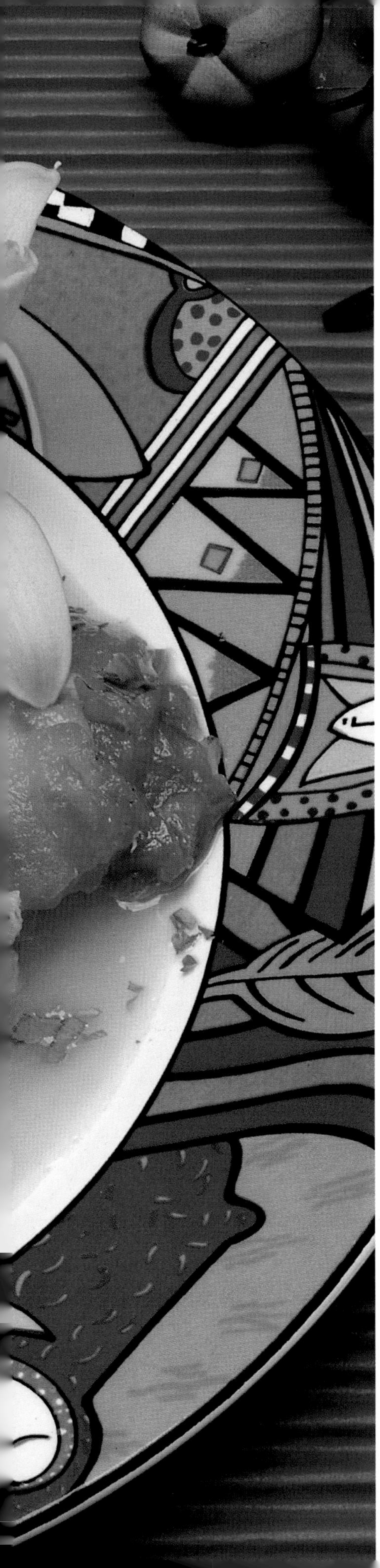

CHICKEN TAGMA

½ lb	225 g	rhubarb
2	2	pared sliced pears
2	2	large pared, sliced cooking apples
1 tsp	5 ml	grated orange rind
¼ cup	60 ml	granulated sugar
⅓ cup	90 ml	Calvados
6-6 oz	6-170 g	boneless, skinless chicken breasts
1½ cups	375 ml	yogurt
4 tbsp	60 ml	fresh chopped basil
3 tbsp	45 ml	fine dry bread crumbs
3 tbsp	45 ml	freshly grated Parmesan cheese
¼ cup	60 ml	white wine

Wash, clean and dice the rhubarb. Place into a sauce pan along with the pears, apples, orange rind, sugar and Calvados. Cover and simmer for 10 minutes; uncover and continue to simmer until the compote is very soft.

Place the chicken in a lightly greased casserole dish.

Combine ¾ cup (190 ml) of the yogurt with 2 tbsp (30 ml) of basil, the bread crumbs and cheese. Spread on the chicken. Bake in a preheated 350°F (180°C) oven for 40 minutes.

Plate the chicken; place 2 tbsp (30 ml) of the fruit compote on top of the chicken. Top with a dollop of the remaining yogurt and a sprinkling of basil. Serve.

SERVES 6

LAPIN FORESTIERE

4 tbsp	60 ml	safflower oil
1½ lbs	675 g	rabbit, cut into quarters
8	8	slices of bacon
20	20	button mushrooms
20	20	pearl onions
3	3	celery stalks, diced
3	3	carrots, diced
4 tbsp	60 ml	flour, all purpose
1 cup	250 ml	tomatoes, peeled, seeded, chopped
2 cups	500 ml	red wine
1 cup	250 ml	Beef Stock (see page 85)
2 tsp	10 ml	Worcestershire sauce
1 tbsp	15 ml	soya sauce
½ tsp	3 ml	Dijon mustard
¼ tsp	1 ml	salt
¼ tsp	1 ml	cracked black pepper
2 tbsp	30 ml	butter
8 oz	225 g	chanterelles

Heat the oil in a large kettle. Add the rabbit and brown. Dice the bacon and add to the rabbit along with the vegetables; sauté for 3 minutes. Sprinkle with flour and cook for 3 minutes. Add the remaining ingredients, except the butter and chanterelles.

Cover and simmer gently for 1½ hours. Heat the butter in a skillet and sauté the chanterelles. Place the rabbit over rice or noodles, and sprinkle with chanterelles.

SERVES 6

Pasta

Every nation of the world holds some kind of "strips of paste" recipes, but the exact origin of pasta is unknown. Pasta has made its mark in cuisine from as far back as the Chinese Ming dynasty. It is thought that Marco Polo introduced "noodles" to Italy upon his return from far away Asiatic countries during his 13th century expedition to China.

Pasta was familiar to Italy before that time, however. When Prince Theodric of the Teutonic tribe from the Vistual area invaded Italy in approximately 405 AD, he brought with him a type of noodle. There is evidence that pasta existed even earlier. Imperial Rome had a noodle very similar to the taglialle noodle (a 1" wide long noodle, also called mafalda) known as laganum. What is known is that upon the return of Marco Polo, the noodle became a popular staple of the Italian people. From Italy, the pasta noodle (tagliarini) spread throughout Europe, becoming the "nouilles" of France, the "fideos" of Spain, the "nudein" of Germany and the "noodle" in England.

Today, pasta has lead the world into new culinary pursuits, and will never be satisfied with being limited to tomato or cream based sauces again. Here in *Simply Delicious Cooking 2*, we have selected a unique and creative array of pasta dishes that even Marco would never have dreamed possible. Such items as Butternut Squash Gnocchi or a Veal Cappelletti with Smoked Chicken, Sun Dried Tomatoes, and Mushrooms in Mornay Sauce would have thrilled the ancient explorer, as they will your guests.

Throughout this chapter, and the publication as a whole, we have presented appetizers, soups, salads, entrées and even dessert pastas. An entire five course gourmet meal focused on pasta may be created from these pasta presentations alone.

You may never have imagined such dishes as Fruit Lobster and Shrimp Manicotti. You will find a recipe for such a masterpiece in this chapter. Or, perhaps you prefer to offer your guests the Chocolate and Curry Fettuccini with Apples and Shrimp. Better yet, use any of our 15 different pasta doughs and create your own special pasta dishes. One thing will always remain constant: the result will be *Simply Delicious*.

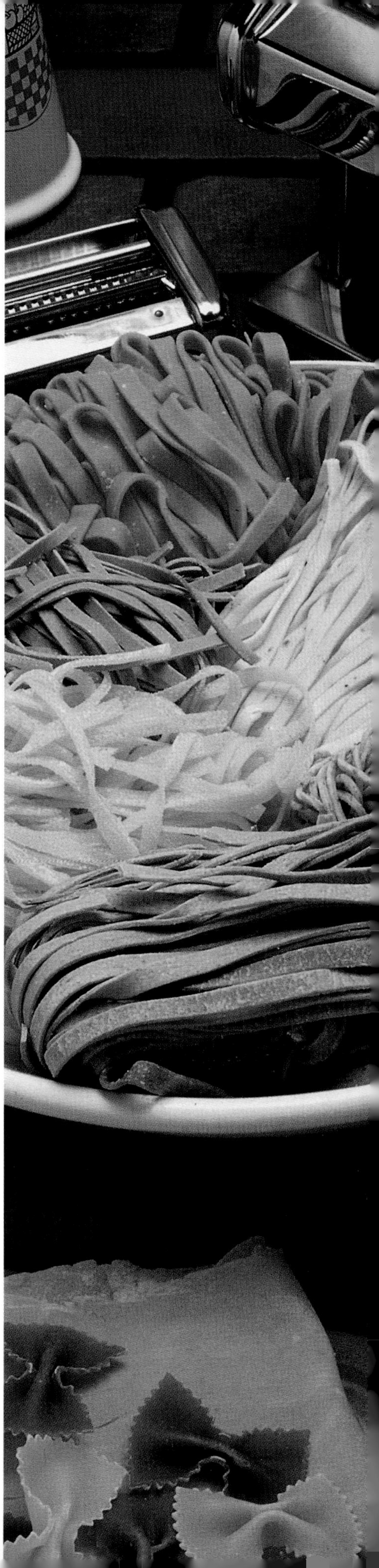

Assorted Pasta

FETTUCCINI WITH SMOKED SALMON

½ lb	250 g	fettuccini
3 tbsp	45 ml	unsalted butter
2 tbsp	30 ml	flour, all purpose
1½ cups	375 ml	light cream
¼ cup	60 ml	sherry
4 oz	120 g	smoked salmon cut in ¼" strips
1 tbsp	15 ml	fresh chopped dill
1 tsp	5 ml	basil
½ tsp	3 ml	cracked black pepper

Cook the noodles al dente in a kettle of boiling salted water.

In a small sauce pan heat the butter. Add the flour and cook for 2 minutes over low heat. Add the cream and simmer until slightly thick. Whip in the sherry and continue to simmer 5 additional minutes.

Place the noodles in a large serving bowl. Pour the sauce over the noodles. Toss with the salmon and herbs. Serve at once.

SERVES 6

SINGAPORE NOODLES

½ lb	225 g	pork tenderloin
3 tbsp	45 ml	light soya sauce
2 tbsp	30 ml	sherry
1 tbsp	15 ml	honey
½ tsp	3 ml	garlic powder
4 drops	4 drops	red food colouring
1 quan	1	Egg Pasta (see page 433)
3 tbsp	45 ml	peanut oil
½ lb	225 g	shrimp
½ cup	125 ml	finely diced onion
½ cup	125 ml	finely diced celery
½ cup	125 ml	finely diced green pepper
2 tsp	10 ml	curry powder

Dice the pork into ½" (1.5 cm) cubes, place in a small mixing bowl.

Blend the soya, sherry, honey, garlic powder and food colouring. Pour over pork and marinate for 3 hours.

In a kettle cook the noodles. Drain and reserve. In a wok or large skillet heat the oil. Quickly fry the pork and shrimp thoroughly. Add the vegetables and fry for 1½ to 2 minutes.

Add the noodles, toss to combine. Sprinkle with curry and fry for 1 minute. Serve.

SERVES 6

BASIC PASTA DOUGH

4 cups	1 L	semolina flour
½ tsp	3 ml	salt
4	4	eggs
1 tbsp	15 ml	oil
⅓ cup	80 ml	ice cold water

Sift the flour and salt together. Place into a mixing bowl. Slowly blend in the eggs one at a time. Add the oil and the water slowly until a smooth soft dough is formed.

Knead the dough for 15 minutes and allow to rest for an additional 15 minutes. Roll out the dough. Lightly dust with flour, fold in three, and roll out again. Repeat 6 to 8 times.

Now pass the dough through the pasta machine setting the rollers gradually down until you reach the desired thickness. The result should be a smooth sheet of dough ready to process as you require.

Pass through a pasta machine, or cut by hand to desired size. If processed by hand, simply roll the dough and cut into thin strips for noodles (fettuccini) or into wider strips for lasagna, cannelloni, ravioli, etc.

Process as any of our recipes direct.

NOTE: Use only enough flour to prevent sticking while rolling.

SERVES 6

Fettuccini with Smoked Salmon

Singapore Noodles

5 Cheese Lasagna

5 CHEESE LASAGNA

1 quan	1 quan	Pasta Verde (see page 436)
2	2	beaten eggs
8 oz	225 g	cream cheese
8 oz	225 g	grated cheddar cheese
8 oz	225 g	grated Havarti cheese
8 oz	225 g	ricotta cheese
1½ cups	375 ml	grated Parmesan cheese
2 tbsp	30 ml	butter
2 tbsp	30 ml	flour, all purpose
1 cup	250 ml	milk
1 cup	250 ml	Chicken Stock (see page 77)
3 cups	750 ml	Chunky Tomato Sauce (see page 117)

Prepare the pasta as directed. Roll into thin sheets. Cut the sheets into 4½ x 11 inches (11.25 x 27.5 cm).

Blend the eggs with the cheeses, reserve ½ cup (125 ml) of Parmesan, chill.

Heat the butter in a sauce pan. Add the flour and cook for 2 minutes. Add the milk and chicken stock. Simmer to a thin sauce.

In a large buttered baking dish place a thin layer of tomato sauce. Top this with a layer of noodles. Spread a layer of white sauce on the noodles topped by a layer of tomato sauce. Spread onto this a layer of cheese topped by another layer of sauces. Repeat this until complete. Be sure to finish with a layer of tomato sauce. Sprinkle with remaining Parmesan.

Cover with foil and bake in a preheated 400°F (200°C) oven for 25 minutes. Remove the foil and continue to bake for 8 minutes more. Serve.

SERVES 8-10

BUCKWHEAT PASTA

1 cup	250 ml	buckwheat flour
½ cup	125 ml	semolina flour
1	1	extra large egg, beaten
¼ cup	60 ml	ice cold milk
		ice water, only if required

Blend the flours in a mixing bowl. Add the egg and milk. Knead into a smooth ball (add small amounts of ice water if required), and process the same as Basic Pasta Dough (see page 426).

NOTE: When cooked this is usually served blended with other types of cooked pasta.

SERVES 6

PENNE CHICKEN CURRY

3 tbsp	45 ml	unsalted butter
1	1	diced green bell pepper
1	1	diced onion
1	1	minced garlic clove
4 oz	120 g	thin sliced mushrooms
3 tbsp	45 ml	flour
1 tbsp	15 ml	curry powder
2 cups	500 ml	diced seeded, peeled, tomatoes
1 cup	250 ml	Chicken Stock (see page 77)
1 cup	250 ml	sour cream
1 lb	450 g	cooked, diced chicken
12 oz	340 g	penne noodles
½ cup	125 ml	toasted sliced almonds

In a sauce pan heat the butter. Sauté the pepper, onion, garlic and mushrooms until tender. Stir in the flour and curry powder. Continue to cook 2 minutes over low heat. Add the tomatoes and simmer for 5 minutes. Add the chicken stock and sour cream, simmer until thickened.

Stir in the cooked chicken. Simmer for 5 additional minutes.

While the sauce is simmering, cook the penne in 3 quarts (3 L) of boiling salted water. Drain and transfer to a serving bowl.

Pour sauce over the noodles, sprinkle with almonds. Serve.

SERVES 6

SPAGHETTI WITH TENDERLOIN TIPS IN MARINARA SAUCE

1 quan	1	Basic Pasta Dough (see page 426)
3 tbsp	45 ml	olive oil
1 lb	450 g	beef tenderloin, diced in ½" cubes
1	1	sliced onion
4 oz	120 g	button mushrooms
½ tsp	3 ml	salt
½ tsp	3 ml	cracked pepper
3 cups	750 ml	Marinara Sauce (see page 111)

Process the pasta as directed. Cut into spaghetti.

In a large skillet heat the oil. Brown the tenderloin. Add the onion and mushrooms and sauté until tender, season with salt and pepper.

Pour the marinara sauce over beef and reduce to a simmer. Simmer for 8-10 minutes.

In a large kettle of boiling salted water cook the pasta al dente, drain and place on serving plates. Ladle generous amounts of sauce over the noodles and serve.

SERVES 6

CILANTRO PASTA

2	2	beaten eggs
1 tsp	5 ml	safflower oil
½ cup	125 ml	chopped cilantro leaves
2 cups	500 ml	semolina flour
		ice water, only if required

Blend the eggs, oil and cilantro together. Add the flour and slowly knead into a soft ball (add small amounts of ice water if required). Process as Basic Pasta Dough (see page 426).

SERVES 6

COCOA PASTA

2 cups	500 ml	semolina flour
2 tbsp	30 ml	cocoa powder
¼ cup	60 ml	granulated sugar
1 tsp	5 ml	vanilla extract
3	3	beaten eggs
		ice water, only if required

Sift together the flour, cocoa and sugar. Mix the vanilla with the eggs. Add flour slowly to the eggs. Knead into a smooth ball (add small amounts of ice water if required), and process the same as Basic Pasta Dough (see page 426).

SERVES 6

Penne Chicken Curry

Chang Yo Mein

HERB PASTA

1 tbsp	15 ml	sage, rosemary, oregano, thyme, chervil, marjoram or basil, choose one or a combination to total weight
3	3	eggs
2¾ cups	675 ml	semolina flour
1 tbsp	15 ml	olive oil
		ice water, only if required

Blend the spices with the herbs. Beat the eggs with the oil. Slowly add the flour and knead into a smooth ball (add small amounts of ice water if required). Process as Basic Pasta Dough (see page 426).

SERVES 6

CORNMEAL PASTA

1½ cups	375 ml	fine ground cornmeal
1½ cups	375 ml	semolina flour
4	4	eggs
1 tbsp	15 ml	safflower oil
		ice water, only if required

Blend the cornmeal and flour together. Beat the oil with the eggs. Place in a mixing bowl. Slowly add the flour. Knead into a smooth ball (add small amounts of ice water if required), and process as in Basic Pasta Dough (see page 426).

SERVES 6

Tomato Gnocchi

CHANG YO MEIN

1 quan	1	Egg Pasta (see page 433)
3 tbsp	45 ml	peanut oil
3 tbsp	45 ml	minced celery
¼ cup	60 ml	minced onion
¼ cup	60 ml	minced green pepper
1 lb	450 g	peeled, deveined shrimp
2 tbsp	30 ml	light soya sauce
2 tbsp	30 ml	sherry

In a wok or large skillet heat the oil. Quickly fry the vegetables and shrimp. Add soya sauce and sherry. Simmer for 1 minute.

Cook the noodles as directed while stir frying the other ingredients.

Transfer hot noodles to a serving plate. Pour the stir fry over the noodles. Serve at once.

SERVES 6

TOMATO GNOCCHI

1 cup	250 ml	Tomato Sauce (see page 106)
1 lb	450 g	potatoes
¼ tsp	1 ml	ground nutmeg
1 tsp	5 ml	chopped basil leaves
2 cups	500 ml	unbleached flour

In a sauce pan gently simmer the tomato sauce, reducing to ½ cup (125 ml) in volume.

Cook the potatoes by steaming them until they are fork tender. Purée the potatoes, blend in the tomato sauce, nutmeg and basil. Slowly add the flour until a soft dough is firm. The dough should hold shape on a teaspoon, place on a floured surface and press with a fork.

Cook the gnocchi in a kettle of boiling water for 3 minutes after they float. Serve with a light tomato sauce, cream sauce or toss with melted butter and sprinkle with Parmesan cheese.

SERVES 6

CALAMARI AND PRAWNS WITH CRACKED PEPPER LINGUINE

1 quan	1	Cracked Black Pepper Pasta (see recipe this page)
¼ cup	80 ml	olive oil
1 tbsp	15 ml	lemon juice
¼ tbsp	1 ml	garlic powder
¼ tsp	1 ml	onion powder
1 tsp	5 ml	oregano leaves
½ tsp	3 ml	cracked black pepper
½ tsp	3 ml	salt
½ lb	225 g	cleaned and sliced squid tubes
½ lb	225 g	peeled & deveined prawns
1	1	garlic clove
1 cup	250 ml	red bell peppers
1 tbsp	15 ml	basil leaves
3 tbsp	45 ml	parsley
3 oz	80 ml	freshly grated Romano cheese
2 tbsp	30 ml	pine nuts

Process the pasta as directed. Cut into linguine.

Blend half the oil with the lemon juice and seasonings. Place squid and prawns in a large mixing bowl, pour the oil lemon marinade over, marinate for 1 hour.

In a food processor or blender purée the garlic and bell peppers in the remaining oil. Add the basil, parsley, cheese and pine nuts. Process into purée.

Remove the seafood and grill over medium coals for 3 minutes per side.

While seafood cooks, boil the linguine in a kettle of boiling salted water al dente. Drain the linguine and toss with pesto, place on serving plates. Top with seafood and serve.

SERVES 6

LEMON PEPPER PASTA

1 tsp	5 ml	fresh cracked black pepper
2 tbsp	30 ml	grated lemon rind
3	3	beaten eggs
2 cups	500 ml	flour, all purpose
		ice water, only if required

Blend the pepper, lemon and eggs together. Place in a mixing bowl. Add the flour slowly and knead into a soft dough ball (add small amounts of ice water if required). Process as Basic Pasta Dough (see page 426).

SERVES 4

CRACKED BLACK PEPPER PASTA

1 tbsp	15 ml	fresh cracked black pepper
3	3	beaten eggs
2 cups	500 ml	semolina flour
		ice water, only if required

In a mixing bowl blend the pepper in the eggs. Slowly add the flour. Knead into a soft ball (add small amounts of ice water if required) of dough, and process the same as Basic Pasta Dough (see page 426).

SERVES 4

Calamari and Prawns with Cracked Pepper Linguine

Agnolotti with Prosciutto & Sausage

AGNOLOTTI WITH PROSCIUTTO & SAUSAGE

1 quan	1	Basic Pasta (see page 426)
6 oz	170 g	fine ground prosciutto
6 oz	170 g	mild Italian sausage meat
4 tbsp	60 ml	unsalted butter
3	3	eggs
½ cup	125 ml	bread crumbs
¼ cup	60 ml	freshly grated Romano cheese
1 tbsp	15 ml	olive oil
1	1	small diced onion
2 cups	500 ml	peeled, seeded and diced tomatoes
1	1	minced garlic clove
2 tsp	10 ml	fresh chopped basil leaves
1 tbsp	15 ml	fresh chopped parsley
3 quarts	4 L	Chicken Stock (see page 77)

Process the pasta into thin sheets. Cut out 36 – 3" (7.5 cm) rounds, cover with a moist cloth to prevent drying.

Blend the meats with 3 tbsp (45 ml) of butter, eggs, bread crumbs and Romano cheese. Mix thoroughly. Chill 1 hour. Place 1 tbsp (15 ml) of filling on each pasta round, moisten the edges and seal by pinching the edges together.

Heat the oil and remaining butter in a sauce pan. Cook the onion with the garlic until tender. Add the tomatoes and herbs. Reduce heat to a simmer, cook for 15 minutes.

Heat the chicken stock in a large kettle. Drop the agnolotti in the stock. Cook each for 3 minutes after they float to the top. Transfer to a serving platter. Pour the sauce over top and serve.

SERVES 6

EGG PASTA

3	3	eggs
2 cups	500 ml	semolina flour

Beat the eggs well. Slowly add the flour. Knead for 10 minutes. Cover and allow to rest for 15 minutes, knead a second time. On a lightly floured dusted board, roll very thin. Dust with flour. Fold and roll again. Repeat this several times. The result will be a smooth sheet of dough. Roll the dough and cut into very thin strips.

In a kettle boil 2 quarts (2 L) of water, cook the noodles for 2-3 minutes. Serve as desired.

SERVES 6

BANANA PASTA

1 cup	250 ml	banana pulp
⅓ cup	80 ml	granulated sugar
1 tsp	5 ml	vanilla extract
1	1	egg
2 cups	500 ml	semolina flour

Blend the banana, sugar, vanilla and egg together. Blend in the flour. Knead the dough into a smooth ball (add small amounts of ice water if required), and process as Basic Pasta Dough (see page 426)

SERVES 6

Ravioli with Fresh Tomato Cream

RAVIOLI WITH FRESH TOMATO CREAM

1 quan	1	Tomato Pasta Dough (see page 440)
1 tbsp	15 ml	olive oil
¾ lb	345 g	shredded beef chuck
2 oz	60 g	minced prosciutto
1	1	egg
½ tsp	3 ml	each of basil and oregano
½ cup	125 ml	freshly grated Romano cheese
2 tbsp	30 ml	butter
2 tbsp	30 ml	flour, all purpose
1 cup	250 ml	half & half cream
2 cups	500 ml	fresh tomato purée

Process the pasta as directed. Roll out into thin sheets. Cover with a moist cloth until required.

Heat the oil in a skillet and brown the beef. Drain oil and allow beef to cool in a large mixing bowl. Blend into the cooled beef the prosciutto, egg, seasonings and cheese.

Place tablespoon amounts of filling evenly over a sheet of dough, moisten the dough surrounding the filling with a little water. Place a second sheet of dough over the first. Cut between the filling with a scalloped edge pastry cutter.

In a sauce pan heat the butter, add the flour and cook for 2 minutes over low heat. Add the cream and simmer into a very thick sauce. Whip in the tomato purée, simmer for 20 minutes.

Cook ravioli in a large kettle of boiling water for 2 minutes, or until they float. Drain and place on serving plates, pour sauce over the ravioli and serve.

SERVES 6

SPINACH GNOCCHI

10 oz	280 g	fresh washed spinach
2 lbs	900 g	potatoes
1	1	beaten egg
1½ cups	375 ml	flour, all purpose

Steam the spinach. Cool. Chop or process until very fine.

Pare the potatoes then steam in a large kettle, until they are fork tender. Drain well, then purée, blend in the spinach.

Place in a mixing bowl. Add the egg and 1 cup (250 ml) flour. Knead the dough adding more flour as required. The gnocchi should be firm yet soft.

Mold 1 tsp (5 ml) of mixture on a spoon. Roll gently in your hands. (Be sure to flour your hands.) Place on a lightly floured surface and press with a fork.

Cook the gnocchi in a large kettle of boiling water. They are done when they float.

Serve with a cream sauce, pesto or a light tomato sauce.

SERVES 6

CRAB VERMICELLI

3 tbsp	45 ml	butter
2 tbsp	30 ml	flour, all purpose
½ cup	125 ml	light cream
1 cup	250 ml	crushed tomatoes
½ tsp	3 ml	fresh cracked black pepper
8 oz	225 g	crab meat
½ cup	125 ml	freshly grated Parmesan cheese
2 tsp	10 ml	basil
1 quan	1	Basic Pasta Dough (see page 426), cut into vermicelli

In a sauce pan heat the butter, add the flour and cook 2 minutes over low heat. Whip in the cream, simmer until a very thick sauce forms.

Whisk the tomatoes and pepper, simmer for 4 minutes. Blend in the crab meat, cheese and basil.

Cook the noodles al dente in a kettle of boiling water, drain and place noodles in a serving bowl and pour sauce over. Serve at once.

SERVES 6

Crab Vermicelli

Chicken Lo Mein

SAFFRON PASTA

¼ oz	8 ml	saffron
¼ cup	60 ml	water
2	2	eggs
2½ cups	625 ml	semolina flour
		ice water, only if required

Boil the saffron in the water, allow to cool completely. Beat the eggs and water together. Place the flour into a mixing bowl. Slowly add the liquid. Knead into a smooth ball (add ice water if required), and process the same as Basic Pasta Dough (see page 426).

SERVES 4

PASTA CAFE

⅓ cup	80 ml	hot water
3 tbsp	45 ml	instant coffee crystals
1	1	egg
2 cups	500 ml	flour, all purpose

Dissolve the coffee crystals in the water, cool. Beat the egg and blend in the coffee. Add the flour and knead into a smooth ball. Process as Basic Pasta Dough (see page 426). Serve with Coffee Chocolate Sauce (see page 112).

SERVES 4

PASTA VERDE

1¼ lbs	625 g	fresh spinach
3 cups	750 ml	semolina flour
4	4	beaten eggs
		ice water, only if required

Wash and rinse the spinach well. Chop the spinach fine. Blend the flour and spinach together. Slowly add the flour into the eggs. Knead into a smooth ball (add small amounts of ice if required), and process as in Basic Pasta Dough (see page 426).

SERVES 6

CHICKEN LO MEIN

1 quan	1	Egg Pasta (see page 433)
3 tbsp	45 ml	peanut oil
½ lb	225 g	diced raw chicken
½ cup	125 ml	sliced mushrooms
1 cup	250 ml	finely diced cabbage
½ cup	125 ml	Chicken Broth (see page 77)
2 tbsp	30 ml	soya sauce
1 tsp	5 ml	cornstarch
2 tbsp	30 ml	red pimento

In a large kettle boil 2 quarts (2 L) water. Add noodles and simmer for 3 minutes. Drain. Transfer to serving plate.

In a wok or large skillet heat the oil. Sauté the chicken until it is cooked thoroughly. Add mushrooms and cabbage. Add chicken broth and simmer for 5 minutes.

Mix the cornstarch with the soya sauce. Add to the chicken and simmer until thickened.

Pour chicken over the noodles, garnish with pimento and serve at once.

SERVES 6

STEAK DOUBLE WONG

1 quan	1	Egg Pasta (see page 433)
4 tbsp	60 ml	peanut oil
1 lb	450 g	shredded flank steak
4 oz	120 g	thinly sliced mushrooms
1 cup	250 ml	thinly sliced onion
3 tbsp	45 ml	soya sauce
1 tbsp	15 ml	honey
2 tbsp	30 ml	sherry
1 tsp	5 ml	cornstarch

In a kettle cook the noodles. Drain and reserve.

In a wok or large skillet heat 2 tbsp (30 ml) of the oil very hot, fast fry the steak. Add the mushrooms and onion, fry 1 minute. Add the remaining oil, continue to fry for 1 minute more.

Add the noodles, fry until brown. Turn the noodles over and fry. Transfer to a serving plate. Reserve hot.

Blend the soya sauce, honey, sherry and cornstarch, heat in a sauce pan until thick. Pour over noodles. Serve.

SERVES 6

Steak Double Wong

Orecchiette in Roasted Red Pepper Sauce

ORECCHIETTE IN ROASTED RED PEPPER SAUCE

1 quan	1	Cornmeal Pasta (see page 431)
1½ lbs	625 g	red bell peppers
2 tbsp	30 ml	olive oil
1	1	diced onion
1	1	minced garlic clove
½ tsp	3 ml	each of salt, basil and thyme
1 tsp	5 ml	cracked black pepper
2 tbsp	30 ml	lemon juice
¼ cup	60 ml	sherry
¼ cup	60 ml	half & half cream

To make orecchiette (little ears) divide the pasta into 2. Roll into a long rope shape, cut into ⅛" (3 mm) thick rounds. Dust each with flour. Place a round in the palm of your hand and indent the centre with your finger. Repeat until all rounds are complete.

Wrap red peppers in foil. Bake in a preheated 400°F (200°C) oven for 15 minutes. Remove foil and peel away the skin from peppers. Core and seed the peppers. Fine dice the peppers.

Heat the oil in a sauce pan and sauté the onion with the garlic until tender. Add the seasonings, lemon juice and peppers. Simmer covered for 45 minutes.

Remove from heat and purée in a food processor, return to sauce pan. Add the sherry and cream.

While the sauce is simmering, cook the pasta in 3 quarts (3 L) of boiling salted water for approximately 9 minutes, drain and transfer to a serving bowl. Toss with sauce and serve.

SERVES 6

Chocolate & Curry Fettuccini with Apples & Shrimp

CHOCOLATE AND CURRY FETTUCCINI WITH APPLES AND SHRIMP

2 cups	500 ml	pared, diced apples
1 quan	1	Basic Pasta Dough, cut into fettuccini (see page 426)
4 tbsp	60 ml	unsalted butter
3 tbsp	45 ml	flour, all purpose
1 tsp	5 ml	curry powder
½ cup	125 ml	half & half cream
1 cup	250 ml	Chicken Stock (see page 77)
4 oz	120 ml	shaved white chocolate
½ lb	225 g	cooked bay shrimp

Soak the apples in a little lemon juice to prevent browning.

In a sauce pan heat the butter, add the flour and curry powder. Cook 2 minutes, do not brown. Add the cream, chicken stock and apples. Simmer gently until thickened. Blend in the chocolate. Simmer for 2 minutes more.

Remove from heat, stir in the shrimp.

While sauce is simmering cook the noodles al dente in a kettle of boiling water. Drain the water, place in a serving bowl, pour sauce over and toss to coat noodles. Serve at once.

SERVES 6

WHOLE WHEAT PASTA

4	4	beaten eggs
1½ cups	375 ml	whole wheat flour
1½ cups	375 ml	semolina flour
2 tbsp	30 ml	olive oil
		ice water, only if required

Place the eggs into a mixing bowl. Sift the flours together. Slowly add the flour to the eggs until they are mixed into a smooth dough. Add the oil until just incorporated (add ice water if required). Process the same as directed in Basic Pasta Dough (see page 426).

SERVES 6

TOMATO PASTA DOUGH

2	2	eggs
¼ cup	60 ml	tomato paste
1 tbsp	15 ml	olive oil
2 cups	500 ml	semolina flour
		ice water, only if required

Blend the eggs, tomato paste and oil together. Place in a mixing bowl. Slowly add the flour. Knead into a smooth ball (add ice water if required), process as Basic Pasta Dough (see page 426).

SERVES 4

BEEF 'N' BROCCOLI NOODLES

1 quan	1	Egg Pasta (see page 433)
2 cups	500 ml	broccoli florets
1 tbsp	15 ml	peanut oil
1 lb	450 g	thin sliced flank steak
3 tbsp	45 ml	oyster sauce

Cook the noodles in a large kettle of boiling water. Drain and transfer to a serving plate, reserve hot.

Blanch the broccoli in boiling water for 2 minutes.

In a wok or large skillet heat the oil. Quickly fry the steak in the oil. Add the broccoli. Fry for 1 minute. Add the oyster sauce. Fry for 1 minute more.

Pour the beef over the noodles and serve at once.

SERVES 6

FARFALLE WESTPHALIAN

1 lb	450 g	farfalle (bow tie shape pasta)
1 lb	450 g	diced ham
4 tbsp	60 ml	unsalted butter
2 tbsp	30 ml	flour, all purpose
1 cup	250 ml	Chicken Stock (see page 77)
½ cup	125 ml	light cream
½ tsp	3 ml	black pepper
¼ cup	60 ml	freshly grated Parmesan cheese
¼ cup	60 ml	fine bread crumbs

In a kettle cook the noodles al dente. Drain and place in a 2 quart (2 L) greased casserole dish. Mix in the ham. Reserve hot.

In a small sauce pan heat ½ the butter. Add the flour and cook for 2 minutes over low heat. Add the chicken stock, simmer for 3 minutes. Add the cream and pepper. Simmer until thick. Pour over noodles. Sprinkle with cheese and bread crumbs. Dot with the remaining butter. Bake in a preheated 500°F (260°C) oven for 7-10 minutes or until golden brown. Serve at once.

SERVES 6

Farfalle Westphalian

Lobster Pirogue with Shrimp Sauce

LOBSTER PIROGUE WITH SHRIMP SAUCE

1 quan	1	any pasta
1 tbsp	15 ml	safflower oil
1	1	finely diced onion
5 oz	150 ml	chopped spinach
¼ tsp	1 ml	black pepper
1½ cups	375 ml	cooked diced lobster
1 cup	250 ml	ricotta cheese
2 tbsp	30 ml	butter
2 tbsp	30 ml	flour, all purpose
1 cup	250 ml	Fish Stock (see page 76)
1 cup	250 ml	light cream
1 cup	250 ml	cooked shrimp meat
½ tsp	3 ml	salt
½ tsp	3 ml	paprika
¼ tsp	1 ml	white pepper

Prepare the pasta as directed. Roll thin. Cut out 36 – 4" (10 cm) round. Cover with a damp cloth until required.

Heat the oil in a skillet, add the onion and sauté until tender. Add the spinach and continue to sauté 2 minutes.

Transfer to a mixing bowl and cool completely. Blend in the black pepper, lobster and ricotta.

Place 1¼ tbsp (20 ml) of filling on each pasta round. Moisten the edges with water, fold in half and pinch to seal. Repeat on each round until complete.

Heat a large kettle with 3 quarts (3 L) boiling salted water. Cook each pirogue until they float, about 3 minutes.

To make sauce heat the butter in a sauce pan, add the flour and cook for 2 minutes over low heat. Whip in the stock and cream. Simmer until thickened. Add the shrimp and seasonings.

Place pirogue on serving plates, smother with sauce and serve.

SERVES 6

FRUIT LOBSTER & SHRIMP MANICOTTI

1⁄2 quan	0.5	Basic Pasta Dough (see page 426), cut for 12 manicotti tubes
1⁄2 cup	125 ml	cottage cheese
1⁄2 cup	125 ml	grated white cheddar
½ cup	125 ml	ricotta cheese
½ cup	125 ml	smoked salmon cream cheese
½ cup	60 ml	freshly grated Parmesan cheese
½ tsp	3 ml	basil leaves
½ tsp	3 ml	cracked black pepper
½ lb	225 g	diced cooked lobster
½ lb	225 g	peeled, deveined cooked shrimp
1 cup	250 ml	diced pineapple
1 cup	250 ml	diced mango
3 tbsp	45 ml	unsalted butter
2 tbsp	30 ml	flour, all purpose
1 cup	250 ml	Chicken Stock (see page 77)
1 cup	250 ml	half & half cream

Begin by blending the cheeses, basil and pepper. Mix into the cheeses the seafood and fruit.

Cook the manicotti tubes in 3 quarts of boiling salted water. Drain and rinse in cold water.

Stuff the manicotti by placing equal amounts of cheese filling in the centre. Roll the pasta. Place the seam end down in a lightly greased casserole dish.

Heat the butter in a sauce pan. Add the flour and cook for 2 minutes over low heat. Add the chicken stock and cream, simmer until thick. Pour the sauce over manicotti. Bake in a preheated 400°F (200°C) oven for 30 minutes. Serve at once.

SERVES 6

Lemon Pepper Vermicelli Primavera

LEMON PEPPER VERMICELLI PRIMAVERA

1 quan	1	Lemon Pepper Pasta (see page 432)
3 tbsp	45 ml	unsalted butter
3 tbsp	45 ml	flour, all purpose
2 cups	500 ml	milk
½ cup	125 ml	Parmesan cheese
2 tsp	10 ml	cracked black pepper
2 tbsp	30 ml	safflower oil
⅓ cup	80 ml	broccoli florets
⅓ cup	80 ml	cauliflower florets
1	1	julienne cut carrot
3 oz	80 g	button mushroom
3 oz	80 g	snow peas
½ cup	125 ml	julienne cut green zucchini
½ cup	125 ml	julienne cut yellow zucchini

Process the pasta as directed. Cut into vermicelli.

In a sauce pan heat the butter, add the flour and cook two minutes over low heat. Add the milk and simmer until sauce thickens. Stir in the cheese and pepper. Simmer for 5 minutes.

Heat the oil in a wok or large skillet. Add the vegetables and sauté until tender. Blend in the sauce. Reserve hot.

In a kettle of boiling water cook the noodles al dente. Drain and transfer to serving plates top with sauce and serve.

SERVES 6

VEAL CAPPELLETTI WITH SMOKED CHICKEN, SUN DRIED TOMATOES & MUSHROOMS IN MORNAY SAUCE

1 quan	1	Basic Pasta Dough (see page 426)
2 tbsp	30 ml	olive oil
¾ lb	345 g	ground veal
2 oz	60 g	minced prosciutto
½ cup	125 ml	freshly grated Parmesan cheese
¼ tsp	1 ml	rosemary
¼ tsp	1 ml	black pepper
1	1	egg
1 tbsp	15 ml	unsalted butter
3 oz	80 g	sliced mushrooms
½ lb	225 g	cooked, smoked, diced chicken meat
6	6	coarsely chopped sun dried tomatoes
3 cups	750 ml	Mornay Sauce (see page 111)

Process the pasta dough and roll out. Cut the dough into 3" (7.5 cm) squares with a scalloped edge pastry cutter. Cover with a damp cloth until required.

Heat the oil in a skillet. Fry the veal until completely cooked through. Drain excess oil, place veal into a large mixing bowl and cool. Blend into the veal the prosciutto, cheese, rosemary, pepper, and the egg.

Place a teaspoon of filling in the centre of each pasta square. Brush the edges with a little water. Fold into a triangle just over the fillings, press to seal. Leave a border of dough around the filling. Wrap the pasta around the index finger. Seal the two sides with your thumb. Curl the overlapping pasta outward. The result should be small pasta hat (cappelletti).

Cook the cappelletti in a large kettle of boiling salted water. When they float they are done. Place onto serving platters, cover with sauce and serve.

TO MAKE THE SAUCE:

Heat the butter in a sauce pan. Sauté the mushrooms in the butter. Add the chicken, tomato and mornay sauce, reduce heat. Simmer for 10 minutes.

SERVES 6

Veal Cappelletti with Smoked Chicken, Sun Dried Tomatoes & Mushrooms in Mornay Sauce

BUTTERNUT SQUASH RICOTTA GNOCCHI

1 lb	450 g	butternut squash
½ lb	225 g	ricotta cheese
2	2	beaten eggs
¼ tsp	1 ml	ground nutmeg
½ tsp	3 ml	ground cinnamon
2 cups	500 ml	flour, all purpose
2 tbsp	30 ml	butter
4 oz	120 g	julienne sliced ham
2 cups	500 ml	julienne sliced radicchio

Cut the squash in half. Cover with foil and bake in a preheated 400°F (200°C) oven for 35-40 minutes, until the flesh is soft. Remove from the oven. Cool and scoop out the flesh.

Blend the squash with the cheese in a food processor into a fine purée. Add the eggs and the spices. Add 1 cup (250 ml) of flour and begin to knead. Slowly add the remaining flour kneading until the mixture becomes a soft dough yet firm enough to hold shape.

Shape the gnocchi by dropping teaspoon size dumpling onto a lightly floured surface, mold into small balls and press down with a fork.

In a large kettle of boiling salted water drop the dumplings into the water. Once the gnocchi float to the top, cook for an additional 3 minutes. Place onto a warm serving plate.

Heat the butter in a skillet. Sauté the ham and radicchio for 1 minute, pour over the gnocchi, toss and serve.

SERVES 6

Butternut Squash Ricotta Gnocchi

CREOLE CHICKEN RAVIOLI

1 quan	1	Cracked Black Pepper Pasta (see page 432)
1 lb	450 g	raw ground chicken
⅓ lb	125 g	hot or spicy Italian sausage meat
½ cup	125 ml	bread crumbs
1 tbsp	15 ml	olive oil
1 cup	250 ml	minced onion
½ cup	125 ml	minced green bell peppers
1	1	minced garlic
2	2	eggs
¼ tsp	1 ml	oregano
⅛ tsp	pinch	cayenne pepper
2 cups	500 ml	hot Creole Sauce (see page 121)

Prepare the pasta according to direction. Roll thin. Cover with a moist cloth until required.

Heat the oil in a skillet, sauté the onion, bell pepper and garlic until tender and all moisture has evaporated. Cool.

Blend the chicken, sausage, bread crumbs, vegetables, eggs and seasonings together.

On a pasta sheet place 1 tbsp (15 ml) size of filling spread evenly over the sheet. Lightly moisten the pasta around the filling. Place a second sheet of pasta over the first. Use a scalloped pastry roll and cut between the filling.

Place the ravioli in a kettle of salted boiling water a few at a time. Cook for 3-4 minutes after each floats. Transfer to a serving platter. Pour the Creole sauce over the ravioli and serve.

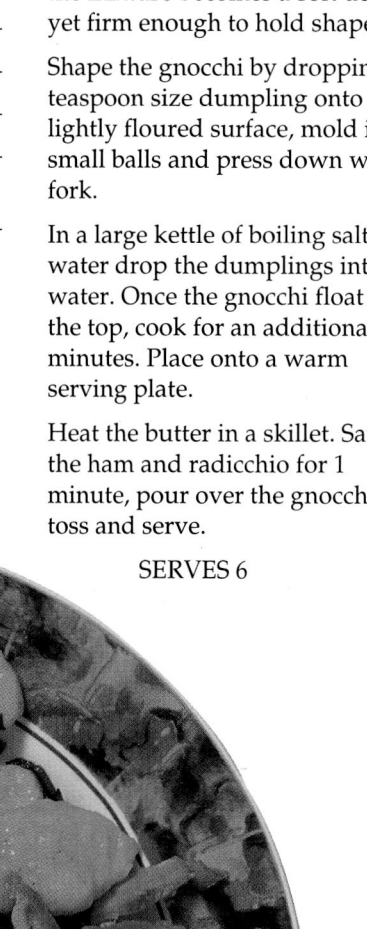

SERVES 6

Creole Chicken Ravioli

Jumbo Shells with Crab Mornay

JUMBO SHELLS WITH CRAB MORNAY

12	12	jumbo pasta shells
3 tbsp	45 ml	unsalted butter
1	1	finely diced onion
½ cup	125 ml	sliced mushrooms
1 lb	450 g	cooked crab meat
½ cup	125 ml	ricotta cheese
1	1	egg
½ tsp	3 ml	black cracked pepper
2 tbsp	30 ml	flour, all purpose
½ cup	125 ml	half & half cream
1 cup	250 ml	Chicken Stock (see page 77)
⅓ cup	80 ml	freshly grated Parmesan cheese

Cook the shells in 4 quarts (4 L) boiling salted water for 12-14 minutes. Rinse under cold water.

Melt 1 tbsp (15 ml) of butter in a large skillet. Sauté the onion and mushrooms until tender and all moisture has evaporated. Allow to cool.

Blend the crab, ricotta, sautéed onion, egg and pepper. Stuff each shell with the mixture pressing into the shell. Place shells in a lightly greased casserole dish.Heat the remaining butter in a sauce pan, add the flour and cook 2 minutes over low heat. Add the chicken stock and cream and simmer until thickened. Add the Parmesan and simmer an additional 2 minutes.

Pour sauce over shells, bake in a preheated 350°F (180°C) oven for 20 minutes. Serve.

SERVES 6

Cilantro Pasta with Blackened Chicken in Ancho Chile Garlic Sauce

CILANTRO PASTA WITH BLACKENED CHICKEN IN ANCHO CHILE, GARLIC SAUCE

1 quan	1	Cilantro Pasta (see page 429)
1 lb	450 g	boneless chicken breast strips
½ tsp	3 ml	each of oregano, basil, thyme, onion powder,
1 tsp	5 ml	garlic powder
¼ tsp	1 ml	each of cayenne pepper, black pepper, white pepper
1 tsp	5 ml	chili powder
1 tsp	5 ml	salt
4 tbsp	60 ml	olive oil
3	3	minced ancho chilies
3	3	minced garlic cloves
2 cups	500 ml	tomato purée

Process the pasta as directed. Cut into desired shape.

Blend all the seasoning together. Reserve 1 tbsp (15 ml) of seasoned blend.

Dust the chicken with the seasonings. Heat 3 tbsp (45 ml) of oil in a skillet to very hot. Fry the chicken a few strips at a time for 2 minutes per side. Once complete reserve hot.

Heat the remaining oil in a sauce pan. Sauté the chili and garlic, add the tomato purée and remaining seasoning. Simmer 20 minutes.

Cook the pasta al dente in a large kettle of boiling water. Drain the pasta and toss with sauce. Top with chicken strips and serve.

SERVES 6

GNOCCHI WITH EMINCE BEEF IN GREEN PEPPERCORN SAUCE

1 quan	1	Gnocchi (choose any of our selections)
3 tbsp	45 ml	olive oil
1	1	fine diced onion
4 oz	120 g	sliced mushrooms
1½ lbs	675 g	ground filet
2 tbsp	30 ml	butter
3 tbsp	45 ml	flour, all purpose
2 cups	500 ml	Beef Stock (see page 85)
¼ cup	60 ml	sherry
2 tsp	10 ml	green peppercorns

Prepare and cook the gnocchi as directed.

Heat the oil in a skillet. Add the onion and mushrooms and sauté until tender. Add the beef and cook until browned.

Stir in the butter and cook for 1 minute. Add the flour and blend thoroughly, continue to cook for 2 minutes. Stir in the beef stock, sherry and peppercorns. Simmer gently until sauce has thicken.

Pour over gnocchi and serve at once.

SERVES 6

Gnocchi with Emince Beef in Green Peppercorn Sauce

SHANGHAI NOODLES

1 lb	450 g	broad noodles
3 tbsp	45 m	peanut oil
2 tsp	10 ml	minced ginger root
1	1	minced garlic clove
1 lb	450 g	pork shredded
½ lb	225 g	shrimp
4 oz	120 g	sliced mushrooms
3 tbsp	45 ml	hoisin sauce
½ tsp	3 ml	cayenne pepper
2 tbsp	30 ml	soya sauce
1 tbsp	15 ml	sherry
2 tsp	10 ml	cornstarch

In a large kettle of boiling water, cook the noodles, drain and reserve.

In a wok heat the oil. Quickly fry the ginger and garlic, add the pork, shrimp and mushrooms, cook thoroughly. Add the noodles and fry 1 minute per side.

Blend the hoisin, cayenne, soya, sherry and cornstarch, pour over noodles. Fry 1-2 additional minutes, serve at once.

SERVES 6

LINGUINE WITH OLIVE OIL, GARLIC AND FRESH HERBS

1 quan	1	Pasta Verde (see page 436)
3	3	minced garlic cloves
4 tbsp	60 ml	olive oil
1 tbsp	15 ml	fresh chopped thyme leaves
2 tbsp	30 ml	chopped cilantro leaves
1 tbsp	15 ml	fresh chopped basil leaves

Process the pasta as directed. Cut into linguine. Cook in a large kettle of boiling salted water. Drain.

In a food processor or blender, purée the garlic, thyme and cilantro. Add the oil, and blend another 10 seconds. Toss the hot noodles in the pesto. Serve.

SERVES 6

Linguine with Olive Oil, Garlic & Fresh Herbs

PIZZA

Take a piece of pan bread, top it with a little sauce and a few other ingredients, and see it sweep the world off its feet. Such is the history and reputation of the pizza.

In France they call it pissaladière, in the Middle East it's a pita, in Mexico it is a tortilla topped with great delights. In essence, a pizza is nothing more than a baked, open-faced sandwich. But, what a sandwich!

Pizza is a culinary invention of Naples, Italy (home of that other popular Italian food, spaghetti), and was first called Pizza Napoletana Verace (the true Neapolitan Pizza). It originally consisted of a base of pan type bread topped with tomato, garlic, olive oil and oregano. The dish was then baked in a hot oven and sold on the street. The addition of cheese came some time later, and with it arrived the first culinary free for all. Soon, no matter what ingredients were on hand, one could put them on a pizza and be well on one's way to culinary success.

Pizza has sustained the poverty ridden (such as the poor street people of Italy), and entertained the well to do (as it does in Wolfgang Puck's restaurant to the stars, Spago). One thing is for certain, however; with pizza, casual entertaining will always be fun, exciting and not expensive. Pizza has become the food to unify friendships forever. As the world's most popular food, every nationality enjoys good fellowship and intimate companionship around this most influential of all cuisines.

Pizzas may come disguised as calzone or panzarotti (a sort of pizza turnover) or a double crust pie with the filling completely enclosed. No matter what name you give it, your guests are going to call it *Simply Delicious*.

Within the pages of this chapter, look forward to a selection of pizzas that may not be found in any restaurant anywhere in the world. Each is an original creation of excitement, which is exactly what your guests will experience when they sample their first bite—utter excitement, coupled with the cry for more.

You may sample such delights as the Calzone Quattro Stagioni. Or plan to intrigue your guests with our Louisiana Scheme Pizza. Why, you may even entertain with dessert pizzas. Or, create your own! All the basic recipes for creative pizzas are found within these pages. The outcome of the party you host will be happy guests, determined to acquire your recipes. They are, after all, *Simply Delicious*.

Quattro Formaggi "Pizza of Four Cheeses"

BASIC PIZZA DOUGH

1 tsp	5 ml	granulated sugar
1 cup	250 ml	warm water
1 tbsp	15 ml	(envelope) of active dry yeast
2 tbsp	30 ml	butter, melted and cooled
3½ cups	875 ml	all purpose flour
⅛ tsp	pinch	salt
2	2	eggs, beaten

In a large bowl, dissolve the sugar in the warm water. Sprinkle with the yeast and let stand 10 minutes or until foamy. Stir in the butter.

Stir in half the flour, pinch of salt and eggs into the yeast mixture. Gradually stir in enough of the remaining flour to make a slightly sticky ball.

Knead the dough on a lightly floured surface until smooth and elastic, about 5 minutes.

Place dough into a greased bowl and let rest 15 minutes. Punch down the dough; cut in half. Roll out each piece of dough into a 11" (28 cm) circle, allow to rise again, 15 minutes.

Place on a greased 14" (35 cm) pizza pan. With finger tips press dough to fill half the pan working from the centre, rest dough for 10 minutes. Press once again until dough covers pan completely.

Dough is now ready for sauce and toppings.

NOTE: To convert basic dough to sweet dough, add these ingredients to the yeast mixture after the first addition of flour. Proceed as directed.

¼ cup	60 ml	granulated sugar
1 tbsp	15 ml	vanilla
1 tbsp	15 ml	lemon peel
1 tsp	5 ml	cinnamon

YIELDS two 14" (35 cm)

BLUEBERRY PIZZA

12 oz	340 g	cream cheese
4	4	eggs
¼ cup	60 ml	heavy cream
2 cups	500 ml	granulated sugar
2 tsp	10 ml	lemon rind
8 cups	2 L	blueberries, fresh
½ quan	0.5	Sweet Dough (see Basic Pizza Dough, preceding recipe)
2 tbsp	30 ml	lemon juice
½ cup	125 ml	apple juice
6 tbsp	90 ml	cornstarch

Preheat oven to 350°F (180°C).

Soften the cream cheese, then beat until very light. Beat the eggs into the cheese 1 at a time. Add the cream, ½ cup (125 ml) sugar and lemon rind, fold in 4 cups (1 L) blueberries and 2 tbsp (30 ml) cornstarch.

*Pan the dough according to instructions.

Pour mixture onto the dough. Bake for 45 minutes. Chill for 4-6 hours before serving.

In a sauce pan, add the remaining blueberries, sugar, lemon juice. Mix the cornstarch with the apple juice, add to the blueberry sauce. Simmer over low heat until mixture thickens. Cool, and ladle over the pizza slices as it is served.

* Use flan pans for fluted edges.

YIELDS two 8" (20 cm) or one 14" (35 cm)

Blueberry Pizza

Pissaladière – French Pizza

PISSALADIÈRE— FRENCH PIZZA

DOUGH:

2 tbsp	30 ml	dry active yeast
¼ cup	60 ml	warm water
2¼ cups	560 ml	unbleached flour
1 tsp	5 ml	salt
⅓ cup	80 ml	olive oil
2	2	eggs

In a large mixing bowl, dissolve the yeast in the water, let it rest 10 minutes. Add 1 cup (250 ml) flour, the salt and oil. Beat into a smooth batter. Add ½ cup (125 ml) flour and the eggs, blend thoroughly.

Turn out onto a floured surface. Knead and gradually add the remaining flour, knead into a smooth ball.

Place into a greased bowl, cover and allow to rise for 1½ hours. Punch down and divide into two. Roll dough into rounds and place into pans. Dough is now ready for topping.

TOPPING:

6	6	large Spanish onions
½ cup	125 ml	olive oil
½ tsp	3 ml	each of basil, oregano, fennel
20	20	anchovy fillets
1 cup	125 ml	black olive slices
½ lb	225 g	grated Gruyere cheese
½ cup	125 ml	grated Parmesan cheese
½ cup	125 ml	grated Romano cheese

While dough is rising for 1½ hours, chop the onions, and heat the oil in a large skillet and gently sauté the onions, cover until soft. Increase the heat, uncover and continue to cook the onions until brown (caramelized). Drain the onions thoroughly.

Sprinkle herbs over dough, then spread the onions over the dough. Add anchovies and olives, then sprinkle the cheese over top.

Bake in a 400°F (200°C) preheated oven for 15 minutes or until golden brown. Serve at once.

YIELDS four 8" (20 cm) or two 10" (25 cm)

HERB CRUST

2 tbsp	30 ml	dry active yeast (2 envelopes)
1½ cups	375 ml	warm water
4 cups	1 L	all purpose flour-approximately
1 tsp	5 ml	salt
½ tsp	3 ml	each of basil, thyme, oregano, garlic powder, onion powder, chervil, black cracked pepper
¼ cup	60 ml	olive oil

In a large mixing bowl, dissolve the yeast in the warm water, rest 10 minutes or until foamy. Stir in 2 cups (500 ml) of flour along with the salt and seasonings. Stir to a smooth batter. Stir in the oil. Add 1 cup (250 ml) flour stirring into a ball. Add enough flour to form a smooth dough. Dough should not be sticky.

Knead the dough for 5 minutes, and allow to rest 15 minutes. Divide into two. Roll out into 11" (28 cm) circles. Rest an additional 15 minutes. Place dough into 14" (35 cm) pizza pans, with finger tips press dough from centre to the edges until pan is completely covered by dough.

Dough is now ready for sauce and toppings.

YIELDS four 8" (20 cm) or two 14" (35 cm)

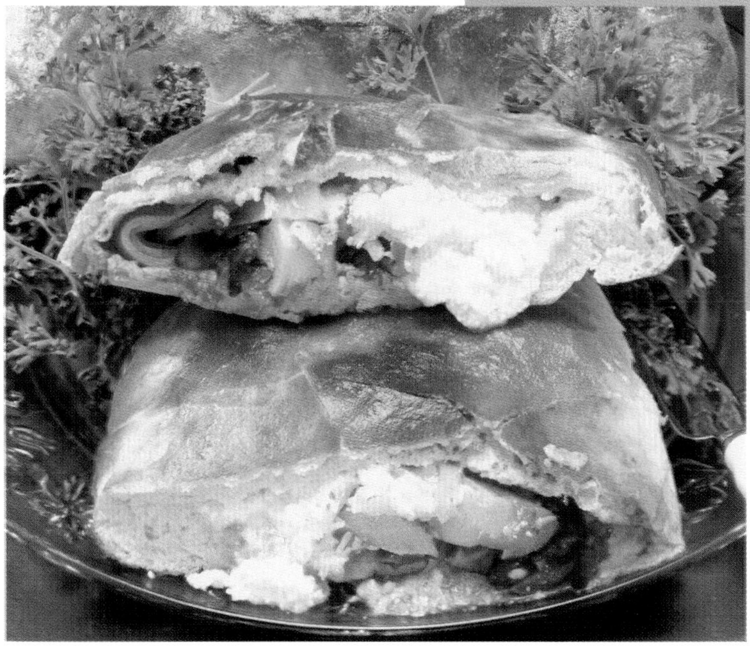

Calzone Quattro Stagioni "Four Season Calzone"

PIZZA SAUCE

3 tbsp	45 ml	vegetable or olive oil
2	2	minced garlic cloves
1	1	finely diced onion
1	1	finely diced celery stalk
½	0.5	finely diced green bell pepper
3 lbs	1.3 kg	peeled, seeded and chopped tomatoes
1 tsp	5 ml	oregano leaves
1 tsp	5 ml	thyme leaves
1 tsp	5 ml	basil leaves
1 tsp	5 ml	salt
½ tsp	3 ml	cracked pepper
1 tbsp	15 ml	Worcestershire sauce
⅔ cup	160 ml	tomato paste

In a large pot heat the oil and sauté the vegetables until tender. Add the tomatoes, seasonings, Worcestershire sauce and tomato paste. Reduce heat and simmer for 2 hours, or until sauce is very thick, stir occasionally. Cool.

Use as required.

YIELDS 2 Cups (500 ml)

QUATTRO FORMAGGI "PIZZA OF FOUR CHEESES"

½ quan	0.5	Basic Pizza Dough (see page 452) or Whole Wheat Crust (see page 456) or Garlic and Parmesan Crust (see page 460) or Herb Crust (see page 453)
2 cups	500 ml	Pizza Sauce (see recipe this page)
1½ cups	375 ml	grated mozzarella
1½ cups	375 ml	grated brick cheese
1 cup	250 ml	grated Parmesan cheese
1 cup	250 ml	grated provolone cheese

Preheat the oven to 450°F (230°C). Pan the dough according to instruction.

Spoon the sauce over the dough to ½" (1.5 cm) from the edge of the pan. Sprinkle evenly with cheeses.

Bake for 15 minutes or until crust is golden. Remove from pan, slice and serve.

YIELDS two 8" (20 cm) or one 14" (35 cm)

CALZONE QUATTRO STAGIONI "FOUR SEASON CALZONE"

1 quan	1	Gourmet Crust (see page 455)
1 cup	250 ml	Pizza Sauce (see recipe this page)
3 oz	80 g	sliced and sautéed mushrooms
6 oz	150 g	julienne cut ham
12 oz	340 ml	julienne cut marinated artichoke hearts drained
½ cup	125 ml	sliced black olives
1 cup	250 ml	ricotta cheese
1 cup	250 ml	grated mozzarella
⅓ cup	80 ml	grated provolone
1	1	egg, beaten

Roll the dough into four rounds. Place two of the rounds into two 8" (20 cm) pizza pans. Preheat the oven to 450°F (230°C).

Sauce each panned round. Cover the sauce with the mushrooms, ham, artichokes, and olives. Blend the cheese's together and place on pizzas.

Place remaining rounds over the pizzas and crimp the edges to seal tightly. Brush with egg. Poke with a fork to allow steam to escape.

Bake for 15-20 minutes or until golden brown.

SERVES 4

TIP: Sauté the mushrooms in the artichoke marinade.

OYSTER & SHRIMP PERNOD PIZZA

4 tbsp	60 ml	butter
2 cups	500 ml	shucked oysters – liquid reserved
2 cups	500 ml	large peeled and deveined shrimp
¼ cup	60 ml	Pernod liqueur
3 tbsp	45 ml	flour
½ cup	125 ml	Chicken Broth (see page 77)
1 cup	250 ml	heavy cream
½ tsp	3 ml	salt
¼ tsp	1 ml	white pepper
¼ cup	60 ml	sherry
1½ cups	375 ml	grated provolone
½ quan	0.5	Basic Pizza Dough (see page 452) or Gourmet Crust (recipe follows)

Heat the butter in a sauce pan, quickly sauté the oysters and shrimp, cook thoroughly, flame carefully with Pernod. Remove the oysters and the shrimp and reserve.

Stir in the flour and cook for 2 minutes over low heat. Add the broth, cream, salt, pepper and sherry. Reduce heat and simmer until thick. Stir in the seafood.

Pan the dough according to instructions. Spoon the mixture over the dough, sprinkle with cheese.

Bake in a preheated 450°F (230°C) oven for 15 minutes or until crust is golden brown. Remove from the pan. Slice and serve.

YIELDS two 8" (20 cm)

GOURMET CRUST

2 tbsp	30 ml	granulated sugar
¼ cup	60 ml	warm water
2 tbsp	30 ml	dry active yeast
2 cups	500 ml	milk
1 tsp	5 ml	salt
3 tbsp	45 ml	butter
6½ cups	1.6 L	flour
1	1	egg, beaten
¼ cup	60 ml	heavy cream

Mix 1 tsp (5 ml) of sugar in the warm water. Dissolve the yeast in the water and let soften 10 minutes.

In a sauce pan combine the milk, remaining sugar, salt and butter. Scald, cool then transfer to a mixing bowl.

Stir in the yeast mixture, and 3 cups (750 ml) of flour. Beat for 2 minutes. Cover. Allow to rise for 1 hour, then beat in the remaining flour, egg and the heavy cream.

Knead in a mixer for 8 minutes, cover and allow to rise.

Divide the dough evenly into either two or four, place into well greased pans (if required by your pizza recipe), allow to rest for 15 minutes. Spread the dough evenly over the pans by pressing it out from the centre with your finger tips (or roll with a rolling pin) covering the entire pan.

Use according to instructions in your recipe.

YIELDS four 8" (20 cm)
or two 14" (35 cm)

SHRIMP PANZAROTTI

½ quan	0.5	Gourmet Crust (preceding recipe)
2 cups	500 ml	Pizza Sauce (see page 454)
½ cup	125 ml	finely diced onions
½ cup	125 ml	finely diced green bell peppers
½ cup	125 ml	sliced mushrooms
2 cups	500 ml	peeled, deveined, cooked shrimp *
2 cups	500 ml	grated mozzarella cheese
1	1	egg beaten

Roll the dough according to instructions except do not pan the dough. Roll four rounds and spread half of each of the rounds with the sauce.

Sprinkle with onions, peppers, mushrooms, shrimp and cheese. Fold in half, crimp the edges to seal. Place on a greased baking sheet, and brush with the egg.

Bake in a preheated 450°F (230°C) oven for 15 minutes or until golden brown. Serve.

*Substitute any other meat desired or omit and use extra or different vegetables.

SERVES 4

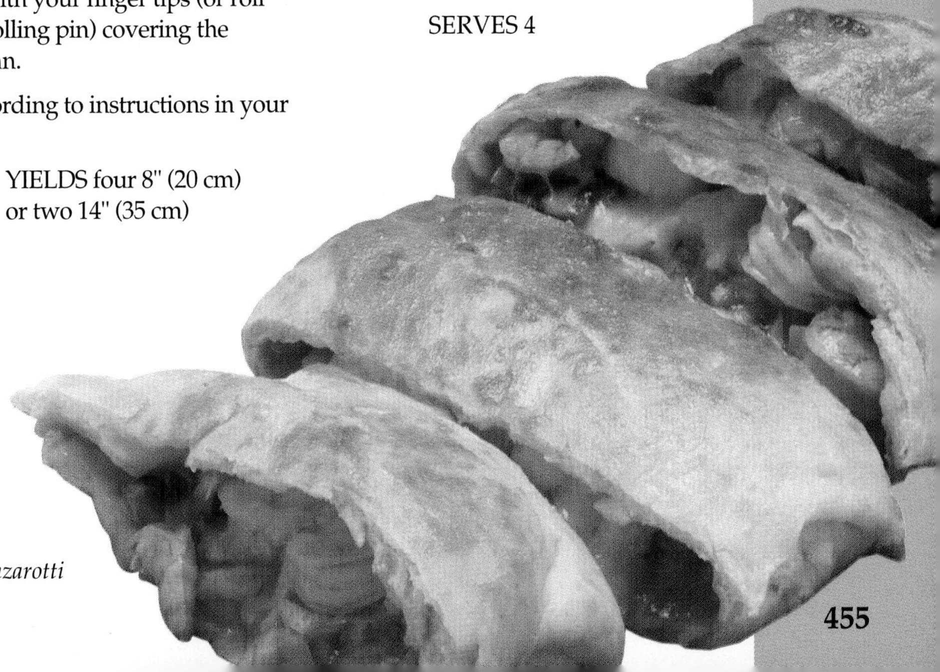

Shrimp Panzarotti

WHOLE WHEAT CRUST

1 tbsp	15 ml	dry active yeast
¾ cup	180 ml	warm water
1 cup	250 ml	whole wheat pastry flour
1½ cups	375 ml	unbleached flour
1	1	egg
½ tsp	3 ml	salt
3 tbsp	45 ml	olive oil

In a large mixing bowl dissolve the yeast in the water, let it rest for 10 minutes or until foamy. Add and stir the whole wheat flour, ½ cup (125 ml) unbleached flour, the egg, salt and oil into a smooth paste.

Gradually knead in the remaining flour and continue to knead into a smooth ball.

Rest the dough for 15 minutes, divide into two. Roll into rounds on a lightly floured surface.

Place into pizza pans, rest 15 minutes longer. With finger tips press dough from centre to the edges until the pan is completely covered by the dough.

Dough is now ready for the sauce and toppings.

YIELDS four 8" (20 cm) or two 14" (35 cm)

CALIFORNIA CHICKEN PIZZA

⅓ cup	80 ml	olive oil
¾ lb	345 g	boneless, diced chicken meat
1 tsp	5 ml	oregano
½ tsp	3 ml	each of basil, thyme, pepper, salt
1 quan	1	Whole Wheat Crust (preceding recipe)
5 oz	150 ml	julienne cut rehydrated sun dried tomatoes
2 cups	500 ml	peeled, deveined and cooked shrimp
1	1	peeled and diced avocado
1	1	fine diced seeded jalapeño pepper
1 cup	250 ml	red currant preserve
3 cups	750 ml	grated Monterey Jack cheese

In a skillet heat half the oil. Brown and cook thoroughly the chicken, seasoning with the herbs and salt. Drain excess oil.

Preheat the oven to 450°F (230°C).

Pan the dough according to instruction. Brush with remaining oil. Spoon the chicken over the dough. Divide the tomatoes, shrimp, avocado, jalapeño over the chicken. Pour the red currant preserves over, and sprinkle with the cheese.

Bake 15-20 minutes or until crust is golden brown. Remove from the pan, slice and serve.

YIELDS two 8" (20 cm) or one 14" (35 cm)

Double Crust Delight

DOUBLE CRUST DELIGHT

3 tbsp	45 ml	olive oil
1 lb	450 g	lean ground beef
¼ lb	115 g	diced bacon
½ lb	225 g	sausage meat
1	1	finely diced onion
1	1	finely diced green bell pepper
2	2	fine diced celery stalks
3 oz	80 g	sliced mushrooms
1	1	minced garlic clove
½ tsp	3 ml	salt
¼ tsp	1 ml	each of basil, oregano, thyme, black pepper
1 cup	250 ml	Pizza Sauce (see page 454)
2 cups	500 ml	grated mozzarella cheese
½ cup	125 ml	freshly grated Parmesan cheese
½ quan	0.5	Gourmet Crust (see page 455)
1	1	egg

In a large pot or Dutch oven heat the oil, and cook the beef, bacon and sausage meat. Drain the excess fat. Add the vegetables and sauté until tender. Add the seasonings and pizza sauce. Reduce heat and simmer for 30 minutes. Cool to room temperature.

Roll out the dough and cut into two. Place half in a 9" (23 cm) spring form pan, fill the pan with mixture, sprinkle with cheese. Cover with remaining dough. Crimp edges to seal. Trim away any excess and use to decorate. Beat the egg and brush on dough. Bake for 25-30 minutes in a preheated 450°F (230°C) oven, or until golden brown. Remove from the pan, slice and serve.

SERVES 8

California Chicken Pizza

Texan Pizza

TEXAN PIZZA

SAUCE:		
½ quan	0.5	Herb Crust (see page 453)
2 lbs	900 g	tomatillos
⅓ cup	80 ml	water
5	5	minced garlic cloves
½ tsp	3 ml	cumin seeds
½ tsp	3 ml	salt
1 tsp	5 ml	cracked black pepper
½ tsp	3 ml	Louisiana hot sauce i.e. Tabasco™
1 tsp	5 ml	Worcestershire sauce
1	1	onion – minced
1 bunch	1 bunch	cilantro chopped

Husk the tomatillos, wash and core them. Cut them into quarters. Place in a sauce pan with the water, garlic, seasonings, hot sauce and Worcestershire sauce. Simmer over medium heat for 30 minutes. Add the onion and cilantro and continue to simmer for an additional 60 minutes, or until sauce is very thick.

TOPPING:		
2	2	red bell peppers
2	2	diced Anaheim peppers
½ lb	225 g	diced smoked beef
1 cup	250 ml	sliced and sautéed shiitake mushrooms
3 cups	750 ml	grated Monterey Jack cheese

Place the peppers on a baking sheet and bake in a preheated 400°F (200°C) oven until the skin blisters, turning often. Place in a paper bag and seal tight, leave for 20 minutes. The skin should be very easily removed, then cut into julienned strips.

Pan the dough according to instruction.

Sauce the dough spreading to ½" (1.5 cm) from the edges of the pan. Cover with diced beef, peppers, chilies, mushrooms and cheese.

Bake in a preheated 450°F (230°C) oven for 15 minutes until crust is golden and cheese is bubbly.

Remove from the pan, slice and serve.

YIELDS two 8" (20 cm) or one 14" (35 cm)

Pone Pie

PONE PIE

3 tbsp	45 ml	olive oil
1¾ lbs	795 g	lean ground pork
1	1	finely diced Spanish onion
2 tsp	10 ml	chili powder
1½ tsp	8 ml	salt
2 cups	500 ml	peeled, seeded and diced tomatoes
2 cups	500 ml	pinto beans, soaked for 8 hours
1 cup	250 ml	Pizza Sauce (see page 454)
½ cup	125 ml	seedless raisins
1½ cups	375 ml	grated cheddar
1½ cups	375 ml	grated Monterey jack
½ quan	0.5	Garlic and Parmesan Crust (see page 460)

Heat the oil in a large skillet, brown the pork and onion. Cook thoroughly then drain excess fat. Add remaining ingredients except the cheese, reduce heat and simmer until very thick.

Preheat oven to 450°F (230°C).

Pan the dough according to instruction. Spread with mixture. Sprinkle with cheeses. Bake for 15 minutes or until the crust is golden. Remove from the pan, slice and serve.

YIELDS two 14" (35 cm) pies

ALMOND RAISIN NUT PIZZA

4 cups	1 L	finely ground almonds
4 cups	1 L	confectioners' sugar
2	2	egg whites
½ cup	125 ml	Amaretto liqueur
½ quan	0.5	Sweet Dough (see Basic Pizza Dough page 452)
1 cup	250 ml	raspberry preserves
1 cup	250 ml	seedless raisins
1 cup	250 ml	roasted almond halves

Blend the ground almonds, sugar, egg whites and liqueur together. Preheat oven to 350°F (180°C). Pan the dough as directed.

Spread with raspberry preserves. Spoon the filling over the dough. Sprinkle with raisins and almonds.

Foil wrap the edges, bake in the centre of the oven for 35-40 minutes or until nicely browned. Chill before serving.

YIELDS two 8" (20 cm) or one 14" (35 cm)

GARLIC AND PARMESAN CRUST

2 tbsp	30 ml	dry active yeast
1 cup	250 ml	warm water
3½ cups	875 ml	unbleached flour-approximately
4	4	minced garlic cloves
½ cup	125 ml	freshly grated Parmesan cheese
2	2	beaten eggs
¼ cup	60 ml	olive oil

In a large mixing bowl dissolve the yeast in the warm water. Rest 10 minutes or until foamy. Stir in 2 cups (500 ml) of flour along with the garlic, Parmesan, eggs and oil forming a smooth batter.

Stir and knead in gradually the remaining flour or enough to form a smooth ball. Place into a greased bowl, cover and rest 15 minutes. Uncover, divide in two and roll into rounds on a lightly floured surface. Place into pans, rest 15 minutes. With finger tips press dough from centre out to cover the entire pan.

Dough is now ready for sauce and toppings.

YIELDS four 8" (20 cm) or two 14" (35 cm)

Almond Raisin Nut Pizza

LOUISIANA SCHEME

3 tbsp	45 ml	olive oil
½ lb	225 g	diced boneless chicken
¼ lb	115 g	diced smoked andouille sausage
2	2	minced garlic cloves
1	1	finely diced medium onion
2	2	finely diced green peppers
1 cup	250 ml	finely diced mushrooms
4	4	large, peeled, seeded, diced tomatoes
½ tsp	3 ml	salt
¼ tsp	1 ml	cracked black pepper
¼ tsp	1 ml	Louisiana hot sauce
½ tsp	3 ml	each of basil, thyme, oregano, paprika, chili powder, garlic powder, onion powder
¼ cup	60 ml	chopped green onions
2 tbsp	30 ml	chopped parsley
2½ cups	625 ml	grated mozzarella
2 cups	500 ml	cooked crayfish tails or shrimp
½ cup	125 ml	freshly grated Parmesan cheese
½ quan	0.5	Garlic and Parmesan Crust (preceding recipe)

Heat oil in a large pot or Dutch oven, and brown the chicken and cook thoroughly. Add the sausage, garlic and vegetables, cook until tender. Add the tomatoes, seasonings and hot sauce. Reduce heat and simmer until sauce is very thick. Stir in the green onions and parsley.

Pan the dough according to instruction.

Spread the mixture over the dough to ½" (1.5 cm) from the edges. Sprinkle with the crayfish tails, cover with the cheese.

Bake in a preheated 450°F (230°C) oven for 15 minutes or until crust is golden brown. Remove from pan, slice and serve.

YIELDS two 8" (20 cm) or one 14" (35 cm)

Louisiana Scheme

CRÊPES

What's small, thin, and oh, so very good? The crêpe, the thin French pancake that no longer has the label of being only a dessert. The crêpe by any other name is still a crêpe and it certainly does have many other names. They range from the Jewish name of blintz, to the Hungarian name palacinken. You may know them as Russian blini or any one of many other names in different countries. They still are delicious in any part of the world.

Crêpes are perfect for any meal. They fit within any budget and therefore are not a menu item which should be overlooked. One may even plan a five course meal all around crêpes. For example:

Appetizer	*Chicken Liver Pâté Roll Ups*
Soup	*Consommé Celestine*
Salad	*Shrimp and Fruit Cheese Logs*
Entrée	*Fajita Crêpes or Coquille St. Jacques Crêpes*
Dessert	*Black Forest Crêpes*

I have given to you more than just a few dessert crêpes. You can choose from hardy fare such as the Rabbit Provencale Crêpes, to such gourmet selections as the Florentine Apple and Smoked Salmon. There are innovative crêpes like our Steak and Mushroom Crêpes and the traditional as in the Crêpes Suzettes.

Crêpes are fast, simple, and, above all, flexible. Creative cooks know that when there are leftovers, a crêpe may be the best way of serving them up, creating a whole new idea in the culinary adventure. Whether the event be formal or casual, one may have complete confidence that with an entrée of crêpes you are serving exactly what everyone requires, something that is *Simply Delicious.*

Crêpes Strawberry Romanoff

SHRIMP & FRUIT CHEESE LOGS

8 oz	225 g	Havarti cheese
8 oz	225 g	cream cheese
8 oz	225 g	cooked, chopped shrimp
¼ cup	60 ml	sherry
½ cup	125 ml	soft dried diced apricots
½ cup	125 ml	soft dried fine diced apple rings
12	12	Crêpes (see Crêpe Batter page 469)

Cream the cheese together, then blend in the shrimp, sherry, apricots and apples.

Spread over the crêpes, roll in jelly roll fashion. Slice into 1" (2.5 cm) thick pieces, serve.

SERVES 6

ASIAN CRÊPES

1½ lbs	675 g	lean, boneless lamb
¼ cup	60 ml	butter
⅓ cup	80 ml	minced onions
⅓ cup	80 ml	Chicken Broth (see page 77)
½ tsp	3 ml	turmeric
1½ tsp	8 ml	ground coriander
½ tsp	3 ml	each of ground cumin, ground ginger, paprika
1 tsp	5 ml	salt
½ cup	125 ml	yogurt
1½ cups	375 ml	tomatoes, peeled, seeded, diced
12	12	Crêpes (see Crêpe Batter page 469)

Trim the lamb of any fat and cut into 2" (5 cm) strips.

Heat the butter in a large skillet and brown the lamb. Add the onion and sauté 3 minutes. Add the broth, seasonings, yogurt and tomatoes. Reduce heat and simmer for 1½ hours or until very thick.

Divide onto crêpes, roll and serve at once.

SERVES 6

SEAFOOD SURPRISE CRÊPES

2 tbsp	30 ml	butter
¼ cup	60 ml	flour, all purpose
2 cups	500 ml	milk
2 cups	500 ml	cooked crab meat
2 cups	500 ml	cooked baby shrimp
16	16	Crêpes (see Crêpe Batter page 469)
½ tsp	3 ml	each of thyme leaves, basil, oregano, pepper
1 tsp	5 ml	paprika
1 tsp	5 ml	salt
3 cups	750 ml	fine bread crumbs
2	2	eggs
4 cups	1 L	safflower oil

In a sauce pan heat the butter, add the flour, reduce heat and cook for 2 minutes. Add 1 cup (250 ml) of milk and cook very slowly over low heat until very thick. Cool.

Add the crab and shrimp, then blend. Divide equally among the crêpes. Roll and refrigerate for 2 hours.

Blend the seasonings in the bread crumbs. Beat the eggs with the remaining milk. Dip the crêpes into the milk, dredge in the bread crumbs.

Heat the oil to 375°F (190°C). Fry the crêpes two at a time. Reserve hot while frying the remaining crêpes. Serve hot. Very good with Sauce Veronique (see page 114).

SERVES 8

Asian Crêpes

Seafood Surprise Crêpes

Black Forest Crêpes

SEAFOOD CRÊPES

2 tbsp	30 ml	olive oil
1	1	finely diced green pepper
1	1	finely diced small onion
1	1	small minced garlic clove
1 cup	250 ml	Tomato Sauce (see page 106)
2 tsp	10 ml	fresh chopped basil
½ tsp	3 ml	salt
¼ tsp	1 ml	pepper
1 cup	250 ml	small broccoli florets
½ lb	225 g	large peeled and deveined shrimp
½ lb	225 g	sea scallops
½ cup	125 ml	sour cream
12	12	Crêpes (see Crêpe Batter page 469)

In a large skillet heat the oil, add the green pepper, onion and garlic, sauté until tender. Add the tomato sauce and seasonings, simmer for 10 minutes.

Add the broccoli and seafood, cover and simmer for 10 minutes. Add the sour cream and continue to simmer for 5 minutes uncovered.

Ladle mixture over the crêpes and roll, serve at once with a salad.

SERVES 6

Crêpes á l'Orange

CRÊPES A' L'ORANGE

3	3	oranges
1 cup	250 ml	apricot preserves
¼ cup	60 ml	Curacao liqueur
12	12	Dessert Crêpes (see Crêpe Batter page 469)
¼ cup	60 ml	confectioners' sugar

Peel and segment the oranges, remove pith and seeds. Heat the apricot preserves and mix in the orange segments with the liqueur.

Spread over the crêpes then roll them up. Dust with confectioners' sugar and serve.

SERVES 6

BLACK FOREST CRÊPES

4 cups	1 L	French vanilla ice cream
2 cups	500 ml	cherry pie filling
12	12	Dessert Crêpes (see Crêpe Batter page 469)
2 cups	500 ml	fudge sauce
1 cup	250 ml	whipped cream

Layer the ice cream and cherry pie filling in the crêpes, and roll. Cover with the sauce and a dollop of whipped cream. Serve.

SERVES 6

Cherries Jubilee Crêpes

CRÊPES A LA CREME PATISSERIE

2 cups	500 ml	half & half cream
1 tsp	5 ml	vanilla extract
5	5	egg yolks
½ cup	125 ml	granulated sugar
4 tbsp	60 ml	flour, all purpose
1 tbsp	15 ml	butter
16	16	Dessert Crêpes (see Crêpe Batter page 469)
2 cups	500 ml	Orange Brandy Sauce (see page 107)

In a double boiler heat the cream and vanilla. Beat the egg yolks with the sugar, slowly add to the hot cream.

Cream the flour with the butter, beat into the cream and strain through a sieve. Beat to cool then chill.

Spread the cream over the crêpes and roll. Place on serving plates and pour orange sauce over. Serve.

SERVES 6

CRÊPES DEJAZET

1½ cups	375 ml	confectioners' sugar
1 tbsp	15 ml	cocoa powder
⅓ cup	80 ml	butter
1 tbsp	15 ml	extra strong cold coffee
12	12	Dessert Crêpes (see Crêpe Batter page 469)
4	4	egg whites
1 cup	250 ml	granulated sugar
1 cup	250 ml	Orange Brandy Sauce (see page 107)

Sift the confectioners' sugar with the cocoa powder three times. Cream the butter with the coffee, fold in the cocoa sugar, beat until very light. Spread on the crêpes and stack.

Whip the egg whites stiff. Gradually add the sugar, whip into a stiff meringue. Pipe the meringue on top of the crêpes, quickly brown under the boiler.

Slice and serve with the orange sauce.

SERVES 6

CHERRIES JUBILEE CRÊPES

1½ cups	375 ml	whipping cream
½ tsp	3 ml	vanilla extract
¼ cup	60 ml	confectioners' sugar
12	12	Dessert Crêpes (see Crêpe Batter page 469)
5 tbsp	75 ml	granulated sugar
4 tbsp	60 ml	butter
2 – 10 oz	2 – 280 ml	cans of cherries
¼ cup	60 ml	cherry brandy
1½ tsp	8 ml	cornstarch

Whip the cream until stiff, and stir in the vanilla. Fold in the confectioners' sugar, and spoon onto the crêpes. Roll the crêpes then refrigerate.

In a sauce pan caramelize the sugar, then add the butter. Drain the cherries reserving the liquid, add the cherries to the sauce pan.

Flame the cherries with the brandy. Mix the cornstarch with the cherry liquid and add to the cherries. Simmer until thick.

Place crêpes on serving plates and spoon over hot cherries. Serve at once.

SERVES 6

CHOCOLATE CREAM ROLLS

2 cups	500 ml	ricotta cheese
1 tsp	5 ml	vanilla extract
¼ cup	60 ml	confectioners' sugar
¼ cup	60 ml	candied fruit
⅓ cup	90 ml	chocolate chips
12	12	Dessert Crêpes (see Crêpe Batter recipe this page)
1 cup	250 ml	Kiwi Papaya Sauce (see page 106)

In a food processor cream the cheese, add the vanilla and sugar and beat. Remove from machine and beat in the fruit and chocolate chips.

Spoon cheese blend onto crêpes and roll. Plate the crêpes and top with sauce, serve at once.

SERVES 6

HUNGARIAN PALACINKEN

1 cup	250 ml	confectioners' sugar
2 tbsp	30 ml	ground cinnamon
1 quan	1	Crêpe Batter (see page 469)
1 cup	250 ml	heated apricot preserves

Sift the sugar together with the cinnamon to blend.

Make the crêpes according to directions. While crêpe is hot, brush with apricot preserves then roll into a cigar shape. Roll through the cinnamon sugar. Serve.

SERVES 6

CRÊPE BATTER

1 cup	250 ml	flour, all purpose
¼ tsp	1 ml	salt
2 tbsp	30 ml	safflower oil
1 cup	250 ml	milk
¼ cup	60 ml	soda water
1	1	egg
½ tsp	3 ml	vanilla extract (for dessert crêpes only)

Sift the flour and salt together, blend in the oil, milk, and water. Beat the egg and add to the liquid. Stir in the vanilla as outlined in making dessert crêpes. Blend in the dry ingredients, beat until a smooth thin batter is formed.

To cook the crêpes, spread about 3 tbsp (45 ml) of batter in a lightly buttered hot skillet. Cook about 1½ minutes, turn the crêpe and cook 1 minute over medium heat. Turn out and use as required.

YIELDS 16

Chocolate Cream Rolls

FAJITA CRÊPES

1½ lbs	675 g	flank steak
3	3	sliced garlic cloves
2	2	sliced Spanish onions
2	2	minced serrano chilies
¼ cup	60 ml	chopped cilantro
⅓ cup	80 ml	lime juice
¼ cup	60 ml	lemon juice
3 tbsp	45 ml	butter
2 tbsp	30 ml	safflower oil
1	1	sliced green bell pepper
1	1	sliced red bell pepper
1	1	sliced yellow bell pepper
3 oz	80 g	sliced mushrooms
1 tsp	5 ml	salt
1 tsp	5 ml	Worcestershire sauce
1 tbsp	15 ml	chili powder
12	12	Crêpes (see Crêpe Batter page 469)
½ cup	125 ml	sour cream
1 cup	250 ml	Guacamole (see page 115)
1 cup	250 ml	Salsa Sauce (see page 115)

Slice the steak into very thin strips. In a casserole dish layer the steak, garlic, 1 onion, chilies and cilantro. Pour over the juices. Cover and refrigerate for 3-4 hours, and drain thoroughly.

In a large skillet heat the butter and oil. Sauté the remaining onion together with the peppers and mushrooms. Season the vegetables with a little salt and the Worcestershire sauce. Transfer to a very hot serving plate and reserve hot.

Cook the steak over a hot grill for 3-4 minutes seasoning with the chili powder and remaining salt. Transfer to a second hot plate.

Serve the steak, vegetables, crêpes, sour cream, guacamole and salsa separately, allowing your guest to "fix em" up how they prefer.

* NOTE: If you choose to use shrimp or lobster, do not marinate. Chicken, however, may follow the same recipe.

SERVES 6

CHICKEN LIVER PÂTÉ ROLL UPS

1 lb	450 g	chicken livers
¾ cup	180 ml	Chicken Broth (see page 77)
½ cup	125 ml	white wine
¼ cup	60 ml	finely minced onion
1 tbsp	15 ml	chopped cilantro
¼ tsp	1 ml	ground ginger
1 tbsp	15 ml	light soya sauce
½ tsp	3 ml	Worcestershire sauce
¼ tsp	1 ml	each of paprika, oregano, thyme, white pepper, basil
½ tsp	3 ml	salt
½ cup	125 ml	softened butter
1 tbsp	15 ml	brandy
8	8	Crêpes (see Crêpe Batter page 469)

Pick through the chicken livers and trim away any fat. Cook the livers in the broth along with the wine, onion, cilantro, ginger, soya sauce and Worcestershire sauce. Allow to cool completely in the liquid. Drain, reserving the liquid.

Put the livers in a food processor, and process with 2 tbsp (30 ml) of reserved liquid. Add the seasonings, butter and brandy, blending until light and smooth. Add more liquid if required to keep mixture soft. Spoon into a chilled bowl and refrigerate until service.

For service, spread the mixture over the crêpes, roll up in jelly roll fashion. Slice into 1" (2.5 cm) thick pieces. Place on a tray and serve.

SERVES 4

Chicken Liver Pâté Rollups

Fajita Crêpes

Orange Brandy Mousse Cups

Grilled Chicken Hollandaise Crêpes

GRILLED CHICKEN HOLLANDAISE CRÊPES

1 lb	450 g	boneless chicken breast
¼ cup	60 ml	safflower oil
1	1	minced garlic clove
2 tbsp	30 ml	lemon juice
2 tbsp	30 ml	white wine
1 tsp	5 ml	salt
½ tsp	3 ml	white pepper
1 tsp	5 ml	chopped basil
8	8	Crêpes (see Crêpe Batter page 469)
¾ cup	180 ml	Hollandaise Sauce (see page 114)

Preheat the oven to 400°F (200°C).

Wash and pat dry the chicken breasts, cut into ½" (1 cm) strips, place into a shallow baking pan.

In a mixing bowl blend the oil, garlic, lemon, wine, salt, pepper and basil together. Pour over the chicken, cover and marinate for 1 hour. Drain.

Cook the chicken over a hot grill for 3-4 minutes. Place in the crêpes and roll.

Place crêpes in a greased casserole dish, cover with hollandaise sauce and bake in oven 7-10 minutes or until golden brown.

SERVES 4

ORANGE BRANDY MOUSSE CUPS

6	6	Dessert Crêpes (see Crêpe Batter page 469)
2 tbsp	30 ml	melted butter
3 oz	90 g	orange flavoured gelatin
½ cup	125 ml	orange brandy
1 cup	250 ml	boiling orange juice
1 cup	250 ml	whipping cream
½ cup	125 ml	orange segments

Place the crêpes into muffin tins and brush with the melted butter. Bake in a preheated 350°F (180°C) oven for 10 minutes. Remove from oven and cool.

Soften the gelatin in the orange brandy, pour in the orange juice and stir until the gelatin dissolves. Chill and allow to almost set but not firm.

Whip the cream and fold into the gelatin, pour into crêpes and allow to set.

Place crêpes on serving plates and garnish with orange segments.

SERVES 6

CONVENT CRÊPES

1 cup	250 ml	water
½ cup	125 ml	granulated sugar
6	6	pears, pared, cored, diced
12	12	Dessert Crêpes (see Crêpe Batter page 469)
1½ cups	375 ml	chocolate fudge sauce
1 cup	250 ml	toasted sliced almonds

In a sauce pan mix the water with the sugar, heat to boil. Reduce to a simmer, poach the pears until tender. Drain and cool the pears.

Place pears in the crêpes and roll. Cover with the sauce, and sprinkle with the almonds, serve.

SERVES 6

COQUILLE ST. JACQUES CRÊPES

1 cup	250 ml	white wine
1 lb	450 g	large sea scallops
¼ cup	60 ml	butter
1	1	diced small onion
3 oz	80 g	sliced mushrooms
3 tbsp	45 ml	flour, all purpose
1 cup	250 ml	heavy cream
⅓ cup	80 ml	sherry
½ tsp	3 ml	salt
½ tsp	3 ml	white pepper
½ tsp	3 ml	paprika
1½ cups	375 ml	cooked small shrimp
12	12	Crêpes (see Crêpe Batter page 469)
½ cup	125 ml	grated Swiss cheese
½ cup	125 ml	grated medium cheddar
¼ cup	60 ml	freshly grated Parmesan cheese

Heat the wine in a sauce pan, add the scallops, simmer for 6 minutes, remove scallops from liquid, reserve the liquid.

In a sauce pan heat the butter, and sauté the vegetables until tender. Add the flour and cook for 2 minutes. Add the cream, sherry and seasonings, simmer until thickened. Drain the scallops and add them to the sauce along with the shrimp, combine thoroughly. Preheat the oven to 400°F (200°C).

Divide the mixture among the crêpes and roll. Place on a greased casserole dish. Sprinkle with the cheeses. Bake for 10 minutes and serve at once.

SERVES 6

Coquille St. Jacques Crêpes

CRÊPES BEEF BURGUNDY

3 tbsp	45 ml	olive oil
20	20	pearl onions
1½ lbs	675 ml	small cubed chuck steak
3 tbsp	45 ml	flour, all purpose
2 cups	500 ml	red wine
1 cup	250 ml	Beef Broth (see page 85)
3 tbsp	45 ml	tomato paste
½ tsp	3 ml	thyme
1	1	bay leaf
1 tsp	5 ml	chopped parsley
½ tsp	3 ml	cracked black pepper
¼ lb	115 g	button mushrooms
12	12	Crêpes (see Crêpe Batter page 469)

In a large kettle or Dutch oven heat the oil, sauté the onions then remove from the pan. Add the beef and brown.

Sprinkle the flour over the beef and cook for 2 minutes. Add the wine, broth, tomato paste, thyme, bay leaf, parsley and pepper, reduce the heat and simmer gently for 1½ hours.

Return the onions and add the mushrooms, continue to simmer for 30 minutes.

Ladle beef onto crêpes and roll together, serve with a rice pilaf.

SERVES 6

CHILI CON CARNE CRÊPES

1 lb	450 g	lean ground beef
5 tbsp	75 ml	butter
2 cups	500 ml	finely diced onions
2	2	minced garlic cloves
2	2	finely diced celery stalks
1	1	finely diced green bell pepper
1 cup	250 ml	sliced mushrooms
3½ cups	875 ml	crushed tomatoes
3 tbsp	45 ml	tomato paste
1½ cups	375 ml	red kidney beans (soaked for 8 hours, or tinned)
½ tsp	3 ml	each of thyme, oregano, chervil, pepper, salt, cumin, onion powder
2 tsp	10 ml	each of paprika, chili powder
5	5 drops	Tabasco™ sauce
1 tsp	5 ml	Worcestershire sauce
12	12	Crêpes (see Crêpe Batter page 469)
1½ cups	375 ml	grated cheddar cheese

In a skillet brown the beef, drain off excess fat.

In a large kettle or Dutch oven, heat the butter and sauté the onions, garlic, celery green peppers, and mushrooms. Stir in the browned beef, tomatoes, tomato paste and beans, simmer for 1 hour. Add the seasonings, Tabasco and Worcestershire. Reduce heat and simmer for 1 hour.

Ladle onto crêpes, place crêpes in a greased casserole pan, sprinkle with cheese and bake in a preheated 400°F (200°C) oven for 15 minutes, serve.

SERVES 6

Chili Con Carne Crêpes

CRÊPES SOUFFLÉ CHEF K

2 cups	500 ml	Fresh Papaya Sorbet (see page 658)
2 cups	500 ml	Lemon Sherbet (see page 547)
2 cups	500 ml	Orange Chocolate Sherbet (see page 571)
12	12	Dessert Crêpes (see Crêpe Batter page 469)
8	8	egg whites
1½ cups	375 ml	granulated sugar
2 cups	500 ml	cherry sauce

Scoop the sorbet and sherbets into four crêpes each. Alternate and stack the crêpes in a pyramid form. Place in the freezer.

Whip the egg whites stiff, gradually beat in the sugar. Pipe the meringue to encase the crêpes. Quickly brown the meringue in a very hot oven.

Slice and serve covered with cherry sauce.

SERVES 6

DURORA CRÊPES

3 cups	750 ml	strawberry ice cream
12	12	Dessert Crêpes (see Crêpe Batter page 469)
2 cups	500 ml	Sabayon (see page 106)
¼ cup	60 ml	Curacao liqueur

Scoop the ice cream over the crêpes, then roll.

Blend the sabayon sauce with the liqueur. Pour over the crêpes and serve.

SERVES 6

Crêpes Cheri Rose

CRÊPES CHERI ROSE

2 cups	500 ml	whipping cream
¾ cup	180 ml	confectioners' sugar
1 tsp	5 ml	rose extract
½ tsp	3 ml	red food colouring
12	12	Dessert Crêpes (see Crêpe Batter page 469)
3 cups	750 ml	washed and hulled sliced strawberries
¼ cup	60 ml	granulated sugar
⅛ tsp	pinch	ground cinnamon

Whip the cream and stir in the sugar, extract and colouring. Spread over the crêpes and roll.

Place crêpes on serving plates and spread with the strawberries. Blend the sugar with the cinnamon and sprinkle over the crêpes. Serve.

SERVES 6

CRÊPES BANANA FOSTER

3	3	bananas
12	12	Dessert Crêpes (see Crêpe Batter page 469)
5 tbsp	75 ml	butter
5 tbsp	75 ml	brown sugar
½ tsp	3 ml	ground cinnamon
3 tbsp	45 ml	banana liqueur
5 tbsp	75 ml	dark rum
¼ cup	60 ml	walnuts

Peel and slice the bananas in quarters. Wrap one crêpe around each banana quarter.

Heat the butter with the brown sugar in a skillet, add the cinnamon and cook until the sugar is dissolved. Add the liqueur and rum, tilt the pan away from you and flambé.

Stir in the nuts. Place the crêpes in the sauce and heat for 2 minutes. Spoon the crêpes onto plates and ladle sauce over the crêpes. Serve at once.

SERVES 6

A TASTE OF ITALY CRÊPES

6 oz	170 g	fine ground prosciutto
6 oz	170 g	cooked mild Italian sausage meat, chopped
4 tbsp	60 ml	unsalted butter
3	3	eggs
½ cup	125 ml	bread crumbs
¼ cup	60 ml	freshly grated Romano cheese
12	12	Crêpes (see Crêpe Batter page 469)
1 cup	250 ml	ricotta cheese
1 tbsp	15 ml	olive oil
1	1	small diced onion
2 cups	500 ml	peeled, seeded and diced tomatoes
1	1	minced garlic clove
2 tsp	10 ml	fresh chopped basil leaves
1 tbsp	15 ml	fresh chopped parsley
½ cup	125 ml	grated provolone

Blend the meats with 3 tbsp (45 ml) of butter, eggs, bread crumbs and Romano cheese. Mix thoroughly. Chill 1 hour.

Place the filling evenly over each crêpe, divide the ricotta over the crêpes and roll together. Place in a greased casserole dish.

Heat the oil and remaining butter in a sauce pan. Cook the onion with the garlic until tender. Add the tomatoes and herbs. Reduce heat to a simmer, cook for 15 minutes. Pour sauce over crêpes. Sprinkle with provolone and bake in a preheated 350°F (180°C) oven for 35 minutes.

SERVES 6

A Taste of Italy Crêpes

Classic Crêpes Suzette

CLASSIC CRÊPES SUZETTE

5 tbsp	75 ml	granulated sugar
5 tbsp	75 ml	butter
1 tbsp	15 ml	lemon and orange rind zest
½ cup	125 ml	Grand Marnier liqueur
1 cup	250 ml	fresh squeezed orange juice
3 tbsp	45 ml	lemon juice
18	18	Dessert Crêpes (see Crêpe Batter page 469)
6 scoops	6	vanilla ice cream

Caramelize the sugar in a sauce pan or skillet, do not burn. Add the butter and fruit zest, stir until melted. Turn the pan away from you and flambé with half the liqueur.

Add the orange and lemon juice, simmer to half the volume. Fold the crêpes to form triangles, simmer in the sauce for 1 minute.

Place 3 crêpes on a single plate, pour equal amounts of sauce over the crêpes. Top with a scoop of ice cream.

Pour the remaining liqueur in a small sauce pan, flambé and pour over crêpes. Serve at once.

SERVES 6

MAPLE WALNUT CRÊPES

4 cups	1 L	French vanilla ice cream
12	12	Dessert Crêpes (see Crêpe Batter page 469)
1 cup	250 ml	walnut pieces
1½ cups	375 ml	hot maple syrup

Scoop the ice cream into the crêpes and roll. Sprinkle with walnuts then pour over the syrup. Serve.

SERVES 6

LASAGNA CRÊPES

1 lb	450 g	Italian sausage
3 tbsp	45 ml	olive oil
1	1	finely diced onion
1	1	finely diced green bell pepper
1	1	finely diced celery stalk
1 cup	250 ml	finely sliced mushrooms
2	2	minced garlic cloves
2 cups	500 ml	Tomato Sauce (see page 106)
2 tsp	10 ml	basil
2 cups	500 ml	ricotta cheese
1	1	egg
¼ cup	60 ml	chopped parsley
¼ cup	60 ml	freshly grated Parmesan cheese
16	16	Crêpes (see Crêpe Batter page 469)
½ cup	125 ml	grated provolone cheese
1¼ cups	310 ml	grated mozzarella cheese

Dice the sausage in small cubes. Heat the oil in a large skillet and brown the sausage, add the onions, green pepper, celery, mushrooms and garlic, sauté until tender. Drain off any excess fat.

Add the tomato sauce and basil. Reduce heat and simmer for 30 minutes.

While sauce simmers, combine the ricotta, egg, parsley and Parmesan cheese.

Ladle a thin layer of sauce on the bottom of a round casserole dish. Place a layer of crêpes, cover with a layer of the cheese blend, top with a layer of crêpes, and add another layer of sauce. Repeat this procedure alternating crêpes, sauce and cheese finishing with a layer of crêpes.

Sprinkle the provolone and mozzarella over the crêpes and bake in a preheated 400°F (200°C) oven for 30 minutes. Serve with Caesar salad.

SERVES 6

Lasagna Crêpes

RABBIT PROVENÇALE CRÊPES

1 lb	450 g	boneless rabbit meat
1 tbsp	15 ml	butter
1 tbsp	15 ml	safflower oil
¼ lb	115 g	diced bacon
1	1	minced garlic clove
1	1	diced Spanish onion
1	1	diced green bell pepper
3 oz	80 g	sliced mushrooms
3 tbsp	45 ml	flour, all purpose
½ tsp	3 ml	fresh chopped basil
½ tsp	3 ml	thyme leaves
½ tsp	3 ml	marjoram
1 tbsp	15 ml	chopped parsley
1 cup	250 ml	tomatoes, peeled, seeded, diced
1½ cups	375 ml	Chicken Broth (see page 77)
2 tsp	10 ml	Dijon mustard
12	12	Crêpes (see Crêpe Batter page 469)

Dice the rabbit into bite size pieces. In a large skillet heat the butter and the oil in the sauce pan, add the rabbit and brown.

Fry the bacon in a second skillet, drain excess fat and add to the rabbit along with the vegetables and sauté until tender. Sprinkle with flour and continue to cook for 2 minutes. Add the seasonings, tomatoes, broth and mustard.

Reduce heat to simmer and cook for 35-40 minutes, or until rabbit is tender and sauce is thickened. Scoop the meat and vegetables into the crêpes, roll and serve.

SERVES 6

FLORENTINE APPLE CRÊPES WITH SMOKED SALMON

10 oz	280 ml	fresh spinach
6 tbsp	90 ml	butter
3 tbsp	45 ml	flour, all purpose
1½ cups	375 ml	light cream
1 tbsp	15 ml	fresh chopped basil
1½ cups	375 ml	apples, pared, cored, diced
2	2	egg yolks
8 oz	225 g	thinly sliced smoked salmon
12	12	Crêpes (see Crêpe Batter page 469)
1½ cups	375 ml	grated Havarti cheese

Wash and dry the spinach, remove the stems. Heat half the butter in a sauce pan, and sauté the spinach until wilted and tender. Set aside to cool.

Heat the remaining butter in a second sauce pan and add the flour and cook for 2 minutes over low heat. Add the cream, basil and apples, simmer until sauce thickens slightly, remove from the heat and whisk in the egg yolks. Stir in the salmon.

Preheat the oven to 400°F (200°C). Divide the mixture equally over the crêpes and roll. Place in a greased casserole dish, sprinkle with cheese and bake for 10 minutes. Serve.

SERVES 6

CRÊPES STRAWBERRY ROMANOFF

2 cups	500 ml	whipping cream
¾ cup	180 ml	confectioners' sugar
¼ cup	60 ml	Grand Marnier liqueur
3 cups	750 ml	washed and hulled sliced strawberries
12	12	Dessert Crêpes (see Crêpe Batter page 469)
24	24	chocolate dipped strawberries

Whip the cream, then fold in the sugar, liqueur and strawberries. Fill and roll crêpes. Place on a serving plate, garnish with the chocolate strawberries. Serve.

SERVES 6

HAZELNUT ROLLS

2 cups	500 ml	whipping cream
¾ cup	180 ml	confectioners' sugar
½ tsp	3 ml	hazelnut or almond extract
12	12	Dessert Crêpes (see Crêpe Batter page 469)
½ cup	125 ml	heated apricot preserves
2 cups	500 ml	coarsely chopped hazelnuts (filberts)

Whip the cream stiff, fold in the sugar and extract. Spoon over the crêpes and roll.

Brush crêpes with apricots and then roll in the nuts. Serve.

SERVES 6

Florentine Apple Crêpes with Smoked Salmon

Hazelnut Rolls

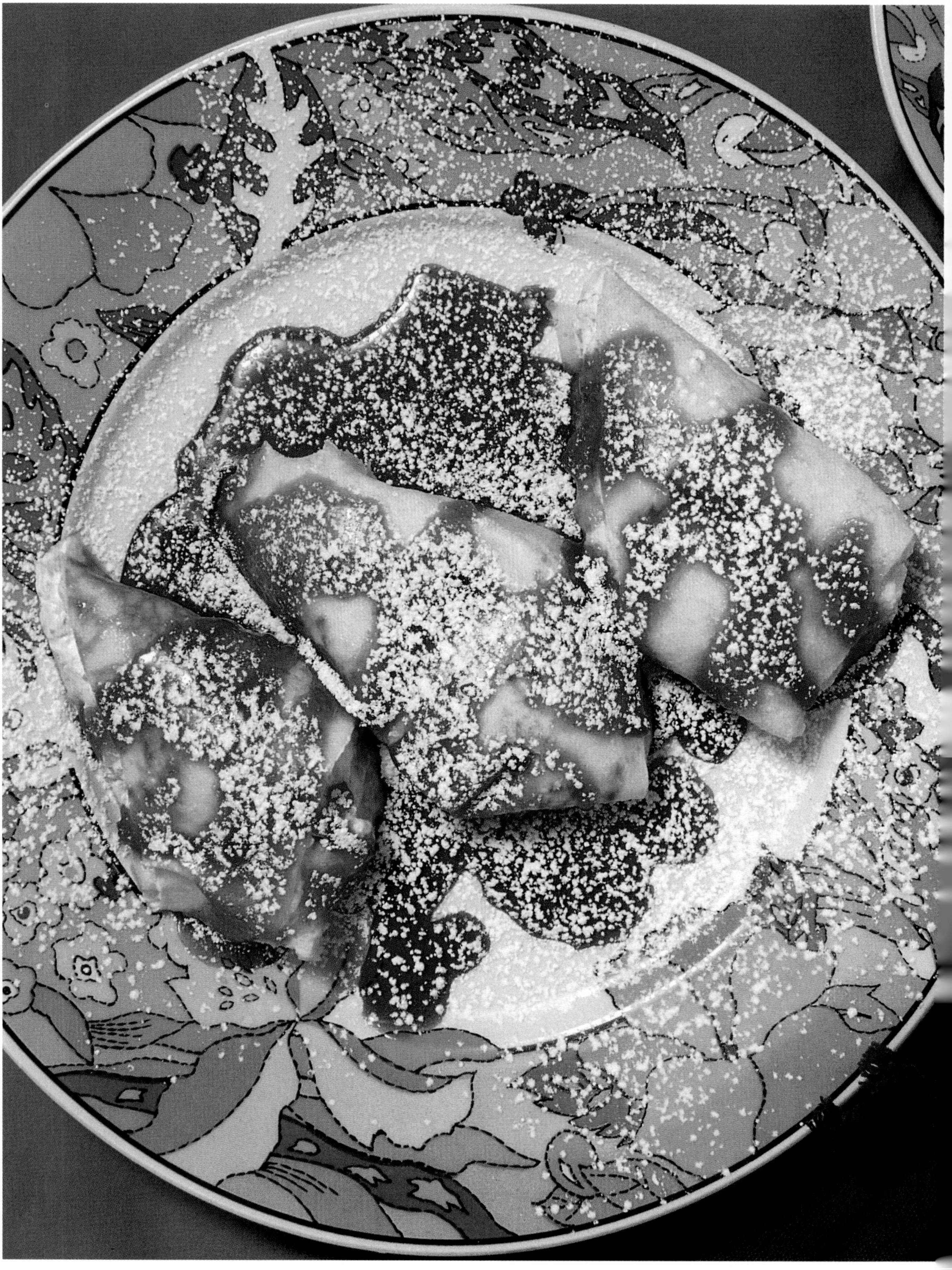

Empire Crêpe

GINGER STEAK CRÊPES

1½ lbs	675 g	New York striploin
2 tbsp	30 ml	butter
1½ tsp	8 ml	fresh, minced ginger root
2 tbsp	30 ml	blanched almonds
1 tsp	5 ml	chili powder
1 tsp	5 ml	fresh, minced garlic
3 tbsp	45 ml	minced onion
3 tbsp	45 ml	flour, all purpose
1½ cups	375 ml	Beef Broth (see page 85)
3 tbsp	45 ml	sherry
3 tbsp	45 ml	plum preserves
12	12	Crêpes (see Crêpe Batter page 469)
		cilantro sprigs for garnish

Cut the steak into 2" (5 cm) strips. Heat the butter in a large skillet, brown the steak in the butter. Add the ginger, almonds, chili powder, garlic and onion, continue to sauté for 2 minutes.

Add the flour, cook for 2 minutes. Add the beef broth, sherry and preserves, reduce heat and simmer until sauce thickens.

Spoon mixture onto crêpes, roll, serve at once garnish with cilantro sprigs.

SERVES 6

Apple Crêpes

APPLE CRÊPES

4	4	large cooking apples
3 tbsp	45 ml	butter
3 tbsp	45 ml	granulated sugar
½ tsp	3 ml	cinnamon
12	12	Crêpes (see Crêpe Batter page 469)
2 cups	500 ml	whipped cream

Peel, core and slice the apples.

In a large skillet heat the butter, add the apples, sugar and cinnamon and cook for 8 minutes over medium heat.

Spoon the apples onto the crêpes, roll and place on serving plates. Top with whipped cream and serve.

SERVES 6

EMPIRE CRÊPES

1½ cups	375 ml	whipping cream
1 tsp	5 ml	vanilla extract
1 cup	250 ml	crushed macaroons
1 cup	250 ml	crushed pineapple, well drained
½ cup	125 ml	confectioners' sugar
12	12	Dessert Crêpes (see Crêpe Batter page 469)
½ cup	125 ml	heated red currant preserves

Whip the cream with the vanilla, fold in the macaroons, pineapple and sugar. Spread on the crêpes and roll.

Brush crêpes with red currant preserves and serve.

SERVES 6

Steak 'n' Mushroom Crêpes

APPLE BLACKBERRY CRÊPES

1½ cups	375 ml	apples, pared, cored, diced
2 tbsp	30 ml	butter
¼ cup	60 ml	granulated sugar
2 cups	500 ml	washed and hulled blackberries
¼ cup	60 ml	apple juice
1 tsp	5 ml	cornstarch
12	12	Dessert Crêpes (see Crêpe Batter page 469)
2 cups	500 ml	whipped cream

Sauté the apples in a skillet with the butter, sprinkle with the sugar and cook for 3 minutes. Add the blackberries continuing to cook for 5 addition minutes.

Mix the apple juice with the cornstarch. Pour the juice over the fruit, bring to a boil and reduce the heat, and simmer until thick. Spread over the crêpes stacking one on top of another. Pour any remaining sauce over the stack. Serve with a dollop of whipping cream on each slice.

SERVES 6

STEAK 'N' MUSHROOM CRÊPES

3 tbsp	45 ml	safflower oil
1 lb	450 g	New York striploin steak – cut in ¼" strips
3 oz	80 g	sliced mushrooms
1 cup	250 ml	Espagnole Sauce (see page 111)
12	12	Crêpes (see Crêpe Batter page 469)

Heat the oil in a large skillet. Quickly fry the steak and mushrooms. Add the espagnole sauce, reduce the heat and simmer for 5-8 minutes.

Spoon mixture evenly into crêpes, roll and serve at once.

SERVES 6

ROYAL PINEAPPLE BANANAS

3 tbsp	45 ml	dark brown sugar
2 tbsp	30 ml	cornstarch
1½ cups	375 ml	crushed pineapple with juice
5 tbsp	75 ml	butter
¼ tsp	1 ml	each of grated lemon and orange peel
6	6	firm ripe bananas
12	12	Dessert Crêpes (see Crêpe Batter page 469)
3 cups	750 ml	Strawberry Banana Ice Cream (see page 641)

In a small sauce pan mix the sugar with the cornstarch. Add the pineapple and 1 tbsp (15 ml) of butter. Bring to a boil and reduce heat and simmer until thick. Remove from heat and stir in the grated citrus peel.

Cut the bananas in half, wrap a crêpe around each half. Heat the remaining butter in a skillet and gently sauté the crêpes to heat the bananas. Place on serving plates, top with ice cream, smother with sauce and serve at once.

SERVES 6

Royal Pineapple Bananas

LOBSTER CHEDDAR CRÊPES

3 tbsp	45 ml	butter
1 lb	450 g	lobster meat
1 cup	250 ml	Mornay Sauce (see page 111)
1 cup	250 ml	grated mild cheddar
8	8	Crêpes (see Crêpe Batter page 469)

Preheat the oven to 350°F (180°C).

Heat the butter in a large skillet, add the lobster, sauté thoroughly. Blend in the mornay sauce and half the cheddar, reduce heat and simmer for 3 minutes.

Spoon the mixture evenly into the crêpes. Roll and place crêpes in a greased casserole dish. Sprinkle with the remaining cheese. Bake in the oven for 15 minutes, serve at once.

SERVES 4

STUFATU CRÊPES

4 tbsp	60 ml	olive oil
1	1	large onion chopped
3	3	minced garlic cloves
12 oz	340 g	cubed lean chuck steak
12 oz	340 g	cubed lean pork
¼ cup	60 ml	diced bacon
2 cups	500 ml	peeled, seeded, chopped tomatoes
½ cup	125 ml	white wine
1 tsp	5 ml	salt
½ tsp	3 ml	cracked black pepper
2 cups	500 ml	Beef Broth (see page 85)
12	12	Crêpes (see Crêpe Batter page 469)
¾ cup	180 ml	grated Gruyere cheese

Heat the oil in a large skillet, sauté the onion and garlic until tender. Add the beef, pork and bacon and brown. Drain excess oil.

Add the tomatoes, wine, seasonings and broth, reduce heat to very low and simmer for 2 hours.

Ladle the meats on to the crêpes and roll. Place into a greased casserole dish, sprinkle with cheese and bake in a preheated 350°F (180°C) oven for 15 minutes. Serve.

SERVES 6

Lobster Cheddar Crêpes

Clam Crêpe Soufflé

SWEET 'N' SOUR CHICKEN CRÊPES

1½ lbs	675 g	boneless chicken, diced into ½" cubes
3 tbsp	45 ml	safflower oil
2 tbsp	30 ml	flour, all purpose
¾ cup	180 ml	pineapple juice
3 tbsp	45 ml	diced green bell pepper
½ tsp	3 ml	prepared hot mustard
2 tbsp	30 ml	garlic wine vinegar
¼ tsp	1 ml	garlic powder
2 tbsp	30 ml	dark soya sauce
1 tbsp	15 ml	molasses
½ cup	125 ml	chili sauce
12	12	Crêpes (see Crêpe Batter page 469)

Heat the oil in a skillet and brown the chicken. Add the flour and cook for 2 minutes. Add the remaining ingredients except the crêpes. Stir, reduce heat and simmer for 15 minutes.

Spoon over crêpes. Roll and serve.

SERVES 6

CLAM CRÊPE SOUFFLÉ

3 tbsp	45 ml	butter
3 tbsp	45 ml	flour, all purpose
1¼ cups	310 ml	Chicken Broth (see page 77)
1¼ cups	310 ml	half & half cream
½ cup	125 ml	freshly grated Parmesan cheese
3	3	slices of bacon
1	1	finely diced small onion
1	1	finely diced celery stalk
1 cup	250 ml	fresh chopped clams
16	16	Crêpes (see Crêpe Batter page 469)
1½ cups	375 ml	grated cheddar cheese

Heat the butter in a sauce pan. Add the flour and cook 2 minutes over low heat.

Stir in the chicken broth and cream. Reduce heat and simmer until thickened. Stir in the cheese and simmer for 2 more minutes.

Dice the bacon and fry in a skillet, add the onions and celery and sauté until tender. Add the clams and cook for 3 minutes, drain excess fat and fold into the sauce.

Layer the crêpes in a round casserole dish alternating with the sauce. Sprinkle with the cheese and bake in a preheated 350°F (180°C) oven for 35 minutes. Serve at once.

SERVES 6

NALESNIKI

2 cups	500 ml	cottage cheese
1 cup	250 ml	ricotta cheese
4	4	eggs
¼ tsp	1 ml	each of salt, pepper, chervil, marjoram, thyme
12	12	Crêpes (see Crêpe Batter page 469)
3 cups	750 ml	bread crumbs
1 tbsp	15 ml	paprika
1 tsp	5 ml	each of oregano, thyme, sage, garlic powder, onion powder, black pepper, marjoram, chili powder
¾ cup	190 ml	milk
2 cups	500 ml	safflower oil
1½ cups	375 ml	diced cooked bacon
1 cup	250 ml	sour cream

Combine the cheeses with 3 eggs and the first seasoning list. Cut the crêpes in half. Ladle the cheese blend onto the crêpes, roll.

Blend the bread crumbs with the remaining seasonings. Beat the remaining egg into the milk. Dip the crêpes in the milk and dredge with bread crumbs.

Heat the oil to 375°F (190°C) and fry the crêpes in small batches, reserve hot while the remainder cook. Transfer to a serving platter, serve with crumbled bacon and sour cream on the side.

SERVES 6

Nalesniki

CRÊPES MARCHAND DE VIN

2 tbsp	30 ml	butter
⅓ cup	80 ml	finely diced ham
⅓ cup	80 ml	finely diced mushrooms
⅓ cup	80 ml	minced green onions
1 cup	250 ml	Demi-Glace (see page 123)
½ cup	125 ml	red wine
4 tbsp	60 ml	safflower oil
1 lb	450 g	beef tenderloin tips
1	1	sliced Spanish onion
8	8	Crêpes (see Crêpe Batter page 469)
3 tbsp	45 ml	chopped parsley

Heat the butter in a sauce pan. Add the ham, mushrooms and green onion, sauté until tender. Add the demi-glace and wine, reduce heat and simmer until sauce yields 1½ cups (375 ml).

Heat the oil in a skillet, sauté the tenderloin tips with the onion to your desired tenderness. Spoon over the crêpes and roll.

Place crêpes on serving plates, cover with the sauce. Garnish with parsley and serve.

SERVES 4

Crêpes Marchand de Vin

Spicy Honey Pork Crêpes

PEACH MELBA CRÊPES

1 cup	250 ml	whipping cream
¼ cup	60 ml	confectioners' sugar
12	12	Dessert Crêpes (see Crêpe Batter page 469)
2 cups	500 ml	heated raspberry preserves
⅓ cup	80 ml	sliced peaches
1½ cups	375 ml	Apricot Raspberry Sauce (see page 108)

Whip the cream and fold in the sugar. Spread the crêpe with raspberry preserves, layer with the peaches and whipped cream. Roll the crêpes, place on serving plates. Cover with the raspberry sauce and serve.

SERVES 6

SPICY HONEY PORK CRÊPES

1½ lbs	675 g	lean pork
½ cup	125 ml	flour, all purpose
2 tbsp	30 ml	safflower oil
1	1	sliced large onion
2	2	minced garlic cloves
3	3	peeled, seeded chopped tomatoes
1	1	seeded finely diced jalapeño pepper
½ tsp	3 ml	salt
¼ tsp	1 ml	each of pepper, chervil, thyme, oregano, cumin, paprika
2 tsp	10 ml	Worcestershire sauce
¼ tsp	1 ml	Tabasco™ sauce
2 cup	500 ml	Chicken Broth (see page 77)
12	12	Crêpes (see Crêpe Batter page 469)
1½ cups	375 ml	grated cheddar cheese

Cut the pork into a 1" (2.5 cm) strips, dust with the flour.

In a large kettle or Dutch oven heat the oil, brown the meat in small batches, remove and reserve. Sauté the onions and the garlic until tender. Stir in the tomatoes, jalepeño, seasonings, Worcestershire, Tabasco and broth, bring to a boil.

Stir in the pork, reduce heat and simmer for 45 minutes.

Spoon filling over crêpes and roll, place in a greased casserole pan. Sprinkle with cheese and bake in a preheated 350°F (180°C) oven for 15 minutes. Serve, with a rice pilaf.

SERVES 6

Peach Melba Crêpes

DESSERTS

Making an extraordinary difference in any meal is always the goal of any good cook, but making the meal memorable is usually left to the finish. The last item your guests dine upon is the one that lasts the longest within their memory, so finish with a memorable dessert.

Finding that dessert is no longer impossible. Just look within the following pages and the search will be complete. The preparation is as easy as finding it. Simply follow the step-by-step procedures and you will end up with an ending for your meal that will be simply delicious. From cakes to cheesecakes, from pies to dessert pastas (yes dessert pastas), memorable desserts are now within your reach.

Simply Delicious Cooking 2's desserts have what it tastes to show your guests that you have what it takes. Great desserts are not impossible, they can be as simple as our Strawberry Fields chocolate drink (see page 769) or as elaborate as our triple layer Banana Split Cheesecake. There is a dessert within for every occasion.

Never think you can't prepare these; we have made them all just right. Our pies will remind you of Mom's, our cakes of that romantic little bistro where just the two of you go. The kids are going to love the cookies. Then, there are the 'just right light' desserts. Our fruit desserts are exactly fresh. There are well over 275, so your favourite is most likely within. If not, we hope you will find a new favourite in this chapter.

Chocolate lovers will not lose their love affair, for our chocolate desserts rate among the finest. Whether the rich Swiss Chocolate Torte or the absolutely decadent White Chocolate Grand Marnier Cheesecake, all chocolate cravings come to an end with one of our desserts.

From Blueberry Ice Cream to Flaming Pears your finale will not be surpassed. Your secret tool will always be *Simply Delicious.*

Raisin Pie

Creme de Menthe Kahlua Swirl Cheesecake

CREME DE MENTHE KAHLUA SWIRL CHEESECAKE

CRUST:		
3½ cups	875 ml	chocolate wafer crumbs
¼ cup	60 ml	melted butter

FILLING:		
15 oz	1250 g	cream cheese
1½ cups	375 ml	granulated sugar
2½ cups	625 ml	heavy cream
4	4	eggs
¼ cup	60 ml	Kahlua liqueur
¼ cup	60 ml	strong coffee
¼ cup	60 ml	Creme de Menthe liqueur

CRUST:

Combine the wafer crumbs with the butter. Press into the bottom and sides of a buttered 10" (25 cm) spring form pan. Chill.

FILLING:

Cream the cheese and sugar until light. Stir in the cream. Add the eggs one at a time beating well after each addition. Divide the batter into two. Stir in the Kahlua and coffee into one batter, and the creme de menthe in the second. Pour the Kahlua batter into the prepared shell. Bake in a preheated 325°F (160°C) oven for 45 minutes. Swirl the creme de menthe batter through the Kahlua batter. Continue to bake for an additional 75 minutes. Turn oven off and prop door open slightly. After 30 minutes transfer to a rack to cool, chill 12 hours or overnight. Serve with a chocolate sauce.

Monkey's Lunch Cake with Banana Kahlua Frosting

MONKEY'S LUNCH CAKE

½ cup	125 ml	butter
¾ cup	180 ml	granulated sugar
2	2	eggs
¾ cup	180 ml	mashed bananas
¼ cup	60 ml	Irish Cream liqueur
1 tsp	5 ml	baking soda
2 cups	500 ml	flour, all purpose
1 tsp	5 ml	baking powder
⅛ tsp	pinch	salt

Cream the butter and sugar until very light and fluffy. Add the eggs one at a time beating well after each addition.

Beat in the banana. Blend in the Irish Cream. Sift together the baking soda, baking powder, flour and salt, fold into the cake.

Pour batter into a 9" (23 cm) buttered and floured spring form pan. Bake in a preheated 350°F (180°C) oven for 40 minutes. Cool 10 minutes then transfer cake to cooling rack, turn cake out and cool completely. Frost with Banana Kahlua Frosting (recipe follows).

BANANA KAHLUA FROSTING

½ cup	125 ml	butter
1¼ cups	310 ml	confectioners' sugar
2	2	eggs
1 cup	250 ml	granulated sugar
¼ cup	60 ml	flour, all purpose
¼ tsp	2 ml	salt
3 tbsp	45 ml	banana liqueur
3 tbsp	45 ml	Irish Cream liqueur
3 oz	90 g	semi-sweet chocolate – melted

In a mixing bowl, cream the butter and whip in the confectioners' sugar.

In a double boiler beat the eggs, sugar, flour, salt, liqueurs and chocolate. Cook 10 minutes, cool. Whip into the cream and butter. Frost cakes.

FRUIT PIZZA

CRUST:		
1 cup	250 ml	white cake crumbs
1 cup	250 ml	macaroons – crushed
¼ tsp	1 ml	cinnamon
¼ cup	60 ml	butter – melted

Combine the ingredients, press into a buttered 9" pie pan. Bake for 5 minutes in a preheated 350°F (180°C) oven.

FILLING:		
1 tbsp	15 ml	gelatin, unflavoured
¼ cup	60 ml	orange juice
6 oz	120 g	cream cheese
1 cup	250 ml	cream whipping
½ cup	125 ml	confectioners' sugar
½ tsp	3 ml	vanilla extract
1 tsp	5 ml	orange rind – grated

Soften the gelatin in the orange juice. Heat the orange juice in a small sauce pan until gelatin dissolves. Cream the cheese, add the orange juice. Whip the cream, fold in the sugar, extract and orange rind. Then fold into the creamed cheese. Pour into the shell and refrigerate for 3 hours.

TOPPING:		
1 cup	250 ml	strawberries – washed, hulled and sliced
1 cup	250 ml	peaches – sliced
1 cup	250 ml	kiwis – pared and sliced or sliced bananas
1 cup	250 ml	red seedless grapes, halved
½ cup	125 ml	apple jelly

Layer the fruit over the chilled filling. Heat the jelly and brush over the fruit. Chill for 1 hour before serving.

SERVES 6

BLUEBERRY CRUSTED ICE BOX CHEESECAKE

1½ tbsp	25 ml	soft butter
2 cups	500 ml	fresh blueberries – divided
½ cup	125 ml	granulated sugar – divided
1	1	envelope unflavoured gelatin
⅔ cup	160 ml	whipping cream – divided
1	1	egg
3	3	(125 g) pkg cream cheese at room temperature
¼ cup	60 ml	icing sugar

Generously butter a 9" (23 cm) pie plate. Gently press about 1½ cups (375 ml) blueberries into the butter to line the pie plate. Sprinkle with 2 tbsp (30 ml) granulated sugar.

Sprinkle the gelatin onto more than ⅓ cup (80 ml) cream in a medium sauce pan to soften. Stir in the egg and the remaining ⅓ cup (80 ml) granulated sugar. Place over medium heat, stirring constantly until mixture thickens slightly and comes to a boil.

Beat the cream cheese until smooth. Slowly add the gelatin mixture, beating until well blended. Beat the remaining ⅓ cup (80 ml) whipping cream until stiff, fold into cream cheese mixture. Pour mixture into blueberry shell and chill 3-4 hours. At serving time sprinkle with remaining blueberries and sifted icing sugar.

Fruit Pizza

Italian Mocha Cake

ITALIAN MOCHA CAKE

6	6	eggs, separated
1 cup	250 ml	granulated sugar
2 tbsp	30 ml	lemon juice
1 tsp	5 ml	lemon rind – grated
1 tsp	5 ml	instant coffee
2 tbsp	30 ml	hot water
½ cup	125 ml	pastry flour
2 tsp	10 ml	baking powder
¼ tsp	1 ml	salt
16	16	chocolate covered coffee beans

Whip the egg yolks, beat in the sugar, lemon juice and rind. Dissolve the coffee in the hot water, then add to the egg yolks.

Sift together the flour, baking powder and salt. Fold into the egg mixture. Beat the egg whites until soft peaks form. Fold into batter. Do not over mix. Pour into 2 – 9" (23 cm) wax paper lined greased and floured round cake pans. Bake in a preheated 350°F (180°C) oven for 20 minutes. Transfer to a cooling rack, cool 10 minutes before removing from pans, cool completely.

Frost and fill with Mocha Cream Fillling (see page 506). Decorate with chocolate coffee beans.

CHOCOLATE SOFTIES

3 oz	80 g	semi-sweet chocolate
1 cup	250 ml	butter
2 cups	500 ml	granulated sugar
2	2	eggs
⅛ tsp	pinch	salt
3¾ cups	930 ml	flour, all purpose
2 tbsp	30 ml	cocoa powder
1 tbsp	15 ml	baking powder
¾ cup	180 ml	milk
1 tsp	5 ml	vanilla extract

Melt the chocolate in a double boiler. Cream the butter, then beat in the sugar and eggs.

Sift together the salt, flour, cocoa and baking powder. Fold into the cream mixture alternating with the milk. Add the vanilla and refrigerate 4 hours. Roll in a cigar shape then cut into rounds.

Bake 10-12 minutes in a preheated 400°F (200°C) oven. Remove from oven and cool.

MAKES 2 DOZEN

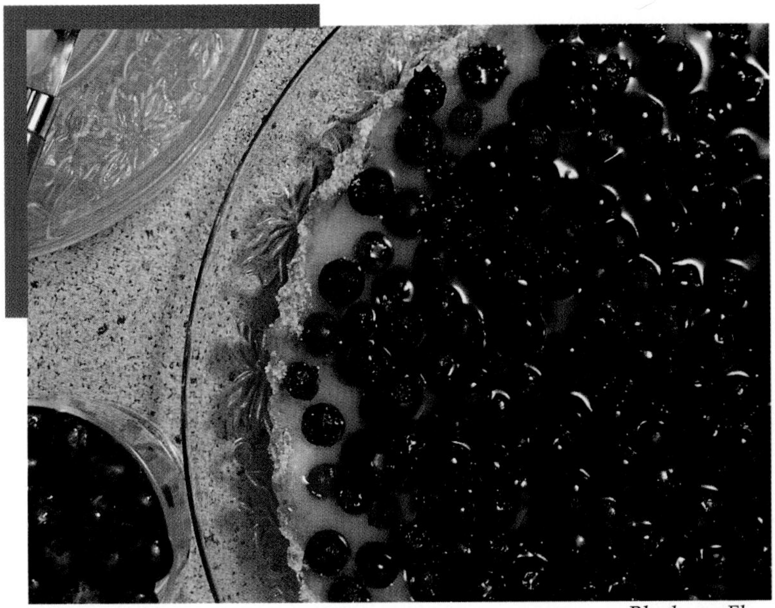

Blueberry Flan

BLUEBERRY FLAN

FLAN:

2½ cups	625 ml	flour, pastry
½ cup	125 ml	granulated sugar
½ cup	125 ml	butter – softened
3	3	egg yolks
1 tsp	5 ml	lemon rind – grated
¼ tsp	1 ml	salt

Place flour in a mixing bowl. Using the dough hook blend in the sugar and butter, add the egg yolks, lemon and salt. Work thoroughly to combine but do not over work pastry. Rest pastry 30 minutes, roll out to ⅛" (3 mm) thick. Fit into a greased 10" (25 cm) flan dish. Bake blind in a 350°F (180°C) oven for 15 minutes.

FILLING:

1¾ cups	430 ml	granulated sugar
¼ cup	60 ml	cornstarch
2	2	eggs
1 tbsp	15 ml	butter
1½ cups	375 ml	milk
1 tsp	5 ml	vanilla extract
3 cups	750 ml	blueberries, fresh
¼ cup	60 ml	apple jelly

Mix 1 cup (250 ml) of sugar, cornstarch and eggs together in a double boiler, add the butter, milk and vanilla, cook until very thick. Pour into the shell. Combine the remaining sugar with the blueberries. Spread over cream filling, return to oven and continue to bake for 25 minutes. Remove from the oven, cool. Heat the apple jelly, brush on blueberries and chill.

SERVES 8-10

FROZEN CHOCOLATE ZABAGLIONE

6	6	egg yolks
½ cup	125 ml	granulated sugar
2 oz	60 g	semi-sweet chocolate
⅓ cup	80 ml	cream sherry
¼ cup	60 ml	heavy cream

In a double boiler over low heat, beat the egg yolks with the sugar until foamy.

Melt the chocolate in a second double boiler. Add the sherry and cream. Slowly pour the chocolate mixture into the eggs. Whisk continuously until mixture thickens, cool then chill. Pour into a ice cream maker and freeze according to manufacturer's instructions.

SERVES 4

GOURMET PUMPKIN PIE

½ quan	0.5	Gourmet Pastry (see page 541)
1¾ cups	430 ml	pumpkin – use canned
½ cup	125 ml	brown sugar – packed
¼ cup	60 ml	honey
½ tsp	3 ml	ginger – ground
1 tsp	5 ml	cinnamon
¼ tsp	1 ml	cloves – ground
2	2	eggs – beaten
1 cup	250 ml	evaporated milk
½ cup	125 ml	water

Roll out the dough and fit into a 9" (23 cm) pie shell. Flute the edges.

Place the pumpkin in a sauce pan and cook for 10 minutes. Blend in the sugar, honey and spices. Remove from heat. Whip in the eggs, milk and the water. Stir until smooth. Pour into the pie shell. Bake in a preheated oven at 450°F (230°C) for 45 minutes, or until a inserted knife comes out clean on the side.

SERVES 6

Gourmet Pumpkin Pie

STRAWBERRY CHEESECAKE

CRUST:		
2 cups	500 ml	white cake crumbs
⅓ cup	80 ml	fine bread crumbs
¼ cup	60 ml	butter – melted

Combine the ingredients together. Press into a buttered 9" spring form pan bottom and top.

FILLING:		
2 cups	500 ml	fresh strawberry purée
1½ lbs	750 g	cream cheese
1½ cups	375 ml	granulated sugar
3	3	eggs
2 tsp	10 ml	vanilla, white

Cream together the strawberries, cheese and sugar. Add the eggs one at a time beating after each addition. Stir in the vanilla, and pour into the shell. Bake for 75 minutes in a preheated 350°F (160°C) oven. Turn oven off, prop door open and leave cake in for 30 minutes. Transfer to a cooling rack and cool to room temperature.

TOPPING:		
2 cups	500 ml	fresh strawberries, cut in half
½ cup	125 ml	apricot preserves

Arrange the strawberries around the cooled cake. Heat the apricots in a small sauce pan and brush over strawberries. Refrigerate cake for 6-8 hours before serving.

Strawberry Cheesecake

B-52 Torte with B-52 Frosting

B-52 TORTE

2 tbsp	30 ml	cocoa powder
2 cups	500 ml	pastry flour
1 tsp	5 ml	baking powder
¼ tsp	1 ml	salt
½ cup	125 ml	butter
1½ cups	375 ml	granulated sugar
2	2	beaten eggs
3 oz	80 g	melted semi-sweet chocolate
⅓ cup	80 ml	milk
⅛ cup	30 ml	orange brandy
⅛ cup	30 ml	Irish Cream liqueur
⅛ cup	30 ml	coffee liqueur

Sift the cocoa powder, flour, baking powder and salt together three times.

Cream the butter with the sugar until very light. Add the eggs one at a time beating after each addition. Mix the chocolate and milk with the liqueurs.

Incorporate the flour and liquid into the creamed mixture in thirds. Pour into 2 – 8" (20 cm) round buttered and floured pans. Bake in a preheated 350°F (180°C) oven for 35-40 minutes.

Cool 10 minutes, turn out onto a cooling rack. Frost and fill with B-52 Frosting (recipe follows).

B-52 FROSTING

3 oz	85 g	semi-sweet chocolate
1 oz	30 ml	Irish Cream liqueur
1 oz	30 ml	orange brandy
1 oz	30 ml	coffee liqueur
1 tsp	5 ml	butter – melted
2	2	egg yolks
2 cups	500 ml	confectioners' sugar

In a double boiler melt the chocolate with the liqueurs and butter. Beat in the egg yolks and cook beating until sauce thickens, remove from heat at once. Place in a mixer and whip in the sugar. Use as directed.

CAPPUCCINO PASTA

½ quan	0.5	Pasta Cafe (see page 436)
½ quan	0.5	Cocoa Pasta (see page 429)
¼ cup	60 ml	granulated sugar
1 cup	250 ml	half & half cream
1 tsp	5 ml	vanilla extract
6 oz	170 g	semi-sweet chocolate

Process the pasta as directed, and cut into capellini.

Dissolve the sugar in the cream, and add the vanilla.

Heat the cream in a double boiler. Add the chocolate to the cream.

Cook the pasta in a large kettle of boiling water. Drain and place on serving plates. Pour sauce over and serve.

SERVES 6

Angel Food Cake

ANGEL FOOD CAKE

10	10	egg whites
1 tsp	5 ml	cream of tartar
1 cup	250 ml	vanilla sugar*
1 cup	250 ml	flour, all purpose
¼ tsp	2 ml	salt
1 tsp	5 ml	vanilla extract

Whip the egg whites until very fluffy. Add the cream of tartar, then the sugar gradually. Sift the flour and salt together 4 times. Fold into the egg whites. Add the vanilla. Fold into an angel food cake pan (do not grease). Bake in a preheated 375°F (190°C) oven for 35-40 minutes. Invert pan over a tube or glass, and allow it to drop on it's own. Once cake has cooled frost with Marshmallow Fudge (page 572), Double Chocolate (page 561) or any of your choice.

* To make vanilla sugar place 2 cups of granulated sugar and 3 vanilla beans in a container. Seal tightly for 2 weeks.

PASTA CAFE FRANGELICO

1 quan	1 quan	Pasta Cafe (see page 436)
¼ cup	60 ml	granulated sugar
1 cup	250 ml	half & half cream
2 tsp	10 ml	instant coffee
2 oz	60 g	Frangelico liqueur
2 oz	60 g	semi-sweet chocolate
¼ cup	60 ml	chopped hazelnuts (filberts)

Process the pasta as directed, and cut into capellini.

In a double boiler, dissolve the sugar in the cream. Add the coffee and liqueur. Melt the chocolate in the same pot.

Cook the pasta in a large kettle of boiling water, then drain.

Pour sauce over pasta, sprinkle with nuts and serve.

SERVES 6

SUGAR BUSH APPLE PIE

1 quan	1 quan	Whole Wheat Pie Crust (recipe follows)
8	8	large tart apples
1 cup	250 ml	maple sugar
1 tbsp	15 ml	flour, all purpose
¼ tsp each	1 ml	nutmeg, cloves
1 tsp	5 ml	cinnamon – ground
2 tbsp	30 ml	butter
1	1	egg – beaten

Roll out half the dough, line a 9" (23 cm) pie pan with the dough. Pare and core the apples. Mix the sugar, flour and spices together. Sprinkle ½ on the pastry. Fill with apples then sprinkle with the remaining sugar. Dot with butter. Roll out the remaining dough, layer on top. Tuck the edges under and flute the sides. Cut the top pastry to allow the steam to escape. Brush with egg. Bake in a preheated 425°F (215°C) oven for 45 minutes or until golden brown. Cool before serving.

SERVES 6

WHOLE WHEAT PIE CRUST

1 cup	250 ml	whole wheat flour
1 cup	250 ml	all purpose flour
1 tsp	5 ml	salt
¾ cup	180 ml	shortening
⅓ cup	80 ml	ice water

Sift the two flours together, twice with salt. Cut the shortening into the flours. Mix the water into the flour a couple of tbsp at a time, until the flour is just moist. Divide into two, cover and chill. Use as required.

Sugar Bush Apple Pie

LEMON OR LIME MERINGUE PIE

½ quan	0.5 quan	Plain Pastry (see page 616)
2¼ cups	560 ml	granulated sugar
⅓ cup	80 ml	cornstarch
1¾ cups	410 ml	boiling water
3	3	eggs – separated
⅓ cup	80 ml	lemon or lime juice and pulp
1 tsp	5 ml	lemon or lime rind grated
1 tbsp	15 ml	butter
2 drops	2 drops	green food colouring – for lime pie

Roll out the pastry and fit into a 9" (23 cm) shell. Flute the edges and blind bake. (See glossary for blind baking). Cool.

Mix 1¼ cups (310 ml) of sugar with the cornstarch. Add the water stirring so no lumps form. Cook on medium heat until mixture thickens. Remove from heat and blend the mixture into the egg yolks a little at a time. Then cook for 2 minutes longer. Add the juice, pulp and butter (colouring for lime).

Cool completely. Pour into the pie shell. Beat the egg whites until stiff. Add the remaining sugar 2 tbsp (30 ml) at a time. Swirl over the pie. Bake for 10-12 minutes in a preheated 450°F (230°C) oven or until meringue turns golden.

SERVES 6

DEVIL'S FOOD CAKE

2 tbsp	30 ml	cocoa powder
2 cups	500 ml	pastry flour
1 tsp	5 ml	baking soda
¼ tsp	2 ml	salt
½ cup	125 ml	butter
1½ cups	375 ml	granulated sugar
2	2	eggs
4 oz	120 g	semi-sweet chocolate – melted
1 cup	250 ml	buttermilk

Sift the cocoa, flour, baking soda and salt together 3 times. Cream the butter and sugar together until very light. Add the eggs one at a time. Add the chocolate. Incorporate the flour and buttermilk in thirds. Pour into 2 – 8" (20 cm) round greased floured cake pans. Bake in a preheated 350°F (180°C) oven for 35-40 minutes. Cool 10 minutes turn out on a cooling rack. Cool and frost with Mocha Cream Filling (recipe follows).

MOCHA CREAM FILLING

½ cup	125 ml	granulated sugar
¼ cup	60 ml	very strong black coffee
¼ cup	60 ml	coffee liqueur
3	3	egg yolks
½ cup + 2 tbsp	155 ml	butter – unsalted

Heat the sugar, coffee and liqueur in a small sauce pan into a thick syrup. Whip the egg yolks, then whip the syrup in slowly.

Cream the butter until light and fluffy. Fold into the egg / coffee mixture. Use as required.

NOTE: To make Irish Cream Filling, substitute the coffee liqueur with Irish Cream.

Lemon or Lime Meringue Pie

Devil's Food Cake with Mocha Cream Filling

Butter Tart Squares

PINA COLADA CHEESECAKE

CRUST:		
1 cup	250 ml	flaked coconut
1 cup	250 ml	roasted filberts – ground
⅓ cup	80 ml	granulated sugar
¼ cup	60 ml	butter – melted

Combine the ingredients. Press onto the bottom of a 9" (23 cm) spring form pan. Refrigerate 10 minutes. Bake 7 minutes in a preheated 350°F (180°C) oven.

FILLING:		
1½ lbs	675 ml	cream cheese
1 cup	250 ml	granulated sugar
¼ cup	60 ml	coconut creme nectar *
1 cup	250 ml	heavy cream
1½ cups	375 ml	crushed pineapple – well drained
3	3	eggs
¼ cup	60 ml	coconut rum (optional)
2 tsp	10 ml	rum extract
1 cup	250 ml	toasted coconut – shredded

Cream the cheese with the sugar until smooth. Blend in the coconut creme, cream and pineapple. Beat in the eggs one at a time. Incorporate rum flavouring. Pour into shell. Bake in a preheated 350°F (160°C) oven for 90 minutes. Turn oven off, prop door open and rest cake for 30 minutes. Sprinkle with coconut. Transfer to a cooling rack, cool to room temperature. Refrigerate 8 hours or overnight before serving.

WHITE CHOCOLATE HONEY TORTE

1¼ cups	310 ml	flour, all purpose
2 tsp	10 ml	baking powder
½ tsp	3 ml	salt
1 cup	250 ml	granulated sugar
3	3	eggs – separated
½ cup	125 ml	milk
¾ cup	180 ml	oil
2 oz	60 g	white chocolate – melted, cooled
1½ tsp	8 ml	white vanilla
¾ cup	180 ml	honey
¼ cup	60 ml	white Creme de Cacao

Sift together the flour, baking powder and salt, twice. Cream the sugar with the eggs until very light. Alternate adding the flour, milk and oil in thirds. Fold in the chocolate and vanilla. Pour batter into a buttered and floured 9" (23 cm) spring form pan. Bake for 30 minutes in a preheated 350°F (180°C) oven. Transfer to a cooling rack. Place the cake on a large platter. Blend the honey with the liqueur, pour over cake and allow to soak in for 24 hours. Serve with unsweetened whipped cream.

BUTTER TART SQUARES

½ cup	125 ml	butter
1 cup	250 ml	flour, all purpose
1¾ cup	430 ml	brown sugar
2	2	eggs, beaten
½ cup	125 ml	oatmeal
¼ tsp	1 ml	salt
½ tsp	3 ml	baking powder
1 tsp	5 ml	vanilla extract
½ cup	125 ml	broken pecan pieces
½ cup	125 ml	raisins

Cut the butter into the flour with 2 tbsp (30 ml) of sugar. Press into a 9" x 9" (22.5 x 23 cm) buttered cake pan. Bake in a preheated 350°F (180°C) oven for 15 minutes.

Beat the eggs with the remaining sugar. Fold in the oatmeal, salt and baking powder, blend well. Stir in the vanilla, nuts and raisins. Pour onto the shell, return to the oven and bake for an additional 20 minutes. Cool before cutting into squares.

YIELDS 20 SQUARES

White Chocolate Honey Torte

WALNUT MANDARIN CAKE

½ cup	125 ml	butter
1 cup	250 ml	granulated sugar
2	2	egg yolks
1½ cups	375 ml	flour, pastry
2¼ tsp	13 ml	baking powder
¼ cup	60 ml	cocoa powder
2 tbsp	10 ml	hot water
½ cup	125 ml	milk
1 tsp	5 ml	vanilla
½ cup	125 ml	walnuts – broken
1 cup	250 ml	Mandarin orange segments

Cream the butter, add the sugar and 1 egg at a time. Beat until very light. Sift together the flour and baking powder. Blend the cocoa powder, hot water, milk and vanilla.

Blend in ⅓rd flour and ⅓rd milk alternating and repeating until complete. Stir in the walnuts and oranges. Fold into 2-9" (23 cm) greased and floured cake pan. Bake in a preheated 350°F (180°C) oven for 25-30 minutes or until an inserted toothpick comes out clean. Cool 10 minutes before removing cakes to cooling rack. Cool completely before frosting with Pineapple Cream Frosting (recipe follows).

PINEAPPLE CREAM FROSTING

1 cup	250 ml	whipping cream
¼ cup	60 ml	confectioners' sugar
2½ cups	625 ml	crushed pineapple with juice
3 oz	90 g	pineapple or vanilla instant pudding

Whip the cream until it forms soft peaks. Whip in the icing sugar. Whip the pineapple together with the pudding until set. Fold in the whipping cream. Frost cake.

CHOCOLATE MOUSSE

6 oz	120 g	semi-sweet chocolate – grated
6	6	large eggs – separated, at room temperature
¼ tsp	1 ml	salt

Melt the chocolate in a double boiler. Cool slightly. Beat the egg yolks until light and thick. Gradually stir in the melted chocolate. Whip the egg whites with the salt until stiff. Gently fold into the mixture. Spoon the mousse into serving dishes, cover with plastic wrap and chill for 6 hours.

SERVES 6

Walnut Mandarin Cake with Pineapple Cream Frosting

B-52 Cheesecake

Sugar 'n' Spice Hermits

RAISIN 'N' NUT OATMEAL COOKIES

1 tsp	5 ml	baking powder
1 tsp	5 ml	baking soda
1 tsp	5 ml	salt
1 cup	250 ml	shortening
1 cup	250 ml	brown sugar – packed
1 cup	250 ml	granulated sugar
2	2	eggs
1 tsp	5 ml	vanilla
2½ cups	625 ml	quick cooking oats
½ cup	125 ml	raisins
½ cup	125 ml	walnut pieces

Preheat oven to 350°F (180°C).

Sift together the baking powder, soda and salt. Cream the shortening and sugars until light and fluffy. Add the eggs one at a time mixing well. Blend in vanilla. Add the dry ingredients to creamed mixture. Stir in the oats, raisins and nuts.

Shape into balls and place on a buttered pastry sheet 2 inches (5 cm) apart. Bake 10-12 minutes.

MAKES 3 DOZEN

SUGAR 'N' SPICE HERMITS

¾ cup	180 ml	butter
1 cup	250 ml	brown sugar
2	2	eggs
¾ tsp	4 ml	baking soda
1 tbsp	15 ml	hot water
2½ cups	625 ml	flour, all purpose
½ tsp	3 ml	salt
1 tsp	5 ml	cinnamon
¼ tsp	2 ml	nutmeg
¼ tsp	2 ml	cloves
1 cup	250 ml	raisins

Cream the butter with sugar. Beat in the eggs, soda and water. Fold in the remaining ingredients. Drop tbsp size dough onto greased cookie sheet 2" (5 cm) apart. Bake in a preheated 350°F (180°C) oven for 10-12 minutes.

MAKES 3⅓ DOZEN

B - 52 CHEESECAKE

CRUST:		
3 cups	750 ml	chocolate wafer crumbs
3 tbsp	45 ml	granulated sugar
¼ cup	60 ml	butter – melted

Combine the ingredients together. Press on the bottom and sides of a buttered 9" spring form pan.

FILLING:		
1¾ lbs	675 g	cream cheese
1 cup	250 ml	granulated sugar
6	6	eggs
3 oz	85 g	semi-sweet chocolate – melted
¼ cup	60 ml	Kahlua liqueur
¼ cup	60 ml	Grand Marnier liqueur
2 tsp	10 ml	orange rind – grated
¼ cup	60 ml	Irish Cream liqueur

Cream the cream cheese and sugar together, beat in the eggs one at a time, divide the batter in 3 parts. In one part blend the chocolate and Kahlua. In the second blend in the Grand Marnier and orange rind. In the last blend the Irish Cream.

Pour the chocolate batter into the shell. Bake for 30 minutes in a preheated 325°F (160°C) oven. Pour over the Irish Cream batter and continue to bake for an additional 20 minutes. Pour the Grand Marnier batter over and finish baking for 45 minutes. Turn the oven off, prop the door open and rest the cake for 30 minutes. Transfer to a cooling rack and cool to room temperature. Refrigerate for 8 hours or overnight. Serve with an Orange Brandy Sauce (see page 107).

FUDGE SQUARES

2 oz	60 g	semi-sweet chocolate
⅓ cup	80ml	butter
1 cup	250 ml	granulated sugar
3	3	eggs
¾ cup	180 ml	flour, all purpose
1 tsp	5 ml	baking powder
1 tsp	5 ml	vanilla
1 cup	250 ml	walnut pieces
1 quan	1 quan	Double Chocolate Frosting (see page 561)

In a double boiler melt the chocolate and the butter, remove from the heat and beat in the sugar and eggs. Sift the flour with the baking powder, fold into mixture. Add the vanilla and walnuts. Pour batter into a 8" (20 cm) square buttered square pan. Bake in a preheated 350°F (180°C) oven for 12-15 minutes. Cool slightly. Frost and cut into squares.

MAKES 2 DOZ

TURTLES SQUARES

¼ cup	60 ml	butter – melted
1 cup	250 ml	chocolate wafer crumbs
1 cup	250 ml	coconut shredded
10 oz	300 g	semi-sweet chocolate chips
6 oz	180 g	caramels
2 cups	500 ml	condensed milk – sweetened
1 cup	250 ml	pecan pieces

Mix the butter with the chocolate crumbs, press into a 13" x 9" (32.5 x 23 cm) buttered pan. Sprinkle with coconut, then half the chocolate chips and caramels. Pour the milk over then sprinkle with nuts. Bake in a preheated 350°F (180°C) oven for 30 minutes. Cool. Melt the remaining chocolate in a double boiler then pour over the squares. Cut into bars once cool.

MAKES 24 SQUARES

PEACH 'N' APPLE PIE

PIE:		
½ quan	0.5	Plain Pastry (see page 616)
4	4	large tart cooking apples, cored, pared, sliced
2 cups	500 ml	fresh peaches – sliced
¼ cup	60 ml	flour, all purpose
½ cup	125 ml	granulated sugar
½ tsp	3 ml	cinnamon

TOPPING:		
½ cup	125 ml	flour, all purpose
½ tsp	3 ml	cinnamon
⅓ cup	80 ml	light brown sugar
⅓ cup	80 ml	butter

PIE:

Roll the pastry out and line a 10" (25 cm) pie pan. Flute the edges.

Mix the apples and peaches together. Blend the flour, sugar and cinnamon together. Toss through the fruit. Pour into pastry shell.

TOPPING:

Mix the flour, cinnamon and sugar together. Cut in the butter until crumbly. Sprinkle on top of the pie. Bake in a preheated 425°F (215°C) oven for 20 minutes, reduce heat to 325°F (160°C) continue to bake for 30 minutes. Remove and cool before serving.

SERVES 6

Peach 'n' Apple Pie

Turtles Squares

Prinzregenten Torte

PRINZREGENTEN TORTE

CAKE:		
1¾ cups	430 ml	granulated sugar
⅓ cup	80 ml	hot water
3 cups	750 ml	pastry flour
1 tbsp	15 ml	baking powder
¼ tsp	2 ml	salt
¾ cup	180 ml	butter
3	3	eggs
1 tsp	5 ml	vanilla
⅔ cup	160 ml	milk

Place ½ cup (125 ml) of sugar in a heavy sauce pan over medium heat cook the sugar stirring constantly until it browns. Remove from heat and add the water allow to cool. Sift the flour, baking powder and salt together. Cream the butter and remaining sugar together until very light.

Beat in the eggs 1 at a time. Mix the cooled syrup with the vanilla and milk. Incorporate the flour and liquid into the creamed mixture in thirds. Cut 8-8" (20 cm) rounds from wax paper and place on pastry sheets. Divide the batter evenly (¾ cup [180 ml] each) over the rounds to 1½" (4 cm) from the edges. Bake 7-8 minutes in a preheated 350°F (180°C) oven. Remove wax paper. Fill and stack each layer after cooling.

FILLING FOR PRINZREGENTEN TORTE

1 cup	250 ml	granulated sugar
¼ cup	60 ml	cornstarch
2	2	eggs
1½ cups	375 ml	milk
1 tsp	5 ml	vanilla
3 oz	85 g	semi-sweet chocolate

In a sauce pan or a double boiler, blend the sugar with the cornstarch and eggs. Whip in the milk and vanilla. Heat over medium heat. Stir in the chocolate, cook until sauce is very thick. Cool and spread over the cakes.

FROSTING:		
10 oz	300 g	semi-sweet chocolate
1½ tsp	8 ml	oil

Melt the chocolate in a double boiler, stir in the oil. Pour over cake while hot. Chill in the refrigerator 1 hour before serving.

Dutch Apple Cheesecake

POMMES A' LA DIABLE

1¼ cups	310 ml	granulated sugar
1¼ cups	310 ml	water
1	1	vanilla bean
6	6	large apples – pared, cored
1½ cups	375 ml	heavy cream
½ cup	125 ml	sour cream
½ cup	125 ml	confectioners' sugar
⅓ cup	80 ml	Calvados liqueur

Boil the sugar, water together with the vanilla bean, reduce heat stirring until sugar has dissolved. Poach the apples until tender. Whip the cream to thick but not stiff, fold in the sour cream and confectioners' sugar. Place apples on plates, smother with cream. Heat the Calvados and ignite, serve at once.

SERVES 6

APPLE 'N' SPICE LOAF

2 cups	500 ml	apple juice
1½ cups	375 ml	granulated sugar
1 cup	250 ml	oil
1 tbsp	15 ml	cinnamon
¾ tsp	4 ml	cloves
1 tsp	5 ml	nutmeg
1 cup	250 ml	raisin
1½ cups	375 ml	apples – pared, cored, shredded
4 cups	1 L	flour, pastry
2 tsp	10 ml	baking powder
1 cup	250 ml	pecans – broken

Simmer the apple juice, sugar, oil, spices, raisins and apples over medium heat for 5 minutes. Remove from heat and cool to room temperature. Blend in the flour, baking powder and nuts. Mix thoroughly. Pour into a 10" x 4" (25 x 10 cm) greased and floured loaf pan. Bake for 1½ hours in a preheated 350°F (180°C) oven. Cool 15 minutes before turning out onto a cooling rack.

DUTCH APPLE CHEESECAKE

CRUST:		
3½ cups	875 ml	graham cracker crumbs
1 tbsp	15 ml	cinnamon
¼ cup	60 ml	melted butter

Combine the ingredients. Press into the bottom and sides of a buttered 10" (25 cm) spring form pan. Chill. Preheat oven to 320°F (160°C).

FILLING:		
2 cups	500 ml	apples – pared, cored, diced
1 cup	250 ml	walnuts – broken
½ cup	125 ml	raisins
1 lb	450 g	cream cheese
¾ cup	180 ml	granulated sugar
4	4	eggs
1 tsp	5 ml	vanilla

Mix the apples with nuts and raisins. Spread over the shell. Cream the cheese with sugar until light and fluffy. Beat in the eggs one at a time mixing well. Stir in the vanilla. Pour over the apples. Bake for 45 minutes.

TOPPING:		
½ cup	125 ml	flour, all purpose
1 tsp	5 ml	cinnamon
⅓ cup	80 ml	light brown sugar
⅓ cup	80 ml	butter

Sift the flour, cinnamon and sugar together. Cream the butter then blend with the flour. Spread on top of cake. Bake for 45 minutes longer. Prop oven door open, turn oven off and leave the cake for 30 minutes. Transfer to cooling rack. Once cool chill 6-8 hours.

Apple 'n' Spice Loaf

Pecan Drops

JUST PEACHY CHEESECAKE

CRUST:		
2 cups	500 ml	white cake crumbs
1 cup	250 ml	fine bread crumbs
¼ cup	60 ml	butter – melted

Combine the ingredients together. Press into the bottom and sides of a buttered 9" (23 cm) spring form pan. Chill 5 minutes, bake 7 minutes in a preheated 350°F (180°C) oven. Chill.

FILLING:		
1½ cups	675 g	cream cheese
1 cup	250 ml	granulated sugar
3	3	eggs
¼ cup	60 ml	cream – heavy
2 cups	500 ml	fresh peach purée
1 tbsp	15 ml	lemon juice
2 tsp	10 ml	vanilla

Cream the cheese with the sugar. Beat in the eggs one at a time. Stir in the cream, peach, lemon and vanilla. Pour into the shell. Bake in a preheated oven at 350°F (180°C) for 70 minutes. Turn oven off, prop door open leave cake in for 30 minutes. Transfer to a cooling rack and cool to room temperature.

TOPPING:		
2 cups	500 ml	fresh sliced peaches
2 tbsp	30 ml	lemon juice
¼ cup	60 ml	apricot preserves

Soak the peaches in the lemon juice for 10 minutes. Then drain any liquid, arrange the peaches on top of the cake. Heat the apricots and brush onto peaches. Chill cake for 6-8 hours before serving.

TIMOTHY'S FRUIT COUPE

CRUST:		
3 cups	750 ml	graham cracker crumbs
½ tsp	3 ml	cinnamon – ground
3 tbsp	45 ml	granulated sugar
¼ cup	60 ml	butter – melted

Combine all the ingredients together. Press into the bottom and sides of a 9" (23 cm) buttered pie plate. Bake 5 minutes in a preheat 350°F (180°C) oven. Cool then chill.

FILLING:		
2 cups	500 ml	cherry pie filling
½ quan	0.5	Kiwi Mango Sorbet (see page 580)
1 quan	1	Strawberry Banana Ice Cream (see page 641)

Spread the shell with the cherry pie filling, alternate layers of sorbet and ice cream. Freeze for 4 hours before serving.

SERVES 8-10

PECAN DROPS

¼ cup	60 ml	butter
½ cup	125 ml	granulated sugar
2	2	eggs – separated
2 tsp	10 ml	baking powder
¼ tsp	2 ml	salt
1 cup	250 ml	flour, all purpose
1 cup	250 ml	pecans – broken
¼ cup	60 ml	milk
1 tsp	5 ml	vanilla

Cream the butter with the sugar, beat in the egg yolks. Whip the egg whites stiff. Sift the baking powder, salt and flour together then the flour into creamed mixture with the egg whites. Stir in the nuts, milk and vanilla. Drop teaspoon sizes onto a buttered pastry sheet. Bake 10-12 minutes in a 350°F (180°C) preheated oven.

MAKES 2½ DOZEN

Timothy's Fruit Coupe

BANANA SPLIT CHEESECAKE

CRUST:		
1 cup	250 ml	flaked coconut
1 cup	250 ml	roasted filberts – ground
⅓ cup	80 ml	granulated sugar
¼ cup	60 ml	butter – melted

Combine the ingredients. Press into a buttered 9" (23 cm) spring form pan. Refrigerate 5 minutes, then bake for 7 minutes in a 350°F (180°C) preheated oven. Cool.

FILLING:		
1½ lbs	675 g	cream cheese
1 cup	250 ml	granulated sugar
3	3	eggs
1 tsp	5 ml	vanilla
½ cup	125 ml	banana – mashed
½ cup	125 ml	strawberry purée
2 oz	60 g	semi-sweet chocolate – melted
1 tbsp	15 ml	cocoa powder

Cream the cheese with the sugar. Beat in the eggs one at a time. Stir in the vanilla. Divide the batter into 3 parts. Blend the banana into one part. Blend the strawberry into a second part, and the chocolate and cocoa into the third part.

Pour the chocolate batter into the shell, bake for 25 minutes. Carefully pour the banana batter over the chocolate and bake for an additional 25 minutes. Pour the strawberry batter over and bake for 30 minutes. Turn oven off, prop the door open and leave the cake in for 30 additional minutes. Transfer to a cooling rack, cool to room temperature. Chill in refrigerator for 8 hours or overnight. Serve with chocolate sauce.

RUM POUND CAKE

8	8	eggs – separated
3 cups	750 ml	granulated sugar
2 cups	500 ml	butter
2 tsp	10 ml	vanilla
3 cups	750 ml	flour, pastry
⅓ cup	80 ml	rum

Whip the egg whites until soft peaks form. Fold in 1 cup (250 ml) sugar gradually forming a stiff meringue. Cream the butter with the remaining sugar. Add one egg yolk at a time beating after each addition. Add the vanilla. Fold in the flour alternating with the rum in one-third additions. Fold into the meringue. Pour into a 4" x 10" (10 x 25 cm) loaf pan. Bake in a preheated 350°F (180°C) oven for 1½ hours. Cool 15 minutes, turn cake out onto a cooling rack. Frost and decorate as desired.

WILD BERRY PIE

1½ quan	1.5 quan	Plain Pastry (see page 616)
4¼ lbs	2 kg	frozen berry mix or 1½ lbs (454 g) each of fresh blueberries, strawberries and loganberries
¾ cup	180 ml	granulated sugar
4 tbsp	60 ml	granulated quick-cooking tapioca
2 tbsp	30 ml	lemon juice
1	1	egg

Roll the pastry out and fit into a 9" (23 cm) pie pan. Wash and sort berries. Mix all the remaining ingredients except the egg together and blend into the berry mix. Pour into the pan shell. Whisk the egg, and moisten the edge of pastry. Add the top crust fluting the edges together. Brush the top with the remaining egg. Cut vent holes for steam to escape.

Bake in a preheated 350°F (180°C) oven for 45 minutes. Cool and Chill.

Rum Pound Cake

Banana Split Cheesecake

Pumpkin Chiffon

PUMPKIN CHIFFON

1 tbsp	15 ml	gelatin – unflavoured
2 tbsp	30 ml	maple syrup
1½ cups	375 ml	pumpkin
¾ cup	180 ml	brown sugar
½ tsp	3 ml	salt
1 tsp	5 ml	cinnamon – ground
¼ tsp	2 ml	cloves
¼ tsp	2 ml	nutmeg
⅓ cup	80 ml	milk
3	3	eggs – separated
⅓ cup	80 ml	granulated sugar
½ cup	125 ml	cream – whipping

Soften the gelatin in the maple syrup. Combine the pumpkin, brown sugar, salt, seasonings and milk in a sauce pan. Bring to a boil over low heat. Beat in the egg yolks and cook for 2 minutes longer. Stir in the maple syrup. Chill until the mixture is nearly set. Whip the egg whites stiff, slowly add the sugar. Fold into the pumpkin. Whip the cream and fold into the pumpkin. Pour into serving glasses and chill until set. Serve very cold.

NOTE: This filling may also be used for pumpkin pie. Prepare ½ quantity of plain pastry (see page 616) and line a 9" (23 cm) pie plate, prepare pumpkin chiffon leaving the gelatin and whipped cream out of filling. Pour filling into pie plate and bake in a preheated 350°F (180°C) oven for 45 minutes. When cool, top with whipped cream and serve.

SERVES 8

Key Lime Cheesecake

KEY LIME CHEESECAKE

CRUST:		
2 cups	500 ml	graham cracker crumbs
¼ cup	60 ml	granulated sugar
⅓ cup	80 ml	butter – melted

Combine the ingredients then press into a buttered 9" (23 cm) spring form pan. Bake 5 minutes in a preheated 350°F (180°C) oven. Cool.

FILLING:		
1½ lbs	675 ml	cream cheese
¾ cup	180 ml	granulated sugar
3	3	eggs
⅓ cup	80 ml	lime juice
1 tsp	5 ml	white vanilla
1 tbsp	15 ml	lime rind – grated
1 tsp	5 ml	lemon extract

Cream the cheese with the sugar. Beat in the eggs one at a time. Stir in the remaining ingredients. Pour into the shell and bake for 35-40 minutes at 350°F (180°C).

TOPPING:		
2 cups	500 ml	sour cream
¼ cup	60 ml	granulated sugar
1 tsp	5 ml	vanilla

Combine the ingredients together. Spread over the cake and continue to bake for 10 minutes. Remove to a cooling rack, cool 1 hour and glaze.

GLAZE:		
½ cup	125 ml	granulated sugar
1½ tbsp	25 ml	cornstarch
¼ tsp	2 ml	salt
½ cup	125 ml	water
½ cup	125 ml	lime juice
2 tsp	10 ml	lime rind – grated
1	1	egg yolk
5 drops	5 drops	green food colouring
1 tbsp	15 ml	butter

In a sauce pan mix the sugar, cornstarch and salt. Place over medium heat combine all the remaining ingredients except the butter, cook until thickened. Whip in butter, cool to warm, pour over cake. Refrigerate 6-8 hours before serving.

LEMON SPONGE

6	6	eggs – separated
3 cups	750 ml	granulated sugar
2 tsp	10 ml	lemon rind – grated
2 tbsp	30 ml	lemon juice
¾ cup	180 ml	water
3 cups	750 ml	flour, pastry
1 tbsp	15 ml	baking powder
½ tsp	3 ml	salt

Whip the egg whites until stiff. Beat the egg yolks until very creamy. Add the sugar, lemon rind, lemon juice, water and the flour, which has been sifted with the baking powder and salt. Fold in the egg whites. Bake in a preheated 350°F (180°C) oven in two 8" (20 cm) greased and floured pans for 30-35 minutes. Cool 10 minutes then turn out on a cooling rack. Cool then fill with Lemon Filling and frost with Lemon Frosting (recipes follow).

LEMON FROSTING

2	2	egg yolks
1¼ cups	310 ml	confectioners' sugar
3 tbsp	45 ml	lemon juice
1 tbsp	15 ml	lemon rind grated

Whip the egg yolks until very smooth. Add the sugar gradually. Add the juice and rind beating until incorporated. Use as required.

LEMON FILLING

2 tsp	10 ml	gelatin
1 tbsp	15 ml	cold water
1½ tbsp	25 ml	hot water
2	2	egg white
¼ cup	60 ml	granulated sugar
2 tbsp	30 ml	lemon juice
1 tbsp	15 ml	lemon rind, grated

Soften the gelatin in the cold water, then blend in the hot water.

Whip the egg whites until soft peaks form then slowly add the sugar. Slowly whip in the gelatin water and the lemon juice and rind. Use to fill cakes.

COCONUT KISSES

1⅓ cups	340 ml	sweetened condensed milk
1 tsp	5 ml	vanilla
3 cups	750 ml	shredded coconut
¼ tsp	1 ml	salt

Blend the milk with the vanilla. Stir in the coconut and salt. Drop teaspoon sizes onto a greased pastry sheet. Bake for 10 minutes in a preheated 350°F (180°C) oven.

MAKES 2½ DOZEN

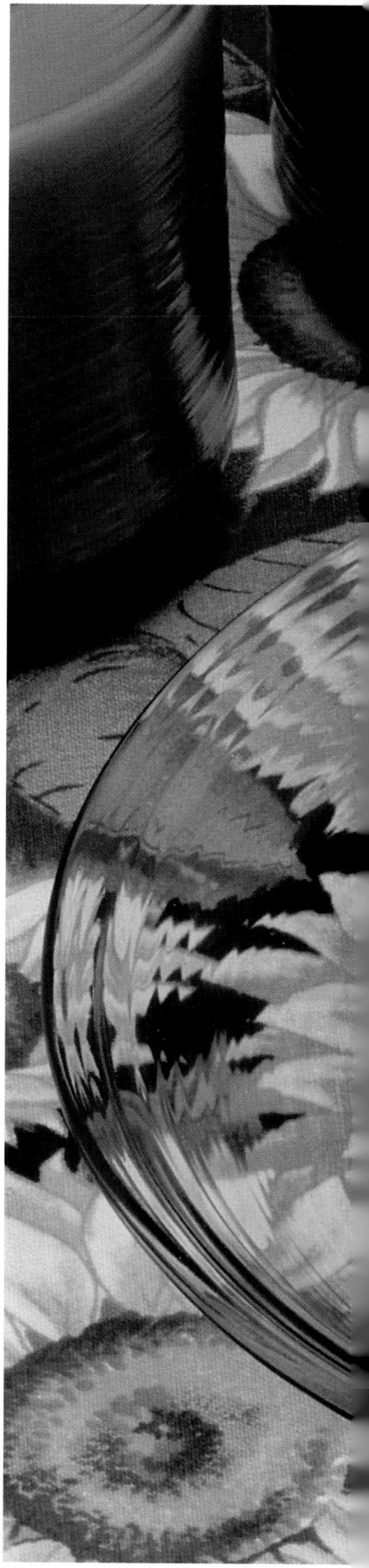

Lemon Sponge

Pamela's Chocolate Nut Fudge

PAMELA'S CHOCOLATE NUT FUDGE

2 oz	60 g	chocolate – bakers
2 cups	500 ml	granulated sugar
1 cup	250 ml	cream – light
1 tsp	5 ml	corn syrup – white
¼ tsp	2 ml	salt
2 tbsp	30 ml	butter
1 tsp	5 ml	vanilla
1 tsp	5 ml	orange rind – grated
½ cup	125 ml	walnuts

Combine the chocolate, sugar, cream, syrup, salt and butter in a sauce pan: over medium heat. Cook with occasional stir to 234°F (111°C) on a candy thermometer. Stir in the vanilla and orange rind. Cool in a pan of cold water to 125°F (50°C). Beat until creamy. Stir in the nuts. Pour into a buttered 8" x 8" (20 x 20 cm) square pan. Mark squares and cool.

YIELDS 1½ LBS

BUTTER PECAN TORTE

1½ cups	375 ml	pastry flour
2 tsp	10 ml	baking powder
¼ tsp	1 ml	salt
⅓ cup	80 ml	butter
¾ cup	180 ml	granulated sugar
2	2	eggs
½ cup	125 ml	milk
1 tsp	5 ml	vanilla
½ cup	125 ml	pecans, broken

Sift the flour, baking powder and salt together, twice.

Cream the butter and the sugar until very light and fluffy. Add the eggs beating well after each. Incorporate the flour and milk in thirds into the cream mixture. Stir in the vanilla and nuts.

Pour into a 8" (20 cm) spring form pan which has been buttered and floured. Bake in a preheated 350°F (180°C) oven for 45 minutes or until an inserted toothpick comes out clean. Transfer the cake to a cooling rack, cool for 10 minutes, turn cake out, cool completely. Frost with Praline Frosting (recipe follows).

Butter Pecan Torte with Praline Frosting

PRALINE FROSTING

PRALINES:

2 cups	500 ml	granulated sugar
¾ cup	190 ml	milk
1 cup	250 ml	honey
2 cups	500 ml	pecan meats, broken

In a heavy sauce pan bring to a boil the sugar, milk and honey. Using a candy thermometer boil to the soft ball stage or 238°F (113°C). Remove from heat, cool to warm beating until very creamy. Stir in the nuts. Spread onto buttered wax paper. Allow to cool and harden then crush and stir into frosting.

FROSTING:

1 cup	250 ml	brown sugar
½ cup	125 ml	boiling water
2	2	egg whites
1 tsp	5 ml	vanilla

In a heavy sauce pan cook the sugar and water to 244°F (116°C) on a candy thermometer or to the soft ball stage. Remove from heat and cool. Whip the egg whites to stiff. Beat in the syrup in a slow thin stream. Add the vanilla and stir in the pralines. Spread on Butter Pecan Torte.

Chocolate Dream Pie

FRESH FRUIT TERRINE

2 tbsp	30 ml	unflavoured gelatin
⅓ cup	80 ml	cold water
¾ cup	180 ml	apricot purée
¾ cup	180 ml	confectioners' sugar
1½ cup	375 ml	whipping cream
1 tsp	5 ml	oil
1½ cups	375 ml	raspberries or blackberries – washed, hulled
1 cup	250 ml	blueberries – washed
1½ cups	375 ml	fresh peach slices
1½ cups	375 ml	strawberry halves

Soften the gelatin in the water. Blend with the apricot purée. Heat in a sauce pan to boiling, remove at once and blend in the sugar. Pour in ¾ cup (180 ml) of cream. Cool and chill to very thick but not set. Whip the remaining cream, fold into the mixture. Line a 7 cup (1.75 L) loaf pan with tight fitting plastic wrap. Brush with oil. Place an assortment of fruit on the bottom and fold the remaining fruit into mixture. Pour into loaf and chill 8 hours. Invert the mold over a platter and carefully remove the wrap. Serve with a Chocolate Raspberry Sauce (see page 115).

CHOCOLATE DREAM PIE

1	1	chocolate wafer crust pie
4 oz	120 g	semi-sweet chocolate
2 tbsp	30 ml	butter
⅓ cup	80 ml	flour, all purpose
1 cup	250 ml	sugar, granulated
¼ tsp	2 ml	salt
2½ cups	625 ml	milk – scalded
3	3	egg yolks
1 tsp	5 ml	vanilla
1 cup	250 ml	whipping cream
¼ cup	60 ml	milk chocolate shavings

In a double boiler melt the chocolate and butter. Mix in the flour, sugar and salt into a smooth paste. Add the milk stirring constantly until sauce thickens. Beat in the egg yolks and continue to cook for 2 minutes. Remove from heat and add the vanilla. Pour into crust and chill. Whip the cream and pipe onto pie. Sprinkle with milk chocolate. Serve.

SERVES 6

CHOCOLATE WHATCHAMACALLITS

⅔ cup	160 ml	sweetened condensed milk
2 cups	500 ml	coconut, medium grind
1 tsp	5 ml	vanilla
⅛ tsp	pinch	salt
½ cup	125 ml	walnut pieces
2 cups	500 ml	chopped dates
¼ cup	60 ml	maraschino cherries
2 oz	60 g	melted semi-sweet chocolate
1½ cups	375 ml	confectioners' sugar
¼ cup	60 ml	butter
½ tsp	3 ml	orange extract
1 tbsp	15 ml	milk
2 oz	60 g	melted white chocolate

Combine the condensed milk, coconut, vanilla, salt, nuts, dates, cherries and semi-sweet chocolate. Pour into a buttered 9" x 9" (22.5 x 23 cm) square pan. Bake for 30 minutes in a preheated 350°F (180°C) oven. Remove from the oven and cool.

Blend the confectioners' sugar with the butter, orange extract and milk. Spread onto the cake. Drizzle with the white chocolate, cool, cut into squares.

YIELDS 36 SQUARES

Fresh Fruit Terrine

Lemon Roll with Lemon Filling

LEMON ROLL

5	5	eggs – separated
¾ cup	180 ml	granulated sugar
¼ tsp	2 ml	salt
½ cup	125 ml	pastry flour
3 tbsp	45 ml	butter – melted
1 tsp	5 ml	vanilla
1 quan	1	Lemon Filling (see page 526)

Whip the egg whites to soft peaks.

Combine the egg yolks with the sugar in a double boiler. Heat to about 140°F (60°C), remove from heat and beat until mixture holds soft peaks. Combine the salt with the flour and fold into mixture. Fold in the butter and vanilla 1 tbsp (15 ml) at a time. Fold in the egg whites. Pour into a wax paper lined 15 x 10 (37.5 x 25 cm) pan. Bake in a preheated oven 350°F (180°C) for 18 minutes.

Remove from oven and turn out on to a wax paper surface dusted with confectioners' sugar. Remove the wax paper from the cake, quickly spread the lemon filling over the cake. Trim the edges even. Roll the cake. Wrap with the wax paper until cool. Remove wax paper once cool dust with confectioners' sugar, serve.

Chocolate Marshmallow Cake with Marshmallow Frosting

CHOCOLATE MARSHMALLOW CAKE

¾ cup	180 ml	butter
2 cups	500 ml	granulated sugar
2 cups	500 ml	pastry flour
4 tsp	20 ml	baking powder
8	8	egg whites
½ cup	125 ml	milk
4 oz	120 g	semi-sweet chocolate – melted
1 tsp	5 ml	vanilla extract

Cream the butter with the sugar until very light and fluffy. Sift the flour with the baking powder. Whip the egg whites into the creamed butter. Add the flour, milk and chocolate, incorporating in thirds. Whip in the vanilla. Pour into 2 – 9" (22.5 cm) buttered and floured cake pans. Bake in a preheated 350°F (180°C) oven for 20-25 minutes. Cool 10 minutes, transfer to cooling rack. Frost with Marshmallow Frosting (recipe follows).

MARSHMALLOW FROSTING

1 cup	250 ml	marshmallows
1 cup	250 ml	granulated sugar
⅓ cup	80 ml	water
2	2	egg whites
2 tsp	10 ml	lemon juice
1 tsp	5 ml	vanilla

Melt the marshmallows in a double boiler. Boil the sugar and water until the syrup threads long. Whip the egg whites until stiff. Slowly pour the syrup into the egg whites, beating rapidly. Add the lemon and vanilla. Whip in the marshmallows. Frost on cake.

CHOCOLATE RASPBERRY ISLANDS

4	4	egg whites
1 cup	250 ml	granulated sugar
¼ cup	60 ml	raspberries
2 oz	60 g	semi-sweet chocolate – melted
2 cups	500 ml	Orange Brandy Sauce (see page 107)

Whip the egg whites stiff, gradually beat in the sugar. Fold in the raspberry preserves and the chocolate. Place heaping tbsp full into simmering water and poach for 2-3 minutes. Float on serving plate covered with Orange Brandy Sauce.

SERVES 6

PEACH BAVARIAN

1 tbsp	15 ml	gelatin – unflavoured
¼ cup	60 ml	cold water
1 cup	250 ml	peaches – fine diced
¼ cup	60 ml	peach syrup
1 tbsp	15 ml	lemon juice
¼ cup	60 ml	granulated sugar
¾ cup	180 ml	whipping cream

Soften the gelatin in the cold water. Place into a small sauce pan along with the peaches, syrup, lemon juice and sugar. Bring to a boil, remove from heat. Cool then chill to thick but not set. Whip the cream and fold into peaches. Pour into a mold or bowl. Chill until set. Unmold and serve.

SERVES 4

Peach Bavarian

CARROT CAKE

4	4	eggs
1 cup	250 ml	granulated sugar
1 cup	250 ml	vegetable oil
2 cups	500 ml	all purpose flour
1½ tsp	7 ml	baking powder
1 tsp	5 ml	salt
2 tsp	10 ml	cinnamon
2 cups	500 ml	carrots – grated
1½ cups	375 ml	apples – pared, cored, grated
1 cup	250 ml	raisins
1 cup	250 ml	slivered almonds

In a large bowl, beat the eggs until very light and frothy. Add the sugar gradually, beating until very light. Gradually whip in the oil.

Sift together the flour with baking powder, salt and cinnamon. Slowly add to the egg mixture. Stir in the carrots, apples, raisins and nuts.

Pour into a greased 9" (22.5 cm) spring form pan and bake in a preheated 350°F (180°C) oven for 1½ to 2 hours or until an inserted toothpick comes out clean.

Cool in the pan 10-15 minutes before removing, turn cake out and cool completely. Frost with Cream Cheese Frosting (recipe follows).

CREAM CHEESE FROSTING

9 oz	255 g	cream cheese – softened
¾ cup	180 ml	butter – softened
1½ tsp	7 ml	vanilla extract
4 cups	1 L	sifted icing sugar (confectioners')

Beat the cream cheese, butter and vanilla until very smooth and fluffy. Gradually beat in the icing sugar until spreading consistency.

Carrot Cake with Cream Cheese Frosting

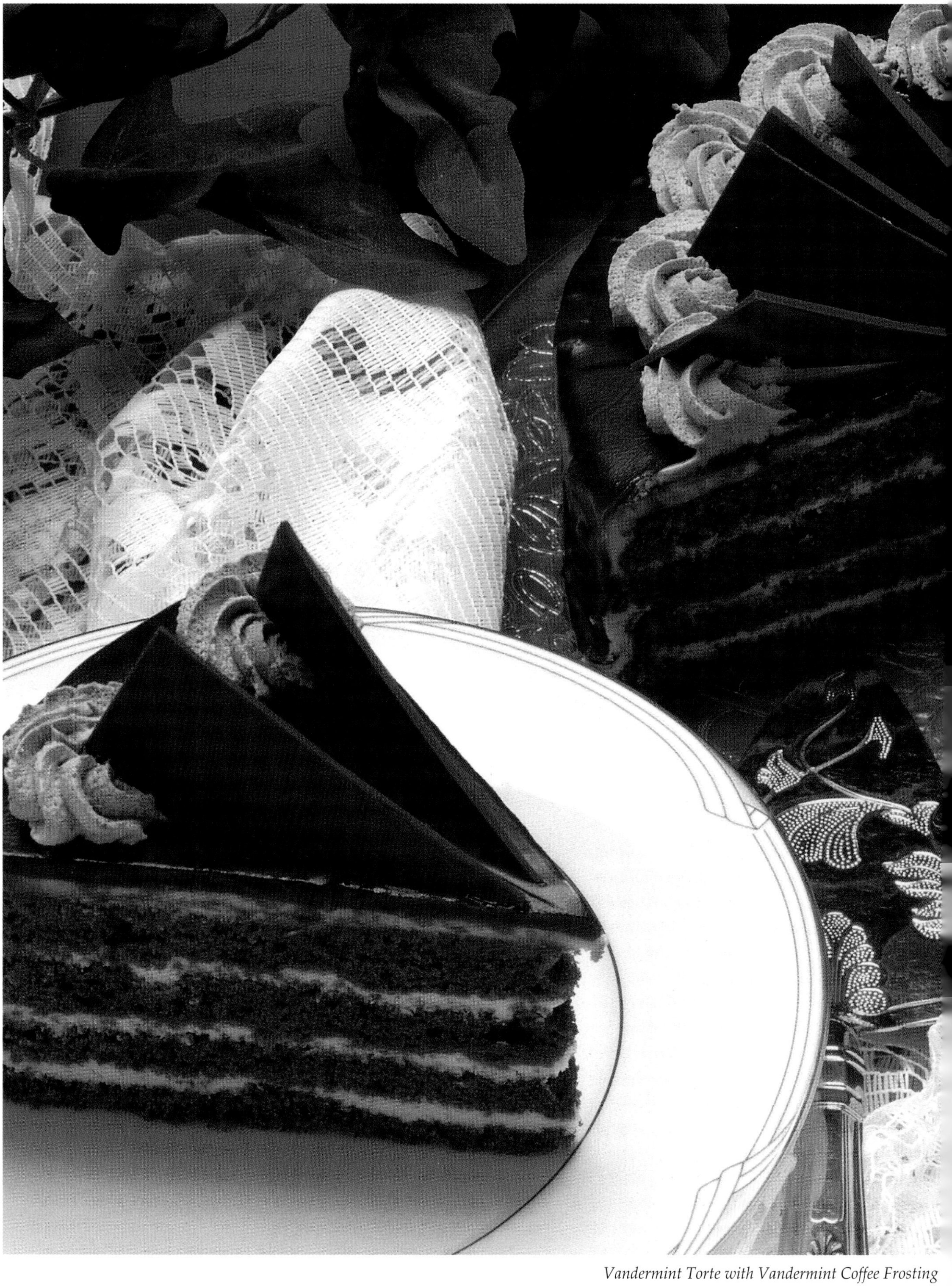

Vandermint Torte with Vandermint Coffee Frosting

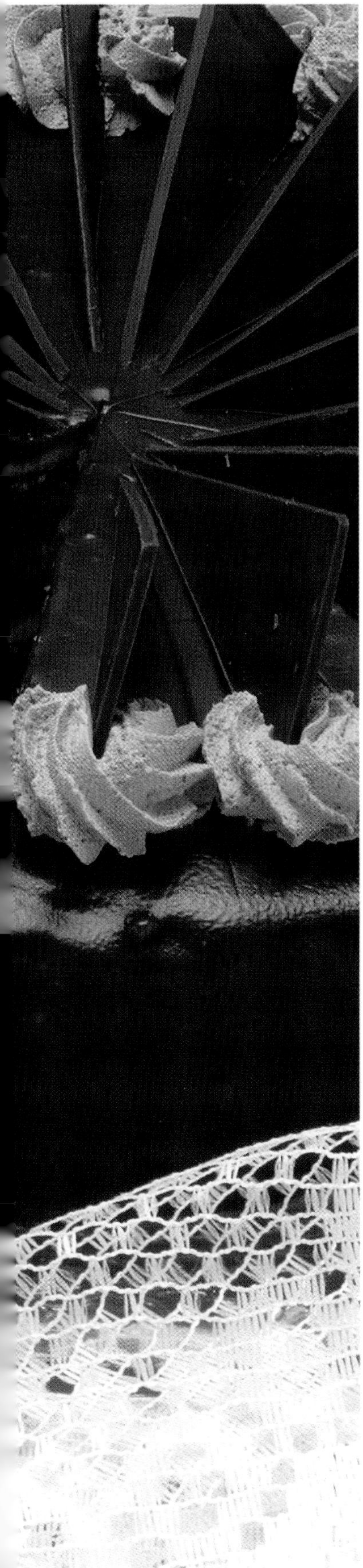

VANDERMINT TORTE

¾ cup	180 ml	butter
1¾ cups	470 ml	brown sugar
3	3	eggs well beaten
½ cup	125 ml	boiling water
¼ cup	60 ml	Vandermint liqueur
3 oz	90 g	bitter sweet chocolate
2¼ cups	560 ml	pastry flour
1½ tsp	8 ml	baking soda
¾ tsp	4 ml	baking powder
¾ tsp	4 ml	salt
¾ cup	180 ml	buttermilk

Cream the butter with the sugar until very light and fluffy. Add the eggs beating well. Pour the water and liqueur over the chocolate in a sauce pan. Heat over medium heat to a thick syrup, cool. Add to egg mixture. Sift the flour, soda, powder and salt together three times. Incorporated the flour and buttermilk into creamed mixture in thirds. Pour batter into 2-9" (23 cm) greased and floured cake pans. Bake in a preheated 350°F (180°C) oven for 25-30 minutes. Cool 10 minutes, transfer cakes to cooling rack. Frost with Vandermint Coffee Frosting (recipe follows).

VANDERMINT COFFEE FROSTING

⅓ cup	80 ml	cream – light
1 cup	250 ml	granulated sugar
3 oz	90 g	bittersweet chocolate
1 tbsp	15 ml	Vandermint liqueur
½ tsp	3 ml	instant coffee
1 tbsp	15 ml	hot water
2 tbsp	30 ml	butter

In a double boiler cook the cream, sugar, chocolate, liquer and the coffee which has been dissolved in the hot water. Add the butter and cook for 6 minutes. Beat until frosting reaches a consistency to spread.

PEANUT BUTTER FUDGE SQUARES

½ cup	125 ml	butter
¾ cup	180 ml	peanut butter – smooth
1½ cup	375 ml	semi-sweet chocolate chips
1 tsp	5 ml	vanilla
2 cups	500 ml	marshmallows – miniature

Combine the butter, peanut butter, chocolate and vanilla together in a double boiler, stir until melted. Remove from the heat, stir in the marshmallows. Pour into a greased 8" x 8" (20 x 20 cm) pan and refrigerate. Cut into squares.

MAKES 20

DUTCH APPLE PIE

PIE:		
½ quan	0.5	Plain Pastry (see page 616)
8	8	cooking apples – cored, pared, sliced
3 tbsp	45 ml	butter – melted
¾ cup	180 ml	granulated sugar
½ tsp	3 ml	cinnamon

TOPPING:		
½ cup	125 ml	flour, all purpose
½ tsp	3 ml	cinnamon
⅓ cup	80 ml	light brown sugar – packed
⅓ cup	80 ml	butter

PIE:

Roll out the pastry and fit into a 9" (23 cm) pie plate. Flute the edges.

Mix the apples, butter, sugar and cinnamon together. Pour into the pastry.

TOPPING:

Sift together the flour, cinnamon and sugar. Cream the butter then add to mixture. Sprinkle over the pie.

Bake pie in a preheated 425°F (215°C) oven for 20 minutes, then reduce heat to 325°F (160°C) continue to bake for 30 minutes. Remove and cool or chill before serving.

SERVES 6

Date Nut Loaf

OLD FASHION APPLE PIE

6	6	large apples
⅔ cup	160 ml	granulated sugar
¼ tsp	1 ml	salt
2 tbsp	30 ml	flour, all purpose
1 quan	1	Plain Pastry (see page 616)
1 tbsp	15 ml	butter
2 tbsp	30 ml	milk

Pare and slice the apples. Sift the sugar, salt and flour together.

Line a 9" (23 cm) pie plate with a round of dough. Sprinkle with half the dry mixture. Sprinkle the remainder into the apples. Fill the pie shell with apples, dot with butter. Cover with top round, seal edges. Cut to allow steam to escape. Brush with milk.

Bake in a preheated 425°F (215°C) oven for 10 minutes. Reduce temperature to 350°F (180°C) and continue to bake for 30 minutes until pie is golden brown. Cool before serving.

DATE NUT LOAF

1 cup	250 ml	butter
2 cups	500 ml	brown sugar
4	4	beaten eggs
3 cups	750 ml	pastry flour
1 tbsp	15 ml	baking powder
¼ tsp	1 ml	salt
1 tsp	5 ml	ground cinnamon
½ tsp	3 ml	ground cloves
½ tsp	3 ml	ground nutmeg
1 cup	250 ml	water
2 cups	500 ml	pitted, chopped dates
2 cups	500 ml	raisins
1 cup	250 ml	walnuts

Cream the butter with the brown sugar, beat in the eggs. Sift the dry ingredients together three times. Incorporate into cream mixture in thirds along with the water.

Fold in the dates, raisins and nuts. Pour into a waxed paper lined 5½" x 10" (13.75 x 25 cm) loaf pan. Bake in a preheated 300°F (150°C) oven for 2 hours or until an inserted toothpick comes out clean.

Cool 15 minutes before transferring the cake to a cooling rack, turn cake out and cool completely.

Dutch Apple Pie & Old Fashion Apple Pie

Dianna's Banana Cream Pie

Jack Daniel's Walnut Pie

DIANNA'S BANANA CREAM PIE

½ quan	0.5	Plain Pastry (see page 616)
5 tbsp	75 ml	flour, all purpose
½ cup	125 ml	granulated sugar
2 cups	500 ml	milk – scalded
2	2	egg yolks
½ tsp	3 ml	banana extract – or vanilla (white)
3	3	ripe bananas – sliced
2 tbsp	30 ml	lemon juice
1 cup	250 ml	whipping cream
¼ cup	60 ml	confectioners' sugar

Roll out the pastry and fit into a 9" (23 cm) pie pan. Blind bake the crust. (See glossary for blind baking). Cool.

Mix the flour, sugar and milk together in a sauce pan, cook over medium heat until mixture thickens. Transfer to a double boiler. Whip in the egg yolks and extract. Cook 2 minutes. Cool to warm. While the mixture cools slice the bananas and soak in the lemon juice. Once mixture is warm stir in the bananas then pour into the pie shell. Cool completely. Whip the cream to stiff. Add the sugar and pipe onto the pie. Serve.

SERVES 6

JACK DANIEL'S WALNUT PIE

½ quan	0.5	Gourmet Pastry (recipe follows)
3	3	eggs
½ cup	125 ml	granulated sugar
1 cup	250 ml	dark corn syrup
3 tbsp	45 ml	Jack Daniels
1½ cups	375 ml	walnut pieces – broken

Roll out the dough and fit into a 9" (23 cm) pie pan. Flute the edges.

Blend the eggs, sugar, syrup and Jack Daniels. Sprinkle pie with nuts, and pour over egg mixture. Bake in a preheated 325°F (160°C) oven for 45 minutes. Cool and chill before serving.

SERVES 6

GOURMET PASTRY

4 cup	1 L	sifted all purpose flour
1 tsp	5 ml	salt
2 tsp	10 ml	baking powder
½ cup	125 ml	shortening
¼ cup	60 ml	hot water
½ cup	125 ml	butter
1 tsp	5 ml	lemon juice
1	1	egg yolk – beaten

Sift the flour, salt and baking powder together. Cut in the shortening. Combine the hot water with the butter and lemon juice, then beat in the egg yolk. Work into the dry ingredients. Chill. Use as required.

CHOCOLATE ROCKY ROAD TERRINE

8 oz	225 g	grated semi-sweet chocolate
¾ cup	180 ml	butter
½ cup	125 ml	confectioners' sugar
3	3	eggs separated, at room temperature
½ tsp	3 ml	vanilla
⅛ tsp	pinch	salt
⅓ cup	80 ml	walnut pieces
1 cup	250 ml	miniature marshmallows
⅓ cup	80 ml	semi-sweet chocolate chips

Melt the grated chocolate in a double boiler and cool.

Beat the butter and sugar until very light. Beat in the egg yolks one at a time, beat until very creamy. Gradually beat in the melted chocolate and vanilla.

Whip the egg whites with the salt until stiff. Fold into the mixture. Fold in the nuts, marshmallows and chocolate chips. Pour into a greased 4 cup (1 L) loaf pan, cover with plastic wrap. Refrigerate overnight.

Unmold, slice and serve with chocolate sauce.

SERVES 6

JEANNIE'S TRIPLE CHOCOLATE CHIP COOKIES

1 cup	250 ml	butter
1 cup	250 ml	granulated sugar
2	2	eggs
2 tsp	10 ml	vanilla flavouring
2 cups	500 ml	flour, all purpose
1 cup	250 ml	cocoa
1 tsp	5 ml	baking soda
1/2 tsp	3 ml	salt
1/2 cup	125 ml	white chocolate chips
1 cup	250 ml	chopped pecans

Cream the butter and sugar together. Slowly add the eggs, one at a time beating well after each addition. Add the flavouring. In a separate bowl combine the flour, cocoa, baking soda, salt, white chocolate chips and pecans. Add to the batter mixing only until thoroughly combined.

Drop from a spoon onto a greased cookie sheet. Ensure each cookie is the size of a walnut, remember the cookies will double in size when baked. Bake in a preheated 350°F (180°C) oven for 12-15 minutes. Remove from oven, remove from pan immediately and place on a cooling rack.

YIELDS 24 COOKIES

STRAWBERRIES VICTORIA

¼ cup	60 ml	butter
¼ cup	60 ml	granulated sugar
3 cups	750 ml	fresh firm strawberries – washed, hulled, halved
⅓ cup	80 ml	Curacao liqueur
½ cup	125 ml	orange juice
2 cups	500 ml	chocolate ice cream
1½ cups	375 ml	Sabayon (see page 106)

Heat the butter with the sugar and caramelize. Toss the strawberries in the hot syrup. Add the liqueur and flame. Pour in the orange juice and simmer for 3 minutes. Scoop ice cream into over-sized champagne glasses, spoon strawberries over ice cream, pour over sabayon. Serve at once.

SERVES 4

Chocolate Rocky Road Terrine

Jeannie's Triple Chocolate Chip Cookies

GRAND MARNIER CAKE

¾ cup	180 ml	butter
1½ cups	375 ml	granulated sugar
8	8	eggs
2¼ cups	560 ml	flour, all-purpose
4 tsp	20 ml	baking powder
1 cup	250 ml	milk
½ cup	125 ml	Grand Marnier liqueur
¼ tsp	1 ml	salt
1 tsp	5 ml	orange extract

Cream the butter and sugar until very light. Beat in the eggs one at a time, incorporating well. Mix the milk with the Grand Marnier and extract.

Sift the flour together with the salt and baking powder.

Blend the flour and liquid into the eggs in thirds incorporating well. Pour into 2 – 9" (23 cm) greased and floured cake pans. Bake in a preheated 350°F (180°C) oven for 20-25 minutes.

Cool 10 minutes, transfer cakes to cooling rack, turn cakes out and cool completely. Frost with Orange Brandy Frosting (recipe follows).

ORANGE BRANDY FROSTING

½ cup	125 ml	butter
1¼ cups	310 ml	confectioners' sugar
2	2	eggs
¼ cup	60 ml	flour, all purpose
1 cup	250 ml	granulated sugar
½ tsp	3 ml	salt
1½ cups	375 ml	scalded milk
¼ cup	60 ml	orange brandy – Grand Marnier
4 oz	120 g	bittersweet chocolate, melted
1 tsp	5 ml	vanilla

Cream the butter, add the confectioners' sugar. Beat the eggs, stir in the flour, granulated sugar, salt, milk, orange brandy and chocolate. Transfer to a double boiler and cook 10 minutes. Cool and whip in the vanilla. Fold into the creamed butter. Use to fill and frost cakes.

FRENCH VANILLA MINT CHEESECAKE

CRUST:		
3½ cups	875 ml	graham cracker crumbs
1 tbsp	15 ml	cinnamon
¼ cup	60 ml	melted butter

FILLING:		
2½ lbs	1 kg	cream cheese
2 cups	500 ml	granulated sugar
1½ cups	375 ml	heavy cream
2 tbsp	30 ml	lemon juice
1 tbsp	15 ml	vanilla
2 tbsp	30 ml	white peppermint extract
4	4	eggs – room temperature
1½ cups	375 ml	sour cream

CRUST:

Combine crust ingredients. Press into the bottom and sides of a buttered 10" (25 cm) spring form pan. Chill. Preheat the oven to 325°F (160°C).

FILLING:

Beat the cream cheese and sugar until smooth. Add the cream, lemon juice, vanilla and peppermint extract, beat until well blended. Add the eggs one at a time, beating well after each addition. Stir in the sour cream.

Pour mixture into prepared shell and bake in the oven until the centre is set, about 90 minutes. Turn off the oven and prop door open slightly.

After about 30 minutes transfer to a rack to cool, chill overnight. Serve as is or with a chocolate mint sauce.

French Vanilla Mint Cheesecake

Grand Marnier Cake

Assorted Ice Cream

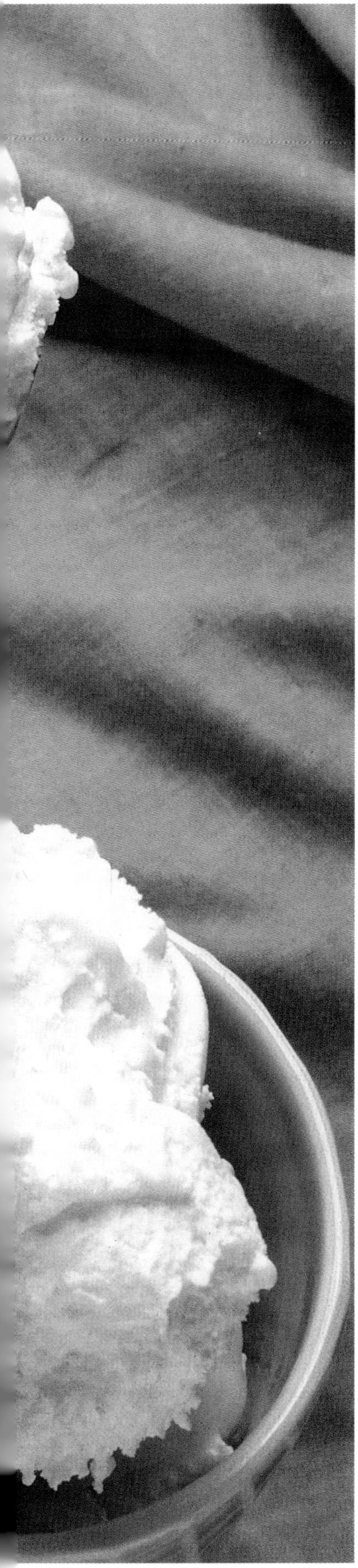

DIANNA'S MAPLE WALNUT ICE CREAM

3 cups	750 ml	cream – half & half
2 tbsp	30 ml	flour, all purpose
3 tbsp	45 ml	maple syrup
3	3	egg yolks
1 cup	250 ml	maple sugar
1½ tsp	8 ml	maple extract
½ cup	125 ml	walnuts – broken

Scald the cream in a double boiler. Blend the flour into the maple syrup and add to cream. Beat the egg yolks with the sugar and add slowly to cream. Cook stirring constantly until mixture is thick. Remove from heat, cool, chill and freeze according to directions of ice cream maker. When mixture is frozen to a slush stage add the extract and nuts, continue to freeze.

YIELDS 5 CUPS (1.25 L)

FRENCH VANILLA OR CINNAMON ICE CREAM

4 cups	1 L	cream – medium
1	1	vanilla bean *
5	5	egg yolks
¾ cup	180 ml	granulated sugar

Scald the cream with the vanilla bean in a double boiler. Beat the egg yolks with the sugar, slowly beat into the cream and cook stirring constantly until thick. (Do not over cook or eggs will cuddle.) Discard vanilla bean. Remove from heat, cool, chill and freeze in ice cream maker according to directions.

*For cinnamon ice cream exchange a cinnamon stick for the vanilla bean.

YIELDS 5 CUPS (1.25 L)

LEMON SHERBET

½ cup	125 ml	lemon juice
½ cup	125 ml	granulated sugar
2 cups	500 ml	milk

Mix the lemon juice with the sugar in a sauce pan. Place over medium heat and boil for 2 minutes. Cool and chill. Add the milk. Pour into a ice cream maker and freeze according to manufacturer's instructions.

YIELDS 3 CUPS (750 ml)

NEAPOLITAN BOMBE

½ quan	0.5	Orange Chocolate Sherbet (see page 571)
½ quan	0.5	Strawberry Banana Ice Cream (see page 641)
½ quan	0.5	Lemon Sherbet (preceding recipe)
½ cup	125 ml	crushed pineapple

Invert a 2 quart (2 L) bombe mold in a bowl of ice. Line the top and side with the orange chocolate sherbet, followed by a layer of strawberry banana ice cream. Finish with lemon sherbet. Place the lid on the mold or cover with wax paper. Freeze 4-6 hours. To unmold dip the mold quickly in hot water, turn out on a serving platter.

SERVES 8

Bavarian Apple Torte

BAVARIAN APPLE TORTE

BASE:		
½ cup	250 ml	soft butter
⅓ cup	75 ml	granulated sugar
¼ tsp	1 ml	vanilla
1 cup	250 ml	all purpose flour
¼ cup	60 ml	raspberry jam

FILLING:		
2	2	(250 g) pkgs cream cheese, at room temperature
½ cup	125 ml	granulated sugar
1 tsp	5 ml	vanilla
2	2	eggs

TOPPING:		
⅔ cup	160 ml	granulated sugar
1 tsp	5 ml	cinnamon
4 cups	2 L	apple slices
1 cup	250 ml	sliced almonds

BASE:

Cream the butter, sugar and vanilla, add the flour and mix well. Press into the bottom of a 10" (25 cm) spring form pan. Spread the crust with jam.

FILLING:

Beat the cream cheese, sugar and vanilla until smooth. Add the eggs one at a time, beating well after each addition. Pour evenly over jam.

TOPPING:

Combine sugar and cinnamon, toss with sliced apples and spoon over cream cheese layer. Sprinkle with almonds and bake in a preheated oven at 350°F (180°C) for 75 minutes or until golden. Chill 8 hours.

Pumpkin Maple Cheesecake

PUMPKIN MAPLE CHEESECAKE

CRUST:		
1½ cups	375 ml	finely crushed gingerbread cookies
⅓ cup	80 ml	butter – melted

FILLING:		
2	2	(250 g) pkgs cream cheese, at room temperature
1 cup	250 ml	maple sugar
½ cup	125 ml	maple syrup
1¼ tsp	6 ml	cinnamon
¾ cup	180 ml	whipping cream
1 tsp	5 ml	vanilla
4	4	eggs
2 cups	500 ml	pumpkin purée
¾ cup	180 ml	sour cream

CRUST:

Combine crushed cookies and butter. Press into the bottom of a greased 9" (23 cm) spring form pan, set aside.

FILLING:

Beat the cream cheese, sugar and cinnamon until smooth. Gradually beat in the maple syrup, whipping cream and vanilla. Add the eggs one at a time, beating well after each addition. Stir in the pumpkin purée and sour cream.

Pour mixture into prepared pan and bake at 325°F (160°C) for 75 minutes. Turn oven off and prop door open slightly. After about 30 minutes transfer to a rack to cool, chill at least 4 hours. Decorate as desired.

Calypso Coffee Pie

MARSHMALLOWS FUDGE ICE CREAM

2 oz	60 g	semi-sweet chocolate chips
2 cups	500 ml	marshmallows – miniatures
2½ cups	625 ml	cream half & half
3	3	egg yolks
¾ cup	180 ml	granulated sugar
2 tsp	10 ml	vanilla

In a double boiler melt the chocolate, marshmallows and scald the cream. Beat the egg yolks with the sugar and slowly add to the cream with the vanilla. Cook until thick, cool, chill then freeze according to directions of ice cream maker. Top with your favourite fruit.

YIELDS 6 CUPS (1 ½ L)

COCONUT SLICES

½ cup	125 ml	butter
1 cup + 2 tbsp	280 ml	flour , all purpose
¼ cup	60 ml	confectioners' sugar
1½ cup	375 ml	brown sugar
¼ tsp	2 ml	salt
1 cup	250 ml	coconut – shredded
2	2	eggs – beaten
¼ tsp	2 ml	baking powder
1 tsp	5 ml	coconut extract
1 cup	250 ml	pecans – broken

Blend the butter, 1 cup flour and the confectioners' sugar. Press onto the bottom of a 13" x 9" (32 x 23 cm) pan. Bake 20 minutes in a preheated oven at 350°F (180°C). Blend the remaining ingredients well. Spread over pastry. Bake for an additional 20 minutes. Cut into squares.

MAKES 32 SQUARES

CALYPSO COFFEE PIE

½ cup	125 ml	butter
1¼ cups	310 ml	confectioners' sugar
2	2	eggs
1 cup	250 ml	sugar – granulated
¼ cup	60 ml	flour, all purpose
¼ tsp	2 ml	salt
1 cup	250 ml	milk – scalded
¼ cup	60 ml	Kahlua liqueur
¼ cup	60 ml	dark rum
¼ cup	60 ml	strong coffee
2 oz	60 g	semi-sweet chocolate
1	1	blind baked pie shell or graham shell
1½ cups	375 ml	sweetened whipping cream, whipped
1 cup	250 ml	chocolate shavings

Cream the butter, add the confectioners' sugar. Beat the eggs, stir in granulated sugar, flour salt, milk, Kahlua, rum, coffee and chocolate. Cook in a double boiler 10 minutes, cool then whip into creamed butter. Pour into a pre-baked pie shell or graham crumb crust. Refrigerate for two hours. Serve covered with sweetened whipped cream and chocolate shavings.

Marshmallow Fudge Ice Cream

Creme au Praline Chocolate Torte

CHEF K'S SCHWARZWALDER KIRSCHENTORTE (BLACK FOREST CAKE)

CAKE:		
2 tbsp	30 ml	cocoa powder
2 cups	500 ml	pastry flour
1 tsp	5 ml	baking powder
¼ tsp	1 ml	salt
4 oz	120 g	semi-sweet chocolate
½ cup	125 ml	butter
1½ cups	375 ml	granulated sugar
2	2	eggs
1 cup	250 ml	milk

Sift the cocoa, flour, baking powder and salt together three times.

Melt the chocolate in a double boiler.

Cream the butter and sugar until very light. Add the eggs one at a time beating after each addition. Stir in the chocolate. Incorporate the flour and milk in ⅓ additions each. Pour batter into 2 – 8" (20 cm) buttered and floured round cake pans. Bake in a preheated 350°F (180°C) oven for 35-40 minutes. Cool 10 minutes then transfer to a cooling rack, turn cake out and cool completely. Frost.

FILLING AND FROSTING:		
2 cups	500 ml	black cherries – pitted, canned
½ cup	125 ml	juice from the cherries
2 tbsp	3 ml	cornstarch
¼ cup	60 ml	Kirsch or cherry brandy
2 cups	500 ml	whipping cream
½ cup	125 ml	confectioners' sugar
1 cup	250 ml	chocolate shavings

Heat the cherries in a sauce pan. Mix the cherry juice with the cornstarch, add to the cherries and boil until thick. Cool to warm.

Sprinkle cakes with kirsch.

Spread the cherries on the first cake and top with the second. Whip the cream, fold in the sugar and spread or pipe onto the cake. Garnish with chocolate.

Chef K's Schwarzwalder Kirschentorte

CREME AU PRALINE CHOCOLATE TORTE

1 quan	1	pralines (see page 529, Praline Frosting)
2 cups	500 ml	half & half cream
1 tsp	5 ml	vanilla extract
5	5	egg yolks
½ cup	125 ml	granulated sugar
¼ cup	60 ml	flour, all purpose
4 oz	115 g	semi-sweet chocolate, melted
16	16	Crêpes (see Crêpe Batter, page 469)

Crush the pralines. In a double broiler, heat the cream with the vanilla. Beat the eggs with the sugar and flour. Slowly pour into the cream, stirring constantly. Stir in the chocolate. Cook mixture until very thick.

Remove from heat and strain mixture through a sieve. Cool. Once cooled, stir in the pralines.

Spread over crêpes, stack crêpes to form a cake. Pour any remaining mixture over crêpes and chill. Slice and serve.

SERVES 8

SUGAR ORANGE CAKE

1 cup	250 ml	butter
1 cup	250 ml	granulated sugar
1 cup	250 ml	orange juice
2	2	eggs
1 tsp	5 ml	vanilla
2½ cups	625 ml	flour, pastry
1 tsp	5 ml	baking soda
1 tsp	5 ml	baking powder
2 tsp	10 ml	orange rind – grated
½ cup	125 ml	walnuts
1 cup	250 ml	orange segments

Cream the butter and sugar until very light. Add the orange juice, eggs and vanilla. Sift together the flour, soda and baking powder. Stir into the liquid. Add the orange rind, walnuts and orange segments. Pour into an oiled bundt pan. Bake in a preheated 350°F (180°C) oven for 50-60 minutes. Cool 10 minutes then remove cake to a cooling rack. Frost with sugar as follows.

1 cup	250 ml	granulated sugar
1 cup	250 ml	orange juice

Combine the orange juice with the sugar and pour over cake.

RASPBERRY MARSHMALLOW FUDGE BOMBE

1 quan	1 quan	Marshmallow Fudge Ice Cream (see page 550)
½ quan	0.5 quan	Raspberry Bavarian (see page 666)

Invert a 2 quart (2 L) bombe mold in a large bowl of ice. Fill the top and sides with the ice cream. Fill the centre with the raspberry bavarian. Spread the remaining ice cream over the bottom. Place the lid of the mold over and seal or line with wax paper. Freeze for 4-6 hours. Dip quickly in hot water to unmold. Slice and serve at table.

SERVES 8

SOUTHERN PEACH ICE CREAM

3 cups	750 ml	cream
2 tbsp	30 ml	flour, all purpose
2 tbsp	30 ml	milk
3	3	egg yolks
1 cup	250 ml	granulated sugar
1 tsp	5 ml	white vanilla
1½ cups	375 ml	peaches – skinned, stoned, puréed

Scald the cream in a double boiler, blend the flour with milk and add to the hot cream. Beat the eggs with the sugar. Slowly add to the hot cream, add the vanilla and cook until thick. Cool, chill, stir in the peaches and freeze according to the directions of the ice cream maker.

YIELDS 6 C (1.5 L)

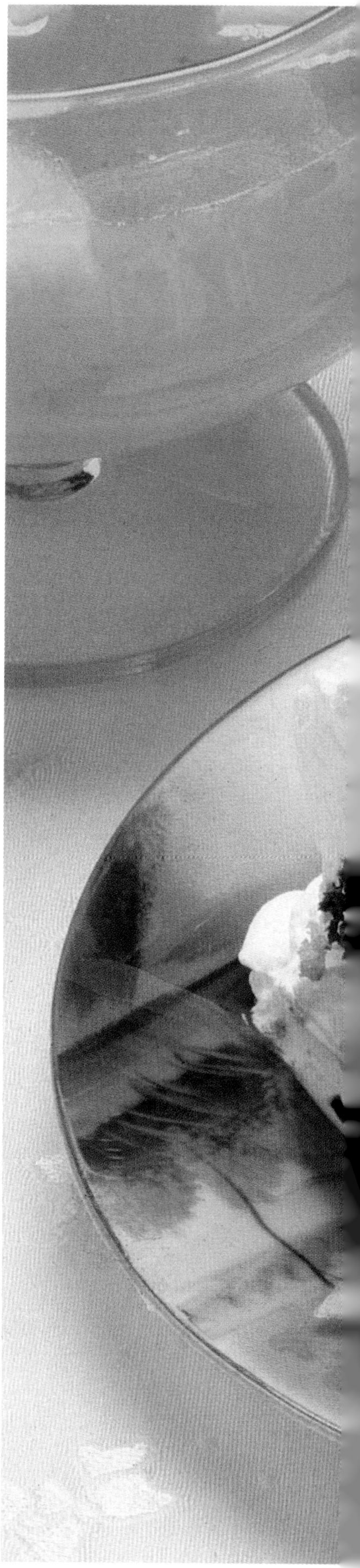

Sugar Orange Cake

Blueberry Spice Cake

BLUEBERRY SPICE CAKE

½ cup	125 ml	butter
2 cups	500 ml	brown sugar
3	3	eggs – separated
2 cups	500 ml	pastry flour
¼ tsp	2 ml	salt
1 tsp	5 ml	baking powder
2 tsp	10 ml	cinnamon – ground
½ tsp	3 ml	cloves
¼ tsp	2 ml	nutmeg
1 cup	250 ml	buttermilk
1 cup	250 ml	fresh blueberries, dusted with flour

Cream the butter with the sugar until light and fluffy. Add the egg yolks one at a time beating after each addition. Whip the egg whites to stiff. Reserve.

Sift together the dry ingredients, twice. Incorporate the flour and the buttermilk in thirds into the creamed mixture. Fold in the egg whites and blueberries. Pour batter into a 9" (23 cm) square buttered, wax paper lines and floured cake pan. Bake in a preheated 350°F (180°C) oven for 60 minutes. Cool 10 minutes. Cut cake and serve hot with hot Spiced Blueberry Sauce (recipe follows), or cold with cold Spiced Blueberry Sauce.

SPICED BLUEBERRY SAUCE

2 lbs	900 g	blueberries
1 tbsp	15 ml	cornstarch
1 tsp	5 ml	cinnamon
¼ tsp	2 ml	cloves
1 tbsp	15 ml	orange juice
¼ cup	60 ml	granulated sugar

Wash and pick through the berries. Reserve 1 cup (250 ml) of the berries then purée the rest in a food processor. Mix the cornstarch with a little of the berry juice. Heat the berries, spices, orange juice and sugar in a sauce pan to a boil. Reduce heat. Stir in the cornstarch, simmer until sauce thickens. Cool to room temperature, stir in the remaining berries. Serve over Blueberry Spice Cake.

MELT IN YOUR MOUTH SHORTBREAD

1 cup	250 ml	butter
¾ cup	180 ml	confectioners' sugar
2¼ cups	560 ml	flour, pastry
½ cup	125 ml	cornstarch

Cream the butter with the sugar until very light.

Sift the flour and cornstarch together, fold into creamed mixture. Roll out the dough and form into desired shapes. Bake in a preheated 225°F (105°C) oven for 35 minutes. Sprinkle with granulated sugar if desired.

SERVES 6

Melt In Your Mouth Shortbread

Oops

OOPS

2 cups	500 ml	miniature marshmallows
2 cups	500 ml	chocolate chips
½ cup	125 ml	peanut butter
2 tbsp	30 ml	butter
2½ cups	650 ml	Rice Krispies™
½ cup	125 ml	raspberry preserves
¾ cup	180 ml	confectioners' sugar

In a double boiler melt the marshmallows, 1 cup (250 ml), chocolate chips and peanut butter. Stir in the Rice Krispies. Press into a 8" x 8" (20 x 20 cm) greased pan.

Melt the remaining chocolate, butter and blend into it the raspberry preserves. Whip in the sugar, pour over the Rice Krispies and spread, refrigerate for 1 hour before cutting.

YIELDS 20 SQUARES

FUDGE BROWNIES

1 cup	250 ml	butter
4 oz	115 g	unsweetened chocolate
4	4	eggs
pinch	pinch	salt
2 cups	500 ml	granulated sugar
1 cup	250 ml	flour, all purpose
1 tsp	5 ml	baking powder
1 tsp	5 ml	vanilla extract
1 cup	250 ml	chopped pecans

Preheat oven to 325°F (170°C). Grease a 9" (23 cm) square baking pan.

Melt butter and chocolate in small saucepan over low heat. Stir to blend and set aside to cool.

Beat eggs until light yellow; add salt, sugar, flour, and baking powder. Beat well. Blend in cooled chocolate, vanilla and pecans. Blend thoroughly.

Pour into prepared pan and bake 35-45 minutes or until knife inserted in centre comes out clean.

Cool before cutting.

YIELDS 36

DOUBLE CHOCOLATE SWIRL CHEESECAKE

CRUST:		
2 cups	500 ml	flour, all purpose
½ cup	125 ml	granulated sugar
1 tsp	5 ml	vanilla
¾ cup	180 ml	butter – melted
1	1	egg yolk

Process the ingredients in a food processor. Press into the bottom and sides of a buttered 10" (25 cm) spring form pan. Bake in a preheated 400°F (200°C) oven for 7 minutes. Remove.

FILLING:		
2 lbs	1 kg	cream cheese
1½ cups	375 ml	granulated sugar
3 tbsp	45 ml	flour, all purpose
1 tbsp	15 ml	orange rind
½ tsp	3 ml	lemon extract
5	5	eggs
½ cup	125 ml	whipping cream
3 tbsp	45 ml	cocoa powder
4 oz	120 g	semi-sweet chocolate – melted
4 oz	120 g	white chocolate – melted

Cream the cheese with the sugar. Beat the flour, orange rind, extract and the eggs one at a time. Stir in the whipping cream. Divide the batter into two parts, ⅔rds and ⅓rd. In the larger amount stir in the cocoa powder and semi-sweet chocolate. Fold the white chocolate into the smaller part. Pour the larger part into the shell bake in a preheated oven at 350°F (160°C) 35 minutes. Swirl the remaining through and continue to bake for 45 minutes, prop oven door open. Turn oven off. Leave cake in for 30 minutes before transferring to a cooling rack. Refrigerate for 8 hours or overnight.

Double Chocolate Swirl Cheesecake

Pineapple Sorbet

THE SOUR CREAM EXTRACT CAKE

1 cup	250 ml	butter
3 cups	750 ml	granulated sugar
6	6	eggs
½ tsp	3 ml	rum extract
¼ tsp	1 ml	almond extract
½ tsp	3 ml	lemon extract
1 tsp	5 ml	vanilla extract
1 tsp	5 ml	butter extract
3 cups	750 ml	flour, pastry
¼ tsp	2 ml	baking powder
1 tsp	5 ml	salt
½ cup	125 ml	milk
1 cup	250 ml	sour cream

Cream the butter and the sugar. Add the eggs one at a time beating after each addition. Beat in the extracts.

Sift the flour, baking powder and salt. Fold into the mixture alternating with the milk and sour cream in thirds. Bake in a well oiled bundt pan in a preheated 300°F (150°C) oven for 1 hour and 10 minutes.

Remove from oven and cool for 10 minutes before turning out onto a cooling rack, turn cake out and cool completely. Frost with Double Chocolate Frosting (recipe follows).

DOUBLE CHOCOLATE FROSTING

2 oz	60 g	bittersweet chocolate
2 oz	60 g	milk chocolate
½ cup	125 ml	cream – heavy
1 tsp	5 ml	butter melted
1	1	egg yolk
2 cups	500 ml	confectioners' sugar
½ tsp	3 ml	vanilla

In a double boiler melt the chocolates. Blend in the remaining ingredients until very smooth. Use as required.

PINEAPPLE SORBET

½ cup	125 ml	granulated sugar
¾ cup	180 ml	water
¼ cup	60 ml	lime juice
2 cups	500 ml	fresh pineapple – pared, diced

In a sauce pan heat the sugar and water. Stir until sugar has dissolved then bring to a boil. Remove from heat, cool then chill. Place the lime and pineapple into a food processor and purée. Scrape into the syrup and mix. Chill thoroughly, then freeze in a ice cream maker according to manufacturer's directions.

YIELDS 3½ CUPS (875 ml)

The Sour Cream Extract Cake

LE GATEAU AU CHOCOLATE BLANC

CRUST:		
1½ cups	375 ml	almonds
2	2	egg whites
¼ cup + 2 tbsp	90 ml	butter
1 cup	250 ml	granulated sugar
1½ tsp	8 ml	flour, pastry
2 tbsp	30 ml	vanilla sugar
1 tsp	5 ml	cinnamon
1 tsp	5 ml	lemon rind – grated
⅛ tsp	pinch	salt

Grind the almonds into a paste in a food processor. Whip the egg whites until stiff and dry.

Cream the ¼cup butter with the sugar. Add the flour, vanilla sugar, cinnamon, lemon rind and salt. Add the egg whites, blend thoroughly.

Blend the almonds, flour, sugar, cinnamon, egg whites, and salt together.

Roll into 1" (2.5 cm) balls, then flatten with your hand, place on a buttered cookie sheet. Bake for 25 minutes in a preheated 350°F (180°C) oven. Do not brown overly. Cool then crush, mix with the remaining butter. Press into the sides and bottom of a buttered 9" (23 cm) spring form pan. Chill.

FILLING:		
6 oz	120 g	grated white chocolate
¾ cup	180 ml	butter – unsalted, no colouring
¾ cup	180 ml	granulated sugar
1 tsp	5 ml	vanilla white extract
¼ tsp	1 ml	salt
6	6	eggs, separated room temperature
		fresh fruit

Combine the chocolate, butter, sugar, vanilla and salt in a double boiler over low heat. When melted remove from the heat. Cool.

Beat in the egg yolks one at a time.

Whip the egg whites until stiff. Fold gently into the batter. Pour into the shell and bake for 40 minutes in a preheated 325°F (160°C) oven. Cool on a rack for 1 hour before serving, or cover and hold overnight, do not refrigerate. Cake may sink slightly as it cools.

Serve covered with fresh fruit.

Le Gateau au Chocolate Blanc

Sugar Cookies

Triple Layer Mint Bars

TRIPLE LAYER MINT BARS

¾ cup	180 ml	butter
¼ cup	60 ml	granulated sugar
1	1	egg
¼ cup	60 ml	cocoa powder
2 cups	500 ml	graham cracker crumbs
1 cup	250 ml	coconut – shredded
½ cup	125 ml	walnut pieces
3 tbsp	45 ml	milk
2 tsp	10 ml	mint extract
2 tbsp	30 ml	instant vanilla pudding powder
2 cups	500 ml	confectioners' sugar – sifted
4 oz	120 g	semi-sweet chocolate
1 tsp	5 ml	oil

In a double boiler blend ½ cup (125 ml) butter, sugar, egg and cocoa powder into a thick sauce. Remove from heat, stir in the cracker crumbs, coconut and nuts, and blend well. Spread into a buttered 9" x 9" (23 x 23 cm) cake pan. Cream the remaining butter, add the milk, mint extract and pudding powder. Blend in the confectioners' sugar. Spread over the base. Melt the chocolate and add the oil, pour over the cake. Chill in the refrigerator for 1 hour. Slice and serve

MAKES 20 SQUARES

MERINGUE COOKIES

4	4	egg whites
½ tsp	3 ml	cream of tartar
¾ cup	180 ml	granulated sugar
¼ tsp	2 ml	almond flavouring, optional
		coloured sprinkles

Preheat over to 400°F (200°C).

Place the egg whites and cream of tarter into mixing bowl. Beat to very soft peaks. Gradually beat in the sugar until meringue is stiff and sugar is completely dissolved. Beat in flavouring (if desired).

Fill a large star tipped pastry bag with the meringue mixture. Pipe 2" (5 cm) diameter cookies onto a greased cookie sheets, swirling for an attractive top.

Sprinkle lightly with the coloured sprinkles. Bake in the preheated over for 7 to 8 minutes or until lightly browned.

Cool at room temperature, away from drafts.

SUGAR COOKIES

1 cup	250 ml	butter
1 cup	250 ml	granulated sugar
2	2	eggs – separated
2 cups	500 ml	flour, pastry
2 tsp	10 ml	baking powder
1 tsp	5 ml	salt
1 tbsp	15 ml	milk
1 tsp	5 ml	white vanilla

Cream the butter until very light. Beat in the sugar and the egg yolks. Whip the egg whites stiff. Sift together the flour, baking powder and salt. Fold into the creamed mixture with the egg whites. Add the milk and vanilla. Roll out the dough and shape into desired forms with cookie cutters. Dust with sugar then bake in a 350°F (180°C) preheated oven. Serve as is or decorate colourfully.

MAKES 2½ DOZEN

CHOCOLATE COCONUT ROAST CAKE

2 cups	500 ml	flour, pastry
1 tsp	5 ml	baking powder
½ tsp	3 ml	salt
1¼ cups	310 ml	granulated sugar
½ cup	125 ml	butter – softened
½ cup	125 ml	sour cream
¼ cup	60 ml	coconut cream nectar
3	3	eggs
3 oz	85 g	semi-sweet chocolate – melted, cooled

Sift the flour, baking powder and salt together, twice. Cream the sugar and butter until very light and fluffy. Blend sour cream and coconut nectar together. Add flour and sour cream alternating in thirds. Beat in the eggs one at a time. Fold in the chocolate. Pour batter into a buttered 8 cup (2 L), bundt pan. Bake for 50-60 minutes in a preheated 350°F (180°C) oven. Cool 10 minutes, transfer cake to cooling rack, frost with Broiled Coconut Frosting (recipe follows).

BROILED COCONUT FROSTING

3 tbsp	45 ml	butter
½ cup	125 ml	icing sugar
4 tbsp	60 ml	sweeten condensed milk
1 cup	250 ml	coconut – shredded
1½ tsp	8 ml	vanilla extract

Cream the butter and sugar. Blend in the remaining ingredients. Pour over cake, run under the oven broiler until golden.

ORANGE CREME BAVARIAN

1 tbsp	15 ml	unflavoured gelatin
¼ cup	60 ml	cold water
1 cup	250 ml	orange juice
2 tsp	10 ml	lemon juice
½ cup	125 ml	granulated sugar
¾ cup	180 ml	whipping cream

Soften the gelatin in cold water. Place in a small sauce pan and heat until gelatin has melted. Add the orange juice, lemon juice and sugar, bring to a boil and remove from heat. Cool and chill until thick but not set. Whip the cream and fold into orange. Pour into a mold or bowl and chill until set. Unmold and serve.

SERVES 4

Orange Creme Bava

Chocolate Coconut Roast Cake

Copacabana

REFRIGERATOR COOKIES

½ cup	125 ml	butter
2 cups	500 ml	brown sugar
2	2	eggs
⅓ cup	80 ml	walnut – pieces
⅓ cup	80 ml	dates – chopped
⅓ cup	80 ml	raisins
1 tsp	5 ml	vanilla
1 tsp	5 ml	cream of tartar
1 tsp	5 ml	baking soda
2½ cups	625 ml	flour, pastry
½ tsp	3 ml	salt

Cream the butter and sugar until light, add the eggs. Sir in the remaining ingredients, blend thoroughly. Shape in rolls 1½" (4 cm) in diameter. Wrap with wax paper. Chill in refrigerator 8 hours or overnight. Slice in 1" (2.5 cm) slice and place on a buttered pastry sheet. Bake in a preheated 400°F (200°C) oven for 10-12 minutes.

MAKES 5-6 DOZEN

Refrigerator Cookies

COPACABANA

6	6	medium size bananas
¼ cup	60 ml	granulated sugar
¼ cup	60 ml	brandy
½ tsp	3 ml	vanilla extract
4 cups	1 L	French Vanilla Ice Cream (see page 547)
1½ cups	375 ml	Chocolate Sauce (see page 123)
½ cup	125 ml	toasted almonds – slices

Place the bananas in a large skillet, add the sugar, brandy and vanilla extract, poach the bananas for 3-5 minutes. Remove, cool then chill. Place on beds of ice cream, smother with chocolate sauce and sprinkle with nuts. Serve at once.

SERVES 6

AMARETTO MOUSSE

2 tsp	10 ml	gelatin unflavoured
¼ cup	60 ml	Amaretto liqueur
4 tbsp	60 ml	butter
5	5	eggs
1 cup	250 ml	granulated sugar
1½ cups	375 ml	whipping cream
½ cup	125 ml	toasted sliced almonds

Soften the gelatin in the liqueur. Melt the butter in a double boiler.

Beat the eggs with the sugar and liqueur. Add to the melted butter and cook stirring constantly until thickened. Cool then chill until very thick. Whip the cream and fold into the mixture. Pour into wine glasses and chill to set. Sprinkle with toasted almonds before serving.

SERVES 8

Mandarin Chocolate Mousse

MANDARIN CHOCOLATE MOUSSE

3 cups	750 ml	miniature marshmallows
½ cup	125 ml	light cream
3 oz	80 g	semi-sweet chocolate
2 tbsp	30 ml	orange juice concentrate
1½ cups	375 ml	whipping cream
2	2	egg whites
1 cup	250 ml	Mandarin orange segments

In a double boiler melt the marshmallows with the cream and chocolate. Stir in the orange juice, remove from the heat and cool.

Whip the cream and fold into cooled mixture. Whip the egg whites stiff and fold into mixture. Fold in the orange segments. Pour into 6 serving dishes or parfait dishes, chill for 3 hours before serving.

SERVES 6

ORANGE CHOCOLATE SHERBET

2 oz	30 g	semi-sweet chocolate
2 tbsp	30 g	cocoa powder
1 cup	250 ml	granulated sugar
2 cups	500 ml	orange juice
4 cups	1 L	milk

Mix the cocoa, sugar and orange juice. Boil 5 minutes. Add milk and boil 7 minutes. Cool. Freeze in ice cream maker according to manufacturers directions.

YIELDS 6 CUPS (1.5 L)

LIME DELICIOUS CHEESECAKE

1¼ cups	310 ml	Zwieback toast crumbs*
2 tbsp	30 ml	granulated sugar
⅓ cup	80 ml	melted butter
1 tbsp	30 ml	unflavored gelatin or 2 envelopes
¼ cup	60 ml	cold water
¼ cup	60 ml	lime juice
3	3	large eggs, separated
½ cup	125 ml	granulated sugar
1½ tsp	8 ml	grated lime peel
16 oz	450 g	light Neufchâtel cheese, soft**
		green food colouring
2 cups	500 ml	thawed whipped topping

Combine crumbs, sugar and butter; press onto the bottom of 9-inch (23 cm) spring form pan. Bake in a preheated 325°F (170°C) oven for 10 minutes. Cool.

Soften gelatin in water, stir over low heat until dissolved. Add juice, egg yolks, ¼ cup (60 ml) sugar and peel; cook, stirring constantly, over medium heat 5 minutes. Cool. Gradually add gelatin mixture to the softened Neufchâtel cheese, mixing until well blended. Stir in a few drops of green food colouring, if desired.

Beat egg whites until foamy; gradually add remaining sugar, beating until stiff peaks form. Fold egg whites and whipped topping into Neufchâtel cheese mixture, pour over crust. Chill until firm. Garnish with additional lime peel , if desired.

SERVES 10

* Slices of Zwieback bread, found in most French bakeries, cut from the loaf and re-baked in the oven then ground to crumbs.

** Small French, loaf-shaped cheese made from skimmed milk. The cheese is a rather dark yellow and is at its best between October and June. Available in most delis.

OLD FASHION GOLD CAKE

¾ cup	180 ml	butter
1 cup	250 ml	granulated sugar
8	8	egg yolks – beaten
2½ cups	625 ml	pastry flour
1 tbsp	15 ml	baking powder
¼ tsp	2 ml	salt
¾ cup	180 ml	milk
¾ tsp	4 ml	vanilla

Cream the butter and the sugar until very light and fluffy. Add the egg yolks continuing to beat. Sift together the flour, baking powder, and salt, twice. Incorporate into the creamed mixture alternating with the milk in ⅓rds. Fold in the vanilla. Pour into 3, 9" (23 cm) round cake pans which have been buttered and floured. Bake in a preheated 350°F (180°C) oven for 20 minutes. Cool 10 minutes then transfer cake to cooling rack. Frost and fill with Marshmallow Fudge (recipe follows) or Praline Frosting (see page 529).

MARSHMALLOW FUDGE FILLING

2 cups	500 ml	granulated sugar
2 cups	500 ml	cream
4 oz	120 g	chocolate – semi-sweet
¼ cup	60 ml	butter
1 tsp	5 ml	vanilla
1 cup	250 ml	marshmallows

Blend the sugar, cream, chocolate, butter and vanilla in a sauce pan. Bring to a boil and cook to a soft ball stage. Melt the marshmallows in a second double boiler and blend into the fudge. Use as required.

APPLES CHATELAINE

1¼ cups	310 ml	water
1¼ cups	310 ml	granulated sugar
1	1	vanilla bean
6	6	large Granny Smith apples – pared, cored
3 tbsp	45 ml	butter – melted
1 cup	250 ml	cherries – halved
½ cup	125 ml	crushed macaroons
¼ cup	60 ml	vanilla sugar
4	4	egg yolks
2 cups	250 ml	milk – scalded

In a sauce pan boil the water, sugar and vanilla bean. Reduce to 1¼ cups (310 ml). Pour into a shallow pan, arrange the apples around the pan. Brush apples with syrup, and butter. Mix the cherries with the macaroons and stuff into the apple core hallow. Bake the apples in a preheated 350°F (180°C) oven for 20 minutes or until apples are tender. Place on a serving platter.

Beat the vanilla sugar in the egg yolks until very light and pale. Whip in the warm milk, cook in a double boiler stirring until thick. Remove from heat, spoon over apples and serve.

SERVES 6

Apples Chatelaine

Old Fashion Gold Cake with Praline Frosting

Raisin 'n' Nut Tumble

JENNIFER'S FUN SQUARES

10 oz	300 ml	sweetened condensed milk
2 oz	60 g	unsweetened chocolate
½ tsp	3 ml	salt
2 cups	500 ml	flaked coconut
½ cup	125 ml	maraschino cherries
½ cup	125 ml	walnut pieces
1 tsp	5 ml	vanilla extract

In a double boiler melt together the milk and chocolate. Blend in the remaining ingredients, pour into a buttered 8" x 8" (20 x 20 cm) square pan. Bake for 18 minutes in a preheated 350°F (180°C) oven. Cool then frost with Jennifer's Fun Frosting (recipe follows).

JENNIFER'S FUN FROSTING

3 tbsp	45 ml	butter
2 cups	500 ml	icing sugar
3 tbsp	45 ml	milk
2 tsp	10 ml	mint extract
1	1	square semi-sweet chocolate
1 tsp	5 ml	oil

Cream the butter, add half the sugar, then alternate the remaining sugar with the milk. Whip until all lumps are gone, stir in the extract. Spread over squares. Melt the chocolate and oil in a double boiler. Drizzle over the icing, cut in squares and serve.

YIELDS 24

RAISIN 'N' NUT TUMBLES

2 tsp	10 ml	baking powder
2¼ cups	560 ml	flour, pastry
½ cup	125 ml	butter
1 cup	250 ml	granulated sugar
2	2	eggs
1 tsp	5 ml	vanilla extract
⅓ cup	80 ml	milk
½ cup	125 ml	raisins
½ cup	125 ml	walnuts
		sugar for dusting

Sift the flour with the baking powder.

Cream the butter until very fluffy. Beat in the sugar and eggs. Stir in the flour, blend in the vanilla and milk . Add the raisins and nuts.

Drop tablespoon size pieces of dough onto a greased baking sheet. Dust with sugar and bake in a preheated 350°F (180°C) oven for 10-12 minutes.

YIELDS 1½ DOZEN

Jennifer's Fun Squares

Dominoes

FROZEN RASPBERRY KIWI SOUFFLÉ

2 cups	500 ml	raspberries
¼ cup	60 ml	granulated sugar
2 tbsp	30 ml	unflavoured gelatin
2 tbsp	30 ml	water – cold
¼ tsp	2 ml	salt
6	6	egg whites
2 cups	500 ml	whipping cream
1½ cups	375 ml	kiwi – pared, chopped

Purée the raspberries in a food processor, strain to remove seeds. Place in a sauce pan and reduce to ¼ cup (60 ml) of sauce. Add the sugar, gelatin which has been softened in the water and salt. Cool to room temperature. Whip the egg whites until stiff and dry. Whip the cream and fold into the egg whites. Fold in the sauce and kiwi. Pour into a 8 cup (2 L) soufflé dish with a 6" (15 cm) foil collar. Freeze 6 hours or overnight. Remove collar and serve.

SERVES 6

CAFE MINT SOUFFLÉ

¼ cup	60 ml	flour, all purpose
1 cup	250 ml	milk
1 cup	250 ml	granulated sugar
3 tbsp	45 ml	butter
1 tsp	5 ml	instant coffee crystals
3 tbsp	45 ml	Kahlua liqueur
3 tbsp	45 ml	Creme de Menthe liqueur
4	4	eggs – separated
2	2	egg whites

Butter a 6 to 8 cups (1.5–2 L) quart soufflé dish. Dust the bottom and side with sugar. In a sauce pan whip the flour into the milk, heat to a boil. Stir in the sugar, butter, coffee, and liqueurs. Remove from the heat, and beat in the egg yolks one at a time. Whip the egg whites stiff and fold into mixture. Bake in a preheat 400°F (200°C) oven for 40 minutes. Serve hot with a chocolate fudge sauce.

SERVES 4

DOMINOES

½ cups	125 ml	chopped walnuts
½ cup	125 ml	sliced almonds
½ cup	125 ml	chopped dates
½ cup	125 ml	almond paste*
1 tsp	5 ml	orange rind – grated
¼ cup	60 ml	orange juice
¼ tsp	2 ml	salt
¼ cup	60 ml	flour, pastry
2 oz	60 g	semi-sweet chocolate – melted
1 tsp	5 ml	butter, melted

In a food processor blend the nuts, dates, almond paste, orange rind, juice and salt. Blend well. Stiffen with the flour only if required.

Shape into squares. Dip into the chocolate blended with the butter.

* Available in most cake decorating stores or at your bakery.

YIELDS 2 DOZEN

Frozen Raspberry Kiwi Soufflé

Refrigerator Chocolate Cheesecak

REFRIGERATOR CHOCOLATE CHEESECAKE

CRUST:		
2 cups	500 ml	chocolate wafer crumbs
2 tbsp	30 ml	granulated sugar
¼ cup	60 ml	butter – melted

Combine the ingredients, press into the bottom of a 9" (23 cm) spring form pan. Chill.

FILLING:		
1 tbsp	15 ml	unflavoured gelatin
⅔ cup	160 ml	water
1 lb	450 g	softened cream cheese
6 oz	170 g	melted chocolate chips
1 cup	250 ml	sweetened condensed milk
1½ tsp	8 ml	vanilla
¾ cup	180 ml	whipping cream, whipped
1 cup	250 ml	chocolate curls
1½ cups	375 ml	Raspberry Sauce (seepage 107)

Soften the gelatin in the water, then heat until gelatin has dissolved, remove from the heat and cool.

Cream the cheese with the chocolate, milk and vanilla. Stir in the gelatin, fold in the whipped cream. Pour into the shell and refrigerate for 4 hours.

Garnish with chocolate curls. Serve with raspberry sauce.

SERVES 8-10

CHEF K'S AMARETTO CHEESECAKE

CRUST:		
3½ cups	875 ml	Italian macaroons, ground
¼ cup	60 ml	butter – melted

Combine the ingredients. Press into the bottom and sides of a buttered 9" (23 cm) spring form pan. Chill. Preheat the oven to 325°F (160°C).

FILLING:		
3 cups	750 ml	cream cheese
¾ cup	180 ml	granulated sugar
4	4	eggs
2 tbsp	10 ml	almond extract
¼ cup	60 ml	Amaretto liqueur

Cream the cheese with the sugar. Beat in the eggs one at a time. Stir in the flavouring and liqueur. Bake in the oven for 90 minutes. Transfer to a cooling rack, cool to room temperature.

TOPPING:		
1 cup	250 ml	clarified butter
8 oz	250 ml	semi-sweet chocolate
½ cup	125 ml	Amaretto liqueur
½ cup	125 ml	sliced, toasted almonds

Combine the butter with the chocolate in a sauce pan, heat but do not boil. Remove pan from the heat and stir in the Amaretto. Pour mixture over the cheesecake. Refrigerate 2 hours. Sprinkle with almonds and continue to refrigerate for 6-8 hours longer.

KIWI MANGO SORBET

¾ cup	180 ml	granulated sugar
¾ cup	180 ml	water
1½ cups	375 ml	kiwis – pared, diced, puréed
1½ cups	375 ml	mango purée
¼ cup	60 ml	lime juice

In a sauce pan combine the sugar and water. Bring to a boil then remove from heat and cool, then chill. Blend the kiwi, mango and lime juice together, chill. Then blend with the syrup. Freeze in a ice cream maker according to manufacturer's directions.

YIELDS 4 CUPS (1 L)

CHOCOLATE CHEESECAKE

CRUST:		
½ cup	125 ml	butter
½ cup	125 ml	granulated sugar
1½ cups	375 ml	graham cracker crumbs
1 tbsp	15 ml	cocoa powder

Blend the butter with the sugar. Add the graham crackers and cocoa powder. Press into a 9" (23 cm) spring form pan. Bake in a preheated 375°F (205°C) oven for 8 minutes. Remove and cool.

FILLING:		
4 oz	125 ml	semi-sweet chocolate
1 lb	450 g	cream cheese
2 cups	500 ml	sour cream
1 cup	250 ml	whip cream
1 cup	250 ml	granulated sugar
1 tsp	5 ml	vanilla
3	3	eggs
3 cups	750 ml	whipping cream, whipped
		chocolate shavings

Melt the chocolate in a double boiler, cool. Beat the cream cheese until fluffy. Add the cooled chocolate, sour cream and whip cream. Blend in sugar, vanilla and 1 egg at a time. Pour into crust. Bake in the centre of a preheated oven at 375°F (205°C) for 50-60 minutes. Remove and chill 6 hours. Spread and decorate with whipped cream. Sprinkle with chocolate shavings. Serve.

Chocolate Cheesecake

Kiwi Mango Sorbet

Blueberry Ice Crean

FIG COOKIES

COOKIES:		
3 cups	750 ml	flour, all purpose
2 tsp	10 ml	baking powder
¼ tsp	1 ml	salt
1 cup	250 ml	granulated sugar
⅓ cup	80 ml	shortening
2	2	eggs
⅓ cup	80 ml	milk
½ tsp	3 ml	vanilla

Sift together the flour, baking powder and salt. Cream the sugar and shortening together. Beat in the eggs, milk and vanilla, fold in the flour and blend thoroughly.

Roll the dough out on a lightly floured dusted surface to ¼" (6 mm) thick. Cut into 4" (10 cm) wide strips and fill with fig filling (recipe follows). Fold over and cut in rounds. Bake 12-15 minutes in a preheated 325°F (160°C) preheated oven. Cool before serving.

FIG FILLING:		
1½ cups	375 ml	granulated sugar
¾ cup	180 ml	water
6 cups	1.5 L	blanched figs
2 cups	500 ml	chopped dates
1 tbsp	15 ml	lemon juice
1 tsp	5 ml	grated lemon rind

In a sauce pan combine the sugar and water, add the figs, dates and lemon. Bring to a boil, reduce heat and simmer gently for 2½ hours or until very thick. Cool before using.

*NOTE: If using dried figs soak in cold water for ½ hour. Reduce cooking time to 20 minutes, then purée in a food processor.

YIELDS 3 DOZEN

Fig Cookies

BLUEBERRY ICE CREAM

3 cups	750 ml	cream – light half & half
2 tbsp	30 ml	flour, all purpose
2 tbsp	30 ml	water
3	3	egg yolks
1 cup	250 ml	granulated sugar
1½ tsp	8 ml	white vanilla – extract
1½ cups	375 ml	blueberries, fresh

In a double boiler, scald the cream. Blend the flour with the water and add to the cream. Beat the egg yolks with sugar, slowly add to the cream with the extract. Cook, stirring constantly until mixture thickens. Remove and chill. Follow manufacturer's directors for the ice cream maker. Add the blueberries just before ice cream is frozen (last 5 minutes of churning).

YIELDS 6 C (1.5 L)

GRANOLA COOKIES

½ cup	125 ml	butter
½ cup	125 ml	oil
½ cup	125 ml	granulated sugar
½ cup	125 ml	brown sugar
1 tsp	5 ml	vanilla
½ tsp	3 ml	cream of tartar
½ tsp	3 ml	baking soda
1	1	egg
1 cup	250 ml	granola
½ cup	125 ml	shredded coconut
½ cup	125 ml	oatmeal
1¾ cups	430 ml	flour, pastry
½ cup	125 ml	raisins
¼ cup	60 ml	walnuts – pieces

Cream the butter with the oil until light. Add the sugar and vanilla. Stir in the tartar, soda and egg. Mix in the remaining ingredients. Drop teaspoon sizes onto a buttered pastry sheet. Bake in a preheated 350°F (180°C) oven for 12-15 minutes.

YIELDS 3 DOZEN

CREOLE PRALINES

1 cup	250 ml	brown sugar
1 cup	250 ml	granulated sugar
½ cup	125 ml	cream – light
2 tbsp	30 ml	butter
1 cup	250 ml	pecans

Dissolve the sugars in the cream in a sauce pan. Heat to 238°F (115°C) on a candy thermometer. Remove from heat, beat in the butter and nuts, continue to beat until thick. Drop on to a pastry sheet lined with buttered wax paper. Leaving enough room between each as they separate.

MAKES 1½ LBS (675 g)

CHRISTMAS EGG NOG PIE

1 tbsp	15 ml	plain gelatin
3 tbsp	45 ml	cold water
1 cup	250 ml	milk
3	3	eggs – separated
1½ cups	375 ml	granulated sugar
2 tsp	10 ml	rum extract
¾ cup	180 ml	whipping cream
½ cup	125 ml	candied fruit – chopped
1	1	Gingersnap Crust (see page 603)
2 tbsp	30 ml	chopped pecans

Soak the gelatin in the water. In a double boiler blend the milk, egg yolks, ½ cup (125 ml) sugar and extract. Remove from heat when mixtures begins to thicken, stir in the gelatin, chill to very thick but not set. Whip the cream and fold into the mixture. Whip the egg whites until stiff. Add the sugar and continue to whip until soft peaks form. Fold into mixture. Mix in the candied fruit. Pour into pie shell and refrigerate until set. Sprinkle with nuts. Serve.

SERVES 6

FRANK'S ITALIAN CHEESECAKE

16 oz	450 g	cream cheese
16 oz	450 g	sour cream
16 oz	450 g	ricotta cheese
4	4	eggs
4 oz	110 g	butter, melted
3 tbsp	45 ml	flour, all purpose
3 tbsp	45 ml	corn starch
1½ cups	375 ml	sugar, granulated
1 tbsp	15 ml	vanilla extract
1 tbsp	15 ml	lemon juice

Line bottom and sides of a 12" (30 cm) spring form pan with foil. Grease foil with butter.

Preheat over to 325°F (170°C). In a large bowl add the cheeses and sour cream and whip until very creamy. Add eggs, one at a time mixing well after each addition. Add melted butter.

Mix the dry ingredients together. Add to the cheese mixture along with vanilla and lemon juice. Mix well. Bake 1½ hours, shut oven off and keep cake in for one more hour (depending upon oven). This is to let cake set.

Refrigerate overnight, sprinkle with icing sugar and serve.

Creole Pralines

Christmas Egg Nog Pie

Grasshopper Pie

GRASSHOPPER PIE

CRUST:		
2 cups	500 ml	chocolate wafer crumbs
⅓ cup	80 ml	butter
¾ cup	180 ml	filberts – ground

Combine the ingredients. Press into the bottom and sides of a 10" (25 cm) buttered pie pan. Bake in a preheated 350°F (180°C) oven for 7 minutes. Cool then chill.

FILLING:		
2 tbsp	30 ml	cold water
1 tbsp	15 ml	unflavoured gelatin
2	2	eggs – separated
½ cup	125 ml	milk
1½ cups	375 ml	marshmallows – miniatures
2 tsp	10 ml	mint extract
1 cup	250 ml	whipping cream
1 tsp	5 ml	green food colouring
1 cup	250 ml	chocolate curls

In the cold water soften the gelatin, transfer to a double boiler. Add the egg yolks and milk and cook to thick. Melt the marshmallows in a second double boiler, fold into the egg mixture and remove from the heat. Stir in the extract. Cool. Whip the cream with the food colouring. Fold into the cooled mixture. Whip the egg whites and fold into the mixture. Pour into the shell. Chill for 4-6 hours. Garnish with chocolate curls before serving.

CHEF K'S WHITE CHOCOLATE GRAND MARNIER CHEESECAKE

CRUST:		
2 cups	500 ml	chocolate wafer crumbs
2 tbsp	30 ml	granulated sugar
¼ cup	60 ml	butter – melted

Combine the ingredients together. Press into the bottom and sides of a buttered 9" (23 cm) spring form pan. Chill. Preheat oven to 350°F (180°C).

FILLING:		
6 oz	180 g	white chocolate
1½ lbs	750 ml	cream cheese
¾ cup	180 ml	granulated sugar
3	3	eggs
⅓ cup	80 ml	Grand Marnier liqueur

Melt the chocolate in a double boiler. Cream the cheese together with the sugar. Beat in the eggs one at a time. Fold in the chocolate and stir in the liqueur. Pour into the shell. Bake 45 minutes.

TOPPING:		
2 cups	500 ml	sour cream
3 tbsp	45 ml	granulated sugar
1 tsp	5 ml	vanilla

Blend the ingredients together until very smooth. Spoon over the cake and continue to bake 10 minutes. Remove to cooling rack, cool 1 hour.

GLAZE:		
½ cup	125 ml	granulated sugar
1½ tbsp	25 ml	cornstarch
¼ tsp	2 ml	salt
½ cup	125 ml	water
¼ cup	60 ml	Grand Marnier liqueur
⅓ cup	80 ml	orange juice
1 tsp	5 ml	orange rind – grated
1	1	egg yolk – beaten
1 tbsp	15 ml	butter, melted

Mix the sugar, cornstarch and salt in a sauce pan. Place over medium heat, whip in the remaining ingredients except the butter. Cool to warm, stir in the butter. Pour over the cake and refrigerate 6 hours.

Chef K's White Chocolate Grand Marnier Cheesecake

CHOCOLATE GRAND MARNIER CREAM

6 oz	120 g	white chocolate – grated
¼ cup	60 ml	Grand Marnier Cream liqueur
¼ cup	60 ml	granulated sugar
2 cups	500 ml	heavy cream
½ tsp	3 ml	orange extract
18	18	chocolate orange segments

Combine the chocolate and liqueur in a double boiler and melt over low heat. Stir in the sugar until dissolved, remove, cool and chill in the refrigerator. Whip the cream with orange extract until thick. Fold into the chocolate mixture. Pour into 6 serving dishes, cover with plastic wrap and refrigerate 8 hours or overnight. Garnish with Chocolate Dipped Orange Segments (recipe follows).

SERVES 6

CHOCOLATE DIPPED ORANGE SEGMENTS

6 oz	120 g	semi-sweet chocolate
1 tbsp	15 ml	butter – melted
40	40	fresh orange segments

In a double boiler over low heat melt the chocolate with the butter. Dip the oranges into the chocolate then transfer to wax paper. Refrigerate 10 minutes then return to room temperature. Serve or use as garnish.

TROPICAL CHEESECAKE

CRUST:

1 cup	250 ml	graham wafer crumbs
3 tbsp	45 ml	brown sugar
¼ cup	60 ml	butter – melted

FILLING:

2	2	envelopes unflavoured gelatin
¼ cup	60 ml	coconut rum
1 can	1 can	(19 oz) crushed pineapple drained
⅓ cup	75 ml	granulated sugar
¼ tsp	1 ml	salt
1	1	egg
1	1	(250 g) pkg cream cheese at room temperature
¾ cup	180 ml	whipping cream

CRUST:

Combine crumbs, sugar and butter. Press into the bottom of a greased 9" (23 cm) spring form pan. Bake in a preheated over at 400°F (200°C) for 5 minutes. Cool.

FILLING:

Sprinkle gelatin over coconut rum in a small dish to soften. Combine pineapple, sugar, salt and egg in a sauce pan. Stir in the softened gelatin and heat, stirring until thickened, set aside to cool at room temperature.

Beat cream cheese and whipping cream just until smooth. Add the pineapple mixture and beat until well blended about 2 minutes. Pour into prepared shell and chill until set, about 4 hours.

Chocolate Grand Marnier Cream with Chocolate Dipped Orange Segments

Neapolitan Cheesecake

COFFEE WALNUT CRUNCH CHEESECAKE

CRUST:		
3 cups	750 ml	chocolate wafer crumbs
2 tbsp	30 ml	granulated sugar
¼ cup	60 ml	butter – melted

Combine all the ingredients together. Press onto the bottom and sides of a 9" (23 cm) spring form pan. Chill 5 minutes bake 7 minutes in a preheated 350°F (180°C) oven.

FILLING:		
1½ lbs	750 g	cream cheese
1 cup	250 ml	granulated sugar
4	4	eggs
½ cup	60 ml	double strength coffee
3 oz	90 g	butterscotch chips – melted
2 oz	60 g	semi-sweet chocolate – melted
½ cup	125 ml	walnuts – broken

Cream the cheese with the sugar, beat in the eggs one at a time. Divide the batter into two parts. Blend the butterscotch chips into one. Add the coffee, chocolate and nuts into the second. Pour the chocolate nut batter into the shell. Bake for 30 minutes in a preheated 350°F (180°C) oven. Pour the butterscotch batter over and continue to bake for 40 additional minutes. Turn oven off, prop open the door and leave cake for 30 minutes. Transfer to a cooling rack. Chill for 8 hours or overnight before serving.

Coffee Walnut Crunch Cheesecake

NEAPOLITAN CHEESECAKE

CRUST:		
3 cups	750 ml	chocolate wafer crumbs
2 tbsp	30 ml	granulated sugar
¼ cup	60 ml	melted butter

Combine the ingredients. Press into a buttered 9" (23 cm) spring form pan. Bake for 5 minutes in a preheated 350°F (180°C) oven. Cool.

FILLING:		
1½ lbs	750 ml	cream cheese
1 cup	250 ml	granulated sugar
3	3	eggs
1 tsp	5 ml	vanilla
2 oz	60 g	semi-sweet chocolate – melted
1 tbsp	15 ml	cocoa powder
1 cup	250 ml	strawberry purée

Cream the cheese and sugar together until very light. Beat in the eggs one at a time. Stir in the vanilla. Divide batter in 3 equal parts. Blend the chocolate and cocoa powder into one part. Mix the strawberries into a second part.

Pour the chocolate batter into the shell. Bake for 20 minutes until sides are set. Gently pour the strawberry portion over the cake and bake for 20 minutes. Pour over the remaining batter continue to bake for 35 minutes. Turn oven off and prop door open, leave cake in for 30 minutes. Transfer to a cooling rack, cool to room temperature. Refrigerate for 6-8 hours before serving. Glaze as follows:

GLAZE:		
½ cup	125 ml	granulated sugar
1½ tbsp	25 ml	cornstarch
¼ tsp	2 ml	salt
½ cup	125 ml	water
½ cup	125 ml	lime juice
2 tsp	10 ml	lime rind – grated
1	1	egg yolk
5 drops	5 drops	green food colouring
1 tbsp	15 ml	butter

In a sauce pan mix the sugar, cornstarch and salt. Place over medium heat combine all the remaining ingredients except the butter, cook until thickened. Whip in butter, cool to warm, pour over cake and serve.

Orange Brandy Sunshine Cake

ORANGE BRANDY SUNSHINE CAKE

8	8	egg whites
½ tsp	3 ml	cream of tartar
½ tsp	3 ml	salt
1½ cups	375 ml	granulated sugar
5	5	egg yolks
1 cup	250 ml	flour, all purpose
2 tbsp	30 ml	water
½ tsp	3 ml	each of almond extract, lemon extract and white vanilla extract

Preheat the oven to 350°F (180°C).

Mix egg whites, cream of tartar and salt together. Beat until very stiff. Beat the sugar and egg yolks together until very light in colour. White beating, slowly add the flour alternating with the water. Add the flavouring. Fold in the egg whites. Pour into an ungreased tube pan. Bake for 60 minutes, remove from oven and invert. When cool, remove cake and frost with Orange Brandy Sauce (recipe follows).

Orange Brandy Sauce:

2 tbsp	30 ml	orange concentrate
2⅓ cups	560 ml	canned Mandarin oranges
½ cup	125 ml	granulated sugar
4 tbsp	60 ml	orange brandy

Place the orange concentrate, drained juice from oranges and sugar in a sauce pan. Boil until thick. Remove from heat, stir in the orange brandy and Mandarin orange segments. Serve warm with cake.

NOTE: You may substitute the orange brandy for 2 tbsp (30ml) of orange brandy flavouring, and 2 tbsp (30 ml) of water.

OLD FASHION BUTTER POUND CAKE

2 cups	500 ml	granulated sugar
1 cup	250 ml	butter
4	4	eggs
2 tsp	10 ml	vanilla
3 cups	750 ml	flour, all purpose
½ tsp	3 ml	baking powder
½ tsp	3 ml	baking soda
½ tsp	3 ml	salt
1 tbsp	15 ml	lemon juice
1 cup	250 ml	milk

Cream the sugar with the butter until smooth. Add the eggs one at a time continuing to beat, add the vanilla. Sift the flour with the baking powder, baking soda and salt. Mix the lemon juice with the milk. Fold in the ⅓ flour and alternate with ⅓ liquid, repeating until finished.

Pour into 4"x10" (10 x 25 cm) greased pan. Bake in a preheated 350°F (180°C) oven for 1 hour and 10 minutes. Cool 10 minutes before removing cake to cooling rack.

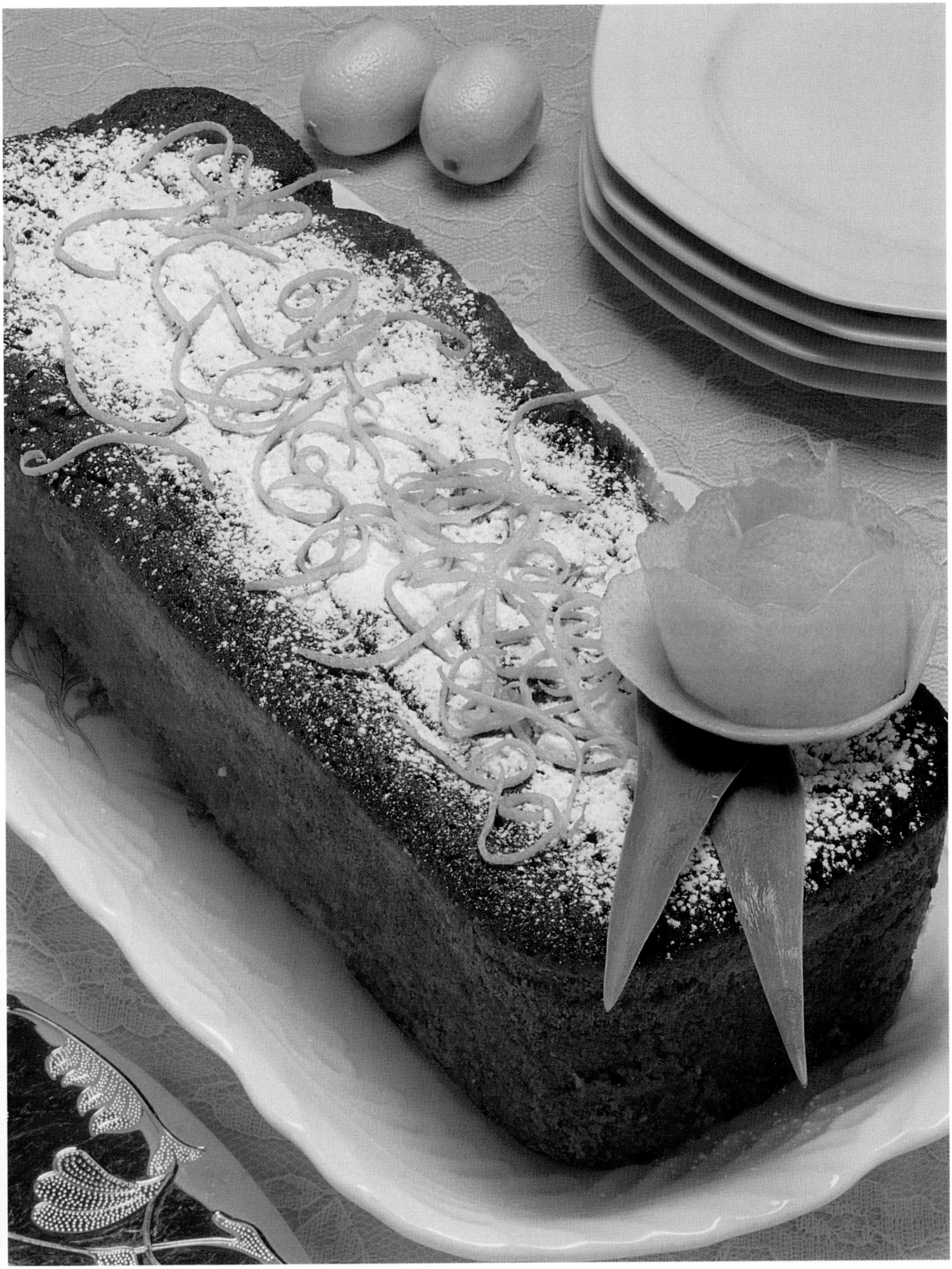

Old Fashion Butter Pound Cake

Sacher Torte Chef K

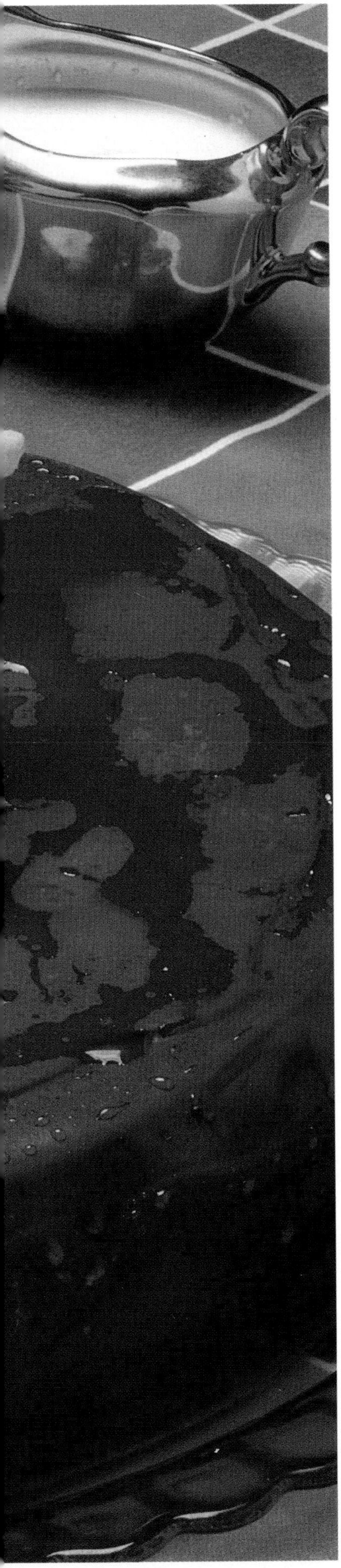

SACHER TORTE CHEF K

CAKE:		
3 oz	85 g	bittersweet chocolate
2 oz	60 g	semi-sweet chocolate
2 cups	500 ml	pastry flour
¼ tsp	2 ml	salt
6	6	eggs, separated
½ cup	125 ml	butter
1½ cups	375 ml	granulated sugar

In a double boiler melt the chocolate. Sift the flour and salt together, twice. Whip the egg whites to soft peaks. Cream the butter with sugar to very light. Add the egg yolks beating after each. Fold in the flour and chocolate in 3 thirds. Fold in the egg whites. Pour into a 9" (23 cm) buttered and floured spring form pan. Bake in a preheated 350°F (180°C) oven for 45 minutes or until an inserted toothpick comes out clean. Cool 10 minutes then transfer cake to cooling rack.

FROSTING:		
½ cup	125 ml	apricot preserve
½ lb	340 g	almond paste *
10 oz	300 g	semi-sweet chocolate
1½ tsp	8 ml	oil
1 cup	250 ml	whipping cream

Heat the apricot until thin, spread on the cake. Roll almond paste thin on a lightly cornstarch dusted surface. Cover the entire cake then trim to fit.

Heat the chocolate in a double boiler. Stir in the oil and pour the chocolate over the cake. Refrigerate 1 hour. Whip the cream and serve on the side with the cake.

* Almond paste may be purchased from any cake decorating store or bakery.

STRAWBERRY SHERBET

2 cups	500 ml	strawberries
2 cups	500 ml	granulated sugar
2 cups	500 ml	milk

Wash and hull the berries. Mash the berries and cook over low-medium heat with the sugar. Bring to a boil, and boil 10 minutes. Purée in a food processor, strain to remove seeds and pulp. Return to a sauce pan, mix in the milk and boil for 5 minutes. Cool and chill. Freeze in ice cream maker according to directions.

YIELDS 6 CUPS (1.5 L)

PEANUT BUTTER CUP CHEESECAKE

CRUST:		
3 cups	750 ml	chocolate wafer crumbs
3 tbsp	45 ml	granulated sugar
¼ cup	60 ml	butter – melted

Combine the ingredients. Press into the bottom and sides of a buttered 9" (23 cm) spring form pan. Chill.

FILLING:		
1½ lbs	750 g	cream cheese
1 cup	250 ml	granulated sugar
4	4	eggs
3 oz	85 g	semi-sweet chocolate – melted
1 tbsp	15 ml	cocoa powder
¾ cup	180 ml	smooth peanut butter

Cream the cheese and sugar together. Beat in the eggs one at a time. Divide the batter in two. Beat the chocolate and cocoa into one half then the peanut butter into the second. Pour the chocolate into the shell and bake 30 minutes in a preheated 350°F (180°C) oven. Pour the peanut butter batter over and continue to bake for an additional 40 minutes. Turn oven off prop the door open and leave cake in for 30 minutes. Transfer to a cooling rack, cool to room temperature, before topping.

TOPPING:		
¼ cup	60 ml	white corn syrup
3 tbsp	45 ml	water
2½ tbsp	38 ml	butter
5 oz	150 g	semi-sweet chocolate chips
½ cup	125 ml	salted peanuts
2 cups	500 ml	whipping cream, whipped

Combine the corn syrup, water and butter in a sauce pan. Bring to a rapid boil, stirring until butter is melted. Remove from heat. Add the chocolate and stir until melted, cool to room temperature.

Pour chocolate over cake. Decorate with whipped cream. Sprinkle with nuts. Serve.

BLUEBERRY PIE

1 quan	1 quan	Plain Pastry (see page 616)
3 cups	750 ml	blueberries
3 tbsp	45 ml	flour, all purpose
¾ cup	180 ml	granulated sugar
2 tbsp	30 ml	lemon juice
1 tsp	5 ml	vanilla
1 tbsp	15 ml	butter
1	1	egg

Roll out half the pastry and fit into a 9" (23 cm) pie pan. Wash and sort the berries. Mix the flour with the sugar then sprinkle half over the pastry in the pan. Add the berries sprinkle with the remaining flour sugar. Sprinkle the lemon juice and vanilla over. Dot with the butter. Roll out the remaining dough and fit on top. Moisten the edges and fold under the bottom layer. Flute the edges. Cut the top to allow steam to escape, brush with beaten egg. Bake in a preheated 450°F (230°C) oven for 15 minutes reduce heat to 325°F (160°C) and continue to bake for 20 minutes. Cool completely before serving.

SERVES 6

Blueberry Pie

Peanut Butter Cup Cheesecake

Swiss Chocolate Torte with Milk Chocolate Frosting

SWISS CHOCOLATE TORTE

¾ cup	180 ml	pastry flour
½ tsp	3 ml	baking powder
¼ tsp	1 ml	baking soda
½ tsp	3 ml	salt
4	4	eggs
¾ cup	180 ml	granulated sugar
3 oz	80 g	grated semi-sweet chocolate
1 tsp	5 ml	vanilla extract
¼ cup	60 ml	cold water

Sift together the flour, baking powder, baking soda and salt, twice.

Beat the eggs and gradually add the sugar beating until 3 times in volume. Fold in the flour.

Melt the chocolate in a sauce pan with the vanilla and water, fold into the batter. Pour the batter into 3-9" (23 cm) buttered and floured cake pans. Bake 18-20 minutes in a preheated 350°F (180°C) oven.

Cool 10 minutes and transfer to a cooling rack, turn cakes out, cool completely. Fill and frost with Milk Chocolate Frosting (recipe follows).

MILK CHOCOLATE FROSTING

4 oz	120 g	milk chocolate
½ cup	125 ml	unsalted butter
3 cups	750 ml	confectioners' sugar
⅓ cup	80 ml	milk
2	2	egg whites, room temperature
½ tsp	3 ml	vanilla extract

Melt the chocolate and butter in a double boiler over low heat. Remove from the heat, whip in remaining ingredients. Place in a bowl of ice and beat until very creamy.

SWEET POTATO PIE

½ cup	125 ml	granulated sugar
¼ tsp	1 ml	salt
1 tsp	5 ml	cinnamon
1 tsp	5 ml	nutmeg
½ tsp	3 ml	ground ginger
2 cups	500 ml	sweet potatoes, boiled and mashed smooth
1 cup	250 ml	milk
2	2	eggs
½ quan	0.5 quan	Plain Pastry (see page 616)
2 cups	500 ml	whipped cream

Combine the dry ingredients. Mix into the sweet potatoes. Blend in the milk and eggs.

Roll out the dough and fit into a 9" (23 cm) pie plate. Pour in potato mixture.

Bake in a preheated 450°F (230°C) oven for 10 minutes. Reduce temperature to 350°F (180°C) and continue to bake for 35 minutes longer. Cool, then chill.

Pipe whipped cream over and serve.

SERVES 8

Sweet Potato Pie

CHOCOLATE PEPPERMINT PATTIES

2 cups	500 ml	condensed milk – sweetened
2 tsp	10 ml	peppermint extract
10 drops	10	green food colouring
32 oz	960 ml	confectioners' sugar
4 oz	120 g	semi-sweet chocolate
1 oz	30 g	edible food wax

Blend the milk, extract and food colouring together. Add the sugar but only enough for mixture to form a firm non-sticky ball. Shape into even size balls. Flatten. Heat the chocolate with the wax. Skewer the patties with a toothpick then dip into the chocolate. Set in a pastry sheet and allow chocolate to harden.

YIELDS 64 PATTIES

PEPPERMINT STICK PIE

CRUST:

3 cups	750 ml	chocolate wafer crusts
3 tbsp	45 ml	granulated sugar
¼ cup	60 ml	butter – melted

Combine the wafers, sugar and butter. Press into the sides and bottom of a 9" (23 cm) spring form pan. Bake in a preheated 350°F (180°C) oven for 7 minutes. Cool then chill.

FILLING:

6 oz	180 g	mint chocolate chips
¼ cup	60 ml	cream
½ quan	0.5 quan	Cafe Mint Ice Cream (see page 669)
½ quan	0.5 quan	French Vanilla Ice Cream (see page 547)

Heat the chocolate chips and cream together in a double boiler, cook until thick. Cool then chill.

Pour half the sauce over the bottom of the shell. Layer four layers of ice cream alternating the cafe mint with vanilla. Pour the remaining sauce over the final layer. Freeze four hours before serving.

SERVES 8-10

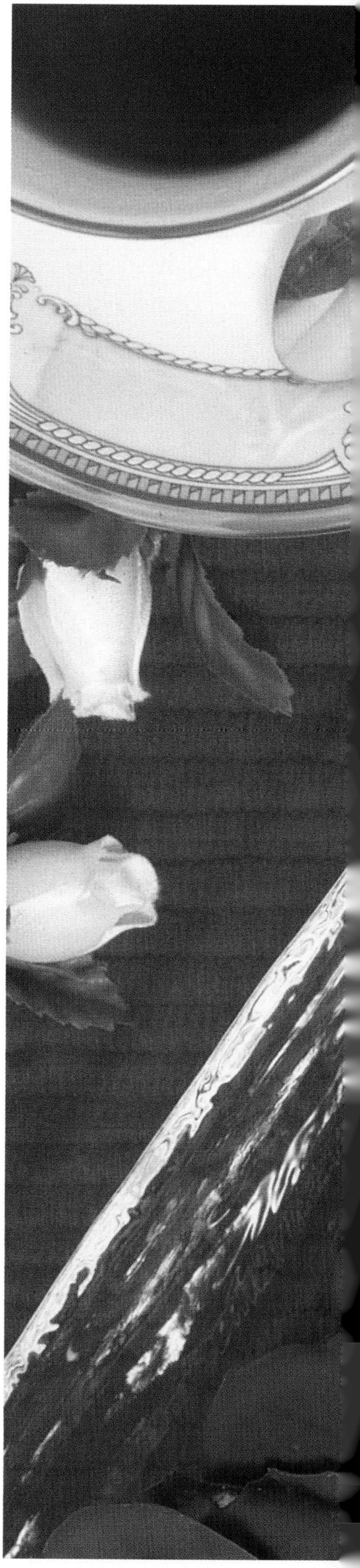

Chocolate Peppermint Patties

Calvados Chocolate Mousse Torte

CALVADOS CHOCOLATE MOUSSE TORTE

CRUST:

2 cups	500 ml	chocolate wafer crumbs
¼ cup	60 ml	butter melted

Combine the ingredients. Press in a 8" (20 cm) spring form pan. Chill.

FILLING:

1 lb	450 g	semi-sweet chocolate – chopped
6	6	large eggs
¼ cup	60 ml	Calvados liqueur, or apple brandy
2 cups	500 ml	cream – whipping
¼ tsp	2 ml	salt

Melt the chocolate in a large bowl, set over simmering water. Cool. Whip 2 eggs plus egg yolks into the chocolate. Add the Calvados blending to smooth. Whip the cream to stiff. Whip four egg whites and salt stiff but not dry. Fold the cream and egg whites in alternating each. Pour into the shell. Freeze 3-4 hours. Spread topping over.

TOPPING:

1 cup	250 ml	cream – whipping
3 tbsp	45 ml	confectioners' sugar
1 tbsp	15 ml	Calvados
½ cup	125 ml	chocolate curls

Whip the cream. Stir in the sugar and liqueur. Spread on the cake and freeze 24 hours. Garnish with curls.

LEMON CHIFFON PIE

1 tbsp	15 ml	unflavoured gelatin
¼ cup	60 ml	cold water
4	4	eggs – separated
¾ cup	180 ml	granulated sugar
¼ tsp	2 ml	salt
¼ cup	60 ml	lemon juice
½ tsp	3 ml	lemon rind – grated
1	1	Gingersnap Crust (recipe follows)

Soak the gelatin in the water. Combine the egg yolks, ½ cup (125 ml) sugar, salt, lemon juice and lemon rind in a double boiler cooking until thick. Cool and refrigerate until thick but not set.

Whip the egg whites until stiff, gradually add the sugar. Fold into the lemon mixture. Pour into the pie shell and set. Once set, cut and serve.

SERVES 6

GINGERSNAP CRUST

1¼ cups	310 ml	gingersnaps – crushed fine
¼ cup	60 ml	butter soft

Blend the gingersnaps with the butter thoroughly. Press into the sides and bottom of a 8" (20 cm) pie pan. Bake 10 minutes in a preheated 350°F (180°C) oven. Use as required.

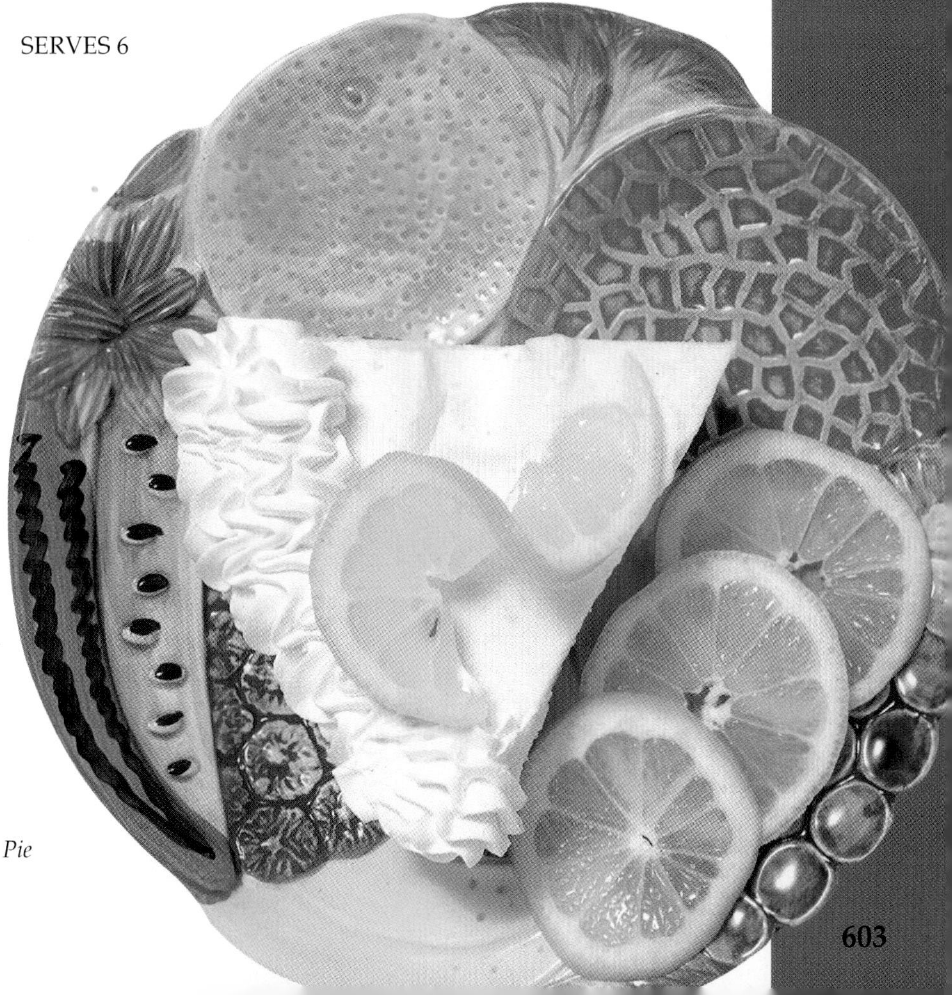

Lemon Chiffon Pie

KAHLUA RUM TORTE

½ cup	125 ml	butter
2 cups	500 ml	brown sugar
3	3	eggs – separated
2 cups	500 ml	pastry flour
¼ tsp	2 ml	salt
2 tsp	10 ml	baking powder
1 tsp	5 ml	cinnamon
½ tsp	3 ml	cloves
¼ tsp	1 ml	nutmeg
¼ cup	60 ml	Kahlua liqueur
¼ cup	60 ml	dark rum
½ cup	125 ml	sour cream

Cream the butter and sugar until very light. Add the egg yolks beating after each addition. Whip the whites stiff and reserve. Sift together the flour, salt, baking powder and spices, twice. Blend the Kahlua, rum and sour cream. Incorporate the flour and liquid into creamed mixture in thirds. Fold in the egg whites. Pour batter into a 9" (23 cm) square buttered cake pan. Bake in a preheated 350°F (180°C) oven for 50 minutes. Cool 10 minutes, transfer cake to cooling rack. Slice cake into 3 layers, frost with Calypso Coffee Frosting when cool (recipe follows).

CALYPSO COFFEE FROSTING

½ cup	125 ml	butter, room temperature
3 cups	750 ml	confectioners' sugar
1 cup	250 ml	cocoa
2 tbsp	30 ml	milk
¼ cup	60 ml	Kahlua liqueur
¼ cup	60 ml	dark rum

Cream the butter, add the confectioners' sugar. Gradually blend in the cocoa with the liquid ingredients alternating in ⅓rds. Once all ingredients are well incorporated, beat on high for 3 minutes until light and creamy. Use as directed, excellent to frost Kahlua Rum Torte.

BRISTOL PEARS

1¼ cups	310 ml	water
1¼ cups	310 ml	granulated sugar
1 tsp	5 ml	vanilla
6	6	pears – pared, cored
3 cups	750 ml	French Vanilla Ice Cream (see page 547)
2 cups	500 ml	Raspberry Sauce (see page 107)
2 cups	500 ml	very small strawberries – hulled, washed
1½ cups	375 ml	whipping cream – whipped

Blend the water, sugar and vanilla in a sauce pan, bring to a boil, reduce to a simmer. Poach the pears in the simmering syrup until tender. Drain, cool and chill. Place ½ cup (125 ml) of ice cream in over sized champagne glasses. Top with a pear, smother with sauce, sprinkle with strawberries. Pipe rosette of whipped cream on and serve.

SERVES 6

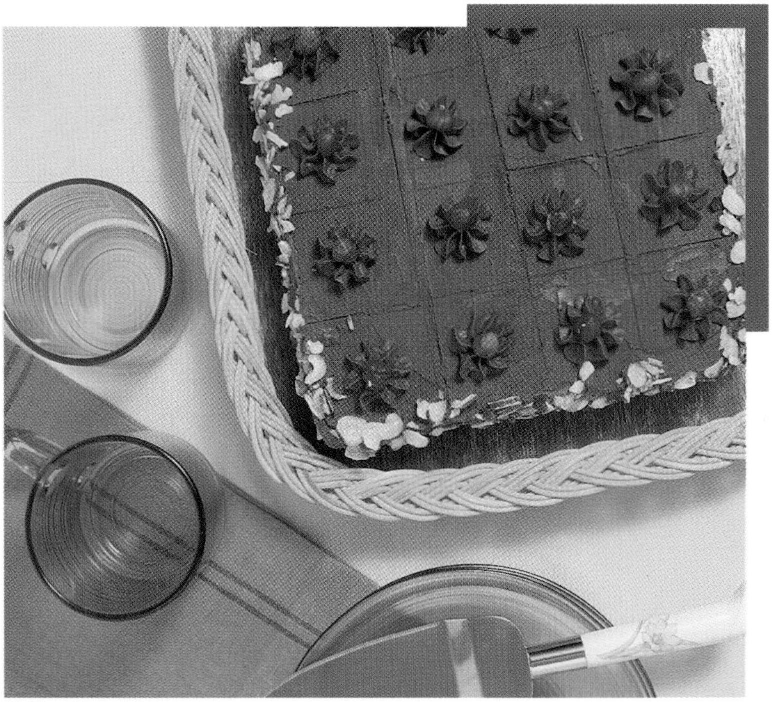

Kahlua Rum Torte

Bristol Pears

Silver Miner's Cak

BUTTERSCOTCH CHOCOLATE CHIP CHEWS

¾ cup	180 ml	butter
¾ cup	180 ml	brown sugar
⅓ cup	80 ml	granulated sugar
1	1	egg
1	1	egg yolk
1½ tsp	8 ml	vanilla
1½ cup	375 ml	flour, pastry
¾ tsp	4 ml	baking soda
¾ tsp	4 ml	salt
¾ cup	180 ml	butterscotch chips
¾ cup	180 ml	chocolate chips
¾ cup	180 ml	walnuts – pieces

Cream the butter, brown sugar and sugar until pale and light. Beat in the egg, egg yolk and vanilla. Sift the flour, soda and salt together, fold into creamed mixture. Fold in the chips and nuts. Pour batter into a 9 x 9" (23 x 23 cm) buttered pan. Bake in a preheated 350°F (180°C) oven for 40-45 minutes or until browned nicely. Cool and cut into squares.

YIELDS 36

HONOLULU BARS

1½ cups	375 ml	granulated sugar
4	4	eggs – beaten
½ cup	125 ml	buttered – melted
1½ cups	375 ml	flour, pastry
½ cup	125 ml	coconut – shredded
¾ cup	180 ml	macadamia nuts – pieces
½ tsp	3 ml	baking soda
½ tsp	3 ml	salt
2 cups	500 ml	pineapple – crushed, drained

In a mixing bowl beat the sugar into the eggs. Whip the butter, then fold in the remaining ingredients. Pour into a greased 13" x 9" (32 x 23 cm) pan. Bake in a preheated 350°F (180°C) oven for 30-35 minutes. Cool before cutting into squares.

MAKES 2 DOZ

SILVER MINER'S CAKE

¾ cup	180 ml	butter
2 cups	500 ml	granulated sugar
2 cups	500 ml	pastry flour
4 tsp	20 ml	baking powder
¼ tsp	2 ml	salt
8	8	egg whites
½ cup	125 ml	milk
1½ tsp	7 ml	almond extract

Cream the butter with the sugar. Whip the egg whites, one at a time into the butter mixture, mixing well after each addition. Sift the flour, baking powder and salt together. Add the flour and milk in thirds incorporating well. Add the extract. Pour into 2-9" (23 cm) buttered and floured round cake pans. Bake in a preheated 350°F (180°C) oven for 20-25 minutes. Cool 10 minutes, turn out onto cooling rack. Fill and frost with your choice of frosting.

Butterscotch Chocolate Chip Chews

Larry Hohn's Rocky Road Squares

LARRY HOHN'S ROCKY ROAD SQUARES

½ cup	125 ml	shortening
2 oz	60 g	bitter sweet chocolate
1 cup	250 ml	granulated sugar
2	2	eggs beaten
½ cup	125 ml	flour, pastry
¼ tsp	1 ml	baking powder
½ tsp	3 ml	salt
1 tsp	5 ml	vanilla extract
½ cup	125 ml	chopped nuts
2 cups	500 ml	miniature marshmallows
3 oz	85 g	semi-sweet chocolate
1 tsp	5 ml	melted butter

In a double boiler melt the shortening and bitter chocolate. Whip in the sugar and eggs then remove from the heat.

Sift the flour, baking powder and salt together then fold into the batter. Stir in the vanilla and nuts. Pour batter into a 8" x 8" (20 x 20 cm) square pan. Bake in a preheated 325°F (160°C) oven for 25-30 minutes.

Remove from the oven. Sprinkle with marshmallows. Melt the semi-sweet chocolate in a double boiler, stir in the butter then pour over the marshmallows. Cut into squares before serving.

YIELDS 20 SQUARES

CHOCOLATE NUT MINT SLICE

1½ cups	375 ml	flour, all purpose
½ cup	125 ml	brown sugar
¾ cup	180 ml	butter
¾ cup	180 ml	coconut shredded
¾ cup	180 ml	walnut – pieces
3 tbsp	45 ml	cream – half & half
1½ cups	375 ml	confectioners' sugar
¾ tsp	4 ml	mint flavouring
½ tsp	3 ml	green food colouring
3 oz	85 g	unsweetened chocolate – grated
2	2	egg yolks
¼cup	60 ml	granulated sugar
3 tbsp	45 ml	water
1 tsp	5 ml	instant coffee crystals

Blend the flour with the brown sugar. Cut in ¾ cup (175 ml) butter. Fold in the coconut and walnuts. Pour batter into a ungreased 9 x 9" (23 x 23 cm) pan. Bake for 30 minutes in a preheated 350°F (180°C) oven. Remove and cool completely.

Blend the cream, confectioners' sugar, mint flavouring and food colouring. Spread over the cake.

Melt the chocolate in a double boiler over very low heat. Beat the egg yolks until foamy.

In a sauce pan boil the sugar, water and coffee, boil rapidly for 1 minute. Remove from the heat. Slowly beat syrup into egg yolks in a slow stream. Cream for 5 minutes. Fold in the chocolate. Pour over the cake and refrigerate until set. Cut into 36 squares.

Chocolate Nut Mint Slice

Blueberry Apples Rocky Mountain

BLUEBERRY APPLES ROCKY MOUNTAINS

6	6	large red apples
3 tbsp	45 ml	lemon juice
1 cup	250 ml	granulated sugar
¼ cup	60 ml	cornstarch
2	2	eggs
1 cup	250 ml	milk
¼ cup	60 ml	Calvados liqueur or apple juice concentrate
¼ tsp	1 ml	salt
2 pints	0.5 L	fresh blueberries – washed, hulled
¼ cup	60 ml	confectioners' sugar

Cut the tops from the apples, scoop out the pulp reserving 2 cups (500 ml). Brush the top and insides of apples with lemon juice. Combine the sugar, cornstarch and eggs together in a double boiler. Add the milk and Calvados, cook stirring until very thick. Stir in the apple pulp, and salt, fill apple shells with mixture. Cool, then chill. Top with mounds of blueberries and dust with confectioners' sugar.

SERVES 6

FRUIT COCKTAIL CAKE

2 cups	500 ml	flour, all purpose
1½ cups	375 ml	granulated sugar
2 cups	500 ml	fruit cocktail
2 tsp	10 ml	baking soda
2	2	eggs, beaten
pinch	pinch	salt
		Fruit Cocktail Cake Icing (recipe follows)

Mix all ingredients by hand in a 9 x 13" (23 x 32 cm) pan. Bake in a preheated 350°F (180°C) oven for about 40 minutes.

SERVES 8

FRUIT COCKTAIL CAKE ICING

1½ cups	375 ml	granulated sugar
6 oz	170 g	butter
1 cup	250 ml	undiluted evaporated milk
½ cup	125 ml	pecans
½ cup	125 ml	coconut, shredded

Cook sugar, butter and milk until thick. Remove from heat and add pecans and coconut. Pour over hot cake.

CHOCOLATE BAVARIAN

1 tbsp	15 ml	unflavoured gelatin
¼ cup	60 ml	cold water
5	5	egg yolks
½ cup	125 ml	granulated sugar
1 cup	250 ml	cream – half & half
1 tsp	5 ml	vanilla
6 oz	120 g	semi-sweet chocolate – grated
2 cups	500 ml	cream – whipping
½ cup	125 ml	toasted almonds

Soften the gelatin in the cold water. Beat the egg yolks until pale with the sugar. Heat the half & half and vanilla in a sauce pan to scalding. Add the gelatin then slowly add the egg. Cook until thick, remove from the heat. Stir in the chocolate, stir until chocolate has melted. Cool then chill until very thick but not set. Whip the cream, fold into the chocolate mixture. Pour into a mold or bowl and refrigerate until set. Unmold and serve sprinkled with toasted almonds.

SERVES 6-8

Chocolate Bavarian

CHEF K'S CHOCOLATE PEAR TORTE

CAKE:		
2 cups	500 ml	flour, pastry
¼ cup	60 ml	granulated sugar
1 cup	250 ml	butter
3	3	egg yolks

Combine the flour and sugar, cut the butter in to form a coarse dough. Beat in the egg yolks. Press into the bottom and 1" (2.5 cm) up the sides of a buttered 10" (25 cm) spring form pan. Bake in a preheated 350°F (180°C) oven for 20-25 minutes. Cool.

FILLING:		
½ cup	125 ml	raspberry preserves
6 oz	180 g	semi-sweet chocolate – grated
6 oz	180 g	cream cheese
3 tbsp	45 ml	milk
3 cups	750 ml	confectioners' sugar
¼ tsp	1 ml	salt
1 tsp	5 ml	vanilla

Spread the preserves over the cake. Melt the chocolate in a double boiler. Cream the cheese with the milk, gradually add the sugar, salt and vanilla. Cream in the chocolate. Spread over the raspberry preserves. Chill.

TOPPING:		
1 cup	250 ml	water
1 cup	250 ml	granulated sugar
1 tsp	5 ml	vanilla extract
5	5	pears – pared, cored, halved
8 oz	225 g	semi-sweet chocolate, melted
1 tbsp	15 ml	butter – melted

Heat the water, sugar and vanilla in a sauce pan, bring to a boil and reduce to a simmer. Poach the pears until tender. Drain and cool. Arrange on top of filling. Pour chocolate mixed with butter over pears. Chill 1 hour before serving.

Chef K's Chocolate Pear Torte

Lemon Cream Dream

Apple Sauce Bars

APPLE SAUCE BARS

⅓ cup	80 ml	butter
1 cup	250 ml	brown sugar – packed
1	1	egg
½ cup	125 ml	applesauce
2 tsp	10 ml	apple juice – concentrated
1¼ cups	310 ml	flour, pastry
1 tsp	5 ml	baking powder
½ tsp	3 ml	baking soda
½ tsp	3 ml	salt
½ cup	125 ml	raisins – seedless
½ cup	125 ml	walnut pieces

Heat the butter and sugar in a saucepan until sugar is dissolved. Whip in the egg, applesauce, and juice. Sift the flour together with the baking powder, baking soda and salt. Stir in the sauce. Fold in the raisins and walnuts. Pour into a greased 9 x 10" (23 x 25 cm) pan. Bake for 25 minutes in a preheated 350°F (180°C) oven. Remove from the oven and glaze with apple glaze. Cut the bars.

APPLE GLAZE:

1½ cups	375 ml	confectioners' sugar
2 tbsp	30 ml	apple juice – concentrate

Blend the ingredients until smooth, pour over bars.

LEMON CREAM DREAM

1 cup	250 ml	granulated sugar
⅛ tsp	pinch	salt
1½ tbsp	25 ml	cornstarch
½ cup	125 ml	cold water
1¼ cups	310 ml	milk
3	3	eggs separated
½ cup	125 ml	lemon juice
1 tsp	5 ml	lemon rind – grated

Blend the sugar, salt and cornstarch. Place in a double boiler and blend in the water and milk. Cook for 15 minutes covered.

Whip in the egg yolks, lemon juice and rind, cook for 2 minutes longer stirring constantly. Cool to room temperature.

Whip the egg whites stiff, fold into the lemon mixture. Pour into wine glasses and chill for 3 hours before serving.

SERVES 4

CARAMELS

2 cups	500 ml	granulated sugar
¼ tsp	1 ml	salt
2 cups	500 ml	corn syrup
½ cup	125 ml	butter
2 cups	500 ml	evaporated milk – sweetened
1 tsp	5 ml	vanilla

In a heavy sauce pan over medium heat combine the sugar, salt and syrup bring to a boil heating to 245°F (118°C) stir occasionally. Slowly add the butter and milk but not fast enough to lose the boil. Continue to cook returning to 245°F (118°C). Remove from heat and stir in the flavouring. Pour into a buttered 9" x 9" (23 x 23 cm) square pan. Cool thoroughly before cutting, then wrap in wax paper.

YIELDS 2 LBS (900 g)

CHEESE CHERRY PIE 1

½ quan	0.5	Plain Pastry (recipe follows)
2½ cups	625 ml	cherry pie filling
½ tsp	3 ml	almond extract
8 oz	225 g	cream cheese
1	1	egg
½ cup	125 ml	granulated sugar
¼ cup	60 ml	toasted sliced almonds

Roll out the pastry and fit into a 9" (23 cm) pie pan. Blind bake the crust. (See glossary for blind baking). Cool the crust.

Mix the cherry pie filling with the almond extract. Spread over pie crust.

Blend the cream cheese, egg and sugar together. Pour over cherry's. Bake for 30 minutes in a preheated 350°F (180°C) oven. Five minutes before completion sprinkle with almonds. Cool, then chill before serving.

SERVES 6

PLAIN PASTRY

1½ cups	375 ml	sifted all purpose flour
¼ tsp	2 ml	salt
½ cup	125 ml	shortening
4-5 tbsp	60-75 ml	water

Sift the flour and salt together into a mixing bowl. Cut shortening into flour with a pastry cutter or fork until pastry forms walnut size. Add the water and toss. However only enough to bind the pastry. Divide pastry in two and chill covered. Use as directed.

CHEESE CHERRY PIE 2

8 oz	225 g	cream cheese
1½ cups	375 ml	sweet condensed milk
⅓ cup	80 ml	lemon juice
1 tsp	5 ml	vanilla
1	1	Rolled Oats Crust (see page 627)
2½ cups	625 ml	cherry pie filling

Whip the cream cheese until very light. Slowly add the milk while beating. Whip in the lemon and vanilla. Fold into the pie shell. Refrigerate 4 hours. Spread cherries over top and serve.

SERVES 6

CHOCOLATE MARSHMALLOW BARS

2 oz	60 g	unsweetened chocolate
½ cup	125 ml	butter
1 cup	250 ml	granulated sugar
2	2	eggs
½ cup	125 ml	flour, pastry
1 tsp	5 ml	vanilla extract
1 cup	250 ml	chopped pecans
16	16	large marshmallows

Preheat oven to 350°F (180°C). Grease an 11 ½ x 7" (29 x 18 cm) baking pan.

Melt chocolate and butter in top of double boiler. Set aside.

Cream sugar and eggs until light and fluffy. Add flour. Beat. Add melted chocolate and butter. Beat well. Mix in vanilla and pecans.

Pour into prepared pan. Bake 18 minutes. Remove from oven and cover with marshmallows. Return to oven and bake until marshmallows are lightly browned.

Cool slightly and cut into bars.

YIELDS 16 BARS

Cheese Cherry Pie I

Southern Peach 'n' Pecan Cookies

PEACH COBBLER

1¾ cups	430 ml	granulated sugar
2 tbsp	30 ml	cornstarch
½ tsp	3 ml	cinnamon – ground
1 cup	250 ml	water
2 tbsp	30 ml	butter
5 cups	1250 ml	fresh peaches – peeled, sliced
1 cup	250 ml	pastry flour
1 tsp	5 ml	baking powder
1 tsp	5 ml	salt
1	1	egg
¼ cup	60 ml	shortening
½ cup	125 ml	cream – light
½ tsp	3 ml	vanilla

Blend 1 cup (250 ml) sugar, cornstarch and cinnamon in the water. Bring to a boil, stirring constantly. Whip in the butter and stir in the peaches. Pour into a shallow buttered 9" x 9" (23 x 23 cm) baking pan. Sift the flour, baking powder, salt together. Stir in the remaining sugar. Beat and cut in the remaining ingredients until very light and smooth. Spread over peaches. Bake in a preheated 350°F (180°C) oven for 35 minutes or until golden brown. Serve warm, with cream.

SERVES 6

Peach Cobbler

SOUTHERN PEACH 'N' PECAN COOKIES

2½ cups	625 ml	peach pulp
½ cup	125 ml	granulated sugar
2 cups	500 ml	flour, all purpose
½ tsp	3 ml	salt
2 tsp	10 ml	baking powder
½ tsp	3 ml	cinnamon
½ cup	125 ml	shortening
1 cup	250 ml	granulated sugar
1	1	egg – beaten
1 cup	250 ml	pecans – broken

In a sauce pan heat the peach pulp and ½ cup (125 ml) of sugar. Simmer gently reducing to ¾ cup (180 ml). Cool to room temperature. Sift the flour, salt, baking powder and cinnamon.

Cream the shortening and sugar until very light. Add the egg and peach sauce, mix well.

Add the flour and nuts mixing well. Drop teaspoon size dough onto a lightly greased pastry sheet. Bake 12-15 minutes in a preheated 400°F (200°C) oven.

MAKES 4 DOZEN

BANANA FETTUCCINI FOSTER

1 quan	1 quan	Banana Pasta (see page 433)
3 tbsp	45 ml	unsalted butter
3 tbsp	45 ml	granulated sugar
2	2	sliced bananas
¼ cup	60 ml	banana liqueur
¼ cup	60 ml	dark rum
½ cup	125 ml	orange juice

Process the pasta as directed, cut into fettuccini.

Heat the butter in a sauce pan. Add the sugar and cook until the sugar turns golden colour (caramelizes).

Add the bananas and cook 1 minute. Add the liqueurs, turn pan away from you and carefully flame. Pour in the orange juice and simmer for 5 minutes.

Cook the pasta in a large kettle of boiling water. Drain. Toss the pasta with sauce. Serve.

SERVES 6

Apricot Torte Chef K

APRICOT TORTE CHEF K

CAKE:		
1 cup	250 ml	granulated sugar
¼ cup	60 ml	water
4 oz	120 g	semi-sweet chocolate – grated
⅓ cup	80 ml	butter
8	8	eggs – separated
1¾ cups	430 ml	ground hazelnuts
2 tbsp	30 ml	fine bread crumbs

In a sauce pan combine the sugar and water, boil until sugar dissolves, remove from heat and stir in chocolate. Cool. Cream the butter until light and pale. Beat in the egg yolks one at a time, be sure each is incorporated before the next addition. Slowly beat in half the chocolate, then alternate for the hazelnuts, finish the chocolate then the hazelnuts and crumbs. Whip the egg whites stiff, fold gradually into batter. Pour into a 10" (23 cm) buttered spring form pan. Bake in a preheated 350°F (180°C) oven for 35-40 minutes, cool 15 minutes transfer to cooling rack, cool for 2-3 hours slicing in half.

FILLING:		
1 cup	250 ml	granulated sugar
¼ cup	60 ml	cornstarch
2	2	eggs
1 cup	250 ml	milk
½ cup	125 ml	apricot preserves
¼ cup	60 ml	peach schnapps liqueur

Blend the sugar, cornstarch and eggs in a double boiler. Stir in the milk, apricots and schnapps, cook slowly until very thick. Cool, spread between and on top of cakes.

TOPPING:		
20	20	apricots – peeled, stoned
⅓ cup	80 ml	apricot preserves – heated

Cut the apricots in half, place on top of cake. Glaze with preserves. Chill one hour before serving.

SERVES 12

ROB BOY COOKIES

½ cup	125 ml	shortening
¾ cup	180 ml	brown sugar
½ tsp	3 ml	salt
¼ tsp	2 ml	cinnamon
¼ tsp	2 ml	cloves – ground
⅛ cup	30 ml	buttermilk
1	1	egg
1 cup	250 ml	flour, pastry
¾ cup	180 ml	rolled instant oats
½ cup	125 ml	walnut pieces
½ cup	125 ml	raisins
½ cup	125 ml	dates – chopped
½ tsp	3 ml	soda

Cream the shortening with the brown sugar, salt and spices. Beat in the milk and egg. Stir in the remaining ingredients.

Drop teaspoon size dough on a greased baking sheet. Bake for 12-15 minutes in a preheated 375°F (190°C) oven.

YIELDS 3 DOZEN

Rob Boy Cookies

Pumpkin Bars

PUMPKIN BARS

2 cups	500 ml	pumpkin
4	4	eggs – beaten
1 cup	250 ml	oil
2 cups	500 ml	flour, all purpose
1 cup	250 ml	brown sugar
1 cup	250 ml	granulated sugar
¼ tsp	2 ml	salt
1 tsp	5 ml	baking powder
1 tsp	5 ml	baking soda
1½ tsp	8 ml	cinnamon
½ tsp	3 ml	cloves
½ tsp	3 ml	nutmeg

Blend the pumpkin, eggs and oil in a mixing bowl. Blend all the dry ingredients together, then fold into the pumpkin. Pour onto a greased large square cake pan. Bake in a preheated 350°F (180°C) oven for 20-25 minutes. Remove from the oven and cool to room temperature before frosting with Cream Cheese Frosting.

CREAM CHEESE FROSTING:		
3 oz	85 g	cream cheese – softened
⅓ cup	80 ml	butter
½ cup	125 ml	confectioners' sugar
½ tsp	3 ml	vanilla
1½ tsp	8 ml	cream – light

Cream the cheese with the butter. Whip in the sugar, vanilla and light cream. Spread on Pumpkin Bars (above).

MAKES 20 SQUARES

CAFE AMARETTO FETTUCCINI

1 quan	1 quan	Pasta Cafe (see page 436)
¼ cup	60 ml	granulated sugar
¾ cup	180 ml	orange juice
1 tbsp	15 ml	lemon juice
1 tbsp	15 ml	unsalted butter
1 tbsp	15 ml	flour, all purpose
1 tbsp	15 ml	orange zest
½ cup	125 ml	chopped, toasted almonds
¼ cup	60 ml	Amaretto liqueur
¼ cup	60 ml	shaved chocolate

Process the pasta as directed and cut into fettuccini.

Dissolve the sugar in the orange and lemon juice. Heat the butter in a sauce pan. Add the flour and cook for 2 minutes. Do not brown. Add the sugared juices. Stir in the orange zest, almonds and Amaretto, reduce heat and simmer to a thin sauce.

In a kettle of boiling water cook the pasta al denté. Toss through sauce. Sprinkle with chocolate and serve.

SERVES 6

Sour Cream Rainbow Spice Cookies

SOUR CREAM RAINBOW SPICE COOKIES

½ cup	125 ml	butter
2 cups	500 ml	brown sugar
2 tsp	10 ml	cinnamon
½ tsp	3 ml	cloves
½ tsp	3 ml	nutmeg
¼ tsp	2 ml	salt
1 tsp	5 ml	vanilla
½ cup	125 ml	sour cream
2	2	eggs
3½ cups	875 ml	flour, all purpose
1 tsp	5 ml	baking powder
1 tsp	5 ml	baking soda
1 cup	250 ml	rainbow chocolate chips

Cream the butter, sugar and spices together. Beat in the salt, vanilla, sour cream and eggs. Sift the flour, powder and soda together. Blend into the creamed mixture, add rainbow chocolate chips.

Place teaspoon sizes of dough on a buttered pastry sheet, bake 10-12 minutes in a preheated 350°F (180°C) oven.

YIELDS 5 DOZEN

GOOSEBERRY FOOL

3 cups	750 ml	gooseberries
¾ cup	180 ml	granulated sugar
1 tsp	5 ml	vanilla extract
1½ cups	375 ml	whipping cream

Heat the gooseberries, sugar and vanilla in a sauce pan over low heat until thick. Purée in a food processor then pass through a sieve. Cool then chill. Whip the cream and fold into the gooseberries. Pour into chilled champagne glasses and serve.

SERVES 6

CREME DE MENTHE KAHLUA BARS

¼ cup	60 ml	butter
1 cup	250 ml	brown sugar – packed
1	1	egg
¼ cup	60 ml	Kahlua liqueur
¼ cup	60 ml	white creme de menthe liqueur
1½ cups	375 ml	flour, pastry
½ tsp	3 ml	baking powder
½ tsp	3 ml	baking soda
1 cup	250 ml	semi-sweet chocolate chips
2 tbsp	30 ml	green creme de menthe liqueur
1 cup	250 ml	confectioners' sugar

Cream the butter, sugar and egg, beating well. Whip in the liqueurs. Sift the flour, baking powder and baking soda together. Stir into creamed mixture, fold in the chocolate chips. Pour batter into a buttered 9" x 9" (23 x 23 cm) pan. Bake in a preheated 350°F (180°C) oven for 20-25 minutes.

Blend the green creme de menthe and confectioners' sugar, smooth over the cake, cool and cut into bars.

YIELDS 20 BARS

Creme de Menthe Kahlua Bars

Flaming Pears

CARROT APPLE SPICE BARS

½ cup	125 ml	butter
1 cup	250 ml	granulated sugar
2	2	eggs
1 cup	250 ml	flour, pastry
1 tsp	5 ml	baking powder
½ tsp	3 ml	baking soda
½ tsp	3 ml	salt
1 tbsp	15 ml	cocoa powder
1 tsp	5 ml	cinnamon
½ tsp	3 ml	nutmeg – grated
¼ tsp	2 ml	cloves
1 cup	250 ml	rolled oats
1 cup	250 ml	apples – pared, cored, grated
¾ cup	180 ml	carrots – pared, grated
½ cup	125 ml	walnuts – pieces

Cream the butter and sugar until very light and fluffy, Beat in the eggs one at a time. Sift together the flour, baking powder, baking soda, salt, cocoa powder and spices. Fold into the creamed mixture along with the oats. Stir in the apples, carrots and nuts. Pour batter into 12" x 16" (30 x 40 cm) greased pan. Bake in a preheated 375°F (190°C) oven for 25 minutes or until an inserted toothpick comes out clean. Frost with Cream Cheese Frosting (see Pumpkin Bars, page 623) before cutting.

MAKES 48

FLAMING PEARS

4	4	Bartlett pears
¼ cup	60 ml	butter
¼ cup	60 ml	granulated sugar
3 tbsp	45 ml	currants
⅓ cup	80 ml	Calvados liqueur
1 tsp	5 ml	cinnamon
2 cups	500 ml	French Vanilla Ice Cream (see page 547)

Pare, core and cut the pears in quarters. Heat the butter in a skillet, saute the pears. Sprinkle with sugar and continue to saute to caramelize. Add the currants, liqueur and cinnamon. Tilt the pan away from self and flame. Serve over the ice cream at once.

SERVES 4

ROLLED OATS CRUST

1 cup	250 ml	rolled oats
⅓ cup	80 ml	all purpose flour
⅓ cup	80 ml	brown sugar – packed
½ tsp	3 ml	salt
⅓ cup	80 ml	shortening – melted

Preheat oven to 375°F (190°C).

Combine rolled oats, flour, sugar and salt in a mixing bowl. Add the shortening and mix until crumbly. Pack into a 9" (23 cm) pie plate on the bottom and side. Place a 8" (20 cm) pie plate filled with dried beans or peas into the 9" (23 cm) plate. Bake 15 minutes. Stand 5 minutes. Remove small plate. Cool, use as required.

Carrot Apple Spice Bars

REFRIGERATOR CHERRY CHEESE CAKE

CRUST:		
2 cups	500 ml	chocolate graham wafer crumbs
2 tbsp	30 ml	granulated sugar
1/3 cup	80 ml	butter, melted

Combine the ingredients, press into an 8" (20 cm) spring form pan and chill.

FILLING:		
1 tbsp	15 ml	unflavoured gelatin
1/3 cup	80 ml	water
1 lb	450 g	cream cheese
1½ cups	375 ml	condensed milk
2 tsp	10 ml	white vanilla flavouring
1 cup	250 ml	whipped whipping cream
32 oz	900 g	cherry pie filling

Soften the gelatin in the water, then heat until the gelatin is dissolved. Remove from heat and cool.

Cream the cheese with the milk and vanilla. Stir in the gelatin. Fold in the whipped cream. Pour into the chocolate shell and refrigerate 4 hours.

Spread the cherry filling over and serve.

SERVES 10

Hazelnut Honey Cookies

HAZELNUT HONEY COOKIES

½ cup	125 ml	butter
¼ cup	60 ml	brown sugar
½ cup	125 ml	honey
1	1	egg
1 tsp	5 ml	vanilla
1½ cups	375 ml	flour, pastry
1 tsp	5 ml	baking powder
½ tsp	3 ml	baking soda
½ cup	125 ml	hazelnut pieces

Cream the butter, sugar, honey and egg together. Stir in the vanilla.

Sift the flour, baking powder and soda together then fold into the mixture with the nuts. Drop teaspoon sizes of dough onto a buttered pastry sheet. Bake in a preheated 400°F (200°C) oven for 12-15 minutes.

YIELDS 3 DOZEN

CARAMEL PUDDING

1 cup	250 ml	brown sugar
2 cups	500 ml	milk
¼ cup	60 ml	flour, all purpose
2	2	eggs
1 cup	250 ml	whipping cream

Blend the sugar into 1½ cup (375 ml) of milk. Scald in a double boiler until sugar is dissolved. Blend the flour in the remaining milk and beaten into egg yolks. Stir into the hot milk then continue to cook until thick. Whip the egg whites and fold into the cooled mixture. Chill until set. Whip cream and serve with pudding.

SERVES 8

Refrigerator Cherry Cheesecake

Dark Fruit Cake

DARK FRUIT CAKE

1 cup	250 ml	shortening
1 cup	250 ml	granulated sugar
4	4	eggs
1 cup	250 ml	molasses
1 cup	250 ml	strong coffee or rum
3½ cups	875 ml	all purpose flour
1 tsp	5 ml	each of salt, nutmeg, baking soda and cinnamon
¼ tsp	2 ml	cloves
1 cup	250 ml	strawberry jam
8 oz	225 g	cherries, glazed
8 oz	225 g	mixed fruit
2 lbs	900 g	each of raisins, dates, currents
1 lb	450 g	almond paste

Cream the shortening and sugar, add beaten eggs, molasses and coffee or rum. Mix well. Add spices to flour and add to mixture. Add strawberry jam and fruit last. Divide into two, five pound pans which have been greased and floured. Bake for 3 hours in a preheated oven at 275-300°F (150-160°C). Roll the almond paste and fit onto the cake. Refrigerate overnight or use as required.

NOTE: If rum is used instead of coffee allow the fruit to soak in it overnight for a better flavour.

PINEAPPLE GRANOLA BAR

5	5	granola bars
¼ cup	60 ml	butter
1½ cups	375 ml	whipping cream
¼ cup	60 ml	confectioners' sugar
½ tsp	3 ml	vanilla
2 cups	500 ml	crushed pineapple drained
4	4	egg whites
1 cup	250 ml	granulated sugar

Crush the granola bars and mix in the butter. Press into the bottom and sides of a buttered 9 x 9" square bake pan. Whip the cream, fold in the confectioners' sugar, vanilla and pineapple. Pour into the shell. Whip the egg white stiff and slowly add the sugar. Fold over the pineapple. Bake for 7-10 minutes in a 500°F (260°C) preheated oven. Serve.

SERVES 6

MERINGUE SHELL

4	4	egg whites
¼ tsp	1 ml	salt
¼ tsp	2 ml	cream of tartar
1 cup	250 ml	sugar - granulated
1 tsp	5 ml	white vanilla

Preheat the oven to 275°F (150°C). Grease a 9" (23 cm) pie pan.

Beat the egg whites with the salt until very foamy, while beating add the cream of tartar until egg whites form soft white peaks. Begin to add the sugar at 2 tbsp (30 ml) intervals. Whipping until all sugar is used and meringue is very thick. Add the vanilla. Pipe onto the pie shell. Cook in the oven for 45 minutes. Do not brown. Loose meringue, remove from pan cool, then fill as required.

NIAGARA PEACH PIE

½ quan	0.5 quan	Plain Pastry (see page 616)
2 lbs	900 g	peaches - peeled, stoned, halved
½ cup	125 ml	granulated sugar
3 tbsp	45 ml	cornstarch
¾ tsp	4 ml	cinnamon
¾ cup	180 ml	cream - heavy
1 tsp	5 ml	vanilla

Roll out the pastry and fit into a 9" (23 cm) pie pan. Flute the edges.

Arrange the peaches into the shell.

Blend the sugar, cornstarch, cinnamon, cream and vanilla, pour over the peaches. Bake in a preheated 400°F (200°C) oven for 40 minutes. Chill before slicing and serving.

SERVES 6

FRESH STRAWBERRY PIE

½ quan	0.5 quan	Plain Pastry (see page 616)
4 cups	1 L	strawberries - washed, hulled, halved
1 cup	250 ml	granulated sugar
1 tsp	5 ml	vanilla - white
⅓ cup	80 ml	cornstarch
1 tbsp	15 ml	lemon juice
1 cup	250 ml	whipped cream
¼ cup	60 ml	confectioners' sugar

Roll out the pastry and fit into a 9" (23 cm) pie pan. Flute the edges and blind bake. (See glossary for blind baking) Cool.

Place the strawberries in a mixing bowl. Sprinkle with sugar and stand refrigerated for 6 hours. Drain off the liquid. Add enough water to bring to 1¾ cups (440 ml) of liquid, add the vanilla.

Blend the cornstarch with the liquid and lemon juice. Cook over direct heat until the sauce thickens and clears. Transfer to a double boiler and continue to cook for 15 minutes.

Pour over the strawberries and cool. Pour into the pie shell. Whip the cream, add the sugar and pipe onto the pie. Garnish with whole strawberries. Serve.

SERVES 6

Fresh Strawberry Pie

Niagara Peach Pie

MARY'S CANDY TRUFFLES

½ cup	125 ml	light corn syrup
¼ cup	60 ml	water
⅓ cup	80 ml	butter
12 oz	340 g	semi-sweet chocolate squares

Combine the corn syrup, water and butter in a sauce pan. Bring to a rapid boil, stirring down the sugar. Boil for 3½ minutes, remove from heat.

Stir in the chocolate, cool slightly than drop the mixture by spoonfuls onto a buttered wax paper, shape them into neat round balls, allow to cool and then chill the truffles for a few hours until they are hard.

VARIATION:

After chocolate candy mixture has cooled slightly, add 1 tablespoon (15 ml) of rum and let mixture cool. Shape the mixture into walnut-sized balls, roll in chocolate pastilles, chill and serve.

OLD FASHION RICE PUDDING

⅓ cup	80 ml	short grain rice
4 cups	1 L	milk
¼ tsp	2 ml	salt
⅓ cup	80 ml	granulated sugar
2 tbsp	30 ml	butter
½ cup	125 ml	raisins
1 tsp	5 ml	cinnamon

Combine all the ingredients except the cinnamon in a 9" x 9" (23 x 23 cm) square baking pan. Bake in a preheated 300°F (148°C) oven for 1½-2 hours. Stir every 15 minutes. Sprinkle with cinnamon and serve hot or cold.

SERVES 6

THE RICHEST TRUFFLES

12 oz	340 g	semi-sweet chocolate
¾ cup	180 ml	butter, unsalted, clarified
¼ cup	60 ml	heavy cream
½ cup	125 ml	cocoa powder for dusting

In a heavy sauce pan heat the chocolate with the butter until it is melted. Do not boil. Allow to cool slightly. Pour the cream into the chocolate blending. Refrigerate several hours (stirring occasionally until chocolate sets hard enough to shape with lightly buttered hands.). Shape into small round irregular balls. Roll in the cocoa powder. Refrigerate. Use directly from refrigerator.

36 PIECES

Mary's Candy Truffles & The Richest Truffles

Old Fashion Rice Pudding

Maple Walnut Blancmange

MARASCHINO SQUARES

1 cup	250 ml	flour, pastry
½ cup	125 ml	butter
2 tbsp	30 ml	confectioners' sugar
1½ cups	375 ml	brown sugar
½ tsp	3 ml	vanilla
2	2	eggs
½ cup	125 ml	maraschino cherries, diced
½ cup	125 ml	coconut – shredded
½ cup	125 ml	pecans – broken
½ tsp	3 ml	baking powder

Blend the flour and butter together with the confectioners' sugar. Spread on a 9" x 9" (23 x 23 cm) cake pan. Bake 10 minutes in a preheated 350 °F (180 °C) oven.

Blend the sugar, vanilla and eggs. Stir in the cherries, coconuts, nuts and baking powder. Pour into shell and bake for 30 minutes at 350°F (180°C). Cool before stirring.

YIELDS 20 SQUARES

PEACHES 'N' CREAM MERINGUE

2 cups	500 ml	peaches – tinned, drained, sliced
1	1	Meringue Shell (see page 632)
3 oz	85 ml	peach gelatin
½ cup	125 ml	orange juice hot
8 oz	225 g	cream cheese
1¾ cups	440 ml	whipping cream
1 cup	250 ml	cracked ice

Line the peaches on the inside of the meringue shell. Blend the gelatin, orange juice, cream cheese in a food processor. With the machine running, slowly add the cream and ice. Mix until very thick. Pour into shell and refrigerate until set. Serve.

SERVES 6

MAPLE WALNUT BLANCMANGE

1¾ cups	440 ml	milk
¼ cup	60 ml	maple syrup
¼ tsp	2 ml	salt
¼ cup	60 ml	maple sugar
2 tbsp	30 ml	cornstarch
1	1	egg – beaten
½ cup	125 ml	whipping cream
½ cup	125 ml	walnuts – broken

Scald 1½ cup (375 ml) of milk in a double boiler. Add the syrup. Blend the salt, sugar and cornstarch with the remaining milk. Stir into milk and cook stirring until smooth. Beat in the egg and remove from the heat. Cool. Whip the cream and fold in half, along with the nuts. Pour into serving dishes and top with the remaining cream. Chill until serving.

SERVES 4

Maraschino Squares

RASPBERRY BLACKBERRY FLAN

CAKE:		
2 cups	500 ml	flour, all purpose
¼ cup	60 ml	sugar
1 cup	250 ml	butter
3	3	egg yolks

Combine the flour and sugar, cut in the butter to form a coarse dough. Beat in the egg yolks. Press into the bottom and up 1½" (4 cm) of the sides of a buttered 10" (23 cm) spring form pan. Bake in a preheated 350°F (180°C) oven for 20-25 minutes. Cool.

FILLING:		
1	1	egg
3	3	egg yolks
½ cup	125 ml	granulated sugar
1 tbsp	15 ml	flour, all purpose
1 cup	250 ml	milk
¾ cup	180 ml	almonds – ground
1 tbsp	15 ml	butter
2 tsp	10 ml	orange extract
1 tsp	5 ml	rum extract

Beat the egg, yolks, sugar and flour smooth. Boil the milk with the almonds, remove from heat and set 10 minutes. Strain through a sieve and beat almonds into the egg mixture. Slowly whip the hot milk into the egg mixture. Place over heat in a double boiler and whip until thick. Beat in the butter and extracts. Pour into shell. Cool and chill.

TOPPING:		
½ lb	225 g	fresh raspberries – washed, hulled
½ lb	225 g	fresh blackberries – washed, hulled
⅓ cup	80 ml	apple jelly, hot

Arrange the berries over the custard. Brush with apple jelly. Refrigerate for 2 hours before serving.

STRAWBERRY BLANCMANGE

1¾ cups	440 ml	milk
¼ cup	60 ml	strawberry syrup
¼ tsp	2 ml	salt
¼ cup	60 ml	granulated sugar
2 tbsp	30 ml	cornstarch
1	1	egg – beaten
½ cup	125 ml	cream – whipping

Scald 1½ cups (375 ml) of milk in a double boiler. Stir in the syrup. Blend the salt, sugar and cornstarch into the remaining milk. Add to scalded milk stirring until very thick and smooth. Remove from heat, and beat in the egg. Cool. Whip the cream, fold half into mixture, pour into serving dishes, top with remaining cream. Chill until served.

SERVES 4

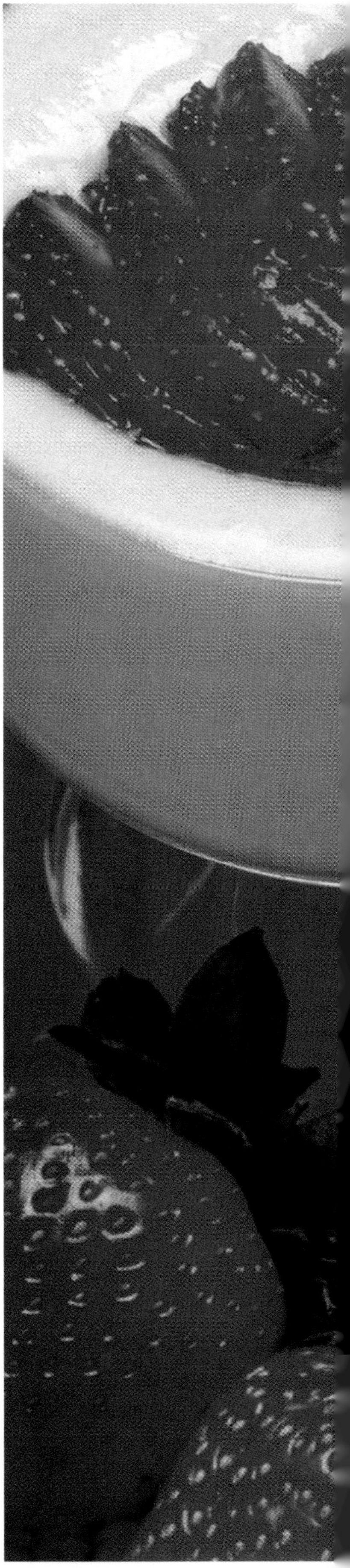

Strawberry Blancmange

Classic Creme Caramel

GRAHAM CRACKER OR CHOCOLATE WAFER CRUSTS

1¾ cups	430 ml	graham crackers or chocolate wafers – crushed into crumbs
¼ cup	60 ml	almonds – ground
½ tsp	3 ml	cinnamon – ground
¼ tsp	1 ml	allspice – ground
½ cup	125 ml	butter – melted

Combine all the ingredients, mix well. Press into the bottom and sides of a 9" (23 cm) spring form pan. Chill and use as required.

MACAROON PIE

1¼ cups	310 ml	soda crackers – crushed fine
½ cup	125 ml	dates – fine chopped
1 cup	250 ml	granulated sugar
1 cup	250 ml	pecans – broken
3	3	egg white

Mix the crackers, dates, sugar and nuts thoroughly together.

Whip the egg whites to very stiff. Fold into the cracker mixture.

Pour into a well greased 9" (23 cm) pie pan. Bake in a preheated 350°F (180°C) oven for 30 minutes. Cool and serve.

SERVES 8

Strawberry Banana Ice Cream

STRAWBERRY BANANA ICE CREAM

3 cups	750 ml	cream – half & half
1 cup	250 ml	bananas – mashed
3	3	egg yolks
¾ cup	180 ml	granulated sugar
1 tsp	5 ml	white vanilla extract
1 cup	250 ml	strawberries – puréed

Scald the cream with the banana in a double boiler. Beat the egg yolks with the sugar. Add slowly to the hot cream, continue to cook until thick. Stir in the vanilla and strawberries. Cool and chill then freeze according to directions of ice cream maker.

YIELDS 6 CUPS (1½ L)

CLASSIC CREME CARAMEL

3¾ cups	940 ml	milk
1½ cups	375 ml	vanilla sugar
5	5	eggs
4	4	egg yolks
1 tbsp	15 ml	vanilla

Scald the milk and allow to cool 20 minutes. In a sauce pan, melt ¾ cup (180 ml) of sugar and cook until dark brown stirring constantly, take care not to scorch. Pour into a warm mold covering the bottom and the sides. Beat the eggs and egg yolks with the remaining sugar. Slowly whip in the milk and vanilla. Pour into the sugar lined mold. Place mold in a second pan fill halfway with hot water. Bake for 45 minutes in a 325°F (160°C) oven. Cool then chill. To serve invert on to a rimmed serving platter.

SERVES 6

Old Fashion Cherry Cobbler

MARY GIFFORD'S CHOCOLATE & MINT CAKE

Need two, 9" (23 cm) chocolate cakes, cut in half horizontally (ending with four halves in total)

FILLING:		
2 cups	500 ml	milk
½ cup	125 ml	cornstarch
1 cup	250 ml	granulated sugar
¼ tsp	2 ml	peppermint extract
		green food colouring
1½ cups	375 ml	butter, at room temperature

Combine ½ cup (125 ml) milk, cornstarch and sugar in a small bowl. In a saucepan bring remaining milk to a boil. Add the cornstarch mixture to the boiling milk, stirring constantly until smooth and thick.

Remove from heat and add extract and food colouring. Cool pudding by placing over ice, stirring constantly.

Whip butter, slowly add the cooled pudding. Place one half, cut side up, on a serving platter. Spread ⅓ of filling over the top of cake. Place another cake half on top. Spread top with ⅓ of filling. Place third half on top and top with remaining filling. Place final cake cut side down on top.

SPECIAL POURED CHOCOLATE ICING:		
1 cup	250 ml	light corn syrup
½ cup	125 ml	water
⅔ cup	160 ml	butter
2–12 oz pkgs	750 ml	semi-sweet chocolate chips

Combine corn syrup, water and butter in a sauce pan. Bring to a rapid boil and continue to boil for 2½ minutes. Remove from heat and stir in the chocolate chips. Cover while icing cools to room temperature. Pour over the Chocolate & Mint Cake.

NOTE: To cut a cream filling cake, dip a sharp bread knife in warm water before making each cut.

OLD FASHION CHERRY COBBLER

½ cup	125 ml	granulated sugar
2 tbsp	30 ml	cornstarch
½ cup	125 ml	cherry juice
2 cups	500 ml	canned sour cherries
1½ cups	375 ml	flour, all purpose
2 tsp	10 ml	baking powder
½ tsp	3 ml	salt
⅓ cup	80 ml	brown sugar
½ cup	125 ml	shortening
1	1	egg, beaten
2 tbsp	30 ml	milk
1 tbsp	15 ml	butter, melted
2 tsp	10 ml	vanilla extract

In a sauce pan, combine the sugar, cornstarch, juice and cherries. Simmer until thick. Pour into a 9"x 9" (23 x 23 cm) buttered pan.

Mix the flour, baking powder and salt together. Blend in 3 tbsp (45 ml) of brown sugar. Cut in the shortening,. Mix the egg with the milk, butter and vanilla, blend into mixture.

Roll out and spread over the cherries. Sprinkle with the remaining sugar.

Bake in a preheated 400°F (200°C) oven for 25-30 minutes or until golden brown.

SERVES 6

Mary Gifford's Chocolate & Mint Cake

Pina Colada Cheesecake with Pineapple Walnut Topping

PINA COLADA CHEESECAKE WITH PINEAPPLE WALNUT TOPPING

CRUST:		
1 cup	250 ml	flaked coconut
1 cup	250 ml	ground roasted filberts
⅓ cup	80 ml	granulated sugar
¼ cup	60 ml	melted butter

FILLING:		
1½ lbs	680 g	cream cheese
1 cup	250 ml	granulated sugar
½ cup	60 ml	coconut cream nectar*
1 cup	250 ml	whipping cream
1½ cups	375 ml	crushed pineapple, well drained
3	3	eggs
2 tsp	10 ml	rum extract

TOPPING:		
1 cup	250 ml	pineapple juice
1 cup	250 ml	brown sugar
6 tbsp	90 ml	cornstarch
6 tbsp	90 ml	pineapple gelatine
1 cup	250 ml	boiling water
3 cups	750 ml	pineapple chunks
1 cup	250 ml	walnut pieces
1½ cups	375 ml	toasted coconut, shredded

CRUST:

Combine all the ingredients together. Press into a greased 9 " (23 cm) springform pan. Refrigerate 10 minutes. Bake in a preheated 350°F (180°C) oven for 7 minutes

FILLING:

Cream the cheese with the sugar until very smooth. Blend in the coconut cream, cream and pineapple. Beat in the eggs, one at a time. Add flavouring, blend well. Pour into shell. Bake in a 350°F (180°C) oven for 90 minutes.

Transfer to a cooling rack. Cool, then chill for 8 hours.

TOPPING:

In a sauce pan, combine the juice, sugar, cornstarch and gelatine. Bring to a boil. Stir in the boiling water, continue to cook until sauce thickens.

Add the pineapple chunks and walnut pieces. Cool. Spread over chilled cake. Sprinkle with toasted coconut. Serve.

SERVES 8

CARAMEL APPLE NUT PIE

½ quan	0.5 quan	Plain Pastry (see page 616)
3 cups	750 ml	apples, sliced
20	20	caramels
½ tsp	3 ml	vanilla
⅓ cup	80 ml	flour, all purpose
¼ tsp	2 ml	cinnamon
3 tbsp	45 ml	granulated sugar
3 tbsp	45 ml	butter
⅓ cup	80 ml	pecans – chopped

Roll out the pastry to fit into a 9" (23 cm) pie pan, flute the edges.

Sprinkle pastry with apples. Melt the caramels in a double boiler stir in the vanilla. Pour over the apples.

Mix the flour, cinnamon and sugar together cut in the butter, add the pecans and mix to crumbly. Sprinkle over the apples and bake in a preheated 350°F (180°C) oven for 40 minutes. Cool before serving.

SERVES 6

MAPLE NUT BRITTLE

1 cup	250 ml	maple sugar
½ cup	125 ml	water
1 tbsp	15 ml	butter
1 tsp	5 ml	salt
1 tsp	5 ml	maple flavouring
½ cup	125 ml	cashews
½ cup	125 ml	peanuts
½ cup	125 ml	filberts

Combine the sugar, water, butter, and salt in a sauce pan. Heat over medium heat to 300°F (149°C) on a candy thermometer. Stir in the nuts. Pour into a greased rim pastry pan. Allow to harden then crack to remove. Stir in maple flavouring after it is cooked.

MAKES 1½ LBS

RAISIN PIE

1 quan	1 quan	Whole Wheat Pie Crust (see page 504)
2 cups	500 ml	seedless raisins
2 cups	500 ml	boiling water
⅓ cup	80 ml	honey
⅓ cup	80 ml	brown sugar
2⅛ tbsp	35 ml	cornstarch
¼ tsp	1 ml	salt
1 tbsp	15 ml	lemon rind – grated
¼ cup	60 ml	orange juice
2 tbsp	30 ml	butter

Roll half the dough and fit into a 9" (23 cm) pastry shell.

In a sauce pan mix the raisins, water and honey. Boil for 5 minutes, mix the sugar, cornstarch and salt. Add to the raisins. Stir and return to a boil cooking for 1 minute. Stir in the lemon rind and orange juice. Pour into the pie shell. Roll out remaining pastry and fit on top. Tuck the edges under and flute the sides. Melt the butter and brush onto the pie. Cut holes to vent the steam. Bake in a preheated 425°F (215°C) oven for 40 minutes. Cool to room temperature before serving.

SERVES 6

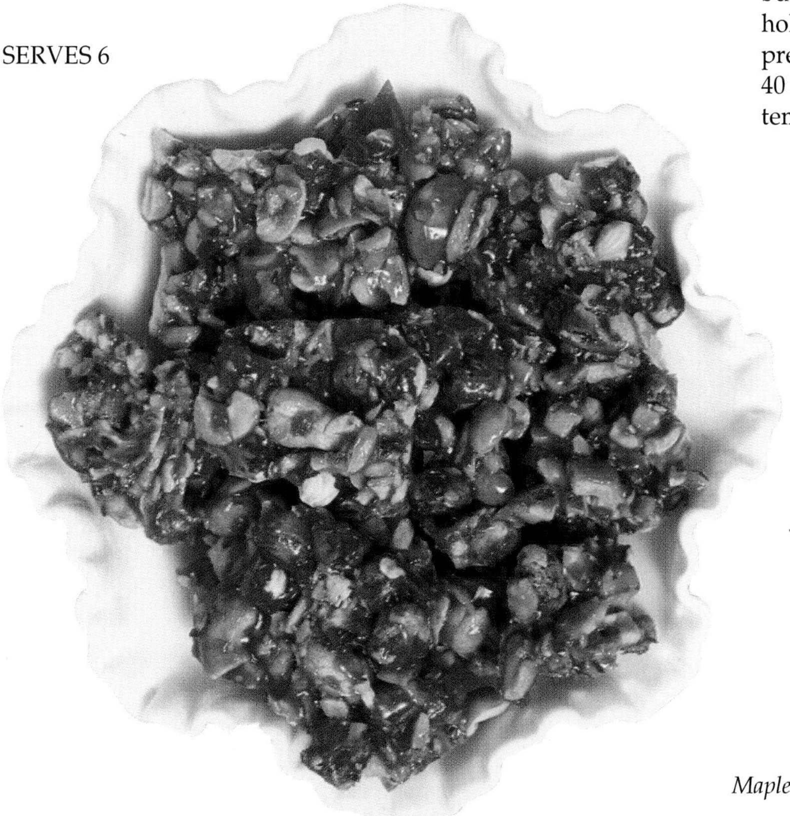

Maple Nut Brittle

Caramel Apple Nut Pie

Date Cookies

CHOCOLATE SOUFFLÉ

2 oz	60 g	semi-sweet chocolate – grated
¼ cup	60 ml	flour, all purpose
1 cup	250 ml	milk
⅓ cup	80 ml	granulated sugar
3 tbsp	45 ml	butter
1 tsp	5 ml	vanilla extract
4	4	eggs – separated
2	2	egg whites

Butter and sugar the bottom and side of 6 to 8 cups (1.5–2 L) soufflé dish. In a sauce pan bring to a boil the chocolate, flour and milk. Stir in the sugar, butter and vanilla and remove from heat. Beat in the egg yolks one at a time. Whip the egg whites stiff. Fold into soufflé dish bake for 40-45 minutes in a preheated 400°F (200°C) oven. Serve with a Raspberry Sauce (see page 107).

SERVES 4

PECAN RAISIN PIE

½ quan	0.5	Plain Pastry (see page 616)
3	3	eggs – separated
3 tbsp	45 ml	butter – melted
1 tsp	5 ml	vanilla
1 cup	250 ml	brown sugar
½ cup	125 ml	raisins
½ cup	125 ml	pecans – broken

Roll out the pastry and fit into a 9" (23 cm) pie pan.

Blend the egg yolks, butter, vanilla, sugar, raisins and pecans. Heat in a double boiler stirring constantly until thick. Remove from heat and cool.

Whip the egg whites until stiff, fold into the egg mixture. Pour into the pie shell. Bake in a preheated 375°F (190°C) oven for 45 minutes. Cool and serve.

SERVES 6

DATE COOKIES

1½ cups	375 ml	brown sugar
1 cup	250 ml	sour cream
2	2	eggs
1 tsp	5 ml	baking soda
⅛ tsp	pinch	salt
2 cups	500 ml	flour, pastry
1 tsp	5 ml	cinnamon
½ tsp	3 ml	cloves
¼ tsp	1 ml	nutmeg
½ lb	225 g	chopped dates
¾ cup	180 ml	pieces walnuts

Whip the sugar, sour cream and eggs together.

Sift together the baking soda, salt, flour and spices. Fold into the creamed mixture, blend in the dates and nuts. Drop teaspoon sizes on a buttered pastry sheet. Bake 10-12 minutes in a preheated 350°F (180°C) oven.

YIELDS 3 DOZEN

Pecan Raisin Pie

CAKE BROWNIES

½ cup	125 ml	butter
½ cup	125 ml	oil
1 cup	250 ml	water
4 tbsp	60 ml	unsweetened cocoa
2 cups	500 ml	flour, all purpose
2 cups	500 ml	granulated sugar
2	2	eggs
1 tsp	5 ml	baking soda
½ cup	125 ml	buttermilk
1 tsp	5 ml	vanilla extract

FROSTING:

½ cup	125 ml	butter
3 tbsp	45 ml	unsweetened cocoa
⅓ cup	80 ml	buttermilk
4 cups	1L	confectioners' sugar
1 cup	250 ml	chopped walnuts
1 tsp	5 ml	vanilla extract

Preheat oven to 350°F (180°C). Grease and flour a 9" x 13" (23 x 33 cm) baking pan.

Mix butter, oil, water and cocoa together in small sauce pan. Bring to boil. Add this mixture to flour and sugar and beat until smooth.

Add eggs, baking soda, buttermilk and vanilla. Mix well. Pour into prepared baking pan. Bake 20 minutes. Prepare frosting while brownies are baking. Put all frosting ingredients in medium saucepan and heat. Do not boil.

Frost immediately after removing from oven. Cut into squares when cool.

YIELDS 24 BROWNIES

Strawberry Meringue Torte

OLD FASHION BLANCMANGE

2 cups	500 ml	milk
¼ tsp	2 ml	salt
¼ cup	60 ml	granulated sugar
1½ tbsp	28 ml	cornstarch
1	1	egg – beaten
1½ tsp	8 ml	vanilla
½ cup	125 ml	cream – whipping

In a double boiler scald 1¾ cup (430 ml) of milk. Blend the remaining milk with salt, sugar and cornstarch, stir into hot milk. Cook until very smooth stirring constantly. Remove from heat. Beat in the egg and vanilla. Cool. Whip the cream and fold half into the mixture. Pour into serving dishes and top with remaining cream. Chill until serving.

SERVES 4

STRAWBERRY MERINGUE TORTE

1	1	Silver Miner's Cake (see page 607)
3 cups	750 ml	strawberries
4	4	egg whites
¼ tsp	1 ml	salt
¼ tsp	2 ml	cream of tartar
1 cup	250 ml	sugar, granulated
1 tsp	5 ml	vanilla
½ cup	125 ml	apricot preserves

Slice the cake in half. Choose 12 of the best strawberries and reserve. Purée the remaining strawberries and spread on half the cake. Place the second half on top.

Whip the egg whites until soft peaks form. Add the salt and cream of tartar. Gradually add the sugar and vanilla. Pipe onto the top, place the strawberries. Place in a 450°F (220°C) oven until the meringue turns golden, remove. Heat the preserves, dip the strawberries in and place in the ring on the cake top.

Old Fashion Blancmange

Chocolate Creme Brulee

Coconut Cream Pie

COCONUT CREAM PIE

¼ cup	60 ml	granulated sugar
¼ cup	60 ml	flour, all purpose
¼ tsp	2 ml	salt
2 cups	500 ml	cream – light
1 tsp	5 ml	vanilla
3	3	egg yolks
1 cup	250 ml	shredded coconut
1	1	Rolled Oats Crust (see page 627)
1 cup	250 ml	whipping cream
¼ cup	60 ml	confectioners' sugar
¼ cup	60 ml	toasted coconut

Combine the sugar, flour, salt and cream in a double boiler, whip until smooth. Add the vanilla, egg yolks and coconut. Cook until thick. Pour into pie shell and chill. Whip the cream, add the sugar and pipe onto the pie. Sprinkle with toasted coconut. Slice and serve.

SERVES 6

CHOCOLATE CREME BRULEE

5	5	egg yolks
4 tbsp	60 ml	granulated sugar
1½ tsp	8 ml	cornstarch
1¼ cups	310 ml	whipping cream
4 oz	120 g	semi-sweet chocolate – grated
¾ cup	180 ml	confectioners' sugar, sifted

Cream the egg yolks with the sugar and cornstarch in a sauce pan over low heat. Slowly stir in the cream and chocolate. Cook for 10 minutes stirring constantly. Pour in molds, cool. Refrigerate until set. Unmold custards onto serving plates, dust with confectioners' sugar or place into parfait glasses alternating layers with whipped cream or vanilla pudding.

SERVES 4

ALMOND COOKIES

2¾ cups	680 ml	flour, pastry
1 cup	250 ml	granulated sugar
½ tsp	3 ml	baking soda
½ tsp	3 ml	salt
1 cup	250 ml	shortening
1	1	egg, slightly beaten
2 tbsp	30 ml	milk
1 tsp	5 ml	almond extract
24	24	blanched almonds, halved

Mix together the flour, sugar, soda and salt. Cut in the shortening until the mixture resembles cornmeal. Combine the egg, milk and extract; add to the flour mixture. Mix well. Shape dough into one-inch balls and place two inches apart on an ungreased cookie sheet. Place an almond half atop each cookie and press to flatten slightly. Bake in a preheated 325°F (170°C) oven for 16-18 minutes.

YIELDS 48 COOKIES

ORANGE CHIFFON CAKE

2 cups	500 ml	flour, all purpose
1½ cups	375 ml	granulated sugar
1 tbsp	15 ml	baking powder
1 tsp	5 ml	salt
½ cup	125 ml	vegetable oil
5	5	unbeaten egg yolks
½ cup	125 ml	orange juice
¼ cup	60 ml	water
1 tsp	5 ml	vanilla
2 tbsp	30 ml	orange rind, finely grated
1 cup	250 ml	egg whites
½ tsp	3 ml	cream of tarter

Preheat the oven to 325°F (170°C). Select a 10" (25 cm) tube pan making sure it is free of any grease.

Blend the flour, sugar, baking powder and salt into a bowl. Add the oil, egg yolks, orange juice, water, vanilla and orange rind. Beat until smooth. In another bowl beat the egg whites until frothy. Sprinkle with the cream of tartar. Continue beating until very stiff peaks form. Do not under beat. Gradually fold batter into the beaten egg whites. Turn batter into the tube pan. Cut through batter with a knife to eliminate air bubbles.

Bake in the oven for 1¼ hours. Invert cake immediately upon removal from the oven. Leave suspended until cold. Loosen with a knife or spatula and carefully shake cake from the pan. Frost with Creamy Orange Frosting (recipe follows).

CREAMY ORANGE FROSTING

2 tbsp	30 ml	butter, softened
½ cup	125 ml	icing sugar
pinch	pinch	salt
1	1	egg yolk
2 tsp	10 ml	orange rind, finely grated
1 tbsp	15 ml	orange juice
1½ cups	375 ml	icing sugar

Cream the butter, add the sugar and salt. Blend until smooth. Add the egg yolk, orange rind, and orange juice beating well. Gradually beat in the sugar. Beat until creamy.

FROSTS 1-9" (23 CM) CAKE

PECAN PIE

½ quan	0.5	Plain Pastry (see page 616)
1 cup	250 ml	light corn syrup
½ cup	125 ml	brown sugar – packed
¼ tsp	2 ml	salt
1 tsp	5 ml	vanilla
1 tbsp	15 ml	lemon juice
3	3	eggs – beaten
1½ cups	375 ml	pecans – broken and whole
2 cups	500 ml	whipped cream

Roll out the pastry and flute the edges. Preheat the oven to 425°F (215°C).

Blend the remaining ingredients together, except whipping cream. Pour into the pie shell. Bake in the oven for 10 minutes. Reduce heat and continue baking for 40 minutes or until filling is set. Pipe whipped cream on top. Cool completely before serving.

SERVES 6

Pecan Pie

Apricot en Chemise

Chocolate Dipped Sugar Rolls

CHOCOLATE DIPPED SUGAR ROLLS

½ cup	125 ml	butter
1 cup	250 ml	confectioners' sugar
½ cup	125 ml	milk
1¾ cups	430 ml	flour, pastry
1 tsp	5 ml	vanilla
¼ tsp	1 ml	salt
3 oz	85 g	semi-sweet chocolate
1 tbsp	15 ml	butter – melted

Cream the butter until light and fluffy. Stir in the sugar and milk. Beat in the flour, vanilla and salt. Spread thin on buttered pastry sheets. Bake in a preheated 400°F (200°C) oven for 8-10 minutes. Melt the chocolate in a double boiler and stir in the butter. Remove the cookies, while pastry is still hot cut into squares and roll in cigar shapes. Dip each end in the melted chocolate.

YIELDS 2 DOZEN

APRICOT EN CHEMISE

12	12	fresh apricots, peeled, stoned, halved
1 cup	250 ml	granulated sugar
1 lb	450 g	Puff Pastry (see page 689)
2	2	eggs
¼ cup	60 ml	milk
¼ cup	60 ml	confectioners' sugar

Dust the apricots with the sugar. Roll out the pastry ¼" thick. Cut in squares and encase the apricot halves within. Fold and seal the edges.

Mix the eggs with the milk, brush on the pastry and bake for 15-20 minutes in a preheated 350°F (180°C) oven. Dust with confectioners' sugar while hot. Serve hot or cold.

YIELDS 24

CHOCOLATE RASPBERRY CHEESECAKE

1½ cups	375 ml	cream filled cookie crumbs*
2 tbsp	30 ml	butter, melted
32 oz	900 g	cream cheese, softened
1¼ cups	310 ml	granulated sugar
3	3	eggs
1 cup	250 ml	sour cream
1 tsp	5 ml	vanilla extract
6 oz	170 g	semi-sweet chocolate chips melted
⅓ cup	60 ml	whipping cream
½ cup	125 ml	fresh raspberries
4	4	fresh mint leaves

Combine crumbs and butter; press onto bottom of 9-inch (23 cm) spring form pan.

Combine ⅔rds of cream cheese and sugar, mixing at medium speed until well blended. Add eggs, one at a time, beating well after each addition. Blend in sour cream and vanilla; pour over crust. Combine remaining cream cheese and melted chocolate, mixing until well blended. Add preserves; mix well. Drop rounded measuring tablespoonfuls of chocolate cream cheese batter over plain cream cheese batter, do not swirl. Bake in a preheated oven at 325°F (170°C) for 1 hour and 25 minutes. Loosen cake from rim of pan; cool before removing rim of pan.

Melt chocolate pieces and whipping cream over low heat stirring until smooth. Spread over cheesecake. Chill. Garnish with additional whipping cream, whipped, raspberries and fresh mint leaves, if desired.

*Cookie crumbs should come from 18 cream filled cookies that have been finely crushed.

SERVES 10

FRESH PAPAYA SORBET

¾ cup	180 ml	granulated sugar
¾ cup	180 ml	water
3 tbsp	45 ml	lemon juice
3 tbsp	45 ml	lime juice
2½ cups	625 ml	papaya puréed

In a sauce pan heat the sugar and water. Stirring constantly bring to a boil. Remove from heat, cool to room temperature. Combine the syrup, lemon and lime, chill to very cold. Stir in the papaya. Pour into a ice cream maker and freeze according to the manufacturer's directions.

YIELDS 4 CUPS (1 L)

OLD FASHION DATE SQUARES

¼ cup	60 ml	butter
1 cup	250 ml	brown sugar
1	1	egg
3 oz	85 g	semi-sweet chocolate – melted
¾ cup	180 ml	flour, all purpose
½ cup	125 ml	pecans – broken
½ cup	125 ml	walnuts – pieces
½ cup	125 ml	almonds – slivered
¼ tsp	2 ml	salt

Cream the butter until light. Beat in the sugar and egg. Stir in the chocolate, flour, nuts and salt mix well. Fold into a 8" (20 cm) buttered cake pan. Bake in a preheated 350°F (180°C) oven for 20 minutes. Remove from the oven and slice while hot in the pan.

YIELDS 2 DOZEN

Old Fashion Date Squares

MOCHA CHOCOLATE CHIP CHEESECAKE

2¼ cups	540 ml	graham cracker crumbs
2 cups	500 ml	semi-sweet chocolate chips
2⅓ cups	580 ml	butter, melted and cooled
½ cup	125 ml	milk
4 tsp	20 ml	instant coffee
1	1	envelope unflavored gelatin
16 oz	450 g	cream cheese, softened
14 oz	400 g	sweetened condensed milk
2 cups	500 ml	whipping cream, whipped

In a large bowl, combine graham cracker crumbs, 1 cup (250 ml) chocolate chips and butter, mix well. Pat firmly into 9-inch (23 cm) spring form pan, covering bottom and 2½ inches (6.5 cm) up sides. Set aside.

In small saucepan, combine the milk and instant coffee, sprinkle gelatin on top. Set aside for 1 minute. Cook over low heat, stirring constantly until gelatin and coffee dissolve. Set aside.

In large bowl, beat cream cheese until creamy. Beat in sweetened condensed milk and gelatin mixture. Fold in whipped cream and remaining 1 cup (250 ml) of chocolate chips. Pour into prepared pan. Chill until firm (about 2 hours). Run knife around edge of cake to separate from pan, remove rim.

SERVES 10

Fresh Papaya Sorbet

Peanut Butter Cookies

NORTHWEST CHEESECAKE SUPREME

1 cup	250 ml	graham cracker crumbs
1 tbsp	15 ml	granulated sugar
1 tbsp	15 ml	butter, melted
32 oz	900 g	cream cheese, softened
1 cup	250 ml	granulated sugar
1 tbsp	15 ml	flour, all purpose
4	4	eggs
1 cup	250 ml	sour cream
1 tsp	5 ml	vanilla extract
21oz (1 can)	605 g	cherry pie filling

Combine crumbs, sugar and butter, press onto the bottom of a 9-inch (23 cm) spring form pan. Bake in a preheated 325°F (170°C) oven for 10 minutes.

Combine cream cheese, sugar and flour, mixing at medium speed until well blended. Add eggs, one at a time, mixing well after each addition. Blend in sour cream and vanilla; pour over crust. Bake in a preheated 450°F (220°C) oven for 10 minutes. Reduce temperature to 250°F (140°C), continue baking for 1 hour. Loosen cake from rim of pan; cool before removing rim of pan. Chill. Top with pie filling just before serving.

VARIATION: Substitute 1½ cups (375 ml) finely chopped nuts and 2 tbsp (30 ml) granulated sugar for graham cracker crumbs and sugar.

SERVES 10

Soufflé Glace Grand Marnier

PEANUT BUTTER COOKIES

1 cup	250 ml	granulated sugar
1 cup	250 ml	brown sugar
1 cup	250 ml	peanut butter
1 cup	250 ml	butter
3	3	eggs
½ tsp	3 ml	salt
2 tsp	10 ml	baking soda
3 cups	750 ml	flour, all purpose
56	56	Hershey's chocolate kisses

Cream the sugars, peanut butter and butter together. Blend in the eggs. Sift the salt, soda and flour together then stir into creamed mixture. Blend. Roll into 1" balls, (2.5 cm) flatten slightly with the palm of your hand as you place on greased cookie sheets. Place a chocolate kiss in the centre of each cookie. Bake in a preheated 325°F (160°C) oven for 15-18 minutes.

YIELDS 4½ DOZEN

SOUFFLÉ GLACE GRAND MARNIER

3 tbsp	45 ml	granulated sugar
2 tbsp	30 ml	unflavoured gelatin
¼ cup	60 ml	Grand Marnier liqueur – cream style
¼ tsp	2 ml	salt
6	6	egg whites
2 cups	500 ml	whipping cream

In a sauce pan combine the sugar, gelatin, liqueur and salt. Cook over low heat stirring until sugar is dissolved. Cool. Whip the egg whites until stiff and dry. Whip the cream then fold into the egg whites. Fold in the liqueur mixture. Pour into a 8 cup (2 L) soufflé dish with a 6" (15 cm) foil collar. Freeze 6 hours or overnight. Remove collar and serve.

SERVES 6

CHOCOLATE CHIP PEANUT BUTTER PIE

1 tbsp	15 ml	unflavoured gelatin
1 cup	250 ml	cold water
3	3	eggs
½ cup	125 ml	honey
½ tsp	3 ml	salt
½ cup	125 ml	smooth peanut butter
½ tsp	3 ml	vanilla
¼ cup	60 ml	granulated sugar
½ cup	125 ml	chocolate chips
1	1	Graham Cracker Crust (see page 641)

Soften the gelatin in ¼ cup (60 ml) water. Combine ¼ cup (60 ml) of water, egg yolks, honey, and salt in a double boiler, blend in the gelatin. Whip until thick and fluffy with a hand rotary blender.

In a mixing bowl whip the peanut butter, ½ cup (125 ml) water and vanilla until smooth. Add the egg mixture and fold together. Chill until thick but not set. Whip the egg whites until stiff then add the sugar gradually. Fold into the peanut mixtures. Fold in the chocolate chips and pour into pie shell. Refrigerate until set. Cut and serve.

SERVES 6

Chocolate Chip Peanut Butter Pie

ALMOND AND APRICOT TARTLETS

TARTLETS:

2½ cups	625 ml	flour, all purpose
½ cup	125 ml	butter
½ cup	125 ml	granulated sugar
1	1	egg
1 tsp	5 ml	lemon rind – grated

Blend the flour with the butter, stir in the sugar, egg and lemon, combine thoroughly but do not over work the dough. Rest dough for 30 minutes, roll out to ⅛" (3 mm) thick square. Cut out rounds with a 2½" (5 cm) pastry cutter. Shape into 1½" (3.75 cm) fluted tartlet shells. Blind bake the tartlets for 15 minutes in a preheated 350°F (180°C) oven. Cool.

FILLING:

1 cup	250 ml	granulated sugar
¼ cup	60 ml	cornstarch
2	2	eggs
1½ cups	375 ml	milk
1 tbsp	15 ml	butter
¼ tsp	1 ml	salt
1 tsp	5 ml	almond extract

Combine the sugar, cornstarch and eggs in a double boiler. Add the butter and milk and cook until very thick. Stir in the salt and extract. Fill tartlets then chill.

TOPPING:

8	8	fresh apricots – peeled, stoned, halved
½ cup	125 ml	apricot preserves
1 cup	250 ml	toasted almonds sliced

Top each tartlet with an apricot half. Glaze with preserves and sprinkle almonds around the edge of the tartlet.

YIELDS 15 TARTLETS

Almond & Apricot Tartlets

Ambrosia

AMBROSIA

2	2	bananas – ripe, sliced
1	1	red apple – cored, unpared, sliced
1	1	pear – cored, unpared, sliced
2	2	oranges – segments
1 cup	250 ml	fresh pineapple chunks
2 tbsp	30 ml	lemon juice
1 cup	250 ml	sabayon – see sauces
1¼ cups	320 ml	flaked coconut

Blend the fruit with the lemon juice. Chill for 1 hour. Stir in the sabayon and coconut just before serving.

SERVES 6

WACKY CAKE

1½ cups	375 ml	flour, all purpose
1 cup	250 ml	granulated sugar
3 tbsp	45 ml	cocoa
1 tsp	5 ml	baking soda
½ tsp	3 ml	salt
1 tsp	5 ml	vanilla extract
1 tsp	5 ml	vinegar
5 tbsp	75 ml	vegetable oil
1 cup	250 ml	cold water

Mix flour, sugar, cocoa, soda and salt. Make three wells in the flour mixture. In one put vanilla; in another the vinegar, and in the third the oil. Pour cold water over all and stir until no lumps remain. No need to beat. Pour into 8" x 8" (20 x 20 cm) pan. Bake in a preheated 350°F (180°C) oven until it springs back, approximately 30 minutes.

SERVES 4

CAPPUCCINO CHEESECAKE

1½ cups	375 ml	finely chopped nuts
2 tbsp	30 ml	granulated sugar
3 tbsp	45 ml	butter, melted
32 oz	900 g	cream cheese, softened
1 cup	250 ml	granulated sugar
3 tbsp	45 ml	flour, all purpose
4	4	eggs
1 cup	250 ml	sour cream
1 tbsp	15 ml	instant coffee granules
¼ tsp	1 ml	cinnamon
¼ cup	60 ml	boiling water

Combine nuts, sugar, and butter; press onto bottom of 9-inch (23 cm) spring form cake pan. Bake in a preheated 325°F (170°C) oven for 10 minutes. Increase oven temperature to 450°F (220°C).

Combine cream cheese, sugar and flour, mixing at medium speed until well blended. Add eggs, one at at time, mixing well after each addition. Blend in sour cream. Dissolve coffee granules and cinnamon in the water. Cool; gradually add to cream cheese mixture, mixing until well blended. Pour over crust. Bake at 450°F (220°C) for 10 minutes. Reduce oven temperature to 250°F (140°C) continue baking 1 hour. Loosen cake from rim of pan; cool before removing rim of pan. Chill. Garnish with whipped cream and whole chocolate covered coffee beans if desired.

SERVES 10

Raspberry Bavarian

RASPBERRY BAVARIAN

3 cups	750 ml	raspberries
1 tbsp	15 ml	gelatin – unflavoured
¼ cup	60 ml	cold water
⅓ cup	80 ml	granulated sugar
¼ tsp	1 ml	salt
¾ cup	180 ml	whipping cream

Purée the raspberries in a food processor, strain to remove the seeds. Place into a sauce pan Heat to reduce to 1 cup (250 ml). Soften the gelatin in the cold water, add it to the raspberry along with the sugar and salt. Remove from heat once it has returned to a boil. Cool and chill until thick but not set. Whip the cream and fold into the mixture. Pour into a mold or bowl, chill until set. Unmold and serve.

SERVES 4

FRESH CHERRY TARTLETS

15	15	tartlets (see Almond and Apricot Tartlets page 662)
½ cup	125 ml	butter
½ cup	125 ml	granulated sugar
1 cup	250 ml	ground almonds
1 tsp	5 ml	flour, pastry
3	3	eggs
3 tbsp	45 ml	cherry brandy
2 cups	500 ml	white cake crumbs
1⅛ lbs	560 g	fresh cherries – pitted
½ cup	125 ml	red currant jelly

Cream the butter with the sugar until light and pale. Fold in the almonds and flour. Beat in the eggs one at a time with 2 tbsp (30 ml) of cherry brandy. Sprinkle the tartlets with cake crumbs, fill with cherries then spoon the almond mixture over the cherries. Bake in a preheated 400°F (200°C) oven for 20 minutes. Cover with foil wrap and bake for an additional 20 minutes or until brown. Heat the jelly with the remaining brandy and sprinkle over tartlets at once.

YIELDS 15

HOLIDAY EGGNOG CHEESECAKE

1 cup	250 ml	graham cracker crumbs
¼ cup	60 ml	granulated sugar
¼ tsp	1 ml	nutmeg
¼ cup	60 ml	butter, melted
1	1	envelope of unflavored gelatin
¼ cup	60 ml	cold water
8 oz	225 g	cream cheese, softened
¼ cup	60 ml	granulated sugar
1 cup	250 ml	eggnog
1 cup	250 ml	whipping cream, whipped

Combine crumbs, sugar, nutmeg and butter; press onto bottom of 9-inch (23 cm) spring form pan.

Soften gelatin in water; stir over low heat until dissolved. Combine cream cheese and sugar until well blended. Gradually add gelatin and eggnog, mixing until blended. Chill until slightly thickened; fold in whipped cream. Pour over crust; chill until firm.

VARIATION: Increase sugar to ⅓ cup (80 ml). Substitute milk for eggnog. Add 1 tsp (5 ml) vanilla and ¾ tsp (4 ml) rum extract. Continue as directed.

SERVES 10

Fresh Cherry Tartlets

Pommes Helene

CAFE MINT ICE CREAM

4 cups	1 L	half & half cream
1½ tbsp	28 ml	instant coffee crystals
1 cup	250 ml	granulated sugar
4	4	egg yolks
2 tsp	10 ml	mint extract

In a double boiler scald the cream with the coffee crystals. Beat the sugar together with the eggs. Slowly add to the cream. Cook until thick, stir the mint extract and cool, chill then freeze according to directions of ice cream maker.

YIELDS 5 CUPS (1¼ l)

POMMES HELENE

1 cup	250 ml	granulated sugar
1 cup	250 ml	water
1 tsp	5 ml	white vanilla
3	3	large apples – pared, cored, halved
3 oz	85 g	semi-sweet chocolate – melted
1 tbsp	15 ml	butter – melted
4 cups	1 L	French Vanilla Ice Cream (see page 547)
1 cup	250 ml	Chocolate Sauce (see page 123)

Boil the sugar, water and vanilla until sugar has dissolved, reduce heat and poach the apples until tender. Remove and drain. Blend the chocolate with the butter, dip apples in chocolate to coat. Scoop the ice cream into large champagne glasses, top with an apple half and serve chocolate sauce separately.

SERVES 6

Cafe Mint Ice Cream

ELIZABETH SQUARES

1 cup	250 ml	boiling water
1 cup	250 ml	dates, chopped
¼ cup	60 ml	butter
½ tsp	3 ml	salt
1 cup	250 ml	granulated sugar
1 tsp	5 ml	baking soda
1	1	egg
1½ cups	375 ml	flour, all purpose
1 tsp	5 ml	baking powder
½ cup	125 ml	nuts, chopped
¾ cup	180 ml	brown sugar
1 tsp	5 ml	vanilla extract
6 tbsp	90 ml	butter
4 tbsp	60 ml	milk
1 cup	250 ml	coconut, shredded

Combine the water and dates in a sauce pan, cook over medium heat until dates are cooked. Allow to cool. Combine the butter, salt, sugar, baking soda, egg, flour, baking powder and nuts. Spread evenly in a greased 9" x 12" (23 x 30 cm) pan. Spread cooled date mixture over the first layer and bake in a preheated 350°F (180°C) oven for 30 minutes. While squares are baking, combine the sugar, vanilla, butter and milk in a sauce pan. Bring to a boil for 5 minutes, remove from heat and stir in the coconut. Take squares out of oven and spread topping evenly over the date mixture. Return to oven for 5 minutes or until mixture is bubbling all over.

Cinnamon Vanilla Custard

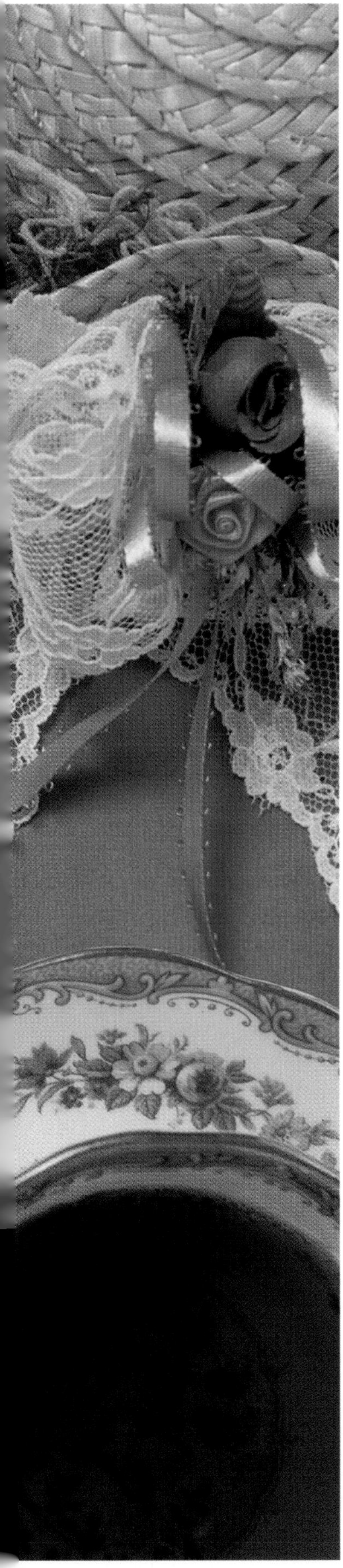

CINNAMON VANILLA CUSTARD

4	4	eggs
2 cup	500 ml	granulated sugar
1 cup	250 ml	cream – light
2 tbsp	30 ml	butter – melted
¼ tsp	2 ml	salt
2 tsp	10 ml	vanilla
½ tsp	3 ml	cinnamon
4 tbsp	60 ml	flour, all purpose

Beat the eggs in a mixing bowl. Beat in the remaining ingredients. Pour into a 9" x 9" (23 x 23 cm) square baking pan and bake 45 minutes in a preheated 300°F (160°C) oven.

SERVES 6

FRESH STRAWBERRY PIE 2

1 qt	1.25 L	fresh strawberries
1¼ cups	310 ml	granulated sugar
1 tbsp	15 ml	cornstarch
1¼ cups	375 ml	water
3 tbsp	45 ml	lemon juice
3 oz (1 pkg)	85 g	strawberry gelatin
1	1	baked 9-inch pie shell

Clean and hull strawberries

In medium saucepan, combine sugar and cornstarch; add water and lemon juice. Over high heat, bring to a boil. Reduce heat; cook and stir until slightly thickened and clear, 4 to 5 minutes. Add gelatin, stir until dissolved. Cool to room temperature. Stir in strawberries; turn into prepared pastry shell. Chill 4 to 6 hours or until set. Serve with whipped cream if desired.

SERVES 6

QUICK GINGERBREAD

3	3	eggs
1 cup	250 ml	granulated sugar
1 cup	250 ml	molasses
1 tsp	5 ml	each cloves, ginger, cinnamon, salt
1 cup	250 ml	salad oil
2⅛ cups	530 ml	flour, all purpose
2 tsp	10 ml	baking soda
2 tbsp	30 ml	warm water
1 cup	250 ml	hot water

Combine the eggs, sugar, molasses, spices, salt and oil. Blend well. Sift in the flour and continue to beat until fluffy. Dissolve the soda in the warm water; add to the mixture and mix well. Lastly add the hot water and beat lightly and quickly. Pour into a greased 9" x 13" (23 x 23 cm) pan and bake in a preheated 350°F (180°C) oven for 40 minutes or until a tooth pick inserted in the centre comes out clean. Serve hot with whipped cream.

VARIATIONS: Bake the gingerbread in layer cake pans for about 25 minutes. As soon as removed from the oven, spread the top of one layer with sliced marshmallows. Place the other cake layer on top and return to over 3 minutes longer. Serve hot with whipped cream.

When blueberries are in season, add to batter 1 cup (250 ml) berries dredged with 1 tbsp (15 ml) all purpose flour.

Praline Chocolate Bon Bons

COCONUT PINEAPPLE FLUFF

1 tbsp	15 ml	gelatin – unflavoured
¼ cup	60 ml	cold water
¾ cup	180 ml	pineapple juice
¼ cup	60 ml	coconut cream nectar
¼ cup	60 ml	granulated sugar
¾ cup	180 ml	whipping cream

Soak the gelatin in the water. Place in a small sauce pan and add the pineapple juice, bring to a boil. Remove from heat and stir in the coconut cream and sugar. Cool and chill to thick but not set. Whip the cream and fold into pineapple. Pour into mold or bowl and chill to set. Unmold and serve.

SERVES 4

PRALINE CHOCOLATE BON BONS

1 cup	250 ml	brown sugar
1 cup	250 ml	granulated sugar
1½ cups	375 ml	chocolate chips
½ cup	125 ml	cream – light
2 tbsp	30 ml	butter
1 cup	250 ml	pecans

Dissolve the sugars and chocolate chips in the cream in a sauce pan. Heat to 238°F (115°C) on a candy thermometer. Remove from heat, beat in the butter and nuts, continue to heat until thick. Drop onto a pastry sheet lined with buttered wax paper, leaving enough room between each as they separate.

YIELDS 2 LBS

APPLE CRUNCH MUFFINS

1½ cups	375 ml	flour, all purpose
½ cup	125 ml	granulated sugar
2 tsp	10 ml	baking powder
½ tsp	1 ml	salt
1½ tsp	8 ml	cinnamon
¼ cup	60 ml	vegetable shortening
1	1	egg, slightly beaten
½ cup	125 ml	milk
1 cup	250 ml	tart apples*
		Nut Crunch Topping

Sift together flour, sugar, baking powder, salt and cinnamon into mixing bowl.

Cut in shortening with pastry blender until fine crumbs form. Combine egg and milk. Add to dry ingredients all at once, stirring just enough to moisten. Stir in apples. Spoon batter into paper-lined 2½" (6.5 cm) muffin pan cups, filling ⅔rds full. Sprinkle with Nut Crunch Topping.

Bake in a preheated 375°F (190°C) oven 25 minutes or until golden brown. Serve hot with butter and home made jelly or jam.

NUT CRUNCH TOPPING: Mix together ¼ cup (60 ml) brown sugar, packed, ¼ cup (60 ml) chopped pecans and ½ tsp (3 ml) ground cinnamon in small bowl.

*Apples are to be washed and cored. Shred the unpeeled apples for recipe.

SERVES 4

Coconut Pineapple Fluff

Raspberry Apricot Soufflé

Pecan Chocolate Dipped Strawberries

MOLASSES REFRIGERATOR MUFFINS

4 cups	1 L	flour, all purpose
2 tsp	10 ml	baking soda
1 tsp	5 ml	each of salt, cinnamon, ginger
¼ tsp	1 ml	each ground cloves, allspice, nutmeg
1⅓ cups	330 ml	vegetable shortening
1 cup	250 ml	granulated sugar
4	4	eggs, slightly beaten
1 cup	250 ml	molasses
1 cup	250 ml	butter
1 cup	250 ml	sour milk
1 cup	250 ml	raisins

Sift together flour, baking soda, salt, cinnamon, ginger, cloves, allspice and nutmeg; set aside.

Cream together shortening and sugar in mixing bowl until light and fluffy. Add eggs, beat well.

Blend in molasses, butter and sour milk. Add dry ingredients all at once, stirring just enough to moisten. Stir in raisins. Spoon into greased 3" (7.5 cm) muffin pan cups, filling ½ full.

Bake in preheated 350°F (180°C) oven 20 minutes or until golden brown. Serve hot with butter and jam.

YIELDS 12

RASPBERRY APRICOT SOUFFLÉ

½ cup	125 ml	granulated sugar
¼ cup	60 ml	flour, all purpose
1 cup	250 ml	milk
½ cup	125 ml	apricots – puréed
¼ cup	60 ml	raspberry preserve
2 tbsp	30 ml	butter
4	4	eggs
2	2	egg whites

Butter a 6 to 8 quart (1.5–2 L) soufflé dish. Dust the sides and bottom with sugar.

In a sauce pan whip the flour into the milk and heat to boiling. Whip in the apricot, raspberry and butter, return to a boil and remove from heat at once. Beat in the egg yolks one at a time. Whip the egg whites stiff and fold into the mixture. Pour into the soufflé dish and bake for 40 minutes in a preheated 400°F (200°C) oven. Serve with an apricot brandy sauce.

SERVES 4

PECAN CHOCOLATE DIPPED STRAWBERRIES

25	25	fresh large strawberries
4 oz	120 g	semi-sweet chocolate – grated
1 tbsp	15 ml	butter – melted
1½ cups	375 ml	pecan pieces chopped fine

Wash the berries then dry them. In a double boiler melt the chocolate and stir in the butter. Dip the strawberries in the chocolate then into the nuts. Place on a sheet of wax paper, allow to harden before removing to a platter. Do not refrigerate.

BANANA PECAN BREAD

½ cup	125 ml	shortening or butter
¾ cup	180 ml	brown sugar
¼ cup	60 ml	granulated sugar
pinch	pinch	salt
1	1	egg
1 cup	250 ml	bananas, over ripe and pureed
1¼ cups	310 ml	flour, pastry
½ tsp	3 ml	baking powder
½ cup	125 ml	butter
1 cup	250 ml	brown sugar
¾ cup	180 ml	pecans, whole

Cream the butter, sugars and salt until light and fluffy. Beat in the egg and bananas. Sift together the flour and baking powder. Fold into the banana mixture.

Heat the butter in a sauce pan and add the brown sugar. Cook until the mixture become smooth. Grease and flour a 9" x 5" (23 x 12 cm) loaf pan and put the sauce into the base. Sprinkle pecans on the sauce followed by the banana bread batter. Smooth the surface and place in a preheated 375°F (190°C) oven for 30-35 minutes.

The caramel that has been formed in the bottom of the pan requires a little time to release itself so you must turn the mold over onto a cake wire, allow to sit for 30 seconds and then remove the mold. The nuts will be encrusted in the base of the bread and the hot caramel will soak into the base of the cake and set.

PINEAPPLE SNOW

1 tbsp	15 ml	gelatin – unflavoured
¼ cup	60 ml	cold water
1 cup	250 ml	crushed pineapple, drained
½ cup	125 ml	syrup from pineapple
½ cup	125 ml	pineapple juice
2 tbsp	30 ml	lemon juice
2	2	egg whites
¼ cup	60 ml	granulated sugar

Soften the gelatin in the cold water. Place in a sauce pan with crushed pineapple, syrup and juices and bring to a boil then remove from heat. Cool and chill to almost set. Whip the egg whites until stiff then gradually add the sugar. Fold into the pineapple, pour in a mold or bowl. Chill until set, unmold and serve.

SERVES 4

BANANA GUMDROP LOAF

1¾ cups	430 ml	unsifted all purpose flour
½ tsp	3 ml	baking soda
1½ tsp	8 ml	baking powder
¾ cup	180 ml	granulated sugar
5 oz	145 g	gumdrops, cut in pieces
1	1	egg, beaten
¼ cup	60 ml	oil
1 cup	250 ml	mashed bananas (approximately 3)
½ cup	125 ml	milk
2 tsp	10 ml	grated orange rind

Measure and sift the dry ingredients in a bowl, stir in the gumdrop pieces. Combine the remaining ingredients and stir into the dry ingredients. Stir until blended and put into a greased 9" x 5" (23 x 12 cm) pan. Bake in a preheated 350°F (180°C) oven for 50 minutes.

YIELD 1 LOAF

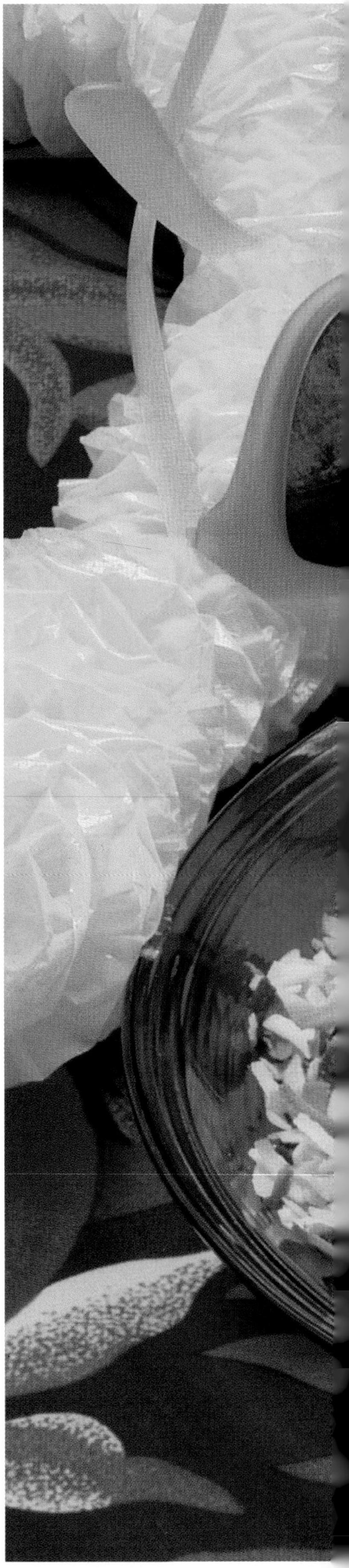

Pineapple Snow

Marshmallow Fudge Bon Bons

Cherry Apple Pie

BLACKBERRY APPLES ROCKY MOUNTAINS

6	6	large red apples
3 tbsp	45 ml	lemon juice
1 cup	250 ml	granulated sugar
¼ cup	60 ml	cornstarch
2	2	eggs
1 cup	250 ml	milk
¼ cup	60 ml	Calvados liqueur or apple juice concentrate
⅛ tsp	pinch	salt
2 pints	0.5 L	fresh washed and hulled blackberries
¼ cup	60 ml	confectioners' sugar

Cut the tops from the apples, scoop out the pulp reserving 2 cups (500 ml). Brush the top and insides of apples with the lemon juice.

Combine the sugar, cornstarch and eggs together in a double boiler. Add the milk and Calvados, cook stirring until very thick. Stir in the apple pulp, and salt, fill apple shells with mixture. Cool, then chill.

Place on serving plates, top with mounds of blackberries and dust with confectioners' sugar.

SERVES 6

CHERRY APPLE PIE

1	1	Plain Pastry (see page 616)
2 cups	500 ml	apples, sliced
2 cups	500 ml	sour red cherries
½ tsp	3 ml	almond extract
⅓ cup	80 ml	flour, all purpose
¼ tsp	2 ml	cinnamon
¾ cup	180 ml	granulated sugar
3 tbsp	45 ml	butter

Roll out half the pastry to fit into a 9" (23 cm) pie pan.

Sprinkle pastry with apples and cherries.

Mix the extract, flour, cinnamon and sugar together, cut in the butter, mixing to crumbly. Sprinkle over the fruit.

Moisten edge of pastry with water. Roll out the remaining pastry and cut into ½" (1.5 cm) strips. Arrange pastry strips on top of pie, lattice style, moistening where necessary to seal. Flute the edges.

Bake in a preheated 350°F (180°C) oven for 45 minutes, or until pastry is golden brown and the cherries are tender. Cool before serving.

SERVES 6

MARSHMALLOW FUDGE BON BONS

2 cups	500 ml	granulated sugar
2 cups	500 ml	cream
8 oz	225 g	chocolate – semi-sweet, melted
¼ cup	60 ml	butter
1 tsp	5 ml	vanilla
1 cup	250 ml	marshmallows
2 oz	60 g	white chocolate, melted

Blend the sugar, cream, 5 oz (120 g) chocolate, butter and vanilla in a sauce pan. Bring to a boil and cook to a soft ball stage (238°F or 114°C). Melt the marshmallows in a double boiler and blend into the fudge.

Pour mixture onto a greased cookie sheet. As mixture cools, break walnut size pieces off and roll to form smooth balls. Place balls back on the cookie sheet and allow to cool. Dip into the remaining chocolate, drizzle with white chocolate.

YIELDS 24 CANDIES

BREADS

Most of us remember the bread grandmother used to bake in her cozy kitchen. Fragrant, golden loaves — crusty, tender and delicious. Home bread-baking is not as common today, and that is a pity, because it is such a pleasant task and surprisingly easy.

The consumption of bread has become almost universal and is an indispensable component of most people's daily diet. Made from wheat, rice, maize (corn) or rye, bread is the only food present on the table from the start to the finish of the meal. Bread constitutes the traditional accompaniment to all dishes, while it slows the assimilation of other foods, making digestion easier and relieving hunger.

There are just two essentials for successful bread-making: Select your ingredients with care and master our simple to follow procedures that guarantee a *Simply Delicious* product. Your outcome will have a crisp crust, an attractive golden colour and a soft crumb — the marks for successful bread making.

In *Simply Delicious Cooking 2*, we have taken the time to provide the guidelines using white bread flour and whole wheat flour to the art of bread making. Once you see the ease in making your own loaves, experiment with different flour types turning your white bread into cracked wheat, Viennese or German, to just 'raise' a few names. Just before panning, place the top side in poppy, sesame or caraway seeds. When making French breads, put a twist into things by braiding the bread and placing on lightly dusted corn meal cookie sheets. The varieties are great, the effort is small, and the result, as always, will be the praise of your guests as they ask; "pass the *Simply Delicious* bread, please."

Bagels

Red Currant Tea Biscuits

DATE BREAD

½ cup	125 ml	molasses
2 cups	500 ml	lukewarm milk
1¾ cups	440 ml	lukewarm water
¼ cup	60 ml	melted butter
3 cups	750 ml	chopped dates
3 tbsp	45 ml	instant yeast
½ tsp	3 ml	salt
6 cups	1.5 L	whole wheat flour
6 cups	1.5 L	bread flour

Blend the molasses, milk, water, butter and dates together.

Combine the yeast and salt.

Mix the flours together, remove 2 cups. Sift the remaining flour together with the yeast. Add the liquid mixture and blend into a soft dough. Add the remaining flour to the dough in small amounts until a firm elastic dough is formed and does not stick to the sides of the bowl (use only sufficient flour to accomplish this dough), knead for 5 minutes.

Place the dough bowl in a pan of warm water, allow the dough to rise to double of its size. Turn out onto a lightly flour dusted surface, punch down, roll the dough in 3 separate loaves. Place into 3 well greased loaf pans, allow to rise to double in size.

Bake in a preheated 350°F (180°C) oven for 40 minutes or until the dough is golden brown and firm in the centre. Remove from oven, let stand for 10 minutes then turn out onto a cooling rack. Cool to room temperature before serving.

YIELDS 3 LOAVES

Date Bread

RED CURRANT TEA BISCUITS

2½ cups	625 ml	bread flour
2 tsp	10 ml	baking powder
½ tsp	3 ml	salt
5 tbsp	75 ml	butter
½ cup	125 ml	milk
1 tsp	5 ml	grated orange rind
1	1	beaten egg yolk
4 tbsp	60 ml	red currant preserves

Sift the flour, baking powder and salt together twice.

Cut in the butter until a fine meal is formed. Remove ⅓ of the mixture, into the remaining blend in the milk, kneading only until a soft dough is formed.

Knead the orange rind, egg and red currant into the remaining dough. Knead the two doughs together slightly. Roll out on a lightly flour dusted surface to ½" (1.5 cm) thick. Cut out with a small flour dusted biscuit cutter.

Bake for 15-18 minutes in a 400°F (200°C) oven.

YIELDS 16 BISCUITS

OLD FASHION CHEDDAR BISCUITS

2 cups	500 ml	bread flour
2 tsp	10 ml	baking powder
⅛ tsp	pinch	salt
2 tbsp	30 ml	butter
1 cup	250 ml	grated medium cheddar
¾ cup	190 ml	milk

Sift the flour, baking powder and salt together. Cut in the butter and cheese. Gradually add the milk until a soft dough is formed.

Turn out on a lightly floured surface and knead slightly (30 seconds). Roll dough into a square ¼" (6 mm) thick. Cut into biscuits with a round biscuit cutter or into even squares.

Place on a ungreased baking sheet, bake in a preheated 400°F (200°C) oven for 15-18 minutes.

YIELDS 12 BISCUITS

STICKY BUN PINWHEELS

1 quan	1 quan	Gourmet Pastry (see page 541)
2 cups	500 ml	brown sugar
5 tsp	25 ml	cinnamon
2 cups	500 ml	pecan, chopped fine

In a 12 cup (3 L) greased medium-size muffin tin, divide ½ cup (125 ml) of brown sugar and ½ cup (125 ml) of pecans evenly, Preheat the oven to 375°F (190°C).

Roll dough onto a lightly floured surface to a 9" (23 cm) square.

Spread rolled dough with 1½ cups (375 ml) of sugar, cinnamon and 1½ cups (375 ml) of pecans. Roll up as for a jelly roll. Seal edges.

Cut into twelve ¾" (2 cm) thick slices and arrange, cut side down, in the greased muffin cups. Bake for 12 to 15 minutes. Remove from pan immediately.

YIELD 12 PINWHEELS

AUSTRIA ROLLS

3¾ cups	940 ml	bread flour
1 tsp	5 ml	salt
1 tbsp	15 ml	instant yeast
1 tsp	5 ml	granulated sugar
1½ cups	375 ml	table cream
1	1	beaten egg
2 tbsp	30 ml	melted butter

Sift the flour, salt, yeast and sugar together. Add the cream and egg and knead into a smooth dough. Cover and allow the dough to rise to double in size.

Turn the dough out on a lightly flour dusted surface, divide the dough into 18 even pieces. Roll the pieces into smooth balls and place on a lightly greased baking sheet, allow to rise to double in size.

Butter the buns with the melted butter, bake buns in a preheated 425°F (220°C) oven for 15-17 minutes. Serve hot or cold.

YIELDS 18 ROLLS

WALNUT CHOCOLATE CRUNCH DOUGHNUTS

1 tbsp	15 ml	cocoa powder
3 cups	750 ml	flour, all purpose
1 cup	250 ml	granulated sugar
¾ cup	180 ml	milk
2	2	eggs
2 tbsp	30 ml	shortening
2 tsp	10 ml	baking powder
1 tsp	5 ml	baking soda
1 tsp	5 ml	salt
2 oz	60 g	semi-sweet chocolate
½ cup	125 ml	walnuts – pieces

Blend the cocoa powder, half the flour and sugar together. Place into a mixing bowl. Beat in the remaining ingredients. Gradually while beating incorporate the remaining flour. Refrigerate for 1 hour, roll the dough out to ¼" (6 mm) thick. Cut into rectangle shapes. Fry in oil at 375°F (190°C). Turning over only once, drain on paper towelling. Dust with granulated sugar.

YIELDS 24

Sticky Bun Pinwheels

Maple Cashew Biscuits

APPLE 'N' SPICE FRITTERS

1¼ cups	310 ml	flour, all purpose
1½ tsp	8 ml	baking powder
3 tbsp	45 ml	sugar
1 tsp	5 ml	cinnamon
2	2	eggs
¼ tsp	2 ml	salt
1 tsp	5 ml	vanilla
½ cup	125 ml	milk
1 cup	250 ml	apples – pared, cored, diced coarse

Sift the flour, baking powder, sugar and cinnamon. Whip the eggs with the salt, vanilla and milk. Stir in the flour, blend in the apples. Drop tablespoon sizes of batter into 375°F (190°C) oil, fry to golden brown on each side. Remove and drain on paper towel. Dust with Cinnamon Sugar (recipe follows) while still hot.

CINNAMON SUGAR:

2 cups	500 ml	confectioners' sugar
1 tbsp	15 ml	cinnamon ground

Blend.

YIELDS 1 DOZ

MAPLE CASHEW BISCUITS

3 tbsp	45 ml	melted butter
½ cup	125 ml	maple syrup
¼ tsp	1 ml	ground cinnamon
2 cups	500 ml	bread flour
1 tbsp	15 ml	baking powder
½ tsp	3 ml	salt
¼ cup	60 ml	butter
⅓ cup	90 ml	milk
½ cup	125 ml	cashew pieces

Combine the butter, syrup and cinnamon together. Place ½ tablespoon (8 ml) in 8 muffin tins.

Blend the flour, baking powder and salt, sift once. Cut the butter into the flour forming a coarse mixture. Fold in the milk.

Turn dough out on a lightly floured surface, knead slightly (30 seconds). Roll into a 9" x 9" (23 x 23 cm) square. Pour the remaining syrup over and sprinkle with nuts. Roll tightly together, cut into eight even pieces.

Place the cut side of each piece into the muffin tins. Bake for 15 minutes in a preheated 400°F (200°C) oven.

YIELDS 8 BISCUITS

BUTTERMILK ROLLS

2 tbsp	30 ml	granulated sugar
2 tbsp	30 ml	brown sugar
2 cups	500 ml	buttermilk
1 tsp	5 ml	salt
2 tbsp	30 ml	instant yeast
5 cups	1.25 L	bread flour
½ tsp	3 ml	baking soda
½ cup	125 ml	melted warm butter

Combine the sugars and buttermilk together.

Sift the salt, yeast, flour and baking soda together, twice.Beat the liquid into the flour until a smooth dough is formed. Brush with butter, cover and allow to rise until twice its size.

Turn the dough out on a lightly floured surface and roll the dough out very thin. Brush with butter and fold three times, cut into 2" (5 cm) strips. Twist the strips and place on a lightly greased baking sheet. Allow to rise to double in size.

Brush with butter and bake for 20-25 minutes in a preheated 375°F (190°C) oven.

YIELDS 3 DOZEN ROLLS

PECAN RAISIN STICKY BUNS

3 cups	45 ml	bread flour
2 tbsp	30 ml	baking powder
2 tbsp	30 ml	granulated sugar
1	1	beaten egg
1 cup	250 ml	table cream
1 tsp	5 ml	salt
⅓ cup	90 ml	butter
1 cup	250 ml	brown sugar
1 tsp	5 ml	ground cinnamon
½ cup	125 ml	chopped pecans
½ cup	125 ml	seedless raisins

Sift the flour, baking powder, sugar and salt together.

Beat the egg into the cream.

Cream ¼ cup (60 ml) of the butter until light, add the flour alternating with the cream in ⅓rds.

Roll dough out on a lightly floured surface. Spread the remaining butter over the dough.

Combine the brown sugar, cinnamon, pecans and raisins, spread over the dough. Roll the dough very tight. Cut into 10-12 pieces, place on a greased baking sheet ¼" (6 mm) apart, bake in a preheated 350°F (180°C) oven for 20-25 minutes. Serve hot or cold.

YIELDS 10-12 LARGE ROLLS

Buttermilk Honey Biscuits

BUTTERMILK HONEY BISCUITS

2 cups	500 ml	bread flour
2 tsp	10 ml	baking powder
¼ tsp	1 ml	baking soda
½ tsp	3 ml	salt
¼ cup	60 ml	shortening
½ cup	125 ml	buttermilk
¼ cup	60 ml	liquid honey

Sift the flour, baking powder, baking soda and salt together. Cut the shortening in until a coarse dough is formed.

Stir in the buttermilk and honey, knead forming a soft dough. Roll the dough into a ½" (1.5 cm) thick square. Cut with a floured biscuit cutter. Bake for 15-18 minutes in a preheated 400°F (200°C) oven.

YIELDS 12 BISCUITS

COTTAGE COUNTRY BISCUITS

1 cup	250 ml	sieved cottage cheese
2 tbsp	30 ml	half & half cream
1	1	beaten egg
2 tbsp	30 ml	butter
⅛ tsp	pinch	basil
2 cups	500 ml	bread flour
½ tsp	3 ml	salt
4 tsp	20 ml	baking powder

Cream the cheese, cream, egg and butter together.

Combine the basil, flour, salt and baking powder together.

Fold the creamed mixture into the flour kneading into a soft dough. Turn the dough out onto a lightly flour dusted surface, roll into a ½" (1.5 cm) square. Cut with a flour dusted biscuit cutter, place on a ungreased baking sheet. Bake for 15-18 minutes in a preheated 400°F (200°C) oven.

YIELDS 12 BISCUITS

Pecan Raisin Sticky Buns

CALIFORNIA SOUR DOUGH BREAD

1 cup	250 ml	Sour Dough Starter (recipe follows)
1½ cups	375 ml	warm water
2 tbsp	30 ml	granulated sugar
6 cups	1.5 L	flour, all purpose
1 tbsp	15 ml	salt
½ tsp	3 ml	baking soda

Combine the starter, water, sugar and 3 cups of flour in a large glass, wooden or plastic mixing bowl. Cover tightly with plastic wrap and allow to stand 8-12 hours or overnight.

Combine the salt and soda with 1 cup (250 ml) of flour, beat into dough. Work in enough of the remaining flour to form a very stiff dough. Knead for 10 minutes. Form into two round balls, place on a baking sheet. With a sharp knife, score top of bread ¼" (6 mm) deep (if desired). Cover the dough and allow to rise for 2 hours.

Sprinkle lightly with water, bake in a preheated 350°F (180°C) oven for 40-45 minutes.

YIELDS 2 LOAF

SOUR DOUGH STARTER

2 cups	500 ml	flour, all purpose
1 tbsp	15 ml	dry yeast
1 tbsp	15 ml	granulated sugar
2 cups	500 ml	potato water

Combine the ingredients in a large glass bowl. Cover and let stand for 48 hours in a warm place. Use as required or cover and refrigerate. To replenish stir in 1 cup (250 ml) of flour and 1 cup (250 ml) of water, allow to stand in a warm place for 48 hours before covering and refrigerating.

California Sour Dough Bread

HONEY ORANGE SOUR CREAM FRITTERS

½ cup	125 ml	honey liquid
2	2	eggs
¼ tsp	2 ml	salt
½ cup	125 ml	sour cream
2 cups	500 ml	flour, all purpose
2 tsp	10 ml	baking powder
1 tbsp	15 ml	orange rind – grated
1 tbsp	15 ml	lemon juice
½ cup	125 ml	orange juice

Blend the honey, eggs, salt and sour cream. Sift together the flour and baking powder, stir in the sour cream. Blend in the orange rind, lemon juice and orange juice. Drop tbsp sizes of batter into oil heated to 375°F (190°C). Fry to golden brown on all sides. Remove and drain on paper towelling. Brush with Orange Glaze (recipe follows).

ORANGE GLAZE:

1 cup	250 ml	granulated sugar
½ cup	125 ml	orange juice

Combine ingredients in a sauce pan, bring to a boil, reduce heat to simmer for 5 minutes. Brush on hot fritters.

YIELDS 24 DOUGHNUTS

SUGAR BUSH AFTERNOON TEA CAKE

¾ cup	190 ml	milk
½ cup	125 ml	butter
¾ cup	190 ml	maple syrup
3½ cups	875 ml	bread flour
1 tbsp	15 ml	instant yeast
½ tsp	3 ml	salt
1	1	eggs
½ cup	125 ml	brown sugar
⅓ cup	90 ml	maple sugar
½ tsp	3 ml	ground cinnamon
½ cup	125 ml	walnuts, chopped

Warm the milk and butter in a small sauce pan along with ¼ cup (60 ml) maple syrup. Cool to room temperature.

Sift together 3 cups (750 ml) of flour, with the yeast and salt.

Beat the eggs then add to the cooled liquid, fold into the flour beating until a smooth batter is formed. Stir in enough of the remaining flour to form a smooth ball of dough. Cover the dough and allow to rise to double it's size.

While the dough rises combine the brown sugar with the maple sugar. Cream the remaining butter and fold in the sugars. Stir in the remaining syrup, 2 tbsp (30 ml) of flour, the cinnamon and nuts.

Divide the dough in half and roll each half into 12" x 12" (30 x 30 cm) squares. Spread with the maple filling, fold in thirds. Roll tightly together, cut each roll into 10 pieces, place the rolls on a greased baking sheet. Allow to rise to twice in size. Bake in a preheated 350°F (180°C) oven for 35-40 minutes. Serve hot or cold.

YIELDS 20 ROLLS

CRANAPPLE BREAD

2 cups	500 ml	bread flour
½ tsp	3 ml	salt
1 tsp	5 ml	baking powder
½ tsp	3 ml	ground cinnamon
½ cup	125 ml	butter
1 cup	250 ml	granulated sugar
1	1	beaten egg
½ cup	125 ml	half & half cream
1 cup	250 ml	pared, cored, thin sliced apples
½ cup	125 ml	fresh or frozen chopped cranberries

Sift together the flour, salt, baking powder and cinnamon.

Cream the butter and sugar until very light and fluffy. Beat in the egg. Fold in the flour in ⅓rds, alternating with the cream. Fold in the apples and the cranberries.

Pour the batter into a well greased 9" loaf pan, bake for 75 minutes in a preheated 350°F (180°C) oven or until an inserted skewer is removed clean. Remove from oven and cool for 10 minutes, turn loaf out and cool to room temperature before serving.

YIELDS 1 LOAF

PUFF PASTRY

2 cups	500 ml	pastry flour
½ cup	125 ml	butter
½ tsp	3 ml	salt
½ cup	125 ml	ice water

Place the flour into a mixing bowl and cut into it 2 tbsp (30 ml) of the butter. Add the salt and stir in just enough water to form a firm dough. Knead the dough for 5 minutes.

Roll the dough out onto a lightly flour dusted surface to ¼" (6 mm) thick, keeping in a rectangle shape. Dot the ⅓rds of the dough with the remaining butter, fold together in thirds (the unbuttered part over the buttered part, the remainder over both). Cover with a towel, chill for 1 hour.

Roll the dough out to ¼" (6 mm) thick and refold, cover and chill for 1 hour, repeat this process 4-8 times depending on how flaky a pastry you desire.

Roll the dough out and use as required, baking at 425°F (215°C) for 5 minutes, reduce temperature to 375°F (190°C) and continue to bake for 25-30 minutes.

Cranapple Bread

Northern Ontario Wild Blueberry Muffins

Bagels

BAGELS

4-5 cups	1-1.25 L	flour, all purpose
1 tbsp	15 ml	instant yeast
2 tsp	10 ml	salt
1½ cups	375 ml	hot water 130°F (55°C)
2 tbsp	30 ml	honey
1	1	egg white
1 tbsp	15 ml	cold water

Sift 4 cups (1 L) of the flour, along with the yeast and salt together. Beat in the hot water and honey, stir in enough of the remaining flour to form a smooth dough ball, knead for 5 minutes.

Cover and allow dough to rest for 15 minutes.

Divide the dough into 12 even portions, roll into balls and then flatten. Poke a hole in the centre, stretch the dough causing the hole to increase to 1½" (3.75 cm) in size. Place on a lightly flour dusted surface, cover and allow to rise for 20 minutes.

In a large kettle or Dutch oven place enough water to cover 2" (5 cm) of the bottom, bring to a boil. Simmer the bagels in the water for 7 minutes a few at a time. Remove from water, pat dry and transfer to a baking sheet.

Mix the egg white with the cold water and brush the bagels, sprinkle with poppy seeds and bake in a preheated 375°F (190°C) oven for 30 minutes or until golden brown or cooked through.

Great with cream cheese and smoked salmon.

YIELDS 12 BAGELS

NORTHERN ONTARIO WILD BLUEBERRY MUFFINS

1 cup	250 ml	granulated sugar
½ cup	125 ml	butter
2	2	eggs
⅓ cup	90 ml	milk
½ tsp	3 ml	vanilla extract
2 cups	500 ml	flour, all purpose
2 tsp	10 ml	baking powder
½ tsp	3 ml	salt
1 cup	250 ml	fresh wild blueberries, washed and picked through

Combine the sugar, butter, eggs, milk and vanilla together.

Sift the flour, baking powder and salt together. Stir the liquids into the flour to form a smooth batter. Fold in the blueberries.

Spoon the batter into 12 well greased muffin tins, bake in a preheated 375°F (190°C) oven for 20-25 minutes. Serve hot or cold.

YIELDS 12 MUFFINS

DATE 'N' NUT BISCUITS

2 cups	500 ml	bread flour
1 tbsp	15 ml	baking powder
¼ tsp	1 ml	salt
¼ cup	60 ml	shortening
¾ cup	190 ml	milk
½ cup	125 ml	chopped dates
¼ cup	60 ml	chopped walnut pieces

Sift together the flour, baking powder and salt.

Cut the shortening into the flour to make a coarse meal. Stir in the milk until dough is soft. Knead for 30 seconds adding the dates and nuts.

Roll the dough out to ¼" (6 mm) thick on a lightly flour dusted surface. Cut the biscuits out with a small flour dusted biscuit cutter. Place on an ungreased baking sheet.

Bake for 15-18 minutes in a preheated 400°F (200°C) oven.

YIELDS 16 BISCUITS

BANANA DOUGHNUTS

2½ cups	625 ml	flour, all purpose
1½ tsp	8 ml	baking powder
½ tsp	3 ml	baking soda
1 tsp	5 ml	salt
½ tsp	3 ml	nutmeg
3 tbsp	45 ml	shortening
½ cup	125 ml	granulated sugar
2	2	eggs
⅓	90 ml	bananas, mashed
¼ cup	60 ml	buttermilk
1 tsp	5 ml	vanilla extract

Sift the flour, baking powder, baking soda, salt and nutmeg together three times. Cream the shortening and sugar, beat in the eggs, bananas, buttermilk and vanilla. Stir in the flour mixture to form a smooth dough, divide the dough in two. Roll to ¼" (6 mm) thick on a flour dusted surface. Cut with 2½" (6 cm) doughnut cutter floured. Fry in a deep fat fryer at 375°F (190°C) to golden brown. Drain on paper towelled surface.

YIELDS 20 DOUGHNUTS

ORANGE PECAN BISCUITS

2 cup	500 ml	bread flour
1 tsp	5 ml	salt
2 tsp	10 ml	baking powder
2 tsp	10 ml	grated orange rind
3 tbsp	45 ml	finely chopped pecan pieces
6 oz	170 g	cream cheese
1 cup	250 ml	butter
½ cup	125 ml	orange juice
18	18	pecan halves

Sift the flour, salt, and baking powder together twice, blend in the orange and chopped pecans.

Cream the cheese and butter together, cut into the flour and knead into a soft dough.

Stir in the orange juice and knead 3 minutes.

Turn dough out onto a lightly floured surface. Roll into a ¼" (6 mm) thick square, cut with a small floured dusted biscuit cutter. Place on a ungreased baking sheet and top each with a pecan half.

Bake in a preheated 400°F (200°C) oven for 15-20 minutes.

YIELDS 12 BISCUITS

PEAR & CARROT PECAN BRAN BREAD

1 cup	250 ml	pared and grated pears
¼ cup	60 ml	pared and grated carrots
2	2	beaten large eggs
1 cup	250 ml	bran
1½ cups	375 ml	bread flour
½ cup	125 ml	granulated sugar
1 tsp	5 ml	baking powder
½ tsp	3 ml	salt
½ tsp	3 ml	baking soda
¼ cup	60 ml	butter
½ cup	125 ml	chopped pecans

Combine the pears, carrots, eggs and bran together and let stand for 15 minutes.

Sift the flour, sugar, baking powder, salt and baking soda together, twice. Cut the butter into the flour until a coarse meal is formed. Stir in the fruit mixture and blend well. Fold in the nuts, pour the batter into a 8½ x 4½ x 2½" (21 x 10 x 5 cm) loaf pan. Allow to stand for 25 minutes.

Bake in a preheated 350°F (180°C) oven for 75 minutes or until a inserted skewer comes out clean. Let stand for 10 minutes, turn out onto a cooling rack and cool completely before serving.

YIELDS 1 LOAF

Orange Pecan Biscuits

Pear & Carrot Pecan Bran Bread

Creole Beignets

Orange Brandy Bread

CREOLE BEIGNETS

1 cup	250 ml	milk – scalded, hot
2 tbsp	30 ml	butter
1 tbsp	15 ml	brown sugar
1 tbsp	15 ml	granulated sugar
3 cups	750 ml	flour, all purpose
1 tsp	5 ml	nutmeg
1 tbsp	15 ml	instant yeast
1 tsp	5 ml	salt
1	1	egg
1 tsp	5 ml	vanilla
1 cup	250 ml	confectioners' sugar

Combine the milk, butter and sugars. Stir until sugar is dissolved. Cool to room temperature. Sift the flour, nutmeg, instant yeast and salt together. Blend half the flour mixture into the milk mixing until smooth. Stir in the egg and the vanilla. Fold in the remaining flour. Cover and place in a warm area. Allow to double in size. Punch dough down and place on a lightly floured surface, cut into squares and allow to rise a second time. Fry in oil at 375°F (190°C). Fry one side to golden brown before turning. Dust with confectioners' sugar, if desired.

YIELDS 24 DOUGHNUTS

OLD FASHION LEFTOVER 'TATER' CHEESE BREAD

¾ cup	190 ml	cold mashed potatoes
¼ cup	60 ml	freshly grated Parmesan cheese
1 cup	250 ml	bread flour
3 tbsp	45 ml	baking powder
1 tsp	5 ml	salt
2 tbsp	30 ml	butter
½ cup	125 ml	cold milk

Blend the potatoes with the cheese.

Sift together the flour, baking powder and salt. Cut the butter into the flour, stir in the potatoes and work the dough into a course meal incorporating the flour and the potatoes completely. Stir in the milk making a soft dough.

Turn the dough out onto a lightly dusted flour surface, roll out to ½" (1.5 cm) thick. Cut into even squares. Place on a ungreased baking sheet and bake for 12-15 minutes in a preheated 400°F (200°C) oven.

YIELDS 12 BISCUITS

ORANGE BRANDY BREAD

1 cup	250 ml	lukewarm water
¼ cup	60 ml	orange brandy (optional, replace with an equal amount of orange juice)
¾ cup	190 ml	orange juice
2 tsp	10 ml	grated orange rind
1 tsp	5 ml	salt
2 tbsp	30 ml	granulated sugar
1	1	beaten egg yolk
1 tbsp	15 ml	instant yeast
4 cups	1 L	bread flour
2 tbsp	30 ml	melted butter

Combine the water, brandy, orange juice, orange rind, salt, sugar and egg together.

Sift the yeast with the flour twice.

Fold into the liquids and knead into a smooth dough. Cover and place the mixing bowl in a bowl of warm water. Allow to rise to double in size, turn dough out and punch down dividing into 2 loaves. Place the loaves in two 9" (23 cm) greased loaf pans and allow to double in size.

Brush the loaves with the melted butter and bake in a preheated 350°F (180°C) oven for 40 minutes or until golden and firm in the centre. Remove from oven, cool for ten minutes, turn the loaf out onto a cooling rack and allow to cool completely before serving.

YIELDS 2 LOAVES

PRESERVES

Nothing captures the taste of freshness like that which is picked from the tree or vine. During long winter months, people long to sample that taste once again. The best way to do so is to preserve that special taste at its peak. Harvest means canning and the fun of choosing the finest fruits and vegetables the market place has to offer.

The best way to have that "just picked freshness" is to do just that: pick it yourself. If this is not possible, hand pick the fruit in your local market, taking care to choose only the very finest. Those with blemishes or bruises must not be used for preserving. Bruising causes flavour distortion which will be enhanced by the canning process. Be sure, as well, that all fruit is thoroughly scrubbed, hulled, washed and cleaned before the canning process begins.

Use your creativity in making preserves. Combine the exotic with the popular and create all new combinations. Keep one rule in mind; "if it's fruit and I enjoy it, it can be preserved." Mixing papayas, mangos, kiwis, star fruit and other exotic fruit with strawberries, raspberries, apples or oranges into marmalades, jam and jellies will be a pleasant surprise to your guest. It will also be a thrill to yourself as you experience their unique combined flavours.

Within this chapter you will gain that information when you sample such preserves as Strawberry and Papaya Jam or Kiwi Apricot Jam. Don't limit yourself to the lowly task of smearing these preserves on toast; use them in all areas of cuisine. A chilled soup made of Choke Cherry Jam and 'kicked' with Jalapeño Jelly as an appetizer will be a sure fire eye-opener to unsuspecting guests, but they'll love it.

So enjoy summer, but be sure to put away a little taste of it making the remaining seasons of the year *Simply Delicious.*

Assorted Preserves

STOCK
BARREL

RASPBERRY JAM

4½ lbs	2 kg	raspberries
2¼ lbs	1 kg	sugar

Wash and pick through the berries. Place in a sauce pan and heat gently and mash. Add the sugar and bring to a boil. Boil for 30 minutes. Pour into sterile jars, seal and label with production date.

YIELDS 8 – 8 oz (250 ml) jars

PRESERVED PEACHES

4½ lbs	2 kg	peaches *
2 cups	500 ml	water
3 tbsp	45 ml	lemon juice
1½ lbs	675 g	granulated sugar

Peel and stone the peaches. Pour the water into a large sauce pan. Add the lemon juice, sugar and peaches. Bring to a boil; reduce heat and simmer until peaches are tender.

Arrange in jars, pour syrup over and seal. Label with production date.

YIELDS 4-6 – 8 oz (250 ml) jars

* NOTE: Works well with apricots, pears, plums or pineapple.

BRANDIED CHERRIES

4½ lbs	2 kg	cherries
2 cups	500 ml	water
3 lbs	1.3 kg	granulated sugar
2 cups	500 ml	brandy

Wash and stone the cherries; place into a sauce pan. Add the water and sugar, stirring until sugar dissolves. Heat to boil and cook 10 minutes. Remove from the heat and let stand 8 hours.

Place the cherries in sterile jars; fill with equal amounts of syrup and brandy. Seal and label the jars with the production date.

Set for a minimum of 2 weeks before using.

YIELDS 4-6 – 8 oz (250 ml) jars

APPLE APRICOT CONSERVE

4 cups	1 L	pared, cored and diced apples
4 cups	1 L	peeled, stoned apricots
4 cups	1 L	sugar
1 tbsp	15 ml	orange zest
1 cup	250 ml	water

Combine all the ingredients in a sauce pan. Stir until sugar dissolves. Bring to a boil, reduce heat and simmer to very thick.

Pour into sterile jars, cover and label with production date.

YIELDS 4 – 8 oz (250 ml) jars

Apple Apricot Conserve

Brandied Cherries

Fruit Cocktail

JALAPEÑO MARMALADE

¾ lb	340 g	oranges
¼ cup	60 ml	lemon juice
3 cups	750 ml	water
8	8	jalapeños
6	6	coriander seeds
1½ lbs	675 g	granulated sugar

Wash the oranges and cut in half. Squeeze all the juices from the oranges and reserve the juice, seeds and pith.

Place the juice in a large sauce pan; add the lemon juice and water.

Slice the jalapeños in half. Discard the seeds. Dice fine.

Tie the orange seeds, pith and coriander in a cheesecloth. Add to the pan. Slice the orange rind into julienne strips. Add to the pan, heat and simmer until volume is reduced by half.

Add the sugar and stir until it has dissolved. Bring to a boil, and boil for 12 minutes. Add the jalapeños; boil 3 minutes longer.

Remove any scum and let stand 15 minutes. Pour into clean, sterile jars. Cool to warm and seal. Label with production date.

YIELDS 4 cups (1 L)

JALAPEÑO JELLY

1 lb	450 g	fresh jalapeños
½ cup	125 ml	wine vinegar
½ cup	125 ml	water
2½ cups	625 ml	granulated sugar

Wash the jalapeños. Cut away the stem. Cut in half lengthwise.

Place in a sauce pan with the vinegar and water. Heat to a boil, reduce heat and simmer until peppers are tender. Pour into a food processor and purée.

Turn in a double thick cheesecloth or jelly bag; let juice drip into a bowl for 8 hours or overnight.

Measure 3 cups (750 ml) of liquid into a sauce pan. Dissolve the sugar in the liquid. Heat to a boil and cook rapidly for 5 minutes. Pour into sterile jars and seal. Be sure to label with production date.

YIELDS 3 – 4 oz (115 ml) jars

CAUTION: Some peppers are high in volatile oils, which causes the peppers' degree of hotness. Handle the peppers with rubber gloves, and thoroughly wash your hands when you are finished handling them.

FRUIT COCKTAIL

½ lb	225 g	stoned cherries
½ lb	225 g	diced pineapple
1 lb	450 g	pared, cored, diced apples
1 lb	450 g	pared, cored, diced pears
½ lb	225 g	peeled, stoned, sliced peaches
½ lb	225 g	mandarin orange sections
¼ cup	60 ml	lemon juice
4 lbs	1.8 kg	granulated sugar
2 cups	500 ml	water

Place all the fruit except the oranges into a large kettle or Dutch oven. Add the lemon juice, sugar and water. Bring to a boil, reduce heat and simmer for 10 minutes.

Add the oranges and continue to simmer for 5 minutes longer.

Pack the fruit into clean, sterile jars. Fill with syrup, seal and label with production date.

YIELDS 8-10 – 8 oz (250 ml) jars

Jalapeño Marmalade

Kiwi and Apricot Jam

BLACKBERRY JAM

4½ lbs	2 kg	blackberries
2¼ lbs	1 kg	sugar

Wash and pick through the berries. Place in a food processor and purée. Pass through a sieve. Place purée in a sauce pan; blend in the sugar. Heat to a boil; cook for 30 minutes.

Pour into sterile jars, seal and label with production date.

YIELDS 8 – 8 oz (250 ml) jars

KIWI AND APRICOT JAM

6 cups	1.5 L	peeled, stoned apricots
5 cups	1.25 L	peeled kiwis
2 tbsp	30 ml	lemon juice
5 cups	1.25 L	granulated sugar

Chop the apricots and kiwis. Sprinkle with the lemon juice. Place in a sauce pan. Stir in the sugar. Bring to a boil, skimming away any scum. Boil for 25 minutes.

Pour in sterilized jars. Seal and label with production date.

YIELDS 4 – 8 oz (250 ml) jars

BLUEBERRY SPICE JAM

4½ lbs	2 kg	blueberries
2¼ lbs	1 kg	granulated sugar
1 tsp	5 ml	ground cinnamon
½ tsp	3 ml	ground allspice
¼ tsp	1 ml	ground cloves

Wash and pick through the berries. Place in a large sauce pan. Add the sugar and spices. Bring to a boil; cook for 30 minutes.

Pour in sterile jars, seal and label with production date.

YIELDS 8 – 8 oz (250 ml) jars

EVELYN HOHN'S GUAVA JELLY

2¼ lbs	1 kg	guavas
15 oz	420 ml	water
2 lbs	900 g	granulated sugar

Cut out the stems and blossoms of the guavas. Do not peel.

Place the guavas and water in a sauce pan. Heat and mash. Cook gently until fruit is tender.

Turn into a cheesecloth or jelly pan. Let juice drip for 8 hours or overnight into a bowl.

Measure 6 cups (1.5 L) of juice and dissolve the sugar in it. Place in a sauce pan and bring to a boil. Boil rapidly for 6-8 minutes. Pour into clean, sterile jars. Seal and label with production date.

YIELDS 6 – 8 oz (250 ml) jars

Blueberry Spice Jam

PIN CHERRY OR CHOKE CHERRY JAM

12 cups	4 L	pin cherries or choke cherries
6 cups	1.5 L	granulated sugar
3 tbsp	45 ml	lemon juice

Wash and pick through the cherries. Place in a sauce pan, heat and mash. Pass through a sieve to remove stones. Return the pulp to the sauce pan. Add the sugar and lemon juice. Heat to a boil; cook for 30 minutes.

Pour into jars, seal and label with production date.

YIELDS 4-6 – 8 oz (225 ml) jars

STRAWBERRY PAPAYA JAM

8 cups	2 L	papaya pulp
1 tbsp	15 ml	lemon juice
8 cups	2 L	washed and hulled strawberries
1 tsp	5 ml	lemon zest
8 cups	2 L	granulated sugar
1 cup	250 ml	apple juice

Soak the papaya in the lemon juice. Place in a large sauce pan with the strawberries. Add the lemon zest, sugar and apple juice. Bring to a boil and cook for 25 minutes.

Pour into sterile jars, seal and label with production date.

YIELDS 8 – 8 oz (250 ml) jars

PEAR PRESERVES

2	2	limes
2¼ lbs	1 kg	pears
1 tsp	5 ml	ground coriander
6	6	cloves
4 cups	1 L	granulated sugar

Wash the limes. Cut in half and squeeze the juice into a large sauce pan.

Pare the pears, remove cores and cut them in quarters. Place into a sauce pan along with enough water to just cover them. Add the coriander and cloves; heat to a simmer and reduce to half the liquid. Remove pears.

Add the sugar. Stir until dissolved. Bring to a boil; boil 15-20 minutes. Replace the pears. Continue to cook until liquid returns to a boil. Remove from the heat.

Spoon into clean sterile jars. Cover with liquid. Seal and label with production date.

YIELDS 4 – 8 oz (250 ml) jars

Pear Preserves

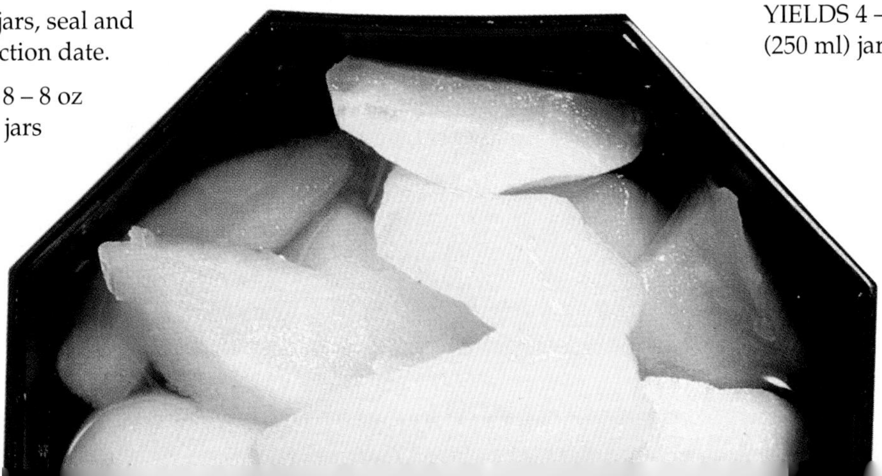

FOUR CITRUS MARMALADE

10 cups	2.8 L	water
1 tsp	5 ml	citric acid
¾ lb	340 g	grapefruit
½ lb	225 g	lemons
1 lb	450 g	clementine oranges
¼ lb	115 g	kumquats
6 lbs	2.75 kg	granulated sugar

Place the water and citric acid in a large sauce pan.

Wash all the fruit. Peel the grapefruit and lemons. Remove the pith. Chop the pulp and peel. Place in the pan. Chop the kumquats and place in the pan.

Cut the oranges in half; squeeze the juice into the pan. Cut the peel into a fine julienne. Place the pith and seeds in a cheesecloth and tie together. Place in the pan.

Bring to boil, reduce heat and simmer. Reduce to half the liquid volume.

Remove the cheesecloth, rinse under cold water, cut open and reserve.

Continue to simmer the remaining fruit for 1½ hours over very low heat.

Add the sugar and reserved orange peel and bring to a boil. Boil rapidly for 20 minutes. Remove any scum. Leave for 30 minutes before placing in jars. Place in jars, cover and label with production date.

YIELDS 4 – 8 oz (250 ml) jars

Four Citrus Marmalade

VEGETABLES, RICE & MEATLESS DISHES

Traditionally, a balanced diet meant regular consumption of the four major food groups; dairy products, meat and eggs, cereals and grains, and fruit and vegetables. This may no longer be the case, however. A balanced meal is one that provides the proper amount of nutrition to the individual. It is now believed that protein-rich vegetables can fulfill many of man's dietary requirements without the need for meats.

Today's progressive cook knows that meat is no longer the main stay of a creative menu. The focus is, as it should always be, on taste and taste does not necessarily require meat. To further understand this principle, see the forward of this book.

The objective in meatless cooking is often one of expression and creativity. The person who prefers meat in every meal has not yet developed an appreciation for a cuisine that is sweeping the entire world. Meatless cookery is the oldest form of food preparation known to man. Adam of the Bible was a vegetarian, for example. Not until after the flood was Noah, and therefore man, given permission to eat meat. Meatless cookery also enjoys a history rich in tradition and style. Oriental countries have cooked with little or no meat in their dishes for over 5000 years. We have learned from these cultures that consuming less fat, fewer calories and less carbohydrates often leads to fewer health related problems. In addition, the use of spices and seasonings from other continents adds to the appeal and interest of many dishes.

The importance of freshness is imperative in the proper cookery of vegetables. Because they are so readily available any time of year, vegetables should be purchased daily whenever possible. Americans can learn from Europeans who purchase much of their food on a daily basis. Immediately, dishes taste fresher, livelier and more nutritious.

In *Simply Delicious Cooking 2*, look forward with anticipation to the most creative, expressive vegetables, rice and meatless dishes you have ever had the opportunity to enjoy. Sample such dishes as Risotto Alla Certosina or Asparagus with Mango Pink Peppercorn Cream. How about a Finocchio with Ginger and Pineapple? There is even a Turtle Bean Stew for the adventurous. All are exquisite complements to your gastronomic repertoire. In other words, they are *Simply Delicious.*

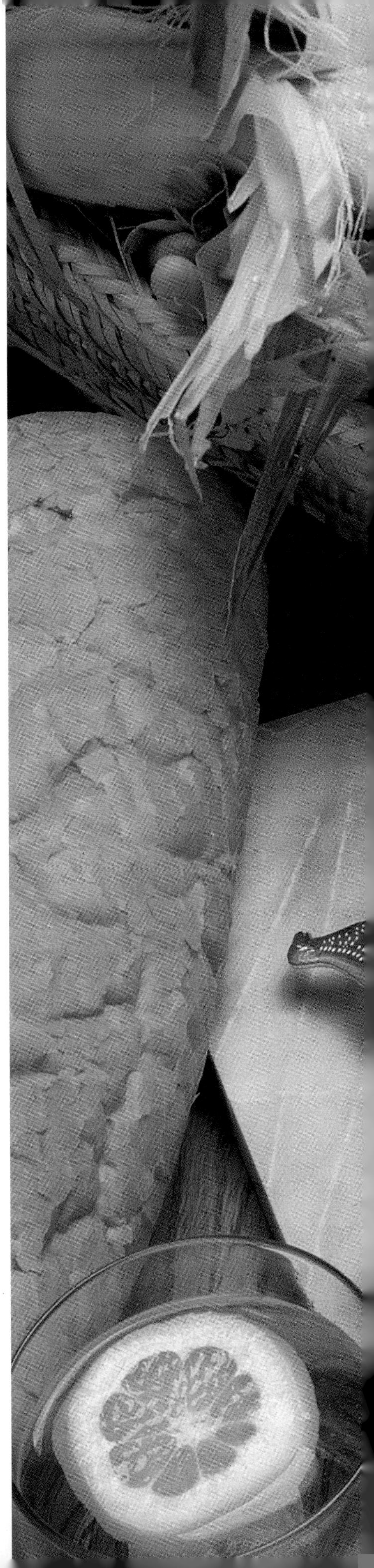

Colourful Veggie Kebabs

Bombay Rice

CURRY RICE

1 cup	250 ml	long grain rice
½ cup	125 ml	brown rice
¼ cup	60 ml	wild rice
4 cups	1 L	Chicken Broth (see page 77)
1½ cups	375 ml	cooked diced chicken
½ cup	125 ml	finely diced onion
½ cup	125 ml	finely diced celery
½ cup	125 ml	finely diced red bell pepper
½ cup	125 ml	finely diced green bell pepper
¼ cup	60 ml	green peas
2 tbsp	30 ml	butter
2 tbsp	30 ml	safflower oil
2 tsp	10 ml	curry powder
¼ cup	60 ml	toasted sliced almonds

Bring the three types of rice to a boil in the chicken broth, and cover.

Simmer until the rice is tender. Drain any excess liquid.

While rice simmers, sauté the chicken and vegetables in the butter and oil. Sprinkle the vegetables with the curry powder.

Stir mixture into rice. Add the almonds, place in a serving bowl and serve.

SERVES 6

FIDDLE HEADS IN CREAM SAUCE

1 lb	454 g	fiddle heads
2 tbsp	30 ml	butter
2 tbsp	30 ml	flour, all purpose
1 cup	250 ml	milk
¼ tsp	1 ml	salt
¼ tsp	1 ml	white pepper
pinch	pinch	nutmeg

Wash the fiddle heads and remove any wilted end pieces. Steam them for 12-15 minutes, transfer to a serving dish.

While the fiddle heads steam, melt the butter in a sauce pan. Add flour and stir into a paste (roux) cook for 2 minutes over low heat.

Add the milk and stir; simmer until thickened. Add the seasonings and simmer 2 additional minutes. Pour sauce over the fiddle heads and serve at once.

SERVES 4

BOMBAY RICE

¼ cup	60 ml	safflower oil
2 cups	500 ml	diced chicken meat
1 cup	250 ml	sliced mushrooms
1	1	diced green bell pepper
1	1	small diced onion
2 cups	500 ml	snow peas
4 cups	1 L	cooked long grain rice
1 tsp	5 ml	curry powder
¼ tsp	1 ml	salt

In a wok or large skillet heat half the oil. Fry the chicken, mushrooms, peppers, onion and peas thoroughly. Remove and reserve hot.

Heat the remaining oil. Add the rice and seasonings fry 3 minutes. Place on a serving platter.

Spoon the chicken and vegetables over the rice. Serve.

SERVES 6

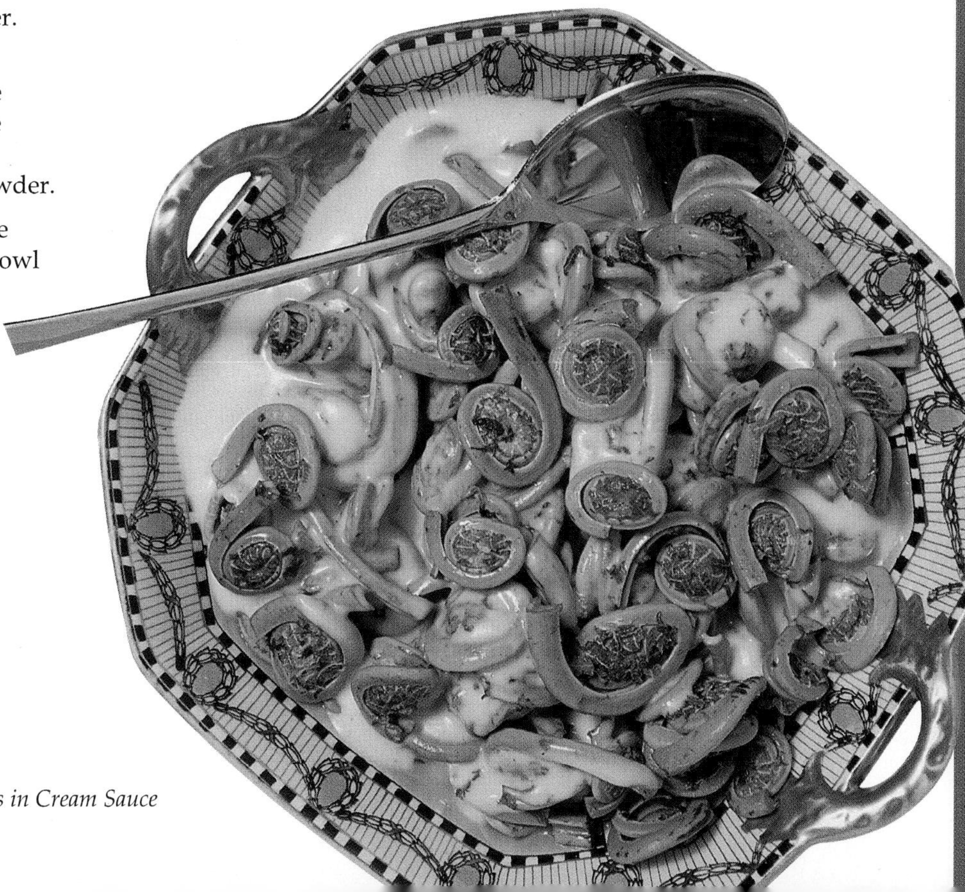

Fiddle Heads in Cream Sauce

Kartoffelpuffer (Potato Pancakes)

ALOO MADARASI

2 tbsp	30 ml	olive oil
1	1	diced Spanish onion
1 tsp	5 ml	English dry mustard
1 tbsp	15 ml	curry powder
3 cups	750 ml	pared, fine diced potatoes
1 cup	250 ml	Vegetable Broth (see page 92)
1 tsp	5 ml	grated lemon peel
1 tsp	1 ml	ground cinnamon
2 tbsp	30 ml	butter

Heat the oil in a sauce pan, add the onion and cook until tender. Sprinkle with mustard and curry powder, cook for 2 minutes over low heat.

Add the potatoes, broth, lemon and cinnamon. Cover and simmer for 15 minutes. Remove cover and simmer an additional 15 minutes.

Transfer to a serving dish, dot with butter and serve.

SERVES 6

KARTOFFELPUFFER (POTATO PANCAKES)

2 tbsp	30 ml	flour, all purpose
1 tsp	5 ml	salt
¼ tsp	1 ml	baking powder
¼ tsp	1 ml	cracked black pepper
6	6	medium potatoes
2	2	eggs
1	1	minced garlic clove
1 tbsp	15 ml	grated onion
¼ cup	60 ml	butter
½ cup	125 ml	crumbled bacon
1½ cups	375 ml	sour cream

Combine the flour, salt, baking powder and pepper together in a mixing bowl.

Pare and grate the potatoes, pat completely dry. Stir into the dry mixture, beat in the eggs. Add the garlic and onion.

Heat the butter in a skillet and fry small pancakes to golden brown on each side. Serve with bacon and sour cream.

SERVES 4

APPLE RICE WITH DATES AND NUTS

1½ cups	375 ml	long grain rice
4 cups	1 L	apple juice
¾ cup	180 ml	chopped pitted dates
½ cup	125 ml	toasted sliced almonds

Bring the rice to a boil in the apple juice, cover and reduce heat to a simmer. Simmer until liquid has been absorbed.

Stir in the dates and almonds. Serve at once.

SERVES 4

FRIED EGGPLANT WITH CILANTRO SAUCE

½ cup	125 ml	sour cream
½ cup	125 ml	whipping cream
2 cups	500 ml	washed and chopped cilantro
2	2	garlic cloves
1 tsp	5 ml	salt
½ tsp	3 ml	cracked black pepper
½ cup	125 ml	flour, all purpose
½ tsp	3 ml	each of thyme, basil, marjoram, salt, paprika, chili powder, onion powder, garlic powder, white pepper
2	2	medium eggplants
2 cups	500 ml	vegetable oil

In a food processor blend the sour cream, whipping cream, cilantro, garlic, salt and cracked black pepper until smooth.

Blend the flour and the seasonings in a small mixing bowl. Peel the eggplant and cut into slices, dredge the eggplant in the flour.

Heat the oil in a large skillet and fry the eggplant slices to golden brown. Place on a hot serving platter. Serve the sauce on the side.

SERVES 6

Apple Rice with Dates and Nuts

CHANCELLOR STYLE POTATOES

1½ lbs	675 g	potatoes
2 tbsp	30 ml	butter
2 tbsp	30 ml	flour, all purpose
1 cup	250 ml	milk
¼ tsp	1 ml	salt
¼ tsp	1 ml	white pepper
pinch	pinch	nutmeg

Pare the potatoes, using a small melon baller cut out small potato balls (Parisian potatoes). Boil in boiling salted water for 15 minutes.

While the potatoes cook, melt the butter in a sauce pan. Add flour and stir into a paste (roux) cook for 2 minutes over low heat.

Add the milk and stir; simmer until thickened. Add the seasonings and simmer 2 additional minutes.

Swirl the sauce through the potatoes and pour into a serving bowl. Serve.

SERVES 4

RUBY RAPINI

1 lb	454 g	rapini florets*
2 tbsp	30 ml	butter
2 tbsp	30 ml	flour, all purpose
½ cup	125 ml	Chicken Stock (see page 77)
¼ cup	60 ml	heavy cream
¼ cup	60 ml	champagne
2 tsp	10 ml	sweet ground paprika

Steam the rapini for 15 minutes, transfer to a serving dish.

While the rapini steams, melt the butter in a sauce pan. Add the flour and stir into a paste (roux) cooking over low heat for 2 minutes.

Add chicken stock, cream, champagne and paprika. Whisk all the ingredients together. Simmer for 10 minutes over medium heat.

Pour sauce over rapini and serve at once.

SERVES 4

*Rapini is Italian broccoli.

Chicken Burgers – Meatless

CHICKEN BURGERS — MEATLESS

⅔ cup	160 ml	vegetable broth, chicken flavoured
3 tbsp	45 ml	ketchup
2 tsp	10 ml	lemon juice
1 tsp	5 ml	Worcestershire sauce
½ tsp	3 ml	each of paprika, rosemary, garlic powder, onion powder, thyme, basil, savory
½ tsp	3 ml	salt
2 tbsp	10 ml	light soya sauce
1 lb	450 g	firm tofu rounds
½ cup	125 ml	whole wheat flour
¼ cup	60 ml	olive oil
4	4	whole wheat kaiser rolls
4	4	lettuce leaves
4	4	sliced tomatoes
⅓ cup	80 ml	mayonnaise

Blend the broth, ketchup, lemon juice, Worcestershire, ¼ tsp (1 ml) of each of the herbs and spices, the salt and soya sauce in a mixing bowl.

Slice the tofu into 4 even rounds. Marinate the tofu in the mixture for 1 hour.

Drain, wrap the tofu in a cloth to dry.

Blend the remaining seasoning with the flour. Dredge the tofu through the seasonings.

Heat the oil in a large skillet, fry the tofu to golden brown on each side.

Cut the kaiser rolls in half.

Serve a tofu slice in each kaiser with a lettuce leaf, tomato slice and a dollop of mayonnaise.

SERVES 4

Apricot Carrots

APRICOT CARROTS

1 lb	454 g	carrots
1 cup	250 ml	dried apricots
1 cup	250 ml	water
2 tbsp	30 ml	granulated sugar
1 tsp	5 ml	cornstarch
1 tbsp	15 ml	lemon juice
¼ cup	60 ml	apple juice

Pare the carrots and cut into sticks. Steam the carrots for 12-15 minutes, transfer to a serving dish and reserve warm.

While carrots steam, boil the apricots in the water for 5 minutes in a small pan. Transfer apricots to a food processor and purée, reserve the water. Stir the sugar into the water. Mix the cornstarch with the lemon juice, add to the water and simmer until thick. Pour over the apricots and blend.

Return to sauce pan and stir in the apple juice, heat but do not boil.

Pour sauce over carrots and serve at once.

SERVES 4

BEETS WITH MUSTARD GREENS

1 lb	454 g	very small beets
1 lb	454 g	mustard greens, washed and trimmed
4 tbsp	60 ml	butter
1 tsp	5 ml	Dijon mustard
1 tsp	5 ml	granulated sugar
1 tbsp	15 ml	lemon juice

Cook the beets until tender in boiling salted water, drain, slip the beet skins off with your fingers, reserve hot.

Heat 3 tbsp (45 ml) of butter in a large skillet, add the mustard greens and sweat until tender. Transfer to a serving platter and top with the beets.

In a small sauce pan heat the remaining butter, swirl in the mustard, sugar and lemon juice. Cook until sugar is dissolved. Pour over the beets and serve at once.

SERVE 6

NOSTIZ POTATOES

1 lb	450 g	potatoes
2 tbsp	30 ml	butter
4	4	eggs
¼ cup	60 ml	heavy cream
1 cup	250 ml	freshly grated Parmesan cheese
1 cup	250 ml	flour, all purpose
½ tsp	3 ml	each of salt, chili powder, pepper, paprika, thyme
2 cups	500 ml	fine bread crumbs
4 cups	1 L	safflower oil

Pare and boil the potatoes. Mash and press through a sieve or process in a food processor until smooth.

Add the butter, 1 egg yolk, cream and cheese; blend until very smooth.

Shape into an even amount of 2" (5 cm) squares. Cool.

Mix the flour with the seasonings. Beat the remaining eggs.

Dust the potatoes with the flour then dip in the eggs and dredge with bread crumbs.

Heat the oil. Deep fry the potatoes until golden brown.

SERVES 6

SKILLET ZUCCHINI WITH FOUR CHEESES

3 tbsp	45 ml	olive oil
1	1	thinly sliced onion
1	1	minced garlic clove
1 tsp	5 ml	basil
3½ cups	875 ml	thinly sliced zucchini
⅓ cup	80 ml	Vegetable Broth (see page 92)
2 tbsp	30 ml	butter
2 tbsp	30 ml	flour, all purpose
1 cup	250 ml	milk
1	1	egg yolk – beaten
2 tbsp	30 ml	whipping cream
3 tbsp	45 ml	freshly grated Parmesan cheese
¼ cup	60 ml	grated cheddar cheese
¼ cup	60 ml	grated mozzarella cheese
¼ cup	60 ml	grated provolone

Heat the oil in a large skillet. Add the onion, garlic, basil and zucchini, and sauté for 3-5 minutes. Add a tablespoon of broth one at a time to prevent vegetables from scorching.

In a sauce pan melt the butter. Add the flour and cook over low heat for 2 minutes.

Pour in the milk and cook stirring constantly until sauce thickens. Remove from the heat.

Whisk the egg yolk with a little sauce. Whisk into the sauce and cook 2 minutes longer, do not boil. Add the cream and cheeses. Pour over zucchini and serve.

SERVES 4-6

Californian Beans

POTATOES NORMANDY

1	1	Spanish onion
1	1	leek
1½ lbs	675 g	potatoes
4 oz	120 g	butter
3 tbsp	45 ml	flour, all purpose
2 cups	500 ml	hot milk
2 tsp	10 ml	salt
½ tsp	3 ml	white pepper
½ cup	125 ml	freshly grated Parmesan cheese

Slice the onion. Wash and chop the leek. Pare and slice the potatoes very thin.

Heat the butter in a large skillet, sauté the onion and leek until tender. Add the flour and continue to cook 2 minutes. Transfer to a greased 2 quart (2 L) casserole dish. Stir in the milk, salt and pepper. Sprinkle with cheese.

Bake in a preheated 375°F (190°C) oven for 45 minutes or until the potatoes are tender.

SERVES 6

CALIFORNIAN BEANS

1 lb	454 g	green beans
3 tbsp	45 ml	olive oil
3 tbsp	45 ml	flour, all purpose
⅔ cup	160 ml	Chicken Broth (see page 77)
⅔ cup	160 ml	light cream
⅓ cup	80 ml	tomato catsup
2 tsp	10 ml	Worcestershire sauce
1 tsp	5 ml	paprika
3 drops	3 drops	Tabasco™ sauce
1 tbsp	15 ml	lemon juice

Wash and trim the beans. Steam them for 15-20 minutes, transfer to a serving dish.

Heat the oil in a sauce pan, add the flour and cook for 2 minutes over low heat.

Whisk in the broth and cream and simmer until thick.

Whisk in the remaining ingredients, continue to simmer for 2 additional minutes.

Pour the sauce over the beans and serve at once.

SERVES 4

Skillet Zucchini with Four Cheeses

Colourful Veggie Kebabs

THREE RICE KOHLRABI ROLLS

⅓ cup	80 ml	brown rice
⅓ cup	80 ml	long grain white rice
⅓ cup	80 ml	wild rice
3 cups	750 ml	Chicken Broth (see page 77)
1	1	finely diced Spanish onion
2	2	finely diced celery stalk
1	1	finely diced green bell pepper
8	8	slices diced bacon
20-25	20-25	large kohlrabi leaves
2 cups	500 ml	Tomato Sauce II (see page 117)

Bring the 3 rices to a boil in the chicken stock, cover and simmer until tender.

While the rice cooks, sauté the onion, celery and green pepper with the diced bacon. Drain excess fat. Blend into the cooked rice.

Trim and wash the kohlrabi leaves. Steam for 1½-2 minutes.

Place 1 heaping tablespoon of rice mixture on each leaf. Fold in half. Fold in the sides then roll together. Place into a lightly greased casserole dish. Pour the tomato sauce over the rolls.

Cover and bake in a preheated 350°F (180°C) oven for 45 minutes. Serve.

SERVES 6

COLOURFUL VEGGIE KEBABS

1	1	green bell pepper
1	1	yellow bell pepper
1	1	red bell pepper
2	2	red onions
2	2	small zucchini, cut into 1" dice
3 oz	80 g	button mushrooms
1 lb	450 g	firm tofu, cut in 1" (2.5 cm) dice
1½ cups	375 ml	wine barbecue sauce

Cut the peppers and onions in wedges. Skewer the zucchini, peppers, onions, mushrooms and tofu, alternating the tofu with the vegetables. Place in a shallow baking dish, cover with the barbecue sauce, marinate for 3 hours.

Grill the kebabs over a hot grill, brushing with the marinade. Grill until lightly browned. Brush one final time before serving with a rice pilaf.

SERVES 4

FIDDLE HEADS A LA POMPADOUR

1 lb	454 g	fiddle heads
¼ lb	115 g	butter
¼ tsp	1 ml	salt
¼ tsp	1 ml	pepper
⅛ tsp	pinch	each of mace and cayenne
1 tsp	5 ml	flour, all purpose
3	3	egg yolks
1 tbsp	15 ml	sherry

Wash and trim the fiddle heads and steam for 15 minutes.

In a double boiler melt the butter and stir in the seasonings.

Whisk in the flour, beat in the egg yolks and sherry. Cook until sauce is thick stirring constantly, remove form heat at once.

Transfer the fiddle heads to a serving platter, ladle the sauce over and serve at once.

SERVES 4

Three Rice Kohlrabi Rolls

Corn Pancakes

CORN PANCAKES

2 cups	500 ml	fresh corn kernels
½ cup	125 ml	table cream
3	3	eggs separated
½ tsp	3 ml	salt
¼ tsp	1 ml	nutmeg

In a mixing bowl blend the corn, cream and egg yolks.

Beat the egg white until stiff and fold into the batter along with the seasoning.

Cook on a well oiled griddle or in a frying pan until golden brown on each side. Serve with maple syrup or Berry Berry Sauce (see page 118).

SERVES 4

FRIJOLES REFRITOS CON QUESO (REFRIED BEANS WITH CHEESE)

2 cups	500 ml	cold Pinto Bean Bake (see page 731)
2 tbsp	30 ml	butter
2 tsp	10 ml	chili powder
1 tsp	5 ml	paprika
1 tsp	5 ml	Worcestershire sauce
½ tsp	3 ml	salt
1 tbsp	15 ml	safflower oil
1 cup	250 ml	grated Monterey jack

Mash the beans. Mix in the butter, seasonings and Worcestershire.

Heat the oil in a skillet, fry the beans until brown.

Sprinkle with cheese, remove from the heat and serve once cheese melts.

SERVES 4

DAUPHINE POTATOES

1⅛ lbs	510 g	potatoes
½ cup	125 ml	butter
7	7	eggs
1¼ tsp	6 ml	salt
½ tsp	3 ml	white pepper
¼ tsp	1 ml	nutmeg
1 cup	250 ml	water
1 cup	250 ml	flour, all purpose
¼ cup	60 ml	melted butter

Pare the potatoes and cook in boiling water until tender. Place in a food processor and blend until smooth.

Add ¼ cup (60 ml) of butter, 1 egg, 2 egg yolks, 1 tsp (5 ml) of salt, pepper and nutmeg. Blend until very smooth.

[FOR CHOUX PASTE] Heat the water to boiling. Add the remaining butter and remaining salt. Stir in the flour.

Cook to the consistency of mashed potatoes.

Add the remaining eggs one at a time beating well after each addition.

Divide the batter into two and blend one half into the potatoes (use the second for Pea Puffs, see page 752). Allow mixture to cool completely.

Divide the potatoe dough into even rounds, place on a baking sheet and brush with the melted butter, Bake in a preheated 350°F (180°C) oven for 15-20 minutes or until golden brown. Potatoes may also be dipped into flour and deep fried. Serve very hot.

SERVES 6

Dauphine Potatoes

BEAN 'N' TOMATOES

10 oz	300 ml	sundried tomatoes
1 lb	454 g	green beans
2 tbsp	30 ml	butter
2 tbsp	30 ml	flour, all purpose
½ cup	125 ml	milk
½ cup	125 ml	Chicken Broth (see page 77)
¼ tsp	1 ml	salt
¼ tsp	1 ml	white pepper

Rehydrate the tomatoes by soaking them in warm water for 20 minutes.

Wash and trim the beans, steam them for 20 minutes.

While beans are steaming, heat the butter in a small sauce pan, add the flour and cook over low heat for 2 minutes. Whip in the remaining ingredients and simmer into a thick sauce.

Chop the tomatoes and stir into the sauce. Transfer the beans to a serving platter, smother with sauce and serve.

SERVES 4

PRALINE TOM THUMB CABBAGES

1½ lbs	625 g	Brussels sprouts
½ cup	125 ml	butter
2 cups	500 ml	dark brown sugar
½ cup	125 ml	whipping cream
1 tbsp	15 ml	lemon juice
¼ cup	60 ml	chopped pecans
1 tsp	5 ml	vanilla extract

Trim the Brussels sprouts of any wilted leaves, cut off the stem end. Steam for 20 minutes.

While the sprouts steam, melt the butter in a double boiler. Blend the sugar with the butter. Whisk in the cream until it blends well. Stir in the lemon juice, cook for 45 minutes over simmering water. Stir occasionally.

Remove from heat, stir in the nuts and vanilla.

Transfer the sprouts to a serving dish, pour the sauce over and serve at once.

SERVES 6

KIWI PAPAYA ENDIVES

6	6	pared, chopped kiwis
2 cups	500 ml	papaya pulp
¼ cup	60 ml	granulated sugar
1½ tbsp	24 ml	cornstarch
⅓ cup	80 ml	apple juice
12	12	Belgian endives
⅓ cup	90 ml	butter
¼ cup	60 ml	water
1 tbsp	15 ml	lemon juice
½ tsp	3 ml	salt
¼ tsp	1 ml	white pepper

Purée the kiwis with the papaya in a food processor. Press through a sieve into a small sauce pan. Stir in the sugar. Mix the cornstarch with the apple juice add to the fruit. Simmer over low heat until sauce is thick. Stir in 2 tbsp (30 ml) of butter.

Trim the endives of any wilted leaves, rinse in cold water.

In a large skillet heat the remaining butter, water, lemon juice, salt and pepper, add the endives and simmer over low heat for 15 minutes. Transfer to a serving platter, smother with sauce and serve at once.

SERVES 6

Praline Tom Thumb Cabbages

Kiwi Papaya Endives

Jacob's Pottage

CHICORÉE DE BRUXELLES À LA POLONAISE

12	12	Belgian endives
½ cup	125 ml	butter
¼ cup	60 ml	water
1 tbsp	15 ml	lemon juice
½ tsp	3 ml	salt
¼ tsp	1 ml	white pepper
3	3	chopped hard cooked eggs
2 tbsp	30 ml	fresh chopped parsley
⅓ cup	90 ml	seasoned bread crumbs

Trim the endives of any wilted leaves, rinse in cold water.

In a large skillet heat ¼ cup (60 ml) of butter, water, lemon juice, salt and pepper, add the endives and simmer over low heat for 15 minutes. Transfer to a casserole dish, sprinkle with the eggs, parsley and bread crumbs.

Melt the remaining butter and pour over the breads crumbs, bake in a preheated 350°F (180°C) oven for 15-20 minutes or until golden brown.

SERVES 6

ASPARAGUS WITH MANGO PINK PEPPERCORN CREAM

2 lbs	900 g	asparagus spears
2 tbsp	30 ml	butter
2 tbsp	30 ml	flour, all purpose
1 cup	250 ml	light cream
1 cup	250 ml	puréed mango pulp
1 tbsp	15 ml	pink peppercorns

Peel the outer skin of the asparagus and trim off the bottom tough ends. Place in a steamer, steam for 8-10 minutes.

While asparagus steams, heat the butter in a sauce pan, add the flour, reduce heat and cook for 2 minutes. Whisk in the cream and simmer until thick.

Whisk in the mango and continue to cook for 3 minutes. Stir in the peppercorns.

Place asparagus on a serving platter, cover with sauce and serve at once.

SERVES 4

JACOB'S POTTAGE

2 cups	500 ml	lentils
6 cups	1.5 L	Chicken Broth (see page 77)
2	2	carrots
1	1	onion
1	1	kohlrabi
1	1	celery stick
3 tbsp	45 ml	olive oil
¾ lb	345 g	diced fine lamb
1	1	garlic clove
1 tsp	5 ml	salt
½ tsp	3 ml	black pepper
1 tbsp	15 ml	flour, all purpose
1	1	bouquet garni (see Glossary)

Wash and rinse the lentils. Place in a large pot with enough broth to cover. Bring to a boil, remove from the heat and drain at once.

Dice the vegetables fine.

Heat the oil in a large pot and brown the lamb. Add the vegetables and garlic continuing to cook until they are tender. Stir in the salt, pepper and flour.

Add the lentils and enough broth to just cover the lentils. Add the bouquet garni. Cover and simmer for 1¼-1½ hours, stir occasionally. Add any broth or water as may be needed to keep the stew from sticking, preventing it from burning.

Discard the bouquet, place in serving bowls. Serve.

SERVES 4

EGGPLANT ROMANIAN

2 tbsp	30 ml	olive oil
2	2	minced garlic cloves
1	1	diced green bell pepper
1	1	diced onion
2	2	diced celery stalks
4 oz	120 g	sliced mushrooms
1 tsp	5 ml	salt
½ tsp	3 ml	pepper
1 tsp	5 ml	basil leaves
½ tsp	3 ml	oregano leaves
½ tsp	3 ml	thyme leaves
½ tsp	3 ml	paprika
¼ tsp	1 ml	cayenne
3 lbs	1.35 kg	peeled, seeded, and chopped tomatoes
6	6	very small eggplants
3 cups	750 ml	sliced onions
2 tbsp	30 ml	butter

In a sauce pan heat the oil. Sauté the garlic, green pepper, onion, celery and mushrooms until tender. Add the seasonings and tomatoes. Simmer for 3 hours.

Cut the root ends from the eggplant and place in a casserole dish. Add half the onions cover with the sauce and bake in a 350°F (180°C) oven for 45 minutes.

While egg plant bakes, heat the butter in a skillet and cook the remaining onions over low heat until golden brown. Make an incision in the egg plants and stuff the golden onions therein, serve the eggplant smothered with the sauce.

SERVES 6

KARTOFFELSPATZEN (POTATO DUMPLINGS)

2 tbsp	30 ml	butter
2 tbsp	30 ml	flour, all purpose
1 cup	250 ml	milk
¼ tsp	1 ml	salt
¼ tsp	1 ml	white pepper
pinch	pinch	nutmeg
4 cups	1 L	cold, cooked, shredded potatoes
½ cup	125 ml	bread crumbs
2	2	eggs
½ cup	125 ml	cooked crumbled bacon
1½ cups	375 ml	sour cream

Melt the butter in a sauce pan. Add flour and stir into a paste (roux) cook for 2 minutes over low heat.

Add the milk and stir; simmer until thickened. Add the seasonings and simmer 2 additional minutes. Blend in the potatoes and bread crumbs. Beat in the eggs.

Drop tablespoon size pieces into boiling salted water, cook dumplings for 2 minutes after they float. Serve with crumbled bacon and sour cream.

SERVES 6

ALMONDS, APPLES, GREEN BEANS WITH MUSTARD CREAM

4 tbsp	60 ml	butter
1 tbsp	15 ml	flour, all purpose
½ cup	125 ml	light cream
1 tbsp	15 ml	Dijon mustard
2	2	large Granny Smith apples
2 cups	500 ml	blanched green beans
⅓ cup	80 ml	toasted sliced almonds

In a sauce pan heat 1 tbsp (15 ml) of butter, sprinkle with the flour, cook over low heat for 2 minutes. Add the cream and mustard and whisk, simmer until thick, reserve warm.

Pare the apples and core them, cut into julienne slices.

Heat the remaining butter in a large skillet, add the apples and beans, sauté for 3 minutes. Add the almonds and continue to sauté for 2 minutes. Transfer to a serving platter, pour sauce over the vegetables and serve.

SERVES 4

Eggplant Romanian

FETA BROWN RICE FLORENTINE

1½ cups	375 ml	brown rice
3 cups	750 ml	Chicken Broth (see page 77)
1	1	Spanish onion
10 oz	280 ml	spinach
3 tbsp	45 ml	butter
1 cup	250 ml	Feta cheese

Bring rice and chicken stock to a boil. Cover and simmer until rice is tender.

While rice cooks, fine dice the onion. Wash and trim the spinach. Heat the butter in a skillet, add the onion and sauté until tender. Add the spinach and cook quickly.

Once rice has cooked, drain any excess liquid. Stir in the onion mixture with the cheese. Serve at once.

SERVES 6

CHERRY BRANDY CARROTS

1 lb	450 g	carrots
1¼ cups	310 ml	Bing cherries – fresh or tinned pitted
¼ cup	60 ml	cherry brandy
3 tbsp	45 ml	cherry liquid or apple juice
1 tbsp	15 ml	lemon juice
2 tbsp	30 ml	granulated sugar

Pare the carrots and cut into slices. Steam the carrots for 10-12 minutes. Transfer to a serving dish, reserve hot.

In a small sauce pan heat the cherries in the cherry brandy over low heat until very tender. Press through the sieve into a second sauce pan.

Add the remaining ingredients, simmer until thick. Pour the sauce over the carrots and serve at once.

SERVES 4

Feta Brown Rice Florentine

ORANGE CASHEW RICE

3 cups	750 ml	orange juice
1¼ cups	310 ml	long grain rice
1½ tbsp	20 ml	butter
2 tbsp	30 ml	granulated sugar
2 tbsp	30 ml	orange peel zest
½ cup	125 ml	unsalted, broken cashew nuts

Bring orange juice to a boil. Add rice, cover and simmer until the liquid has been absorbed.

Stir in the butter, sugar, orange peel and nuts. Serve.

SERVES 4

FIVE CHEESE RICE

1 cup	250 ml	long grain rice
3 cups	750 ml	milk
½ cup	125 ml	each of grated cheddar, mozzarella, Havarti cheeses
¼ cup	60 ml	each of freshly grated Parmesan, Romano cheese
½ tsp	3 ml	salt
1 tbsp	15 ml	chopped chives
1 tbsp	15 ml	chopped parsley

Simmer the rice in the milk until liquid is absorbed.

Stir in the remaining ingredients. Serve.

SERVES 4

Orange Cashew Rice

Asparagus Smitane

No Beef Steaks

ASPARAGUS SMITANE

1 lb	454 g	asparagus spears
1 tbsp	15 ml	butter
2 tbsp	30 ml	grated onion
½ cup	125 ml	white wine
1¼ cups	310 ml	sour cream
⅓ cup	90 ml	cooked crumbled bacon
¼ cup	60 ml	freshly grated Parmesan cheese

Pare the asparagus and remove the root end. Cook the asparagus in boiling salted water for 15 minutes, keep the tips above the water*. Drain and reserve hot.

In a small sauce pan heat the butter and sweat the onions (cook until tender and transparent in colour). Add the wine and simmer until all liquid has evaporated. Stir in the sour cream, bring to a boil, reduce heat and simmer for 3 minutes. Strain through a fine sieve.

Transfer asparagus to a serving platter, smother with sauce and sprinkle with bacon and cheese before serving.

SERVES 4

*To keep the tips above the water as asparagus simmers, simply tie then together in small bundles and stand then upright as they cook.

BEETS IN ORANGE APRICOT SAUCE

1 lb	450 g	very tiny beets
3	3	oranges
1 cup	250 ml	apricot preserves
¼ cup	60 ml	Curacao liqueur

Cook the beets until tender in boiling salted water, drain, slip the beet skins off with your fingers, reserve hot.

Zest and segment the oranges, remove pith and seeds.

In a small sauce pan heat the apricot preserves and mix in the orange segments with the liqueur, simmer for 3 minutes.

Place the beets in a serving dish, smother with sauce, garnish with orange zest.

SERVES 4

NO BEEF STEAKS

⅓ cup	80 ml	brown sugar
1 tsp	5 ml	ground ginger
½ tsp	3 ml	garlic powder
1 cup	250 ml	Vegetable Broth (see page 92)
⅓ cup	80 ml	soya sauce low sodium
1 tsp	5 ml	dry mustard
1 lb	450 g	firm tofu
1 tbsp	15 ml	cornstarch
2 tbsp	30 ml	sherry

In a mixing bowl, dissolve the sugar, ginger and garlic in the vegetable broth and soya sauce. Add the mustard.

Cut the tofu into 8 slices. Place in the marinade, cover and refrigerate for 1½ hours.

Drain marinade into a sauce pan, heat to a boil. Mix the cornstarch in the sherry and add to sauce. Simmer until thick.

Broil the tofu for 3 minutes per side, brushing several times with marinade. Serve at once.

SERVES 4

CARROT AND CAULIFLOWER LOAF

2 cups	500 ml	cooked cauliflower florets
2 cups	500 ml	cooked diced carrots
1½ cups	375 ml	whipping cream
1 cup	250 ml	grated Jarlsberg cheese
5	5	beaten eggs
3 tbsp	45 ml	butter
1	1	finely diced small onion
1	1	pared, cored, finely diced apple
2 tbsp	30 ml	flour, all purpose
1 tbsp	15 ml	curry powder
¼ cup	60 ml	coconut milk
⅔ cup	160 ml	Chicken Broth (see page 77)
½ cup	125 ml	light cream
½ tsp	3 ml	salt
¼ tsp	1 ml	white pepper

Preheat the oven to 350°F (180°C).

In a food processor purée the cauliflower and carrots together.

Transfer to a mixing bowl and stir in the cream, cheese and eggs. Combine thoroughly. Pour mixture into a 9" (22 cm) greased loaf pan.

Bake for 40-45 minutes in a hot water bath.

Heat the butter in a sauce pan, add the onion and apple and sauté until tender. Add the flour and curry and continue to cook 2 minutes over low heat. Stir in the coconut milk, broth and cream, continue to simmer until sauce thickens. Stir in salt and pepper.

Remove the loaf from the oven, turn out on a serving tray. Cover with the sauce and serve.

SERVES 6

Carrot and Cauliflower Loaf

PINEAPPLE MANGO CARROTS

1 lb	450 g	pared, julienne cut carrots
1 cup	250 ml	crushed pineapple, drain and reserve juice
1 cup	250 ml	mango pulp
¼ cup	60 ml	granulated sugar
1½ tbsp	24 ml	cornstarch

Steam the carrots for 12-15 minutes, transfer to a serving dish.

Purée the pineapple with the mangoes in a food processor, press through the sieve into a small sauce pan. Stir in the sugar.

Blend the cornstarch into ¼ cup (60 ml) of reserved pineapple juice. Add to fruit. Cook over low heat until sauce thickens.

Pour the sauce over the carrots and serve at once.

SERVES 4

BELGIAN ENDIVES IN PLUM BRANDY CREAM

12	12	small Belgian endives
3 tbsp	45 ml	butter
¼ tsp	1 ml	salt
3 tbsp	45 ml	granulated sugar
4	4	egg yolks
1¾ cups	430 ml	warm light cream
¼ cup	60 ml	plum brandy preserves, or plum jam

Trim the endives of any wilted leaves. Blanch in salted water for 5-6 minutes. Heat the butter in a sauce pan, reduce heat, add endives and simmer for 30 minutes.

While endives are simmering, beat the salt and sugar into the egg yolks. Place over a double boiler and whisk in cream. Whisk until sauce has thicken, remove from the heat. Whisk in preserves.

Transfer endives to a serving platter, cover with the sauce. Serve at once.

SERVES 4

Pineapple Mango Carrots

Broccoli Almandine

PINTO BEAN BAKE

1 lb	450 g	pinto beans
⅓ cup	80 ml	brown sugar
½ cup	125 ml	liquid honey
⅓ cup	80 ml	maple syrup
2 tsp	10 ml	dry mustard
½ tsp	3 ml	each of cinnamon, all spice, ginger, nutmeg
1 tsp	5 ml	cracked black pepper
1	1	diced onion
8 oz	225 g	diced smoked ham
1	1	smoked ham hock, cracked
6 oz	170 g	salt pork, or bacon

Soak the beans for 8 hours or overnight. Drain. Place the beans in a sauce pan, cover with water, bring to a boil, remove from heat. Stand 1 hour. Drain. Reserve the water, spoon the beans into a crock pot.

Stir in the sugar, honey, syrup, mustard, seasonings, onion and ham. Place the ham hock in the centre and cover with mixture. Layer the salt pork on top. Cover tightly.

Bake in a preheated 275°F (140°C) oven for 6-8 hours. Check periodically to prevent drying, add enough reserve water to cover when needed. Remove salt pork, dice and stir into the beans if desired. Serve.

SERVES 6

CAULIFLOWER IN AURORA SAUCE

2 tbsp	30 ml	butter
2 tbsp	30 ml	flour, all purpose
1 cup	250 ml	Chicken Broth (see page 77)
½ tsp	3 ml	salt
¼ tsp	1 ml	white pepper
3 tbsp	45 ml	whipping cream
3 tbsp	45 ml	tomato paste
3 cups	750 ml	cauliflower

Heat the butter in a sauce pan. Add the flour and cook for 2 minutes over low heat. Add the broth, salt and pepper, simmer into a thick sauce. Whip in the cream and tomato paste.

Steam the cauliflower while you prepare the sauce.

Place cauliflower in a serving bowl, cover with the sauce and serve at once.

SERVES 4

BROCCOLI ALMANDINE

1 lb	454 g	broccoli florets
¼ cup	60 ml	butter
⅓ cup	90 ml	slivered almonds
2 tbsp	30 ml	lemon juice
1 tsp	5 ml	grated orange rind

Steam the broccoli for 15 minutes or until tender.

In a small sauce pan heat the butter, add the almond and sauté until golden brown. Swirl in the lemon juice and orange rind.

Transfer broccoli to a serving dish and pour sauce over, serve at once.

SERVES 4

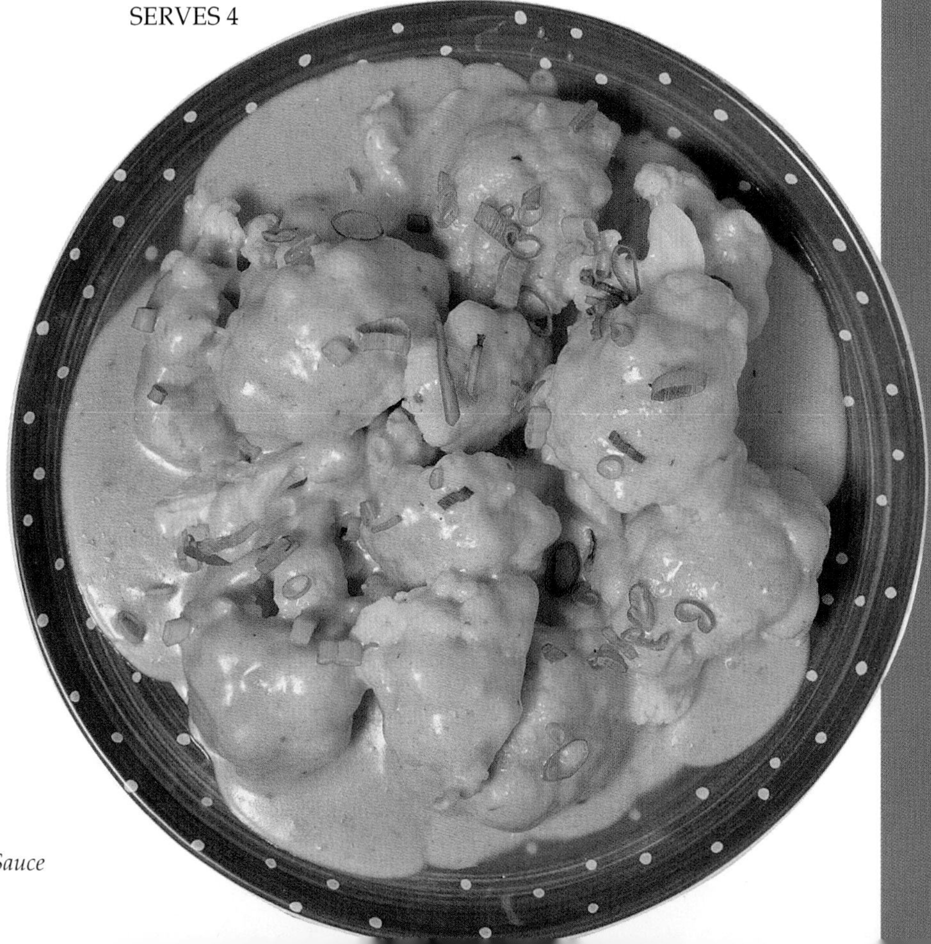

Cauliflower in Aurora Sauce

ARTICHOKES WITH CURRY EGG SAUCE

8	8	small artichokes
3	3	hard cooked egg yolks
1 tsp	5 ml	Dijon mustard
1 cup	250 ml	olive oil
1½ tbsp	20 ml	wine vinegar
1 tbsp	15 ml	curry powder
3 tbsp	45 ml	whipped whipping cream

Trim the artichokes, cut off their stems from the base. Trim and round the leaves, (scissors work best). Wash the artichokes. Place in a large kettle of boiling salted water. Cook for 30-45 minutes, until they are tender. Drain and cool.

In a blender process the egg into a smooth paste with the mustard. Slowly add the oil with the machine running. Blend in the vinegar slowly. Pour sauce into a small mixing bowl. Stir in the curry, then fold in the cream.

Place artichokes on a serving platter, cover with sauce and serve.

SERVES 4

CORN PUDDIN'

2 tbsp	30 ml	butter
2 tbsp	30 ml	flour, all purpose
1 cup	250 ml	milk
¼ tsp	1 ml	salt
¼ tsp	1 ml	white pepper
pinch	pinch	nutmeg
2 cups	500 ml	fresh corn kernels
2	2	eggs

Melt the butter in a sauce pan. Add flour and stir into a paste (roux) cook for 2 minutes over low heat.

Add the milk and stir; simmer until thickened. Add the seasonings and simmer 2 additional minutes.

Stir the corn into the sauce and beat in the eggs. Transfer to a small casserole dish. Set the dish into a second pan of hot water and bake in a preheated 350°F (180°C) oven for 35 minutes. Serve from the casserole dish.

SERVES 4

EGGPLANT HOTEL STYLE

3	3	eggplants
4	4	peeled, seeded, diced tomatoes
1	1	small finely diced onion
4 tbsp	60 ml	olive oil
¼ tsp	1 ml	each of thyme, chervil, basil, marjoram, white pepper
1 tsp	5 ml	salt
2 cups	500 ml	fine dry bread crumbs
2	2	eggs
¼ cup	60 ml	freshly grated Parmesan cheese
2 tbsp	30 ml	melted butter

Pare one of the eggplants and chop into a fine dice. Mix the egg plant with the tomatoes and onions.

Heat the oil in a large skillet and sauté the chopped vegetables until all moisture has evaporated, place into a mixing bowl. Add the seasonings, bread crumbs, eggs and cheese, combine thoroughly.

Pare and slice the remaining eggplants into thick lengthwise pieces. Brush with butter and top with mounds of mixture. Place on a baking sheet and bake in a preheated 350°F (180°C) oven for 20-25 minutes or until golden brown.

SERVES 6

Artichokes with Curry Egg Sauce

Eggplant Hotel Style

BROCCOLI WITH SAUCE MOUSSELINE

1 lb	450 g	broccoli florets
½ cup	125 ml	butter
2	2	egg yolks
2 tsp	10 ml	lemon juice
pinch	pinch	cayenne pepper
¼ cup	60 ml	whipping cream

Steam the broccoli for 15 minutes.

While the broccoli steams, melt the butter to very hot.

Place the egg yolks in a double boiler over low heat. Add lemon juice slowly, be sure its thoroughly incorporated. Remove from heat, slowly whisk in the hot butter.

Add the cayenne and the whipping cream.

Place broccoli in a serving platter, pour sauce over and serve at once.

SERVES 4

Broccoli with Sauce Mousseline

CHAMPAGNE CARROTS

1 lb	454 g	carrots
3 tbsp	45 ml	butter
3 tbsp	45 ml	flour, all purpose
1½ cups	375 ml	Chicken Stock (see page 77)
½ cup	125 ml	heavy cream
½ cup	125 ml	champagne

Pare carrots and cut into sticks. Steam the carrots for 15 minutes.

While the carrots are steaming, melt the butter in a sauce pan. Add the flour and stir into paste (roux) cooking over low heat.

Add chicken stock, cream and champagne. Whisk all the ingredients together.

Simmer for 10 minutes over medium heat. Pour sauce over carrots and serve.

SERVES 4

MUSHROOM CRAB CUTLETS

½ lb	225 g	mushrooms
3 tbsp	45 ml	olive oil
2 tbsp	30 ml	butter
2¼ cups	560 ml	flour, all purpose
1 cup	250 ml	milk
¼ tsp	1 ml	salt
¼ tsp	1 ml	white pepper
½ tsp	3 ml	each of thyme, marjoram, basil
½ lb	225 g	cooked crab meat
2	2	eggs
¼ cup	60 ml	light cream
2 cups	500 ml	fine bread crumbs
1 cup	250 ml	safflower oil

Wash and chop the mushrooms very fine.

Heat the oil in a large skillet and sauté the mushrooms until all liquid has evaporated.

Melt the butter in a sauce pan. Add ¼ cup (60 ml) of the flour and stir into a paste (roux) cook for 2 minutes over low heat.

Add the milk and stir; simmer until thickened. Add the seasonings and simmer 2 additional minutes.

Fold the mushrooms and crab into the sauce and blend thoroughly. Cool to room temperature.

Shape into 8 round patties, place on a waxed paper lined baking sheet and chill for 2 hours.

Beat the eggs with the cream. Dust the patties with the remaining flour, dip into the eggs and dredge through the bread crumbs.

Heat the oil in a large skillet and shallow fry the cutlets to golden brown.

Serve with Madeira Wine Sauce (see page 112).

SERVES 4

BELGIAN ENDIVES AROMATE

12	12	small Belgian endives
½ tsp	3 ml	each of marjoram, sage, basil, chives, peppercorns, thyme
1 tbsp	15 ml	minced shallots
¼ cup	60 ml	white wine
3 tbsp	45 ml	butter
3 tbsp	45 ml	flour, all purpose
¾ cup	180 ml	Chicken Stock (see page 77)
½ cup	125 ml	light cream
1 tbsp	15 ml	fresh chopped chervil

Trim the endives of any wilted leaves. Blanch in boiling salted water for 5-6 minutes. Drain. Reserve hot.

In a small sauce pan combine the seasonings, shallots and wine. Boil and reduce to half the liquid. Strain through a cheese cloth or fine strainer. Reserve the liquid.

Heat the butter in a second sauce pan, add the flour and cook 2 minutes over low heat. Add the reserved liquid, stock, and cream, simmer until thick. Stir in the chervil.

Pour sauce over the endives and serve.

SERVES 4

Brussels Sprouts in Suzette Sauce

RICE WITH FINE HERBS

2 tbsp	30 ml	butter
⅓ cup	80 ml	finely diced onion
¼ cup	60 ml	finely diced celery
¼ cup	60 ml	finely diced red bell pepper
5 cups	1.25 L	Chicken Broth (see page 77)
2 cups	500 ml	long grain rice
½ tsp	3 ml	each of basil, thyme, oregano, chervil
1 tbsp	15 ml	chopped chives
2 tbsp	30 ml	chopped parsley

In a sauce pan heat the butter. Add the vegetables and sauté until tender. Add the chicken broth and rice. Bring to a boil, reduce to a simmer, cook until rice has absorbed the liquid.

Blend in the herbs and serve.

SERVES 6

BRUSSELS SPROUTS IN SUZETTE SAUCE

1 lb	450 g	Brussels sprouts
1	1	orange
½ cup	125 ml	butter
½ cup	125 ml	granulated sugar
3 tbsp	45 ml	orange brandy

Wash the sprouts and trim any wilted leaves, cut away the stem end. Cook the sprouts in boiling salted water for 10 minutes. Drain and reserve hot in a serving bowl.

While sprouts cook, zest the orange peel, and squeeze the juice from the orange and reserve.

Heat the butter in a sauce pan, stir in the sugar, cook until sugar caramelizes. Add the orange zest. Turn pan away from and flame with the brandy. Pour in the juice of the orange, cook for 2 minutes over low heat. Pour over sprouts and serve.

SERVES 4

Roasted Peppers with Sautéed Mushrooms

ROASTED PEPPERS WITH SAUTÉED MUSHROOMS

1	1	red bell pepper
1	1	yellow bell pepper
1	1	green bell pepper
3 oz	80 g	button mushrooms cut into halves
3 tbsp	45 ml	butter
1 cup	250 ml	Ailloli Sauce (see page 102)

Preheat the oven to 400°F (200°C). Place the peppers on a baking sheet. Bake in the oven for 20 minutes, turning frequently. Remove from the oven and place in a paper bag. Seal tightly. Keep enclosed for 20 minutes or until skin sweat off. Peel away loose skin. Slice in half and discard the seeds and membranes. Cut into julienne strips.

While peppers are sweating, heat the butter in a sauce pan. Add the mushrooms and sauté until no moisture is left. Add the peppers and sauté for 2 minutes.Place peppers and mushrooms on a platter, cover with the ailloli sauce and serve.

SERVES 4

COMMANDER AND CHIEF TWICE BAKED POTATOES

6	6	large baked potatoes
5 oz	140 g	fresh spinach
3 tbsp	45 ml	butter
1	1	minced garlic clove
½ tsp	3 ml	each of basil, thyme, oregano
2 tsp	10 ml	salt
1 tsp	5 ml	pepper
1 cup	250 ml	freshly grated Parmesan cheese

While hot, cut the tops from the potatoes, scoop out the pulp, mash and reserve.

Wash the spinach and remove the stems. Chop fine.

Preheat the oven to 450°F (230°C).

Heat the butter in a skillet and sauté the spinach with the garlic clove. Stir into the potatoes with the seasonings and cheese. Restuff the potato skins.

Place on baking sheet and bake until heated through and golden brown.

SERVES 6

POTATOES KALENUIK STYLE

1½ lbs	675 g	pared potatoes
⅓ lb	150 g	diced bacon
1	1	diced Spanish onion
½ cup	125 ml	diced green bell pepper
1 cup	250 ml	sliced mushrooms
4 tbsp	60 ml	butter
3 tbsp	45 ml	flour, all purpose
1 cup	250 ml	peeled, seeded, chopped tomatoes
1½ cup	375 ml	Beef Broth (see page 85)
¼ cup	60 ml	sherry
1 tsp	5 ml	Worcestershire sauce
1 tbsp	15 ml	soya sauce
1 tsp	5 ml	salt
½ tsp	3 ml	pepper
¼ tsp	1 ml	each of thyme, basil, oregano, paprika, chili powder, onion powder, garlic powder
1 cup	250 ml	sharp cheddar cheese – grated

Cut the potatoes in slices, par boil, drain and place into a 12 cup (3L) greased casserole dish.

In a skillet fry the bacon, drain excess fat. Reserve 2 tbsp (30 ml).

In a sauce pan sauté the onion, pepper and mushrooms in the butter and reserved fat. Add the bacon, and sprinkle with flour and cook for 2 minutes. Add the remaining ingredients, except the cheese. Reduce heat, stir, simmer until sauce thickens.

Pour over the potatoes. Bake in a preheated 375°F (190°C) oven for 15 minutes. Sprinkle with cheese and bake 5 minutes longer. Serve.

SERVES 6

LEMON NUT BROCCOLI

1 lb	454 g	broccoli florets
2 tsp	10 ml	cornstarch
¾ cup	180 ml	granulated sugar
1¾ cups	430 ml	boiling water
¼ cup	60 ml	lemon juice
1 tbsp	15 ml	grated lemon rind
2 tbsp	30 ml	butter
¼ cup	60 ml	toasted sliced almonds

Steam the broccoli for 12-15 minutes, transfer to a serving dish.

Blend the cornstarch with the sugar. Whisk into the boiling water, simmer until thick. Whip in the juice, and rind, simmer until the sauce thickens again.

Remove from heat and whip in the butter. Pour sauce over the broccoli, sprinkle with nuts and serve.

SERVES 4

SWEET 'N' SOUR PRAWNS (MEATLESS)

1 lb	450 g	firm tofu
2 tbsp	30 ml	olive oil
1	1	garlic clove
1	1	diced small onion
1	1	diced small green bell pepper
¼ cup	60 ml	peeled, seeded, diced tomatoes
4 tsp	20 ml	brown sugar
4 tsp	20 ml	light soya sauce
⅔ cup	160 ml	Chicken Broth (see page 77)
1 tbsp	15 ml	lemon juice
1 tbsp	15 ml	rice wine (optional)
⅔ cup	160 ml	diced pineapple
2 tsp	10 ml	cornstarch
2 tsp	10 ml	water

Wrap the tofu in a cloth to drain excess moisture. Cut into 1" (2.5 cm) dice.

Heat the oil in a wok, add the garlic, onion, and pepper, fry quickly. Add the tofu and fry 1 minute. Stir in the tomato, sugar, soya, broth, lemon juice and wine. Bring to a boil. Add the pineapple.

Mix cornstarch with the water and add to the mixture. Cook until thick.

Serve over rice.

SERVES 4

Lemon Nut Broccoli

Marinated Vegetable Gri

MARINATED VEGETABLE GRILL

1	1	egg plant
1	1	large zucchini
1	1	red bell pepper
1	1	yellow bell pepper
2	2	large pared carrots
1	1	Spanish onion
¾ cup	190 ml	olive oil
¼ cup	60 ml	lemon juice
1 tbsp	15 ml	grated onion
1	1	minced garlic clove
½ tsp	3 ml	salt
¼ tsp	1 ml	each of basil, thyme, oregano, paprika, pepper
1 tbsp	15 ml	sherry
1 tsp	5 ml	Worcestershire sauce

Trim the vegetables and cut into large slices, place in a mixing bowl.

Combine the remaining ingredients and pour over vegetables, marinate for 1 hour.

Grill the vegetables over medium coals for 10 minutes, brushing several times with the marinade. Brush one final time and serve.

SERVES 4

Brussels Sprouts Aegir

BRUSSELS SPROUTS AEGIR

1 lb	450 g	Brussels sprouts
½ cup	125 ml	butter
2	2	egg yolks
2 tsp	10 ml	lemon juice
1 tsp	5 ml	dry English mustard
pinch	pinch	cayenne pepper

Trim the stem end of the sprouts along with any wilted leaves. Cook for 10 minutes in boiling salted water.

Melt the butter to very hot.

While sprouts cook, place the egg yolks in a double boiler over low heat. Add the lemon juice and mustard, incorporate well. Cook whisking constantly until thick and creamy. Remove from the heat at once.

Whisk in the melted butter gradually into the eggs. Add the cayenne.

Place sprouts on a serving platter, pour sauce over sprouts and serve at once.

SERVES 4

ENDIVES BEULEMANNS

12	12	Belgian endives
¼ cup	60 ml	butter
¼ cup	60 ml	water
1 tbsp	15 ml	lemon juice
½ tsp	3 ml	salt
¼ tsp	1 ml	white pepper
½ cup	125 ml	finely diced ham
1 cup	250 ml	cooked sliced mushrooms
1 cup	250 ml	Demi-Glace Sauce (see page 123)
¼ cup	60 ml	heavy cream

Trim the endives of any wilted leaves, rinse in cold water.

In a large skillet heat the butter, water, lemon juice, salt and pepper, add the endives and simmer over low heat for 15 minutes.

In a small sauce pan simmer together the ham, mushrooms, demi-glace and cream.

Transfer the endives to a serving dish, smother with sauce and serve.

SERVES 6

COUNTRY CARROTS

1½ lbs	675 g	carrots
4 tbsp	60 ml	butter
3 tbsp	45 ml	flour, all purpose
1 cup	250 ml	milk
1 cup	250 ml	Chicken Broth (see page 77)
½ tsp	3 ml	salt
¼ tsp	1 ml	black cracked pepper

Pare the carrots and cut into sticks, steam the carrots for 15 minutes, transfer to a serving dish.

In a sauce pan heat the butter, add the flour and cook for 2 minutes over low heat. Whisk in the milk, broth, salt and pepper, reduce heat and simmer until smooth.

Pour sauce over carrots and serve at once.

SERVES 8

ORANGE BRANDY ASPARAGUS

1 lb	450 g	asparagus spears
2 tsp	10 ml	cornstarch
½ cup	125 ml	granulated sugar
1½ cups	375 ml	orange juice
½ cup	125 ml	Grand Marnier liqueur
2 tsp	10 ml	grated orange rind
1½ tbsp	24 ml	butter

Pare the asparagus and remove the root end. Cook the asparagus in boiling salted water for 15 minutes, keep the tips above the water. Drain and reserve hot.

Blend the cornstarch with the sugar. Heat the orange juice and liqueur to boiling. Stir in the sugar, reduce heat and simmer until thick. Remove from heat and stir in the rind and butter.

Transfer the asparagus to a serving dish, pour the sauce over and serve at once.

SERVES 4

RISOTTO ALLA CERTOSINA

1	1	finely diced Spanish onion
3 tbsp	45 ml	extra virgin olive oil
1 cup	250 ml	long grain rice
1 cup	250 ml	orzo*
4 cups	1 L	Fish Stock (see page 76)
½ cup	125 ml	finely diced red bell pepper
½ cup	125 ml	finely diced green bell pepper
3 tbsp	45 ml	butter
2 tbsp	30 ml	flour, all purpose
2 cups	500 ml	cooked shrimp meat
2 cups	500 ml	half and half cream
¼ tsp	1 ml	each of salt, basil, chervil, marjoram
¼ tsp	1 ml	white pepper
⅔ cup	160 ml	grated Parmesan cheese
2 tbsp	30 ml	chopped parsley

In a large skillet or sauce pan sauté the onion in the oil. Add the rice and orzo and sauté stirring until they turn golden in colour. Add the fish stock, cover and simmer until all the liquid is absorbed.

In a small sauce pan sauté the red and green peppers in the butter. Sprinkle with flour, cook for 2 minutes over low heat. Add the shrimp, cream and seasonings. Simmer for 8-10 minutes. Blend in the cheese.

Stir the sauce into the rice. Place into a serving bowl. Sprinkle with parsley and serve.

SERVES 6

*Orzo is a dried, rice shaped pasta found in the pasta section of most grocery stores.

Orange Brandy Asparagus

Risotto Alla Certosina

POMME DE TERRE À LA BARBANÇONNE

2¼ lbs	1 kg	potatoes
3 tbsp	45 ml	butter
3 tbsp	45 ml	flour, all purpose
1¼ cups	310 ml	Chicken Broth (see page 77)
1¼ cups	310 ml	half & half cream
½ cup	125 ml	freshly grated Parmesan cheese
3 tbsp	45 ml	minced chives
3 tbsp	45 ml	chopped fresh parsley

Pare the potatoes and cut into thick slices. Boil the potatoes in salted water until cooked but still firm, drain.

Heat the butter in a sauce pan. Add the flour and cook 2 minutes over low heat. Stir in the chicken broth and cream. Reduce heat and simmer until thickened. Stir in the cheese, chives and parsley and simmer for 2 more minutes.

Place alternate layers of potatoes and sauce in a large charlotte mold and bake in a preheated 350°F (180°C) oven fro 35 minutes. Turn out of mold and serve.

SERVES 6

CHINESE SEAFOOD RICE

¼ cup	60 ml	safflower oil
¼ lb	60 g	peeled and deveined shrimp
¼ lb	115 g	lobster meat
¼ lb	115 g	crab meat
1	1	finely diced medium onion
1	1	finely diced red bell pepper
20	20	button mushrooms
4 cups	1 L	cooked long grain rice
1 tbsp	15 ml	soya sauce
1 tbsp	15 ml	sherry

In a wok or large skillet heat half the oil. Add the seafood and fry quickly. Remove from wok and reserve hot.

Add the remaining oil to the wok. Fry the onion, pepper and mushrooms. Add the rice fry 1 minute. Return the seafood, mix.

Pour the soya sauce and sherry over. Stir to blend. Serve.

SERVES 6

COCONUT RICE

1 cup	250 ml	long grain rice
3½ cups	875 ml	milk
¾ cup	180 ml	flaked coconut
¼ cup	60 ml	granulated sugar

Bring rice and milk to a boil, stir in the coconut and sugar. Cover and simmer until the liquid has been absorbed. Serve with Polynesian dishes.

SERVES 4

Pomme de Terre à la Barbançonne

Coconut Rice

POTATOES DAUPHIN

8	8	pared large potatoes
½ tsp	3 ml	salt
½ tsp	3 ml	white pepper
⅔ cup	160 ml	melted butter

Preheat the oven to 400°F (200°C).

Cut the potatoes in fine julienne slices. Rinse in cold water. Drain.

Arrange the potatoes in layers in a square casserole dish. Season.

Pour the melted butter over the potatoes. Bake in the oven for 30-45 minutes until tender. Turn out onto a square serving platter. Serve hot.

SERVES 6

FINOCCHIO (FENNEL) WITH GINGER & PINEAPPLE

8	8	small finocchio (fennel)
4 tbsp	60 ml	butter
½ cup	125 ml	apple juice
2 tbsp	30 ml	lemon juice
2 tsp	10 ml	grated ginger root
3 tbsp	45 ml	cornstarch
1 tbsp	15 ml	brown sugar
½ cup	125 ml	diced pineapple

Trim the finocchio of all the green stalks and cut off the base. Remove wilted outer leaves.

Place the butter in a sauce pan, add apple juice and the finocchio, reduce heat and simmer for 20 minutes.

While finocchio simmers, blend the lemon juice and ginger. Mix the cornstarch and sugar together. Blend into the liquid. Heat to a boil, add the pineapple, reduce heat and simmer until sauce thickens.

Transfer finocchio to a serving platter, cover with the sauce and serve.

* Excellent side dish for fish.

SERVES 4

POMME DE TERRE BERNY

1 lb	454 g	potatoes
2 tbsp	30 ml	butter
4	4	eggs
¼ cup	60 ml	cream
1 cup	250 ml	flour, all purpose
1¼ tsp	6 ml	salt
½ tsp	3 ml	white pepper
¼ tsp	1 ml	nutmeg
¼ cup	60 ml	milk
2 cup	500 ml	slivered almonds
¼ cup	60 ml	melted butter

Pare the potatoes and cook in boiling water until tender. Place in a food processor and blend until smooth.

Add the butter, 1 egg yolk and cream; blend until very smooth.

Divide into rounds on a waxed paper lined baking sheet, cool completely. Shape the rounds in cigar shapes.

Mix the remaining flour with the seasonings. Beat the remaining eggs with the milk.

Roll the potatoes in the flour, dip into the milk and roll through the almonds. Place on a baking sheet, brush with the butter and bake in a preheated 350°F (180°C) oven for 15-20 minutes or until golden brown. Potatoes may also be deep fried.

SERVES 4

Pomme de Terre Berny

NADINE POWERS' CARROT PIE

½ quan	0.5	Gourmet Pastry (see page 541)
1¾ cups	430 ml	puréed cooked carrots
½ cup	125 ml	packed brown sugar
¼ cup	60 ml	maple syrup
½ tsp	3 ml	ground ginger
1 tsp	5 ml	ground cinnamon
pinch	pinch	ground cloves
2	2	beaten eggs
1 cup	250 ml	evaporated milk
½ cup	125 ml	water

Roll the dough and fit into a 9" (22 cm) pie pan. Flute the edges.

Place the carrot purée in a food processor, blend in the sugar, syrup and spices. Whip in the eggs, milk and water. Purée until smooth.

Pour into the pie shell, bake in a preheated 450°F (230°C) oven for 10 minutes. Reduce the temperature to 300°F (140°C) and continue to bake for 45 minutes or until an inserted knife comes out clean.

Remove from the oven cool before servings. Nice with whipped cream.

SERVES 6

Nadine Powers' Carrot Pie

SUNCHOKES GRATINATED

1½ lbs	675 g	Jerusalem artichokes
2 tbsp	30 ml	butter
2 tbsp	30 ml	flour, all purpose
1 cup	250 ml	Chicken Broth (see page 77)
½ cup	125 ml	half & half cream
¼ cup	60 ml	freshly grated Parmesan cheese
1 cup	250 ml	grated medium cheddar
¼ cup	60 ml	dry bread crumbs

Pare the artichokes and cut into thick slices, steam for 15 minutes.

While artichokes steam, heat the butter in a sauce pan. Add the flour and cook 2 minutes over low heat for 2 minutes.

Stir in the chicken broth and cream. Reduce heat and simmer until thickened. Stir in the Parmesan cheese and simmer for 2 more minutes.

In a greased casserole dish, alternate layers of artichokes and sauce finishing with the sauce. Sprinkle with cheddar cheese and bread crumbs. Bake in a preheated 350°F (180°C) oven for 35 minutes. Serve.

SERVES 4

RAPINI MORNAY

1 lb	454 g	rapini florets
2 tbsp	30 ml	butter
2 tbsp	30 ml	flour
1 cup	250 ml	Chicken Broth (see page 77)
½ cup	125 ml	half & half cream
¼ cup	60 ml	freshly grated Parmesan cheese

Steam the rapini for 15 minutes, transfer to a serving dish.

While the rapini steams, heat the butter in a sauce pan. Add the flour and cook 2 minutes over low heat for 2 minutes.

Stir in the chicken broth and cream. Reduce heat and simmer until thickened. Stir in the cheese and simmer for 2 more minutes.

Pour sauce over the rapini and serve at once.

SERVES 4

Broccoli Soufflé

POTATOES SAVOYARDE

⅔ lb	150 g	bacon
1	1	Spanish onion
3 tbsp	45 ml	butter
1 lb	450 g	pared, sliced potatoes
2 cups	500 ml	Vegetable Broth (see page 92) or Beef Broth (see page 85)
½ tsp	3 ml	salt
½ tsp	3 ml	pepper
1 cup	250 ml	grated Parmesan cheese
1 cup	250 ml	grated Gruyere cheese

Dice the bacon and fry in a large skillet. Drain the fat.

Slice the onion and sauté in the skillet with the butter. Add the potatoes and cook for 10 minutes tossing. Transfer to a greased 8 cup (2L) casserole dish.

Cover with the broth, season and stir in the Parmesan. Bake in a preheated 375°F (180°C) oven for 20 minutes. Sprinkle the Gruyere and continue to bake for an additional 15 minutes, or until potatoes are tender.

SERVES 6

PAMELA'S BLACK EYED PEAS

1½ lbs	675 g	black eyed peas
4 cups	1 L	Chicken Broth (see page 77)
3 cups	750 ml	hot Mornay Sauce (see page 111)
1½ cups	375 ml	cooked diced chicken
1½ cups	375 ml	cooked crayfish tails
1 tsp	5 ml	paprika
2 tbsp	30 ml	chopped parsley

Simmer the peas in the broth for 1-1½ hours until tender. Drain. Place into a 8 cup (2L) casserole dish.

Preheat the oven to 350°F (180°C).

Mix the mornay sauce with the chicken and crayfish. Ladle over the peas. Sprinkle with paprika. Bake for 30 minutes.

Remove from oven, sprinkle with parsley and serve.

SERVES 6

BROCCOLI SOUFFLÉ

3 tbsp	45 ml	butter
3 tbsp	45 ml	flour, all purpose
1¼ cups	310 ml	milk
1 cup	250 ml	grated Swiss cheese
⅓ cup	80 ml	grated Parmesan cheese
½ tsp	3 ml	salt
¼ tsp	1 ml	pepper
6	6	large, separated, eggs room temperature
1 cup	250 ml	steamed broccoli florets

Preheat the oven to 375°F (190°C).

In a sauce pan heat the butter, add the flour and cook for 2 minutes over low heat. Stir in the milk and simmer until sauce thickens. Stir in the cheeses, salt and pepper. Remove from the heat, cool.

Butter a 2½ quart (2.5L) soufflé dish.

In a mixing bowl beat the egg yolks. Whisk the egg into the sauce, then fold in the broccoli.

Whip the egg whites until stiff. Fold into the mixture. Pour mixture into the soufflé dish. Bake for 40 minutes or until soufflé rises high. Serve at once, (quickly).

SERVES 4

Pamela's Black Eyed Peas

Riz Saint Denis

SPICE 'N' CHICKEN RICE

1 cup	250 ml	long grain rice
¾ cup	180 ml	orzo
3 tbsp	45 ml	safflower oil
1	1	small finely diced onion
1	1	celery stalk finely diced
1 cup	250 ml	sliced mushrooms
½ cup	125 ml	finely diced green bell pepper
4 cups	1 L	hot Chicken Stock (see page 77)
1½ cups	375 ml	cooked diced chicken meat
½ tsp	3 ml	salt
¼ tsp	1 ml	each of garlic powder, onion powder, paprika, chili powder, oregano leaves, thyme leaves, basil leaves
⅛ tsp	pinch	each of black pepper, white pepper, cayenne pepper
2 tbsp	30 ml	butter

In a large sauce pan or skillet, brown the rice and orzo in the oil. Add the onion, celery, mushrooms and green pepper. Sauté until tender. Pour the chicken stock over, cover. Reduce to a simmer, cook until the liquid has been absorbed.

Stir the chicken, seasonings and butter into the hot rice. Place into serving bowls and serve.

SERVES 6

Spanish Rice

RIZ SAINT DENIS

4 oz	120 g	mushrooms
2 cups	500 ml	long grain rice
4 cups	1 L	Beef Broth (see page 85)
2 cups	500 ml	hot Demi-Glace Sauce (see page 123)
⅔ cup	160 ml	freshly grated Parmesan cheese

Wash and trim the mushrooms, then dice them. Place in a sauce pan, add the rice and beef broth. Bring to a boil, cover and reduce to a simmer. Cook the rice until tender and the liquid has been absorbed.

Place in a mound on a round serving dish. Pour the demi glace around the borders of the dish. Sprinkle with cheese and serve.

SERVES 6

SPANISH RICE

8	8	diced bacon slices
1	1	large finely diced Spanish onion
1	1	finely diced green bell pepper
2	2	celery stalk
2 cups	500 ml	Chicken Stock (see page 77)
1 cup	250 ml	long grain rice
2 cups	500 ml	peeled, seeded and chopped tomatoes
2 tsp	10 ml	chili powder
½ tsp	3 ml	salt
¼ tsp	1 ml	each of pepper, paprika

In a large sauce pan fry the bacon. Add the vegetables and sauté until tender.

Add the chicken stock, rice, tomatoes and seasonings. Cover, bring to a boil, reduce to a simmer. Cook until liquid is absorbed. Serve.

SERVES 4

TOM THUMB CABBAGES 2

1 lb	454 g	Brussels sprouts
⅓ cup	90 ml	butter
1 tsp	5 ml	lemon juice
1 tbsp	15 ml	fresh chopped chervil
2	2	hard cooked grated eggs

Cut off the root stem end of the sprouts and trim the outer leaves. Steam the sprouts for 10 minutes. Transfer to a serving dishes.

Heat the butter in a small sauce pan until foamy, add the lemon juice and chervil, cook for 1 minute. Pour over sprouts.

Sprinkle with grated eggs and serve.

SERVES 4

MAPLE WALNUT CARROTS

2	2	egg yolks
½ cup	125 ml	maple syrup
½ cup	125 ml	whipping cream – whipped
¼ cup	60 ml	broken walnut pieces
1 lb	454 g	pared, julienne cut carrots

Beat the egg yolks. Whip in the syrup, place over a double boiler and cook until thick, remove from heat and cool to room temperature.

Fold in the cream and nuts.

Steam the carrots for 12 minutes, transfer to a serving dish. Pour sauce over carrots and serve at once.

SERVES 4

TURTLE BEAN STEW

1½ lbs	675 g	black beans
¼ lb	115 g	diced coarse ham
¼ lb	115 g	diced bacon
2	2	minced garlic clove
1	1	sliced onion
2	2	diced celery stalks
2 cups	500 ml	peeled, seeded, chopped tomatoes
4 cups	1 L	Beef Broth (see page 85)
1 tsp	5 ml	Worcestershire sauce
¼ tsp	1 ml	Tabasco™ sauce
¼ tsp	1 ml	each of pepper, oregano, thyme, onion powder, basil, cayenne
1 tsp	5 ml	each of paprika, salt
½ tsp	3 ml	chili powder

Soak the black beans 8 hours or overnight.

In a large kettle fry the ham and bacon. Sauté the garlic, onion, and celery until tender. Add the tomatoes, broth, beans, Worcestershire, Tabasco™ sauce and seasonings. Bring to a boil, reduce to simmer for 2½-3 hours. Serve.

SERVES 6

Tom Thumb Cabbages 2

Turtle Bean Stew

POMME DE TERRE BOULANGERE

¼ cup	60 ml	butter
1	1	sliced Spanish onion
1 lb	450 g	pared, sliced potatoes
2 cups	500 ml	Chicken Broth (see page 77)
½ tsp	3 ml	salt
½ tsp	3 ml	white pepper

Heat the butter in a large skillet and sauté the onion. Add the potatoes, cook for 10 minutes tossing. Transfer to a 8 cup (2L) casserole dish.

Cover with the broth and season with the salt and pepper. Bake in a preheated 375°F (180°C) oven for 45 minutes or until potatoes are tender.

SERVES 6

BRUSSELS SPROUTS LYONNAISE

1 lb	450 g	Brussels sprouts
½ cup	125 ml	milk
½ cup	125 ml	light cream
¼ tsp	1 ml	nutmeg
¼ tsp	1 ml	salt
¼ tsp	1 ml	white pepper
1	1	medium Spanish onion
3 tbsp	45 ml	butter
3 tbsp	45 ml	flour, all purpose
⅓ cup	80 ml	sweet white wine

Trim the sprouts of any wilted leaves, cut away the end bottoms. Cook in boiling salted water for 10 minutes. Drain, reserve hot in a serving bowl.

Combine the milk, cream, nutmeg, salt, pepper and onion in a sauce pan. Bring to a boil and cook until onions are soft.

In a second sauce pan melt the butter, stir in the flour and cook for 2 minutes over low heat stirring constantly. Add the onion cream and wine, simmer for 8-10 minutes or until thick. Pour over sprouts and serve at once.

SERVES 4

PEA PUFFS

½ quan	0.5	Choux Paste (see Dauphine Potatoes, page 719)
2 tbsp	30 ml	butter
2 tbsp	30 ml	flour, all purpose
1 cup	250 ml	milk
¼ tsp	1 ml	salt
¼ tsp	1 ml	white pepper
pinch	pinch	nutmeg
1½ cups	375 ml	cooked peas
½ cup	125 ml	minced ham (optional)

Preheat the oven to 400°F (200°C).

On a lightly greased baking sheet, drop 1 tbsp (15 ml) of choux pastry 2" (5 cm) apart.

Bake in the oven for 20 minutes or until golden brown.

While the pastry bakes, melt the butter in a sauce pan. Add flour and stir into a paste (roux) cook for 2 minutes over low heat.

Add the milk and stir; simmer until thickened. Add the seasonings and simmer 2 additional minutes. Blend in the peas and ham.

Cut the tops from the puffs, fill with the creamed pea mixture, replace the tops and serve.

SERVES 4

Pea Puffs

Chef K's Cassoulet

CHEF K'S CASSOULET

¼ lb	115 g	pinto beans
¼ lb	115 g	large lima beans
¼ lb	115 g	black beans
1½ lbs	675 g	diced lamb
¾ lb	345 g	smoked sausage
¼ cup	60 ml	olive oil
4 cups	1 L	Beef Broth (see page 85)
3 tbsp	45 ml	brown sugar
½ tsp	3 ml	dry mustard
½ tsp	3 ml	salt
¼ tsp	1 ml	cracked black pepper
1	1	onion sliced rings
1 cup	250 ml	Tomato Sauce (see page 106)

Soak the beans in water for 8 hours or overnight. Cook in a large kettle of boiling water until half tender.

In a large skillet brown the lamb and sausage in the oil. Cover with 2 cups (500 ml) of broth and simmer until tender.

Transfer to a casserole dish. Drain the beans and mix with the meats. Add the remaining broth and other ingredients. Blend thoroughly.

Bake in a preheated 350°F (180°C) oven for 1½ hours. Remove from oven and serve.

SERVES 6

HOT SUNCHOKE AND GREEN BEAN SALAD

¾ lb	345 g	Jerusalem artichokes*
¾ lb	345 g	green beans
3 tbsp	45 ml	fine diced sweet red bell pepper
1 tsp	5 ml	each of chopped, chives, parsley, chervil, capers and gherkins
½ cup	125 ml	olive oil
3 tbsp	45 ml	lemon juice

Pare and slice the artichokes, steam them for 10 minutes or until tender.

Wash and trim the green beans and steam them for 20 minutes.

In a small sauce pan heat (but do not boil) the remaining ingredients.

Mix the beans with the artichokes in a serving dish, pour the sauce over and serve. May also be chilled in the marinade before serving.

SERVES 4

*A Jerusalem artichoke or sunchoke is not related to the artichoke family at all. It is the tubular root of the sunflower plant.

RAPINI ALLA ROMANA

4 cups	1 L	rapini florets*
4 tbsp	60 ml	olive oil
½ cup	125 ml	diced onions
½ cup	125 ml	diced red bell peppers
2 tsp	10 ml	minced garlic
3 tbsp	45 ml	lemon juice
1 cup	250 ml	peeled, seeded, chopped tomatoes
1 tsp	5 ml	sweet basil
½ tsp	3 ml	salt
¼ tsp	1 ml	pepper
½ cup	125 ml	freshly grated Parmesan cheese

Blanch the rapini in boiling salted water for 2 minutes. Drain and reserve.

Heat the oil in a sauce pan, add the onion, red pepper, garlic and sauté until tender. Stir in the lemon juice, tomatoes, basil, salt and pepper. Reduce the heat and simmer for 10 minutes.

Stir in the rapini and continue to simmer for 5 minutes. Transfer to a serving dish. Sprinkle with the cheese and serve.

SERVES 6

*Rapini is Italian broccoli.

Delmonico Potatoes

POMME DE TERRE ALPHONSE

6	6	large potatoes
4 tbsp	60 ml	butter
¼ tsp	1 ml	each of basil, oregano, thyme, sage, black pepper
1 tsp	5 ml	salt
1½ cups	375 ml	grated Gruyere cheese

Wash and scrub the potatoes, then par boil the potatoes. Drain, cool, and reserve skins, then slice.

Preheat the oven to 400°F (200°C).

Place the potatoes in a greased casserole dish. Dot with the butter and sprinkle with the seasonings. Bake for 20 minutes.

Sprinkle with cheese and continue to bake 5 minutes longer. Serve.

SERVES 4

DELMONICO POTATOES

1½ lbs	675 g	potatoes
2 tbsp	30 ml	butter
2 tbsp	30 ml	flour, all purpose
1 cup	250 ml	milk
¼ tsp	1 ml	salt
¼ tsp	1 ml	white pepper
pinch	pinch	nutmeg
¼ cup	60 ml	diced pimento
½ cup	125 ml	bread crumbs
¼ cup	60 ml	butter

Pare the potatoes, cut into ½" dice. Boil in boiling salted water for 15 minutes.

While the potatoes cook, melt the butter in a sauce pan. Add flour and stir into a paste (roux) cook for 2 minutes over low heat.

Add the milk and stir; simmer until thickened. Add the seasonings and simmer 2 additional minutes. Blend in the pimento.

Swirl the sauce through the potatoes and pour into a greased casserole dish. Sprinkle with bread crumbs and dot with butter. Bake in a preheated 350°F (180°C) oven for 30 minutes. Serve.

SERVES 4

ENDIVES A LA MORNAY

12	12	Belgian endives
⅓ cup	90 ml	butter
¼ cup	60 ml	water
1 tbsp	15 ml	lemon juice
½ tsp	3 ml	salt
¼ tsp	1 ml	white pepper
2 tbsp	30 ml	flour, all purpose
1 cup	250 ml	Chicken Broth (see page 77)
½ cup	125 ml	half & half cream
¼ cup	60 ml	freshly grated Parmesan cheese

Trim the endives of any wilted leaves, rinse in cold water.

In a large skillet heat ¼ cup (60 ml) of butter, water, lemon juice, salt and pepper, add the endives and simmer over low heat for 15 minutes.

While endives simmer, heat the remaining butter in a sauce pan. Add the flour and cook 2 minutes over low heat for 2 minutes.

Stir in the chicken broth and cream. Reduce heat and simmer until thickened. Stir in the cheese and simmer for 2 more minutes.

Transfer the endives to a serving platter, smother with sauce and serve.

SERVES 6

Endives a la Mornay

Rice Matriciana

Raspberry Asparagus with Baby Shrimp

RICE MATRICIANA

8	8	slices of bacon
1	1	minced garlic clove
1	1	finely diced smal onion
2 cups	500 ml	peeled, seeded and chopped tomatoes
2 cups	500 ml	long grain rice
4 cups	1 L	Chicken Stock (see page 77)
2 cups	500 ml	tomato juice
1 tsp	5 ml	chervil
½ tsp	3 ml	salt
¼ tsp	1 ml	pepper

Fine dice the bacon and sauté along with the garlic and onion. Add the tomatoes, cook gently until most of the moisture has evaporated.

Stir in the rice. Add the chicken stock, tomato juice and seasonings. Cover and simmer until the rice is tender and liquid has been absorbed. Serve.

SERVES 6

RASPBERRY ASPARAGUS WITH BABY SHRIMP

6 tbsp	90 ml	raspberry vinegar
4 tsp	20 ml	Dijon mustard
4 tsp	20 ml	granulated sugar
¾ tsp	4 ml	salt
¼ tsp	1 ml	pepper
¾ cup	190 ml	olive oil
1½ lbs	675 g	asparagus spears
2 cups	500 ml	cooked baby shrimp

Blend together the vinegar, mustard, sugar, salt and pepper. Very slowly whisk in the oil.

Pare the asparagus and remove the tough root ends, blanch for 7 minutes without allowing the tips to touch the water. Rinse under cold water and pat dry.

Place the asparagus on a serving plate. Pour the dressing over and allow to marinate refrigerated.

Sprinkle the shrimp over the salad and serve.

SERVES 4

BEVERAGES

What's a meal without an excellent beverage? Lonely! That's why I've presented an interesting selection of beverages for today's lifestyle, some without any alcohol, others with.

Fresh, fruity drinks, healthy drinks, party drinks and quiet time drinks. All found in the next few pages are absolutely *Simply Delicious*. Coffees and chocolates like no others have ever been offered, and like you have never tasted. You'll become as popular as your favourite restaurant's mixologist.

Taste, of course, is the final rule and these beverages meet all the requirements of taste. Even a drink can be a failure, though, if the proper ingredients are not used. Follow the recipe and avoid defeat. Each drink is designed for the best in flavour; a little more or less of an ingredient can reduce a great beverage to mediocre. By all means experiment with your beverages. Use your creativity to ensure the best for yourself and your guests.

Many consider their beverage least of all in the making of a great meal, yet the beverage is upon the lips of a guest for a longer time than any other course offered throughout the meal. Therefore, it should be given at least equal consideration. When selections of fine beverages are offered during the evening meal, the meal is made that much more memorable.

During a five-course dinner one may consume as many as four different wines. Why not exchange the wines for four different beverages? They are sure to gain compliments and provide something your guest will look forward to more than just the popping of a cork.

Simply Delicious Beverages will enliven any party, take the chill off a cold winter night or bring the heat down on a scorching 100 degree day. There are more than forty drinks to choose from, and vary so that you may serve just the right drink with the right occasion. Just keep in mind that the best drinks are the ones that are *Simply Delicious*.

Northern & CNR

CROSSING
ROAD
STOP
WHEN
SWINGING
LIONEL
CANADIAN
NATIONAL
CN 290205
CN
BUDDY
LIONEL LI
RAIL
CROSSING
ROAD
246

YO YO

1 oz	30 ml	dark rum
1 oz	30 ml	Tia Maria
1	1	maraschino cherry

Build in a rock glass over ice. Garnish with the cherry and serve.

SERVES 1

MELON BALL

½	0.5	honeydew melon, seeded
½	0.5	cantaloupe, seeded
1	1	orange

Spoon melons into a blender. Process lightly, section the orange and add to the drink. Serve.

SERVES 2

BEAUTIFUL CHOCOLATE

2 oz	60 g	semi-sweet chocolate, grated
¼ cup	60 ml	granulated sugar
½ cup	125 ml	boiling water
2½ cups	625 ml	milk, scalded
1 tbsp	15 ml	instant coffee crystals
⅓ cup	80 ml	cognac
⅓ cup	80 ml	Amaretto liqueur
½ cup	125 ml	whipping cream
¼ cup	60 ml	toasted sliced almonds

In a small sauce pan combine the chocolate, sugar and water, bring to a boil, reduce heat and simmer for 2 minutes.

Whisk in the milk, coffee, cognac, Amaretto and simmer for 2 more minutes.

Pour into four mugs. Whip the cream and float on top of the chocolate drink. Sprinkle with the almonds and serve.

SERVES 4

Yo Yo

LICORICE STICK

3 oz	80 g	white chocolate, grated
¼ cup	60 ml	granulated sugar
2 cups	500 ml	milk
1 cup	250 ml	half & half cream
¼ cup	60 ml	Pernod liqueur
¼ cup	60 ml	Anisette liqueur
6	6	black strap licorice sticks

In a small sauce pan combine the chocolate, sugar, milk, cream and liqueurs. Heat, but do not boil. Pour into mugs, garnish with licorice sticks and serve.

SERVES 4

ALMOND CHEESECAKE

2 oz	60 ml	Amaretto liqueur
½ cup	125 ml	light cream
1 cup	250 ml	almond nut ice cream
2 tbsp	30 ml	simple syrup
¼ tsp	1 ml	almond extract
2 tsp	10 ml	toasted sliced almonds

In a blender combine the liqueur, cream, ice cream, syrup and extract, blend until smooth.

Pour into 2 collins glasses, garnish with sliced almonds and serve.

SERVES 2

Melon Ball

Aw Nuts

50-50 BAR

3 oz	80 g	semi-sweet chocolate, grated
2 cups	500 ml	milk
1 cup	250 ml	half & half cream
¼ cup	60 ml	Galliano liqueur
¼ cup	60 ml	Triple Sec liqueur
¼ cup	60 ml	orange juice concentrate
½ cup	125 ml	whipping cream
4	4	orange chocolate candy sticks

In a sauce pan combine the chocolate, milk, cream, liqueurs and orange juice. Heat but do not boil.

Pour into mugs.

Whip the cream and float it on top of the beverage. Garnish with a chocolate stick, serve.

SERVES 4

50-50 Bar

CUBAN COCKTAIL

⅔ oz	20 ml	brandy
⅓ oz	10 ml	apricot brandy
1 tsp	5 ml	lime juice
2 dashes	2 dashes	orange bitters

Pour the ingredients over crushed ice in a shaker glass. Stir, strain into a cocktail glass.

SERVES 1

AW NUTS

¼ cup	60 ml	blanched almonds
½ cup	125 ml	pineapple yogurt
½ cup	125 ml	pineapple juice
1 drop	1 drop	almond extract
1 tsp	5 ml	toasted sliced almonds

Combine all ingredients in a blender, process until smooth. Pour into a champagne glass and serve.

SERVES 1

KAHLUA DREAMS

2 oz	60 ml	Kahlua liqueur
1 tbsp	15 ml	powdered sugar
2 tbsp	30 ml	extra strong cold coffee
½ cup	125 ml	light cream
1 cup	250 ml	coffee ice cream

Combine the ingredients in a blender and blend until smooth. Pour in 2 collins glasses and serve.

SERVES 2

PEACH DREAM

2 tbsp	30 ml	honey
1 cup	250 ml	sliced fresh peaches
½ cup	125 ml	plain yogurt
1 cup	250 ml	apricot or peach nectar

Place all ingredients in a blender, process until smooth. Pour into large rock glasses and serve.

SERVES 2

AGGRAVATION

1 oz	30 ml	scotch
1 oz	30 ml	Kahlua
1 oz	30 ml	cream

Build in a rock glass over ice. Serve.

SERVES 1

RUSSIAN BANANA

3 oz	80 g	semi-sweet chocolate, grated
1½ cups	375 ml	strong coffee
1 cup	250 ml	half & half cream
¼ cup	60 ml	granulated sugar
¼ cup	60 ml	vodka
¼ cup	60 ml	Kahlua
2	2	bananas, mashed
½ cup	125 ml	whipping cream
¼ cup	60 ml	chocolate shavings

In a sauce pan combine the chocolate, coffee, cream, sugar, liqueurs and bananas. Heat but do not boil.

Pour into mugs. Whip the cream, float on top of the beverage. Garnish with the chocolate shavings and serve.

SERVES 4

CAFE MEXICO

3 cups	750 ml	coffee
⅓ cup	80 ml	tequila
⅓ cup	80 ml	Kahlua liqueur
¼	0.25	lemon
¼ cup	60 ml	granulated sugar
½ cup	125 ml	whipping cream
12	12	chocolate covered coffee beans

Heat the coffee with the tequila and Kahlua. Rim the mugs with lemon then dip into the sugar. Fill with coffee. Whip the cream and float on top. Garnish each drink with 4 coffee beans and serve.

SERVES 4

HONOLULU LADY

2 oz	60 ml	Calvados
1 oz	30 ml	coconut milk
1 oz	30 ml	lemon juice
1 tbsp	15 ml	Grenadine
3 oz	90 ml	lemon lime soda
½ tsp	3 ml	powdered sugar
1	1	pineapple stick
1	1	maraschino cherry

Fill a collins glass half full of crushed ice, pour the liquids over, add the sugar and stir. Skewer the pineapple stick and the cherry with a toothpick, use to garnish the drink.

SERVES 1

Peach Dream

Cafe Mexico

LADY BUG CHOCOLATE

3 oz	80 g	white chocolate, grated
¼ cup	60 ml	granulated sugar
2 cups	500 ml	milk, scalded
1 cup	250 ml	half & half cream
⅓ cup	80 ml	Creme de Bananas liqueur
⅓ cup	80 ml	Triple Sec liqueur
1 tbsp	15 ml	Grenadine
¼ cup	60 ml	chocolate shavings

Combine the chocolate, sugar and milk in a small sauce pan and heat but do not boil. Add the cream and liqueurs, simmer for 3 additional minutes.

Run four stripes of Grenadine along the inside of crystal mugs. Fill with beverage and float chocolate shavings on top. Serve.

SERVES 4

Lady Bug Chocolate

BROWN FOX

1¼ oz	35 ml	bourbon
½ oz	15 ml	Benedictine
1	1	maraschino cherry

Build in a rock glass over ice. Garnish with the sherry and serve.

SERVES 1

BEE'S KNEES

1 oz	30 ml	vodka
½ oz	15 ml	honey
½ oz	15 ml	lime juice

Pour the liquids over crushed ice in a shaker glass. Shake well, strain into a cocktail glass, serve.

SERVES 1

SIDECAR

1 oz	30 ml	Cointreau
1 oz	30 ml	brandy
1 oz	30 ml	lemon juice

Pour the liquids over crushed ice in a shaker glass. Shake well, strain into a cocktail glass, serve.

SERVES 1

ALEXANDER COCKTAIL

2 oz	60 ml	Créme de Cacao
4 oz	120 ml	gin
2 oz	60 ml	heavy cream

Pour the ingredients over crushed ice in a shaker. Shake well, strain into 2 cocktail glassed.

SERVES 2

BOURBON CASSIS

1 oz	30 ml	bourbon
½ oz	15 ml	dry vermouth
1 tsp	5 ml	Creme de Cassis
1 tsp	5 ml	lemon juice
1	1	lemon twist

Build in a rock glass over ice. Garnish with a lemon twist.

SERVES 1

COCONUT DREAM

2 oz	60 g	semi-sweet chocolate, grated
¼ cup	60 ml	coconut nectar creme
2 cups	500 ml	milk
¾ cup	180 ml	half & half cream
¼ cup	60 ml	coconut rum
½ cup	125 ml	whipping cream
⅓ cup	80 ml	toasted coconut flakes

In a small sauce pan combine the chocolate, coconut nectar, milk, cream and rum. Heat but do not boil.

Pour into crystal mugs. Whip the cream, and float it on the beverage, sprinkle with toasted coconut. Serve.

SERVES 4

POMEGRANATE APPLE

3	3	pomegranates
1½ cups	375 ml	apple juice

Cut the pomegranates in half, scoop the seed pulp into a food processor. Blend for 1 minute. Strain, reserving the liquid. Blend the pomegranate liquid with the apple juice. Pour over crushed ice filled collins glasses. Serve.

SERVES 2

GRAND GALLIANO COFFEE

3 cups	750 ml	coffee
¼ cup	60 ml	Grand Marnier liqueur
¼ cup	60 ml	Galliano liqueur
½ cup	125 ml	whipping cream
¼ cup	60 ml	chocolate shavings

Heat the coffee and liqueurs together. Pour into sugar rimmed glasses. Whip the cream and float it on top of the coffee. Top with chocolate shavings. Serve.

SERVES 4

Coconut Dream

Strawberry Fields

Vandermint Chocolate Coffee

STRAWBERRY FIELDS

3 oz	80 g	white chocolate, grated
2 cups	500 ml	milk
1 cup	250 ml	half & half cream
¼ cup	60 ml	granulated sugar
1 cup	250 ml	strawberry purée
½ cup	125 ml	whipping cream
4	4	large fresh strawberries

In a small sauce pan combine the chocolate, milk, cream, sugar and purée. Heat but do not boil. Pour into 4 mugs.

Whip the cream, and float on top of the beverage. Garnish with a strawberry and serve.

SERVES 4

VANDERMINT CHOCOLATE COFFEE

2 oz	60 g	semi-sweet chocolate, grated
2 cups	500 ml	coffee
¼ cup	60 ml	granulated sugar
1 cup	250 ml	half & half cream
⅓ cup	80 ml	Vandermint chocolate liqueur
¼ cup	60 ml	Creme de Cacao liqueur
½ cup	125 ml	whipping cream
4	4	maraschino cherries
4	4	chocolate mint sticks

In a sauce pan combine the chocolate, coffee, sugar and cream. Bring to a boil, than reduce the heat and simmer for 2 minutes. Stir in the liqueurs, and simmer 1 additional minute.

Pour into mugs. Whip the cream and float it on top of the drink. Garnish with a cherry and a mint stick, serve.

SERVES 4

XYZ COFFEE

3 cups	750 ml	black coffee
⅓ cup	80 ml	Benedictine liqueur
⅓ cup	80 ml	bourbon
¼	0.25	orange
¼ cup	60 ml	granulated sugar
½ cup	125 ml	whipping cream
4	4	maraschino cherries

In a small sauce pan heat the coffee and liqueurs. Rim four mugs with the orange, dip into the sugar. Fill with coffee.

Whip the cream, and float it on top of the coffee. Garnish with a cherry and serve.

SERVES 4

APPLE BLOSSOM

2 oz	60 ml	Calvados
1 tbsp	15 ml	lime juice
1 tsp	5 ml	lemon juice
4 oz	120 ml	apple juice
1	1	fresh cut apple slice

Fill a collins glass half full of crushed ice, pour the liquids over, garnish with the apple slice.

SERVES 1

FRENCH 95

1¼ oz	35 ml	bourbon
2 tbsp	30 ml	lemon juice
½ oz	15 ml	soda
3 oz	80 ml	champagne
1	1	lime slice

Build over crushed ice in a collins glass. Garnish with the lime slice and serve.

SERVES 1

GRAND ORANGE MILKSHAKE

2 oz	60 ml	Grand Marnier liqueur
2 oz	60 ml	orange juice concentrate
½ cup	125 ml	light cream
1 cup	250 ml	orange sherbet
2	2	slices fresh oranges

In a blender combine the liqueur, concentrate, cream and sherbet, blend until smooth.

Pour into collins glasses, garnish with orange slice and serve.

SERVES 2

CHERRY BLOSSOM

1 oz	30 ml	brandy
¾ oz	20 ml	cherry brandy
1 tsp	5 ml	Curacao
1 tsp	5 ml	Grenadine
3 oz	80 ml	soda
1	1	maraschino cherry

Build in a Collins glass over crushed ice. Garnish with the cherry and serve.

SERVES 1

THE FOURTH DEGREE

⅓ oz	10 ml	white vermouth
⅓ oz	10 ml	red vermouth
⅓ oz	10 ml	gin
1 tsp	5 ml	Anisette

Pour the ingredients over crushed ice in a shaker. Shake well, strain into a cocktail glass.

SERVES 1

Blueberry Cheesecake

WHITE DESTRUCTION

3 oz	85 g	white chocolate, grated
2 cups	500 ml	milk, scalded
1 cup	250 ml	half & half cream
¼ cup	60 ml	granulated sugar
¼ cup	60 ml	brandy
¼ cup	60 ml	white Creme de Cacao
¼ cup	60 ml	white Creme de Menthe
½ cup	125 ml	whipping cream

In a small sauce pan combine the chocolate, milk, cream, sugar and liqueurs. Heat, but do not boil. Pour into mugs.

Whip the cream and float on top of the beverage. Serve.

SERVES 4

BLUEBERRY CHEESECAKE

½ cup	125 ml	washed and cleaned blueberries
½ cup	125 ml	light cream
1 cup	250 ml	vanilla ice cream
2 oz	60 ml	Parfait Amour liqueur
¼ cup	60 ml	softened cream cheese

Reserve a dozen blueberries and place the rest in a blender. Add the remaining ingredients, blend until smooth.

Pour into 2 collins glasses, garnish with the reserved berries and serve.

SERVES 2

Cherry Blossom

COINTREAU COCKTAIL

1 oz	30 ml	Cointreau
1 oz	30 ml	brandy
1 oz	30 ml	lemon juice
		orange peel twist

Pour the ingredients over crushed ice in a shaker glass. Shake well, strain into a cocktail glass. Garnish with the orange peel.

SERVES 1

BANANA COFFEE

¼ cup	60 ml	Creme de Bananas liqueur
¼ cup	60 ml	Creme de Cacao liqueur
3 cups	750 ml	hot coffee
¼	0.25	lemon
¼ cup	60 ml	granulated sugar
½ cup	125 ml	whipping cream

Heat the liqueurs and blend with the coffee. Rim crystal four coffee mugs with the lemon, dip the rims into the sugar.

Fill the mugs with coffee. Whip the cream and float on top of the coffee.

SERVES 4

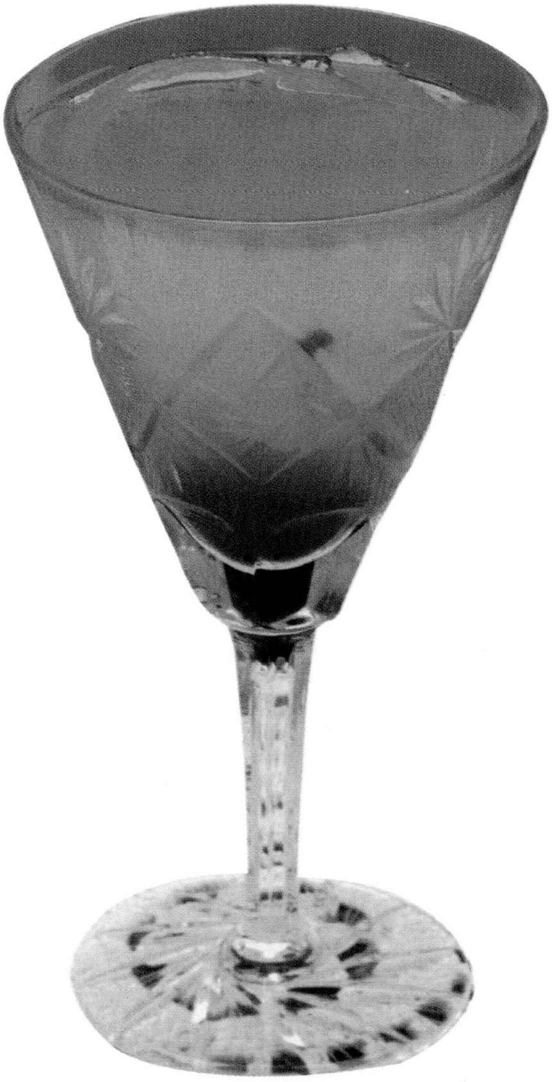

Cointreau Cocktail

VERY RICH HOT CHOCOLATE

3 oz	80 ml	semi-sweet chocolate, grated
¼ cup	60 ml	granulated sugar
1 cup	250 ml	water
½ cup	125 ml	sweetened condensed milk
2 cups	500 ml	milk, scalded
⅛ tsp	pinch	salt
¼ tsp	1 ml	vanilla extract
½ cup	125 ml	whipping cream

In a sauce pan combine the chocolate, sugar, water and condensed milk. Bring to a boil, than reduce the heat and simmer for 2 minutes. Add the milk, salt and vanilla. Whip with a mixer for 1 minute.

Pour into 4 mugs. Whip the cream and float on top of the beverage. Serve.

SERVES 4

APPLE KICKER

2	2	eggs
1½ cups	375 ml	apple juice
½ cup	125 ml	light cream
2 tsp	10 ml	honey
½ tsp	3 ml	cinnamon

Combine all the ingredients in a blender until smooth. Pour into rock glasses and serve.

SERVES 2

Apple Sunrise

APPLE SUNRISE

1¼ oz	35 ml	Calvados
1¼ oz	35 ml	orange juice
2 oz	30 ml	lemon juice
2 oz	30 ml	lime cordial
1 tsp	5 ml	Grenadine
1	1	apple wedge

Build in a collins glass over crushed ice, float Grenadine on top. Garnish with the apple wedge and serve.

SERVES 1

HONEY NOG

1 cup	250 ml	cold milk
1	1	egg
1½ tbsp	22 ml	honey
1 tsp	5 ml	vanilla extract

Pour the ingredients over a little crushed ice in a blender. Blend until smooth, strain in a crystal mug and serve.

SERVES 1

SOUTH AFRICA SUNDOWNER

1½ oz	45 ml	brandy
½ oz	15 ml	white vermouth
½ oz	15 ml	lemon juice
½ oz	15 ml	orange juice

Pour the liquids over crushed ice in a shaker glass. Shake well, strain into a cocktail glass, serve.

SERVES 1

Chocolate Grasshopper

CHOCOLATE GRASSHOPPER

3 oz	80 ml	white chocolate, grated
¼ cup	60 ml	granulated sugar
2 cups	500 ml	milk
1 cup	250 ml	half & half cream
¼ cup	60 ml	green Creme de Menthe liqueur
¼ cup	60 ml	white Creme de Cacao liqueur
¼ tsp	1 ml	green food colouring
½ cup	125 ml	whipping cream
4	4	candied mint leaves
4	4	chocolate mint sticks

In a small sauce pan combine the chocolate, sugar, milk, cream, liqueurs and food colouring. Heat but do not boil. Pour into the mugs.

Whip the cream and float it on top of the drinks. Garnish with mint leaves and chocolate sticks, serve.

SERVES 4

APPLE SAUCE

1 oz	30 ml	gin
1 oz	30 ml	Calvados
1 tbsp	15 ml	lemon bar mix crystals
1 tbsp	15 ml	lime bar mix crystals
1 oz	30 ml	orange juice
2 oz	60 ml	crushed ice
1	1	cherry

Combine all the ingredients except the cherry in a blender. Pour into a sour glass. Garnish with the cherry.

SERVES 1

MINT JULEP

1¼ oz	35 ml	bourbon
1 tsp	5 ml	green Creme de Menthe
1 tsp	5 ml	soda water
		mint sprig

Build in a high ball glass over crushed ice. Garnish with a mint sprig.

SERVES 1

MOSS LANDING COFFEE

3 cups	750 ml	coffee
⅓ cup	80 ml	Grand Marnier liqueur
⅓ cup	80 ml	Creme de Bananas liqueur
½ cup	125 ml	whipping cream
¼ cup	60 ml	chocolate shavings

Heat the coffee and liqueurs together. Pour into sugar rimmed glasses. Whip the cream, float it on top of the coffee. Garnish with chocolate shavings.

SERVES 4

AVOCADO APHRODISIAC

1	1	medium-sized avocado
1	1	long English cucumber
¼ cup	60 ml	lemon juice
2 tsp	10 ml	Worcestershire sauce
2 cups	500 ml	crushed ice

Peel and stone the avocado. Zest the cucumber and slice it. Place cucumber into a food processor, reserving two slices for garnish. Add the avocado along with remaining ingredients and purée.

Pour into large fluted glasses, garnish with the zest and the slices of the cucumber.

Serve.

SERVES 2

Avocado Aphrodisiac

BARRACUDA

¾ oz	20 ml	Jack Daniel's whiskey
1 tsp	5 ml	Orgeat
1 oz	30 ml	orange juice
1 tbsp	35 ml	lemon bar mix crystals
1	1	orange wedge

Combine all the ingredients in a blender. Pour into a collins glass filled with crushed ice. Garnish with an orange wedge and serve.

SERVES 1

THE STINGER

1 oz	30 ml	Creme de Menthe
1 oz	30 ml	brandy

Pour the liquids over crushed ice in a shaker glass. Shake well, strain into a cocktail glass, serve.

SERVES 1

BLOODY CAESAR

1	1	slice lemon
½ tsp	3 ml	salt
1 tbsp	35 ml	vodka
2 oz	60 ml	clam nectar
2 oz	60 ml	tomato juice
¼ tsp	1 ml	Worcestershire sauce
drop	drop	Tabasco™ sauce
pinch	pinch	pepper
pinch	pinch	Cajun spice blend
1	1	celery stick

Rim a high ball glass with the lemon slice, then dip in the salt. Fill the glass with crushed ice. Pour in the vodka, clam nectar, juice, sauces, pepper and spice. Stir. Garnish with the celery stick and serve.

SERVES 1

Lemon Spumante

NORTHERN & CNR

1 oz	30 ml	dark rum
1 oz	30 ml	brandy
2 oz	60 ml	pineapple juice
1 tbsp	15 ml	lemon juice

Pour the ingredients over crushed ice in a shaker glass. Shake well, strain into a cocktail glass.

SERVES 1

LEMON SPUMANTE

6 tbsp	90 ml	powdered sugar
1 cup	250 ml	water
½ cup	125 ml	lemon juice
4 cups	1 L	Asti Spumante

In a small sauce pan combine the sugar, water and lemon juice, bring to a boil, cool to room temperature. Pour into ice cube trays and freeze.

Remove lemon ice cubes and place into 6 collins glasses, pour the wine over the ice and serve.

SERVES 6

BROADWAY MELODY

½ oz	15 ml	gin
½ oz	15 ml	white vermouth
½ oz	15 ml	Grand Marnier

Pour the ingredients over crushed ice in a shaker glass. Shake well, strain into a cocktail glass.

SERVES 1

GRAPE RENEW

1 cup	250 ml	grape juice concentrate
2 cups	500 ml	water
4 cups	1 L	Asti Spumante

Blend the grape concentrate with the water, pour into ice cube trays and freeze.

Remove grape ice cubes and place into 6 collins glasses, pour the wine over the ice and serve.

SERVES 6

Grape Renew

HEALTH DRINK

1 cup	250 ml	orange segments
1 cup	250 ml	milk
1	1	egg
1	1	banana
½ cup	125 ml	orange juice
½ cup	125 ml	pineapple juice
1 tsp	5 ml	maple syrup
1 tbsp	15 ml	wheat germ

Place the ingredients in a blender, and blend until smooth. Pour into large rock glasses and serve.

SERVES 2

ROYAL ALEXANDER

1 oz	30 ml	Créme de Cacao
1 oz	30 ml	brandy
1 oz	30 ml	fresh cream
½ oz	15 ml	dry white vermouth

Pour the ingredients over crushed ice in a shaker glass. Shake well, strain into a cocktail glass.

SERVES 1

KING OF HEARTS CHOCOLATE

2 oz	60 g	semi-sweet chocolate, grated
2 cups	500 ml	coffee
¼ cup	60 ml	granulated sugar
1 cup	250 ml	half & half cream
¼ cup	60 ml	vodka
¼ cup	60 ml	Galliano liqueur
¼ cup	60 ml	Grand Marnier liqueur
½ cup	125 ml	whipping cream
¼ cup	60 ml	chocolate shavings

In a small sauce pan combine the chocolate, coffee and sugar. Bring to a boil, than reduce the heat and simmer for 2 minutes. Add the cream and liqueurs, continue to simmer for 3 minutes. Pour into mugs.

Whip the cream and float on top of the chocolate. Garnish with chocolate shavings, serve.

SERVES 4

CALYPSO COFFEE

1 tbsp	15 ml	granulated sugar
3 cups	750 ml	coffee
⅓ cup	80 ml	rum
⅓ cup	80 ml	Kahlua
½ cup	125 ml	whipping cream
4	4	maraschino cherries, stem on

Heat the sugar, coffee, rum and kahlua together. Pour into sugar rimmed mugs. Whip the cream and float on the coffee. Garnish with a cherry and serve.

SERVES 4

Pinemelon

HAWAIIAN WAHOO

2 oz	60 ml	gin
2 oz	60 ml	cherry brandy
2 oz	60 ml	pineapple juice
1 tsp	5 ml	Grenadine
1	1	wedge of fresh pineapple

Pour the liquids over crushed ice in a shaker glass. Shake well, strain into a jumbo champagne glass, garnish with a pineapple.

SERVES 1

STRAWBERRY FLIP

1 cup	250 ml	sliced fresh strawberries
½ cup	125 ml	strawberry yogurt
1 cup	250 ml	milk
½ cup	125 ml	apple juice

Place all ingredients in a food processor, blend thoroughly. Pour into highball glasses and serve.

SERVES 2

PINEMELON

1 cup	250 ml	pineapple juice
1 cup	250 ml	cubed honeydew melon
1 cup	250 ml	cubed cantaloupe melon

Place the ingredients in a blender, process until smooth. Pour into 2 rock glasses and serve.

SERVES 2

NORTH OF 49TH PARALLEL

2 tbsp	30 ml	maple syrup
1 cup	250 ml	washed blueberries
½ cup	125 ml	yogurt
1 cup	250 ml	apple juice

Place all ingredients in a blender, process until smooth. Pour into large rock glasses, serve.

SERVES 2

CANADIAN QUIZ

1 cup	250 ml	yogurt
2 cups	500 ml	pineapple juice
1 cup	250 ml	blueberries
2 tbsp	30 ml	maple syrup

Place the ingredients in a blender, process until smooth. Pour into rock glasses and serve.

SERVES 2

TIGER PAW

3 oz	80 ml	white chocolate
2 cups	500 ml	milk
1 cup	250 ml	half & half cream
⅓ cup	80 ml	Anisette liqueur
⅓ cup	80 ml	orange juice concentrate
¼ cup	60 ml	granulated sugar
1 tbsp	15 ml	Grenadine
1 tbsp	15 ml	molasses

In a small sauce pan combine the chocolate, milk, cream, liqueur, orange concentrate and sugar. Heat, but do not boil.

Run strips of grenadine and molasses inside crystal mugs, fill with the beverage and serve.

SERVES 4

CAPTAIN MORGAN

1 oz	30 ml	dark rum
1 tsp	5 ml	lime juice
½ tsp	3 ml	Cointreau
1	1	olive, green

Pour the liquids over crushed ice in a shaker glass. Shake well, strain into a cocktail glass, garnish with the olive.

SERVES 1

Hawaiian Wahoo

Glossary of Cooking Terms

The following are definitions of common terms used in the preparation of food:

AGING:	A term applied to meat held at a temperature of 34°F to 36°F (1-2 °C) to improve its tenderness, for 14-21 days.
A' LA' CARTE:	French — "According to the menu."
A' LA' MODE:	"In the fashion" — means a certain way a dish is served, e.g. - pie or pot roast.
ALBUMEN:	The major component of egg white.
ANCHOVY:	A small herring type fish, usually canned in highly spiced oil.
ANDOUILLE SAUSAGE:	Highly spiced, Creole Cajun sausage. Available from most meat purveyors through special order.
APPLES VARIETIES:	Baldwin, Cortland, Empire, Golden & Red Delicious, Gala, Granny Smith, Gravenstein, Greening, Ida Red, Jonathan, Lodi, Macintosh, Macoun, Milton, Newton, Pippin, Northern Spy, Rome Beauty, Russet, Stayman, Winesap, York Imperial, all are excellent eating, most will do for baking and cooking, always use the finest, freshest available.
ASPIC:	A highly flavourful gelatin made from meat or vegetable stock in which such foods have been set and molded.
AU GRATIN:	Foods; seafoods, chicken or vegetables prepared with a sauce, covered with buttered crumbs, or buttered crumbs and cheese, and browned in the oven.
AU JUS:	The natural juice of roasted meat.
BAIN MARIE:	French term for double boiler.
BAKE:	To cook by indirect dry heat, usually in an oven: when applied to meats, it is called roasting.
BAKING POWDER:	SAS Phosphate: often referred to as double action. Reacts when first incorporated into the batter and then once again during cooking or baking.
BAKING SODA:	Bicarbonate of soda — used with baking powder or alone to leaven cakes, etc. Must be baked immediately.
BARBECUE:	To roast slowly over coals, or on a spit. Usually basting with a highly seasoned sauce: also refers to smoked foods in central and south United States.

BASTE: To moisten the outer layers of foods during cooking, to prevent drying, improve flavour and appearance.

BATTER: A blended mixture of flour, liquid and other ingredients, used in cakes, fritters, griddle cakes, etc.

BEAT: To mix energetically, using a rotary and lifting motion with spoon or whip.

BEURRE: Butter (French term).

BISQUE: A thick and creamy shellfish soup.

BLANCH: To rinse in boiling water, then in cold water.

BLANC MANGE: French word "blanc" means white plus "mange" — to eat. Usually a pudding thickened with cornstarch.

BLEND: To combine two or more ingredients thoroughly.

BLIND BAKE: To bake a pie shell empty. Flute the edge of the pastry in your favourite way. Prick (dock) with a fork at 1" (2.3 cm) intervals. Bake in a preheated 450°F (220°C) oven for 10 to 12 minutes or until golden brown. Cool before adding the filling.

BOIL: The cooking action of any liquid, the temperature of boiling water is 212°F (100°C) at sea level.

BOUCHÉE: Small choux paste pastry shell filled with meat, poultry or fish.

BOUILLON A clear meat soup, usually made from beef stock.

BOUQUET-GARNI: A combination of herbs used to flavour meat, soup etc. usually tied together in cheesecloth. For the recipes in this book, use 2 tsp each of parsley, thyme and marjoram, ½ tsp of whole black peppercorns and 1 bay leaf unless otherwise specified in the recipe.

BRAISE: To brown in a hot container, in a small amount of fat followed by slow cooking, covered, in a small amount of liquid.

BRAN: Skin or outer covering of the wheat grain, removed during milling.

BREAD: (Cookery term) — to coat with breadcrumbs, cornmeal or crackers.

BREAD RUSKS: Rounds of bread lightly toasted.

BRINE: A solution of salt in water, with, or without, other preservations; used for preserving meats, vegetables etc.

BROIL: To cook by direct heat from hot coals obtained from a gas, electric or coal flames.

BROTH: The same as stock or bouillon, liquid in which meat, fish or vegetable have been cooked; a thin soup.

BRUNOISE: Food cut into small dice — ⅛ of an inch (.32 cm).

BRUSH: To spread with butter, egg, etc., thinly with a brush or a small paper or cloth.

CALORIE:	A unit which measures heat or energy generated in the body caused by food.
CANAPÉ:	An appetizer. Always prepared on a base, such as bread, toast or crackers with a flavoured butter.
CANDY:	To conserve or preserve by boiling with sugar; to encrust or coat with sugar.
CANE SUGAR:	A sweet carbohydrate obtained from unrefined or refined sugar cane plant.
CARAMELIZE:	To heat sugar, or food containing sugar, until dark brown and a peculiar 'buttery nut flavour' develops.
CAVIAR:	Eggs or roe of fish, black is usually sturgeon, red is often salmon.
CÉPES:	Species of mushrooms.
CHAMPIGNONS:	Mushrooms. (French term).
CHANTERELLES:	Species of mushrooms.
CHÂTEAUBRIAND:	16 oz (450 g) tenderloin steak.
CHILI CON-CARNI:	Spanish, meaning peppers with meat.
CHOP:	1. To cut food into smaller pieces. 2. A certain cut of meat; i.e. pork chop, lamb chop.
CLARIFIED BUTTER:	Butter which has been melted, the curd removed leaving only the golden fat.
CLARIFY:	To clear by removing scum, small particles, and fat from soup stock.
COAT:	To cover the complete surface of food .
COCKTAIL:	An appetizer, can be made of seafood, served in small quantities.
CODDLE:	To cook slowly just below the boiling point.
COLE SLAW:	A salad of finely cut cabbage, carrots in a vinegar dressing.
COMBINE:	To mix ingredients.
COMPOTE:	A combination of fruits.
CONCASSE OF TOMATO:	Peeled, seedless tomato, cut into dice ¼ of an inch (.64 cm).
CONDIMENTS:	Food seasonings such as salt, pepper, vinegar, herbs and spice.
CONSOMMÉ:	A clear soup made from meat and vegetables, seasoned, strained and clarified.
CORNED:	A method used to preserve beef in brine.
CORNSTARCH:	The refined starch of corn, used to thicken puddings.
COURT BOUILLON:	An aromatic liquid in which meat, fish and various vegetables are cooked together with wine, citrus fruit and bouquet garni.

CREAM: To soften a fat with a spoon or beater; also to combine thoroughly, the softened fat with sugar.

CREAM OF TARTAR: A residue of wine that is an acid substance used extensively before baking powder became common. It is an essential ingredient when using egg whites in baking.

CROQUETTES: A combination of chopped or ground cooked foods, bound together by eggs or a thick cream sauce, shaped, then dipped into egg and crumbs and fried.

CROUTONS: Small cubes of crisp toasted bread.

CUBE: To cut into approximately ¼ inch (0.64 cm).

CUT: To incorporate firm fat into dry ingredients with little blending permitting the fat to remain in small particles; to divide foods with a knife or scissors.

CUTLETS: A small, boneless slice of meat.

DEGLACER: To dilute a pan roast's juices with a liquid.

DÈGRAISSER: To skim off excess fat — from stocks, sauce, soups, stews.

DICE: To cut into ¼ inch (0.64 cm) or smaller cubes.

DISSOLVE: The absorbtion of a solid within a liquid.

DOT: To place small pieces of butter, cheese etc., over the surface of food.

DRAIN: To free solid food from liquid.

DRAWN BUTTER: Melted butter, with the milk curd removed.

DREDGE: To sprinkle with or roll lightly in bread crumbs or other fine grained ingredients.

DRIPPINGS: The remnant of roasted meats left in the pan.

DRY HEAT: A term used when cooking with no liquid.

DUST: To sprinkle lightly with flour or sugar.

DUXELLES: Chopped onions and mushrooms sautèed in butter and oil, until all the moisture has completely evaporated.

EMINCÈ: Cut fine.

EMULSION: The binding together of two or more liquids not mutually soluble. If the two liquids are thoroughly beaten together, one will divide into globules that will be completely surrounded by the other. As egg surround melted butter in a hollandaise.

EN BROCHETTE: On a skewer.

ENTRÉE:	In North America it is the main course of a dinner. In France it is an appetizer.
ETAMINE:	Cheesecloth, straining cloth.
FILLET, FILET:	A boneless piece of lean meat or fish.
FINES HERBES:	Finely chopped herbs, parsley, chives, chervil.
FINNAN HADDIE:	Smoked haddock or cod (fish).
FLAKE:	To break into small light pieces.
FLEURONS:	Crescents and similar shapes baked of puff pastry.
FOIE GRAS:	Fatted goose liver.
FOLD:	To combine using two motions, cutting vertically through the mixture and turning over and over by sliding the implement across the bottom of the mixing bowl with each turn.
FOND:	Basic stock for sauces and soups.
FRICASSEE:	To cook by sautéing, then stewing in stock or sauce.
FRITTERS:	A batter of eggs, flour, and milk into which meat, fruit or vegetables have been incorporated then deep fried.
FROST:	To cover cakes or cookies with a confectioners' sugar icing.
FROMAGE:	Cheese (French term).
FRY:	To cook in hot fat. Pan-fry or sauté is to cook in small amount of fat; deep-fry is to cook in fat sufficient to cover the food.
GARLIC:	A strong, aromatic member of the onion family.
GARNISH:	To decorate the main course with small, contrasting eye-pleasing food particles.
GELATIN:	Is made from animal bones and marrow. Used in dessert jellies, aspics and molded meats and salads.
GHERKINS:	Small, sweet, pickled cucumbers.
GIBLETS:	The heart, liver and gizzard of poultry.
GLAZE:	A shiny coating of a sugar substance such as red currant preserves applied to food for decorating purposes.
GLUTEN:	A substance found in wheat flour which gives dough its tough, elastic quality.
GOURMET:	A person who likes fine foods and drinks.
GRATE:	To obtain small particles of food by rubbing it on a grater.
GREASING:	Spreading a film of fat on a surface.
GRILL:	To cook by indirect heat on a solid top.
GRIND:	To chop food into small pieces by putting through a food chopper.

GUMBO:	A type of soup or stew that is slightly thickened with okra. The South American word for okra.
HORS D'OEUVRES:	Small, savory portions of food served as an appetizer.
HUMIDITY:	Amount of moisture in the air which may affect the outcome of some bakery products.
ICE:	The application of a confectioner sugar icing or frosting; certain types of frozen desserts.
INFUSION:	Liquid impregnated by with the essence of a solid by steeping, ie. tea, coffee.
INGREDIENT:	A food material.
INVERT SUGAR:	A simple sugar, a mixture of glucose and levulose; e.g. honey.
JULIENNE:	Vegetable cut into match-like pieces. Comes from the name of French Chef "Jean Julienne."
KIPPERED HERRING:	Dried or smoked herring.
KNEAD:	To work dough with a stretching, beating action, folding and refolding the dough into itself.
LARD:	Made of the rendered fat of a hog. Also, to cover lean meat, poultry or fish with strips of fat before cooking, or to insert fat with a skewer or larding needle.
LEAVENING:	Raising or lightening a product by air, steam or gas (carbon dioxide), usually accomplished with yeast, baking powder or soda.
LEEK:	A member of the onion family, long, thin plants.
LÈGUMES:	Vegetables. Also refers to such dried foods as beans, peas and lentils.
LENTIL:	Flat red or green seed. Used for soups.
LIAISON:	Binding with mixture of cream and yolks of eggs.
MACEDOINE:	A mixture of vegetables or fruits cut into definite shapes.
MARINADE:	An acidic aromatic liquid, used for soaking food so that the food absorbs the flavour of the liquid.
MELBA:	Food created by Auguste Escoffier to honour opera star Nellie Melba.
MELT:	To liquefy by heat.
MELTING POINT:	The temperature at which a solid becomes a liquid.
MERINGUE:	Stiffly beaten egg whites and sugar.
MILK:	The natural food product of the cow. May be found in various forms such as buttermilk, condensed, dry or powdered, evaporated, etc.
MILK SOLIDS:	All of milk except water.
MINCE:	To chop or cut into very fine pieces.

MIREPOIX:	A mixture of onions, carrots, celery and peppers, usually diced.
MISE - EN - PLACE:	To prepare ahead (stocks, sauces, meat, vegetables, dough).
MIX:	To combine two or more ingredients.
MOCHA:	A variety of coffee used to flavour foods. May also refer to a combination of chocolate and coffee.
MOUSSE:	Frozen dessert of whipped cream.
M.S.G.:	(Monosodium Glutamate) — a chemical used to enhance the flavours of foods, derived from sugar beets, corn and wheat. Care must be used in the amounts used in food preparation.
ORANGE ROUGHY:	A small, tender white fish from Australia, similar to pompano.
ORANGES VARIETIES:	Seville, Valencia, Navel, Temple, Tangerine, Clementine, Mandarin, Satsuma, Kumquat, Ugli (Tangelo).
PAN - BROIL:	To cook, uncovered, in a hot pan or on a griddle, removing fat as it collects.
PARBOIL:	To boil or simmer until partially tender; cooking is usually completed by some other method.
PARE:	To remove the skin from potatoes, apples, etc., with a sharp knife.
PARFAIT:	A dessert of ice cream, fruit and whipped cream.
PASTE:	1. A mixture of flour or cornstarch and water. 2. A mixture of ground food combined together until creamy.
PÂTÉ:	Fine ground foods held together with a binding agent.
PEEL:	To remove skin.
PETIT:	Small.
PETITS - FOURS:	Individual fancy cakes, iced all over.
PIQUANT:	Highly seasoned foods or sauces, a name for "hot" salsa sauce.
PLANKED:	To broil meat and serve on a board made for the purpose.
POACH:	To cook under the boiling point (simmer) in enough hot liquid to cover.
POULTRY:	A general term, includes all domestic birds, chickens, turkey, hens, geese, etc.
POT ROAST:	To cook a large piece of meat by braising.
POTAGE:	French term for a thick soup.
PRAWN:	A shellfish which looks like a shrimp but is much larger.
PRINTAINER:	This usually means a garnish of filling of early spring vegetables cut in various shapes.
PURÈE:	To put through a sieve.
REDUCE:	To reduce the volume of a liquid by simmering.

RENDER:	To melt fat by heating slowly.
ROAST:	The same as bake but applies to meats.
ROE:	Fish eggs.
ROMAINE:	A type of lettuce used in salads.
ROULADE:	Rolled meat with a stuffing.
ROUX:	A cooked mixture of flour and fat used to thicken soups and sauces.
SALAMANDER:	The broiler of an oven, under which foods are placed to brown.
SALPICON:	A compound of various products cut into dice and generally combined with a sauce.
SAUTÈ:	To pan fry in small amounts of fat.
SAUTEUSÉ:	Sauté pan.
SCALD:	The cooking of food at the boiling point. Milk that has reached at least 185°F (85°C).
SCALLOP:	To bake food in a cream sauce or other liquid. A type of shellfish.
SEAR:	To brown the surface of meat quickly over intense heat.
SHALLOT:	Vegetable of the onion family.
SHRED:	To cut into thin strips.
SIFT:	To put dry ingredients through a fine sieve or sifter.
SIMMER:	To heat a liquid to 185°F (85°C), or to cook a food in the same.
STEAM:	To cook in steam with or without applied pressure.
STEEP:	To extract flavour by adding boiling water and allowing to stand.
STEW:	To simmer in liquid until tender.
STOCK:	The liquid obtained by simmering meat, bones or vegetables: for use in soups, gravies or sauces.
SULTANA RAISINS:	Raisins made from seedless grapes.
SUPRÉME:	Best, most delicate, also name given to filet or breast of chicken.
TEXTURE:	Interior grain or structure of a product; the feeling of a substance under the fingers or in the mouth.
TOAST:	To brown the surface of food by application of direct heat.
TOSS:	To mix lightly as in making salads.
TRUFFLES:	Black fungus-like mushroom grown underground, usually very costly.
TRUSS:	To bind or fasten together.
VOL-AU-VENT:	A puff pastry shell of various sizes depending upon the recipe required.

WASH: A liquid brushed on the surface of an unbaked product; a liquid or mixture of liquids (e.g. - egg wash) into which a food is dipped before cooking.

WHIP: To beat rapidly, with a lifting motion to increase volume by incorporating air.

WINE GRAPES: Gamay, red wine grape, used for Beaujolais and rosé.
Pinot Noil, red wine grape, also used in Champagne.
Sémillion, white wine grape, used in Sauternes.
Chenin Blanc, white wine grape.
Riesling white wine grape.
Chardonnay, white wine grape, used in white Burgundy and Champagne.
Muscat, sweet white wine grape.
Grenache, sweet red wine grape.
Cabernet Sauvignon, red wine grape.
Sauvignon Blanc, white wine grape.
Zinfadel, red wine grape.

YEAST: Leavening agent, available in dry active, instant, and compressed cakes, 1 tbsp of dry or instant equals 1 oz (30 ml) compressed cake, instant may be used directly into the product required without standing in warm sugar water. 1 oz (30 ml) of yeast will rise approximately 3 ½ lbs (1.6 kg) of flour.

ZESTE: French for "peel", the outermost coloured, glossy film of the rind of a citrus fruit.

ZWIEBACK: German for twice baked, a sweetened bread dough baked, cut into slices and toasted.

MEASUREMENT CONVERSION CHART

Imperial	American	Metric	Australian
1 tbsp	1 tbsp	15 ml	20 ml
¼ cup	¼ cup	60 ml	2 tbsp
⅓ cup	⅓ cup	80 ml	¼ cup
½ cup	½ cup	125 ml	⅓ cup
⅔ cup	⅔ cup	170 ml	½ cup
¾ cup	¾ cup	190 ml	⅔ cup
1 cup	1 cup	250 ml	¾ cup
1¼ cup	1¼ cup	310 ml	1 cup

OVEN TEMPERATURES

Electric	F	C
very slow	250	120
slow	300	150
mod slow	325	160
moderate	350	180
mod hot	425	210
hot	475	240
very hot	525	260

Gas	F	C
very slow	250	120
slow	300	150
mod slow	325	160
moderate	350	180
mod hot	375	190
hot	400	200
very hot	450	230

INDEX

APPETIZERS

BARBECUE

BEEF AND VEAL

BEVERAGES

BREADS

CHEF K'S SPECIALTIES

CRÊPES

DESSERTS

EASY GOURMET

EGG DISHES

GAME

PASTA

PÂTÉS

PIZZA

PORK AND LAMB

POULTRY

PRESERVES

SALADS

SAUCES

SEAFOOD

SOUPS

VEGETABLES, RICE & MEATLESS DISHES

Acknowledgements

We would like to thank the following sponsors for their generous donations.

SYLVIA COOK *Sherwood Park*

KIM GRIFFITHS *Edmonton*

ASHBROOKS *Edmonton*

BOWRINGS LTD. *Edmonton*

COUNTRY'S REACH *Sherwood Park*

DANSK GIFTS/HIEDI ROSS *Edmonton*

LE GNOME GALLERIA INC. *Edmonton*

LONDON DRUGS LTD. *Sherwood Park*

EATONS OF CANADA *Edmonton*

STOKES INC. *Edmonton*

WOODCRAFTERS/HOME ACCENTS *Edmonton*

TOTALLY TROPICAL INTERIORS INC. *Edmonton*

HALLMARK CARD SHOPS *Sherwood Park/Edmonton*

PRINCESS HOUSE OF CANADA/ELAINE VADER *Sherwood Park*